STATISTICS USING STATA

Engaging and accessible to students from a wide variety of mathematical backgrounds, *Statistics Using Stata* combines the teaching of statistical concepts with the acquisition of the popular Stata software package. It closely aligns Stata commands with numerous examples based on real data, enabling students to develop a deep understanding of statistics in a way that reflects statistical practice. Capitalizing on the fact that Stata has both a menu-driven "point and click" and program syntax interface, the text guides students effectively from the comfortable "point and click" environment to the beginnings of statistical programming. Its comprehensive coverage of essential topics gives instructors flexibility in curriculum planning and provides students with more advanced material to prepare them for future work. Online resources – including complete solutions to exercises, PowerPoint slides, and Stata syntax (Do-files) for each chapter – allow students to review independently and adapt codes to solve new problems, reinforcing their programming skills.

Sharon Lawner Weinberg is Professor of Applied Statistics and Psychology and former Vice Provost for Faculty Affairs at New York University. She has authored numerous articles, books, and reports on statistical methods, statistical education, and evaluation, as well as in applied disciplines, such as psychology, education, and health. She is the recipient of several major grants, including a recent grant from the Sloan Foundation to support her current work with NYU colleagues to evaluate the New York City Gifted and Talented programs.

Sarah Knapp Abramowitz is Professor of Mathematics and Computer Science at Drew University, where she is also Department Chair and Coordinator of Statistics Instruction. She is the coauthor, with Sharon Lawner Weinberg, of *Statistics Using IBM SPSS: An Integrative Approach, Third Edition* (Cambridge University Press) and an Associate Editor of the *Journal of Statistics Education*.

Statistics Using Stata

AN INTEGRATIVE APPROACH

SHARON LAWNER WEINBERG

New York University

SARAH KNAPP ABRAMOWITZ

Drew University

CAMBRIDGE
UNIVERSITY PRESS

CAMBRIDGE
UNIVERSITY PRESS

One Liberty Plaza, 20th Floor, New York NY 10006, USA

Cambridge University Press is part of the University of Cambridge.

It furthers the University's mission by disseminating knowledge in the pursuit of education, learning, and research at the highest international levels of excellence.

www.cambridge.org
Information on this title: www.cambridge.org/9781107461185

First published 2016

Printed in the United States of America by Sheridan Books, Inc.

A catalogue record for this publication is available from the British Library.

Library of Congress Cataloguing in Publication Data
Names: Weinberg, Sharon L. | Abramowitz, Sarah Knapp, 1967–
Title: Statistics using stata: an integrative approach / Sharon Lawner Weinberg, New York University, Sarah Knapp Abramowitz, Drew University.
Description: New York NY: Cambridge University Press, 2016. | Includes index.
Identifiers: LCCN 2016007888 | ISBN 9781107461185 (pbk.)
Subjects: LCSH: Mathematical statistics – Data processing. | Stata.
Classification: LCC QA276.4.W455 2016 | DDC 509.50285/53–dc23
LC record available at http://lccn.loc.gov/2016007888

ISBN 978-1-107-46118-5 Paperback

Additional resources for this publication are at www.cambridge.org/Stats-Stata.

To our families

Contents

Preface

This text capitalizes on the widespread availability of software packages to create a course of study that links good statistical practice to the analysis of real data, and the many years of the authors' experience teaching statistics to undergraduate students at a liberal arts university and to graduate students at a large research university from a variety of disciplines including education, psychology, health, and policy analysis. Because of its versatility and power, our software package of choice for this text is the popularly used Stata, which provides both a menu-driven and command line approach to the analysis of data, and, in so doing, facilitates the transition to a more advanced course of study in statistics. Although the choice of software is different, the content and general organization of the text derive from its sister text, now in its third edition, *Statistics Using IBM SPSS: An Integrative Approach*, and as such, this text also embraces and is motivated by several important guiding principles found in the sister text.

First, and perhaps most important, we believe that a good data analytic plan must serve to uncover the story behind the numbers, what the data tell us about the phenomenon under study. To begin, a good data analyst must know his/her data well and have confidence that it satisfies the underlying assumptions of the statistical methods used. Accordingly, we emphasize the usefulness of diagnostics in both graphical and statistical form to expose anomalous cases, which might unduly influence results, and to help in the selection of appropriate assumption-satisfying transformations so that ultimately we may have confidence in our findings. We also emphasize the importance of using more than one method of analysis to answer fully the question posed and understanding potential bias in the estimation of population parameters.

Second, because we believe that data are central to the study of good statistical practice, the textbook's website contains several data sets used throughout the text. Two are large sets of real data that we make repeated use of in both worked-out examples and end-of-chapter exercises. One data set contains forty-eight variables and five hundred cases from the education discipline; the other contains forty-nine variables and nearly forty-five hundred cases from the health discipline. By posing interesting questions about variables in these large, real data sets (e.g., Is there a gender difference in eighth graders' expected income at age thirty?), we are able to employ a more meaningful and contextual approach to the introduction of statistical methods and to engage students more actively in the learning process. The repeated use of these data sets also contributes to creating a more cohesive presentation of statistics; one that links different methods of analysis to each other and avoids the perception that statistics is an often-confusing array of so many separate and distinct methods of analysis, with no bearing or relationship to one another.

Third, to facilitate the analysis of these data, and to provide students with a platform for actively engaging in the learning process associated with what it means to be a good researcher and data analyst, we have incorporated the latest version of Stata (version 14), a popular statistical software package, into the presentation of statistical material using a highly integrative approach that reflects practice. Students learn Stata along with each new statistical method covered, thereby allowing them to apply their newly-learned knowledge to the real world of applications. In addition to demonstrating the use of Stata within each chapter, all chapters have an associated .do-file, designed to allow students not only to replicate all worked out examples within a chapter but also to reproduce the figures embedded in a chapter, and to create their own.do-files by extracting and modifying commands from them. Emphasizing data workflow management throughout the text using the Stata.do-file allows students to begin to appreciate one of the key ingredients to being a good researcher. Of course, another key ingredient to being a good researcher is content knowledge, and toward that end, we have included in the text a more comprehensive coverage of essential topics in statistics not covered by other textbooks at the introductory level, including robust methods of estimation based on resampling using the bootstrap, regression to the mean, the weighted mean, and potential sources of bias in the estimation of population parameters based on the analysis of data from quasi-experimental designs, Simpson's Paradox, counterfactuals, other issues related to research design.

Fourth, in accordance with our belief that the result of a null hypothesis test (to determine whether an effect is real or merely apparent) is only a means to an end (to determine whether the effect is important or useful) rather than an end in itself, we stress the need to evaluate the magnitude of an effect if it is deemed to be real, and of drawing clear distinctions between statistically significant and substantively significant results. Toward this end, we introduce the computation of standardized measures of effect size as common practice following a statistically significant result. Although we provide guidelines for evaluating, in general, the magnitude of an effect, we encourage readers to think more subjectively about the magnitude of an effect, bringing into the evaluation their own knowledge and expertise in a particular area.

Finally, we believe that a key ingredient of an introductory statistics text is a lively, clear, conceptual, yet rigorous approach. We emphasize conceptual understanding through an exploration of both the mathematical principles underlying statistical methods and real world applications. We use an easy-going, informal style of writing that we have found gives readers the impression that they are involved in a personal conversation with the authors. And we sequence concepts with concern for student readiness, reintroducing topics in a spiraling manner to provide reinforcement and promote the transfer of learning.

Another distinctive feature of this text is the inclusion of a large bibliography of references to relevant books and journal articles, and many end-of-chapter exercises with detailed answers on the textbook's website. Along with the earlier topics mentioned, the inclusion of linear and nonlinear transformations, diagnostic tools for the analysis of model fit, tests of inference, an in-depth discussion of interaction and its interpretation in both two-way analysis of variance and multiple regression, and nonparametric statistics, the text provides a highly comprehensive coverage of essential topics in introductory statistics, and, in so doing, gives instructors flexibility in curriculum planning and provides students with more advanced material for future work in statistics.

The book, consisting of seventeen chapters, is intended for use in a one- or two-semester introductory applied statistics course for the behavioral, social, or health sciences at either the graduate or undergraduate level, or as a reference text as well. It is not intended for readers who wish to acquire a more theoretical understanding of mathematical statistics. To offer another perspective, the book may be described as one that begins with modern approaches to Exploratory Data Analysis (EDA) and descriptive statistics, and then covers material similar to what is found in an introductory mathematical statistics text, designed, for example, for undergraduates in math and the physical sciences, but stripped of calculus and linear algebra and grounded instead in data examples. Thus, theoretical probability distributions, The Law of Large Numbers, sampling distributions and The Central Limit Theorem are all covered, but in the context of solving practical and interesting problems.

Acknowledgments

This book has benefited from the many helpful comments of our New York University and Drew University students, too numerous to mention by name, and from the insights and suggestions of several colleagues. For their help, we would like to thank (in alphabetical order) Chris Apelian, Ellie Buteau, Jennifer Hill, Michael Karchmer, Steve Kass, Jon Kettenring, Linda Lesniak, Kathleen Madden, Isaac Maddow-Zimet, Meghan McCormick, Joel Middleton, and Marc Scott. Of course, any errors or shortcomings in the text remain the responsibility of the authors.

CHAPTER ONE

Introduction

Welcome to the study of statistics! It has been our experience that many students face the prospect of taking a course in statistics with a great deal of anxiety, apprehension, and even dread. They fear not having the extensive mathematical background that they assume is required, and they fear that the contents of such a course will be irrelevant to their work in their fields of concentration.

Although it is true that an extensive mathematical background is required at more advanced levels of statistical study, it is not required for the introductory level of statistics presented in this book. Greater reliance is placed on the use of the computer for calculation and graphical display so that we may focus on issues of conceptual understanding and interpretation. Although hand computation is deemphasized, we believe, nonetheless, that a basic mathematical background – including the understanding of fractions, decimals, percentages, signed (positive and negative) numbers, exponents, linear equations, and graphs – is essential for an enhanced conceptual understanding of the material.

As for the issue of relevance, we have found that students better comprehend the power and purpose of statistics when it is presented in the context of a substantive problem with real data. In this information age, data are available on a myriad of topics. Whether our interests are in health, education, psychology, business, the environment, and so on, numerical data may be accessed readily to address our questions of interest. The purpose of statistics is to allow us to analyze these data to extract the information that they contain in a meaningful way and to write a story about the numbers that is both compelling and accurate.

Throughout this course of study we make use of a series of real data sets that are located in the website for this book and may be accessed by clicking on the Resources tab using the URL, www.cambridge.org/Stats-Stata. We will pose relevant questions and learn the appropriate methods of analysis for answering such questions. Students will learn that more than one statistic or method of analysis typically is needed to address a question fully. Students also will learn that a detailed description of the data, including possible anomalies, and an ample characterization of results, are critical components of any data analytic plan. Through this process we hope that this book will help students come to view statistics as an integrated set of data analytic tools that when used together in a meaningful way will serve to uncover the story contained in the numbers.

THE ROLE OF THE COMPUTER IN DATA ANALYSIS

From our own experience, we have found that the use of a statistics software package to carry out computations and create graphs not only enables a greater emphasis on conceptual understanding and interpretation but also allows students to study statistics in a way that reflects statistical practice. We have selected the latest version of Stata available to us at the time of writing, version 14, for use with this text. We have selected Stata because it is a well-established comprehensive package with a robust technical support infrastructure that is widely used by behavioral and social scientists. In addition, not only does Stata include a menu-driven "point and click" interface, making it accessible to the new user, but it also includes a command line or program syntax interface, allowing students to be guided from the comfortable "point and click" environment to the beginnings of statistical programming. Like MINITAB, JMP, Data Desk, Systat, SPSS, and SPlus, Stata is powerful enough to handle the analysis of large data sets quickly. By the end of the course, students will have obtained a conceptual understanding of statistics as well as an applied, practical skill in how to carry out statistical operations.

STATISTICS: DESCRIPTIVE AND INFERENTIAL

The subject of statistics may be divided into two general branches: descriptive and inferential. *Descriptive statistics* are used when the purpose of an investigation is to *describe* the data that have been (or will be) collected. Suppose, for example, that a third-grade elementary school teacher is interested in determining the proportion of children who are firstborn in her class of thirty children. In this case, the focus of the teacher's question is her own class of thirty children and she will be able to collect data on all of the students about whom she would like to draw a conclusion. The data collection operation will involve noting whether each child in the classroom is firstborn or not; the statistical operations will involve counting the number who are, and dividing that number by thirty, the total number of students in the class, to obtain the proportion sought. Because the teacher is using statistical methods merely to describe the data she collected, this is an example of descriptive statistics.

Suppose, by contrast, that the teacher is interested in determining the proportion of children who are firstborn in *all* third-grade classes in the city where she teaches. It is highly unlikely that she will be able to (or even want to) collect the relevant data on all individuals about whom she would like to draw a conclusion. She will probably have to limit the data collection to some randomly selected smaller group and use *inferential statistics* to generalize to the larger group the conclusions obtained from the smaller group. *Inferential statistics* are used when the purpose of the research is not to describe the data that have been collected but to generalize or make inferences based on it. The smaller group on which she collects data is called the *sample*, whereas the larger group to whom conclusions are generalized (or inferred), is called the *population*. In general, two major factors influence the teacher's confidence that what holds true for the sample also holds true for the population at large. These two factors are the method of sample selection and the size of the sample. Only when data are collected on *all* individuals about whom a conclusion is to be drawn (when the sample *is* the population and we are therefore in the realm of descriptive statistics), can the conclusion be drawn with 100 percent certainty. Thus, one of the major goals of inferential statistics is to assess the degree of certainty of inferences when such inferences are drawn from sample data. Although this text is divided roughly into two parts, the first on descriptive statistics and the second on inferential statistics, the second part draws heavily on the first.

VARIABLES AND CONSTANTS

In the previous section, we discussed a teacher's interest in determining the proportion of students who are firstborn in the third grade of the city where she teaches. What made this question worth asking was the fact that she did not expect everyone in the third grade to be firstborn. Rather, she quite naturally expected that in the population under study, birth order would vary, or differ, from individual to individual and that only in certain individuals would it be first.

Characteristics of persons or objects that vary from person to person or object to object are called *variables*, whereas characteristics that remain constant from person to person or object to object are called *constants*. Whether a characteristic is designated as a variable or as a constant depends, of course, on the study in question. In the study of birth order, birth order is a variable; it can be expected to vary from person to person in the given population. In that same study, grade level is a constant; all persons in the population under study are in the third grade.

. . . .

EXAMPLE 1.1. Identify some of the variables and constants in a study comparing the math achievement of tenth-grade boys and girls in the southern United States.

Solution. *Constants:* Grade level; Region of the United States
 Variables: Math achievement; Sex

. . . .

EXAMPLE 1.2. Identify some of the variables and constants in a study of math achievement of secondary-school boys in the southern United States.

Solution. *Constants:* Sex; Region of the United States
 Variables: Math achievement; Grade level

Note that grade level is a constant in Example 1.1 and a variable in Example 1.2. Because constants are characteristics that do not vary in a given population, the study of constants is neither interesting nor informative. The major focus of any statistical study is therefore on the variables rather than the constants. Before variables can be the subject of statistical study, however, they need to be numerically valued. The next section describes the process of measuring variables so as to achieve that goal.

THE MEASUREMENT OF VARIABLES

Measurement involves the observation of characteristics on persons or objects, and the assignment of numbers to those persons or objects so that the numbers represent the amounts of the characteristics possessed. As introduced by S. S. (Stanley Smith) Stevens (1946) in a paper, "On the theory of scales of measurement," and later described by him in a chapter, "Mathematics, Measurement, and Psychophysics," in the *Handbook of Experimental Psychology*, edited by Stevens (1951), we describe four levels of measurement in this text. Each of the four levels is defined by the nature of the observation and the way in which the numbers assigned correspond to the amount of the underlying characteristic that has been observed. The level of measurement of a variable determines which numerical operations (e.g., addition, subtraction, multiplication, or division) are permissible on that variable. If other than the permissible numerical operations are used on a variable given its level of measurement, one can expect the statistical conclusions drawn with respect to that variable to be questionable.

Nominal Level. The nominal level of measurement is based on the simplest form of observation – whether two objects are similar or dissimilar; for example, whether they are short versus nonshort, male versus female, or college student versus noncollege student. Objects observed to be similar on some characteristic (e.g., college student) are assigned to the same class or category, while objects observed to be dissimilar on that characteristic are assigned to different classes or categories. In the nominal level of measurement, classes or categories are *not* compared as say, taller or shorter, better or worse, or more educated or less educated. Emphasis is strictly on observing whether the objects are similar or dissimilar. As befitting its label, classes or categories are merely named, but not compared, in the *nominal* level of measurement.

Given the nature of observation for this level of measurement, numbers are assigned to objects using the follow simple rule: if objects are dissimilar, they are assigned different numbers; if objects are similar, they are assigned the same number. For example, all persons who are college students would be assigned the same number (say, 1); all persons who are noncollege students also would be assigned the same number different from 1 (say, 2) to distinguish them from college students. Because the focus is on distinction and not comparison, in this level of measurement, the fact that the number is 2 is larger than the number 1 is irrelevant in terms of the underlying characteristic being measured (whether or not the person is a college student). Accordingly, the number 1 could have been assigned, instead, to all persons who are noncollege students and the number 2 to all persons who are college students. Any numbers other than 1 and 2 also could have been used as well.

Although the examples in this section (e.g., college student versus noncollege student) may be called *dichotomous* in that they have only two categories, nominal variables also may have more than two categories (e.g., car manufacturers – Toyota, Honda, General Motors, Ford, Chrysler, etc.):

Ordinal Level. The ordinal level of measurement is not only based on observing objects as similar or dissimilar but also on ordering those observations in terms of an underlying characteristic. Suppose, for example, we were not interested simply in whether a person was a college student or not but, rather, in ordering college students in terms of the degree of their success in college (e.g., whether the college student was below average, average, or above average). We would, therefore, need to observe such ordered differences among these college students in terms of their success in college and we would choose numbers to assign to the categories that corresponded to that ordering. For this example, we might assign the number 1 to the below average category, the number 2 to the average category, and the number 3 to the above average category. Unlike in the nominal level of measurement, in the ordinal level of measurement, it is relevant that 3 is greater than 2, which, in turn, is greater than 1, as this ordering conveys in a meaningful way the ordered nature of the categories relative to the underlying characteristic of interest. That is, comparisons among the numbers correspond to comparisons among the categories in terms of the underlying characteristic of success in college. In summary, the ordinal level of measurement applies two rules for assigning numbers to categories: (1) different numbers are assigned to persons or objects that possess different amounts of the underlying characteristic, and (2) the higher the number assigned to a person or object, the less (or more) of the underlying characteristic that person or object is observed to possess. From these two rules it does *not* follow, however, that equal numerical differences along the number scale correspond to equal increments in the underlying characteristic being measured in the ordinal level of measurement. Although the differences between 3 and 2 and between 2 and 1 in our college student success example are both equal to 1, we cannot infer from this that the difference in success between above average college students and average college students equals the difference in success between average college students and below average college students.

We consider another example that may convey more clearly this idea. Suppose we line ten people up according to their size place and assign a number from 1 to 10, respectively, to each person so that each number corresponds to the person's size place in line. We could assign the number 1 to the shortest person, the number 2 to the next shortest person, and so forth, ending by assigning the number 10 to the tallest person. While according to this method, the numbers assigned to each pair of adjacent people in line will differ from each other by the same value (i.e., 1), clearly, the heights of each pair of adjacent people will not necessarily also differ by the same value. Some adjacent pairs will differ in height by only a fraction of an inch, while other adjacent pairs will differ in height by several inches. Accordingly, only some of the features of this size place ranking are reflected or modeled by the numerical scale. In particular, while, in this case, the numerical scale can be used to judge the relative order of one person's height compared to another's, differences between numbers on the numerical scale cannot be used to judge how much taller one person is than another. As a result, statistical conclusions about variables measured on the ordinal level that are based on other than an ordering or ranking of the numbers (including taking sums or differences) cannot be expected to be meaningful.

Interval Level. An ordinal level of measurement can be developed into a higher level of measurement if it is possible to assess how near to each other the persons or objects are in the underlying characteristic being observed. If numbers can be assigned in such a way that equal numerical differences along the scale correspond to equal increments in the underlying characteristic, we have, what is called an *interval level of measurement*. As an example of an interval level of measurement, consider the assignment of yearly dates, the chronological scale. Because one year is defined as the amount of time necessary for the earth to revolve once around the sun, we may think of the yearly date as a measure of the number of revolutions of the earth around the sun up to and including that year. Hence, this assignment of numbers to the property *number of revolutions of the earth around the sun* is on an interval level of measurement. Specifically, this means that equal numerical differences for intervals (such as 1800 C.E. to 1850 C.E. and 1925 C.E.to 1975 C.E.) represent equal differences in the number of revolutions of the earth around the sun (in this case, fifty). In the interval level of measurement, therefore, we may make meaningful statements about the amount of *difference* between any two points along the scale. As such, the numerical operations of addition and subtraction (but not multiplication and division) lead to meaningful conclusions at the interval level and are therefore permissible at that level. For conclusions based on the numerical operations of multiplication and division to be meaningful, we require the ratio level of measurement.

Ratio Level. An interval level of measurement can be developed into a higher level of measurement if the number zero on the numeric scale corresponds to zero or "not any" of the underlying characteristic being observed. With the addition of this property (called an *absolute zero*), ratio comparisons are meaningful, and we have, what is called the *ratio level of measurement*. Consider once again the chronological scale and, in particular, the years labeled 2000 C.E. and 1000 C.E. Even though 2000 is numerically twice as large as 1000, it does not follow that the number of revolutions represented by the year 2000 is twice the number of revolutions represented by the year 1000. This is because on the chronological scale, the number 0 (0 C.E.) does not correspond to zero revolutions of the earth around the sun (i.e., the earth had made revolutions around the sun many times prior to the year 0 C.E.). In order for us to make meaningful multiplicative or ratio comparisons of this type between points on our number scale, the number 0 on the numeric scale must correspond to 0 (none) of the underlying characteristic being observed.

In measuring height, not by size place, but with a standard ruler, for example, we would typically assign a value of 0 on the number scale to "not any" height and assign the other numbers according to the rules of the interval scale. The scale that would be produced in this case would be a ratio scale of measurement, and ratio or multiplicative statements (such as "John, who is 5 feet tall, is *twice* as tall as Jimmy, who is 2.5 feet tall") would be meaningful. It should be pointed out that for variables to be considered to be measured on a ratio level, "not any" of the underlying characteristic only needs to be meaningful theoretically. Clearly, no one has zero height, yet using zero as an anchor value for this scale to connote "not any" height is theoretically meaningful.

Choosing a Scale of Measurement. Why is it important to categorize the scales of measurement as nominal, ordinal, interval, or ratio? If we consider college students and assign a 1 to those who are male college students, a 2 to those who are female college students, and a 3 to those who are not college students at all, it would not be meaningful to add these numbers nor even to compare their sizes. For example, two male college students together do not suddenly become a female college student, even though their numbers add up to the number of a female college student (1 + 1 = 2). And a female college student who is attending school only half-time is not suddenly a male college student, even though half of her number is the number of a male college student (2/2 = 1). By contrast, if we were dealing with a ratio-leveled height scale, it would be possible to add, subtract, multiply, or divide the numbers on the scale and obtain results that are meaningful in terms of the underlying trait, height. In general, and as noted earlier, the scale of measurement determines which numerical operations, when applied to the numbers of the scale, can be expected to yield results that are meaningful in terms of the underlying trait being measured. *Any numerical operation can be performed on any set of numbers; whether the resulting numbers are meaningful, however, depends on the particular level of measurement being used.*

Note that the four scales of measurement exhibit a natural hierarchy, or ordering, in the sense that each level exhibits all the properties of those below it (see Table 1.1). Any characteristic that can be measured on one scale listed in Table 1.1 can also be measured on any scale below it in that list. Given a precise measuring instrument such as a perfect ruler, we can measure a person's height, for example, as a ratio-scaled variable, in which case we could say that a person whose height is 5 feet has twice the height of a person whose height is 2.5 feet. Suppose, however, that no measuring instrument were available. In this situation, we could, as we have done before, "measure" a person's height according to size place or by categorizing a person as tall, average, or short. By assigning numbers to these three categories (such as 5, 3, and 1, respectively), we would create an ordinal level of measurement for height.

TABLE 1.1. Hierarchy of scales of measurement
1. Ratio
2. Interval
3. Ordinal
4. Nominal

In general, it may be possible to measure a variable on more than one level. The level that is ultimately used to measure a variable should be the highest level possible, given the precision of the measuring instrument used. A perfect ruler allowed us to measure heights on a ratio level, while the eye of the observer allowed us to measure height only on an ordinal level.

If we are able to use a higher level of measurement but decide to use a lower level instead, we would lose some of the information that would have been available to us on the higher level. We would also be restricting ourselves to a lower level of permissible numerical operations.

• •

EXAMPLE 1.3. Identify the level of measurement (nominal, ordinal, interval, or ratio) most likely to be used to measure the following variables:

1. Ice cream flavors *nominal*
2. The speed of five runners in a one-mile race, as measured by the runners' order of finish, first, second, third, and so on. *ordinal*
3. Temperature measured in Centigrade degrees. *interval*
4. The annual salary of individuals.

Solution.

1. The variable ice cream flavors is most likely measured at the nominal level of measurement because the flavors themselves may be categorized simply as being the same or different and there is nothing inherent to them that would lend themselves to a ranking. Any ranking would have to depend on some extraneous property such as, say, taste preference. If numbers were assigned to the flavors as follows,

Flavor	Number
Vanilla	0
Chocolate	1
Strawberry	2
etc.	etc.

   meaningful numerical comparisons would be restricted to whether the numbers assigned to two ice cream flavors are the same or different. The fact that one number on this scale may be larger than another is irrelevant.

2. This variable is measured at the ordinal level because it is the order of finish (first, second, third, and so forth) that is being observed and not the specific time to finish. In this example, the smaller the number the greater the speed of the runner. As in the case of measuring height via a size place ranking, it is not necessarily true that the difference in speed between the runners who finished first and second is the same as the difference in speed between the runners who finished third and fourth. Hence, this variable is not measured at the interval level. Had time to finish been used to measure the speed of the runners, the level of measurement would have been ratio for the same reasons that height, measured by a ruler, is ratio-leveled.

3. Temperature measured in Centigrade degrees is at the interval level of measurement because each degree increment, no matter whether from 3 to 4 degrees Centigrade or from 22 to 23 degrees Centigrade, has the same physical meaning in terms of the underlying characteristic, heat. In particular, it takes 100 calories to raise the temperature of 1 mL of water by 1 degree Centigrade, no matter what the initial temperature reading on the Centigrade scale. Thus, equal differences along the Centigrade scale correspond to equal increments in heat, making this scale interval-leveled. The reason this scale is not ratio-scaled is because 0 degrees Centigrade does not correspond to "not any" heat. The 0 degree point on the Centigrade scale is the point at which water freezes, but even frozen water contains plenty of heat. The point of "not any" heat is at −273 degrees Centigrade. Accordingly, we cannot make meaningful ratio comparisons with respect to amounts of heat on the Centigrade scale and say, for example, that at 20 degrees Centigrade there is twice the heat than at 10 degrees Centigrade.

4. The most likely level of measurement for annual salary is the ratio level because each additional unit increase in annual salary along the numerical scale corresponds to an equal additional one dollar earned no matter where on the scale one starts, whether it be, for example, at $10,000 or at $100,000; and, furthermore, because the numerical value of 0 on the scale corresponds to "not any" annual salary, giving the scale a true or absolute zero. Consequently, it is appropriate to make multiplicative comparisons on this scale, such as "Sally's annual salary of $100,000 is twice Jim's annual salary of $50,000."

DISCRETE AND CONTINUOUS VARIABLES

As we saw in the last section, any variable that is not intrinsically numerically valued, such as the ice cream flavors in Example 1.3, may be converted to a numerically valued variable. Once a variable is numerically valued, it may be classified as either discrete or continuous.

Although there is really no exact statistical definition of a discrete or a continuous variable, the following usage generally applies. A numerically valued variable is said to be *discrete* (or *categorical* or *qualitative*) if the values it takes on are integers or can be thought of in some unit of measurement in which they are integers. A numerically valued variable is said to be *continuous* if, in any unit of measurement, whenever it can take on the values a and b, it can also theoretically take on all the values between a and b. The limitations of the measuring instrument are not considered when discriminating between discrete and continuous variables. Instead, it is the nature of the underlying variable that distinguishes between the two types.

☞ **Remark.** As we have said, there is really no hard and fast definition of discrete and continuous variables for use in practice. The words discrete and continuous do have precise mathematical meanings, however, and in more advanced statistical work, where more mathematics and mathematical theory are employed, the words are used in their strict mathematical sense. In this text, where our emphasis is on statistical practice, the usage of the terms discrete and continuous will not usually be helpful in guiding our selection of appropriate statistical methods or graphical displays. Rather, we will generally use the particular level of measurement of the variable, whether it is nominal, ordinal, interval, or ratio.

X= region
x finite
x = discrete

EXAMPLE 1.4. Let our population consist of all eighth-grade students in the United States, and let X represent the region of the country in which the student lives. X is a variable, because there will be different regions for different students. X is not naturally numerically valued, but because X represents a finite number of distinct categories, we can assign numbers to these categories in the following simple way: 1 = Northeast, 2 = North Central, 3 = South, and 4 = West. X is a discrete variable, because it can take on only four values. Furthermore, because X is a nominal-leveled variable, the assignment of 1, 2, 3, and 4 to Northeast, North Central, South, and West, respectively, is arbitrary. Any other assignment rule would have been just as meaningful in differentiating one region from another.

1. NE
2. N.C.
3. S.
4 W.

EXAMPLE 1.5. Consider that we repeatedly toss a coin 100 times and let X represent the number of heads obtained for each set of 100 tosses. X is naturally numerically valued and may be considered discrete because the only values it can take on are the integer values 0, 1, 2, 3, and so forth. We may note that X is ratio-leveled in this example because 0 on the numerical scale represents "not any" heads.

EXAMPLE 1.6. Consider a certain hospital with 100 beds. Let X represent the percentage of occupied beds for different days of the year. X is naturally numerically valued as a proportion of the number of occupied beds. Although X takes on fractional values, it is considered discrete because the proportions are based on a count of the number of beds occupied, which is an integer value.

EXAMPLE 1.7. Let our population consist of all college freshmen in the United States, and let X represent their heights, measured in inches. X is numerically valued and is continuous because all possible values of height are theoretically possible. Between any two heights exists another theoretically possible height. For example, between 70 and 71 inches in height, exists a height of 70.5 inches and between 70 and 70.5 exists a height of 70.25 inches, and so on.

☞ **Remark.** Even if height in Example 1.7 were reported to the nearest inch (as an integer), it would still be considered a continuous variable because all possible values of height are theoretically possible. Reporting values of continuous variables to the nearest integer is usually due to the lack of precision of our measuring instruments. We would need a perfect ruler to measure the exact values of height. Such a measuring instrument does not, and probably cannot, exist. When height is reported to the nearest inch, a height of 68 inches is considered to represent all heights between 67.5 and 68.5 inches. While the precision of the measuring instrument determines the accuracy with which a variable is measured, it does not determine whether the variable is discrete or continuous. For that we need only to consider the theoretically possible values that a variable can assume.

☞ **Remark.** In addition to the problem of not being able to measure variables precisely, another problem that often confronts the behavioral scientist is the measurement of traits, such as intelligence, that are not directly observable. Instead of measuring intelligence directly, tests have been developed that measure it indirectly, such as the IQ test. While such tests report IQ, for example, as an integer value, IQ is considered to be a continuous trait or variable, and an IQ score of 109, for example, is thought of as theoretically representing all IQ scores between 108.5 and 109.5.

Another issue, albeit a more controversial one, related to the measurement of traits that are not directly observable, is the level of measurement employed. While some scientists would argue that IQ scores are only ordinal (given a good test of intelligence, a person whose IQ score is higher than another's on that test is said to have greater intelligence), others would argue that they are interval. Even though equal intervals along the IQ scale (say, between 105 and 110 and between 110 and 115) may not necessarily imply equal amounts of change in intelligence, a person who has an IQ score of 105 is likely to be closer in intelligence to a person who has an IQ score of 100 rather than to a person who has an IQ score of 115. By considering an IQ scale and other such psychosocial scales as ordinal only, one would lose such information that is contained in the data and the ability to make use of statistical operations based on sums and differences, rather than merely on rankings.

Another type of scale, widely used in attitude measurement, is the Likert scale, which consists of a small number of values, usually five or seven, ordered along a continuum representing agreement. The values themselves are labeled typically from strongly disagree to strongly agree. A respondent selects that score on the scale that corresponds to his or her level of agreement with a statement associated with that scale. For the same reasons noted earlier with respect to the IQ scale, for example, the Likert scale is considered by many to be interval rather than strictly ordinal.

• •

EXAMPLE 1.9. For each variable listed, describe whether the variable is discrete or continuous. Also, describe the level of measurement for each variable. Use the following data set excerpted from data analyzed by Tomasi and Weinberg (1999). The original study was carried out on 105 elementary school children from an urban area who were classified as learning disabled (LD) and who, as a result, were receiving special education services for at least three years. In this example, we use only the four variables described below.

Variable Name	What the Variable Measures	How It Is Measured
SEX		0 = Male
		1 = Female
GRADE	Grade level	1, 2, 3, 4, or 5
AGE	Age in years	Ages ranged from 6 to 14
MATHCOMP	Mathematical comprehension	Higher scores associate with greater mathematical comprehension. Scores could range from 0 to 200.

Solution. The variable SEX is discrete because the underlying construct represents a finite number of distinct categories (male or female). Furthermore, individuals may be classified as either male or female, but nothing in between. The level of measurement for SEX is nominal because the two categories are merely different from one another.

The variable GRADE is discrete because the underlying construct represents a finite number (five) of distinct categories and individuals in this study may only be in one of the five grades. The level of measurement for GRADE is interval because the grades are ordered and equal numerical differences along the grade scale represent equal increments in grade.

The variable AGE is continuous even though the reported values are rounded to the nearest integer. AGE is continuous because the underlying construct can theoretically take on any value between 5.5 and 14.5 for study participants. The level of measurement for AGE is ratio because higher numerical values correspond to greater age, equal numerical differences along the scale represent equal increments in age within rounding, and the value of zero is a theoretically meaningful anchor point on the scale representing "not any" age.

The variable MATHCOMP, like AGE, is continuous. The underlying construct, mathematical comprehension, theoretically can take on any value between 0 and 200. The level of measurement is at least ordinal because the higher the numerical value, the greater the comprehension in math, and it is considered to be interval because equal numerical differences along the scale are thought to represent equal or nearly equal increments in math comprehension. Because individuals who score zero on this scale do not possess a total absence of math comprehension, the scale does not have an absolute zero and is, therefore, not ratio-leveled.

SETTING A CONTEXT WITH REAL DATA

We turn now to some real data and gain familiarity with Stata. For this example and for others throughout the book, we have selected data from the National Educational Longitudinal Study begun in 1988, which we will refer to as the *NELS* data set.

In response to pressure from federal and state agencies to monitor school effectiveness in the United States, the National Center of Education Statistics (NCES) of the U.S. Department of Education conducted a survey in the spring of 1988. The participants consisted of a nationally representative sample of approximately 25,000 eighth graders to measure achievement outcomes in four core subject areas (English, history, mathematics, and science), in addition to personal, familial, social, institutional, and cultural factors that might relate to these outcomes. Details on the design and initial analysis of this survey may be referenced in Horn, Hafner, and Owings (1992). A follow-up of these students was conducted during tenth grade in the spring of 1990; a second follow-up was conducted during the twelfth grade in the spring of 1992; and, finally, a third follow-up was conducted in the spring of 1994.

For this book, we have selected a sub-sample of 500 cases and 48 variables. The cases were sampled randomly from the approximately 5,000 students who responded to all four administrations of the survey, who were always at grade level (neither repeated nor skipped a grade) and who pursued some form of post-secondary education. The particular variables were selected to explore the relationships between student and home-background variables, self-concept, educational and income aspirations, academic motivation, risk-taking behavior, and academic achievement.

Some of the questions that we will be able to address using these data include: Do boys perform better on math achievement tests than girls? Does socioeconomic status relate to educational and/or income aspirations? To what extent does enrollment in advanced math in eighth grade predict twelfth-grade math achievement scores? Can we distinguish between those who use marijuana and those who don't in terms of self-concept? Does owning a computer vary as a function of geographical region of residence (Northeast, North Central, South, and West)? As you become familiar with this data set, perhaps you will want to generate your own questions of particular interest to you and explore ways to answer them.

As shown below, Stata, which must be obtained separately from this text, opens with five sub-windows contained within one large window. Collectively, these windows help us to navigate between information about the variables in the data set and statistical output based on analyses that have been carried out on that data set. The largest (the area that contains the word *Stata*), is called the *Results* or *Output Window* as it will contain the results or output from our analyses. Directly below the *Output Window* is the *Command Window* headed by the word, Command. It is in this window that we enter the commands we want Stata to execute (run). The window on the upper right is the *Variables Window,* headed by the word Variables. This window displays a list of all variable names and labels for the active dataset; that is, the dataset we currently are analyzing. Directly below the *Variables Window* is the *Properties Window* headed by the word, Properties. This window lists the properties of each of the variables in our data set (e.g., their formats, variable labels, value labels, data types and so on) as well as the properties of the data set itself (e.g., its filename, number of variables, number of observations, and so on). On the extreme left is the *Review Window*, headed by the word Review. This window gives a history of the commands that we have executed to date. Because we have not yet executed any commands, the Review Window currently contains the message, "There are no items to show."

Across the top of the screen, is a list of eight words (*File, Edit, Data, Graphics, Statistics, User, Window, Help*) that when clicked may be used to navigate the Stata environment. We will refer to this list as comprising the *main menu bar*. By clicking **File**, for example, we would obtain a drop-down menu covering the variety of Stata activities that are at the file level, such as **File/Open** and **File/Save**. If we were to click **Window** on the main menu bar, we would see a listing of all of Stata's windows, the first five of which are those just described above. In addition to these, there are five other windows that we do not see when we open Stata (*Graph, Viewer, Data Editor, Do-file Editor,* and *Variables Manager*). These will be discussed later in the text as needed.

It is important to note that Stata is case-sensitive, which means that Stata will interpret a lowercase m, for example, as different from an uppercase M. In addition, all commands entered into the Command Window must be in lowercase. Stata will not understand a command typed with an uppercase letter. It also means that a variable name with only lower case letters must be typed in the Command Window with only lower case letters, a variable name with only upper case letters must be typed in the Command Window with only upper case letters, and a variable name with a combination of lower and upper case letters must be entered in the Command Window with that exact combination of upper and lower case letters.

After typing a command, Stata will execute that command after we press **Enter**. Although the results of executing that command will appear in the *Output Window*, Stata does not automatically save the contents of the *Output Window*. To keep a permanent copy of the contents of the *Output Window*, we should begin each data analytic session by creating a *log file*. When a log file is created, Stata outputs results to both the Output Window and the log file. All of this will become quite clear when you do the end-of-chapter Exercises of Chapter 1, which includes opening the *NELS* data set in Stata.

A description of the *NELS* data set may be found in Appendix A. Material for all appendices, including Appendix A, may be found online at www.cambridge.org/Stats-Stata. Descriptions of the other real data sets we use throughout this text are also found in Appendix A.

Exercise 1.9 introduces you to some of the variables in the *NELS* data set without the use of Stata. Exercise 1.10 shows you how to open the *NELS* data set in Stata and Exercise 1.15 shows you how to enter data to create a new data set in Stata. These exercises also review how to start a log file in Stata.

Once we have completed our analyses and saved our results, and are now ready to close Stata, we may do so by clicking on the main menu bar **File/Exit** or by typing in the Command Window the **exit** and hitting Enter.

☞ **Remark.** Although we have described four levels of measurement in this chapter, you should not confuse this with the "Data Type" that Stata specifies. Stata characterizes each variable in the data set as either an alphanumeric variable (i.e., a "string" variable), or a numeric variable. Numeric variables are stored in one of several ways depending upon how much precision is desired by the analyst when carrying out computations. For our purposes, in this book, we will not be concerned about a numeric variable's storage type, but will simply use the storage type assigned by Stata for that variable.

☞ **Remark.** There is an important distinction to be drawn between the numerical results of a statistical analysis and the *interpretation* of these results given by the researcher. Methods involved in the interpretation of results, such as researcher judgment, are not statistical operations. They are extra-statistical. For instance, to determine on the basis of having administered the same standardized test to a group of boys and girls that the girls attain, on average, higher scores than the boys is a statistical conclusion. However, to add that the reason for this difference is that the test is biased toward the girls is a researcher based, not a statistically based, conclusion. In offering such an interpretation, the researcher is drawing on non-statistical information. It is important to be able to separate statistical conclusions from researcher-inferred conclusions. The latter may not justifiably follow from the former; and unfortunately, the latter are the ones that are usually remembered and cited.

EXERCISES

1.1. Suppose Julia is a researcher who is gathering information on the yearly income and number of years of experience of all female doctors practicing in the United States. Identify each of the following as either a constant or variable in this study. If your answer is variable, identify its most likely level of measurement (nominal, ordinal, interval, or ratio).

    a) Sex
    b) Yearly income as reported on one's tax return
    c) Ethnicity
    d) Profession (not specialty)
    e) Number of years of experience

1.2. Given the population of all clowns in the Ringling Brothers, Barnum and Bailey Circus, identify the following as either constant or variable. If your answer is variable, identify its most likely level of measurement (nominal, ordinal, interval, or ratio).

    a) Height
    b) Profession
    c) Age
    d) Eye color

1.3. Identify each of the following numerical variables as either discrete or continuous and identify their most likely levels of measurement (nominal, ordinal, interval, or ratio).

    a) Percentage of high school seniors each year who report that they have never smoked cigarettes
    b) Annual rainfall in Savannah, Georgia, to the nearest inch
    c) Number of runs scored in a baseball game
    d) Weight
    e) Verbal aptitude as measured by SAT verbal score
    f) Salary of individual government officials

1.4. Identify the following numerical variables as either discrete or continuous and identify their most likely levels of measurement (nominal, ordinal, interval, or ratio).

    a) Number of students enrolled at Ohio State University in any particular term
    b) Distance an individual can run in five minutes
    c) Hair length
    d) Number of hot dogs sold at baseball games
    e) Self-concept as measured by the degree of agreement with the statement, "I feel good about myself," on a five-point scale where 1 represents strongly disagree, 2 represents disagree, 3 represents neutral, 4 represents agree, and 5 represents strongly agree
    f) Lack of coordination as measured by the length of time it takes an individual to assemble a certain puzzle

1.5. Identify the following numerical variables as either discrete or continuous and identify their most likely levels of measurement (nominal, ordinal, interval, or ratio).

    a) Baseball jersey numbers
    b) Number of faculty with Ph.D.'s at an institution
    c) Knowledge of the material taught as measured by grade in course

d) Number of siblings
e) Temperature as measured on the Fahrenheit scale
f) Confidence in one's ability in statistics as measured by a yes or no response to the statement, "I am going to do very well in my statistics class this semester"

1.6. A survey was administered to college students to learn about student participation in University sponsored extra-curricular activities. Identify the most likely level of measurement of each of the following variables taking into account the coding used.

Variable Name	Question Asked	Coding (if any)
AGE	How old are you in years?	
EXTRAC	At which type of extra-curricular activity do you spend most of your time?	1 = Sports 2 = Student Government 3 = Clubs and organizations 4 = None
TIME	How much time do you spend weekly on University sponsored extracurricular activities?	0 = None 1 = 1–2 hours 2 = 3–5 hours 3 = 6–10 hours 4 = 10–20 hours 5 = More than 20 hours

a) AGE
b) EXTRAC
c) TIME

1.7. The Campus Survey of Alcohol and Other Drug Norms is administered to college students to collect information about drug and alcohol use on campus. Identify the most likely level of measurement of each of the following variables from that survey taking into account the coding used.

Variable Name	Question Asked	Coding (if any)
ABSTAIN	Overall, what percentage of students at this college do you think consume no alcoholic beverages at all?	
LIVING	Living arrangements	1 = House/apartment/etc. 2 = Residence Hall 3 = Other
STATUS	Student status:	1 = Full-time (12+ credits) 2 = Part-time (1–11 credits)
ATTITUDE	Which statement about drinking alcoholic beverages do you feel best represents your own attitude?	1 = Drinking is never a good thing to do. 2 = Drinking is all right but a person should not get drunk

Variable Name	Question Asked	Coding (if any)
		3 = Occasionally getting drunk is okay as long as it doesn't interfere with academics or other responsibilities.
		4 = Occasionally getting drunk is okay even if it does interfere with academics or other responsibilities.
		5 = Frequently getting drunk is okay if that's what the individual wants to do.
DRINK	How often do you typically consume alcohol (including beer, wine, wine coolers, liquor, and mixed drinks)?	0 = Never
		1 = 1–2 times/year
		2 = 6 times/year
		3 = Once/month
		4 = Twice/month
		5 = Once/week
		6 = 3 times/week
		7 = 5 times/week
		8 = Every day

a) ABSTAIN
b) LIVING
c) STATUS
d) ATTITUDE
e) DRINK

Exercise 1.8 includes descriptions of some of the variables in the Framingham data set. The Framingham data set is based on a longitudinal study investigating factors relating to coronary heart disease. A more complete description of the Framingham data set may be found in Appendix A.

1.8. For each variable described from the *Framingham* data set, indicate the level of measurement.

    a) CURSMOKE1 indicates whether or not the individual smoked cigarettes in 1956. It is coded so that 0 represents no and 1 represents yes.

    b) CIGPDAY1 indicates the number of cigarettes the individual smoked per day, on average, in 1956.

    c) BMI1 indicates the body mass index of the individual in 1956. BMI can be calculated as follows:

    d) $BMI = \left(\dfrac{Weight\_in\_Pounds}{\left(Height\_in\_inches\right) \times \left(Height\_in\_inches\right)} \right) \times 703$

e) SYSBP1 and DIABP1 indicate the systolic and diastolic blood pressures, respectively, of the individuals in 1956. Blood is carried from the heart to all parts of your body in vessels called arteries. Blood pressure is the force of the blood pushing against the walls of the arteries. Each time the heart beats (about 60–70 times a minute at rest), it pumps out blood into the arteries. Your blood pressure is at its highest when the heart beats, pumping the blood. This is called systolic pressure. When the heart is at rest, between beats, your blood pressure falls. This is the diastolic pressure.

Blood pressure is always given as these two numbers, the systolic and diastolic pressures. Both are important. Usually they are written one above or before the other, such as 120/80 mmHg. The top number is the systolic and the bottom the diastolic. When the two measurements are written down, the systolic pressure is the first or top number, and the diastolic pressure is the second or bottom number (for example, 120/80). If your blood pressure is 120/80, you say that it is "120 over 80." Blood pressure changes during the day. It is lowest as you sleep and rises when you get up. It also can rise when you are excited, nervous, or active. Still, for most of your waking hours, your blood pressure stays pretty much the same when you are sitting or standing still. Normal values of blood pressure should be lower than 120/80. When the level remains too high, for example, 140/90 or higher, the individual is said to have high blood pressure. With high blood pressure, the heart works harder, your arteries take a beating, and your chances of a stroke, heart attack, and kidney problems are greater.

Exercise 1.9 includes descriptions of some of the variables in the NELS data set. The NELS data set is a subset of a data set collected by the National Center for Educational Statistics. They conducted a longitudinal study investigating factors relating to educational outcomes. A more complete description of the NELS data set may be found in Appendix A.

1.9. Read the description of the following variables from the *NELS* data set. Then, classify them as either discrete or continuous and specify their levels of measurement (nominal, ordinal, interval, or ratio). The variable names are given in capital letters.

a) GENDER. Classifies the student as either male or female, where 0 = "male" and 1 = "female."

b) URBAN. Classifies the type of environment in which each student lives where 1 = "Urban," 2 = "Suburban," and 3 = "Rural."

c) SCHTYP8. Classifies the type of school each student attended in eighth grade where 1 = "Public," 2 = "Private, Religious," and 3 = "Private, Non-Religious."

d) TCHERINT. Classifies student agreement with the statement "My teachers are interested in students" using the Likert scale 1 = "strongly agree," 2 = "agree," 3 = "disagree," and 4 = "strongly disagree."

e) NUMINST. Gives the number of post-secondary institutions the student attended.

f) ACHRDG08. Gives a score for the student's performance in eighth grade on a standardized test of reading achievement. Actual values range from 36.61 to 77.2, from low to high achievement.

g) SES. Gives a score representing the socioeconomic status (SES) of the student, a composite of father's education level, mother's education level, father's occupation, mother's occupation, and family income. Values range from 0 to 35, from low to high SES.

h) SLFCNC12. Gives a score for student self-concept in twelfth grade. Values range from 0 to 43. Self-concept is defined as a person's self-perceptions, or how a person feels about himself or herself. Four items comprise the self-concept scale in the *NELS* questionnaire: I feel good about myself; I feel I am a person of worth, the equal of other people; I am able to do things as well as most other people; and, on the whole, I am satisfied with myself. A self-concept score, based on the sum of scores on each of these items, is used to measure self-concept in the *NELS* study. Higher scores associate with higher self-concept and lower scores associate with lower self-concept.

i) SCHATTRT. Gives the average daily attendance rate for the school.

j) ABSENT12. Classifies the number of times missed school. Assigns 0 to Never, 1 to 1–2 times, 2 to 3–6 times, etc.

Exercises 1.10–1.13 require the use of Stata and the NELS data set.

1.10. Follow the instructions given below to access the *NELS* data set from the website associated with this text.

Open Stata and begin a log file to keep a permanent copy of your results. To begin a log file, click **File/Log/Begin on the main menu bar**. A window will then appear prompting you to give the log file a name and save it in a location of your choosing. Log files are denoted in Stata by the extension .smcl added to their filename. It is a good idea to save the log file in a folder that is associated with the analysis you will doing using this data set. For example, you might want to save it in a folder labeled Exercise 1.10.

Open the NELS data set by clicking File/Open on the main menu bar, browsing to locate the NELS data set (this data set, along with all other data sets for this text, is located under the Resources tab on the book's website, www.cambridge.org/Stats-Stata) and clicking Open. The NELS data set will now be in active memory and you will see something like the following on your computer screen:

Notice that the Variables Window now contains the complete list of variable names and labels for each variable in the NELS data set, and the Output Window contains the command (**use**) that was used to open the data set itself. The word **clear** at the end of the **use** command clears any data that currently may be in Stata's active memory so that we may begin with a clean slate. The command **use** is followed by quotes within which appears the address of the location of the NELS.dta data set.

To see the complete data set displayed on the screen, on the main menu bar click **Data/Data Editor/Data Editor(Edit)**. More simply, you may type the command **edit** in the Command Window and hit **Enter**. A spreadsheet containing the NELS data set will appear on the screen, and you will now be able to edit or modify the data in the dataset. If you do not want to edit the data at this time and want to avoid the risk of changing some values by mistake, you can go into browse mode instead of edit mode by clicking **Data/Data Editor/Data Editor(Browse)**. More simply, you may type the command **browse** in the Command Window and hit **Enter**.

a) What is the first variable in the *NELS* data set? ~~Name~~ *id*   *Adv. Math*
   advmath8; take 8th
b) What is the <u>second variable</u> in the data set and what is its <u>variable label</u>? ~~label~~ *grade; case number*
c) What are the <u>value labels</u> for this variable? That is, how is the variable coded?
   (HINT: You may use one of the following four approaches to answer this question.)
   1. On the main menu bar, click **Data/ Data Utilities/ Label Utilities/List Value Labels** and select the desired variable from the drop-down list. Click **OK** and the value labels (codes) for this variable will appear on the screen in the Output Window. If no specific variable is selected from the drop-down list, the value labels for all the variables in the dataset will appear in the Output Window when **OK** is clicked.
   2. Alternatively, type the command **label list** in the Command Window and hit **Enter** to view the value codes for all the variables in the dataset. If you only want the value codes for a particular variable, you would type the name of that variable following the command **label list** in the Command Window and hit **Enter**. For example, you would type **label list advmath8** and hit **Enter** to view the value codes for only the variable advanced math in 8th grade.

   advmath8
   0 No
   1 yes
   8 missing

   3. And still another approach would be to type the command **edit** in the Command Window, hit **Enter** to view the complete set of data in the Data Editor Window, and click the variable advmath8 in the Variables Window. Notice that the Properties Window now contains information about the variable advmath8. In the row labeled Value Label within the Properties Window, the variable name advmath8 is followed by three dots (…).

If you click on those three dots, the following window will appear on your screen.

If we were to click the + sign next to advmath8, the value labels for this variable would appear on the screen. If, instead, we were interested not only in viewing the value labels, but also in editing (changing) them, we would click Edit Label on this screen and the following window would appear, allowing us to make the changes we wished.

4. Finally, and perhaps, most simply, type the command **codebook** in the Command Window and hit **Enter** to view the value codes for all the variables in the dataset. If you only want the value codes for a particular variable, you would type the name of that variable following the command **codebook** in the Command Window and hit **Enter**. For example, you would type **codebook advmath8** and hit **Enter** to view the value codes for only the variable advanced math in 8th grade

d) What is the Type entered for this variable in Stata? (Hint: The Variables Window contains a listing of the variable names and their labels. To view the Type for this variable, click on the variable name in the Variables Window and refer to the Properties Window below to view this variable's Type. Because all the variables in the NELS data set are numeric, one of the following will be listed as the Type of that variable – *byte*, *int*, *long*, *float*, or *double*. These numeric Types are listed in order of increasing precision, but as was mentioned earlier, for our purposes we do not need to pay much attention to these different numeric Types. *numeric (double)*

e) What is the variable label for the variable famsize? *Family size*

f) Why are there no value labels for this variable? *It could be a huge range or no fam @ all*

g) How many variables are there in the *NELS* data set? (Hint: On the main menu bar, click **Data/ Describe Data/Describe data in memory**. Then click **OK**. Or, more simply type the command **describe** in the Command Window and hit **Enter**. A full description of all the variables in the data set will appear in the Output Window along with information at the top of the Window regarding the total number of observations (Obs:) in the dataset and the total number of variables (Var:) in the

^500   *^48*

dataset. Information regarding the number of variables and observations in the data set may also be obtained by looking under Data in the Properties Window.

h) You may now close Stata by typing **exit** in the Command Window and hitting **Enter**.

1.11. Click **Data/Data Editor/ Data Editor (Browse)** on the main menu bar or type the command **browse** in the Command Window to view the full NELS data set on the screen. Refer to this data set to answer the following questions.

4 a) How many people are in the family (famsize) of the first student (ID=1) in the *NELS* data set?

yes b) Did the first student in the *NELS* data set (id = 1) take advanced math in eighth grade (advmath8)?

missing c) Did the second student in the *NELS* data set (id = 2) take advanced math in eighth grade (advmath8)?

500 d) How many people are in the *NELS* data set? (See the Hint given for Exercise 1.10(g))

? **1.12.** The variable late12 gives the number of times a student has been late for school in twelfth grade using the following coding: 0 = never, 1 = 1–2 times, 2 = 3–6 times, 3 = 7–9 times, 4 = 10–15 times, and 5 = over 15 times. Although a code of 0 indicates that the student was never late, late12 is not measured on a ratio scale. Explain. Identify the level of measurement used. Describe how the variable might have been measured using a higher level of measurement.

ratio interval **1.13.** The variable expinc30 gives, for each student in the *NELS*, the expected income at age 30 in dollars. Identify the level of measurement used. Describe how the variable might have been measured using a lower level of measurement.

Exercise 1.14 requires the use of Stata and the States data set. The States data set contains educational information for the 50 states and Washington DC. A more complete description of the States data set may be found in Appendix A.

1.14. In this exercise, we introduce the notion of Type in the Properties Window and review some of the other information that may be obtained in Stata's Data Editor Window. Load the *States* data set into active memory by clicking on the main menu bar **File/Open** and then open the Data Editor Window in browse mode by clicking **Data/Data Editor/ Data Editor(Browse)**.

a) Verify that the string (alphanumeric) variable state has Type *str42* and the numeric variable stut each has Type *double*. The number 42 following *str* indicates that the state with the longest name has 42 letters/characters. Which state is it? What is the data Type for the variable enrollmnt?

b) Value labels typically are used for variables at the nominal and ordinal levels to *South* remind us which values have been assigned to represent the different categories of these variable. For the variable region, which region of the country has been assigned a value of 3?

    [Hint: One way is to click on the main menu bar, Data/Data Utilities/List Value Labels, and select the variable region from the drop-down list.] What are three other ways to find the answer to this problem? [Another Hint: See Exercise 1.10(c).]

c) What is the difference between Variable Labels and Values?

d) Why does the variable region have no label? *it has a value label*

e) In which region is Arizona? *West*

Exercise 1.15 provides a tutorial on data entry and requires the use of Stata.   ✱

1.15. In this exercise, we will enter data on 12 statisticians who each have contributed significantly to the field of modern statistics. We have provided a table of variable descriptions and a table of data values and detailed instructions on how to proceed. In most cases, we provide the commands that are needed to execute the steps, but we also provide the main menu point and click steps when those are easy and not cumbersome to carry out.

a) The data, given near the end of this exercise relate to the variables described in the table below. We will enter these data into Stata using the steps provided.

Name	Type	Label	Values
Statistician	String		
Gender	float		1 = Female
			2 = Male
Birth	float	Year of birth	
Death	float	Year of death	
AmStat	float	Number of references in The American Statistician, 1995–2005	

Use the following steps to enter the data:

To enter these data into Stata, we need to be in edit mode in the Data Editor Window. To do so, click on **Data/Data Editor/Data Editor(Edit)** or type the command **edit** in the Command Window and hit **Enter**. A new, blank datasheet will appear ready to receive the data you wish to enter. Remember that Stata is case-sensitive and all commands must be written in lowercase.

A copy of the spreadsheet with the data is given at the end of this exercise. Begin to enter the data per cell as shown below for the first row:

var1	var2	var3	var4	var5
Sir Francis Galton	2	1822	1911	7

To select a location on your computer in which you would like to save this file, on the main menu bar click **File/Change Working Directory**, and select the location in which you would like to save this file. To save the file with the data entered so far, and to give it the filename Statisticians, type **save** Statisticians in the Command Window and hit **Enter**. Alternatively, on the main menu bar, click **File/Save As** and browse for the location in which you would like to save the file, give the file a name (e.g., Statisticians) and hit **Save**. This data file, as well as all other Stata data files, will have the extension .dta added to its filename to distinguish it as Stata data file.

Once the data are entered, we might wish to make changes to the dataset. For example, if we wished to give each variable a name other than the generic name it has been initially assigned by Stata (var1, var2, etc.), we would click on the main menu bar **Data/Data Utilities/Rename Groups of Variables**. In the panel labeled, "Existing variable names," we would type var1 var2 var3 var4 var5. In the panel labeled, "New variable names," we would type Statistician Gender Birth Death

AmStat, and then click **OK**. Alternatively, we could type **rename (var1 var2 var3 var4 var5) (Statistician Gender Birth Death AmStat)** in the Command Window and hit **Enter**.

If we wished to give the dataset a label in addition to its filename, on the main menu bar, we would click **Data/Data Utilities/Label Utilities/Label Dataset** and type the label you wish in the space provided (e.g., **Statisticians Data – Exercise 1.15) and click OK.** Alternatively, we could type **label data "Statisticians Data – Exercise 1.15"** in the Command Window and hit **Enter**.

To label individual variables (e.g., AmStat) with labels in addition to their variable names, on the main menu bar, we would click **Data/Data Utilities/Label Utilities/ Label Variable**, select the variable we wished to label (AmStat) from the drop-down menu and type the label itself in the space provided (# of references in the *American Statistician*, 1995–2005). Alternatively, we could type **label variable AmStat "# of references in the *American Statistician*, 1995–2005"** and hit **Enter**.

To define value labels and then assign these labels to the variable Gender, on the main menu bar, we would click **Data/Variables Manager**, and click on the variable Gender and in the Properties Window to the right, click **Manage** and then **Edit Labels** in the new screen that appears and add the desired label values. Alternatively, we could type the following two commands in the Command Window, hitting Enter after each:

> **label define sex 2 "Male" 1 "Female"**
> **label values Gender sex**

We could then type the command **codebook Gender** to confirm that what we did was correct.

To view how all the data in this file are represented or described internally in the computer, we could type **describe** in the Command Window and hit **Enter**.

Once you are finished with the task of creating your dataset, you will want to save it, but since we already saved a portion of these data and the file Statisticians .dta already exists, rather than simply typing in the Command Window **save Statisticians**, we would type **save Statisticians, replace.** Alternatively, on the main menu bar, we could click **File/Save.** At this point, Stata will ask whether we want to overwrite the existing file, and we would click **Yes**.

To list the contents of the data set on the screen (in the Output Window), type list in the Command Window.

Statistician	Gender	Birth	Death	AmStat
Sir Francis Galton	2	1822	1911	7
Karl Pearson	2	1857	1936	16
William Sealy Gosset	2	1876	1937	0
Ronald Aylmer Fisher	2	1890	1962	5
Harald Cramer	2	1893	1985	0
Prasanta Chandra Mahalanobis	2	1893	1972	0
Jerzy Neyman	2	1894	1981	7
Egon S. Pearson	2	1895	1980	1

Statistician	Gender	Birth	Death	AmStat
Gertrude Cox	1	1900	1978	6
Samuel S. Wilks	2	1906	1964	1
Florence Nightingale David	1	1909	1995	0
John Tukey	2	1915	2000	12

To log out of Stata, type **exit** in the Command Window and hit **Enter**.

CHAPTER TWO

Examining Univariate Distributions

As noted in Chapter 1, the function of descriptive statistics is to describe data. A first step in this process is to explore how the collection of values for each variable is distributed across the array of values possible. Because our concern is with each variable taken separately, we say that we are exploring *univariate distributions*. Tools for examining such distributions, including tabular and graphical representations, are presented in this chapter along with Stata commands for implementing these tools. As we noted in Chapter 1, we may enter Stata commands either by using a menu-driven point and click approach or by directly typing the commands themselves into the Command Window and hitting Enter. Because directly typing the commands is simpler and less cumbersome than the menu-driven approach, in only the first chapter do we provide both the menu-driven point and click approach and the command-line approach. In this and succeeding chapters we focus on the command-line approach, but provide in this chapter, instructions for how to obtain the particular sequence of point and click steps on the main menu bar that would be needed to run a command.

COUNTING THE OCCURRENCE OF DATA VALUES

We again make use of the *NELS* data set introduced in Chapter 1, by looking at various univariate distributions it includes. To begin our exploration, we ask the following questions about two of them. How many students in our sample are from each of the four regions of the country (Northeast, North Central, South, and West)? How are the students distributed across the range of values on socioeconomic status (ses)? By counting the number of students who live within a region, or who score within a particular score interval on the ses scale, we obtain the *frequency* of that region or score interval. When expanded to include all regions or all score intervals that define the variable, we have a *frequency distribution*. Frequency distributions may be represented by tables and graphs. The type of table or graph that is appropriate for displaying the frequency distribution of a particular variable depends, in part, upon whether the variable is discrete or continuous.

WHEN VARIABLES ARE MEASURED AT THE NOMINAL LEVEL

The variable REGION in the *NELS* data set is an example of a discrete variable with four possible values or categories: Northeast, North Central, South, and West. To display the number of student respondents who are from each of these regions, we may use frequency and percent tables as well as bar and pie charts.

FREQUENCY AND PERCENT DISTRIBUTION TABLES

MORE Stata: To create frequency and percent distribution tables

We type the following command in the Command Window and hit **Enter**: **tabulate region**

☞ **Remark.** As described, we can type in the variable name **region** in the above command, or we can click on the variable **region** in the Variable Window located in the top right corner of the Stata screen (see later). An arrow will appear as shown. Place your cursor wherever you want the variable to appear on the command line (after the command **tabulate**, in this case) and click on the arrow.

Variables		
Variable	**Label**	
id	Case Number	
advmath8	Advanced Math T...	
urban	Urbanicity	
region	Geographic Regio...	
gender	Gender	
famsize	Family Size	
parmarl8	Parents' Marital St...	
homelang	Home Language ...	
slfcnc08	Eighth Grade Self-...	
slfcnc10	Tenth Grade Self ...	
slfcnc12	Twelfth Grade Self...	
schtyp8	School Type in Eig...	

The result, as given in Table 2.1, will appear on your screen in the Output Window.

In Table 2.1, the first column lists the four possible categories of this variable. The second column, labeled "Freq.", presents the number of respondents from each region. From this column, we may note that the fewest number of respondents, 93, are from the West. Note that if we sum the frequency column we obtain 500, which represents the total number of respondents in our data set. This is the value we should obtain if an appropriate category is listed for each student and all

Table 2.1. Frequency distribution for region

Geographic Region of School	Freq.	Percent	Cum.
Northeast	106	21.20	21.20
NorthCentral	151	30.20	51.40
South	150	30.00	81.40
West	93	18.60	100.00
Total	500	100.00	

students respond to one and only one category. If an appropriate category is listed for each student and all students respond to one and only one category, we say the categories are *mutually exclusive and exhaustive*. This is a desirable, though not essential property of frequency distributions.

While the frequency of a category is informative, so is also the *relative frequency* of the category; that is, the frequency of the category relative to (divided by) the total number of individuals responding. The relative frequency represents the *proportion* of the total number of responses that are in the category. The relative frequency of student respondents from the West, for example, is 93/500 or .186.

Relative frequencies can also be converted easily to *percents* by multiplying the relative frequency by 100. Making this conversion, we find that 18.6 percent ($.186 \times 100$), or close to 20 percent of our sample is from the West. The full percent distribution relative to all four regions may be found in the third column of Table 2.1, labeled "Percent". Note that the sum of values in this column equals 100 percent, as one would expect. In some cases, however, when round-off error is incurred in converting fractions to percents, a sum slightly different from 100 percent may be obtained.

The last column, "Cum." (to denote Cumulative Percent), is described in the section on accumulating data in this chapter. For reasons that will be discussed at that time, this column is meaningless because the region data are nominal.

MORE Stata: The command **tab1**

The **tab1** command may be used in the same way as tabulate, but it is especially useful when we wish to obtain a series of frequency distribution tables on different variables. For example, **tab1 ses region** would produce two frequency distribution tables, one for ses and the other for region. *Ses — Socio economic status*

BAR CHARTS

In addition to a tabular format, frequency and percent distributions of nominal data may be represented visually in the form of a bar chart. Figure 2.1 contains a bar chart depicting the frequency of each region.

MORE Stata: To generate the bar chart of Figure 2.1

We type **graph bar (count), over(region) ytitle(frequency)** in the Command Window and hit **Enter.**

Note: The option **ytitle(frequency)** labels the y (or vertical) axis with the word, frequency.

As depicted in Figure 2.1, the values of the variable region are represented by points along the category (or horizontal or x) axis, whereas the frequencies (or counts) are represented by points along the vertical axis, labeled frequency. In other cases, relative frequencies or percents are represented along the vertical axis. The ordering of the categories along the category axis follows the ordering of the numerical values assigned to the categories when the data were entered originally. Recall that as noted in Example 1.4 in Chapter 1, a 1 is assigned to the category northeast, 2 to north central, and so on. Because region is a nominal-leveled variable, this assignment of numbers to region categories is arbitrary.

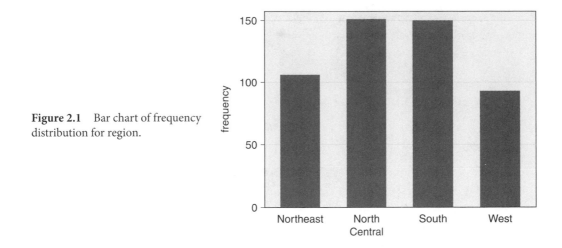

Figure 2.1 Bar chart of frequency distribution for region.

Accordingly, in the case of Figure 2.1, the ordering of the regions along the category axis is arbitrary. For ordinal-, interval-, or ratio-leveled variables, however, the inherent ordering of the variable itself dictates the ordering of categories along the horizontal axis. The importance of this distinction will become clear when we discuss cumulative distributions.

A bar chart is characterized by *unconnected* bars or rectangles of equal width, each of whose height reflects the frequency of the category it represents. For example, the height of the bar labeled South reaches a count of 150, indicating that the frequency of that category is 150. Furthermore, because the heights of the bars labeled North Central and South are approximately equal we may infer that the frequencies for those two categories are approximately equal as well.

☞ **Remark.** A nice property of this chart is that the vertical axis starts at 0. As discussed in Chapter 1, frequency, like height, may be considered to be a ratio-leveled variable. As a ratio-leveled variable, we may make multiplicative or ratio comparisons between different values along the frequency scale. Because height, as another ratio-leveled variable, is used to represent frequency in a bar chart, for such ratio comparisons to be meaningful using the heights of the bars, a bar with zero height should represent a category with zero frequency. Fortunately, this is the case in Figure 2.1. Before using the heights of the bars alone in a bar chart to make ratio comparisons between categories along the horizontal axis, check that the vertical axis actually begins at the value zero – that a bar of zero height would represent a category with zero frequency.

Although we have illustrated the use of bar charts to depict frequency distributions, we may also use bar charts to depict percent distributions.

MORE Stata: To generate a bar chart by percents instead of counts

We replace the word **count** with the word **percent** and change the title of the y-axis using the option **ytitle** as shown here:

graph bar (percent), over(region) ytitle(percent)

Or, equivalently we may type the following because the bar graph with percents is Stata's default:

graph bar, over(region) ytitle(percent)

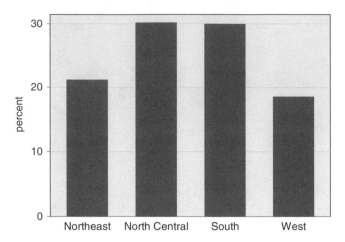

Figure 2.2   Bar chart of percent distribution for region.

To create a percent bar graph of a different nominal variable, simply substitute the name of that variable for the variable region whenever region appears in these commands.

We may use the command **help graph bar** to learn more about the options available for constructing bar graphs and also, if interested, to learn what the sequence of points and clicks on the main menu bar would be for constructing this bar graph. For this command, this sequence appears under the heading **Menu** on this help page and is given as **Graphics > Bar chart**.

Notice that the relative standing of the heights of the bars in Figure 2.2 is the same as that in the chart in Figure 2.1. This is because the percent scale differs from the frequency (or count) scale in terms of a constant of proportionality only. To obtain each percent value, we simply divide each frequency value by the sample size (500, in this case) and then multiply by 100. Effectively, then, each frequency value is multiplied by the constant of proportionality, one-fifth (100/500) to obtain the corresponding percent value, in this case.

MORE Stata: Ordering the bars by height

To put the bars of a bar graph in height order with the shortest first, we would type:

graph bar (percent), over(region, sort(1)) ytitle(percent)

To put the bars in height order with the tallest first, we would type:

graph bar (percent), over(region, sort(1) descending) ytitle(percent)

Because the sorting relates to how the regions are to be drawn, the word **sort** appears within the parentheses related to region. The number 1 within the ()'s following **sort** refers to the fact that the first (and, in this case, only) variable (namely, region) is to be used for sorting the heights of the bars.

MORE Stata: Orienting the direction of the bars

To orient the bars horizontally, instead of vertically as has been shown, we use the command **graph hbar** instead of **graph bar**:

graph hbar (count), over(region) ytitle(frequency)

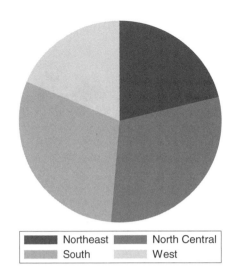

Figure 2.3   Pie chart of frequency distribution for region.

PIE CHARTS

Pie charts may be used to depict frequency and percent distributions in the discrete variable case as long as the categories are exhaustive. Pie charts are particularly useful for depicting each category relative to the entire set of categories. A pie chart of the frequency distribution for region is given in Figure 2.3.

MORE Stata: To create a pie chart of the variable region, for example

We type **graph pie, over(region)** in the Command Window and press **Enter**.

In a pie chart, the larger frequencies are indicated by larger slices. Notice that the two regions of approximately equal numbers of students, South and North Central, are represented by approximately equal-sized slices. And that these two regions account for more than half of the students who are in our sample. Just as bar charts may be misleading if their vertical axes do not start at zero, pie charts may be misleading if the categories they depict are not exhaustive. Consider the case illustrated in Figure 2.4 depicting the annual number of deaths in New York City: Tobacco vs. Other.

Notice that this pie chart misleads the viewer into thinking that tobacco is the greatest cause of death. However, not included in the list of causes considered are, for example, heart disease and cancer unrelated to tobacco use, which are known leading causes of death. In this example, the categories are not exhaustive, and clearly for a reason. This pie chart was created as part of an anti-smoking campaign.

WHEN VARIABLES ARE MEASURED AT THE ORDINAL, INTERVAL, OR RATIO LEVEL

In the previous section we discussed ways to explore univariate distributions of variables that are measured at the nominal level. In this section, we present analogous tools for variables that are measured at the ordinal, interval, or ratio level.

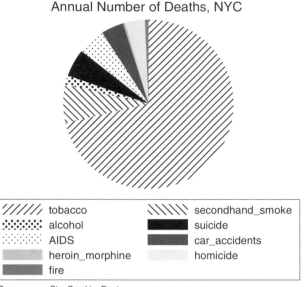

Figure 2.4 Annual number of deaths in New York City for different causes.

Source: www.StopSmokingDoctors.com

FREQUENCY AND PERCENT DISTRIBUTION TABLES

Because a variable often has many distinct values in its distribution, a frequency distribution table with each category representing one value is often too unwieldy to be informative. Table 2.2 contains such a table generated by Stata for socioeconomic status (ses), a variable that is part of the *NELS* data set. ses ranges from 0 to 35 with higher scores associated with higher ses. ses is a composite of parents' education level, occupation, and family income. Notice that while we have not lost any information contained in the original data set with this tabular representation, the number of categories is too large for easy interpretation.

MORE Stata: To construct a frequency distribution table for the variable ses, for example We type **tabulate ses** in the Command Window and press Enter.

Because we are tabulating one variable only (ses), we may type **help tabulate one-way** to learn more about this command and also, as noted earlier, if interested, to learn what the sequence of points and clicks on the main menu bar would be for obtaining a frequency distribution for a single variable. Under the heading **Menu** on this help page, we note that the required sequence of points and clicks on the main menu bar would be: **Statistics > Summaries, tables, and tests > Frequency tables > One-way table**

In Table 2.3, the data have been grouped into categories defined by intervals of values, and the number of categories, therefore, has been reduced. Notice that unlike the frequency distribution for region, where each of the small number of categories contains a single value (Northeast, North Central, South, and West), each category for ses is actually a range of ses values represented by its midpoint. For example, the first category, represented by its midpoint 1.5, contains all values from 0 to 3. Six students, representing 1.2 percent,

Table 2.2 Frequency distribution for socio-economic status (ses)

Socio-Economic Status	Freq.	Percent	Cum.
0	1	0.20	0.20
1	1	0.20	0.40
2	2	0.40	0.80
3	2	0.40	1.20
4	4	0.80	2.00
5	1	0.20	2.20
6	12	2.40	4.60
7	7	1.40	6.00
8	15	3.00	9.00
9	9	1.80	10.80
10	18	3.60	14.40
11	22	4.40	18.80
12	16	3.20	22.00
13	15	3.00	25.00
14	19	3.80	28.80
15	24	4.80	33.60
16	18	3.60	37.20
17	33	6.60	43.80
18	28	5.60	49.40
19	39	7.80	57.20
20	24	4.80	62.00
21	22	4.40	66.40
22	19	3.80	70.20
23	22	4.40	74.60
24	14	2.80	77.40
25	21	4.20	81.60
26	20	4.00	85.60
27	16	3.20	88.80
28	16	3.20	92.00
29	12	2.40	94.40
30	16	3.20	97.60
31	8	1.60	99.20
32	3	0.60	99.80
35	1	0.20	100.00
Total	500	100.00	

[handwritten margin note: grouped frequency distribution]

have ses values within this range. Because the ses scale is constructed so that a lower score corresponds to a lower socioeconomic status, these students are the most socioeconomically disadvantaged in our sample.

Each ses category defines an interval of values in Table 2.3; the values are said to be grouped together. Accordingly, this type of frequency distribution is often referred to as a *grouped frequency distribution*.

Table 2.3. Grouped frequency distribution of socio-economic status (ses)

categories	Freq.	Percent	Cum.
0	10	2.00	2.00
5	44	8.80	10.80
10	90	18.00	28.80
15	142	28.40	57.20
20	101	20.20	77.40
25	85	17.00	94.40
30	27	5.40	99.80
35	1	0.20	100.00
Total	500	100.00	

MORE Stata: Grouped Frequency Distribution in tabular form

To obtain the grouped frequency distribution in Table 2.3, we use the **cut()** function in combination with the command **egen** to generate or create a new variable that contains the grouped frequencies at cut points 0 to 40 by increments of 5. We then use the **tabulate** command to display the values as a frequency distribution as follows:

at (0(5)40)

egen categories = cut(ses), at((5)40)
tabulate categories

In creating grouped frequency tables, in general, the following advice is offered. For variables that are at least ordinal and have many distinct values, grouped frequency tables should be created so that:

1. The number of categories is sufficiently small to reduce the data and make them more understandable, yet sufficiently large so as to retain much of the specific information contained in the data. Considering both clarity and retention of information, the number of categories typically is between 6 and 12 inclusive.
2. The categories are mutually exclusive and exhaustive (i.e., each piece of data must fall into one and only one category).
3. The categories are all of equal size so as to achieve a clear picture of the data.

Note that in Table 2.3 there are eight mutually exclusive and exhaustive categories defined by intervals of equal size, beginning, respectively, at the values 0, 5, 10, and so on.

☞ **Remark.** To uphold the principle that all categories should be mutually exclusive, we may consider the interval that begins with 5, for example, to include the values 5 up to just less than the value 10. The value 10 would be included in the next interval that begins with 10.

The grouped as opposed to the ungrouped frequency distribution often reflects more clearly the distribution's three major properties, its *level* (the magnitude of a "typical" value in the distribution), its *spread* (how far apart the values are from one another), and its *shape* (the extent to which the values of the distribution are balanced on either side of the typical value). The level of a distribution also may be viewed as a way of describing the *location* of the distribution relative to the entire set of values in the data set.

In Chapter 3 and later in this chapter we elaborate on these three properties and provide ways for characterizing them statistically.

STEM-AND-LEAF DISPLAYS

An alternative technique for describing data that are at least ordinal is the stem-and-leaf display. In this display, the digits of each data value are separated into two parts, called a stem and a leaf. For distributions of values between 0 and 100, the stem contains all but the units (rightmost) digit of each data value, and the leaf contains only the units (rightmost) digit. The stems are ordered numerically in a column from smallest to largest and the leaves are listed to the right of their associated stems, also in increasing order from left to right.

Our first example of a stem and leaf will relate to the *States* data set, which includes different educational measures of the 50 states. In this case, we will create a stem-and-leaf plot of pertak, a variable that gives, for each state, the percentage of high school seniors who took the SAT in that state in 2012. These data are from *The 2014 World Almanac and Book of Facts.*

MORE Stata: To obtain a stem-and-leaf display of pertak, for example

We type the following command in the Command Window and hit **Enter: stem pertak**

We may type **help stem** to learn more about this command and its options. We note that the sequence of points and clicks on the main menu bar needed to run this command is: **Statistics > Summaries, tables, and tests > Distributional plots and tests > Stem-and-leaf display**

Table 2.4 contains a stem-and-leaf display of the variable pertak.

This stem and leaf sorts the 50 values into eleven groupings. The first grouping includes the values from 0 to 9 only, the second grouping includes the values from 10 to 19, the third grouping includes the values from 20 to 29, and so on. We know this to be the case because each leaf value replaces the single asterisk that appears at the end of each stem value. The asterisk may be thought of as a placeholder for the units digit. Accordingly, the lowest value of 0*3 represents the number 03 or, more simply, 3. Likewise, the highest value of 10*0 represents the number 100, and so on. We see that there are three instances of 0*6 or 06 or, more simply, 6 indicating that three states have only 6 percent of their high school seniors taking the SAT tests.

Because of the relatively small size of this data set (50 cases), there is only one line per stem. The first line contains the leaves for those states whose stem is 0, that is, whose percentage of high school seniors taking the SAT is less than 10. By counting the occurrences in that

Table 2.4. Stem-and-leaf display of pertak

Stem-and-leaf plot for pertak
Percentage of Eligible Students Taking the SAT, 2012)

0*	3334444555556666789
1*	03779
2*	078
3*	
4*	9
5*	4578
6*	2668999
7*	234458
8*	1389
9*	03
10*	0

row, we see that there are 18 such states. The second line contains the leaves for those states whose stem is 1, that is, whose percentage of high school seniors taking the SAT is greater than or equal to 10, but less than 20. We see that there are 5 such states.

If we define the typical percentage of high school seniors who take the SAT per state as the most frequently occurring percentage of high school seniors who take the SAT per state, we may note that that value is 5 percent, according to the stem and leaf display. This is because the pertak value of 5 percent (appearing in row one of the display) occurs five times, more than any other percentage value in the distribution. Accordingly, using this definition of typical, we may say that the value 5 percent represents the level of the pertak distribution or its location relative to the entire set of pertak values in the distribution. Other, and perhaps better, ways of defining the level or location of a distribution are presented later in this chapter and in Chapter 3.

To determine how spread out the pertak values in this distribution are, we simply may compute the range of percentage values in this distribution, obtained by subtracting the lowest (or minimum) value from the highest (or maximum) value, or $100 - 3 = 97$. In this case, a range of 97 suggests a large spread given that as percentages, the values in this distribution can range only from 0 to 100. Again, other, and perhaps better, ways of defining the spread of a distribution of values are presented later in this chapter and in Chapter 3.

Finally, we may note that the percentage values in this distribution do not appear to be balanced around the typical percentage value of 5. By contrast, the distribution of pertak values separates into two clusters of states, one cluster having fewer than 30 percent of its students taking the SAT and the other cluster having 49 percent or more of its students taking the SAT. Describing the shape of a distribution will be discussed in greater detail later in this chapter and in Chapter 3.

Another stem and leaf display is presented to exemplify a situation in which the values of the distribution are not between 0 and 100. This example also comes from the *States* data set. In this case, we will create a stem-and-leaf plot of satm, a variable that gives, for each state, the average math SAT score of high school seniors in that state. Table 2.5 contains this stem and leaf plot.

In Table 2.5, as in Table 2.4, the stem represents the beginning digits of the values in the distribution and because there is only one asterisk at the end of each stem value, the leaf represents the units place. For example, 61*7 represents the value 617, the highest satm average of all 50 states. Exercise 2.31 gives an example of a stem and leaf display in which there are three asterisks at the end of each stem, serving as placeholders for the hundreds, tens, and units digits, respectively.

Table 2.5. Stem-and-leaf of satm

Average SAT Math in 2013 Stem-and-Leaf Plot

Stem-and-leaf plot for SATM (Average SAT Math in 2013)

```
45* | 79
46* | 67
47* |
48* | 77
49* | 0049
50* | 00114456
51* | 2249
52* | 023889
53* | 4
54* | 057
55* | 36
56* | 699
57* | 0
58* | 1348
59* | 55
60* | 11489
61* | 07
```

Table 2.6. Stem-and-leaf of display of ses

Stem-and-leaf plot for ses (Socio-Economic Status)

```
0*  │ 01
0t  │ 2233
0f  │ 44445
0s  │ 6666666666667777777
0.  │ 888888888888888999999999
1*  │ 000000000000000000111111111111111111111111
1t  │ 2222222222222222333333333333333
1f  │ 44444444444444444455555555555555555555555
1s  │ 6666666666666666667777777777777777777777777777777
1.  │ 8888888888888888888888888888899999999999999999999999999999999999999
2*  │ 000000000000000000000000111111111111111111111111
2t  │ 2222222222222222223333333333333333333333
2f  │ 44444444444444455555555555555555555555
2s  │ 66666666666666666666667777777777777777
2.  │ 8888888888888888999999999999999
3*  │ 0000000000000000011111111
3t  │ 222
3f  │ 5
```

With larger data sets, such as the *NELS*, the stem-and-leaf displays can be more complicated. To show this, Table 2.6 contains a stem-and-leaf display of the variable ses, representing the socioeconomic status of the 500 individuals in the *NELS* data set. Based on this display, we can see that the ses distribution ranges from 0 to 35.

Each stem in Table 2.6 occupies five lines to accommodate the many values in our large data set. Each of the five lines contains one-fifth, or two, of the possible leaf values per stem in the display. In our example, the top line of each stem contains the leaves 0 and 1, the second line contains the leaves 2 and 3, and so forth. Rather than asterisks alone, there are letters and other symbols after the numbers in the stem to refer more specifically to the numbers that are contained in the corresponding leaf; * = 0, t = 2, f = 4, s = 6, . = 8.

HISTOGRAMS

Another graphic for representing data that are at least ordinal is the *histogram*. Figure 2.5 illustrates the use of a histogram to represent ses data from our *NELS* data set. Along the horizontal axis of Figure 2.5 are the midpoints of the intervals whose frequencies are represented by the heights of the bars. The histogram differs from a bar chart in that no spaces appear between the bars unless categories with zero frequency occur. Eliminating the spaces between bars in a histogram makes the chart convey a feeling of continuity that reflects the ordinal nature of the variable. Bar charts, by contrast, include spaces between the bars to avoid the interpretation of a trend in the case of nominal-leveled data. The ordering of categories from nominal-leveled data would be arbitrary along the horizontal axis.

MORE Stata: To generate a histogram of ses, for example, with frequencies on the y-axis
We type the following in the Command Window and hit Enter: **histogram ses, frequency**
To learn more about this command and its options, we may type **help histogram**. We note that the sequence of points and clicks on the main menu bar needed to run this command is: **Graphics > Histogram**

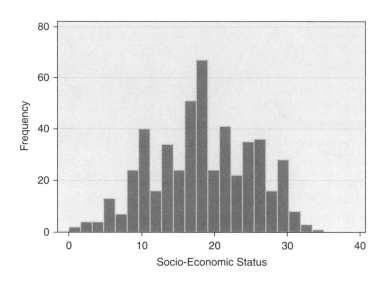

Figure 2.5   Default histogram of ses.

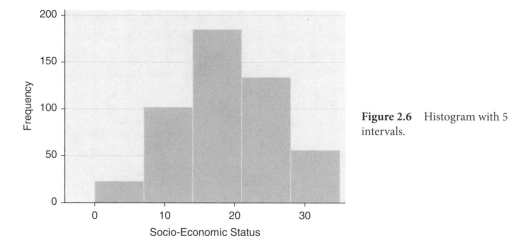

Figure 2.6   Histogram with 5 intervals.

We note that a histogram is affected by the number of bars (or bins) chosen. Figure 2.5 has 21 bins by default. This default value, creating Figure 2.5, appears to provide a good balance between summarizing the data and providing details about the distribution.

MORE Stata: To edit the number of bins of a histogram
  We type the following to obtain Figure 2.6 with 5 bins: **histogram ses, bin(5) frequency**
  To obtain Figure 2.7 with 30 bins, we type: **histogram ses, bin(30) frequency**

MORE Stata: To generate a histogram with percents on the y-axis to obtain Figure 2.8
  We type: **histogram ses, percent**.

The shape of the histogram in Figure 2.8 defined by percents is identical to that of the default histogram in Figure 2.5

Figure 2.7 Histogram with 30 intervals.

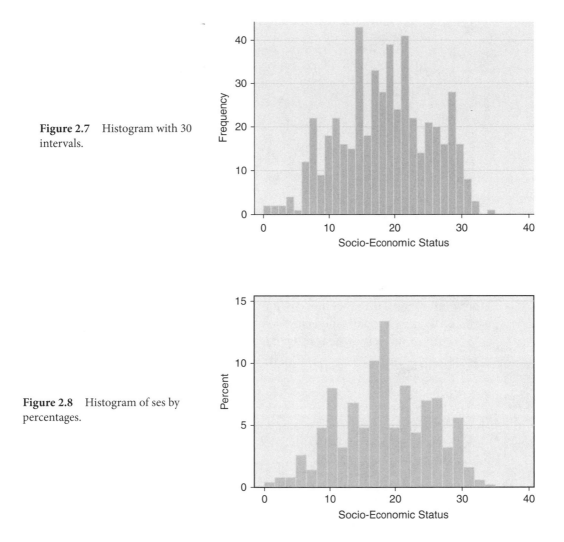

Figure 2.8 Histogram of ses by percentages.

A histogram differs from a stem-and-leaf display in that the latter uses the leaf values themselves to create the bars of the display. As a result, the stem-and-leaf display provides more information about the original set of data than the histogram.

LINE GRAPHS

Another type of graph that is often used to represent data that are at least ordinal is the *line graph* or *polygon*. Figure 2.9 illustrates a frequency polygon for our socioeconomic status variable from the *NELS* data set.

MORE Stata: To construct a line graph

The simplest way to do this is by recasting the histogram as a line graph with frequencies on the y-axis, and typing the following command:

twoway histogram ses, recast(line) lcolor(gs9) lwidth(medium) freq

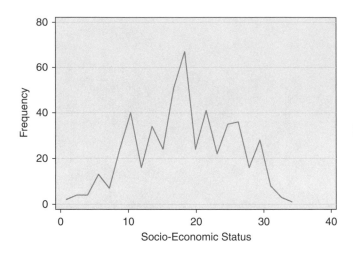

Figure 2.9   Line graph of ses.

The option **lcolor** sets the color of the line to gray scale 9 and the option **lwidth** sets the width of the line to medium as shown. To learn more about the histogram command and its options, we may type **help twoway histogram**.

For percents on the y-axis instead of frequencies, we type:

twoway histogram ses, recast(line) lcolor (gs9) lwidth(medium) percent

To obtain a smoothed version of the line graph we may type **kdensity ses, bwidth(.75)**

In the **kdensity** command, **bwidth** represents the bandwith (i.e., the width of the interval of ses values) used for obtaining the proportions. For more smoothing, we would use a larger bandwidth value (e.g., **bwidth(2)**).

As one would expect, the stem-and-leaf display, the histogram, the line graph, and kdensity graphs all bear a strong resemblance to each other in their depiction of ses frequencies. While, as noted, there may be some advantages of one type of display over another, the ultimate choice of which display to use belongs to the researcher.

Line graphs are often used when we are depicting two variables, and one represents time. An example is given in Figure 2.10 that is taken from the *Marijuana* data set. The figure shows, for the years 1987–2012, the percentage of high school seniors who said that they had ever used marijuana. These data are from *The 2014 World Almanac and Book of Facts*.

MORE Stata: To create the two-variable line graph of Figure 2.10

We type the following: **twoway line marij year**

To learn more about this command and its options, we may type **help twoway line**. We note that the sequence of points and clicks on the main menu bar needed to run this command is: **Graphics > Twoway graph (scatter, line, etc.)**

MORE Stata: Line options to customize the line pattern, width, and color

To customize Figure 2.10, we may make the line color blue, the line dashed, the line width medium, and also add a title to the graph itself, as follows:

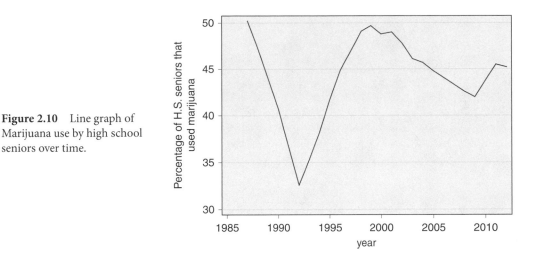

Figure 2.10 Line graph of Marijuana use by high school seniors over time.

twoway (line marij year, lcolor(blue) lpattern(dash) lwidth(medium)), title(Marijuana Usage by Year)

Notice that the options that relate to the line itself (**lcolor, lpattern, lwidth**) are placed within the first set of parentheses since these options are modifying the line to be drawn. The option **title**, relates to the entire twoway graphic and so it is placed outside those parentheses. For more information about the variety of line colors, patterns, and widths that may be chosen, type

help colorstyle; help linepatternstyle; and help linewidthstyle, respectively.

DESCRIBING THE SHAPE OF A DISTRIBUTION

A curve is said to be *symmetric* if, when folded from left to right along its vertical axis of symmetry (its middle), one-half of the curve overlaps the other. Two symmetric curves are shown in Figure 2.11 and differ because the graph on the left is single-peaked and the one on the right is double-peaked. In Chapter 3, we introduce other words to describe the shape of the curve based on its peaks. If, on the other hand, overlapping does not result, the curve is said to be *asymmetric*.

Another characteristic often used to describe the shape of a frequency or percent distribution graph is the *skewness*. For our purposes, the term skewness will refer to the distribution of the graph's area about its mean. For example, the histogram for self-concept in grade 12 (slfcnc12) from our *NELS* data set (Figure 2.12) is asymmetric. The bulk of its scores ranges from 25 to 45 and its tail is to the left of this bulk (or in a negative direction). That is, the bulk of the data consists of relatively high scores, yet there are a few relatively low scores. Accordingly, we say that these data are *skewed to the left,* or *skewed negatively*. Thus, most students in our sample have higher values of self-concept and only relatively few have lower values of self-concept.

If the graph looked like Figure 2.13 instead, with its tail to the right of the main bulk (or in a positive direction from the main bulk), we would say that the graph is *skewed to the right,* or *skewed positively*. The skewness of a graph is the direction in which its tail lies

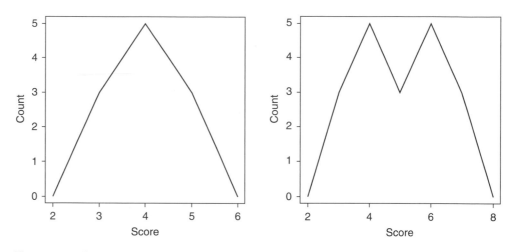

Figure 2.11   Symmetric curves.

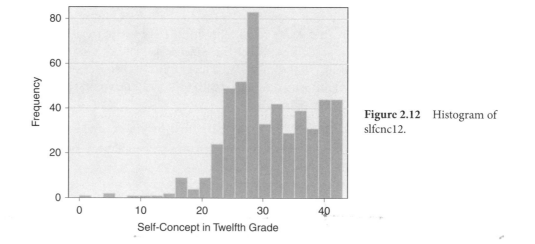

Figure 2.12   Histogram of slfcnc12.

relative to its main bulk. Figure 2.13 depicts for our sample the frequency distribution of responses to the question: "What annual income do you expect to have at the age of thirty?" Clearly, the bulk of students expect incomes less than or equal to $150,000 per year, while only a relative few expect incomes in excess of $150,000 and one student, in fact, expects an income of $1,000,000. Where would your response fit within this depiction, within the bulk of the responses, or in the tail?

☞ **Remark.** Extreme values, such as the $1,000,000 expected income, are called *outliers*. For reasons that will become clear in the next chapter, one of the key jobs of a data analyst is to learn how to identify and handle such outliers.

☞ **Remark.** Figure 2.13 is noticeably more skewed than Figure 2.12.

It is possible for a graph to be asymmetric without being noticeably skewed either to the left or to the right. In this case, we would simply say that the graph is asymmetric and leave it at that.

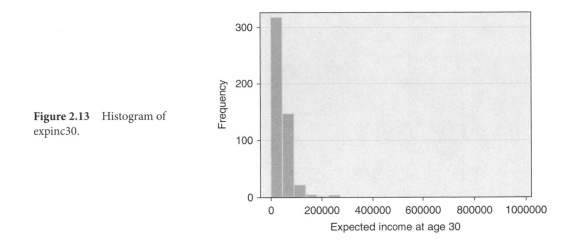

Figure 2.13 Histogram of expinc30.

ACCUMULATING DATA

When data are at least ordinal, the inherent ordering of the values allows us to accumulate the data in ways that make sense. We can look at the percentage (or number) of scores below a given score. For example, we can find the percentage of students in the *NELS* data set who have socioeconomic status ratings of 9 or lower. We can also look at the score below which a certain percentage of scores fall. For example, we can ask what is the socioeconomic status score below which 25 percent of the students in the *NELS* data set fall?

CUMULATIVE PERCENT DISTRIBUTIONS

Up to now, the vertical axis has represented either frequency or percent. There are other possibilities to be considered. Referring once again to the grouped frequency distribution of ses (Table 2.3), suppose we want to know at a glance the percent of students in our sample who have socioeconomic status ratings of 9 or lower. While we could sum the percents associated with the categories 0–3, 3–6, and 6–9, respectively, to obtain the sum 10.8 percent (1.2 percent, 3.4 percent, 6.2 percent), a more direct solution is available from the column labeled *Cumulative Percent* in Table 2.3. This column contains the cumulative percent distribution for SES and may be used to obtain the percent of students whose ses values fall *at or below* a certain point in the distribution.

Table 2.3 is useful in finding the cumulative percent of a value of 9, because 9 is the uppermost value of one of the categories, 6–9, contained in this table. Had we been interested in the cumulative percent of a value of 8, on the other hand, Table 2.3 would not have been useful because we do not know from this table how many of the 31 students with ses between 6 and 9 actually have an ses value at or below 8. By grouping the data into larger than unit intervals, we lose the specific information needed to answer this question exactly. Based on Table 2.3 alone, then, we do not know whether all, none, or some of the 31 students have ses values between 8 and 9 and should not be counted in answering this question. Because there is no way to determine the true situation from only the grouped distribution given in Table 2.3, to determine the percent of students with SES values at or below 8, for example, we make use of the ungrouped percent distribution found in Table 2.2. In so doing, we find that 9 percent of the students have SES values at or below 8 in this distribution.

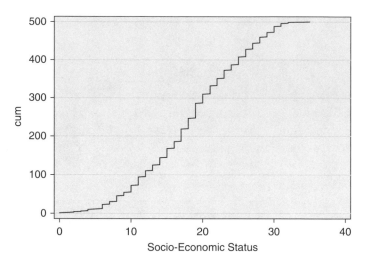

Figure 2.14 Cumulative percent distribution of SES.

OGIVE CURVES

A line graph representing a cumulative frequency or percent distribution is called an *ogive curve* (the g is pronounced as a j) or *S curve* because the curve often looks like an elongated S. Ogive curves are always nondecreasing, because they represent accumulated values. The graph of the cumulative percent SES distribution appears in Figure 2.14. As noted, the curve does take on the appearance of an elongated S.

MORE Stata: To obtain the Ogive of Figure 2.14

We first use the **cumul** command to generate a new variable, which we call cum, that contains the cumulative frequency distribution of ses. The word **capture** placed before cumul allows the execution of the **cumul** command to continue even if the variable cum already exists in our database. The option **freq** specifies that we want cum to contain cumulative frequencies as opposed to cumulative relative frequencies, which would be the default.

capture cumul ses, gen(cum) freq

Now that we have created the variable cum, we may plot the ogive by first sorting the values of cum from lowest to highest, using the command **sort cum** to ensure a one-to-one match between the cumulative frequencies of ses and the values of ses themselves. As one variable (cum) goes from lowest to highest, so does the other (ses). By placing cum before ses in the command **twoway line**, as shown below, Stata, by convention, will place cum on the y-axis and ses on the x-axis.

sort cum
twoway line cum ses

We could create a more customized ogive by using the following twoway line command instead:

twoway line cum ses, ytitle(cumulative frequency) title(Cumulative Frequency /// Distribution) subtitle(SES – NELS data)

This command produces a title for the y-axis and a title and subtitle for the graph overall.

MORE Stata: Options that apply to all two-way graphs – titles, labels, and legends

In addition to the default title provided by Stata, each graph can have a customized **title()** and **subtitle()** as shown in the previous command. These typically appear at the top of the graph. For additional graph documentation, we could add text at the bottom of the graph in the form of a **legend()**, **note()**, and **caption()**. To learn more about these options and about adding text to a graph, in general, we may type **help title_options**. And to learn more about how that text may appear (its font type and size, etc.), we may type **help graph text**.

☞ **Remark.** Like many continuous variables, ses is measured using a scale of integer values. Hence, anyone with ses greater than or equal to 24.5 but less than 25.5 will be recorded to have ses equal to 25. If the measure had been more precise, for example, if it had been recorded to two decimal places, the cumulative SES distribution would probably have been a straight line, because no two people would have had exactly the same ses.

PERCENTILE RANKS

The *percentile rank* of a given raw score is the percent of scores falling below that raw score in a specified distribution. As discussed previously, the cumulative percent of a given raw score is the percent of scores falling at or below that raw score in a specified distribution. The difference between these two statistics, that one reports the percent *below* a given raw score, whereas the other reports the percent *at or below* a given raw score, rests in the distinction between continuous and discrete variables. Technically the percentile rank is more appropriate for variables that are continuous, and the cumulative percent is more appropriate for variables that are discrete.

Because many discrete variables, however, like income, property value, and frequency data, share many of the properties of a continuous variable, the percentile rank and the cumulative percent, when applied to such variables, will provide similar results. Likewise, when applied to continuous variables, in practice, the cumulative percent and the percentile rank will provide similar results. Given their respective definitions, the cumulative percent value will, in general, be larger than the percentile rank. In this book, for simplicity, we shall not compute the exact values of percentile ranks; rather we shall estimate them using cumulative percents based on an ungrouped frequency distribution such as the one in Table 2.2.

EXAMPLE 2.1. Use the cumulative percent to estimate the percentile rank of an SES value of 13 for the sample of 500 students under study.

Solution. We obtain an estimate of the percentile rank of 13 by using the cumulative percent distribution in Table 2.2. We find that one-fourth (25 percent) of the students in our sample have SES scores equal to or below 13; so that an estimate of the percentile rank of an SES score of 13 is 25th.

As the example illustrates, the percentile rank makes raw score data more meaningful by allowing us to know the relative standing of a single score within a set of scores. From another viewpoint, knowing that your raw score on an exam is 90, for example, has little meaning, because the exam could have been out of 100 points or it could have been out of 500 points. Knowing that your percentile rank on an exam is 90, however, means that 90 percent of the people taking the exam received scores below yours.

Often, we seek to know an individual's raw score corresponding to a particular percentile rank. For example, suppose you were told that your percentile rank on an exam was 90, and you wanted to find your raw score. In so doing, you would be finding the 90th percentile, or that raw score corresponding to the 90th percentile rank (that raw score with 90 percent of the scores below it).

PERCENTILES

In general, a percentile is that theoretical raw score that would correspond to a given percentile rank in a specified distribution. From Example 2.1, for example, we know that approximately one-fourth of these students' SES values are below the value of 13; that the value of 13 is at the 25 percentile in the SES distribution. Just as the value of 13 has approximately one-fourth of the distribution below it, it also has approximately three-fourths (75 percent) of the distribution above it. Accordingly, the value of 13 may be said to divide the SES distribution into two groups of students: one group that contains 25 percent or 125 students, and the other group that contain 75 percent or 375 students.

☞ **Remark.** The percentile is often referred to as a centile and is denoted by the letter C. The 25th percentile, therefore, is denoted as C_{25}.

For a fuller understanding of what centiles represent in terms of an underlying distribution, we shall examine the set of centiles $C_1, C_2, C_3, \ldots, C_{99}$. These percentiles are the 99 theoretically possible raw scores that divide a distribution into 100 equal parts. That is, between any two consecutive centiles there will be 1 percent of all the scores in the distribution. For example, if, as in our SES distribution, there are 500 raw scores, then between any two consecutive centiles, there will be 1 percent of the 500 scores, or $(0.01)(500) = 5$ scores.

☞ **Remark.** C_{100} is not necessary because only 99 points are needed to divide a set of scores into 100 intervals with equal frequencies. The scores from C_{99} to the maximum value in the distribution define the 100th interval.

· ·

EXAMPLE 2.2. How many of the raw scores in a distribution made up of 500 raw scores will fall:

a. Between C_{40} and C_{41}
b. Between C_{40} and C_{50}
c. Below C_{25}
d. Below C_{10}

Solution.
a. Because C_{40} and C_{41} are consecutive percentiles, there will be 1% of the total number of scores in the distribution, or $(0.01)(500) = 5$ scores between them.
b. Because C_{40} and C_{50} differ by 10 percentiles $(50 - 40 = 10$ percentiles), there will be $(10)(1\%) = 10\%$ of the total number of scores in the distribution between them. This would be $(0.10)(500) = 50$ scores.

c. Because C_{25} is by definition the raw score having 25% of the total number of scores in the distribution below it, C_{25} would have $(0.25)(500) = 125$ scores below it. C_{25} is commonly referred to as the *1st quartile* and denoted by the symbol Q_1. C_{50} is commonly referred to as the *2nd quartile* and denoted by the symbol Q_2, and C_{75} is commonly referred to as the *3rd quartile* and denoted by the symbol Q_3. Therefore, $Q_1 = C_{25}$, $Q_2 = C_{50}$, and $Q_3 = C_{75}$. Because no reference is made to a 100th percentile, C_{100}, we likewise make no reference to a 4th quartile, Q_4.

d. Because C_{10} is by definition the raw score having 10% of the total number of scores in the distribution below it, C_{10} would have $(0.10)(500) = 50$ scores below it. C_{10} is commonly referred to as the *1st decile* and denoted by the symbol D_1. Similarly, C_{20} is commonly referred to as the *2nd decile* and denoted by the symbol D_2, and so on. Therefore, $D_1 = C_{10}$, $D_2 = C_{20}$, $D_3 = C_{30}$, $D_4 = C_{40}$, $D_5 = C_{50}$, $D_6 = C_{60}$, $D_7 = C_{70}$, $D_8 = C_{80}$, and $D_9 = C_{90}$. Because no reference is made to a 100th percentile, C_{100}, we likewise make no reference to a 10th decile, D_{10}.

☞ **Remark.** We will make most use of quartiles. Another way of thinking of quartiles is that Q_2 divides the entire distribution in half, Q_1 divides the bottom half in half, and Q_3 divides the top half in half.

☞ **Remark.** Like percentile ranks, percentiles are appropriately defined on distributions of continuous variables, and may be thought of as cut points that divide a distribution into a given number of groups of equal frequency. The set of three quartiles represents the three cut points that will divide a distribution into four groups of equal frequency; the set of nine deciles represents the nine cut points that will divide a distribution into ten groups of equal frequency, and so on. To divide a distribution into a given number of groups of equal frequency, each cut point or percentile, by definition, is a theoretically possible value, which may or may not be one of the actual values from the scale of measurement used to measure the variable. Because for most applications, however, estimates of percentiles suffice, Stata does not calculate percentiles exactly; it only estimates them. As a result, the groups defined by these estimated percentiles will not necessarily have equal frequencies, although their frequencies will be approximately equal.

☞ **Remark.** Be careful not to confuse the raw score with the percentile. For example, a person who gets a 75 percent on a test is probably not at the 75th percentile. For example, if 10 people took the test and 9 people get 100 percent and one person gets 75 percent, the percentile rank of the score of 75 percent is 0.

• •

EXAMPLE 2.3. Using Stata, find the three quartiles of the SES distribution – those values that divide the distribution into four (approximately) equal groups. Because there are 500 values in the SES distribution, each group should contain approximately 125 values. Use Table 2.2 to determine how many values are actually in each of the four groups.

Solution.

MORE Stata: To find the quartiles of the SES distribution, we may type either of the following commands in the Command Window and hit Enter after each one:

columns(variable)

tabstat ses, stats (n p25 p50 p75) ~~column~~(variable)
summarize ses, detail

Note: the option **column(variable)** in the **tabstat** command instructs Stata to present the results in a table with the variables organized as columns rather than as rows (inserting the word **row**, rather than column, would orient the table horizontally). The output given below is from the **tabstat** command with the option column(variable). To learn more about the **tabstat** command and its options, we may type **help tabstat**. To navigate using the main menu bar, we would use the following steps: **Statistics > Summaries, tables, and tests > Other tables > Compact table of summary statistics.** To learn more about the **summarize** command and its options, we may type **help summarize**. To navigate using the main menu bar, we would use the following steps: **Statistics > Summaries, tables, and tests > Summary and descriptive statistics > Summary statistics**

stats	ses
N	500
p25	13.5
p50	19
p75	24

The 25th, 50th, and 75th percentiles, corresponding to the first, second, and third quartiles, are given as 13.5, 19, and 24, respectively. If these percentiles were exact, then exactly 25 percent of the distribution (or 125 scores) would fall below 13.5, exactly 25 percent would fall between 13.25 and 19, exactly 25 percent would fall between 19 and 24, and, exactly 25 percent would fall at or above 24. But, these percentiles are not exact, and, as we shall see, the four groupings are only approximately equal to each other.

MORE Stata: Obtaining additional percentiles

If we want percentiles other than those given as part of the **tabstat** command, which only reports the percentiles p1, p5, p10, p25, p50, p75, p90, p95 and p99, or the quartiles, we use the **centile** command. For others, one should use centile as shown in this exercise. For example,

centile ses, c(20 40 60 80)

Gives the 20th 40th 60th and 80th percentile of ses

☞ **Remark.** By Stata convention, to determine how many scores fall between two percentiles, we include the frequency of the lower percentile, but not the frequency of the upper percentile.

Using Table 2.2 we find that 125 students (1+1+2+2+4+1+12+6+16+9+18+22+16+15) have ses ratings in the first quartile (below a score of 13.5), 122 students have ses ratings between the first and second quartiles (greater than or equal to 13.5 but less than 19), 126 students have ses ratings between the second and third quartiles (greater than or equal to 19 but less than 24), and finally, 127 students have ses ratings at or above a score of 24.

Notice that just as the three quartiles, as a set, divide the ses distribution into (approximately) equal quarters, the second quartile, labeled as the 50th percentile, divides the ses distribution into (approximately) equal halves. There are 247 scores below 19 and 253 scores at 19 or above. As such, the score of 19 is the middle score in the distribution, the score that locates the distribution's center.

Notice also that the middle 50 percent of the distribution is contained between the first and third quartiles, 13.5 and 24. Said differently, the middle 50 percent of this distribution lies between 13.5 and 24, and therefore, extends over 10.5 ses values (24 − 13.5). If the distribution were such that the value of 19 were again at its center, but the first and third quartiles were at 8 and 29, respectively, then the middle 50 percent of this distribution would extend over 21 ses values (29 − 8). We would say, in this case, that relative to the first distribution, the second distribution has a greater spread about its center, or a greater *interquartile range(IQR)* or *midspread.* We could say, equivalently, that the second distribution is less densely concentrated about its middle than the first distribution.

As this example illustrates, a lot can be learned about the location (level), shape, and form of a distribution by finding the quartiles of that distribution. The second quartile tells us something about its location, and the first and third quartiles tell us something about its spread. With the addition of two more points, the distribution's lowest value, its *minimum*, and its highest value, its *maximum*, a more complete picture may be obtained.

FIVE-NUMBER SUMMARIES AND BOXPLOTS

A five-number summary of a distribution includes the three quartiles, Q_1, Q_2, and Q_3 as well as the minimum and maximum values. While the three quartiles summarize distributional characteristics about the center, the minimum and maximum characterize the tails of the distribution. We may obtain the five-number summary from a cumulative percent distribution (e.g., Table 2.2), or from a stem-and-leaf display (e.g., Table 2.4), or more directly, by using either of the following two commands.

MORE Stata: To find the five-number summary of the ses distribution, for example. We may type either of the following two commands in the Command Window:

tabstat ses, statistics(count min max p50 p75 p25) column(variable)
summarize ses, detail

Using the **tabstat** command, we obtain Table 2.7.

From this five-number summary, we know that the ses distribution extends from a minimum value of zero to a maximum value of 35, with its center at 19 and its center bulk of 50 percent situated over the interval 13.5 to 24.

A graphical representation of the five-number summary is given by a *boxplot,* also called a *box-and-whiskers plot*. Figure 2.15 is a boxplot for our SES data. The box depicts the middle 50 percent of the distribution, which ranges from $Q_1 = 13.5$ to $Q_3 = 24$. The middle line in the

Table 2.7. Five-number summary for ses

stats	ses
N	500
min	0
max	35
p25	13.5
p50	19
p75	24

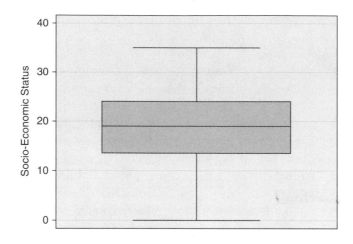

Figure 2.15   Boxplot of ses.

box represents Q_2, the middle score of the distribution, which is equal to 19. The whiskers extend out from the box on both ends. From the end representing lower values, the whisker extends to the minimum value of 0 and from the end representing higher values, it extends to the maximum value of 35. The advantage of a boxplot is that it provides in one graphic information about the level (location), spread, and shape of a distribution.

The 50th percentile, or middle score, is another way of defining the typical score for the distribution. In this case, we see that the typical SES value in the NELS data set is 19. There are two measures of spread easily obtained from the boxplot. The first, the range, is, as noted earlier, the maximum value minus the minimum value, or in this case, 35 − 0 = 35. The range is often not the best measure of spread because it is based on only two values and they are the two most extreme or unusual values in the distribution. A better measure is the range of the middle 50 percent of the data, called the *interquartile* range. The interquartile range is the box height or $Q_3 − Q_1$. In this case, we have 24–13.5 or 10.5. In terms of the shape, notice in this representation, that the distance from Q_3 to Q_2 approximately equals the distance from Q_2 to Q_1, and that the whiskers are of about equal length, suggesting that this distribution is reasonably symmetric, as we know it to be.

MORE Stata: To obtain a box-plot for ses, for example

We type the following in the Command Window; **graph box ses**

To learn more about this command, we may type **help graph box**. To navigate using the main menu bar, we would follow the sequence: **Graphics > Box plot**

In comparing the boxplot to either the stem-and-leaf display (Table 2.4) or the histogram (Figure 2.6) of these data, we observe, that with only five numbers, the boxplot captures well the important features of this distribution. Characterizations that summarize data well with only a small number of values are called *parsimonious*. As you will learn, one of the goals of statistics is parsimony.

It is instructive to examine the boxplots for both self-concept in twelfth grade and expected income at age 30 that appear in Figures 2.16 and 2.17, respectively, and to

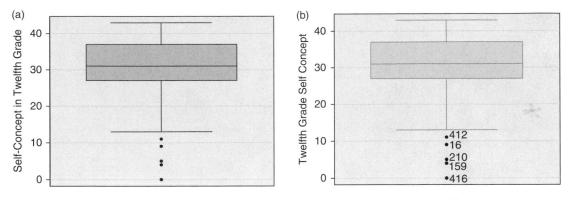

Figure 2.16   (a) Boxplot of slfcnc12. (b) Boxplot of slfcnc12 with outliers identified by id.

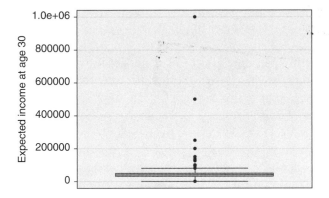

Figure 2.17   Boxplot of expinc30.

compare these boxplots to the corresponding histograms of these variables that appear in Figures 2.12 and 2.13.

In Stata, we notice that in Figures 2.16 (a) and 2.17 extreme values in the boxplots are provided. We may modify the instructions for creating a boxplot to identify the extremes by a variable such as id. Such a modified boxplot is reproduced as Figure 2.16 (b).

MORE Stata: To create a boxplot for which outliers are identified by a variable

In this example, we use the variable id to identify the outliers in the example with slfcnc12.

We type the following:

graph box slfcnc12, marker(1, mlabel(id))

Note: The option **marker(1, mlabel(id))** instructs Stata to label each outlier with its identification number. If you would prefer to label the outliers by some variable other than id, simply replace the variable name id with the name of that other variable. The number 1 tells Stata that the labelling should be applied to the first (and, in this case, only) variable (namely, slfcnc12) graphed in the command.

If we included another variable in this graph with the same metric (e.g., slfcnc08), and wanted to label the extreme values for both variables, we would add a second **marker** option and type:

✳ **graph box slfcnc12 slfcnc08, marker(1, mlabel(id)) marker(2, mlabel(id))**

Notice first, that like the boxplot of ses, depicted in Figure 2.15, the boxplots of self-concept and expected income capture the essential features of their corresponding histograms. By looking at these boxplots alone, we should have no problem visualizing the complete distributions of these variables. In Figure 2.16, the several outliers, or extreme values, at the bottom of the plot (the lower tail of the distribution), suggest negative skewness. Add to that the fact that the distance between the end of the top whisker and Q_2 is smaller than the distance between the end of the bottom whisker and Q_2, that is, that the bulk of the distribution of self-concept is relatively high, we have a rather full picture of the shape of the distribution of this variable.

There are four ways that the boxplot can indicate skewness of the distribution, listed from least serious, to most serious skew. First, the middle line, or 50th percentile, can be unevenly spaced within the box. Second, the box can be unevenly spaced between the whiskers. Third, there are asymmetric outliers, that is, points that lie beyond the whiskers on one side of the distribution, indicated by a circle on the boxplot.

Expected income at age 30 is more extremely skewed than self-concept. The greater concentration of values between 0 and 150,000 coupled with the larger number of more extreme outliers, located in the more positive direction, characterize this distribution as highly positively skewed. In fact, case number 102 is highly optimistic. He (this person actually is male) expects to earn $1 million! Exercise 2.23 asks you to determine this individual's self-concept relative to the sample. Once again, we may notice that this boxplot summarizes well the histogram depicted in Figure 2.13.

The skew of the distributions of expected incomes (Figure 2.17) is considered to be more extreme than the skew of the distributions of self-concept (Figure 2.16), because there are more outliers on one side of the graph and they are further away from the bulk of the scores in terms of *IQR* units.

☞ **Remark.** To allow the full range of values to be displayed in the boxplot of Figure 2.17, the vertical scale must extend from the minimum of 0 to the maximum of 1,000,000, thanks to our optimist. Because of the presence of outliers, in this case, the bulk of the distribution, as depicted by the box, appears to be quite compact relative to the full range. To alleviate the influence of outliers on the graph, we may delete these cases from consideration, or we may change the scale of measurement from dollars to some other unit that preserves the ordinality of these data. Ordinality is an essential feature of these data, which makes the boxplot meaningful. Changing from one scale of measurement to another is called *transforming* or *re-expressing* the data. More will be said about this in Chapter 4.

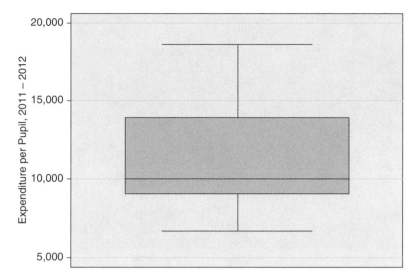

Figure 2.18   Boxplot of educexpe.

☞ **Remark.** A distribution can be skewed even though no outliers are present, when the box is not centered between the whiskers or when the middle line is unevenly spaced within the box. In such cases, skewness tends not to be severe. We illustrate in Figure 2.18 with the variable educational expenditure per pupil, educexpe, from the *States* data, which gives the average educational expenditure per pupil by state. Educexpe is positively skewed.

• •

EXAMPLE 2.4. Use Stata to construct four side-by-side boxplots based on the *States* data set showing the states' average educational expenditure per pupil by region. Use the graph to determine (1) whether there are differences in the level of educational expenditures by region, (2) whether there are differences in the spread of the educational expenditures by region, and (3) whether there are differences in the shape of the educational expenditures by region.

Solution.

MORE Stata: To obtain a single graphic that contains the boxplots of the educational expenditure by region, for example:
    We type the following:

graph box educexpe, over(region) marker(1, mlabel(state))

The result is the following set of boxplots with extreme values labelled by state:

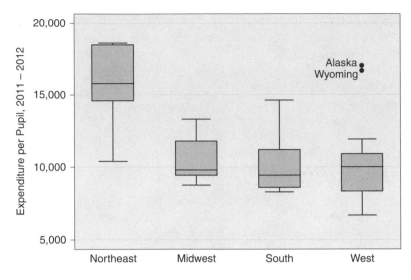

1. According to the heights of the 50th percentiles for the four regions, the Northeast has the highest overall level of educational expenditures per pupil, followed by the West, the Midwest, and the South.

2. According to the interquartile ranges, the educational expenditures are most spread out in the Northeast, followed by the West, the South, and the Midwest.

3. The distributions of educational expenditures are skewed in all regions. They are probably most skewed in the West because there are outliers that represent unusually high expenditures. In the Northeast the distribution is negatively skewed because the bottom whisker is longer than the top one. In the Midwest and South the distributions are positively skewed because the top whisker is longer.

☞ **Remark.** Both the stem-and-leaf display and the boxplot are inventions of John Tukey (1915–2000), which he described, along with other such novel and ingenious methods of data analysis, in his highly influential work *Exploratory Data Analysis* (1977). In this book, and elsewhere, Tukey promoted a very practical approach to data analysis, one that emphasizes an examination of the data themselves, rather than prior assumptions about the data, as the starting point for choosing an appropriate data analytic model. Because of his creative genius and versatility, demonstrated over a long and active career in statistics, Salsburg (2001) quite appropriately calls him "the Picasso of Statistics" (pp. 229–236).

MODIFYING THE APPEARANCE OF GRAPHS

In addition to typing additional options in the command line, we can edit the appearance of graphs and plots to customize its font, color, and overall appearance by using Stata's Graph Editor. When the graph appears as its own window, click File → Start Graph Editor. The functions included in this editor allow us to change the fonts, colors, and appearance of our graphs.

SUMMARY OF GRAPHICAL SELECTION

You should know how to create each of the displays in this chapter and under what circumstances it is appropriate to use each of them.

If your variable is nominal or ordinal with only few categories, a frequency distribution table, bar graph, or pie graph (given that set of categories is exhaustive) are all appropriate methods for summarizing the data.

If your variable is ordinal with many categories or it is a scale variable, a frequency distribution table (unless there are too many values and the table becomes unwieldy), a stem and leaf plot, histogram, line graph, or boxplot are all appropriate methods for summarizing the data.

SUMMARY OF STATA COMMANDS IN CHAPTER 2

These are the command lines used to generate the tables and graphs in Chapter 2 and for some of the exercises. In Chapter 4, we will introduce Do-files, which provide another way to summarize all of the commands from each chapter. Once you learn about Do-files, you should access a complete listing of all Stata commands associated with this chapter in the Do-file for Chapter 2 located on the text website.

COMMANDS FOR FREQUENCY AND PERCENT DISTRIBUTION TABLES

Create	Command Lines
Frequency and percent distribution tables of region (Table 2.1)	**tabulate region**
Frequency and percent distribution tables of both ses and region	**tab1 ses region**
– Grouped frequency distribution for ses (Table 2.3)	**egen categories = cut(ses), at(0(5)40)** **tabulate categories**

BAR AND PIE GRAPHS

Create	Command Lines
Bar chart of region by counts (Figure 2.1)	**graph bar (count), over(region) ytitle("frequency")**
Bar chart of gender with bars labeled by counts (Exercise 2.4)	**graph bar (count) id, over(gender) blabel(total)**
Bar chart of region by percents (Figure 2.2)	**graph bar (percent), over(region)**
Bar graph with bars in height order with the shortest first	**graph bar (percent), over(region, sort(1)) ytitle("percent")**
Bar graph with bars in height order with the tallest first	**graph bar (percent), over(region, sort(1) descending) ytitle("percent")**
Bar graph with bars oriented horizontally	**graph hbar (count), over(region) ytitle("frequency")**
Grouped bar graph with bars labeled with counts (Exercise 2.5)	**graph bar (count), over(alcbinge) over(gender) blabel(total) ytitle("alcbinge frequency")**

Create	Command Lines
Bar chart with bars ordered (Exercise 2.6)	**graph bar amstat, over(statistician, sort(1))**
Bar chart based on the values of individual cases for amstat by statistician (Exercise 2.6)	**graph bar amstat, over(statistician)**
Pie chart of region (Figure 2.3)	**graph pie, over(region)**
To add labels to each slice in a pie chart (Exercise 2.7)	**graph pie, over(urban) plabel(_all sum)**
	OR
	graph pie, over(urban) plabel(_all percent)

STEM AND LEAF DISPLAYS

Create	Command Lines
Stem-and-leaf of pertak (Table 2.4)	**stem pertak**
Stem and leaf plots separately for a grouping variable (Exercise 2.13)	**by sex, sort: stem sysbp1**

HISTOGRAMS

Create	Command Lines
Histogram of ses (Figure 2.5)	**histogram ses, frequency**
Edit the scale of the horizontal axis of a histogram of ses (Figures 2.6 and 2.7)	**histogram ses, bin(5) frequency** for Figure 2.6
	histogram ses, bin(30) frequency for Figure 2.7
Histogram with percents represented by the vertical axis (Figure 2.8)	**histogram ses, percent**
Histogram of ses by computer (Exercise 2.15)	**histogram ses, by(computer)**

LINE GRAPHS

Create	Command Lines
Line graph of counts of ses (Figure 2.9)	**twoway histogram ses, recast(line) lcolor(gs9) lwidth(medthick) freq**
Line graph of percentages	**twoway histogram ses, recast(line) lcolor (gs9) lwidth(medthick) percent**
Smoothed line graph	**kdensity ses, bwidth(.75)**
Line graph of marij by year (Figure 2.10)	**twoway line marij year**
Ogive graph of ses (Figure 2.14)	**capture cumul ses, gen(cum) freq**
	sort cum
	twoway line cum ses

PERCENTILES

Create	Command Lines
Quartiles of ses (Example 2.3)	**tabstat ses, stats (n p25 p50 p75) column (variable)**
	OR
	summarize ses, detail
Five-number summary of ses (Table 2.7)	**tabstat ses, statistics(count min max p50 p75 p25) columns(variables)**
	OR
	summarize ses, detail
Other percentiles	**centile ses, c(20 40 60 80)**

BOXPLOTS

Create	Command Lines
Boxplot of ses (Figure 2.15)	**graph box ses**
Boxplot of slfcnc12 with outliers labeled by id (Figure 2.16 (b))	**graph box slfcnc12, marker(1, mlabel(id))**
Boxplot of two variables with outliers labeled by id for each	**graph box slfcnc12 slfcnc08, marker(1, mlabel(id)) marker(2, mlabel(id))**
Boxplots of educexpe by region (Example 2.4)	**graph box educexpe, over(region) marker(1, mlabel(state))**
Boxplots of educexpe by region in two separate panels	**graph box educexpe, by(region) marker(1, mlabel(state))**
To obtain a boxplot for slfcnc08, slfcnc10, and slfcnc12 (Exercise 2.24)	**graph box slfcnc08 slfcnc10 slfcnc12**
To obtain a boxplot for slfcnc08, slfcnc10, and slfcnc12 separated by gender (Exercise 2.27)	**graph box slfcnc08 slfcnc10 slfcnc12, over(gender)**

EXERCISES

Exercises 2.1 through 2.3 involve questions about frequency and percent distribution tables of variables in the NELS data set.

2.1. Create a frequency distribution table of the variable absent12, which gives the number of times a student was absent in twelfth grade. Use the frequency distribution to answer the following questions.

    a) How many students in the *NELS* data set were absent 3–6 times in twelfth grade?

    b) How many students in the *NELS* data set were absent exactly 3 times in twelfth grade?

    c) What percentage of students in the *NELS* data set was absent 3–6 times in twelfth grade?

    d) What percentage of students in the *NELS* data set was absent 6 or fewer times in twelfth grade?

    e) How would you describe the shape of the distribution of absences in twelfth grade – positively skewed, negatively skewed, or reasonably symmetric? Explain.

2.2. Create a frequency distribution table of the variable parmarl8, which gives the marital status of the parents when the student was in eighth grade. Use it and the Data Editor window to answer the following questions.

    a) What does a score of 3 indicate on the variable parmarl8?

    b) For how many students in the *NELS* data set was parmarl8= 3?

    c) For what percent of students was parmarl8 = 3?

    d) What is the most frequently occurring marital status for parents of students in the *NELS*?

2.3. Create a frequency distribution table of the variable famsize, which represents the number of people in a student's household when the student was in eighth grade. Use the frequency distribution table to answer the following questions.

    a) What was the greatest number of people in a household for all the students in the *NELS* data set?

    b) How many students lived in households with only three members?

    c) How many students lived in households with at most three members?

    d) What percentage of the students lived in households with only three members?

    e) What percentage of the students lived in households with at most three members?

    f) Estimate Q_2 for famsize.

Exercises 2.4 through 2.5 involve questions about bar graphs of variables in the NELS data set. Exercise 2.6 involves questions about bar graphs of variables in the Statisticians data set.

2.4. Create a bar chart summarizing the variable gender. Use it to answer the following questions.

In order to get the bars labeled with the counts, use the following command: **graph bar (count) id, over(gender) blabel(total)**

    a) Why is a bar chart an appropriate display in this case?

    b) Are there more males or females in the *NELS*?

    c) According to the graph, approximately what percentage of students is female?

    d) Would a pie chart be appropriate to depict these data?

2.5. In this exercise, we will make a bar graph clustered by males and females of the variable, ALCBINGE, which indicates whether a student has ever binged on alcohol.

To create a percent bar chart by a grouping variable with the bars labeled with counts, type the command:

graph bar (count), over(alcbinge) over(gender) blabel(total) ytitle("alcbinge frequency")

a) What percentage of males in the *NELS* data set has ever binged on alcohol?

b) Which gender, males or females, has more of a tendency to have ever binged on alcohol?

c) If we reverse the order of the variable in the "over" commands, what is the effect on the graph? That is, how does the graph generated using the Stata command **graph bar (count), over(gender) over(alcbinge) blabel(total) ytitle("alcbinge frequency")** differ from the one we first generated in this exercise?

2.6. Create a bar chart for average daily school attendance rate given by the variable schattrt in the *NELS* data set. Use the bar chart to answer the following questions.

a) What appears to be problematic with the way in which the values are set along the x-axis of the bar chart?

b) What is a type of graph that could be selected to display schattrt that does not have that problem?

c) What is the shape of the distribution of schattrt?

2.7. This exercise is based on the *Statisticians* data set created in Exercise 1.15.

a) Create a bar chart indicating the number of recent citations for each of the statisticians.

Type in the Command Window: **graph bar (asis) amstat, over(statistician)**.

(Note: to change the labels on the x-axis so that they are more legible, right click on the bar chart that has been created and click **Start Graph Editor**. Then right click on the x-axis and select **axis properties**. Click on **label properties** and change the angle to **45 degrees**. Click **OK** and then **OK** once again.

---

b) How did Stata determine the ordering of categories along the *x*-axis?

c) Use the bar chart to approximate the number of citations of Ronald A. Fisher.

d) Construct a new bar graph with statisticians ordered on the x-axis according to their respective number of citations.

Type in the Command Window: **graph bar amstat, over(statistician, sort(amstat))**.

The graph will now show statisticians in ascending order by their respective number of recent AMSTAT citations.

---

e) What is a useful feature of this ordered graph?

f) Of the twelve statisticians, where in the ranking (from the top) is Ronald A. Fisher?

g) The bar graphs constructed in parts a) and d) of this exercise depict the number of recent citations considered individually for each statistician listed separately. Construct a different type of graphic that depicts the shape, location, and spread of the number of recent citations considered collectively across all twelve statisticians.

h) Describe the shape of this distribution. Where does the center of this distribution appear to be located and what is its spread, from the minimum to the maximum value?

Exercise 2.8 involves questions about a pie chart of a variable in the NELS data set.

2.8. Construct a pie chart of the variable urban, which indicates whether in eighth grade the student lived in an urban, suburban, or rural area in the United States.
   a) Edit the graph so the slices are labeled by counts (sums) and by percents.

Type in the Command Window **graph pie, over(urban) plabel(_all sum)** or **graph pie, over(urban) plabel(_all percent)**.

---

   b) How many students come from an urban area? What percentage of students comes from an urban area?
   c) Use Stata to construct the associated bar chart.
   d) Compare the two charts. Which do you prefer? Why?
   e) What have you learned about the distribution of students in this sample across urban, suburban, and rural areas?

Exercises 2.9 through 2.13 involve questions about stem-and-leaf graphs of variables from different data sets.

2.9. Create a stem-and-leaf of the variable mathcomp from the *learndis* data set. Use it to answer the following questions.
   a) What is another type of graph that could be used to depict these data?
   b) What is the total number of scores in this distribution?
   c) How many scores are in the seventies?
   d) Are there any outliers (i.e., extreme values) in this distribution?
   e) How would you describe the shape of this distribution? Explain.
   f) What is the 50th percentile?
   g) What is/are the most frequently occurring score(s) in this distribution? How many times does it/do they occur?
   h) What is the highest score in this distribution?
   i) Can we use this stem-and-leaf to obtain the original set of values for this variable?

2.10. Create a stem-and-leaf of the variable birth from the *Statisticians* data set that you entered in Exercise 1.15. Use it to answer the following questions.
   a) How many people in the data set were born in 1900?
   b) Are there any outliers (i.e., extreme values) in this distribution?
   c) How would you describe the shape of this distribution? Explain.
   d) What is/are the most frequently occurring score(s) in this distribution? How many times does it/do they occur?
   e) What is the highest score in this distribution?
   f) Can we use this stem-and-leaf to obtain the original set of values for this variable?

2.11. Create a stem-and-leaf of the variable total cholesterol, given by the variable totchol1 found in the *Framingham* data set. Use it to answer the following questions.
   a) What is the lowest score in this distribution?
   b) Are there any outliers (i.e., extreme values) in this distribution? Describe them.
   c) How would you describe the shape of this distribution? Explain.

    d) What is the 50th percentile of these data?

    e) What is the highest score in this distribution?

    f) Can we use this stem-and-leaf to obtain the complete set of original values for this variable?

2.12. Create a stem-and-leaf of eighth grade math achievement scores given by the variable achmat08 in the *NELS* data set. Use the stem-and-leaf to answer the following questions.

    a) According to the stem-and-leaf plot, what is the lowest eighth grade math achievement score?

    b) According to the stem-and-leaf graph, approximately how many students received the lowest eighth grade math achievement score?

    c) According to the stem-and-leaf plot, are there any outliers (extreme values) in this distribution?

    d) According to the stem-and-leaf plot, how would you characterize the shape of this distribution – negatively skewed, approximately symmetric, or positively skewed?

    e) According to the stem-and-leaf plot, which eighth grade math achievement score occurs most often?

    f) What type of question is better answered with a stem-and-leaf and what type of question is better answered by a frequency distribution table?

2.13. Follow the instructions to create separate stem-and-leaf graphs of sysbp1 (systolic blood pressure) for men and women (sex) using the *Framingham* data set.

Type in the Command Window the following syntax.

by sex, sort: stem sysbp1

    a) In which distribution (male or female) do we find the lowest systolic blood pressure value? Explain.

    b) In which distribution is the most frequently occurring systolic blood pressure value higher? Explain.

    c) In which, if either, distribution does systolic blood pressure have a greater spread? Explain.

    d) In which, if either, distribution is systolic blood pressure more skewed? Explain.

Exercises 2.14 through 2.15 involve questions about histograms of variables in the NELS data set.

2.14. Create a histogram of the twelfth grade math achievement given by the variable achmat12 in the *NELS* data set. Use the histogram to answer the following questions.

    a) According to the histogram, what is the smallest twelfth grade math achievement score in the *NELS* data set? Approximately how many times does that score occur?

    b) According to the histogram, what is the most frequently occurring twelfth grade math achievement score interval?

    c) According to the histogram, what is the shape of the distribution? Explain.

2.15. Follow the instructions to create two side-by-side histograms for socioeconomic status, given by the variable ses in the *NELS* data set. Let one histogram represent those did not own a computer in eighth grade and the other represent histogram represent those who did own a computer in eighth grade (computer). Use it to answer the following questions.

To create histograms of ses by computer, type in the Command Window the following syntax:

histogram ses, by(computer)

---

    a) Which computer group has the single highest ses score?
    b) Would you say that ses is higher for the group that owns a computer? Why or why not?
    c) Do the ses values have more spread for one group over another?

2.16. Create two histograms, one for a student's self-concept in eighth grade as given by the variable clfcnc08 in the *NELS* data set and the other for a student's self-concept in twelfth grade as given by the variable slfcnc12 in the *NELS* data set. Edit the histograms so that they each have the same scale and range of values on both the horizontal and vertical axes, and use them to answer the following questions.
    a) For which grade (eighth or twelfth) is the overall level of self-concept higher?
    b) For which grade is the spread of self-concept scores less?
    c) For which grade is self-concept more skewed, and in which direction?

Exercises 2.17 through 2.19 involve questions about line graphs of variables in the NELS data set.

2.17. Create a line graph for average daily attendance rate per school as given by the variable schattrt in the *NELS* data set. According to the line graph, is schattrt negatively skewed? Explain.

2.18. Create an ogive or cumulative line graph for the distribution of schattrt. Use it to answer the following questions.
    a) Approximately how many students attend schools where the average daily attendance rate is less than 90 percent?
    b) Based on the ogive or cumulative line graph, would you describe the distribution as positively skewed, negatively skewed, or symmetric?

2.19. In this exercise we will see that the interpretation of a line graph can change with a change in the scale of the vertical and horizontal axes.
    a) Use the *Marijuana* data set and Stata to construct a line graph depicting the percentage of students who have ever tried marijuana by year.
    b) Use the following instructions to compress the scale on the vertical axis.

Right click on the graph and select Start Graph Editor. Double click on any value on the vertical axis to bring up the **Axis Properties** box. Click Range/Delta and type the value **0** for the minimum, **60** for the maximum, and **10** for the delta. Click **OK**.

What is the effect of this change on the interpretation of the graph?

c) Use the following instructions to restrict the range of values on the horizontal axis to 1992 through 1999 in the uncompressed graph. Provide an interpretation of the graph.

To limit the graph to show only the years 1992 through 1999 type in the Command Window:

twoway (line marij year if year >= 1992 & year <= 1999).

Exercises 2.20 through 2.22 involve questions percentiles and percentile ranks of variables in the NELS data set. In these exercises, we use the cumulative percent to estimate the percentile rank.

2.20. Find the following values for a student's expected income at age 30 given by the variable expinc30 in the *NELS* data set.
   a) What is the exact value of the 15th percentile, according to Stata?
   b) What is the exact value of the 50th percentile, according to Stata?
   c) What is the approximate percentile rank of an expected income of $50,000?

2.21. Why is the calculation of percentiles not appropriate for the variable parmarl8?

2.22. This question relates to the optimist who is expecting to earn $1,000,000 per year at age 30 (expinc30 = 1,000,000).
   a) What is this student's ID?
   b) What was this student's eighth grade self-concept score (slfcnc08)?
   c) What is the percentile rank of his eighth grade self-concept score? Is it what you expected?
   d) Use percentile ranks to determine the grade (eighth, tenth, or twelfth) in which this student was least self-confident relative to his peers.

Exercise 2.23 deals with questions about a boxplot of a single variable from the NELS data set.

2.23. Create a boxplot that shows the number of times a student in twelfth grade was recorded late for school as given by the variable late12. Note that the level of measurement of late12 is ordinal. Use the boxplot and the scoring information in the data set to answer the following questions.
   a) Estimate and interpret the value of the 50th percentile for late12, represented by the line in the middle of the box.
   b) Estimate the *IQR* of this distribution.
   c) What is the shape of this distribution? Explain by referring to the boxplot.
   d) What is the significance of the fact that the graph has no bottom whisker?

Exercise 2.24 deals with questions about boxplots of more than one ordinal or scale variable constructed on the same axes.

2.24. Create one graph that has three boxplots, one for each of the distributions of self-concept scores for eighth, tenth, and twelfth grades, respectively. Use this graph to answer the following questions.

To obtain a boxplot for slfcnc08, slfcnc10, and slfcnc12, type in the Command window:

graph box slfcnc08 slfcnc10 slfcnc12.

---

a) How would you describe the shape of the distribution of self-concept in eighth grade?
b) For which grade is the self-concept distribution most nearly symmetric?
c) Overall, which of the three grades has the highest level of self-concept?
d) Which of the three grades contains the highest single self-concept score? And, what is your estimate of that score?
e) Based on the interquartile range, which distribution appears to have the highest spread?

Exercises 2.25 through 2.26 involve boxplots of a single variable for different sub-groups.

2.25. Create four boxplots on the same axis, one for each region, that plots the number of years of math taken in high school as given by the variable unitmath of the *NELS* data set. Use the graph to answer the following questions.

To create a boxplot of unitmath by region, type in the Command Window:

graph box unitmath, over(region)

---

a) Which region is most symmetric with respect to the distribution of units (years) of math taken in high school?
b) In which of the four regions is the overall level of unitmath lowest?
c) Which of the four regions contains the student with the single lowest number of units of math taken in high school? And, what is that number?
d) In which region, if any, is the spread of unitmath smallest?
e) How many of the 106 students in the Northeast have unitmath scores between Q_1 and Q_2? Is this number confined to unitmath scores or does it generalize to all variables in this data set?

2.26. Construct four side-by-side boxplots of the number of AP classes offered at a student's school (apoffer), one for each of the four types of high school programs (hsprog) represented in the *NELS* data set.
a) How might one explain that there are academic program schools that offer many AP courses, but not any rigorous academic program schools that offer more than 20?
b) What would be a better way to represent AP courses offerings other than by their number per school?

Exercise 2.27 involves boxplots of more than one ordinal, interval, or ratio variable broken down by a grouping variable.

2.27. Make four side by side boxplots showing the distributions of slfcnc08, slfcnc10, and slfcnc12, the self-concept scores in eighth, tenth, and twelfth grades, respectively, by gender.

To obtain a boxplot for slfcnc08, slfcnc10, and slfcnc12 separated by gender, type in the Command Window:

graph box slfcnc08 slfcnc10 slfcnc12, over(gender)

---

  a) Does self-concept generally appear to be increasing from eighth to twelfth grade for both sexes?
  b) What is most noticeable about these boxplots when comparing males to females?
  c) If not for the female outliers in 12th grade, would you say that males and females are comparable in their homogeneity of self-concept in 12th grade?

Exercises 2.28–2.30 involve a variety of boxplots.

2.28. In this exercise, we review the construction of the four different types of boxplots using the *NELS* data set.
  a) Construct a boxplot of eighth grade reading achievement (achrdg08).
  b) Construct, within one set of axes, two boxplots of eighth grade reading achievement, one for males and the other for females using the variable gender.
  c) Construct, within one set of axes, three boxplots, respectively, of eighth, tenth, and twelfth grade reading achievement.
  d) Construct, within one set of axes, boxplots of eighth, tenth, and twelfth grade reading achievement, separately for males and females.

2.29. Describe the shape of each the following distributions denoted a, b, c, d, e, and f.

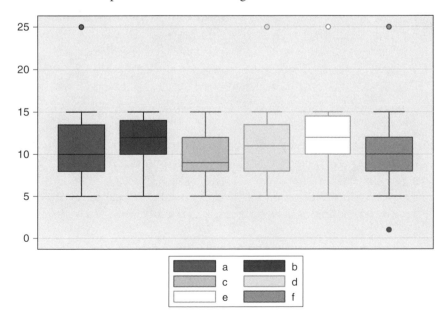

2.30. This exercise is based on the States data set, but does not require the use of Stata. The boxplots below show, for each of the four regions, the average educational expenditure for the states in that region. The four stem-and-leaf displays, labeled A, B, C, and D show the same. Match the letter associated with each stem-and-leaf to the appropriate boxplot.

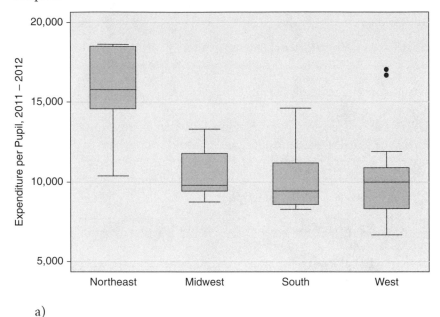

a)

```
Expenditure per Pupil, 2011-2012 Stem-and-Leaf Plot for
region= A
Stem-and-leaf plot for educexpe (Expenditure per Pupil,
2011-2012)
8***  | 285,436,492,498
8***  | 577,597,776
9***  | 060,440
9***  | 586,847,998
10*** |
10*** |
11*** | 192
11*** | 777
12*** |
12*** |
13*** |
13*** | 952
14*** | 396
14*** | 616
```

b)

```
Expenditure per Pupil, 2011-2012 Stem-and-Leaf Plot for
region= B
Stem-and-leaf plot for educexpe (Expenditure per Pupil,
2011-2012)
10*** | 396
11*** |
12*** |
13*** | 904
14*** | 587,938
15*** | 790
16*** | 683
17*** |
18*** | 485,571,616
```

c)

```
Expenditure per Pupil, 2011-2012 Stem-and-Leaf Plot for
region= C
Stem-and-leaf plot for educexpe (Expenditure per Pupil,
2011-2012)
6*** | 683,849
7*** |
8*** | 247,323
9*** | 053
10*** | 000,001,203,309,897
11*** | 906
12*** |
13*** |
14*** |
15*** |
16*** | 666
17*** | 032
```

d)

```
Expenditure per Pupil, 2011-2012 Stem-and-Leaf Plot for
region= D
Stem-and-leaf plot for educexpe (Expenditure per Pupil,
2011-2012)
8*** | 757
9*** | 218,402,435
```

```
9***  | 518,760,842
10*** |
10*** | 820
11*** | 398
11*** |
12*** | 172,455
12*** |
13*** | 313
```

Exercise 2.31 involves questions about selection of appropriate graphical displays.

2.31. For the following variables in the *NELS* data set, indicate whether the most appropriate types of graphical displays are (1) bar chart or pie chart, or (2) histogram, line graph, stem-and-leaf plot, or boxplot.

    a) gender

    b) urban

    c) schtyp8

    d) tcherint

    e) numinst

    f) achrdg08

    g) schattrt

    h) absent12

Exercises 2.32–2.33 involve a number of different topics.

2.32. The following questions pertain to the tenth grade social studies achievement score for students as given by the variable achsls10 in the *NELS* data set.

    a) What is the highest tenth grade social studies achievement score in the *NELS* data set?

    b) How many students obtained the highest score?

    c) What is the most frequently occurring score in this distribution?

    d) What is the 50th percentile of the distribution?

    e) What is the 67th percentile?

    f) What percentage of students scored 70 or below?

    g) What is the shape of the distribution?

2.33. The following questions pertain to the amount of time spent weekly on extracurricular activities in twelfth grade as given by excurr12 in the *NELS* data set.

    a) What does the value 2 represent?

    b) How many students in the *NELS* data set answered excurr12 that they spent 1 to 4 hours per week on extracurricular activities?

    c) What is the value at the 50th percentile?

    d) What is the shape of this distribution?

Exercises 2.34–2.36 involve reading and interpreting graphs.

2.34. The line graphs below show the number of jobs in thousands and the unemployment rate for part of the time president George W. Bush was in office. The graph was released

by the US Treasury Department and a good analysis of it may be found at http://www
.brendan-nyhan.com/blog/2005/12/the_treasury_de.html. Answer the following questions.

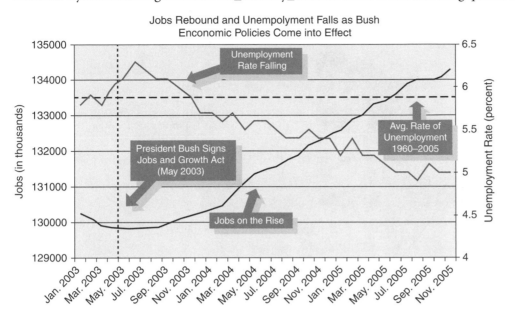

a) The vertical line represents what month? Why is this month highlighted?
b) What was the approximate number of jobs in March 2003? What was the approximate unemployment rate?
c) Give the month and year of the lowest unemployment rate.
d) Based on this graph, is it fair to say that President George W. Bush's Jobs and Growth Act helped create jobs and lower unemployment? Explain.

2.35. The following graph gives the relative average speed of Mets' baseball pitcher R.A. Dickey's knuckleball velocity in 2012 and 2013. (http://www.huffingtonpost.com/raviparikh/lie-with-data-visualization_b_5169715.html). The graphic is reproduced here as a bar chart. Comment upon the design of this graphic.

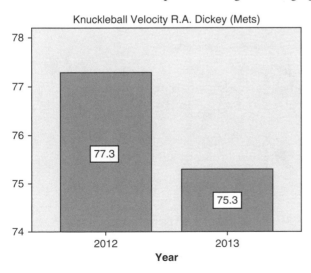

2.36. On June 3, 2014, H&R Block (http://blogs.hrblock.com/2014/06/03/the-things-you-can-do-but-what-should-you-do-infographic/) published pie and bar charts, indicating the best and worst college majors in terms of employment prospects.

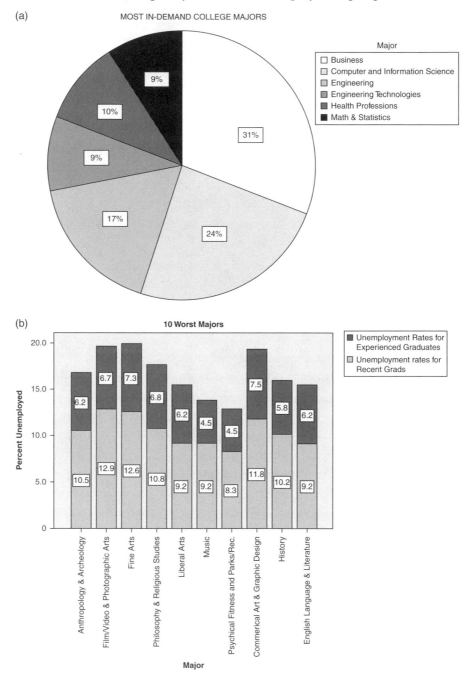

a) In the pie chart, what is the interpretation of the 31 associated with the business major?
b) What would be an advantage of using a bar chart instead of a pie chart to depict the most in-demand college majors?

    c) What percentage of recent grads who majored in anthropology and archeology are unemployed?

    d) Why does it make sense for this bar chart to be stacked?

Exercises 2.37–2.47 check your conceptual understanding of the material in this chapter, without the use of Stata.

2.37. Assuming the statistics are all calculated on the same set of data, rank the following from numerically smallest to numerically largest: C_{50} C_4 D_1 D_3 Q_1 Q_3

2.38. Determine what, if anything, is wrong with the following statement: A raw score of 75 is always surpassed by 25 percent of the scores in the distribution from which it comes.

2.39. Determine what, if anything, is wrong with the following statement: A 90-item test was scored by giving one point for each correct answer so that possible scores ranged from 0 to 90. On this test, the highest percentile rank possible is 90.

2.40. Determine what, if anything, is wrong with the following statement: On a certain English exam, Alice's score is twice as high as Ellen's. Therefore, Alice's percentile rank on the exam must be twice Ellen's percentile rank.

2.41. Determine what, if anything, is wrong with the following statement: If it takes 10 raw score points to go from a percentile rank of 50 to a percentile rank of 58, then it must also take 10 raw score points to go from a percentile rank of 90 to a percentile rank of 98.

2.42. Determine what, if anything, is wrong with the following statement: Scott, who scored at the 85th percentile in a math achievement test given to everyone in his school, and at the 95th percentile in a science test given to all students in the city in which the school is located, is doing better in science than in math.

2.43. Determine what, if anything, is wrong with the following statement: In a recent door-to-door survey, only five of the people questioned said they were opposed to a proposed school bond issue. The local school board publicized the results of this survey as evidence of tacit approval of the proposal.

2.44. Are the following, possible values for percentiles: 50, -2, 512? Are they possible values for percentile ranks?

2.45. Explain how a symmetric distribution can have outliers in its boxplot.

2.46. Explain how a boxplot could have only one whisker.

2.47. Draw a picture of two side-by-side boxplots so that

    a) The one on the left clearly has scores that are typically at a higher level and the one on the right has scores that are clearly less consistent. The graphs you create indicate that higher scores do not necessarily mean more spread.

    b) The one on the left is clearly less spread out and the one on the right is clearly less skewed. The graphs you create indicate that more skew does not necessarily mean more spread.

CHAPTER THREE

Measures of Location, Spread, and Skewness

In our examination of univariate distributions in Chapter 2, three summarizing characteristics of a distribution were discussed. First, its shape (as denoted by its skewness or its symmetry, by how many peaks and/or outliers it has, and so on). Second, its location (as denoted by its middle score, Q_2). Third, its spread (as denoted by both the range of values and the interquartile range, which is the range of values within which its middle 50 percent falls). In this chapter, we will expand upon that discussion by introducing other summary statistics for characterizing the location, spread, and shape of a distribution.

CHARACTERIZING THE LOCATION OF A DISTRIBUTION

When we speak of the location of a univariate distribution, we mean the point or number between the smallest and largest values of the distribution that best represents the distribution's "center." It is a single value that connotes the typical or "average" value in the distribution, the point around which most values are centered. For this reason, measures of location are also known as measures of *central tendency*. In this section, we discuss three commonly used measures of location: mode, median, and mean. These measures can be used to answer questions like: "Do seniors typically have higher grade point averages than freshmen?" "Do union workers have a higher overall income than nonunion workers?" "Does female self-concept change, on average, from eighth grade to twelfth grade?"

THE MODE

The *mode* is that data value that occurs most often in a distribution and can be found for any distribution. The mode is easy to compute and simple to interpret. The mode of the distribution for homelang (Home language background) for the 500 students in our *NELS* sample (see Table 3.1 for the frequency distribution) is English Only because that category occurs more often than any other in the distribution. That is, most students in our sample come from home backgrounds in which English is the only language spoken. Because relatively few students come from different home language backgrounds, the mode, English Only, best describes the typical home language background for this sample. As such, the category, English Only, is an effective measure of location for this distribution. In other situations, however, the mode is not so effective as a measure of a distribution's location.

Consider the frequency distribution of region presented in Table 2.1 of Chapter 2 and represented here as the bar graph of Figure 3.1. Notice that the frequencies of the

Table 3.1. Frequency distribution of home language background

Home Language Background	Freq.	Percent	Cum.
Non-English Only	15	3.00	3.00
Non-English Dominant	35	7.00	10.00
English Dominant	47	9.40	19.40
English Only	403	80.60	100.00
Total	500	100.00	

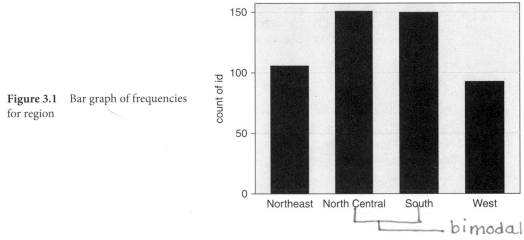

Figure 3.1 Bar graph of frequencies for region

bimodal

categories, North Central and South are approximately equal; North Central outnumbers South by only one case. Accordingly, it would be misleading to report North Central as the only mode of this distribution. A more appropriate characterization would be to report both North Central and South as modes in this case. Distributions that have two modes are called *bimodal.*

In Figure 3.1, the two peaks, one above each mode, are adjacent to each other. Because region is a nominal-leveled variable, and the order of categories in the distribution is arbitrary, the fact that the two modes are adjacent to each other is arbitrary as well.

When variables are ordinal-leveled or higher, however, and the order of categories in the distribution is not arbitrary, bimodal frequency distributions typically contain two peaks that are separated from each other by a gap in between. Figure 3.2 is an example of a bimodal distribution of 100 scores on a test of Spanish fluency.

Notice that most students either speak Spanish fluently (and receive very high scores on the test) or hardly at all (and receive very low scores on the test); a small number of students can speak some Spanish (and receive scores in the middle range).

Another distribution that has been suggested as being bimodal is that of the intelligence quotients (IQs) of viewers of the television show *Court TV*. Viewers of *Court TV* are purported to have either very high IQs or very low IQs; a small number of viewers are

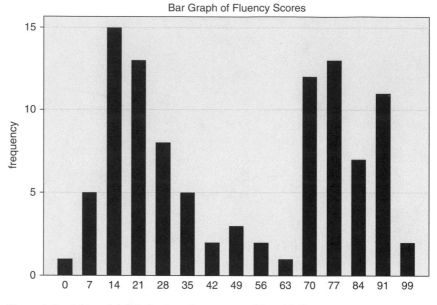

Figure 3.2 A bimodal distribution of test scores of Spanish fluency

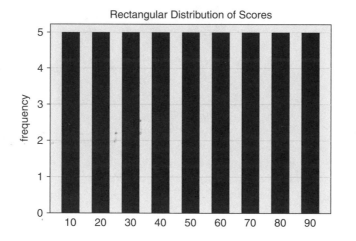

Figure 3.3 A rectangular distribution

reported as having IQs in the middle range. Can you think of other examples of bimodal distributions?

Some distributions are trimodal (three modes), and by extension, it is possible to have a distribution in which every category has the same, and therefore the largest, frequency. Such distributions are called *uniform* or *rectangular* distributions and are not well characterized by the mode. Figure 3.3 is an example of a rectangular distribution. In this distribution, each score category contains exactly five cases.

While homelang was at least ordinal and region was nominal, and both had fewer than five categories, we may obtain the modes of distributions of any level of measurement which take on any number of possible values. As in the previous cases, however, the effectiveness of a mode as a measure of a distribution's location, depends on the shape of

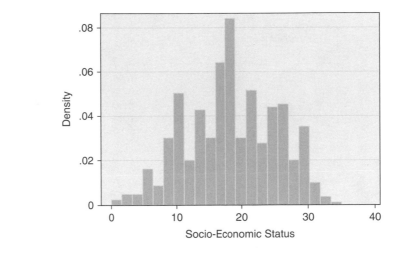

Figure 3.4   Histogram of socioeconomic status

the distribution itself. Where distributions are skewed or contain gaps in the middle, the effectiveness of the mode as a measure of location is diminished. Where the distribution is reasonably symmetric, and *unimodal* (one mode, or *single-peaked*), however, the mode is useful in characterizing the location, or center, of a distribution.

Recall that the frequency distribution of socioeconomic status, ses, presented in Table 2.2 of Chapter 2, and reproduced here as Figure 3.4 in its histogram form, is reasonably symmetric and unimodal. From the histogram, the mode of this distribution appears to be contained in the category with midpoint value 20 since that category occurs most often among the students in our sample of 500. Notice that because the distribution is reasonably symmetric and single-peaked, the mode is an effective numerical summary of the location of the ses distribution on the continuum from lowest to highest possible values.

The mode of a variable also may be obtained directly from Stata.

MORE Stata: To find the mode of ses, for example
   We type the following command in the Command Window and hit **Enter**:

tabulate ses

   We also may use the **egen mode** command as shown below when the variable has no missing values and when there is only one mode.

egen sesmode = mode(ses)

list sesmode if id ==1

Using the **tabulate** command we obtain:
In so doing, we find the mode to be 19, since 19 is the single value that occurs most frequently in the SES distribution. Scanning the numbers under frequencies reveals that there are 39 cases where SES is equal to 19.

Socio-Economic Status	Freq.	Percent	Cum.
0	1	0.20	0.20
1	1	0.20	0.40
2	2	0.40	0.80
3	2	0.40	1.20
4	4	0.80	2.00
5	1	0.20	2.20
6	12	2.40	4.60
7	7	1.40	6.00
8	15	3.00	9.00
9	9	1.80	10.80
10	18	3.60	14.40
11	22	4.40	18.80
12	16	3.20	22.00
13	15	3.00	25.00
14	19	3.80	28.80
15	24	4.80	33.60
16	18	3.60	37.20
17	33	6.60	43.80
18	28	5.60	49.40
19	39	7.80	57.20
20	24	4.80	62.00
21	22	4.40	66.40
22	19	3.80	70.20
23	22	4.40	74.60
24	14	2.80	77.40
25	21	4.20	81.60
26	20	4.00	85.60
27	16	3.20	88.80
28	16	3.20	92.00
29	12	2.40	94.40
30	16	3.20	97.60
31	8	1.60	99.20
32	3	0.60	99.80
35	1	0.20	100.00
Total	500	100.00	

Using the **egen** and **list** commands we obtain the same result:

	sesmode
1.	19

THE MEDIAN

median = Q_2

The *median* is defined as any theoretically possible data value in a distribution of a continuous variable below which 50 percent of all data values fall. Intuitively, then, the median may be thought of as the middle point in a distribution or as that point which divides a distribution into two equal halves. Since Q_2 (the second quartile, or, equivalently, the 50th percentile) also is defined as the middle point in a distribution, the median is another name for Q_2.

To approximate the median of a variable in a small data set, order the values in magnitude from lowest to highest. <u>If the data set contains an odd number of values, the median is simply the middle value</u>. If, on the other hand, the <u>data set contains an even number of values, the median is the average of the two middle values</u> obtained by summing the two middle values and dividing by 2.

EXAMPLE 3.1. National data for the United States on the number of home accident deaths from firearms for years 1990 to 1996 are given in the *2006 World Almanac and Book of Facts*. Approximations to these data are given here by year. What is the median number of deaths?

Year	Number of accidental deaths due to firearms
1997	981
1998	866
1999	824
2000	776
2001	802
2002	800
2003	700

Solution. To find the median number of home accident deaths in the United States due to firearms during the period from 1997 to 2003, we order the data from its lowest to highest value as follows:

700   776   800   802   824   866   981
                         ∧
                      median

Given that there are an odd number of values in this distribution, the median is simply the middle value, or 802. Notice that on both sides of this middle value, there is an equal number of values.

To find the median of a variable in a large data set, like ses, for example, we make use of a software package, like Stata, and obtain Q_2 as shown in Chapter 2.

MORE Stata: To find the median of ses, for example

We may type either of the following commands in the Command Window and hit **Enter**:

tabstat ses, stats(median)
summarize ses, detail

The option **detail** in the summarize command instructs Stata to calculate the median, among several other summary statistics.

tabstat may be used to calculate many other statistics in addition to the median. A listing of these statistics may be obtained by typing **help tabstat** in the Command Window. As noted in Chapter 2, the **help** command is very useful for obtaining information about any command as long as you know the command's name.

The **tabstat** command produces the following output. Both the **tabstat** and **summarize** commands refer to the median as the 50th percentile or, in shortened form as p50. The median of ses is 19, which is the same value as the mode of ses.

variable	p50
ses	19

Recall that the median is defined as that point below which are half the values in the distribution and above which also are half the values in the distribution. As a result, the median is meaningful only when it makes sense to order the values in a data set from low to high, that is, when the variable is at least ordinal-leveled. A median is not meaningful on data that are nominal-leveled because such data would be ordered arbitrarily and different orderings would give rise to different medians. For nominal-leveled data, the mode, then, is the only appropriate measure of location.

Suppose we are interested in knowing the incomes of three individuals, and we are told that one of these individuals has an income of $0, another has an income of $5,000, and the median income for all three individuals is also $5,000. Because the median can be thought of as the middle or central point in a distribution, it might seem reasonable to suppose that the third individual has an income of $10,000. In reality, the third individual's income could be any value above $5,000 and still be consistent with the given information. The third individual's income could, for example, be $1,000,000, and the three incomes of $0, $5,000, and $1,000,000 would still have a median of $5,000. Thus, because the total number of data values above the median equals the total number of data points below the median, the median is not particularly sensitive to the exact values of each data value in a distribution. Changing one of the data values may or may not have any effect on the value of the median.

THE ARITHMETIC MEAN

The *arithmetic mean* (or simply the *mean*) is the most frequently used measure of location and is especially useful in inferential statistics. If we denote the ith observation of the variable X by X_i, the mean (denoted $\overline{X}$) is the sum of all the data values of the distribution (Denoted $\sum X_i$, where the upper-case Greek letter sigma Σ represents the operation of summation) divided by N, the total number of data values in the distribution. The definition of the mean may be translated into the following mathematical equation:

$$\overline{X} = \frac{\sum X_i}{N}$$

(3.1)

. . . .

EXAMPLE 3.2. Find the mean number of home accident deaths due to firearms in the United States from the years 1997 to 2003.

Solution. Following Equation 3.1, we obtain,

$$\frac{700+776+800+802+824+866+981}{7} = \frac{5749}{7} = 821.29$$

The mean for these data equals approximately 821 deaths.

To find the mean using Stata, we can type either of the following commands in the Command Window and then hit Enter:

MORE Stata: To find the mean of ses, for example
  We may type either of the following commands:

tabstat ses, stat(mean)
summarize ses

The output from using the summarize command is:

Variable	Obs	Mean	Std. Dev.	Min	Max
ses	500	18.434	6.924271	0	35

We find the mean ses to be 18.43. Recall that the median and mode for these data were both equal to 19. *not sensitive*

Unlike the mode and the median, the mean is sensitive to any change in the data values of the distribution. Thus, if one value in the distribution is increased (or decreased), the mean of the distribution will increase (or decrease), but not by the same amount. If, for example, we increase one of the values in the ses distribution by 25 points, the new mean will equal 18.93, an increase of 0.5 points. Try it on your data, using any one of the values in the ses distribution. Be sure to replace the altered value by the original one once you have finished this check.

Of course, if more than one data value in a distribution is changed with some values increased and some values decreased, the changes can cancel out each other's effects on the mean and leave the mean unchanged.

There is another property of the mean worth mentioning. If for each X value in the distribution, $\bar{X}_i$, we calculate its difference from the mean, $(X_i - \bar{X})$, then these differences, summed across all data values, will be equal to zero. The difference, $X_i - \bar{X}$, may be thought of, as well, as the deviation or distance of the value from the mean. This property may be expressed in terms of the following equation:

$$\sum \left(X_i - \bar{X} \right) = 0 \tag{3.2}$$

Equation 3.2 shows that when distance is measured from the mean, the total distance of points above the mean equals the total distance of points below the mean. As a result, a point that is far from the others in a distribution (e.g., an outlier) would pull the mean closer to it so as to balance the negative and positive differences about the mean. Further, because the mean relies on distances to find a distribution's center, means should be computed only on variables that are at least interval-leveled. A mean of region or homelang (home language background), for example, would be meaningless.

EXAMPLE 3.3. Verify that $\sum \left(X_i - \bar{X} \right) = 0$ for the deaths due to firearms data.

Solution.

$(700 - 821.29) + (776 - 821.29) + (800 - 821.29) + (802 - 821.29) + (824 - 821.29) +$
$(866 - 821.29) + (981 - 821.29)$

$$= (-121.29) + (-45.29) + (-21.29) + (-19.29) + (2.71) + (44.71) + (159.71) = -207.16$$
$$+ 207.13 = -0.03.$$

This value is within rounding of 0.

☞ **Remark.** Most statistical software packages will compute any measure of location on any set of numerical values, regardless of how meaningful or meaningless these values are in measuring the underlying trait in question. Stata, for example, will readily compute a mean of the variable region in the *NELS* data set because numerical values have been assigned to the variable region's different categories. Using the Stata Summary Statistics procedure, we see that the mean of region is 2.46, which is the average of all 500 of the values that region assumes, where each value is between 1 and 4. The value 2.46 does not have a meaningful interpretation because the variable region is measured at the nominal level with more than two categories. The onus is on the researcher, then, to know which summary measures are appropriate in which circumstances. Without good judgment and thought in data analysis, interpretations of results may often be meaningless.

Interpreting the mean of a dichotomous variable

Although the mean is usually meaningless when calculated on a nominal leveled variable, it is meaningful when calculated on a dichotomous variable (a variable with only two categories) when those categories are coded as 0 and 1. In particular, in this situation, the mean of the variable will be equal to the proportion of cases in the category assigned the value of 1.

• •

EXAMPLE 3.4. Find the mean of gender in our *NELS* data set of 500 cases.

Solution. Recall that gender is a dichotomous variable with the two categories, male and female. In the *NELS* data set, the category female is assigned the value of 1 while the category male is assigned the value of 0.

MORE Stata: To find the mean of gender, together with a frequency distribution
We type the following two commands in the Command Window, hitting **Enter** after each.

summarize gender
tabulate gender

We obtain the following result:

Variable	Obs	Mean	Std. Dev.	Min	Max
gender	500	.546	.4983781	0	1

Gender	Freq.	Percent	Cum.
Male	227	45.40	45.40
Female	273	54.60	100.00
Total	500	100.00	

Notice that the mean of gender equals .55 (rounded to two decimal places), which is equal to the proportion of females in our sample of 500 cases.

The Weighted Mean

In Example 3.2, each value (number of accidental deaths due to firearms) occurs once and therefore has a frequency equal to 1. If, instead, however, each value in the distribution occurred a different number of times, as in the case of the ses variable (see the frequency distribution for ses given in Table 2.2), we could use a modification of Equation (3.1) that takes into account the varying frequencies (f_i) of each value of ses (X_i) to represent the mean of the ses distribution. This equation is given by Equation (3.3).

$$\bar{X} = \frac{\sum_1^k X_i f_i}{N} \tag{3.3}$$

In Equation (3.3), the value of k above the summation sign represents the number of distinct values in the distribution. In the ses example, $k = 36$, because as shown in Table 2.2, there are 36 distinct values in the ses distribution (labeled 0 to 35), and $N = 500$, the number of individuals in the data set with nonmissing ses values. We know from our previous work that the mean of the ses distribution equals 18.43.

Suppose, instead, we were told that the ses distribution was divided into three mutually exclusive and exhaustive categories that represented low, middle, and high ses groupings, respectively. Suppose we also were told that the low ses category consisted of 168 individuals with ses mean equal to 10.6, the middle ses category consisted of 276 individuals with ses mean equal to 20.92, and the high SES category consisted of 56 individuals with ses mean equal to 29.55. If we did not already know that the overall mean of the ses distribution was 18.43, what procedure might we use to arrive at that value?

Because each ses category contains a different number of individuals, rather than add up the three means (10.6, 20.92, and 29.55) and divide by 3, our procedure would need to take into account the different sizes of each category and weigh the means of the three categories accordingly. Because the middle ses group is largest, its mean should be weighted more heavily than the mean of the next largest group (the low ses group), which, in turn, should be weighed more heavily than the mean of the smallest group (the middle ses group).

Analogous to having weighed each X value (X_i) by its frequency (f_i) in Equation (3.3) to obtain the overall mean, we now weigh each mean value ($\bar{X}_j$) by the size of its group (n_j), to obtain what is called the *weighted mean*. Just as the sum of the frequencies f_i equals N, so does the sum of the group sizes n_j equal N. The resulting equation for the weighted mean is given by Equation (3.4).

$$\text{Weighted Mean} = \frac{\sum_1^k \bar{X}_j n_j}{N} \tag{3.4}$$

Using Equation (3.4), we compute the weighted mean for ses as follows:

$$\text{SES Weighted Mean} = \frac{10.6 \times 168 + 20.92 \times 276 + 29.55 \times 56}{500} = 18.43.$$

We can use Stata to calculate the weighted mean by creating a new data set and weighting cases by frequency. Detailed information about how to do this may be found in Chapter 17.

COMPARING THE MODE, MEDIAN, AND MEAN

As we have noted in earlier sections of this chapter, the mode, median, and mean measure different aspects of the location of a distribution of data values. Depending upon the particular shape of a distribution, the numerical values of these three measures may be the same or different. Conversely, knowing the values of these three measures relative to one another can often provide us with a better understanding of the shape of the underlying distribution.

When a distribution is symmetric, the mean will be equal to the median (see Figure 3.5 (A) and (B)). When a distribution is symmetric and also unimodal, the mode will equal the mean and the median as well. The distribution of our data in Example 3.1 on home accident deaths due to firearms is symmetric and unimodal, which explains why the mode, median, and mean were all equal to each other.

If a distribution is highly negatively skewed, in general, the mean will be smaller than the median, because the value of the mean is more influenced than the value of the median by the extreme low values present in such a distribution. Analogously, for a distribution that is highly positively skewed, in general, the mean will be larger than the median, because it is more influenced than the median by the extreme high values present in such a distribution. Because of the differential influence of extreme scores on the mean and median, the mean of a highly skewed distribution will lie in the direction of skewness (the direction of the tail) relative to the median. This relationship between the mean and the median is illustrated in Figures 3.6 and 3.7, which depict unimodal continuous distributions. Exercise 3.6 illustrates that in the case of discrete distributions or multimodal continuous distributions counter-examples exist. In fact, they are not uncommon in those circumstances. When, however, a distribution is severely skewed and unimodal continuous, we can expect the mean and median to differ in a predictable way.

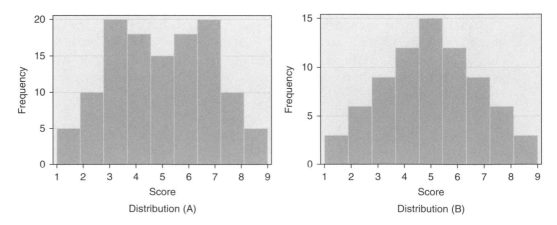

Figure 3.5   Histograms of two symmetric distributions.

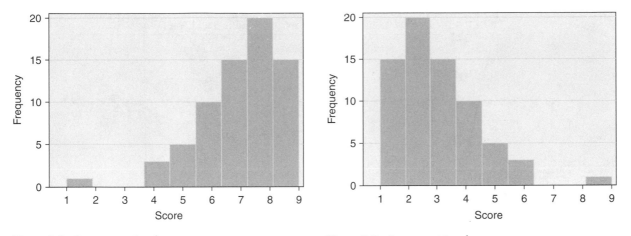

Figure 3.6 Severe negative skew

Figure 3.7 Severe positive skew

☞ **Remark.** The converse is not true, however. That is, if the mean and the median are different from each other, the distribution need not be skewed. Analogously, if the mean is equal to the median, the distribution need not be symmetric.

EXAMPLE 3.5. Compare the values of the mode, median, and mean for (a) ses (b) expinc30 (expected income at age 30), (c) schattrt (School attendance rate, which measures the average daily attendance rate of the high school that each student attended; and (d) slfcnc08 (self-concept score in eighth grade. Explain the direction of difference that exists among these three measures of location. Note that by calculating the mean of these variables, we are treating them as at least interval-leveled.

Solution.

MORE Stata: To generate a single table with the mean and median of more than one variable
  We type: **tabstat ses expinc30 schattrt slfcnc08, stat(mean median)**

The resulting Stata output is reproduced below. Note that the order in which the variables are displayed is the order in which they are listed in the drop down menu or syntax.

stats	ses	expinc30	schattrt	slfcnc08
mean	18.434	51574.73	93.64988	21.062
p50	19	40000	95	21

Recall that the distribution of ses is reasonably symmetric. We see that the two measures of location (central tendency) are approximately equal. On the other hand, we know from our earlier work that expected income at age 30 is highly positively skewed. Not

TABLE 3.2. Average monthly temperature of Springfield and San Francisco

Month	Springfield temperature	San Francisco temperature
Jan	32	49
Feb	36	52
Mar	45	53
Apr	56	55
May	65	58
Jun	73	61
Jul	78	62
Aug	77	63
Sep	70	64
Oct	58	61
Nov	45	55
Dec	36	49

surprisingly, the value of the mean is quite a bit higher than the value of the median. From Exercise 2.15c) we know that average daily school attendance rate is highly negatively skewed, which explains why the mean is smaller than the median in this case.

CHARACTERIZING THE SPREAD OF A DISTRIBUTION

When we speak of the spread of a univariate distribution, we mean the extent to which the values in the distribution vary from its "average" and from one another. Instead of the word spread, we may use, equivalently, the words, *variability, dispersion, heterogeneity, inconsistency,* and *unpredictability.* Several different summary statistics exist to measure spread: the range, interquartile range, variance, and standard deviation. As we shall see, each of these summary statistics taps a different aspect of spread. Measures of spread may be used to answer the following sample questions: "Are females more variable than males in their self-concept?" "Are reading scores more homogeneous in private schools than in public schools?" "Are home insurance fees more consistent in California than in New York?"

We present a variation of an example from Burrill and Hopfensperger (1993), to illustrate more clearly what it is that measures of spread capture about a set of numbers, as opposed to, for example, measures of location.

● ●

EXAMPLE 3.6. Congratulations! You have just won a trip to one of two cities in the United States that have similar average annual temperatures (approximately 57 degrees): San Francisco, CA or Springfield, MO. The prize also includes a wardrobe of clothes that would be suitable, from the point of view of warmth, for visiting the city of your choice any time during the year.

Would the same clothes be suitable for both cities at any time during the year? For which city would the wardrobe of clothing necessarily be more extensive? The average monthly temperatures (in Fahrenheit) for the two cities are given in Table 3.2 and are saved in the *TEMP* data set.

Solution. Because a more extensive wardrobe would be required by the city that has a greater variability in temperature across the months of the year, we explore the relative variability in monthly temperature for the two cities using boxplots.

☞ **Remark.** There are two ways to enter these data as two variables. First, we could enter the data just as they are entered in the table naming the second two columns spring and sanfran. The first gives the Springfield temperature and the second the San Francisco temperature. Second the data could be reorganized. We could use two variables, city and temp. City is a dichotomous variable with two categories (Springfield, assigned the value of 1, and San Francisco, assigned the value of 2) while temp is a continuous variable of temperature in degrees Fahrenheit for each month. The second is the way the data are displayed in the data file *Temp* located on the text website. An excerpt of the data file is presented.

city	temp
1	32
2	49
1	36
2	52
1	45
2	53
etc.	etc.

The resulting graphs and statistics are the same regardless of the format of the data, but because the methods for obtaining them differ slightly, both are presented. For example, the way to create side-by-side boxplots giving the temperatures for the two cities differs depending on the layout of the dataset. The first is based on the first layout for the data.

MORE Stata: Constructing boxplots of different variables in one or more separate panels

If the temperatures are given for the two cities, one column per city, each labeled spring and sanfran, for example,

We would type: **graph box spring sanfran**

If, instead, the values of the temperature for both cities are in one column labeled temp, and there is an associated column labeled city that is a grouping variable indicating from which city the corresponding temperature is from (San Francisco or Springfield), we use either of the following commands to generate the boxplots. To obtain the box-plots of the different groups (city, in this case)

within separate frames or panels, we would type: **graph box temp, by(city)**

within the same frame or panel, we would type: **graph box temp, over(city)**

The command **graph box temp, by(city)** produces the following result:

From the boxplot display, we may observe that while the cities share the same typical or "average" temperature across the twelve months of the year (the median is approximately 57 degrees), they differ quite markedly in terms of the temperature spread. For Springfield, the temperature varies from a low of 32 to a high of 78, whereas for San Francisco the temperature varies only from a low of 48 to a high of 64. What this suggests is that while

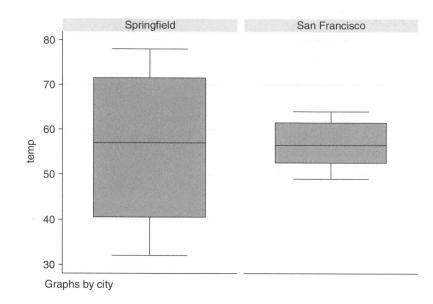

Graphs by city

for San Francisco, middle-weight clothes would be suitable for all months of the year, for Springfield, light-, middle-, and heavy-weight clothes are necessary. Said differently, Springfield requires the more extensive wardrobe of the two cities.

More formally, we may characterize the variability in temperature using one of several numeric summaries of spread.

THE RANGE AND INTERQUARTILE RANGE

The *range* of a distribution is simply the difference between the highest and lowest values in the distribution. The range is easy to compute and simple to interpret. For San Francisco, the range is 64–49 or 15 degrees Fahrenheit, while for Springfield, the range is 78–32 or 46 degrees Fahrenheit. As 46 degrees is greater than 15 degrees, the range correctly captures the relative spread for the data of these two distributions. However, because the range depends upon the highest and lowest values of a distribution, and because these values tend to be the least stable values of a distribution, the range is not usually the best measure of a distribution's spread.

For example, the interquartile range, introduced in Chapter 2, is less sensitive than the range to changes in the extreme values, or, more generally, to changes in the shape of the tails of a distribution. The *interquartile range* is the difference between the third quartile, Q_3, and the first quartile, Q_1, and as such, equals the distance covered by the middle 50 percent of the distribution.

Because the interquartile range is based on the values near the center of the distribution, it is not sensitive to the small number of values in the tails. Statistics, such as the interquartile range, which are not sensitive to changes in a small number of values within a distribution, are called *resistant statistics*. The median is another example of a resistant statistic because unlike the mean, the median is not sensitive to extreme values in either tail of the distribution.

To estimate the interquartile range for both cities, we first order the 12 temperature values from lowest to highest for each city.

For Springfield, the ordered temperature values are:

32   36   36   45   45   56   58   65   70   73   77   78
                              ^

The median is therefore 57. Because we may think of Q_1 as that value that divides the lower half of the distribution in half, a good estimate for Q_1 is the middle value of the six values, 32, 36, 36, 45, 45, 56, or that value that has three values below it and three values above it. An estimate of that value is halfway between 36 and 45, or 40.5. Likewise, a good estimate for Q_3 is that value halfway between 70 and 73, or 71.5. An estimate of the interquartile range is therefore $Q_3 - Q_1 = 71.5 - 40.5 = 31$.

For San Francisco, the ordered temperature values are:

49   49   52   53   55   55   58   61   61   62   63   64
                              ^

The median for these data is 56.5, an estimate of $Q_1 = 52.5$, and an estimate of $Q_3 = 61.5$. Therefore, an estimate of the interquartile range is $Q_3 - Q_1 = 61.5 - 52.5 = 9$.

We may use Stata to obtain an estimate of the interquartile range that is based on a somewhat different set of assumptions about the data. The interquartile range from Stata will not necessarily be equal to the value obtained by our estimation procedure.

MORE Stata: To obtain the interquartile ranges for distributions of a single variable for different sub-groups, defined in this case by the variable city.

Type the following in the Command Window and hit **Enter**.

by city, sort: summarize temp, detail

The prefix to the command, **by city, sort,** sorts our data into subgroups defined by city before summary statistics of temp are calculated. This sorting operation is only temporary. Once the **summarize** command is executed, the data return to their original order in our data file

A shortened, yet equivalent form of this command is:

by city: summarize temp, detail

Instead, we also could have used the following **tabstat** command:

tabstat temp, stats(iqr) by(city)

In using the two summarize commands, we would need to calculate the *IQR* from the given quartiles. The results using the first summarize command are given below and agree with our own earlier estimates. For Springfield, the $IQR = 71.5 - 40.5 = 31$ and for San Francisco, the $IQR = 61.5 - 52.5 = 9$. The interquartile range values are ordered in a way that we would expect based on our visual examination of the data using the boxplot.

.by city, sort: summarize temp, detail

```
--> city = Springfiel
                                    temp

              Percentiles      Smallest
    1%             32              32
    5%             32              36
   10%             36              36        Obs                    12
   25%            40.5             45        Sum of Wgt.            12

   50%             57                        Mean             55.91667
                                Largest      Std. Dev.        16.82238
   75%            71.5             70
   90%             77              73        Variance         282.9924
   95%             78              77        Skewness        -.0679089
   99%             78              78        Kurtosis         1.531904


--> city = San Franci
                                    temp

              Percentiles      Smallest
    1%             49              49
    5%             49              49
   10%             49              52        Obs                    12
   25%            52.5             53        Sum of Wgt.            12

   50%            56.5                       Mean             56.83333
                                Largest      Std. Dev.        5.390789
   75%            61.5             61
   90%             63              62        Variance         29.06061
   95%             64              63        Skewness        -.1552291
   99%             64              64        Kurtosis         1.610694
```

The **tabstat** command outputs the *IQR* directly as shown below:

Summary for variables:
temp by categories of: city

city	iqr
Springfield	31
San Francisco	9
Total	14.5

THE VARIANCE

If we conceptualize the spread of a distribution as the extent to which the values in the distribution differ from the mean and from each other, then a reasonable measure of spread might be the average deviation, or difference, of the values from the mean. In notation form, this may be expressed as:

$$\frac{1}{N} \sum \left(X_i - \bar{X} \right) \tag{3.3}$$

Although at first glance, this might seem reasonable, using Equation 3.2, this expression always equals 0, regardless of the actual spread of the data values in the distribution. Recall that this occurs because the negative deviations about the mean always cancel out the positive deviations about the mean, producing a sum or average of 0.

To avoid this cancellation effect, one may simply drop any negative signs from the deviation values before averaging. In mathematical terminology, dropping the negative sign of a number is called taking that number's absolute value. The mean of the absolute values of the deviations is called the mean deviation. Although the mean deviation is a good measure for describing the spread of a given set of data, it is not often used because the concept of absolute value does not lend itself to the kind of advanced mathematical manipulation necessary for the development of inferential statistical equations.

The usual method for avoiding such cancellation is, therefore, to square the deviations rather than taking their absolute values. In so doing, we obtain a measure that is sensitive to differences in spread and is easy to work with mathematically in the development of inferential statistical equations. The average of the squared deviations about the mean is called the *variance.* It is denoted by the symbol SD^2 and is given by Equation 3.4.

$$SD^2 = \frac{\sum(X_i - \bar{X})^2}{N} \tag{3.4}$$

The variance of the distribution of Springfield temperatures is 259.41 while the variance of San Francisco temperatures is 26.64. These values are consistent with our observation that Springfield has a larger temperature spread than San Francisco, or that the distribution of Springfield temperatures is more variable (less homogeneous, or more heterogeneous) than the distribution of San Francisco temperatures.

While this book has a noncomputational focus, we believe that seeing a worked-out example for computing the variance using Equation 3.4 will aid many of you in conceptualizing this statistic.

• •

EXAMPLE 3.7. Use Equation 3.4 to find the mean and variance of the San Francisco monthly temperature. (Recall that these values are approximately 56.83 and 26.64, respectively.)

Solution. We denote the temperature variable as X.

X	$X - \bar{X}$	$\left(X - \bar{X}\right)^2$
49	−7.83	61.31
52	−4.83	23.33
53	−3.83	14.67
55	−1.83	3.35
58	1.17	1.37
61	4.17	17.39
62	5.17	26.73
63	6.17	38.07
64	7.17	51.41
61	4.17	17.39
55	−1.83	3.35
49	−7.83	61.31
Total: 682		**Total: 319.67**

$$\text{Mean} = \bar{X} = \frac{\sum X_i}{N} = \frac{682}{12} = 56.83$$

$$\text{Sum of Squares} = SS = \sum (X_i - \bar{X})^2 = 319.67$$

$$\text{Variance} = SD^2 = \frac{SS}{N} = \frac{\sum (X_i - \bar{X})^2}{N} = \frac{319.67}{12} = 26.64$$

According to Equation 3.4, the more the values of the distribution tend to differ from the mean, the larger the variance. But, how large is a large variance? Unfortunately, there is no simple answer. Variances, like other measures of spread, are used primarily to compare the spread of one distribution to the spread of another and not to judge, offhand, whether or not a single distribution has a large spread. However, a variance of zero, the smallest possible value, indicates that there is no spread, that is, that all of the scores are the same.

The numerical value of a variance of a distribution also depends upon the unit of measurement used. As we will formalize in the next chapter, the variance of a distribution of heights measured in inches, for example, will be considerably larger than the variance of the same distribution of heights measured in feet. When comparing the variances of two or more distributions, therefore, for comparability, the unit of measurement should be the same for all distributions.

The earlier output from the two **summarize** commands provides the variance of temperature values for each city. For San Francisco, the variance is 29.06, which is different from our hand calculation of 26.64.

☞ **Remark.** A problem with Stata is that it does not calculate the variance as it is defined in Equation 3.4. Rather than calculating it as the sum of squared deviations about the mean divided by N, it calculates it as the sum of squared deviations about the mean divided by $N-1$. While dividing by $N-1$ will make sense in the context of inferential statistics, when we seek to obtain a variance estimate based on sample data, in the context of descriptive statistics it does not. To obtain the variance, as it is defined, you need only to multiply the value obtained from Stata by $(N-1)/N$. Alternatively, you may reason that, especially when N is large, the value obtained from Stata will be close enough to the correct value to forego making this adjustment. For descriptive purposes, we shall adjust the value obtained from Stata by multiplying by $(N-1)/N$, whenever N is less than 30. With an N of 30 or more, the adjustment factor $(N-1)/N$ is close enough to one not to matter in practice.

Based on this remark, to obtain the value of the variance as defined by Equation 3.4, we simply multiply 29.06 by $(N-1)/N$, or, in this case, 11/12, to obtain 26.64.

☞ **Remark.** While the range and interquartile range for our temperature example are in terms of degrees Fahrenheit, the original units of measurement, this is not the case for the variance. The variance is expressed in terms of squared units as opposed to the original units of measurement. This means that for this example, the variance is expressed in terms of squared degrees Fahrenheit, rather than in degrees Fahrenheit. To see that this is the case we need only to review Example 3.7 in which the variance of the distribution of San Francisco temperatures is calculated. In Example 3.7, the mean (in degrees Fahrenheit) is subtracted from the value of each temperature to obtain a deviation, $X - \bar{X}$, in degrees Fahrenheit, for each month. But, then these deviations are squared. The squared deviations are in squared degrees Fahrenheit rather than in degrees Fahrenheit. The variance, which is the average of these squared deviations, is then also in squared degrees Fahrenheit.

THE STANDARD DEVIATION

Because the variance is expressed in squared units rather than in the original units of measurement, the variance value cannot meaningfully be related to the original set of data. The variance may be expressed in terms of the original units of measurement, however, if we take the positive square root of the variance. This new measure is called the *standard deviation*. It is denoted by the symbols *SD* or *S*, and is given by the following equation:

$$SD = +\sqrt{SD^2} \tag{3.5}$$

Because the standard deviation is a measure of spread in terms of the original units of measurement, it may be directly related to the original set of data. The standard deviation of the San Francisco temperatures is 5.16. If we order the temperatures from lowest to highest, we have the following:

San Francisco temperatures in order of magnitude: 49, 49, 52, 53, 55, 55, 58, 61, 61, 62, 63, 64

The values within 57 ± 5.16 are the values within the interval 51.84 to 62.16. These are the values 52, 53, 55, 55, 58, 61, 61, and 62. Hence, 8 of the 12 values, or 67 percent, fall within one standard deviation of the mean. All values fall within two standard deviations of the mean for this distribution. The number of values that fall within one standard deviation of the mean in a distribution will vary somewhat from distribution to distribution; so will the number of standard deviations needed to capture all the values of a distribution.

☞ **Remark.** One may also describe the standard deviation as that distance from the mean (in both directions) within which the majority of values of a distribution fall. The distance will be shorter in distributions that are clustered tightly about the mean, and longer in distributions that are not clustered so tightly about the mean.

☞ **Remark.** While, as noted earlier, the interquartile range is a resistant statistic, the variance and standard deviation are not. The variance is conceptualized as the average of squared deviations about the mean and the standard deviation as the square root of that. Cases with extreme deviations, therefore, are highly influential as they enter the calculation as the deviation squared, rather than as the deviation itself. Because a deviation of 10 adds 100 points to the calculation while a deviation of 20 adds 400 points, for example, the more extreme the deviation, the greater the increase in its influence on the variance and standard deviation. As a result, the variance and standard deviation are especially sensitive to the influence of extreme values, and are considered to be highly nonresistant statistics.

☞ **Remark.** The standard deviation obtained from Stata is also not consistent with the convention used in this text. While the Stata variance is off by a factor of $(N-1)/N$, the Stata standard deviation is off by a factor of $\sqrt{(N-1)/N}$. Thus, Stata reports the standard deviation of the San Francisco temperatures as 5.39, rather than 5.16.

MORE Stata: To find the standard deviation of the variable temp by city
  We may use any of the following commands:

by city, sort: summarize temp, detail
by city, sort: summarize temp
by city, sort: tabstat temp, stats(sd)
tabstat temp, stats(sd) by(city)
tabulate city, summarize(temp)

  Note: The first three commands with the prefix **by city, sort:** organize the results into two separate tables, one for each city; the last two commands organize the results into a single table. The prefix in the first three commands may be shortened to simply **by city:**

CHARACTERIZING THE SKEWNESS OF A DISTRIBUTION

In the previous chapter we described the shape of a distribution as symmetric, or as positively or negatively skewed. Our description was based on "eyeballing" the data represented visually. Often one may be interested in a numerical summary of skewness for the purpose of comparing the skewness of two or more distributions or for evaluating the degree to which a single distribution is skewed. The *skewness statistic* is such a numerical summary. Equation 3.6 gives the expression for the skewness statistic as calculated by Stata and the standard error of the skewness.

$$\text{Skewness} = \frac{\sum (X_i - \bar{X})^3 / N}{\left(\sqrt{\dfrac{\sum (X_i - \bar{X})^2}{N}}\right)^3} \tag{3.6}$$

$$\text{Standard Error Skewness} = \sqrt{\frac{6N(N-1)}{(N-2)(N+1)(N+3)}}$$

While the variance is based on the sum of squared deviations about the mean, the skewness statistic is based on the sum of cubed deviations about the mean. And while the variance can only be positive or zero (since it is based on the sum of *squared* deviations), the skewness statistic may be either positive, zero, or negative (since it is based on the sum of *cubed* deviations). The skewness statistic is positive when the distribution is skewed positively and it is negative when the distribution is skewed negatively. If the distribution is perfectly symmetric, the skewness statistic equals zero. The more severe the skew, the more the skewness statistic departs from zero.

  To compare the skewness of two distributions of relatively equal size, one may use the skewness values themselves. To compare the skewness of two distributions that are quite unequal in size, or to evaluate the severity of skewness for a particular distribution when that distribution is small or moderate in size, one should compute a skewness ratio. The skewness ratio is obtained as the skewness statistic divided by the standard error of the skewness statistic. Although the meaning of the standard error will be discussed in Chapter 9, we note simply for now that the standard error is a function of the sample size.

● ●

EXAMPLE 3.8. Use Equation 3.6 to calculate the skewness and standard error of the skew for the San Francisco monthly temperature.

Solution. We denote the temperature variable as X. Recall that according to the output obtained using Stata, $\bar{X} = 56.83$ and SD = 5.39 for San Francisco.

X	$X - \bar{X}$	$(X - \bar{X})^3$
49	−7.83	−480.05
52	−4.83	−112.68
53	−3.83	−56.18
55	−1.83	−6.13
58	1.17	1.60
61	4.17	72.51
62	5.17	138.19
63	6.17	234.89
64	7.17	368.60
61	4.17	72.51
55	−1.83	−6.13
49	−7.83	−480.05
	Total: −256.08	

$$\text{The skewness} = \frac{\sum (X_i - \bar{X})^3 / N}{\left(\sqrt{\frac{\sum (X_i - \bar{X})^2}{N}} \right)^3} = \frac{-256.08 / 12}{\left(\sqrt{\frac{319.67}{12}} \right)^3} = \frac{-21.34}{5.16^3} = \frac{-21.34}{137.39} = -0.155$$

$$\text{The standard error of the skewness} = \sqrt{\frac{6N(N-1)}{(N-2)(N+1)(N+3)}} = \sqrt{\frac{6(12)(11)}{(10)(13)(15)}} = .637$$

And, the skewness ratio of temp for San Francisco is −0.155/.637 = −.243.

MORE Stata: To find the standard error of skewness using **display**
  display is Stata's built-in calculator command. We type:

display sqrt((6*12*11)/(10*13*15))

  Note that the results obtained (.637) appear only in the Output Window and do not affect our data in our Data Editor.

Even when using **display**, the computation of the standard error of the skew can be cumbersome. Accordingly, we have created a program consisting of a series of Stata commands that calculates not only the standard error of the skewness, but also the skewness, and the ratio of the skewness divided by the standard error of the skewness. The name of the program is **summskew**.

MORE Stata: To find the skewness, standard error of skewness, and the skewness ratio using **summskew**.

Because this is a command that, by default, is not part of Stata, we first need to install it.

Instructions for doing so may be found under the Resources tab in "Instructions for downloading and saving the files in the additional-files.zip folder" on the book's website www.cambridge.org/Stats-Stata.

Once you have completed these instructions, you are set to use **summskew**. You also are set to use the **summskewcell** program referenced in a later chapter of this book. There is no need to go through this process again.

To use **summskew**, we type, for this example:

summskew temp, by(city)

Note: **by()** is an option for the **summskew** command that we would include if there is a grouping variable (e.g., city) and we would like to compute the skewness statistics for each sub-group defined by that grouping variable. On the other hand, we would omit the **by()** option if we were interested in computing the skewness statistics not by sub-group, but overall.

We obtain the following result:

For city = 1: skewness = −.06790885; seskew = .63730198; skewness ratio = −.106
For city = 2: skewness = −.15522906; seskew = .63730198; skewness ratio = −.243

By convention, when this ratio exceeds 2.00 for small- and moderate-sized samples, one should consider the distribution to be highly skewed. In our case, these statistics corroborate our impressions from the boxplot that these distributions are not skewed.

Because many summary statistics (e.g., the mean, variance, and standard deviation) are sensitive to extreme values, and because distributions which are skewed often contain extreme values, we routinely should check a distribution for the severity of its skewness. It is often possible to reduce the skewness of a distribution by expressing the data of that distribution in an alternative form. Ways for doing so are covered in the next chapter.

MORE Stata: (OPTIONAL) The set of commands upon which the **summskew** program is based for calculating the standard error of skewness and the skewness ratio *when there is a grouping variable*

For the reader who is interested in learning some Stata programming skills, we present the set of commands upon which the program **summskew** is based in terms of the example at hand. For this example, we seek to calculate the standard error of skewness (seskew) and the skewness ratio for the temp data, which has two variables, city and temp. City is a grouping variable and temp is a scale variable. At this point, without knowledge of what is called a Do-file, to be introduced in the next chapter, we would need to enter each command individually in the Command Window, and press Enter at the end of each. Since it would be far too annoying to do that, we present this program for heuristic reasons only.

```
summarize city, detail
display "maximum number of groups = " r(max)
display "minimum number of groups = " r(min)
global k = r(max)
global m = r(min)
forval i = $m (1) $k {
quietly summarize temp if city == `i', detail
capture drop n skew seskew skew_ratio
local n = r(N)
local skew = r(skewness)
local seskew = sqrt((6*(`n')*(`n' - 1))/((`n' - 2)*(`n' +
1)* (`n' + 3)))
local skew_ratio = `skew'/`seskew'
display "For city = " `i' ": skewness = " `skew' "; seskew =
" `seskew' "; skewness ratio = " `skew_ratio'
}
```

MORE Stata: (OPTIONAL) Explaining the commands used in the program to compute the skewness ratio *when there is a grouping variable*

The set of commands begins with the **summarize city, detail** command and uses several statistical results produced by this command and stored as **r()** variables to calculate the skewness ratio. In particular, **r(max)** contains city's maximum value label, equal to 2, representing San Francisco, and **r(min)** contains the city's minimum value label, equal to 1, representing Springfield. By the statement **global m = r(max)**, we assign the value 2 to the global variable **m** and analogously, by the statement **global k = r(max)**, we assign the value 1 to the global variable **k**. By Stata convention, as "global" variables, m and k must be referred to as **$m** and **$k**, respectively, in future references to them. The line, **forval i = $m (1) $k {**, and the last line of the set,**},** are bookends that define, what is called a *loop* in programming. A loop is a series of commands that is to be repeated some number of times as defined, in this case, by the **forval** statement. If we substitute the actual values for **$m** and **$k** into the **forval** command, we note that **forval** simply directs Stata to execute the series of commands between the open and closed brackets when **i** (an index that may be thought of as a counter) equals 1, and when incremented by 1 (the value in parentheses), **i** equals 2. Accordingly, the seven command lines beginning with **quietly ...** and ending with **display ...** are executed twice. Once when **i**=1 and again when **i**=2. Within the body of the loop, the index **i** must be referred to within open and closed quotes as follows: `i'. The particular open quote used may be found on the same key as ~ on the keyboard and the particular closed quote used is the apostrophe. In addition, all variables defined as **local variables** must be referred to within the same open and closed quotes as `i'. Local variables are not saved in the data set, but are used only locally within the program itself.

MORE Stata: (OPTIONAL) To calculate the skewness, standard error of skewness and skewness ratio with a separate set of command lines *when there is NO grouping variable*

If there were no grouping variable for the problem, we would not need a loop and we could use the following set of commands to find the seskew and skewness ratio of

varname. In running the syntax, we would need to replace **varname** with the actual name of the variable of interest (e.g., slfcnc08). Note that n, like other **local variables**, must be placed within open and closed quotes, `n`, once it is defined. Given our ability to obtain the skewness statistics much more simply, however, using **summskew**, the program below is included for heuristic reasons only.

```
summarize varname, detail
quietly {
local n = r(N)
local skew = r(skewness)
local seskew = sqrt((6*(`n')*(`n' - 1))/((`n' - 2)*(`n' +
1)*(`n' + 3)))
local skew_ratio = `skew'/`seskew'
}
display "skewness = " `skew' "; seskew = " `seskew' ";
skewness ratio = " `skew_ratio'
```

SELECTING MEASURES OF LOCATION AND SPREAD

Table 3.3 provides a summary of the relationship between the level of measurement of a variable and the generally appropriate measures of central tendency and spread. In the case of interval- or ratio-leveled variables, the shape of the distribution influences whether one chooses a resistant measure (i.e., median and interquartile range) or a nonresistant measure (i.e., mean, standard deviation, and range) to summarize the data. If a distribution is not severely skewed, either may be appropriate. If the distribution is severely skewed, however, resistant measures are generally more appropriate. As discussed in this chapter, resistant measures are not as influenced by outliers as nonresistant measures and, therefore, will provide better summary characterizations of the data when data are severely skewed.

APPLYING WHAT WE HAVE LEARNED

Suppose we wish to know the extent to which eighth grade males expect larger incomes at age 30 than eighth grade females, and the extent to which there is lack of consensus among eighth grade males in their expectations of income at age 30 relative to females. We make use of the statistics presented thus far to find answers to our questions.

While quick answers might be obtained by comparing the numerical summaries of location and spread for expinc30 for both males and females, to be confident of their

TABLE 3.3. Guidelines for selecting appropriate measures of location and spread based on a variable's level of measurement and other characteristics.

Variable Characteristics	Appropriate Measures of	
	Location	**Spread**
Nominal with more than 2 categories	Mode	Frequency distribution table
Ordinal with fewer than 5 categories	Mode	IQR
Ordinal with more than 5 categories	Median	IQR
Scale (interval or ratio) and severely skewed	Median	IQR
Scale (interval or ratio) and not severely skewed	Mean	SD

accuracy, we need first to examine the data that are being summarized. A good way to do so is with the help of two side-by-side boxplots, one for males and one for females. The Explore procedure in Stata can be used to generate both summary statistics and associated graphs and is especially useful when comparing two or more groups on the same variable.

MORE Stata: To obtain boxplots, organized into separate panels, and statistics for a variable by subgroups.

Type:

graph box expinc30, by(gender)

by gender, sort: summarize expinc30, detail

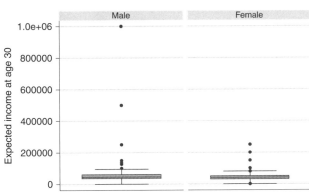

Graphs by Gender

```
–> gender = Male
                            Expected income at age 30

          Percentiles        Smallest
   1%        10000               1
   5%        25000            10000
  10%        30000            10000        Obs                  215
  25%        35000            20000        Sum of Wgt.          215

  50%        45000                         Mean            60720.93
                             Largest        Std. Dev.       79258.87
  75%        60000           250000
  90%       100000           250000        Variance         6.28e+09
  95%       125000           500000        Skewness         8.801321
  99%       250000          1000000        Kurtosis         97.53704


–> gender = Female
                            Expected income at age 30

          Percentiles        Smallest
   1%            0               0
   5%        20000               0
  10%        25000               0        Obs                  244
  25%        30000               0        Sum of Wgt.          244

  50%        40000                        Mean            43515.57
                             Largest       Std. Dev.       26965.09
  75%        50000           150000
  90%        70000           200000        Variance         7.27e+08
  95%        80000           200000        Skewness         3.792478
  99%       200000           250000        Kurtosis         25.20726
```

From the boxplots we notice that with the exception of two outliers, the distributions of expinc30 are similar in shape for males and females.

MORE Stata: Modifying the box plot

To identify the outliers in your data set by id and, in addition, to place the two box plots within the same frame or panel, rather than in different frames or panels as before, we may use the option **over** instead of **by**. We also may modify the command to add marker labels as follows:

graph box expinc30, over(gender) marker(1, mlabel (id))

The 1 refers to the first (and only) variable to be plotted in this boxplot (namely, expinc30). If we were creating a boxplot of a second variable on the same coordinate axes, we would add the option **marker(2, mlabel(id))** as follows:

graph box slfcnc08 slfcnc10, over(gender) marker(1, mlabel (id)) marker (2,mlabel(id))

Plotting more than one variable on the same set of coordinate axes, whether in the same panel or not, makes most sense when the variables share a common metric.

Because of the presence of many more extreme outliers in the male distribution, we can expect the male, female differences with respect to the mean, range, and standard deviation to be more pronounced than those based on the median and interquartile range as these latter statistics are more resistant to being influenced by extreme values.

From the table of summary statistics we may note that the skewness of the male distribution is approximately 8.801 whereas the skewness of the female distribution is approximately 3.792.

Because the *NELS* data set has different numbers of males ($n = 215$) and females ($n = 244$), we calculate the skewness ratio for each group by using the command **summskew, by(gender)** and obtain the following results:

For gender = 0: skewness = 8.801321; seskew = .16590399; skewness ratio = 53.05
For gender = 1: skewness = 3.7924776; seskew = .15585993; skewness ratio = 24.3

These summary statistics corroborate our graphical impressions that both distributions are severely positively skewed and that the male distribution is far more positively skewed than the female distribution.

Notice that, as expected, the male mean is considerably higher than the female mean. On average, the 215 males who responded to this question expect an income at age 30 of $60,721, while the 244 females who responded to this question expect an income at age 30 of only $43,516. Notice also that the male median is $45,000 while the female median is $40,000. Thus, whether one uses the mean or the median, males are shown to have higher expected incomes at age 30 than females. However, the magnitude of difference is considerably greater between the sexes when one uses the mean rather than the median as a measure of location. This attests more to the fact that the distribution of expinc30 is more positively skewed for males than for females than to some essential truth about the difference in expected income between the majority of males and females.

Comparing the spread of the male and female distributions, we find again that different summary statistics lead to different interpretations. The difference in expected income variability between males and females is most pronounced when nonresistant measures are used (e.g., the range, variance, and standard deviation) and less pronounced when more resistant measures of spread are used (e.g., the interquartile range). When a non-resistant statistic, like the standard deviation, is used to compare the spreads of the male and female distributions, males, with $SD = 79,259$, are shown to have much greater lack of consensus than females with $SD = 26,965$. When a resistant statistic like the interquartile range is used, the degree of discrepancy between the genders is diminished. While males, with $IQR = 25,000$, are again shown to have a greater lack of consensus than females, with $IQR = 20,000$, the degree of difference in consensus is far smaller.

☞ **Remark.** Note that because the values of the variance are large for the two distributions, scientific notation was used by Stata to express these values. This is often the case when values are either very large or very small. To understand this format, we translate the value of the variance for males from scientific to standard notation. The value in scientific notation is 6.3E+09. This is equivalent to 6.3×10^9 or 6,300,000,000.

Because of the extreme outliers in the male distribution, the more resistant statistics, not being so influenced by these two extreme cases, are more accurate in describing the extent of difference between males and females relative to the bulk of the cases in our data set. Had we not examined the data initially, we might have characterized the magnitude of the difference between the bulk of males and females as being greater than it actually is, both in terms of level and spread.

We might also explore the extent to which our summary statistics would change if these two male outliers were removed from the analysis. By eliminating these two outliers, we can expect our numerical summaries to represent with greater accuracy the bulk of cases in our sample. The following table contains the new statistics calculated on the male group without cases 102 and 494, obtained using the following command line in Stata

by gender, sort: summarize expinc30 if expinc30 < 450000, detail

Alternatively, we could use the following command (note that!= means not equal to):

by gender, sort: summarize expinc30 if id!=102 & id!= 494, detail

Notice that the skewness of this "new" male distribution is now quite similar to the skewness of the original female distribution. Notice also that the resistant statistics have not changed at all, and that the nonresistant statistics all have moved quite a bit closer to the resistant statistics. In short, by eliminating two of the 500 cases, we have convergence in our results. We know now the extent to which males have higher expected incomes at age 30 and the extent to which they have less consensus on their income expectations relative to females. The reason why we know the extent of outlier influence in this example is because two separate analyses were carried out, one with and one without the outliers. Whenever outliers are eliminated from a data set, standard practice should be to carry out one analysis on all data points, including outliers, and another analysis on the subset of data points excluding outliers. Then, the results of the original analyses can be reported along with the extent to which these results have been influenced by the outliers.

In practice, one should not eliminate data points indiscriminately to achieve a "better" result. One should not report that "the average expected income for the males in

```
-> gender = Male
                        Expected income at age 30

           Percentiles      Smallest
    1%        10000              1
    5%        25000          10000
   10%        30000          10000      Obs                 213
   25%        35000          20000      Sum of Wgt.         213

   50%        45000                     Mean            54248.83
                             Largest    Std. Dev.        35034.2
   75%        60000         150000
   90%       100000         250000      Variance         1.23e+09
   95%       100000         250000      Skewness        2.999023
   99%       250000         250000      Kurtosis        15.50133


-> gender = Female
                        Expected income at age 30

           Percentiles      Smallest
    1%            0              0
    5%        20000              0
   10%        25000              0      Obs                 244
   25%        30000              0      Sum of Wgt.         244

   50%        40000                     Mean            43515.57
                             Largest    Std. Dev.       26965.09
   75%        50000         150000
   90%        70000         200000      Variance         7.27e+08
   95%        80000         200000      Skewness        3.792478
   99%       200000         250000      Kurtosis        25.20726
```

this sample is \$54,248," without adding that "two subjects with extremely high expected incomes were excluded."

If outliers are present, one needs to understand why they are there. Perhaps they represent errors in data entry, or perhaps they belong to persons who are not part of the population identified for study. Additionally, it may be that they represent a segment of the population underrepresented in your study and that through further sampling these cases will no longer be extreme. While we eliminated the two outliers in this example, other ways for reducing the effects of outliers are presented in the next chapter.

MORE Stata: Operators and Expressions

In addition to <, &, and!=, a more complete set of standard arithmetic, logical and relational operators that may be used in expressions is given below:

Arithmetic: + (add); − (subtract); * (multiply); / (divide); ^ (exponentiate)
Logical:! or ~ (not); | (or); & (and)
Relational: == (equal to);!= or ~= (not equal to); < (less than); > (greater than); <= (less than or equal to); >= (greater than or equal to)

SUMMARY OF STATA COMMANDS IN CHAPTER 3

Once you learn about Do-files, you should access a complete listing of all Stata commands associated with this chapter in the Do-file for Chapter 3 located on the text website.

Create	Command Lines
Calculate the mode of ses or any variable with no missing values and one mode	**egen sesmode = mode(ses)** **list sesmode if id ==1**
Calculate the median of ses (Example 3.1)	**tabstat ses, stat(median)** OR **summarize ses, detail**
Calculate the mean of ses (Example 3.2)	**tabstat ses, stat(mean)** OR **summarize ses**
To find the mean of gender, together with a frequency distribution table (Example 3.4)	**summarize gender** OR **tabstat gender** AND **tabulate gender**
To generate a single table with summary statistics for each of the three variables, ses, expinc30, and schattrt (Example 3.5)	**tabstat ses expinc30 schattrt slfcnc08, statistics(mean median)**
To obtain the interquartile ranges for distributions of the single variable temp for different sub-groups by city	**tabstat temp, stats(iqr) by(city)**
To obtain the standard deviations for distributions of the single variable temp for different sub-groups by city	**by city, sort: summarize temp, detail** **Or** **by city, sort: tabstat temp, stats(sd)** **Or** **tabstat temp, stats(sd) by(city)** **Or** **tabulate city, sum(temp)**
To calculate the skewness ratio for the variable slfcnc08	**summskew slfcnc08**
To calculate the skewness ratio for the variable expinc30 broken down by the grouping variable gender	**summskew expinc30, by(gender)**
To obtain descriptive statistics for the variable expinc30 broken down by gender subgroups	**by gender, sort: summarize expinc30, detail**
To obtain descriptive statistics for the variable expinc30 broken down by gender subgroups and omitting some cases	**by gender, sort: summarize expinc30 if expinc30 < 450000, detail** **by gender, sort: summarize expinc30 if id!=102 & id!= 494, detail**

HELPFUL HINTS WHEN USING STATA

Stata is very user-friendly. Commands can be executed either by using the menus, or by directly typing syntax into the Command Window or.do file. Learning a new programming language, however, is always a bit challenging. Here are some hints that should help users become more comfortable with Stata.

Online Resources

There are a variety of resources available online that can help if a problem is encountered using Stata. Visit the following websites if you require additional resources when using Stata.

- http://www.ats.ucla.edu/stat/stata/
- http://statcomp.ats.ucla.edu/stata/
- http://www.stata.com/links/

In addition, we can simply pose a question on google, such as "stem and leaf plot in Stata," and a number of resources will pop up that should contain an answer to our question.

Finally, as a last resort, we can send an email message to tech-support@stata.com. In our own experience, we have found that responses from Stata's tech support are extremely prompt and helpful.

The Stata Command

Stata offers a variety of commands that allows us to work with and analyze our data. As noted earlier in the text, all commands must be written in lower case unless otherwise noted, and variable names must be typed in a case sensitive manner. That is, if a variable has been given the name MathAch, Stata will understand that we are referring to that variable as long as we type the M and A as upper case and the remaining letters as lower case. To make the job of writing syntax easier, we recommend that variables names contain lower case letters only.

Stata's commands generally have the following syntax or form:

[prefix command:] command [varlist] [if] [in] [, options]

The items enclosed in square brackets are not necessary to run the command and are optional. To run a Stata command, all we need is the command itself.

We describe each of the items in square brackets and illustrate by using the command **summarize** introduced in Chapter 2, applied to one of our smaller data sets, icecream.dta, which contains four variables, id (for identifying the day on which data were collected, ranging from 1 to 30), temp (for day's highest temperature), barsold (for number of ice cream bars sold that day), and relhumid (for day's relative humidity).

We assume that the icecream.dta file is now open and in active memory.

Typing **summarize** without a *varlist*, will produce descriptives (number of observations, mean, standard deviation, minimum, and maximum) on all of the variables in the ice cream data set.

Typing **summarize temp relhumid** will produce descriptives only on the variables temp and relhumid.

Including *if* in the command line restricts the analysis to those observations that have a particular value or values on one of the variables in the data set.

For example, typing **summarize temp relhumid if barsold > 170** will produce descriptives on temp and relhumid based only on those days for which the number of ice cream bars sold exceeds 170. As we may verify, only ten days satisfy this condition.

Including *in* in the command line restricts the analysis to those observations whose order in the dataset corresponds to the range of numbers listed. The range may be a single number, or a range of numbers. Specifying 5/10, for example, restricts the analysis to six observations in the data set, those that represent the 5th, 6th, 7th, 8th, 9th, and 10th observations; specifying 8/L, for example, restricts the analysis to the 8th through the last observation in the data set; and, specifying F/25, for example, restricts the analysis to the first through the 25th observation in the data set.

For example, typing **summarize temp relhumid in 5/10** will produce descriptives on temp and relhumid based only on the observations collected on the fifth through the tenth day of data collection.

Stata commands have *options* that may be used depending upon the situation. To find out which options are available for each command, it is often helpful to make ample use of Stata's **help** command. For example, if you do not recall the options that may be used with the command **summarize**, type **help summarize** in the Command Window and hit Enter.

By typing **help summarize** the Viewer Window opens with lots of information about the command **summarize**. An excerpt of that information is provided below:

```
Title
[R] summarize - Summary statistics
Syntax
  summarize [varlist]
  [if] [in] [weight]
  [, options]
 options               Description
 Main
 detail                display additional statistics
 meanonly              suppress the display; calculate only
                       the mean; programmer's option
 format                use variable's display format
 separator(#)          draw separator line after every #
                       variables; default is separator(5)
 display_options       control spacing, line width, and base
                       and empty cells
 varlist may contain factor variables; see fvvarlist.
 varlist may contain time-series operators; see tsvarlist.
 by, rolling, and statsby are allowed; see prefix.
Menu
Statistics > Summaries, tables, and tests > Summary and
descriptive statistics > Summary statistics
Description
summarize calculates and displays a variety of univariate
summary statistics. If no varlist is specified, summary
statistics are calculated for all the variables in the
dataset.
```

According to the above excerpt, there are several *options* that may be used with this command. One of these is**, detail**, which, if included on the command line, will produce additional summary statistics on the variables of interest. Note that options are separated from the main part of the command by a comma.

Typing **summarize temp relhumid, detail** will not only produce the usual five (number of observations, mean, standard deviation, minimum, and maximum), but also an array of other statistics, including percentiles, the iqr, range, and so on.

These are *prefix* commands that may be included before the command of interest to modify the dataset temporarily to support the proper execution of the command itself. In Chapter 2, we introduced an example of a prefix command (**by ses, sort:**).

STATA TIPS

Before we open a data file, it is a good idea to type the command **clear** in the Command Window to clear Stata's active memory of data and to start with a clean slate. Once Stata's active memory is cleared, we may now load our data set into the computer's active memory as described in Chapter 1.

A useful command for getting to know our data is **describe**. The **describe** command produces a description of the dataset that currently is in memory, listing all the variable names and their labels.

Another useful command for getting to know our data, including the numeric values assigned to the different categories of a categorical variable and the frequencies of those categories, is **codebook**. To obtain information about all the variables in our active dataset, simply type the command **codebook**. To obtain information on a particular variable or variables, follow the command **codebook** with the name(s) of those variables.

The **drop** command will delete variables from the dataset. To drop variables temporarily from the data set, type the command **preserve** before typing the command **drop**. With **preserve** typed before drop, we may reinstate the dropped variables by typing **restore**.

In the following example, we temporarily **drop** the variable temp from the ice cream dataset and then **restore** it to the dataset after we have run the **summarize** command. The summarize command will compute descriptives on all the variables in the data set, with the exception of temp, since temp had been dropped from the dataset prior to running **summarize**.

```
preserve
drop temp
summarize
restore
```

When typing commands in the Command Window, you may navigate more efficiently through the Output Window by hitting the **Page Up** button on your keyboard to reach the results of each of the previously run commands.

Sometimes commands are too long to fit on one line or, for some other reason, we would like a command to span two or more lines. To do so, we add three forward slashes /// at the end of each line that we wish to have continued to the next, leaving a space before and after ///.

EXERCISES

Exercises 3.1–3.7 involve measures of central tendency and require the use of Stata.

3.1. For the following variables from the *NELS* data set, what are the appropriate measures of central tendency (mean, median, mode) and why? Use Stata to calculate the values of these measures and interpret the results.

a) gender
b) urban
c) schtyp8
d) tcherint
e) numinst
f) achrdg08
g) schattrt
h) absent12

3.2. These questions involve the variable late12 from the *NELS* data set.

a) How many students in the data set were never late to school?
b) How often was the first person in the data set late to school?
c) What is a typical number of times students were late to school?

3.3. For the following variables in the *NELS* data set, indicate the most appropriate set of summary statistics for summarizing the distribution: (1) frequencies or percentages and mode, (2) median and interquartile range, (3) median, interquartile range, and skewness ratio, (4) mean, standard deviation, and skewness ratio. Your answers should depend upon the level of measurement of the variable as well as the extent to which extreme values are present in the distribution to influence unduly the value of these summary statistics.

a) gender
b) urban
c) schtyp8
d) tcherint
e) numinst
f) achrdg08
g) schattrt
h) absent12

3.4. Cigarette is a dichotomous variable coded 0 for those who have not smoked and 1 for those who have.

a) Compute the proportion of those that ever smoked based on the number from the frequency distribution.
b) Compute the mean of cigarette. Interpret the mean in view of the result of part (a).
c) Do a greater proportion of males or females report having ever smoked?

3.5. In this exercise, we examine measures of central tendency for the variable CIGSPDAY1 in the *Framingham* data set.

a) Create a boxplot showing the distribution of the number of cigarettes smoked per day (CIGPDAY1). Comment upon the presence of outliers in the distribution. Based on the graph, how many cigarettes per day do you think a typical person in the data set smokes?

b) Calculate and report the values for the mean and median of CIGPDAY1.

c) Which measure of central tendency gives a better description of the number of cigarettes smoked per day by people in the *Framingham* data set? Why do you suppose that is?

3.6. In this exercise, we examine the gender difference in the number of cigarettes smoked per day in the *Framingham* data set, taking into account the presence of one extreme male outlier.

a) Create a boxplot showing the distribution of the number of cigarettes smoked per day (CIGPDAY1) by gender (SEX). Comment upon the presence of outliers in the two distributions.

b) Are there gender differences in the number of cigarettes smoked per day? Provide statistical support for your answer.

3.7. It was noted in this chapter that when a unimodal continuous distribution is positively skewed, the mean is generally larger than the median given that extreme values influence the value of the mean more than they do the value of the median. While there are rare exceptions to this rule in the case when a variable is many-valued, in other cases, as exemplified by this exercise, exceptions are more common.

a) Create a histogram of the variable tcherint from the *NELS* data set, which contains only four possible values. According to the histogram, what is the shape of the distribution?

b) Which is larger, the mean of tcherint, or the median?

Exercise 3.8 involves measures of dispersion and the NELS data set.

3.8. Which measure(s) of dispersion or variability (range, Interquartile range, standard deviation, or variance), if any, may be used appropriately to measure the spread of the following variables from the *NELS* data set? Report these values. In stating your answer, take into account both the level of measurement of the variable and whether there are extreme values in its distribution that could unduly influence the value of certain dispersion statistics, making them less representative of the distribution as a whole.

a) gender

b) urban

c) numinst

d) achrdg08

e) schattrt

f) absent12

Exercises 3.9–3.14 involve selecting a relevant Stata procedure and calculating and interpreting a variety of appropriate summary statistics using variables from the NELS data set.

3.9. Use Stata to find the following summary descriptive statistics for a student's self-concept in eighth grade (slfcnc08).

a) Minimum

b) Maximum

c) 40th percentile

d) 25th percentile

e) Mean

f) Median

g) Mode

  h) Range
  i) Interquartile range
  j) Variance
  k) Standard deviation
  l) Skewness
  m) Standard error of the skewness (seskew)

3.10. The following questions investigate how, among the students in the *NELS* data set, tenth grade math achievement (achmat10) is related to whether or not the student's family owned a computer when he or she was in eighth grade (computer). Use Stata to generate the values of appropriate statistics to answer the related questions.

  a) Compare the shape of the distributions of achmat10 for those who did and those who did not own a computer in eighth grade. Begin by constructing boxplots of achmat10, one for each value of computer and follow up by calculating skewness ratios.

  b) Is tenth grade math achievement typically higher or lower for students whose families owned a computer when they were in eighth grade than students whose families did not own a computer when they were in eighth grade? Explain and support your answer with the value of at least one appropriate descriptive statistic, indicating if any other statistics contradict your conclusion.

  c) Among students in the *NELS* data set, is tenth grade math achievement more or less variable for students whose families owned a computer when they were in eighth grade? Explain and support your answer with the value of at least one appropriate descriptive statistic, indicating if any other statistics contradict your conclusion.

3.11. This exercise addresses differences in socioeconomic status (ses) by urbanicity (urban) for students in the *NELS* data set. Use Stata to generate the descriptive statistics that will be used for answering the following questions.

  a) Describe the shape of ses for each of the three levels of urban.

  b) What type of student has the highest typical socioeconomic status, those from urban, suburban, or rural settings? Support your answer with appropriate descriptive statistics, indicating whether all such statistics support your conclusion.

  c) For what type of setting is the socioeconomic status of the students most dispersed, those from urban, suburban, or rural settings? Support your answer with appropriate descriptive statistics, indicating whether all such statistics support your conclusion.

  d) In what type of setting does the person with the highest socioeconomic status live, urban, suburban, or rural?

3.12. Answer the following questions to compare eighth grade self-concept (slfcnc08) to twelfth grade self-concept (slfcnc12) for students in the *NELS* data set.

  a) Is the distribution of self-concept scores in the *NELS* data set severely skewed in either eighth or twelfth grade? If the distribution is severely skewed, indicate the direction of the skew. If the distributions are severely skewed, indicate which is more skewed. Explain and support your answer using the value(s) of at least one appropriate statistic.

  b) Do students in the *NELS* data set typically have higher self-concept scores in eighth or twelfth grade? Explain and support your answer with the value(s) of at least one appropriate statistic.

c) Are the self-concept scores of students in the *NELS* data set more heterogeneous in eighth or twelfth grade? Explain and support your answer with the value(s) of at least one appropriate statistic.

3.13. In this exercise, we explore differences between males and females on three variables in the *NELS* data set, one affective, another cognitive, and the third, behavioral.

a) Are males and females similar in terms of the extent to which they believe teachers show an interest in them (tcherint)? Begin by considering similarities in their distributions by constructing boxplots. Follow up by using Stata to obtain a comparison of measures of central tendency for these interest scores across gender.

b) Do males and females display similar patterns of change in achievement in reading across eighth (achrdg08), tenth (achrdg10), and twelfth grades (achrdg12)? Begin with boxplots, and, then use Stata to obtain a comparison of measures of central tendency for these achievement scores across grades.

c) Do males and females have similar patterns of school attendance in grade 12 as measured by absent12, cuts12, and late12? Does one gender report greater incidents of absenteeism than the other? Begin by constructing boxplots. Given the ordinal nature of these three variables, follow-up with Stata to calculate medians, *IQR's*, and skewness for all three variables by gender.

Ex.

3.14. Taking advanced math in eighth grade is often thought to be a proxy for being a more serious student, who is on a college bound track. In this exercise we explore differences on a number of academic and nonacademic variables between those who did and did not take advanced math in eighth grade (advmath8).

a) Do those who took advanced math in eighth grade report having spent more time per week on homework outside of school in twelfth grade (hwkout12) than those who did not take advanced math in eighth grade? Construct a boxplot for each group and follow-up with appropriate descriptive statistics for this ordinal variable.

b) Do those who took advanced math in eighth grade report typically fewer incidents of absenteeism in twelfth grade (absent12) than those who did not take math in eighth grade? Construct a boxplot for each group and follow-up with appropriate descriptive statistics for this ordinal variable.

c) Is there a difference between those who took advanced math in eighth grade and those who did not in terms of the number of post-secondary institutions they attended (numinst). Recall that numinst is a ratio-leveled variable. Begin by constructing histograms and then follow-up with descriptive statistics using Explore.

Exercises 3.15–3.16 are based on data sets other than the NELS and relate to a variety of summary statistics.

3.15. Create a stem-and-leaf plot of the variable readcomp from the *Learndis* data set. Use it to answer the following questions.

a) What term best describes the shape of this distribution: positively skewed, negatively skewed, or symmetric?

b) What is the mode reading comprehension score for these students? If there is more than one mode, report them all.

c) What is the maximum reading comprehension score for these students?

d) Without calculating, which is probably larger for these students, the mean reading comprehension score or the median comprehension score? Explain.

e) Without calculating it, which statistic would probably be best to summarize the spread of this distribution? Explain.

f) Which boxplot below (A, B, or C) best describes the data in the stem-and-leaf plot?

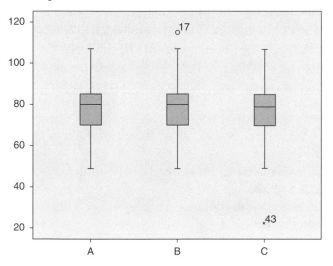

3.16. This question explores variables from the *Framingham* data set. Provide a demographic assessment by sex of this sample of individuals at baseline with respect to the following variables.

a) Age (AGE1)

b) Total Serum Cholesterol (TOTCHOL1)

c) Blood Pressure (Systolic and Diastolic) (SYSBP1 and DIABP1)

d) BMI (BMI1)

e) Current Cigarette Smoker (CURSMOKE1)

f) Number of Cigarettes Smoked Per Day (CIGPDAY1)

Exercises 3.17–3.19 require some computation by hand to reinforce your understanding of how the values provided by Stata are derived. In so doing, we believe that your conceptual understanding of these descriptive statistics will be enhanced.

3.17. Use the *Statisticians* data set in this exercise.

a) Calculate the mean, median, mode, range, interquartile range, variance, and standard deviation of the variable amstat by hand.

b) Use Stata to check your answers to part a).

c) Demonstrate that the sum of the deviations about the mean equals 0.

3.18. The following distribution of initial blood pressure values comes from the *Blood* data set.

| 107 | 110 | 123 | 129 | 112 | 111 | 107 | 112 | 135 | 102 | 123 |
| 109 | 112 | 102 | 98 | 114 | 119 | 112 | 110 | 117 | 130 | |

a) Calculate the mean, median, mode, range, interquartile range, variance, and standard deviation of the distribution by hand.

b) Calculate the mean, median, mode, range, interquartile range, variance, and standard deviation of the distribution using Stata.

3.19. Create a frequency distribution table of the variable grade from the *Learndis* data set. Use it to answer the following questions.

a) Estimate Q_1, Q_2, and Q_3 for this distribution based on the frequency distribution table.

b) Estimate the interquartile range for this distribution.

c) Suppose an error were found in the data, and two of the cases classified as second graders were really first graders. After the data is corrected, which of the mode, median, and mean will have changed, and in which direction?

Exercises 3.20–3.39 test your conceptual understanding and do not require the use of Stata.

3.20. For a sample of size 12, the mean is 4, the median is 5, and the mode is 6. Is it true that the sum of the raw scores is 36?

3.21. For each of parts (a)–(g), create a (possibly different) data set with five numbers from –5 to 5 (with repeats allowed) for which

a) The mean, median, and mode are all equal.

b) The mean is greater than the median.

c) The mode is higher than the median or mean.

d) The mean is 0.

e) The standard deviation is as small as possible.

f) The distribution is negatively skewed.

3.22. Three different people correctly report the typical wage of a group of five wage earners to be $5,000, $7,000, and $10,000. Explain how this is possible. Find a set of five wages that can correctly be said to have these three measures of location.

3.23. Show that a distribution with a higher mean does not necessarily have a higher standard deviation. Construct two distributions, X and Y, with two scores each, so that X has the larger mean and Y has the larger standard deviation.

3.24. Show that a distribution with a higher mean does not necessarily have a higher median. Construct two distributions, X and Y, so that X has the larger mean and Y has the larger median.

3.25. Show that a distribution with more values does not necessarily have a higher standard deviation. Construct two distributions, X and Y, so that X has more values in its distribution, but Y has the larger standard deviation.

3.26. Construct a distribution X for which the mode is not the majority response.

3.27. Is it possible for the standard deviation of a distribution to be more than half the range? Explain.

3.28. Show that a symmetric distribution exists for which the mean does not equal the mode, by sketching the graph of such a distribution.

3.29. Show that a distribution can have outliers and still be symmetric, by sketching the graph of such a distribution.

3.30. Show that a distribution with a higher maximum does not necessarily have a higher mean. Construct two distributions, X and Y, so that X has a higher maximum value, but Y has a higher mean.

3.31. Show that a skewed distribution can be consistent. Construct two distributions, X and Y, so that X is less skewed, but Y is more consistent.

3.32. Show that a skewed distribution can contain low typical scores. Construct two distributions, X and Y, so that X is more skewed, but Y has a larger mean.

3.33. Answer the following questions about statistics reported in the March 2013 article, "TheKnot.com and WeddingChannel.com Reveal Results of Largest Wedding Study of its Kind, Surveying more than 17,500 Brides." The relevant information is contained in the questions themselves, but the interested reader may look up the article at http://www .prnewswire.com/news-releases/theknotcom-and-weddingchannelcom-reveal-results-of-largest-wedding-study-of-its-kind-surveying-more-than-17500-brides-195856281.html.

    a) According to the survey, the average wedding budget in 2012 was $28,427, excluding honeymoon. If someone wanted to encourage you to spend as much as possible on your wedding, which would be better to report, the mean or the median? Explain.

    b) The average marrying age for brides in the US is 29. Do you think that the standard deviation is closer to 3 days, 3 months, or 3 years? Explain.

3.34. Consider the distribution, for all children in the United States, of the ages at which they enter kindergarten. Do you think that the standard deviation of this distribution is closer to 5 years or 5 months? Explain.

3.35. Assume that on a final exam, the raw scores for student performance were severely negatively skewed.

    a) What is probably true about the performances of the students in the class on the exam?

    b) If the exam were to be curved, which is preferable from a student perspective, that the median be set to a B- or that the mean be set to a B-?

3.36. Match each set of summary statistics (A, B, C, D, E) with the corresponding histogram (X1, X2, X3, X4, X5) below. Computations are not necessary to complete this exercise.

	A	B	C	D	E
Mean	4.5	5	5	5.5	6
Standard Deviation	1.96	1.23	.82	1.96	1.23

3.37. The following excerpt was taken from an editorial by Paul Krugman in the New York Times on January 21, 2003 (p. 23):

"On Saturday, in his weekly radio address, George W. Bush declared that 'the tax relief I propose will give 23 million small-business owners an average tax cut of $2,042 this year.' That remark is intended to give the impression that the typical small-business owner will get $2,000. But as the Center on Budget and Policy Priorities points out, most small businesses will get a tax break of less than $500; about 5 million of those 23 million small businesses will get no break at all. The average is more than $2,000 only because a small number of very wealthy businessmen will get huge tax cuts."

    a) What is the shape of the distribution of tax cuts for small business owners?

    b) What would you guess is the value of the median of the distribution of tax cuts for small business owners?

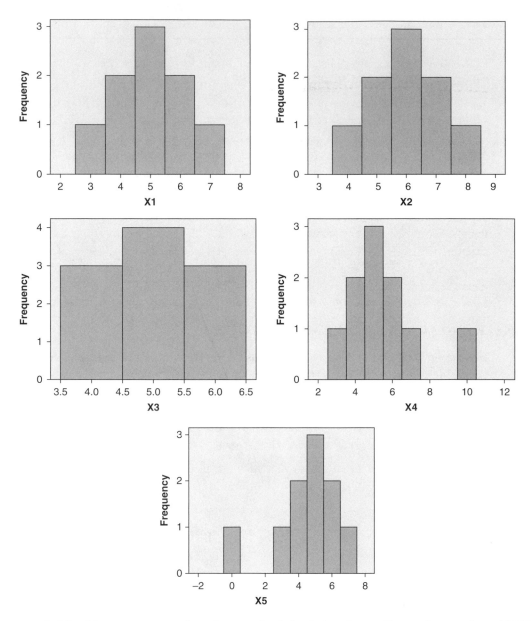

c) Would you suppose that the standard deviation is smaller or larger than $500? Explain.

3.38. Among women in the U.S. aged 40–49, would you expect the mean number of living children per woman to be less then, greater than, or about the same as the median number of living children per woman? Explain your answer.

3.39. Assume your course average is based on a midterm exam worth 100 points and a final exam that also is worth 100 points. Assume also that the midterm exam counts 40 percent of your course average and the final exam counts 60 percent of your course average. If you scored 80 on the midterm exam and 85 on the final exam, what is your average grade for the course?

CHAPTER FOUR

Reexpressing Variables

Often, variables in their original form do not lend themselves well to comparison with other variables or to certain types of analysis. In addition, often we may obtain greater insight by expressing a variable in a different form. For these and other reasons, in this chapter we discuss four different ways to re-express or transform variables: applying linear transformations, applying nonlinear transformations, recoding, and combining. We also describe how to use syntax files to manage your data analysis.

LINEAR AND NONLINEAR TRANSFORMATIONS

In Chapter 1 we discussed measurement as the assignment of numbers to objects to reflect the amount of a particular trait such objects possess. For example, a number in inches may be assigned to a person to reflect how tall that person is. Of course, without loss of information, a number in feet or even in meters, can be assigned instead.

What we will draw upon in this section is the notion that the numbers themselves used to measure a particular trait, whether they be in inches, feet, or meters, for example, are not intrinsic to the trait itself. Rather, they are mere devices for helping us to understand the trait or other phenomenon we are studying. Accordingly, if an alternative numeric system, or *metric* (as a numeric system is called), can be used more effectively than the original one, then this metric should be substituted, as long as it retains whatever properties of the original system we believe are important. In making this change on a univariate basis, each number in the new system will correspond on a one-to-one basis to each number in the original system. That is, each number in the new system will be able to be matched uniquely to one and only one number in the original system.

The rule that defines the one-to-one correspondence between the numeric systems is called the *transformation*. Transformations may be classified according to the properties they retain of the original system. When transformations retain the order of data points in the original system, they are called *monotonic transformations*. In this chapter, we will confine discussion of transformations to monotonic transformations because, in the work we do in the behavioral and social sciences, ordinality is an important feature of a data set worth retaining. This section is devoted to two types of monotonic transformation: *linear* and *nonlinear*. In short, a linear transformation preserves or reflects the shape of the original distribution while a nonlinear transformation is often used to change the shape of the original distribution.

LINEAR TRANSFORMATIONS: ADDITION, SUBTRACTION, MULTIPLICATION, AND DIVISION

heights

Linear transformations are defined by rules that include only a combination of multiplication, division, addition, and subtraction to set up the one-to-one correspondence between numeric systems. For example, suppose we are interested in studying the relative heights of professional basketball players in the United States and Italy. If we used the original numbers for measuring the players' heights in both countries, these numbers would not be comparable because of the different measurement systems used in the two countries. (In the United States, height is measured in inches or feet, in Italy, it is measured in centimeters or meters.) *To obtain comparability of measures*, a more appropriate approach might be to express the heights of the U.S. players in centimeters rather than in inches. To do so, we need only multiply the values of height in inches by 2.54 since there are 2.54 centimeters per inch.

• •

EXAMPLE 4.1. Use the *Basketball* dataset to re-express in centimeters the heights of the 20 scoring leaders, 10 each from the U.S. Women's and Men's National Basketball Association, for the 2012–2014 season. Use the following arithmetic operation to do so.

Height (in centimeters) = height (in inches) * 2.54

Solution. The heights in inches and the heights re-expressed in centimeters are presented below.

Name	Height in Inches (heightin)	Height in Centimeters (heightcm)
Maya Moore	72	182.88
Skylar Diggins	69	175.26
Candace Parker	76	193.04
Angel McCoughtry	73	185.42
Tina Charles	76	193.04
• Diana Taurasi	72	182.88
Seimone Augustus	72	182.88
Nneka Ogwumike	74	187.96
Odyssey Sims	68	172.72
Chiney Ogwumike	76	193.04
Kevin Durant	81	205.74
Carmelo Anthony	80	203.2
LeBron James	80	203.2
Kevin Love	82	208.28
James Harden	77	195.58
Blake Griffin	82	208.28
Stephen Curry	75	190.5
LaMarcus Aldridge	83	210.82
DeMarcus Cousins	83	210.82
DeMar DeRozan	79	200.66

We may use Stata to perform the computation to re-express the original values of height.

MORE Stata: To transform height in inches (heightin) to height in centimeters (heightcm)

After opening the *basket* data set, we type **generate heightcm = heightin * 2.54** in the Command Window and hit Enter.

gen

The variable heightcm will be added to your data set as the last variable.

Note that the command **generate** may be shortened to **gen**. Most Stata commands have a shortened form, which may learn by typing the relevant **help** command.

Because the rule for re-expressing inches as centimeters involves multiplying every value in the distribution by a positive constant, it is an example of a *linear transformation*. Notice that the order of data points has been retained under this transformation. Lisa Leslie is taller than Diana Taurasi regardless of whether their heights are measured in inches or in centimeters.

While this linear transformation involves multiplication only, linear transformations may involve multiplication, addition, or a combination of multiplication and addition. The general form of a linear transformation may be expressed as:

$$X_{new} = K * X_{old} + C \tag{4.1}$$

where K and C are constants and $K \neq 0$. It is worth pointing out that K represents both multiplication and division. For example, when $K = 1/2$, multiplication by K is equivalent to division by 2. Also, C represents both addition and subtraction. For example, when $C = -4$, adding C units is equivalent to subtracting 4 units. K changes the scale of the original values, either by stretching (when K is less than -1 or greater than 1) or compressing (when K is between -1 and $+1$) the horizontal axis, while C translates the location of the original values either up (when C is positive) or down (when C is negative) along the horizontal axis. Figure 4.1 illustrates a linear transformation where $K = 2$ and $C = 10$. Notice that the scale of the new values is doubled (with each unit increase in X, there is a two unit increase in $2X+10$) and the location of the new values is shifted in a positive direction along the horizontal axis from 2 to 14 ($2*2 + 10$).

Linear transformations are so named because, as Equation 4.1 suggests, the new values are a linear function of the original values.

THE EFFECT ON THE SHAPE OF A DISTRIBUTION

Linear transformations not only retain the order of points in a distribution, but they also retain the relative distance between points in a distribution. That is, two points that are far from one another under the original numeric system will be as far from one another to the same relative extent under the new system. In our example, Diana Taurasi's height is closer to Cappie Pondexter's height than to Lisa Leslie's height to the same relative extent in both inches and centimeters. Because relative distance does not change under linear transformation, neither does the general shape of a distribution under linear transformation.

. . . .

EXAMPLE 4.2. Construct boxplots of both distributions of height (in inches and in centimeters). Comment on the shape of these two distributions as represented by the histograms.

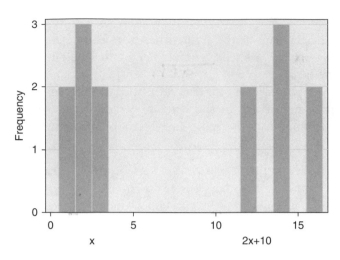

Figure 4.1 Histograms of original values and linearly transformed values (2X+10).

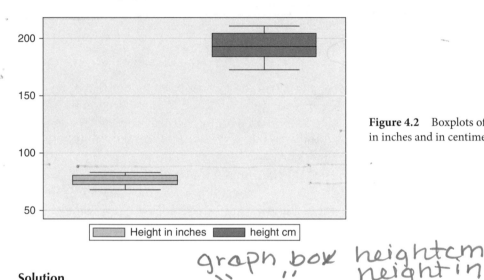

Figure 4.2 Boxplots of height in inches and in centimeters.

Solution.

Create boxplots of heightin and heightcm using Stata.

Clearly, the two boxplots have the same shape. By transforming the data linearly from inches to centimeters, the general shape of a distribution remains the same, although the central tendency and spread can change, as they have in this example.

THE EFFECT ON SUMMARY STATISTICS OF A DISTRIBUTION

While under linear transformation, the general shape of a distribution remains the same, the summary characteristics of a distribution do not. Notice the difference in central tendency or level and spread values for the two boxplots pictured in Figure 4.2. More specifically, the mean height in centimeters (193.29) equals the mean height in inches (76.10) multiplied by 2.54, and the standard deviation of the height in centimeters (9.99) equals the standard deviation of the height in inches (3.93) multiplied by 2.54. In other words, both the mean and standard deviation are multiplied by 2.54, the value by which the heights themselves were multiplied.

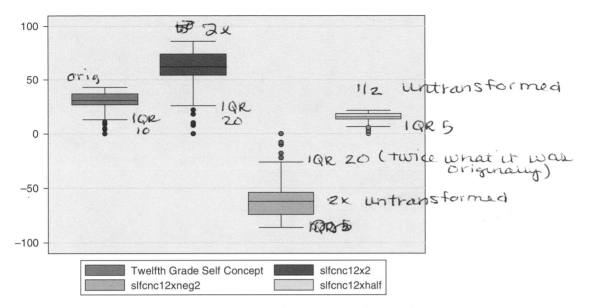

Figure 4.3   An example of a multiplicative linear transformation using the *NELS* data set.

While the new standard deviation is larger than the original standard deviation by a factor of 2.54, the new variance will be larger than the original variance by a factor of 2.54^2, or 6.45. Because the old variance was 3.93^2 or 15.46, the new variance, equals 6.45*15.46 or 99.76.

The boxplots depicted in Figure 4.3 give another example of a multiplicative transformation. In this case, we have created side by side boxplots of slfcnc12, the self-concept scores of the students in the *NELS* data set from twelfth grade, 2* slfcnc12, (–2)* slfcnc12, and (1/2)* slfcnc12. Looking at the level, spread, and shape of these boxplots, we can see certain patterns emerging. The level, or central tendency of the distribution is given by the median of the boxplot. Here we see that the operation that was performed on every score was also performed on the median. So, the median of the original untransformed variable slfcnc12 is about 30. After multiplying every score in the distribution by two to obtain the second boxplot from the left, we see that the median is now around 60, which is twice what it was for the untransformed variable. Similarly the median for the third boxplot from the left is approximately –60 or negative two times the untransformed median and the median for the fourth boxplot is approximately 15 or one half times the untransformed median. The spread is given by the *IQR* of the distribution. Here we see that when multiplying every score by a number, the *IQR* is then multiplied by the absolute value of that number. In the case of the untransformed self-concept given in the leftmost boxplot, the *IQR* is approximately 10. When every score is multiplied by two, resulting in the second boxplot from the left, the *IQR* is approximately 20. In the third boxplot from the left we note that the *IQR* is still positive, even though the distribution has been multiplied by a negative number. All measures of spread are always positive numbers. Even though every score was multiplied by negative 2, the resulting *IQR* is now 20, or twice what it was originally. Finally, the *IQR* for the fourth boxplot is 5 or one half the untransformed value. We can look intuitively at the shape, because it is not possible to estimate the size of the skewness or skewness ratio from the boxplot. In this case we see that when K is positive, the direction of the skew is preserved, and then K is negative, the direction of the skew is reversed. In fact, the magnitude of the skew does not change under a linear transformation, only, potentially, the sign.

More generally, the effects on the measures of central tendency, spread, and shape of a distribution when multiplying all the values in a distribution by a nonzero constant, K, are summarized as follows.

When $X_{New} = K^*X_{Old}$

1. For measures of central tendency:
   $\text{Mode}_{New} = K^* \text{Mode}_{Old}$
   $\text{Median}_{New} = K^* \text{Median}_{Old}$
   $\text{Mean}_{New} = K^* \text{Mean}_{Old}$
2. For measures of spread:
   $\text{IQR}_{New} = |K|^*\text{IQR}_{Old}$
   $\text{SD}_{New} = |K|^*\text{SD}_{Old}$
   $\text{Range}_{New} = |K|^*\text{Range}_{Old}$
   $\text{Variance}_{New} = K^2 *\text{Variance}_{Old}$
3. For measures of shape the result depends on the sign of K:
   If K is positive
   $\text{Skewness}_{New} = \text{Skewness}_{Old}$
   $\text{Skewness Ratio}_{New} = \text{Skewness Ratio}_{Old}$
   If K is negative
   $\text{Skewness}_{New} = (-1)^*\text{Skewness}_{Old}$
   $\text{Skewness Ratio}_{New} = (-1)^*\text{Skewness Ratio}_{Old}$

The boxplots depicted in Figure 4.4 give an example of an additive transformation. In this case, we have created side by side boxplots of slfcnc12, the self-concept scores of the students in the *NELS* data set from twelfth grade, slfcnc12+5 and slfcnc12-5. Looking at the level, spread, and shape of these boxplots, we can see certain patterns emerging. The level, or central tendency of the distribution is given by the median of the boxplot. Here we see that the operation that was performed on every score was also performed on the median. So, the median of the original untransformed variable slfcnc12 is about 30. After adding 5 to every score to obtain the second boxplot from the left, we see that the median is now around 35, which is five more than what it was for the untransformed variable. Similarly the median for the third boxplot from the left is approximately 25 or five less than the untransformed median. The spread is given by the *IQR* of the distribution. Here we see that when adding or subtracting we do not change the spread of the distribution. In the case of the untransformed self-concept given in the leftmost boxplot, the *IQR* is approximately 10 and it is the same for both of the transformed boxplots as well. Similarly, the shape of the boxplot is unchanged by the transformation and we see that both the skewness and skewness ratio of the transformed variables are the same as for the original.

We see that another type of linear transformation is adding a constant, C, to all values in a distribution. The effects on summary statistics of this type of transformation are summarized as follows.

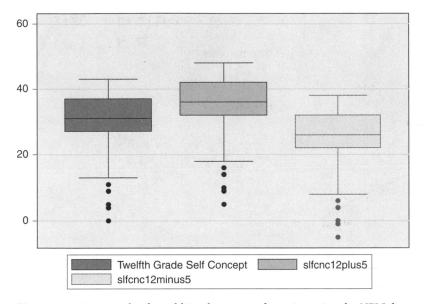

Figure 4.4 An example of an additive linear transformation using the *NELS* data set.

When $X_{New} = X_{Old} + C$

1. For measures of central tendency:
   $\text{Mode}_{New} = \text{Mode}_{Old} + C$
   $\text{Median}_{New} = \text{Median}_{Old} + C$
   $\text{Mean}_{New} = \text{Mean}_{Old} + C$

   $C = constant$

2. For measures of spread:
   $\text{IQR}_{New} = \text{IQR}_{Old}$
   $\text{SD}_{New} = \text{SD}_{Old}$
   $\text{Range}_{New} = \text{Range}_{Old}$
   $\text{Variance}_{New} = \text{Variance}_{Old}$

3. For measures of shape:
   $\text{Skewness}_{New} = \text{Skewness}_{Old}$
   $\text{Skewness Ratio}_{New} = \text{Skewness Ratio}_{Old}$

COMMON LINEAR TRANSFORMATIONS

In this section we present examples of three common types of linear transformation: Translation, reflection, and standard scores. Among standard scores, we will make the most use of *z*-scores.

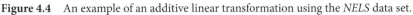

EXAMPLE 4.3. Using the data set 1, 2, 2, 3, show graphically and numerically the effects of adding 4 to all points in this data set.

Solution. Let $X_{OLD} = 1, 2, 2, 3$ and $X_{NEW} = 5, 6, 6, 7$. A graphical representation of the distributions of X_{OLD} and X_{NEW} are given in Figure 4.5.

xnew is xold shifted 4pts
along axis
to the right

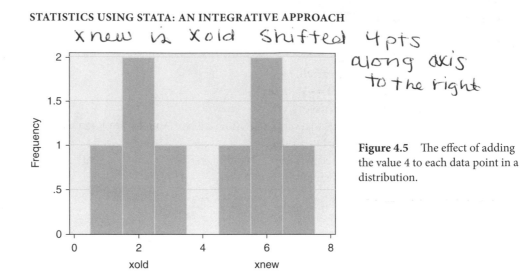

Figure 4.5 The effect of adding the value 4 to each data point in a distribution.

Notice that the distributions are identical but for their location. In particular, the standard deviation, range, interquartile range, and variance of X_{NEW} equal the respective standard deviation and variance of X_{OLD}, but the mean, median, and mode of X_{NEW} are 4 points higher than the respective mean, median, and mode of X_{OLD}. In other words, X_{NEW} is X_{OLD} shifted along the axis 4 points to the right.

A linear transformation that shifts a distribution along the horizontal axis is called a *translation*. One type of translation that we will make use of in Chapter 15 is called *centering*, in which the mean of the distribution is subtracted from each of the scores.

• •

EXAMPLE 4.4. Given that a survey was administered to 30 individuals that included the following as one of its items measuring assertiveness (the data for this item are contained in the file *Likert.dta*):

Circle one value along the five-point scale below to indicate your degree of agreement with the statement: "I have the ability to stand up for my own rights without denying the rights of others."

strongly agree	agree	neutral	disagree	strongly disagree
1	2	3	4	5

Notice that on this scale, high scores are associated with low levels of assertiveness. This scoring could be considered to be illogical. Find a linear transformation that reverses the scores on this scale so that, instead, high scores associate with high levels of assertiveness and low scores associate with low levels of assertiveness. Keep the range of values from 1 to 5.

Solution. Multiplying all values in the distribution by –1 will convert the scale scores from 1 to 5 to –5 to –1 so that, now, the higher (the less negative) the value, the more assertive the response. Adding 6 to each value shifts the scale along the horizontal axis from –5 to –1 to 1 to 5, as desired. On this new scale, a value of 5 now corresponds to the response "strongly agree" and a response of 1 now corresponds to a response of "strongly disagree." On this new scale, the higher the score, the greater the assertiveness. Alternatively, we could have achieved the same result by subtracting each value in the scale from the value 6.

MORE Stata: To reflect the variable assert

We may type **gen assertref = –1 * assert + 6** in the Command Window and press Enter.

Or, equivalently type **gen assertref = 6 – assert**

The new variable assertref will be added as a new variable to the *Likert.dta* dataset.

Although assert has value labels attached to it (e.g., 1 = SD, 2 = D, etc.), the new variable assertref will be generated without value labels. To add value labels to assertref we type the following two commands:

label define likertref 1 "SD" 2 "D" 3 "N" 4 "A" 5 "SA"
label value assertref likertref

Note: Another approach is to use the **recode** command as discussed later in this Chapter.

☞ **Remark.** Any time the values of a scale are multiplied by –1, the new values on the scale will be mirror images, of the original values. As a result, this type of transformation is called a *reflection*. Values that were low on the original scale are now high on the new scale and values that were high on the original scale are now low on the new scale. Because the values on the new scale are based on a reversed direction of scoring, caution must be exercised when interpreting results based on scales that have been reflected.

STANDARD SCORES

In addition to enhancing the comparability of values measured in different units, data are often linearly transformed to give meaning to individual scores within a distribution. For example, an SAT verbal score of 750 carries with it its own meaning relative to the distribution of individuals who have taken this test. Said differently, if you were told that on a recently administered SAT test you scored 750, you would not ask, "Is that a good score?" You would know already, by the score itself, that you performed better than the vast majority of other SAT test-takers. You would know this because SAT scores are an example of what are called *standard scores*. By contrast to raw scores that reveal nothing about the relative standing of a score within a distribution, standard scores convey meaning about relative standing because they are linked directly to the mean and standard deviation of the distribution of which they are a part.

In short, a standard score conveys how far above or below a raw score is from the mean of its distribution relative to the standard deviation of that distribution. Because the vast majority of scores of most distributions are clustered within two standard deviations of their means, scores that are approximately two standard deviations above the mean in a distribution are considered to be extremely high. Analogously, scores that are approximately two standard deviations below the mean in a distribution are considered to be extremely low. Scores that are at the mean fall zero standard deviations from the mean, and are considered to be average, or typical scores in a distribution, and scores that fall between zero and two standard deviations away from the mean are considered to be somewhere between average and extreme.

TABLE 4.1. Means and standard deviations of commonly-used standard score systems

Standard Score System	Mean	Standard Deviation
Graduate Record Exam (GRE)	500	100
Intelligence Quotient (IQ)	100	15
Scholastic Aptitude Test (SAT)	500	100
T Scores	50	10
z-scores	0	1

Standard score systems, like the SAT, each has a specified mean and standard deviation. Table 4.1 provides the mean and standard deviation of each of several commonly used standard score systems.

To determine how many standard deviations from the mean the SAT score of 750 actually falls, we need to transform the SAT score linearly by performing a simple arithmetic operation. That is, we need to first subtract 500, the mean of the SAT score distribution, from 750 to find out how many SAT score units the score of 750 falls from the mean of 500. We then need to divide that difference by 100, the standard deviation of the SAT distribution, to determine how many standard deviations from the mean the score falls. This arithmetic operation is expressed as

$$\frac{750-500}{100} = \frac{250}{100} = 2.5. \tag{4.2}$$

According to Equation 4.2, an SAT verbal score of 750 is 2.5 standard deviations above the SAT verbal mean. A score that is 2.5 standard deviations above its mean surpasses the vast majority of scores in its distribution and is considered to be extremely high. This explains why, of course, a score of 750 would make some SAT test-taker quite happy.

Z-SCORES

Knowing the number of standard deviation distances a score is from the mean is quite informative and useful for locating a score within its distribution. Scores that have been re-expressed in terms of standard deviation distances from the mean are given a special name: *z-scores*. Because *z*-scores themselves convey the number of standard deviations a score is from the mean, a distribution of *z*-scores has, as Table 4.1 indicates, a mean of 0 and a standard deviation of 1. Any score may be re-expressed as a *z*-score by using Equation 4.3.

$$z = \frac{X - \bar{X}}{S} \tag{4.3}$$

A comparison of Equation 4.3 with that of 4.2 suggests that in Equation 4.2 we converted the SAT verbal score of 750 to a *z*-score so that we could obtain the number of standard deviations the score was far from the mean of 500. To convert an individual raw score to a *z*-score, one only needs the mean and standard deviation of the distribution of which the raw score is a part.

EXAMPLE 4.5. Determine the number of standard deviations away from the mean the following standard scores are: (a) an IQ score of 110; (b) a GRE score of 450; (c) a *z*-score of −2.

Solution.

a) From Table 4.1, we know that the mean and standard deviation of an IQ scale are 100 and 15, respectively. We use Equation 4.3 to find that the z-score of an IQ score of 110 is

$$z = \frac{110-100}{15} = 0.67.$$

In other words, an IQ score of 110 is .67 standard deviations above the IQ mean.

b) From Table 4.1, we know that the mean and standard deviation of the GRE scale are 500 and 100, respectively. We use Equation 4.3 to find that the z-score of a GRE score of 450 is

$$z = \frac{450-500}{100} = -0.50.$$

In other words, a GRE score of 450 is one-half standard deviations below the GRE mean.

c) A z-score of –2 may be interpreted directly as being 2 standard deviations below the mean.

EXAMPLE 4.6. Determine the number of standard deviations away from the mean the following scores are: (a) a score of 90 on a test of Spanish fluency that has a mean of 85 and a standard deviation of 10; (b) a score of 30 on the SES scale from the *NELS* data set; (c) all scores on the SES scale from the *NELS* data set; (d) verify that the z-score distribution has mean 0 and standard deviation 1.

$$\frac{90-85}{10} \quad .5$$

Solution.

a) To find the number of standard deviations away from the mean a score of 90 is on a Spanish fluency test, we use Equation 4.3.

$$z = \frac{90-85}{10} = 0.50.$$

A score of 90 on this test is one-half standard deviations above the mean in the distribution of Spanish fluency test scores.

b) Using Stata, we compute the mean and standard deviation of the SES distribution to be 18.43 and 6.92, respectively, when rounded to two decimal places. From Equation 4.3, we find the z-score equivalent of an SES score of 30 to be

$$z = \frac{30-18.43}{6.92} = 1.67.$$

Command Summarize SES

mean 18.434
SD 6.924
Score 30
$$\frac{30-18.43}{6.92} = 1.67$$

c) To transform all scores in the SES distribution to z-scores using Stata we use the **egen** command.

MORE Stata: To create a standardized variable

To standardize ses, for example, and to generate a new variable that contains the standardized values for ses, we type **egen zses = std(ses)** in the Command Window and press **Enter**. The new variable called zses will be added to our dataset.

---

d) To verify that zses has mean 0 and standard deviation 1, we type **summarize zses** in the Command Window and press Enter. In the output you see that the mean is given as 5.78E-04, which is scientific notation for the number 0.000578, which is equal to zero when rounded to two decimal places. Also, the standard deviation is 1.0006, which is equal to one when rounded to two decimal places.

Thus, by transforming the scores of a distribution linearly into z-scores, we gain knowledge as to the placement of each score in that distribution relative to the mean and standard deviation of the scores in that distribution. Because conversion to z-scores involves a linear transformation, and because all linear transformations are monotonic, the order of scores in the original distribution is preserved in the z-score distribution. If Carolyn's score is higher than Allison's in the original distribution, it will still be higher than Allison's in the z-score distribution. In addition, because linear transformations preserve the relative distance between points in a distribution, the shape of a z-score distribution will be the same as that of the original distribution, except for possible stretching or shrinking along the horizontal axis.

Just as we can transform raw (or standard) scores to z-scores knowing the mean and standard deviation of the original distribution, we also can use Equation 4.3 to transform z-scores to raw (or standard scores) knowing the mean and standard deviation of the new distribution. Equation 4.3 can also be re-expressed so that it can be used directly to convert any z-score to its corresponding original score. Thus, any z-score may be converted to its corresponding raw score by using Equation 4.4.

$$X = Sz + \overline{X} \tag{4.4}$$

• •

EXAMPLE 4.7. Transform the following z-scores to raw scores within a distribution with a given mean and standard deviation: (a) a z-score of -2.5 on a test of Spanish fluency with mean 85 and standard deviation 10; (b) a z-score of -3 on the SES scale from the *NELS* data set; (c) a z-score of 0 on the SES scale from the *NELS* data set.

Solution.

a) We use Equation 4.4 to find the Spanish fluency raw score equivalent of a z-score of −2.5 in a distribution with mean and standard deviation 85 and 10, respectively.

   X = 10(–2.5) + 85
   X = 60

b) We use Equation 4.4 to find the *NELS* SES raw score equivalent to a z-score of -3. Recall that the mean and standard deviation of the *NELS* SES distribution are 18.43 and 6.92, respectively.

   X = 6.92(–3) + 18.43
   X = –2.33

c) A z-score of 0 is at the mean of the z-score distribution. Therefore, the equivalent raw SES score would be equal to the mean of the SES distribution, 18.43. Of course, we could use Equation 4.4 to verify that this is the case.

Using *z*-Scores to Detect Outliers

In our discussion of boxplots in Chapter 2, we noted that Stata defines an outlier as a score that falls more than 1.5 *IQRs* beyond the 75th or 25th percentile. Because boxplots are based on resistant statistics, including the median, it makes sense to measure outliers in terms of *IQR* distances. In other contexts, when the location of a distribution is measured in terms of the mean, it makes sense to measure outliers in terms of standard deviation distances. Again, while there are no set conventions for defining outliers in terms of standard deviations, a reasonable approach is to call a score an outlier if it falls more than two standard deviations away from its distribution's mean; that is, if its *z*-score is greater than 2 in magnitude.

· ·

Example 4.8. Using the variable slfcnc12 in the NELS data set, which indicates the students' self-concept scores in twelfth grade, find the number of outliers in the distribution using (a) the boxplot criterion (at least 1.5 *IQRs* above the 75th percentile or below the 25th percentile) and (b) the *z*-score criterion (at least two standard deviations away from the mean).

Solution.

(a) We create the boxplot (obtained using the command: **graph box slfcnc12**), depicted below and count the number of circle and starred outliers. In this case, we see that there are 5.

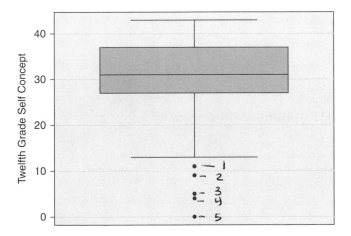

(b) First we use the command **egen zslfcnc12 = std(slfcnc12)** to convert all of the scores in the slfcnc12 distribution to z-scores and create a new variable (placed at the end of the data set) called zslfcnc12 that contains these scores. We then create a frequency distribution of zslfcnc12 and add the frequencies for the entries that are less than -2 and greater than 2. In this case, we see that there are 17(1+1+1+1+1+1+2+4+5). Alternatively, and more efficiently, we may run the command **tabulate zslfcnc12 if abs(zslfcnc12) > 2**. Note that **abs** represents the absolute value of the variable in parentheses (namely, zslfcnc12) and the command is instructing Stata to create a frequency distribution of those values of zslfcnc12 that have absolute value greater than 2.

Standardized values of (slfcnc12)	Freq.	Percent	Cum.
–4.353361	1	0.20	0.20
–3.800202	1	0.20	0.40
–3.661912	1	0.20	0.60
–3.108753	1	0.20	0.80
–2.832174	1	0.20	1.00
–2.555594	1	0.20	1.20
–2.279015	2	0.40	1.60
–2.140725	4	0.80	2.40
–2.002435	5	1.00	3.40
–1.725856	4	0.80	4.20
–1.587566	3	0.60	4.80
–1.449276	6	1.20	6.00
–1.310987	6	1.20	7.20
–1.172697	18	3.60	10.80
–1.034407	3	0.60	11.40
–.8961174	46	9.20	20.60
–.7578277	5	1.00	21.60
–.619538	47	9.40	31.00
–.4812483	11	2.20	33.20
–.3429585	72	14.40	47.60
–.2046688	9	1.80	49.40
–.0663791	24	4.80	54.20
.0719107	15	3.00	57.20
.2102004	27	5.40	62.60
.3484901	10	2.00	64.60
.4867798	19	3.80	68.40
.6250696	16	3.20	71.60
.7633593	23	4.60	76.20
.9016491	14	2.80	79.00
1.039939	17	3.40	82.40
1.178228	14	2.80	85.20
1.316518	30	6.00	91.20
1.593098	44	8.80	100.00
Total	500	100.00	

Standardized values of (slfcnc12)	Freq.	Percent	Cum.
–4.353361	1	5.88	5.88
–3.800202	1	5.88	11.76
–3.661912	1	5.88	17.65
–3.108753	1	5.88	23.53
–2.832174	1	5.88	29.41
–2.555594	1	5.88	35.29
–2.279015	2	11.76	47.06
–2.140725	4	23.53	70.59
–2.002435	5	29.41	100.00
Total	17	100.00	

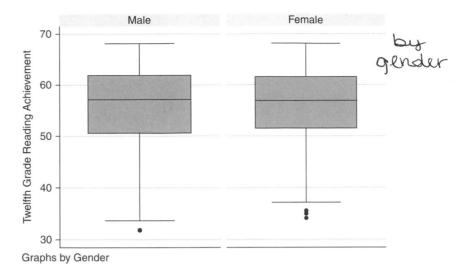

by gender

Figure 4.6 Boxplot of 12th grade reading achievement by gender.

MORE Stata: Combining Statements Using the Relational Operators **&** and **|**

We may form expressions that combine statements using the relational operators **&** (and) and **|** (or). For example, instead of having used the command **tabulate zslfcnc12 if abs(zslfcnc12) > 2**, equivalently, we could have used the command **tabulate zslfcnc12 if zslfcnc12 > 2 | zslfcnc12 < −2.**

Using *z*-Scores to Compare Scores in Different Distributions

In addition to using *z*-scores to determine the relative standing of a raw score within its own distribution, *z*-scores are often used to compare raw scores from different distributions. For such comparisons to be meaningful, however, the underlying raw score distributions must have similar shapes.

The boxplots in Figure 4.6 (obtained using the command **graph box achrdg12, by(gender)**) show the distributions of twelfth grade reading achievement by gender. Notice both distributions are negatively skewed.

In order to find the means and standard deviations of a distribution broken down by subgroups, we may use the following summary statistics commands.

MORE Stata: To find means and standard deviations by subgroups

We may type either command into the Command Window and press **Enter**:

table gender, contents(mean achrdg12 sd achrdg12) or

tabulate gender, summarize(achrdg12)

Gen	mean	SD
m	55.310352	8.560149
f	55.844286	7.480346

The output from the tabulate command is given in Table 4.2.

Consider Pat who scored 65. Did Pat score better relative to the males or the females in the data set? Pat scored above the mean in both groups, and scored more points above

Table 4.2. Means and standard deviations of 12th grade reading achievement by gender.

Gender	Summary of Twelfth Grade Reading Achievement		
	Mean	Std. Dev.	Freq.
Male	55.310352	8.560149	227
Female	55.844286	7.4803663	273
Total	55.60188	7.9849236	500

the male mean than the female mean. However, when deciding in which group the score is further above the mean *relative to the scores in the group*, we should take into consideration the spread of the scores in the distributions. One way to do so is to calculate z-scores.

$$\text{Relative to the males: } z = \frac{65 - 55.3104}{8.5601} = 1.13$$

$$\text{Relative to the females: } z = \frac{65 - 55.8443}{7.4804} = 1.22$$

Because 1.22 exceeds 1.13, we see that Pat performed better relative to the females. The score of 65 is 1.22 standard deviations above the mean for the females and only 1.13 standard deviations above the mean for the males.

Relating z-Scores to Percentile Ranks

In the previous section, we looked at the use of z-scores to compare scores in different distributions. Recall that for such comparisons to be meaningful, however, the underlying raw score distributions must have similar shapes. It is not even enough, as the following example illustrates, for the two raw score distributions to have the same mean and standard deviation. If the raw score distributions do not have similar shapes, the same z-scores may correspond to different percentile ranks, undermining the utility of z-scores in comparing raw scores from different distributions. Consider that two tests, math and English, have been administered to the same individuals and that their score distributions are as in Table 4.3.

These two distributions do not have similar shapes. The math distribution is positively skewed; the English distribution is negatively skewed. (You might want to construct a histogram for each distribution to convince yourself of this.) Both math and English distributions have means of 5 and standard deviations of 2.72. (You may want to convince yourself of this as well.) Therefore, in each distribution, a raw score of 8 corresponds to a z-score of

TABLE 4.3. Distributions of Math and English achievement

Math Achievement	English Achievement
2 3 3 3 4 4 4 8 9 10	0 1 2 6 6 6 7 7 7 8

$$z = \frac{X - \bar{X}}{S} = \frac{8 - 5}{2.72} = \frac{3}{2.72} = 1.10$$

But, in the math distribution, the percentile rank of a score of 8 is 70 (as estimated by the cumulative percent), whereas in the English distribution the percentile rank of a score of 8 is 90. While a comparison based on z-scores suggests that an individual with a raw score of 8 on both math and English tests has the same performance on these exams relative to the two distributions, this is not the case. Because these two distributions are dissimilar in shape, the more appropriate comparison of performance is based on percentile ranks. Based on percentile ranks, a score of 8 represents a higher score in English than in math for this group of students.

In sum, when the shapes of distributions are not known to be similar, percentile ranks are a better scoring system than z-scores for comparing scores between distributions.

NONLINEAR TRANSFORMATIONS: SQUARE ROOTS AND LOGARITHMS

As we have seen, statistics, like the mean and standard deviation, do not characterize well the bulk of values in a highly skewed distribution. To remedy this situation, in the previous chapter, we eliminated the two extreme values in the right tail of the expected income at age 30 distribution. In so doing, we shortened the long right tail and made this once highly positively skewed distribution more symmetric. As a result, the mean and standard deviation corroborated with the other, more resistant numeric summaries of location and spread, making the job of describing the bulk of our data easier and more accurate.

By making a distribution more symmetric, we avoid the problem of having a small number of extreme values highly influence the numeric summaries that characterize a data set. For this reason and others, it is advantageous to symmetrize distributions. But, as we have observed previously, we are often not justified in making distributions more symmetric by merely eliminating extreme values.

An approach that is preferred, because it does not entail the elimination of points from a distribution, is the *monotonic nonlinear transformation*. Like the linear transformation, the monotonic nonlinear transformation retains the order of values in a distribution. Unlike the linear transformation, however, the monotonic nonlinear transformation changes the relative distances between the values in a distribution, and in so doing, effects a desired change in the shape of the distribution. Two commonly used monotonic nonlinear transformations are the square root and logarithm base 10.

☞ **Remark.** Logarithms are defined by exponents. The logarithm of the value 8 using the base 2 equals 3 since $2^3 = 8$. This statement can be expressed as $\log_2 8 = 3$. Likewise, the logarithm of 16 base 2 equals 4 since $2^4 = 16$, i.e. $\log_2 16 = 4$. And, the logarithm of 100 base 10 equals 2 since $10^2 = 100$, i.e. $\log_{10} 100 = 2$. What is $\log_{10} 1,000,000$? — 6

☞ **Remark.** Examples of logarithmic scales used in practice are the Richter scale to measure the motion of the ground due to earthquakes, decibels to measure the energy intensity of sound, and pH to measure the acidity of a substance. For example, an earthquake that measures 4 on the Richter scale is 10 times more powerful than one that measures 3 and 100 times more powerful than one that measures 2. In other words, an increase in the Richter scale of k units indicates that the earthquake is more powerful by a factor of 10^k. Decibels compare the level of pressure from a sound (represented by p_1) to the level of pressure from the smallest noise audible to a person with normal hearing (represented by p_0). The decibel is then given by $D = 10\log(p_1/P_0)$. Finally, the acidity, or pH of a substance is found by the formula pH = $-\log(H^+)$ where (H^+) represents the concentration of the hydrogen ion. If the pH is less than 7, the solution is said to be acid. If the pH equals 7, the solution is said to be neutral. If the pH is greater than 7, the solution is said to be basic.

Example 4.8 illustrates how a monotonic nonlinear transformation changes the relative distance between the values in a distribution and, in so doing, changes the shape of the distribution.

EXAMPLE 4.8. Given the following set of data points: 1 4 16 64 256

a) Compute the distances between the adjacent points in the data set. Would you say the distribution is skewed? Why? Compute the skewness of these data using Stata.
b) Transform the data set linearly by multiplying each value by 1/2. Compute the distances between the adjacent points in the data set. Compare the distances and skewness of the distribution to those obtained in part a). What does this result imply about the effect of a linear transformation on the skewness and relative distances between points in a distribution?
c) Transform the data set nonlinearly by taking the square root of each value. The command for calculating a new variable that is the square root of another variable, x, is **gen newvar = sqrt(x)**.
d) Compute the distances between the adjacent points in the data set. Have the relative distances between adjacent points changed? In what way? Is the square root–transformed data set less positively skewed than the original data set?
e) Transform the data set nonlinearly by taking the logarithm (using base 2) of each value.
f) Compute the distances between the adjacent points in the data set. Have the relative distances between adjacent points changed? In what way? Is the logarithmic-transformed data set less positively skewed than the original data set? Is it less positively skewed than the square root–transformed data set?

Solution.

a) The original values along with their adjacent distances are:

Values:	1		4		16		64		256
		v		v		v		v	
Adjacent distances:		2		12		48		192	

Because these distances between adjacent points increase as the values themselves increase, the distribution appears to be skewed positively. Using Stata, we find that the distribution is positively skewed with skew = 1.96.

b) The new values, linearly transformed by multiplication by 1/2, along with their adjacent distances are:

Values:	5		2		8		32		128
		v		v		v		v	
Adjacent distances:		1.5		6		24		96	

Notice that the transformed scores and their adjacent distances are both 1/2 as large as the original scores and their adjacent distances. Relative to the new scale then, the distances between points remain the same and the skewness, therefore, remains the same. Using Stata, we find that the linearly transformed distribution has skew = 1.96, as before. What this implies is that linear transformations do not change the relative distances between points, and hence, do not change the shape of the distribution, including its skew.

c) The original distribution, transformed by its square root, is: 1 2 4 8 16.

d) The transformed values from (c) along with their adjacent distances are:

Values:	1	2	4	8	16
	v	v	v	v	
Adjacent distances:	1	2	4	8	

The relative distances between the values have changed as a result of this square root transformation. In particular, the square root transformation has reduced the distances between adjacent values in a nonuniform way. The higher the value, the more the reduction in distance between it and its adjacent points. The most extreme distance of 192 units in the original distribution is reduced to a distance of only 8 units after square roots are taken; the next most extreme distance of 48 units in the original distribution is reduced to a distance of 4 units after square roots are taken. Because a nonlinear transformation, such as the square root transformation, reduces differentially the distances between points in a distribution, with greatest reduction occurring in the right tail, the shape of the distribution changes. Such a transformation has the effect of "bringing in" the right tail and making the distribution more symmetric as the new skew value of 1.33 (obtained from Stata) indicates.

e) The original distribution, transformed by the logarithm base 2, is: 0 2 4 6 8.

f) The log-transformed values along with their adjacent distances are:

Values:	0	2	4	6	8
	v	v	v	v	
Adjacent distances:	2	2	2	2	

Notice that, in contrast to the other cases in this example, the log-transformed distribution is symmetric about the value of 4 and the adjacent distances are all equal to one another. Using Stata, we find that the skew value for these log-transformed values is, in fact, 0. A log transformation will not usually make a distribution perfectly symmetric. Because the log transformation has a greater impact on extreme scores than the square root transformation, it is often the case that for highly skewed data, the log transformation will be more effective than the square root transformation for making a distribution more symmetric. It is often a good idea to try both types of transformation to see which of the two produces more symmetric results and to use the one that does.

☞ **Remark.** While we used a base 2 logarithm in Example 4.8, other positive values except 1 may be used as bases. A logarithmic transformation, whether its base is 2.7, 3, 4, 5, or 10, for example, will reduce the skewness of a distribution by the same amount and change the shape of the distribution to the same extent. Two commonly used logarithmic bases are e (approximated by 2.7), associated with what is called the natural logarithm, and 10,

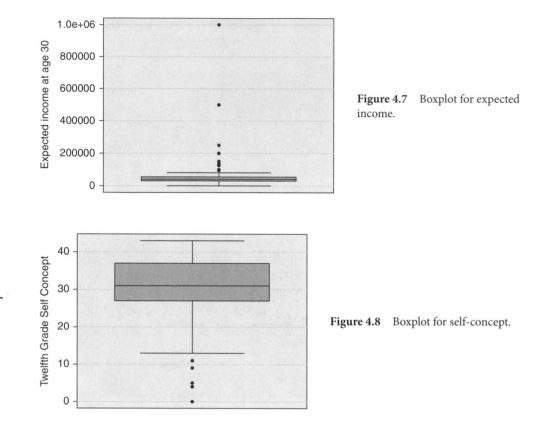

Figure 4.7 Boxplot for expected income.

Figure 4.8 Boxplot for self-concept.

associated with what is called the common logarithm. Stata denotes these two logarithm systems as **ln**(x) and **log10**(x), respectively. In this text, we make use of log10.

☞ **Remark.** For the type of data we encounter in the behavioral and social sciences, square roots are defined only on values greater than or equal to 0, while logarithms are defined only on values greater than 0. Thus, to apply a square root transformation to data that ranges from –12 to 5 we would first add 12, for example, to all values in the distribution, so that the values are all greater than or equal to 0. Likewise, to apply a logarithmic transformation to data that ranges from –12 to 5, we would first need to add 13, for example, to all values in the distribution so that the values are all greater than 0.

In Example 4.9, we illustrate with *NELS* data the effects on the shape and skewness of a distribution of using the square root and common logarithms. Through this example, you will learn that we may often need to apply a combination of transformations in our efforts to reduce the skew of a distribution. In this example, the square root and log transformations are used in conjunction with a reflection and a translation.

EXAMPLE 4.9. As we have observed, and as is indicated in Figures 4.7 and 4.8, the distribution of expected income at age 30 is positively skewed and the distribution of self-concept in grade 12 is negatively skewed. Use appropriate transformations to make both distributions more symmetric.

Solution. The descriptive statistics for these two variables are as follows. They are generated using the Stata command:

summarize expinc30 slfcnc12, detail

(handwritten: expinc30)

Expected income at age 30				
	Percentiles	Smallest		
1%	1	0		
5%	20000	0		
10%	25000	0	Obs	459
25%	30000	0	Sum of Wgt.	459
50%	40000		Mean	51574.73
		Largest	Std. Dev.	58265.76
75%	55000	250000		
90%	80000	250000	Variance	3.39e+09
95%	100000	500000	Skewness	10.89864
99%	250000	1000000	Kurtosis	162.8027

(handwritten: pos pointing to Skewness 10.89864)

(handwritten: slfcnc12)

Twelfth Grade Self Concept				
	Percentiles	Smallest		
1%	12	0		
5%	21	4		
10%	23	5	Obs	500
25%	27	9	Sum of Wgt.	500
50%	31		Mean	31.48
		Largest	Std. Dev.	7.231195
75%	37	43		
90%	41	43	Variance	52.29018
95%	43	43	Skewness	−.3825967
99%	43	43	Kurtosis	3.581335

(handwritten: neg pointing to Skewness −.3825967)

In symmetrizing the income at age 30 distribution, which is positively skewed, we try both the square root and logarithm (base 10) transformations. Because the minimum value of expected income is 0, and because the logarithm of 0 is undefined, we first add some small quantity, like 1, to each value, and then we take the logarithm of each value. The numeric expression for carrying out the logarithm transformation is log10(expinc30 + 1). Although it would be meaningful to take the square root of 0, for consistency, we also compute the square root of the translated expected income.

(handwritten: log10(expinc30+1))

MORE Stata: To transform a variable (expinc30) using logs and square roots

To add 1 to each value of expinc30, we type **gen expincpl = expinc30+1** in the Command Window and press Enter.

For the log transformation, we type **gen expinclg = log10(expincpl)** in the Command Window and press Enter.

For the square root transformation, we type **gen expincsq = sqrt(expincpl)** in the Command Window and press Enter.

Descriptive statistics for the log10 and sqrt transformed variables are output as follows.

expinclg				
	Percentiles	Smallest		
1%	.30103	0		
5%	4.301052	0		
10%	4.397957	0	Obs	459
25%	4.477136	0	Sum of Wgt.	459
50%	4.602071		Mean	4.590111
		Largest	Std. Dev.	.5261862
75%	4.740371	5.397942		
90%	4.903095	5.397942	Variance	.2768719
95%	5.000004	5.698971	Skewness $(-)$	−6.866786
99%	5.397942	6	Kurtosis	60.6735

expincsq				
	Percentiles	Smallest		
1%	1	0		
5%	141.4214	0		
10%	158.1139	0	Obs	459
25%	173.2051	0	Sum of Wgt.	459
50%	200		Mean	214.5201
		Largest	Std. Dev.	74.61886
75%	234.5208	500		
90%	282.8427	500	Variance	5567.975
95%	316.2278	707.1068	Skewness $(+)$	3.720272
99%	500	1000	Kurtosis	34.7838

Notice that the log transformation over-compensates for the positive skew as it results in a highly negatively skewed distribution. In this case, the square root transformation is the better of the two as Figure 4.9 illustrates.

As we have seen, the logarithm and square root transformations may be used to symmetrize a positively skewed distribution. If the logarithm or square root transformation is applied to a negatively skewed distribution, however, the effect will be to make that distribution even more negatively skewed. Accordingly, when a distribution is negatively skewed, a first step in symmetrizing such a distribution would be to reflect it so that it becomes positively skewed. Because the square root is not defined on negative values and

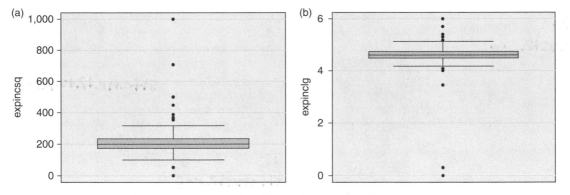

Figure 4.9 Boxplots of square root (top) and log10 (bottom) transformations of expected income at age 30.

the logarithm is not defined on negative or zero values, if there are negative or zero values in the distribution, the next step would be to add a constant to each value in the distribution to eliminate such negative or zero values. The third step would be to apply the logarithm or square root transformation as before.

Self-concept in grade 12 (slfcnc12) is an example of a negatively skewed distribution.

MORE Stata: To reflect the variable, slfcnc12

We multiply slfcnc12 by –1 and create a new variable, called slfcnc12ref, by typing in the Command Window and pressing **Enter**:

gen slfcnc12ref = (–1) * slfcnc12

In preparation for taking the logarithm and square root transformations, we want all the values of slfcnc12ref to be greater than 0. To accomplish this, we add 44 to each value of slfcnc12ref value because 44 equals 1 more than the maximum value of slfcnc12ref. This type of variable transformation is called a **translation**.

MORE Stata: To translate the variable, slfcnc12ref

We type in the Command Window and press **Enter**:

gen slfcnc12reftr = slfcnc12ref + 44

A new variable called slfcnc12reftr will appear as the last variable in your dataset.

☞ **Remark.** Through this numeric operation, on this new scale, scores that were originally high are now low, and scores that were originally low are now high. As a consequence, higher self-concept is represented by lower scores and lower self-concept is represented by higher scores.

The distribution of slfcnc12 is presented on the left hand side of Figure 4.10, with slfcnc12ref in the middle and slfcnc12reftr on the right hand side.

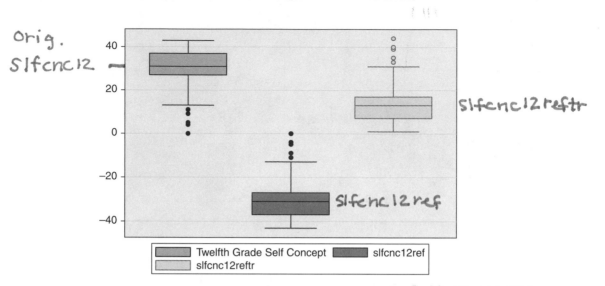

Orig. Slfcnc12

slfcnc12reftr

Slfcnc12ref

Figure 4.10 Preparing a negatively skewed distribution for a square root and logarithmic transformation (from left to right).

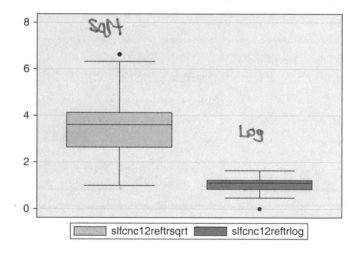

Sqrt

Log

Figure 4.11 The distributions of the square root (left) and log (right) transformed variables.

The distributions of the square root and log transformed variables are shown in Figure 4.11 on the left and right hand sides, respectively. The skewness of these two new variables are −.4953 and −1.396, respectively.

Because the two new variables are more negatively skewed than the original slfcnc12 variable (original skew = −.383), neither transformation serves to improve symmetry. Accordingly, the best course of action, in this case, would be to leave slfcnc12 in its original form.

NONLINEAR TRANSFORMATIONS: RANKING VARIABLES

Sometimes we may be interested in knowing the ranking of scores in a distribution and working with those rather than the scores themselves. For example, while we may have information on each student's grade point average in a particular graduating class, we also may be interested in their class ranking; that is, whether they placed 1st, 50th, or in some other position. To transform scores to ranks, we shall assign a 1 to the highest score, a 2 to the next highest, and so on. In the case of tied scores, each score is assigned the mean of the ranks that would have been assigned those scores had they not been tied. We illustrate the ranking procedure in Example 4.10 with the *Hamburger* data from McDonald's on the number of grams of fat and calories contained in each of five types of hamburger sold.

EXAMPLE 4.10. Rank the five hamburgers by their (a) fat content and (b) calorie content using Stata. In both instances, assign the value 1 to the hamburger with the highest value. Assign the mean ranking in the case of ties.

MORE Stata: To transform scores to ranks.

To transform the variables, fat and calories, into new variables whose scores are now ranks, we use the **egen** command and the Stata **rank** function, as follows.

egen rfat = rank(fat)
egen rcalories = rank(calories).

The **rank** function assigns a rank of 1 to the variable's highest value. If, instead, we want the variable's lowest value to be assigned a rank of 1, we would subtract the ranked values from one more than the number of values in the data set as follows:

gen rkfat = 6 − rfat
gen rkcalories = 6 − rcalories

Although the distinction between the commands **egen** and **gen** is not so clear cut, in general, **egen** (as opposed to **gen**) is used when the expression following the equal sign is more complicated (e.g., does not include simple mathematical operators, such as plus, minus, sqrt, etc.).

The two new ranked variables, named rkfat and rkcalories, will appear in your data editor as shown below. Notice that in the case of fat, where there are no ties (each hamburger has a unique fat content), the rankings are the whole numbers 1 to 5. From this ranking we know, for example, that a Quarter Pounder with Cheese ranks number 1 in fat relative to the other hamburgers and that a Hamburger ranks last. In the case of CALORIES, there is a tie between the Quarter Pounder with Cheese and the Big Mac. Accordingly, these two types of hamburger share the 1st and 2nd place rank and so are assigned the mean of 1 and 2, which is, of course, 1.5.

name	fat	calories	rkfat	rkcalories
Hamburger	10	270	5.0	5.0
Cheeseburger	14	320	4.0	4.0
Quarter Pounder	21	430	3.0	3.0
Quarter P. w/ c	30	530	1.0	1.5
Big Mac	28	530	2.0	1.5

We may note that a rank transformation preserves the ordinality of the values, but that is all. The interval or ratio properties that might have existed in the original data are now lost.

☞ **Remark.** Rankings provide the ordinal position of a value in a distribution. From rankings we may know, for example, that a value is 100th in a distribution, but from that rank alone, we do not know how many other, or what percentage of, values are below that value. For this information, we use the percentile ranking introduced in Chapter 2.

OTHER TRANSFORMATIONS: RECODING AND COMBINING VARIABLES

RECODING VARIABLES

Variables may be recoded for at least two reasons: to transform variables and to collapse or combine categories. In Example 4.4, we reflected the Likert scale used to measure assertiveness so that lower scores no longer associated with agreement, but rather with disagreement and higher scores no longer associated with disagreement, but rather with agreement. In particular, we applied the linear transformation (6 – assert) to achieve the desired transformation of this five-point scale. In Example 4.11 we provide another way to achieve this same result via recoding.

••

EXAMPLE 4.11. Using recoding, reflect the Likert-scaled variable assert that is scored using the five-point scale shown below.

strongly agree	agree	neutral	disagree	strongly disagree
1	2	3	4	5

MORE Stata: To recode a variable into a variable with a different name

We use a series of **replace** commands and press Enter after each line to create the recoded variable, assertrec, in our dataset that represents a reflected version of assert. The data for this example are from the *Likert.dta* file.

```
gen assertrec = 0
replace assertrec = 1 if assert == 5
replace assertrec= 2 if assert == 4
replace assertrec = 3 if assert == 3
replace assertrec = 4 if assert == 2
replace assertrec = 5 if assert == 1
replace assertrec =. if assert ==.
```

Because Stata represents the missing values of a numeric variable by a dot, the last line ensures that missing values continue to be coded as missing.

Note that the first line assigns all individuals the value of 0 on the new variable assertre. The next line replaces the value of 0 on assertre with the value of 1 for those individuals who have an assert value equal to 5; the next line after that replaces the value of 0 on assertre with the value of 2 for those individuals who have an assert value equal to 4, and so on. Finally we replace the value of 0 on assertre with the missing value code (.) for those individuals whose assert value is missing.

Although assert has value labels attached to it (e.g., 1 = SD, 2 = D, etc.), the new variable assertrec will be generated without value labels. To add value labels to assertrec we type the following two commands:

define labels (handwritten)

label define likertrec 1 "SD" 2 "D" 3 "N" 4 "A" 5 "SA"
label value assertrec likertrec

Note: The first command (**label define**) defines a label to be associated with each of the values on the Likert scale and creates a variable (in this case likertrec) to house these labels; the second command (**label value**) assigns the value labels housed in the variable likertrec to the values on the Likert-scaled variable assertrec.

___

The next example uses recode to collapse categories of a variable.

• •

EXAMPLE 4.12. In the frequency distribution of eighth grade school type, SCHTYP8 given below, we may note that school type is described as: 1 = public, 2 = private (religious), and 3 = private (nonreligious). If we are interested in distinguishing between 1 = public and 2 = private types only, then we may use the Recode procedure to collapse these three categories into two in the following way.

Solution.

___

MORE Stata: To reduce the number of categories of a variable by collapsing some

To collapse the three categories of schtyp8 into two categories: public and private, we type the following series of **gen** and **replace** commands into the Command Window, and press Enter after each line.

capture gen schtypre = 0
replace schtypre = 1 if schtyp8 == 1
replace schtypre = 2 if schtyp8 == 2 | schtyp8 == 3
replace schtypre =. if schtyp8 ==.

Note that, as before, we begin by assigning all individuals the value of 0 on the new variable schtypre. We then replace the value of 0 on schtypre with the value of 1 for those individuals who have schtyp8 equal to 1; we next replace the value of 0 on schtypre with the value of 2 for those individuals who have schtyp8 equal to 2 or to 3; and, finally we replace the value of 0 on schtypre with the missing code (.) for those individuals whose schltyp8 value is missing.

___

Whenever a variable is treated as if it were continuous, it is preferable to retain as much of the variability in the scores as possible, which implies continuing to measure the variable on a many-valued scale. Sometimes, however, researchers choose to dichotomize such variables to simplify interpretation, among other reasons, using a _median split_. The Bem Sex-Role Inventory (1977), for example, uses two median splits, one on each of two continuous variables, Masculinity and Femininity, to divide the scores on each into two categories: low and high Masculinity and low and high Femininity. The low Femininity-low Masculinity category is labeled Undifferentiated, the low Femininity-high Masculinity category is labeled Masculine, the high Femininity-low Masculinity category is labeled Feminine, and the high Femininity-high Masculinity category is labeled Androgynous.

median split (handwritten)

Simply stated, a median split transforms a many-valued variable into two categories, one that includes all scores above the median and the other which includes all scores below the median. The scores at the median typically are assigned arbitrarily to one of the two categories. Note that if the variable is skewed originally, in taking a median split, the new variable will be symmetric. Although we do not recommend the median split, the next example describes how to split a variable at its median to create a dichotomous variable from one that is originally continuous.

. . . .

EXAMPLE 4.13. Find the median of self-concept in eighth grade SLFCNC08 and transform this variable using a median split procedure.

Solution.

The median of slfcnc08 is 21, obtained using **summarize slfcnc08, detail**.

MORE Stata: To obtain a median split of a variable.

To obtain the median split of slfcnc08, we once again use the **gen** and **replace** commands as follows, pressing Enter after each line is typed.

gen slfcn8ms = 0
replace slfcn8ms = 1 if (slfcnc08 <= 21)
replace slfcn8ms = 2 if (slfcnc08 >= 22)
replace slfcn8ms =. if slfcnc08 ==.

We begin by assigning all individuals the value of 0 on the new variable slfcn8ms. We then replace the value of 0 with the value of 1 for those individuals whose slfcnc08 is less than or equal to the median (21); we next replace the value of 0 with the value of 2 for those individuals whose slfcnc08 is greater than or equal to 22; and, finally we replace the value of 0 with a missing code (.) for those individuals whose slfcnc08 is missing. The new variable, slfcn8ms, will be added as the last variable in the dataset.

The frequency distribution of slfcn8ms is given below.

slfcn8ms	Freq.	Percent	Cum.
1	266	53.20	53.20
2	234	46.80	100.00
Total	500	100.00	

The decision whether to lump all scores that equal the median value in the lower or upper category needs to be made by the researcher. Because there are 30 individuals who scored at the median of 21, the two categories do not each constitute 50 percent of the distribution. In this case, the median value of 21 was placed in the lower category. The upper category started at 22 because the distribution takes on only integer values.

☞ **Remark.** To repeat, when recoding a distribution with missing values, it is important that missing values continue to be coded as missing. It also is important to define and assign new value labels to the new categories created. Exercise 1.15 in Chapter 1 illustrates how to do this and Exercise 4.26 at the end of this chapter gives additional practice.

COMBINING VARIABLES

While variables may be combined in a variety of ways, in this book we will be concerned with combining variables using the operations of addition, subtraction, multiplication and division. For example, using the _NELS_ data set, suppose we wished to construct a variable that represented the combined number of years of math and English courses the student took in high school. The _NELS_ data set has two variables that are relevant: the number of years of math taken, unitmath, and the number of years of English taken, unitengl. In Example 4.14, we construct a new variable that represents the combined number of years of math and English.

unitmath
unite ngl

• •

EXAMPLE 4.14. Construct a new variable, sumunits, which represents the combined number of years of math and English taken in high school.

Solution.

MORE Stata: To create a new variable as the sum of two variables
   The following command will create the new variable, sumunits, as the sum of the unitmath and unitengl:

gen sumunits = unitmath + unitengl

DATA MANAGEMENT FUNDAMENTALS – THE DO-FILE

One of the most important tasks as a data analyst is to keep a permanent and detailed record of the steps you take in carrying out the data analysis portion of your project, including documentation on how variables were re-expressed and created, which specific analyses were carried out, and the order in which they were carried out. The final product of such documentation should be so detailed that if we were to lose the entire set of output in connection with your project, we could, with a click or two, reproduce what was done in a matter of minutes, if not seconds.

To keep a permanent and detailed record of such documentation, we need to create and save a file, called a _Do-file_ that contains all the commands we executed, whether they relate to variable creation or modification, data selection, graphical display, or to the analyses themselves. These commands include those we type directly into the Command Window, as well as those generated by Stata when we use its point and click, menu-driven approach.

To create a new Do-file, on the main menu bar, we would click, **Window/Do-file Editor/ New Do-file Editor**; we also could type the command **doedit** directly into the Command Window. In each case, a new Do-file Editor Window will appear, and you may begin typing your commands directly into that Window. Periodically, and, certainly when you are finished typing your commands into the Do file, you will need to save the file in a location and name of your choosing. To do so, on the Do-file Editor Window menu, click **File/Save as**, browse to a location of your choosing on your computer, give your file a name, and click **Save**. The Do-file will have the extension **.do** to distinguish it from other file types.

To open an existing Do-file, on the main menu bar, we would click **File/do**, browse to the location of the file, highlight the filename, and click **Open**; we also could type the command **doedit** directly into the Command Window, and when the Do-file Editor Window opens, click **File/Open/File** on the Do-file Editor Window menu bar, browse to the location of the file on your computer, highlight the filename, and click **Open**.

To execute the commands in your Do-file, whether all, or a selection of them, highlight the chosen commands, and on the Do-file Editor Window menu bar, we would click **Tools/Execute** or press **Control + d** on our computer keyboard.

Comments that describe the work we are undertaking are critical components to a Do-file. Without them, we would most certainly not remember, by the next time we opened the Do-file, which might not happen for several weeks, why we included the commands we did. To create such descriptive comments, we may type one or more asterisks,*, at the beginning of a line, or we may enclose our comment at any point on the line with /* and */ as bookends. The following illustrates both ways to include comments in a Do-file.

*** The following syntax generates descriptive statistics for temp, relhumid, and barsold.

> **summarize temp relhumid barsold /*barsold represents the number of ice cream sales*/**

A Do-file for each of the chapters in this text has been created that contains the Stata commands used to execute the analyses and construct the figures of that chapter. Once you have had a chance to create your own Do-file in Exercise 4.15, it would be a good idea to open the Do-file associated with this chapter and run the commands contained in it so that you can see first-hand how to re-create the Stata output we obtained in this chapter. You also may wish to go back to Chapters 2 and 3 and do the same thing with respect to those chapters. Going forward, we recommend that you adopt a more interactive way of reading this text by opening the Do-file associated with the chapter you currently are reading and executing, in turn, the Stata commands in that Do-file so as to re-create the Stata output contained in the text of the chapter itself.

• •

Example 4.15. Consider the situation of Example 4.14 in which we are interested in creating a new variable, sumunits as the sum of the two variables, unitmath and unitengl, and computing summary statistics on that new variable as well as a stem and leaf display and boxplot. Rather than typing each of the necessary commands into the Command Window directly and pressing Enter at the end of each line, in this example, we will carry out this work using a Do-file.

MORE Stata: To create and save a Do-file
   We would:

Open the NELS data set by clicking **File/Open** on the main menu bar and browsing to the location of the NELS data set on our computer or on the text's website. Click **Open** and **OK**.

Highlight the **use** command that appears in the Output Window signifying that the NELS data set is now loaded into active memory copy the highlighted command using either **Ctrl+C** or by clicking **Edit/Copy**.

Open the Do-file Editor Window by either typing in the Command Window **doedit** or by using the main menu bar and clicking **Window/Do-file Editor/New Do-file Editor**. Once the Do-file Editor Window opens, paste the **use** command into it by either using **Ctrl+V** or by clicking on the Do-file Window menu bar **Edit/ Paste**.

We are now ready to type the remaining commands into our Do-file to carry out what we wish to do. We type the following lines as shown, which includes both documentation and commands:

***Create the variable sumunits

capture gen sumunits = unitmath + unitengl

***Create a box plot of sumunits

graph box sumunits

***Create a stem and leaf display of sumunits

stem sumunits

***Generate summary statistics for the variable sumunits

tabstat sumunits, stats(n min max mean p50 sd iqr)

Save the Do-file in a location and filename of your choosing

Highlight the commands in the file you want to execute, starting with the gen command.

Execute these commands from the Do-file by pressing **Control+d**, or click Tools/ Execute listed on the Do-file Editor Window menu.

NOTE: Because sumunits already exists in our data set from our work on Example 4.14, we use the word **capture** to overwrite that variable in the data set and prevent execution of the commands in the Do-file from stopping.

The boxplot will pop up on the screen from the Graphic Editor Window and the stem and leaf display and summary statistics will be printed in the Output Window, as usual. We may copy and paste the box plot into a Word file by clicking **Edit/Copy** in the Graphic Editor Window, opening Word and clicking **Paste** or **Paste Special** in the desired Word file.

MORE Stata: The word **more** printed along with output

Notice that the printing of output stops and the word **more** appears in the Output Window. In order to get the next batch of output to appear in the Output Window, we need to point and click on the word **more**. To avoid having to do that each time it appears, you may type the following as the first command in the.do file: **set more off** and highlight this command along with the others before pressing **Control+d**.

☞ **Remark.** In addition to having the ability to make a permanent record of your work in the service of reproducibility, because a Do-file may be edited much like a Word file, you can avoid the often laborious sequence of clicks necessary to conduct an analysis or series of analyses when using the menu-driven option within Stata.

As you continue to work through this text, it will become increasingly clear how the ability to create, modify, and save Do-files provides flexibility and power in carrying out the work of a data analyst.

SUMMARY OF STATA COMMANDS IN CHAPTER 4

For a complete listing of all Stata commands associated with this chapter, you may access the Do-file for Chapter 4 located on the text website.

Create	Command Lines
Calculate a new variable (Examples 4.1 and 4.4)	**generate heightcm = heightin * 2.54**
	OR
	gen assertre = –1 * assert + 6
Create the standardized variable for ses (Example 4.5)	**egen zses = std(ses)**
List all outliers in the data set according to the *z*-score criterion (Example 4.8)	**tabulate zslfcnc12 if abs(zslfcnc12) > 2**
Take the log of the variable expinc30 (Example 4.9), but first add 1 to each value	**gen expincpl = expinc30 + 1**
	gen expinclg = log10(expincpl)
Take the square root of the variable expinc30 (Example 4.9)	**gen expincsq = sqrt(expincpl)**
Rank a variable assigning 1 to the highest value (Example 4.10)	**egen rfat = rank(fat)**
Recoding (Example 4.11)	**gen assertre = 0**
	replace assertre = 1 if assert == 5
	replace assertre = 2 if assert == 4
	replace assertre = 3 if assert == 3
	replace assertre = 4 if assert == 2
	replace assertre = 5 if assert == 1
	replace assertre =. if assert ==.
Reflect and translate variable assert on a 1 to 5 scale (Example 4.11)	**gen assertre = 6-assert**
Collapse cells in schtyp8 (Example 4.12)	**gen schtypre = 0**
	replace schtypre = 1 if schtyp8 == 1
	replace schtypre = 2 if schtyp8 == 2 | schtyp8 == 3
	replace schtypre =. if schtyp8 ==.

Perform a median split on slfcnc08   **gen slfcn8ms = 0**
(Example 4.13)   **replace slfcn8ms = 1 if (slfcnc08 <= 21)**
                                            replace slfcn8ms = 2 if (slfcnc08 >= 22)
                                            replace slfcn8ms =. if slfcnc08 ==.
Combine variables (Example 4.14)   **gen sumunits = unitmath + unitengl**
Create and save a Do-file (Example 4.15)   **See the text**

EXERCISES

Create a.do file for each Exercise that requires the use of Stata. Run the commands from the. do file by highlighting them and hitting **Control+d***. Save each.do file using a name associated with the Exercise for which it was created. The first exercise that requires Stata is 4.4. It is recommended that you review the Do-file for* Chapter 4 *located on the textbook's website before completing these exercises. To facilitate doing each exercise, it may be helpful to copy and paste relevant commands from the Do-file for* Chapter 4 *into your own Do-file and modify them as needed.*

Exercises 4.1–4.8 involve the effects of linear transformations on the summary statistics of a distribution.

4.1. In this series of exercises, we find the summary statistics of distributions that are linear transformations of original distributions. These exercises do not require the use of Stata.

  a) If each value in a distribution with mean equal to 5 has been tripled, what is the new mean?
  b) If each value in a distribution with standard deviation equal to 5 has been tripled, what is the new standard deviation?
  c) If each value in a distribution with skewness equal to 1.14 has been tripled, what is the new skewness?
  d) If each value in a distribution with mean equal to 5 has the constant 6 added to it, what is the new mean?
  e) If each value in a distribution with standard deviation equal to 5 has the constant 6 added to it, what is the new standard deviation?
  f) If each value in a distribution with skewness equal to 1.14 has the constant 6 added to it, what is the new skewness?
  g) If each value in a distribution with mean equal to 5 has been multiplied by –2, what is the new mean?
  h) If each value in a distribution with standard deviation equal to 5 has been multiplied by -2, what is the new standard deviation?
  i) If each value in a distribution with skewness equal to 1.14 has been multiplied by –2, what is the new skewness?
  j) If each value in a distribution with mean equal to 5 has had a constant equal to 6 subtracted from it, what is the new mean?

    k) If each value in a distribution with standard deviation equal to 5 has had a constant equal to 6 subtracted from it, what is the new standard deviation?

    l) If each value in a distribution with skewness equal to 1.14 has had a constant equal to 6 subtracted from it, what is the new skewness?

4.2. Consider a situation in which you would like to measure the amount of time it takes children in grades 4 and 6 to complete a task. This exercise does not require Stata.

    a) The grade 4 teacher found that the average time to complete a task was 20 minutes with a standard deviation of 7 minutes. The grade 6 teacher found that the average time was .25 hours to complete a task with a standard deviation of .09 hours. In which grade were the students faster? In which grade were the students more similar in the amount of time taken to complete the task?

    b) The grade 4 teacher found that the average time was 20 minutes with a standard deviation of 7 minutes and the grade 6 teacher found that the average time was 22 minutes with a standard deviation of 5 minutes. If the grade 6 teacher had included reading the instructions, which took four minutes, in his calculation of the time to complete the task. After adjusting for this additional time to make the two classes comparable, in which grade were the students faster? In which grade were the students more similar in the amount of time taken to complete the task?

4.3. Assume that you are studying college students and have measured a variable called credits that gives the number of credits taken by a part-time or full-time student during the current semester. For the individuals you are studying, the number of credits taken ranges from 4 to 26, with a mean of 16.26, a standard deviation of 2.40, and a skewness ratio of −12.05. This exercise does not require Stata.

    a) Assuming that, on average, each class is worth 3 credits, define a Stata generate statement to create a variable called classes as a linear transformation of credits that estimates the average number of classes taken during the current semester.

    b) What is the mean of classes?

    c) What is the standard deviation of classes?

    d) What is the shape of the distribution of classes? Explain and support your answer with an appropriate descriptive statistic. Be sure to indicate whether or not the distribution is *severely* skewed.

    e) Why do you suppose the skewness is so severe in the negative direction?

4.4. The variable schattrt in the *NELS* data set gives the average daily attendance rate for the school that the student attends.

    a) What are the mean, median, standard deviation, variance, range, interquartile range, and skewness of schattrt?

    b) Compute a new variable schattpp that expresses the average daily attendance as a decimal instead of as a percentage, i.e., that gives the average daily attendance proportion for the school that the student attends. What is the numeric expression you used?

    c) Based on the summary statistics for schattrt that you generated in part a), find the mean, median, standard deviation, variance, interquartile range, and skewness of schattpp.

    d) Use Stata to calculate the mean, median, standard deviation, variance, range, interquartile range, and skewness of schattpp.

4.5. The variable expinc30 in the *NELS* data set measures the expected annual income at age 30 of students in the eighth grade.

a) What are the mean, median, standard deviation, variance, range, interquartile range, and skewness of expinc30?

b) Compute a new variable, expcents, which gives the expected income at age 30 in terms of pennies, not dollars. What is the numeric expression you used?

c) Based on the summary statistics for expinc30 that you generated in part a), find the mean, median, standard deviation, variance, interquartile range, and skewness of expcents.

d) Use Stata to calculate the mean, median, standard deviation, variance, range, interquartile range, and skewness of expcents.

4.6. The variable computer in the *NELS* data set indicates whether the student's family owned a computer when the student was in eighth grade. The variable is coded so that $0 = $ No and $1 = $ Yes.

a) Verify that in using this coding, the mean equals the proportion of Yes's, or, in this case, 1's. What is that value?

b) Use Stata to compute the standard deviation of the variable computer?

c) What is the linear transformation to convert computer into comp1, which is coded 1 for No and 2 for Yes.

d) What is the linear transformation to convert computer into comp2, which is coded 0 for Yes and 1 for No.

e) Use the rules for the effects of linear transformations on summary statistics to determine the means and standard deviations of the variables comp1 and comp2.

4.7. The variable CIGPDAY1 from the *Framingham* data set gives the number of cigarettes smoked per day by the respondents at first examination in 1956. Assume that the values of CIGPDAY1 are then multiplied by negative 2 and then 3 is added to each value to create the variable CIGTRANS.

a) What are the values of the mean, standard deviation, and skewness of CIGPDAY1?

b) What is the value of the mean of CIGTRANS?

c) What is the value of the new *SD*?

d) What is the value of the new skewness statistic?

4.8. In the *Framingham* data set, SEX is coded so that $1 = $ Men and $2 = $ Women. What is the mean of SEX? Apply appropriate linear transformations to interpret the mean of SEX as a proportion of women.

Exercises 4.9–4.17 involve z-scores.

4.9. Consider the variable, number of members in a student's household, given by the *NELS* variable, famsize (family size).

a) If a student has a *z*-score of -1.28, how many members are in her household?

b) What is the *z*-score for a student with 6 members in her household?

c) Using the *z*-score criteria for outliers, that is, that a score is an outlier if its associated *z*-score is less than -2 or greater than 2, how many outliers are in this distribution?

4.10. Consider the variable, self-concept in eighth grade, given by the *NELS* variable, slfcnc08.

   a) Find the mean and standard deviation of slfcnc08.
   b) Write down a Stata **gen** statement to calculate the *z*-score distribution for slfcnc08 and call the variable zslfcnc08ver1. You will need to look up the mean and the standard deviation of the variable
   c) Use the Stata command **egen zslfcnc08ver2 = std(slfcnc08)** to create the *z*-score distribution for slfcnc08.
   d) Without computing, what are the means and standard deviations of zslfcnc08ver1 and zslfcnc08ver2?
   e) If a new variable, slf08p5, were created by adding 5 points to the eighth grade self-concept score for each student in the *NELS* data set, what would be the mean and standard deviation of slf08p5?

4.11. The variable unitengl in the *NELS* data set gives the number of years of English taken in high school. The variable unitmath gives the number of years of math taken in high school. Advanced course work enabled some of the recorded values of these two variables in the data set to exceed four.

   a) What is the *z*-score of a student who took 5.5 years of high school English?
   b) How many years of high school English did a student with a *z*-score of –1.71 take?
   c) Using the *z*-score criteria for outliers, that is, that a score is an outlier if its associated *z*-score is less than –2 or greater than 2, how many outliers are in the distribution unitengl?
   d) According to cumulative percentages, if a student took 5.5 years of both math and English, relative to his classmates, is that more unusual for English or math?
   e) According to z-scores, if a student took 5.5 years of both math and English, relative to his classmates, is that more unusual for English or math?

4.12. The variables slfcnc08, slfcnc10, slfcnc12 in the *NELS* data set, measure self-concept in eighth, tenth, and twelfth grade, respectively. A self-concept score of 25 is relatively highest in which of these distributions?

   a) Base your answer on cumulative percentages.
   b) Base your answer on z-scores.

4.13. Does an eighth grade self-concept (slfcnc08) score of 25 represent a higher level of eighth grade self-concept for males or for females? Use as criteria (a) cumulative percentages and (b) z-scores. Create separate frequency distributions and summary statistics for males and female students in the *NELS*, using the following commands:

by gender, sort: tabulate slfcnc08
by gender, sort: summarize slfcnc08

4.14. Who scores higher in science achievement in eighth grade (achsci08) relative to his or her gender, a female who scores 58, or a male who scores 63? Use as criteria (a) cumulative percentages and (b) z-scores. As in 4.13, create separate frequency distributions for males and female students in the *NELS* dataset.

4.15. Determine the number of standard deviations away from the mean a score of 89 is on a test with mean 92 and variance 4.

4.16. If Steve's z-score on a test is +1.5, what is his raw score if the mean of the test is 75 and the standard deviation is 10?

4.17. Given a unimodal, symmetric distribution, rank from numerically smallest to numerically largest the following values from that distribution:

$$z = +1 \quad \bar{X} \quad Q_1$$

Exercises 4.18–4.20 involve a mixture of topics about linear transformations and some review topics.

4.18. The following questions involve the variable grade from the *Learndis* data set.
   a) What are the mean, standard deviation, and skewness ratio of the variable grade?
   b) Assume that students start first grade at age 6 and go up one grade each year. Use a linear transformation to convert grade to age, the approximate age of the student in that grade.
   c) Use the information about the distribution grade to find the mean age for students in the data set.
   d) Use the information about the distribution grade to find the standard deviation for age.
   e) Use the information about the distribution grade to find the skewness ratio for age. How would you describe the shape of the age distribution?

4.19. Compare the distribution of reading comprehension scores (readcomp) in the *Learndis* data set by whether the student was assigned part time to the resource room for additional instruction (placement = 0) or full time in a self-contained classroom (placemen = 1).
   a) Is either of the two distributions severely skewed? If so, which one(s) and what is the direction of the skew? Explain and support your answer with appropriate descriptive statistics.
   b) In which type of placement do these students have a higher overall level of reading comprehension? Explain and support your answer with an appropriate descriptive statistic taking into account the varying degrees of skewness in the two distributions. Is there another statistic that suggests an alternative conclusion?
   c) For which type of placement are the reading comprehension scores more consistent? Explain and support your answer with an appropriate descriptive statistic taking into account the varying degrees of skewness in the two distributions. Is there another statistic that suggests an alternative conclusion?
   d) Does the student with the highest reading comprehension score in the data set have a resource room or a self-contained classroom placement? Provide statistical support your answer.
   e) What is the z-score corresponding to a reading comprehension score of 75 for a student with a resource room placement?
   f) What is the reading comprehension score corresponding to a z-score of 2 for a student with a resource room placement?
   g) Would a student with a reading comprehension score of 75 be more unusual (further from the bulk of the scores in standard deviation units) relative to the resource

room students or to the self-contained classroom students? Explain and support your answer.

h) Can a percentile in the distribution of reading comprehension scores for the students with a resource room placement have the value 103? Explain.

4.20. Consider the variable AGE1 in the *Framingham* data set, which gives a respondent's age in 1956, the first year of the study.

a) How many people in the dataset were 40 years old in 1956?

b) What percentage of people in the dataset were younger than or equal to 40 in 1956?

c) Is 40 years old above or below the median in this data set? Explain.

d) Is 40 years old above or below the mean in this data set? How many standard deviations is 40 years old above or below the mean?

e) If we consider a score to be an outlier if its associated z-score is less than –2 or greater than 2, how many outliers are there in the AGE1 distribution?

f) What is the breakdown of outliers by men and women?

g) Write the formula for linearly transforming the variable AGE1 to the new variable BIRTHYR, which gives the year in which the person was born.

h) What is the median of the variable BIRTHYR?

i) What is the standard deviation of the BIRTHYR?

Exercises 4.21–4.23 involve square root and logarithmic transformations.

4.21. Consider the two achievement measures in the tenth grade, achmat10 and achrdg10, in the *NELS* data set. Determine their skewness and a nonlinear transformation (e.g., log, square root) that will be useful in symmetrizing the variable if it is highly skewed.

4.22. For each of the following variables from the *NELS* data set, determine whether the variable is skewed, and, if so, whether a log or square root transformation is effective in symmetrizing the variable.

a) apoffer

b) famsize

c) schattrt

d) What would be the effect, if any, of a nonlinear transformation on a dichotomous variable, such as cigarett?

4.23. For each of the following variables from the *Learndis* data set, determine whether the variable is skewed, and, if so, whether a log or square root transformation is effective in symmetrizing the variable.

a) grade

b) mathcomp

c) readcomp

Exercises 4.24–4.28 involve recoding and combining variables.

4.24. In the *NELS* data set, unitmath represents the total number of units (in years) of mathematics taken in high school, while unitcalc represents the number of units (in years) of calculus taken.

a) Create the variable unitmnc to represent the number of units of noncalculus mathematics taken.

b) What is the largest number of units of noncalculus math taken by a student in the *NELS* data set? How many student(s) took that amount of noncalculus math?

4.25. There are four variables in the *NELS* data set that describe different types of achievement in twelfth grade: achmat12, achrdg12, achsci12, and achsls12.

a) Create a composite variable, achtot12 that represents the sum of a student's achievement on all four tests.

b) Describe the shape of the distribution of achtot12.

c) On average, do boys score higher on achtot12 than girls? Support your answer with appropriate descriptive statistics and indicate if different statistics lead to different conclusions.

4.26. The variable apoffer gives the number of Advanced Placement (AP) courses offered by the school that the student attends in the *NELS* data set.

a) Create a new variable, apoffyn, that indicates whether a school offers any AP courses. Make sure that missing values on apoffer continued to be coded as missing on apoffyn. Define and label new value labels so that 0 = no and 1 = yes on apoffyn.

b) How many schools in the *NELS* data set do not offer AP courses?

c) How may we interpret the mean of this 0–1 coded dichotomous variable apoffyn?

4.27. In Exercise 1.15, you created the *Statisticians* data set. Using the variables in that data set, create the following new variables and answer related questions about them.

a) Create the variable alive, representing how long each statistician lived. Who lived the longest?

b) Create the variable old, that indicates how old each statistician would be now, if they were still living. Who is the "youngest" statistician in the data set?

★ **4.28.** Use the *Framingham* data set to determine if after experiencing a coronary heart disease event (CHD), individuals reduce their weight (as measured by BMI) and cigarette smoking (as measured by CIGPDAY). Consider the initial period as period 1 (1956) and the final period as period 3 (1968). The variable ANYCHD4 indicates whether a person in the study experienced a CHD during the study.

a) Create two new variables that reflect the difference in BMI and CIGDAY from period 1 to period 3; e.g., BMIDIFF = BMI3 – BMI1 and CIGPDIFF = CIGDAY3 – CIGDAY1. Looking at the frequency distribution of these two variables, how many individuals lost weight? How many reduced their cigarette smoking?

b) What is the change in BMI, on average, from period 1 to period 3 for those who experienced a CHD event during this time period as compared to those who did not experience a CHD event during this time period?

c) What is the change in CIGDAY, on average, from period 1 to period 3 for those who experienced a CHD event during this time period as compared to those who did not experience a CHD event during this time period?

Exercises 4.29–4.32 make use of the Do-files for Chapters 2 *and* 3.

4.29. Use the Do-file for Chapter 2 to reproduce Table 2.1 and Figures 2.1, 2.2, 2.3, and 2.4 in the text by highlighting the relevant command lines in the Do-file and pressing **Control+d**. Be sure to open the relevant data set first.

4.30. Use the Do-file for Chapter 2 to obtain the results of Example 2.3 and to reproduce Figures 2.15, 2.16(a), 2.16(b), and 2.17 in the text by highlighting the relevant command lines in the Do-file and pressing **Control+d**. Be sure to open the relevant data set first.

4.31. Use the Do-file for Chapter 3 to reproduce the mean and median results of Example 3.5 in the text by highlighting the relevant command lines in the Do-file and pressing **Control+d**. Be sure to open the relevant data set first.

4.32. Use the Do-file for Chapter 3 to duplicate the analysis described under the section, "Applying What We Have Learned" as it regards the variable expinc30 from the *NELS* data set by highlighting the relevant command lines in the Do-file and pressing **Control+d**. Be sure to open the relevant data set first.

CHAPTER FIVE

Exploring Relationships between Two Variables

Up to this point, we have been examining data univariately; that is, one variable at a time. We have examined the location, spread, and shape of several variables in the *NELS* data set, such as socioeconomic status, mathematics achievement, expected income at age 30, and self-concept. Interesting questions often arise, however, that involve the relationship between two variables. For example, using the *NELS* data set we may be interested in knowing if self-concept relates to socioeconomic status; if gender relates to science achievement in twelfth grade; if sex relates to nursery school attendance; or if math achievement in twelfth grade relates to geographical region of residence.

When we ask whether one variable relates to another, we are really asking about the shape, direction, and strength of the relationship between the two variables. We also find it useful to distinguish among the nature of the variables themselves; that is, whether the two variables in question are both measured either, at least, at the interval level, or are both dichotomous, or are a combination of the two. For example, when we ask about the relationship between socioeconomic status and self-concept, we are asking about the relationship between two at least interval-leveled variables. When we ask about whether sex relates to nursery school attendance, we are asking about the relationship between two dichotomous variables. And, when we ask about whether sex relates to twelfth grade science achievement, we are asking about the relationship between one dichotomous variable and one at least interval-leveled variable.

WHEN BOTH VARIABLES ARE AT LEAST INTERVAL-LEVELED

While the questions posed in the introductory paragraph of this chapter are motivated by our familiarity with the *NELS* data set, for heuristic reasons, we have chosen much smaller, yet real, data sets, to introduce the important ideas associated with the concept of relationship between two continuous variables.

Do hamburgers that have more fat tend to have more calories? Table 5.1 contains the fat grams and calories associated with the different types of hamburger sold by McDonald's. The data are from McDonald's Nutrition Information Center and are saved in the *Hamburg* data set.

Does a state's average SAT Critical Reading score relate to the percentage of students who have taken the SAT in that state? Data on the percentage of students who took the SAT in 2012 in each state along with the average SAT Critical Reading score is taken from the *States* data set. The source for these data is *The World Almanac and Book of Facts 2014*.

For bills of $20 or lower, is there an association between the value of the bill and the total number in circulation? Table 5.2 contains for the smaller bill denominations, the

TABLE 5.1. Fat grams and calories by type of McDonald's hamburgers

Type of McDonald's Hamburger	Grams of fat (X)	Calories (Y)
Hamburger	10	270
Cheeseburger	14	320
Quarter Pounder	21	430
Quarter Pounder w/ cheese	30	530
Big Mac	28	530

TABLE 5.2. Value and total circulation of United States currency

Denomination	Total circulation ($)	Number in circulation
$1	10,334,000,000	10,334,000,000
$2	2,009,000,000	1,004,500,000
$5	12,025,000,000	2,405,000,000
$10	17,332,000,000	1,733,200,000
$20	148,219,000,000	7,410,950,000

value of the bill and the total circulation in dollars. These values are saved in the *Currency* data set. We use the methods of Chapter 4 to calculate the total number of bills in circulation by dividing the total circulation in dollars by the bill value, given as the last column in Table 5.2. The source for these data is *The World Almanac and Book of Facts 2014*.

Finally, what is the pattern of marijuana use by twelfth graders from 1987 through 1996? We answer this question using data from the *Marijuana* data set, which gives the year and the percentage of twelfth graders who report that they have ever used marijuana. The source for these data is *The World Almanac and Book of Facts 2014*.

SCATTERPLOTS

With any of these data sets, a natural question is, how may we describe the relationship between the two variables? While the relationship may often be grasped by inspecting the table of pairs of data values, a better approach is to use a graphic that depicts each pair of (X,Y) values as a separate point in an (X,Y) coordinate plane. Such a graphic is called a *scatterplot*. The scatterplots for the data in our four examples are given in Figures 5.1 through 5.4, respectively.

MORE Stata: To obtain the scatterplot in Figure 5.1, for example
    We type the following in the Command Window and press **Enter**:

twoway (scatter calories fat)

MORE Stata: To obtain a scatterplot on a restricted set of data as in Figure 5.4
    We use an "if" statement to limit the values on the x-axis to the years 1987 through 1996; that is, to the years greater than or equal to 1987 and less than or equal to 1996.

twoway (scatter marij year) if (year >=1987) & (year <=1996)

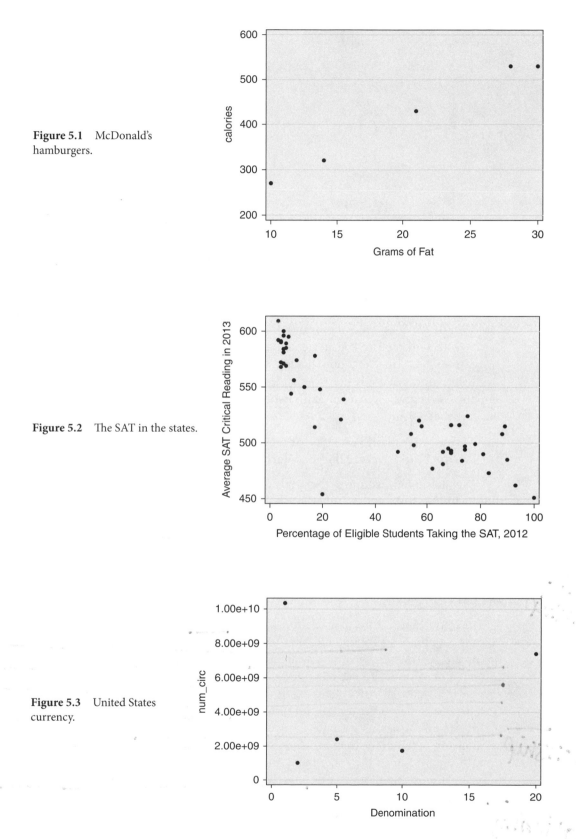

Figure 5.1 McDonald's hamburgers.

Figure 5.2 The SAT in the states.

Figure 5.3 United States currency.

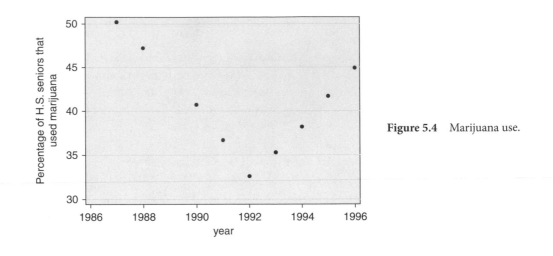

Figure 5.4   Marijuana use.

MORE Stata: Customizing our graphic.

A title may be added to a graph as an option. We could also specify the font size and color of the title. To generate the graph of Figure 5.4 with a title that has medium large font (instead of large font as the default) and is in the color red, we would use the following command. Notice that both the font size and color are placed within the parentheses for title to show that it is the title that font size and color are describing. Because title is an option relative to the command **twoway,** it sits outside the parentheses that contain **scatter marij year.**

twoway (scatter marij year) if (year >=1987) & (year <=1996), title (Marijuana Usage Across Years, size(medlarge) color(red))

We also could customize the symbol, color, and size of the points in the scatterplot by including **msymbol** (marker symbol), **mcolor** (marker color), and **msize** (marker size) in our command. Because these options relate to the scatter itself, they must be placed within the parentheses that define the scatterplot of marijuana vs. year:

twoway (scatter marij year if (year >=1987) & (year <=1996), title(Marijuana Usage Across Years, size(medlarge) color(red)) msymbol(D) mcolor(blue) msize(large))

An important feature of a relationship is its *shape.* Notice that in the scatterplots of Figures 5.1 and 5.2, although all points do not exactly fall along a single straight line, the points are represented well by a straight line. Accordingly, the relationships between fat content and calories and between the percentage of students taking the SAT exam and the average SAT math score for states in the western United States are said to be linear. By contrast, the variables of the scatterplot of Figures 5.3 are not systematically related because the points follow neither a single straight line nor a simple curve. We say that there is no relationship between the denomination of the bill and the number of such bills in circulation. In Figure 5.4, on the other hand, the variables are systematically related because the points of this scatterplot are best represented by a simple curve, not by a single straight line. Marijuana use is relatively high in the late 1980's and early 1990s, decreases until 1992 and then increases again through 1996. This particular type of curvilinear relationship is called *quadratic* because it has an approximately parabolic shape and parabolic curves are represented by quadratic functions.

Another important feature of a relationship is its *direction*. Because the straight line representing the points of Figure 5.1 has positive slope, the linear relationship is said to be positive; that is, the higher the fat content, the higher the number of calories (and the lower the fat content, the lower the number of calories). On the other hand, because the straight line representing the points of Figure 5.2 has negative slope, the linear relationship is said to be negative. That is, the states with higher percentages of students taking the SAT tend to have lower average SAT Critical Reading scores (and the states with lower percentages of students taking the SAT tend to have higher average SAT Critical Reading scores). Because Figure 5.3 suggests no simple systematic relationship between the two variables in question (currency value and number in circulation), the notion of a direction of relationship is not meaningful. Finally, in the quadratic relationship of Figure 5.4 the direction of the relationship changes from negative to positive. For years 1988 through 1992, the earlier years are associated with higher marijuana use while the later years are associated with lower marijuana use. For years 1992 through 1996, the earlier years are associated with lower marijuana use while the later years are associated with higher marijuana use.

Relationships also may be characterized by their *strength*. Simply stated, the closer the points in the scatterplot are to the straight line (or curve) that best represents the points, the stronger the relationship between the two variables. If all the points in the scatterplot fall exactly on the line (or curve) that best represents the points, we would say that a perfect linear (or nonlinear) relationship exists between the two variables. The farther the points in the scatterplot are from the line (or curve), the weaker the linear (or nonlinear) relationship between the two variables.

Figures 5.5(A) through (I) provide a series of scatterplots varying in the direction and strength of the linear relationships they depict. They include as well fit lines superimposed on the graphs to accentuate the strength and direction of the relationship.

The data for Figure 5.5(A) through Figure 5.5(I) are located in the file, Figures5.5.dta.

MORE Stata: To superimpose a fit line on a scatterplot as illustrated in Figure 5.5(A)

graph twoway (scatter ay ax) (lfit ay ax)

The Do-file associated with this chapter contains the code used to generate Figures 5.5(A) through 5.5(I) with the superimposed fit lines.

Figures (A) through (D) depict increasingly weaker negative linear relationships because the points in these figures depart increasingly from the straight line that best represents them. While Figure 5.5(A) represents a perfect negative linear relationship because all points fall exactly on the straight line, Figures (B) through (D) do not. Figure (E) depicts no relationship between the two variables and Figures (F) through (I) depict increasingly stronger positive linear relationships.

A scatterplot may be used to depict the shape, direction, and, to a lesser extent, the strength of the relationship between two variables, but summary statistics may also be used to quantify the strength and direction of relationships. In the case of two continuous variables, when both are on at least interval scales of measurement, the direction and strength

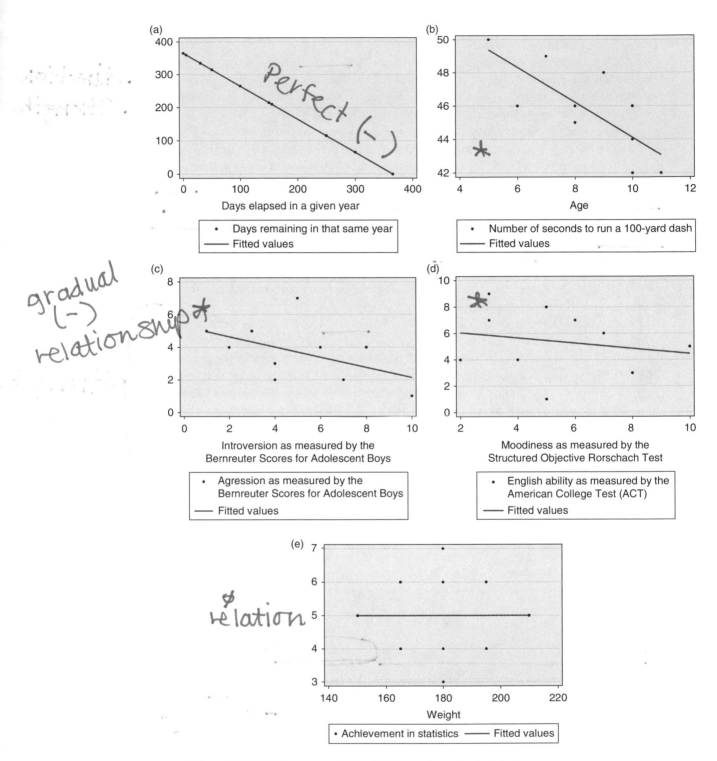

Figure 5.5 (A) The passage of time. (B) Elementary school students.
(C) Adolescent boys. (D) College freshmen. (E) Male college students.
(F) College students. (G) Children in grades K – 3. (H) Elementary school students. (I) Dimensions of a tree.

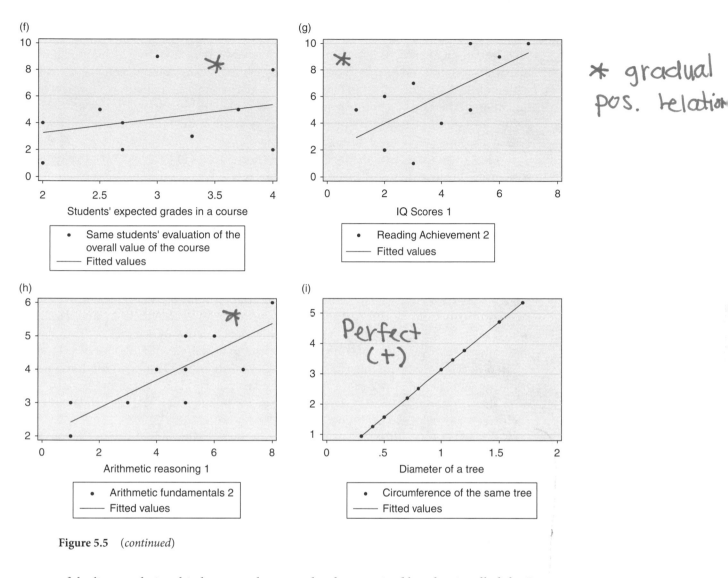

Figure 5.5 *(continued)*

of the linear relationship between them may be characterized by what is called the *Pearson Product Moment Correlation Coefficient.*

☞ **Remark.** The Pearson Correlation Coefficient is named after Karl Pearson, who in 1896 published the first mathematically rigorous treatment of this index. It was Sir Francis Galton, however, a cousin of Charles Darwin, who in the 1870's first conceptualized the notion of correlation and regression (to be covered in the next chapter) through his work in genetics; and, in particular, by examining two-dimensional scatterplots of the relationship between the sizes of sweet pea plants of mother-daughter pairs (Stanton, 2001).

While indices exist to represent the strength of nonlinear relationships, these are beyond the scope of our discussion, which, in this section, is confined to linear relationships only. For a more advanced treatment of correlation, including nonlinear relationships, the interested reader is referred to Cohen, Cohen, West and Aiken (2003).

THE PEARSON PRODUCT MOMENT CORRELATION COEFFICIENT

The strength of a linear relationship is characterized by the extent to which a straight line fits the data points. That is, by the extent to which high scores on one variable are paired with high scores on the other and low scores on one variable are paired with low scores on the other, in the case of a *positive*, or *direct*, linear relationship. Or, by the extent to which high scores on one variable are paired with low scores on the other and vice versa in the case of a *negative*, or *indirect*, linear relationship.

To illustrate, we refer to the fat content (X) and calories (Y) values of the five types of hamburger given in Table 5.1 that we have observed to have a positive linear relationship. For convenience, as shown in Table 5.3, we index the values by a subscripting letter rather than by the type of hamburger itself.

We may determine whether high scores on fat content are paired with high scores on calories and whether low scores on fat content are paired with low scores on calories by first determining if each type of hamburger's fat content value is high or low *within the set of fat content values*. And we can do likewise for each type of hamburger's value on calories. Once we have labeled each fat content value and calorie value as either high or low within its own distribution, we can compare one to the other for each type of hamburger. In so doing, we may determine the extent to which high fat content values tend to be paired with high calorie values and low fat content values tend to be paired with low calorie values.

In order to label a particular fat content value as either high or low within its own distribution, we calculate the z-scores for each fat and calorie value within its own distribution. These z-scores, as calculated using the Stata commands **egen zfat = std(fat)** and **egen zcalories = std(calories)**, are shown in Table 5.4 for both X and Y.

To determine whether a high fat content is paired with a high calorie count, and whether a low fat content is paired with a low calorie count, we form the product of the two z-scores for each hamburger type. If both X *and* Y scores are high with regard to their respective distributions, then both terms in the product will be positive and the product itself will be positive. Likewise, if both the X *and* Y scores are low with regard to their respective distributions, then both terms in the product will be negative and the product will again be positive.

Notice that all the products in Table 5.5 are positive. A positive product results when either both terms are positive or both terms are negative.

☞ **Remark.** When one (but not both) of the differences is negative, signifying either a high *X* value paired with a low *Y* value or a low *X* value paired with a high *Y* value, a negative product results.

TABLE 5.3. Fat content and calories of five hamburger types

Type of McDonald's Hamburger (indexed)	Grams of fat (X)	Calories (Y)
1	$X_1 = 10$	$Y_1 = 270$
2	$X_2 = 14$	$Y_2 = 320$
3	$X_3 = 21$	$Y_3 = 430$
4	$X_4 = 30$	$Y_4 = 530$
5	$X_5 = 28$	$Y_5 = 530$

TABLE 5.4. Difference about the mean for grams of fat content and calories

Type of McDonald's Hamburger (indexed)	fat (X)	calories (Y)	zfat	zcalories
1	$X_1 = 10$	$Y_1 = 270$	−1.226	−1.226
2	$X_2 = 14$	$Y_2 = 320$	−.763	−.806
3	$X_3 = 21$	$Y_3 = 430$	.046	.118
4	$X_4 = 30$	$Y_4 = 530$	1.087	.957
5	$X_5 = 28$	$Y_5 = 530$	.856	.957

TABLE 5.5. Taking the product of the difference terms

Fat (X)	Calories (Y)	z_x	z_y	$z_x z_y$
$X_1 = 10$	$Y_1 = 270$	−1.226	−1.226	1.503
$X_2 = 14$	$Y_2 = 320$	−.763	−.806	.615
$X_3 = 21$	$Y_3 = 430$	.046	.118	.005
$X_4 = 30$	$Y_4 = 530$	1.087	.957	1.041
$X_5 = 28$	$Y_5 = 530$	.856	.957	.819

In order to obtain a summary measure that incorporates all types of hamburger and all types of fat content and calorie count values, we can approximate the *average* tendency of the values to have positive (or negative) products by dividing the sum of the products by $N - 1$.

$$r = \frac{\sum z_x z_y}{N - 1} \tag{5.1a}$$

Equation 5.1a is called the *Pearson Product Moment Correlation Coefficient*, denoted by the symbol r_{xy} or the letter r. N represents the number of pairs of fat content and calorie count values in the data set. In the McDonald's example, N equals 5 because there are five pairs of values. For these data, $r = .996$.

MORE Stata: Using Stata to compute r as given by Equation (5.1a)
    We first transform the fat and calories values to z-scores

egen zfat = std(fat) egen zcalories = std(calories)

    We then generate the product terms zfat*zcalories: **gen prod = zfat*zcalories**
    We then obtain the sum of the products: **summarize prod, detail**
    And then list the post-estimation statistics created by the summarize command

return list

    Note: A **return list** command lists in the Output Window the array of statistics, called **post-estimation statistics**, that are estimated, but not necessarily printed, when we run a command, such as **summarize prod, detail**. The particular array of post-estimation statistics is unique to each command, and is represented by variables of the form r(). For the **summarize prod, detail** command, for example, this array of variables include: r(N), r(sum), r(mean), r(var), r(sd), r(skewness), r(kurtosis), r(min), r(max), r(p1), r(p5), and so on. The variable r(N) contains the size of the sample used to compute the summary statistics for prod, and r(sum) contains the sum of the values of prod, which is the sum we need for computing Equation 5.1(a). The nice part about these post-estimation statistics, is that we may use them directly using their r() variable name, as we do in the **display** command line below, or we may save them in our dataset under a new variable name for future use (e.g., **gen sum_prod = r(sum)**).

Finally, we calculate and display the results of Eq. 5.1(a) in the Output Window
display "Pearson Product Moment Correlation Coefficient=" r(sum)/(r(N) − 1)

Had we not used Stata to calculate the *z*-scores, it is likely that we would have divided by *N* in calculating the standard deviation values upon which the *z*-scores are based. In this case, the Pearson Product Moment Correlation Coefficient is expressed as Equation 5.1b.

$$r = \frac{\sum z_x z_y}{N} \tag{5.1b}$$

When *N* is large, results from Equations 5.1a and 5.1b will be only negligibly different.

The sign of the correlation indicates the direction of the relationship; the magnitude of the correlation indicates the strength. The correlation is bounded between −1.00 and +1.00 inclusive. A correlation value of −1.00 indicates a *perfect negative linear relationship*, while a Pearson Correlation value of +1.00 indicates a *perfect positive linear relationship*. A correlation value of 0 indicates no linear relationship.

As expected, the sign of the correlation between fat and calories is positive, suggesting that hamburgers with low fat content tend to have low calorie counts and hamburgers with high fat content tend to have high calorie counts. Furthermore, because the magnitude of this correlation is so close to 1.00, we may infer that the relationship between fat content and calorie count is very strong.

☞ **Remark.** The calculation of *z*-scores in Equations 5.1(a) and 5.1(b) requires that we divide by both S_x and S_y. Because division by 0 is not defined, we must impose the restriction that whenever either $S_x = 0$ or $S_y = 0$ (all the X values are the same or all the Y values are the same) or both, the Pearson Correlation Coefficient will be undefined. Conceptually, the Pearson Correlation Coefficient should not be defined in this case. For example, suppose we wanted to determine the relationship between age rounded to the nearest year (*X*) and income (*Y*), and the data consisted only of 25 year olds. Because there is no variability on age for such data, the standard deviation of age would be zero, and there would be no way to determine whether in fact income varies with age.

MORE Stata: To obtain the correlation coefficient between two variables (fat and calories)

We may use either of the following commands:

correlate calories fat
pwcorr calories fat, obs

Note: the **pw** in **pwcorr** stands for pairwise and the option **obs** after the comma instructs Stata to output the number of observations on which the correlation is based

The output from the pwcorr command is reproduced below.

(obs=5)

The output is formatted as a two-by-two table called a matrix. The upper left and bottom right cells form what is called the _main diagonal_ of the matrix. The cells in the main diagonal contain the correlations of each variable with itself. Because a variable is always perfectly positively correlated with itself, these correlations (the first value in each cell) equal 1.00. The lower left and upper right cells form what is called the _off-diagonal_ of the matrix. The correlation in the

	calories	fat
calories	• 1.0000	
fat	0.9957	• 1.0000

upper right cell is the correlation between CALORIES and FAT while the correlation in the lower left cell is the correlation between FAT and CALORIES. Notice that in both cells, this correlation equals .996. These correlations are equal because the bivariate correlation is a symmetric measure of a linear relationship. That is, $r_{xy} = r_{yx}$.

• •

EXAMPLE 5.1. Given the data corresponding to Figures 5.2 through 5.4, find and interpret the correlations between (a) the percentage of students taking the SAT and the average Critical Reading SAT score in the United States; (b) the currency value of a bill and the total number of such bills in circulation; (c) percentage marijuana use among twelfth graders and year from 1987 through 1996.

Solution. Using Stata we obtain the following results.

(a) $r = -.86$ suggesting that states with larger percentages of students taking the SAT tend to have lower average Critical Reading SAT scores, and vice versa.

(b) $r = .13$, suggesting that the currency value of a bill is only weakly positively linearly related to the total number of such bills in circulation. From the scatterplot of Figure 5.3, we may conclude further that knowing the currency value of a bill tells us almost nothing about how many such bills are in circulation.

(c) $r = -.42$ suggesting that percentage of marijuana use is negatively linearly related to the year of observation, from 1987 to 1996. However, we know from looking at the scatterplot of Figure 5.4, that correlation, which measures the strength and direction of the linear relationship, is not a good statistic to use to describe the relationship between these two variables. Over the entire span of years measured, the relationship is better described as quadratic, not linear. Alternatively, one could compute two correlations, one based on the data from 1992 and earlier, and the other on the data from 1992 and later. These two correlations would better reflect the strong relationship between marijuana use and year of use, negative before 1992 and positive after 1992.

☞ **Remark.** When describing the nature of the linear relationship between two variables, you need to be careful to avoid causal language. For example, when we are looking at the positive relationship between weight and height among adults, it might be tempting to write, "As weight goes up, height goes up." However, that statement is not correct because plenty of adults gain weight as they age and their height does not change. A correct statement is, "Adults who are heavier tend to be taller and adults who weigh less tend to be shorter." When writing up these descriptions, we recommend that you start the sentence with the unit of analysis of the data set. So, for the Hamburg data set we write, "Hamburgers with low fat content tend to have low calorie counts and hamburgers with high fat content tend to have high calorie counts." For the States data set we write, "States with larger percentages of students taking the SAT tend to have lower average Critical Reading SAT scores, and vice versa."

EXAMPLE 5.2. The following table gives the correlation coefficient for each of the scatterplots depicted in Figures 5.5(A) through 5.5(I). Do the magnitude and direction of these relationships corroborate the impressions obtained from the scatterplots?

Figure letter	Correlation, r
A	−1.00
B	−0.76
C	−0.50
D	−0.20
E	0.00
F	+0.32
G	+0.65
H	+0.82
I	+1.00

Solution. The correlations (A) through (D) are increasingly less negative and corroborate the fact that the points in these figures depart increasingly from the negatively sloped straight line that best represents them. As expected, the correlation of Figure (E) is zero, and the correlations (F) through (I) are increasingly more positive.

Interpreting the Pearson Correlation Coefficient

Judging the Strength of the Linear Relationship. Whether a Pearson Correlation Coefficient value r is to be judged unusually strong or unusually weak depends on the situation in which the correlation has been computed.

For example, if we administered the Stanford-Binet Intelligence Test to a group of elementary school children and then re-administered the test to these same children a week later, the correlation value we would expect to obtain between the two testings is approximately $r = 0.90$. Under these circumstances, the correlation value of $r = 0.90$ would not be considered unusually strong; it would be considered typical. This is because, given the relatively short time between testings, it is unlikely that anything has happened to alter substantially the responses to the test.

Under different circumstances, a correlation value of $r = 0.90$ might be considered unusually strong. If, for example, two different tests had been used instead of only one (a test of intelligence and a test of creativity, for example), then a correlation of $r = 0.90$ might be considered unusually strong. Thus, the terms *strong and weak* are used to compare descriptively the obtained correlation value to the value we would expect under the given circumstances.

Within an applied psychology framework, specific criteria for categorizing the magnitude of linear relationships as strong, moderate, and weak were first introduced by Cohen (1988) and are now widely used in behavioral science research. The strength of the correlation also is known as its *effect size*.

TABLE 5.6. Correlation coefficients for selected variables

Variables	Correlation Coefficient
Heights of identical twins	.95
Intelligence test scores of identical twins	.88
Reading test scores grade 3 versus grade 6	.80
Rank in high school class versus teachers' rating of work habits	.73
Height versus weight of 10-year-olds	.60
Arithmetic computation test versus nonverbal intelligence test (grade 8)	.54
Height of brothers, adjusted for age	.50
Intelligence test score versus parental occupational level	.30
Strength of grip versus speed of running	.16
Height versus Binet IQ	.06
Ratio of head length to width versus intelligence	.01
Armed Forces Qualification Test scores of recruits versus number of school grades repeated	−.27
Artist interest versus banker interest	−.64

According to an often-cited publication by Cohen (1988), Pearson correlation values approximately equal to:

$r = \pm 0.50$ are considered strong;

$r = \pm 0.30$ are considered moderate;

$r = \pm 0.10$ are considered weak.

Cohen's classification of a correlation of ± 0.50 as strong, comes from his assertion that "workers in personality-social psychology, both pure and applied (i.e., clinical, educational, personnel), normally encounter correlation coefficients above the .50–.60 range only when the correlations are measurement reliability coefficients" (1969, p. 75).

Based on these criteria, case (H) of Example 5.2 ($r = 0.82$) indicates a *very strong* linear relationship between the two variables, whereas case (F) ($r_{xy} = 0.32$) indicates only a *moderate* linear relationship between the two variables. However, both are examples of typical correlation values within their respective contexts.

Because the sign of the correlation value indicates only the nature of the relationship between the two variables (whether it is positive or negative) and not its magnitude, a Pearson correlation value of +0.50 indicates a linear relationship of the same strength as a Pearson Correlation Coefficient value of −.50. Likewise, a correlation of -0.76 represents a stronger linear relationship than a correlation of 0.65.

To get a sense of some of the correlation values that appear in the literature, Table 5.6 gives correlation coefficients for selected variables (Thorndike and Hagen, 1969).

The Correlation Scale Itself Is Ordinal. One may ask whether an increase in correlation values of 0.10 units represents a constant increase in the strength of the relationship regardless of the values of the correlations themselves. Because the Pearson Correlation Coefficient as a measure of linear relationship is on an ordinal level of measurement, it does not. Whereas a correlation value of +0.50 represents a stronger relationship between two variables than a correlation value of +.30, and a correlation value of +.30 represents a stronger relationship between two variables than a correlation value of +.10, the increase in strength from +0.10 to +0.30 is not the same as (and is actually smaller than) the increase in strength from +.30 to +0.50.

Correlation Does Not Imply Causation. Another important consideration in interpreting a Pearson Correlation Coefficient value is that, in general, the existence of a correlation between two variables does not necessarily imply the existence of a causal link between these two variables.

For example, suppose we obtain a correlation of $r = +0.60$ between the number of television sets in various countries at a particular time and the number of telephones in the same countries at the same time. This correlation does not necessarily imply that a causal relationship exists between the number of televisions and the number of telephones in a country. For example, importing a million television sets into a country will not automatically increase that country's number of telephones. Similarly, importing a million telephones into a country will not automatically increase that country's number of television sets.

It is possible that the values of both of these variables are due to a common third variable (such as the industrial level of the country or its gross national product) and that this third variable causes both the other two variables. If this is true, an artificial increase in either the number of television sets or the number of telephones will not cause a change in the other variable, because the real cause of normal changes, the third variable, has remained the same. In general, causal links cannot be deduced merely from the existence of a correlation between two variables. All that can justifiably be said is that the two variables are related. We need more information than the existence of a correlation to establish a cause-and-effect relationship.

The Effect of Linear Transformations. Another important point in interpreting a Pearson Correlation Coefficient relates to the units of measurement employed. Suppose you compared the heights of individuals measured in inches to the weights of the same individuals measured in pounds and found a Pearson correlation value of $r = 0.30$. Would you expect the correlation value to change if you re-computed the correlation, measuring the heights of the individuals in feet and the weights of the individuals in ounces, and could get all measurements perfectly? We do not suppose you would. If a person's height is high relative to that of others in the group when the heights are measured in inches, it should be just as high relative to the others when the heights are measured in feet. That is, the position of an individual relative to his or her group will remain the same, despite the fact that the scores of the group are transformed into some other scale or frame of reference. In this example, each original height score, measured in inches, was converted to feet by dividing by 12. In addition, each original weight score, measured in pounds, was converted to ounces by multiplying by 16.

Had a constant value been added to either height or weight or both, in addition to the multiplication or division that was done, the relative standing of individuals within each group would still have been the same, and the correlation value would have remained the same. Thus, linear transformations of the X variable and/or Y variable do not change the magnitude (size) of the Pearson Correlation Coefficient. The sign of the coefficient will be reversed only if one but not both of the sets of scores (X *or* Y) is multiplied or divided by a negative number. For example, if the correlation between X and Y is $r_{xy} = 0.70$ and if all the X scores are multiplied by -2, the new correlation coefficient will have the same magnitude but a reversed sign. That is, the new correlation coefficient value will be $r_{xy} = -0.70$.

Restriction of Range. When a correlation is computed on a subset of the natural range of one or both variables, the magnitude of the correlation may be either smaller or larger than the correlation computed on the entire range.

Suppose, for example, that we are interested in the correlation coefficient between Age X and Weight Y for a group of individuals whose ages range from 1 year to 15 years. A correlation coefficient calculated on only the very youngest and the very oldest of the individuals (say, on only those individuals who are 3 or younger or 12 or older), will result in a stronger correlation than one based on the entire set of data. This is because, in this subset, there is a greater tendency for the younger group to have lower weight and for the older group to have higher weight than for the entire set of individuals taken as a whole.

Analogously, if we calculate the correlation coefficient on a restricted, more homogeneous subset of the entire range (such as on only those individuals with ages between X = 9 and X = 11 years of age), then we can expect the correlation to be weaker (closer to 0) than if it were calculated on the entire set of data. This is because, with all the individuals in this subset being so similar to each other in age relative to the entire group, there will be less of a tendency for differences in age among the individuals to correspond to systematic differences in weight.

We present another example of restriction of range involves the elimination of the middle values of the distribution. The *Brainsz* data set, taken from the DASL (Data Sets and Stories Library) website, is based on a study by Willerman et al. (1991) in which such a method was used. The purpose of the study was to examine the relationships between brain size, gender, and intelligence. The research participants consisted of 40 introductory psychology students who were selected from a larger pool of psychology students with total Scholastic Aptitude Test Scores higher than 1,350 or lower than 940, where these scores were used to measure intelligence. In other words, students with moderate intelligence scores were omitted from the study. The result was that the correlations between gender and intelligence and brain size and intelligence were inflated.

The conclusion to be drawn from this discussion is that you should not expect the correlation between two variables to be the same in a large group as it is in a subset of that group if the subset is either more or less homogeneous than the larger group in one or both of the variables under study. By eliminating the middle group, the subset becomes less homogeneous than the original, larger group.

The Shape of the Underlying Distributions. Another factor that affects the size of a correlation is the relative similarity or dissimilarity of the shapes of the X and Y distributions. Simply stated, a perfect positive correlation between X and Y ($r = +1$) can only occur when the X and Y distributions have exactly the same shape. For example, if X were positively skewed and Y were negatively skewed, we would expect this difference in shape to result in a weaker positive correlation than if the two distributions had the same shape. If one or both of the variables is skewed, one should consider applying a nonlinear transformation (e.g., square root or logarithm) to symmetrize the distribution(s) prior to calculating *r*.

The Reliability of the Data. A third factor that affects the size of *r* concerns the reliability of the X and Y values or, in other words, the extent to which the X and Y values consistently reflect the amounts of the characteristics they are supposed to represent. The less reliable a measure, the greater the amount of error in each of its observed values. Because error, by definition, is random and does not correlate with anything, the more error a variable contains, the less we can expect that variable to correlate with any other variable. Consequently, it is important to check the reliability of any measuring instruments used, and to employ those instruments with a high reliability. A more complete discussion of reliability is beyond the scope of this book. The interested reader should consult a text on tests and measurement. One such example is, Cohen and Swerdlik (2005).

WHEN AT LEAST ONE VARIABLE IS ORDINAL AND THE OTHER IS AT LEAST ORDINAL: THE SPEARMAN RANK CORRELATION COEFFICIENT

Spearman Rank correlation coefficient

The Spearman Rank Correlation Coefficient measures the strength of the linear relationship between two variables when the values of each variable are rank-ordered from 1 to N, where N is the number of pairs of values. The formula for the Spearman Correlation Coefficient, given as Equation (5.4), and denoted by r_s, ρ, or *rho*, may be obtained as a special case of the Pearson Correlation Coefficient when the N cases of each variable are assigned the integer values from 1 to N inclusive and no two cases share the same value.

$$r_s = 1 - \frac{6 \sum d_i^2}{N^3 - N} \tag{5.4}$$

where d_i represents the difference between ranks for each case. As a special case of the Pearson Correlation Coefficient, r_s is interpreted in the same way as the Pearson. For example, notice that when the ranks for the two variables being correlated are identical, the differences between them will be zero and the Spearman Correlation Coefficient will be 1.00, indicating a perfect positive correlation between the variables.

· ·

EXAMPLE 5.3. Consider the McDonald's hamburger data. Suppose we are not convinced that our measure of fat is interval-leveled. That is, while we believe that the Quarter Pounder™, with 21 grams of fat, has more fat than the Cheeseburger, with 14 grams of fat, and less fat than the Big Mac™, with 28 grams of fat, we are not convinced that, in terms of fat, the Quarter Pounder™ is midway between the other two types of hamburger. Accordingly, we decide to consider the fat scale as ordinal, and transform the original data to ranked data. To find the relationship between fat and calories, we compute the Spearman Correlation Coefficient on the ranked data instead of the Pearson Correlation Coefficient on the original data.

☞ **Remark.** The formula for the Spearman is derived as a special case of the Pearson formula by taking advantage of the fact that the data are rankings from 1 to N. We may note that the Spearman Correlation Coefficient on the ranked data will give the identical result as the Pearson Correlation Coefficient on the ranked data.

Solution. To obtain the ranked data by hand, we simply rank order the five types of hamburger in terms of fat, and assign a value from 1 to 5 to each hamburger to denote its place in that ranking. Then, we assign ranked values to the five types of hamburger in terms of calories. The original data, together with their rankings, are provided in the first five columns of Table 5.7. The last two columns contain the difference and squared difference between the ranks for each hamburger, respectively.

Notice that the Quarter Pounder with Cheese™ and the Big Mac™ have the same original calorie count of 530. Accordingly, they are tied for first and second place in the rankings. We,

TABLE 5.7. Original and ranked data for hamburger fat and calories

Hamburger Type	Grams of fat (X)	Ranked Fat	Calories (Y)	Ranked Calories	d_i	d_i^2
Hamburger	$X_1 = 10$	5	$Y_1 = 270$	5	0	0
Cheeseburger	$X_2 = 14$	4	$Y_2 = 320$	4	0	0
Quarter Pounder™	$X_3 = 21$	3	$Y_3 = 430$	3	0	0
Quarter Pounder w/Cheese™	$X_4 = 30$	1	$Y_4 = 530$	1.5	−.5	.25
Big Mac™	$X_5 = 28$	2	$Y_5 = 530$	1.5	.5	.25

therefore, assign the average of these two ranks, 1.5, to each of them. The same procedure is used whenever ties occur.

The Spearman Correlation Coefficient equals, in this case, $r_s = 1 − 6(.50)/(125 − 5) = .975$, suggesting that there is a very strong linear relationship between fat and calories expressed in ranked form. Notice that this value is slightly different from the Pearson Correlation Coefficient of $r = .996$, because the Quarter Pounder with Cheese™ and the Big Mac™ are tied in their numbers of calories.

MORE Stata: To obtain the Spearman Correlation Coefficient (between calories and fat)

spearman calories fat

☞ **Remark.** The Pearson Correlation Coefficient measures the direction and strength of the linear relationship between the _numerical values_ assigned to the variables in question. Because these numerical values may take on many forms, including rankings and dichotomies, we need to be sensitive to the nature of these numerical values when interpretations are made.

WHEN AT LEAST ONE VARIABLE IS DICHOTOMOUS: OTHER SPECIAL CASES OF THE PEARSON CORRELATION COEFFICIENT

In measuring the correlation between two variables when one is at least interval and the other is dichotomous or when both are dichotomous, we may use the Pearson Correlation Coefficient. In these cases, however, the Pearson Correlation Coefficient is often given a different name to reflect the type of data being analyzed.

The _Point Biserial Correlation Coefficient_ is the name given to the special case of the Pearson for measuring the direction and strength of the linear relationship between two variables when one is dichotomous and the other is at least interval. The _Phi Coefficient_ is the name given to the special case of the Pearson for measuring the direction and strength of the linear relationship between two dichotomous variables.

THE POINT BISERIAL CORRELATION COEFFICIENT: THE CASE OF ONE AT LEAST INTERVAL AND ONE DICHOTOMOUS VARIABLE

EXAMPLE 5.4. Use the McDonald's data set to perform a correlation analysis to determine whether there is a relationship between the calorie count of a burger and whether or not it

TABLE 5.8. Calories and cheese for McDonald's hamburgers

Hamburger Type	Calories (Y)	Cheese (0 = "no, 1 = "yes")
Hamburger	270	0
Cheeseburger	320	1
Quarter Pounder™	430	0
Quarter Pounder w/Cheese™	530	1
Big Mac™	530	1

comes with cheese and if there is one, to describe it. In other words, we will perform a correlation analysis to determine whether there is a difference in the average number of calories between those hamburgers with and those without cheese. Table 5.8 contains, for each of the five types of hamburger, the calories and whether or not the burger has cheese.

Solution. Cheese is a dichotomous variable as it takes on two values (no, yes) while the variable calories is measured at the ratio level. We use Stata to obtain the Pearson Correlation Coefficient because we know that the Pearson will give the identical numerical result as the Point Biserial Correlation Coefficient, the special case of the Pearson when one variable is at least interval and the other is dichotomous.

As in the case of two at least interval variables, we first depict the relationship between these two variables using a scatterplot. If we proceed as shown earlier to obtain the scatterplot with cheese as the X variable and calories as the Y variable, the result appears as in Figure 5.6. Recall that for these data, hamburgers without cheese are assigned the value 0 on cheese and hamburgers with cheese are assigned the value 1.

Because cheese is dichotomous, the scatterplot does not appear as a cloud of points as it does in Figures 5.1 through 5.4, but rather, as two vertical columns of points centered, respectively, over 0 (for no cheese) and 1 (for cheese). By inspecting the scatterplot and, in particular, the locations of the two vertical columns relative to the calorie scale (the Y axis), we may infer that, for these McDonald's hamburgers, hamburgers with cheese have more calories, on average, than those without cheese.

Furthermore, because hamburgers without cheese are assigned a value of 0 and hamburgers with cheese a value of 1, we may note that low scores on cheese (no cheese) associate with low scores on calories and high scores on cheese (cheese) associate with high scores on calories. Given the coding of our variables, then, we should expect to obtain a positive correlation between calorie and cheese content for these hamburgers. Using Stata, we find the correlation between cheese and calories is $r = .506$, a strong positive correlation.

☞ **Remark.** Had the coding scheme been reversed for the variable cheese so that hamburgers with no cheese were assigned a 1 and hamburgers with cheese a 0, the sign of the correlation coefficient would have changed from positive to negative, leaving the interpretation of the direction of the relationship unchanged. While the coding reversal changes the sign of the correlation, it does not affect the magnitude.

Notice that the horizontal axis of the scatterplot given in Figure 5.6 is treating cheese as if it were continuous. It makes more sense to have a discrete horizontal axis with two

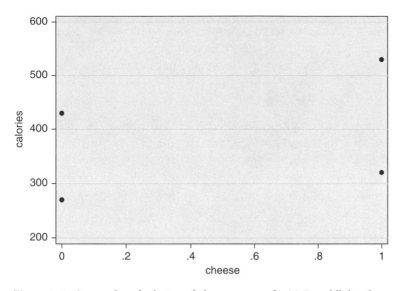

Figure 5.6   Scatterplot of calorie and cheese content for McDonald's hamburgers.

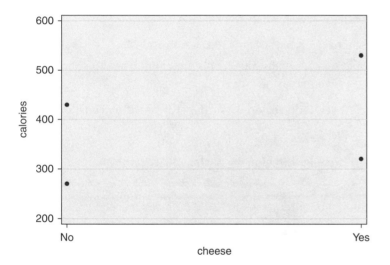

Figure 5.7   Scatterplot of calorie and cheese content for McDonald's hamburgers.

categories representing the two types of cheese content. Such a graph is obtained using the following Stata command and is provided as Figure 5.7.

MORE Stata: To create a scatterplot with labels when one of the variables is at the nominal level

twoway scatter calories cheese, xlabel(0 1, valuelabel)

Note: the option **xlabel(0 1, valuelabel)** instructs Stata to label the x-axis not with 0 and 1, but with the labels associated with 0 and 1 for the cheese variable. Because cheese is the second variable listed after **scatter**, it defines the x-axis.

• •

EXAMPLE 5.5. Use the *NELS* data set to determine the correlation for students in the West between (1) gender and achievement in science in twelfth grade, and (2) gender and achievement in reading in twelfth grade. Our focus on the students in the West in this example is for heuristic reasons.

Solution.

1) Gender is a dichotomous variable as it takes on two values (male, female) while achievement in science in twelfth grade is a continuous variable. We use Stata to obtain the Pearson Correlation Coefficient because we know that the Pearson will give the identical numerical result as the Point Biserial Correlation Coefficient, the special case of the Pearson when one variable is continuous and the other is dichotomous.

Given our question, we first need to select the students in the West so that our analysis will be confined to those students only.

MORE Stata: To obtain a correlation on a subset of the data

We use an "if statement" as part of the command to select the subset of students in the West.

correlate achsci12 gender if region == 4

Note: **pwcorr** would have given the same result as **correlate**.

MORE Stata: Labelling the x-axis with value labels (for gender, as shown in Figure 5.8)
We may add labels for gender using either:

twoway scatter achsci12 gender if region == 4, xlabel(0 "Male" 1 "Female")

Or

twoway scatter achsci12 gender if region == 4, xlabel(0 1, valuelabel)

MORE Stata: Using the option **jitter** to separate the points in a scatterplot and the option **ytitle** to add a title on the y-axis

Given how clumped the points are in Figure 5.8, especially for females, we may use an option related to scatter that randomly jitters the points by some small amount to separate them out from one another.

twoway scatter achsci12 gender if region == 4, xlabel(0 1, valuelabel) jitter(5) ytitle(achievement in science)

By inspecting the scatterplot and, in particular, the locations of the two vertical columns relative to the achievement in science scale (the Y axis), we may infer that, for students in the West, males do slightly better in science achievement in twelfth grade than females.

Furthermore, because males are assigned a value of 0 and females a value of 1, we may note that low scores on GENDER (males) associate with high scores on achievement in science and high scores on GENDER (females) associate with low scores on achievement in science. Given the coding of our variables, then, we should expect to obtain a negative correlation between gender and achievement in science in twelfth grade. Using Stata, we

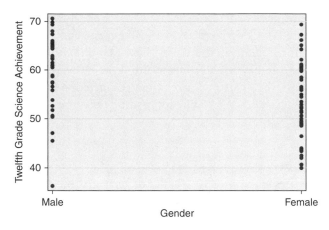

Figure 5.8 Scatterplot of gender and 12th grade science achievement for students in the West.

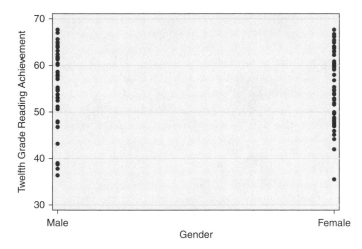

Figure 5.9 Scatterplot of gender and reading achievement in 12th grade for students in the West.

find that for the 93 students in the West, the correlation between gender and achievement in science in twelfth grade is $r = -.395$, a moderately strong negative correlation.

☞ **Remark.** Notice the outlier in the distribution of male science achievement scores in Figure 5.8. Checking further, we find that this outlier score belongs to case number 194. (The series of steps needed to obtain this case number is the focus of Exercise 5.5.) To see to what extent score 194 influences the result, we re-compute the correlation between gender and achievement in science on these data, but without the score for this individual. The result is $r = -.443$, suggesting an even stronger relationship between gender and science achievement in twelfth grade for students in the West without this outlier.

    2) We use the command **twoway scatter achrdg12 gender if region == 4, xlabel(0 "Male" 1 "Female") to obtain the scatterplot** for gender and achrdg12 for students in the West and obtain Figure 5.9.

Notice that in Figure 5.9, the locations of the two vertical columns relative to the achievement in reading scale (Y-axis) are not as different from one another as they are in Figure 5.8 (relative to science achievement). In fact, they are hardly different from one another at all, suggesting that there is little or no relationship between gender and achievement in reading in twelfth grade for students in the West. That is, boys do not appear to do better or worse than girls in reading achievement in the twelfth grade. Using Stata, we find that for the 93 students in the West, the Pearson Correlation Coefficient between sex and reading achievement in the twelfth grade, is $r = -.021$, confirming our impressions of little or no relationship.

☞ **Remark.** From the above two results, we may infer that the stronger the correlation between a dichotomous variable and a continuous one, the greater the separation between the two groups, designated by the dichotomous variable, in terms of the values on the continuous measure. On average, the reading achievement distributions for boys and girls were quite similar, whereas the science achievement distributions for boys and girls were not. Conceptually, therefore it should make sense that a point biserial correlation reflects the degree to which the means of the two groups on the continuous measure are different. The formula for the point biserial correlation coefficient, given as Equation 5.5, makes this interpretation clear.

$$r_{pb} = \frac{(\overline{Y}_1 - \overline{Y}_0)S_X}{S_Y} \tag{5.5}$$

where $\overline{Y}_1$ and $\overline{Y}_0$ are the Y means of the groups designated by the dichotomous variable. S_X and S_Y represent the standard deviations of X and Y, respectively. Note that because X is dichotomous and takes on the values 0 and 1, S_X can be expressed as $\sqrt{pq}$, where p and q are the respective proportions of the total for each of the two groups. From Equation 5.5 we realize that when there is no separation between the two groups on the continuous measure, Y (i.e., when $\overline{Y}_1 = \overline{Y}_0$), r_{pb} will equal zero. Likewise, the larger the separation between the two groups relative to the spread (i.e., the more discrepant 1 and 0 relative to the spread), the stronger the correlation, r_{pb}, will be.

THE PHI COEFFICIENT: THE CASE OF TWO DICHOTOMOUS VARIABLES

As noted earlier, when both variables are dichotomous the Pearson Correlation Coefficient may be expressed in a simplified, numerically equivalent form, called the Phi Coefficient.

• •

EXAMPLE 5.6. Use the *NELS* data to determine the correlation between (1) nursery school attendance and gender for students in the South and (2) nursery school attendance and computer ownership for students in the West.

Solution.

1) To select students from the South only, we must use the if statement at the end of the command; and, in particular, **if region == 3.** We then proceed with the solution to the problem.

While scatterplots were useful in depicting the types of bivariate relationship discussed earlier in this chapter, as Figure 5.10 illustrates, they are not useful when the two variables in question are both dichotomous.

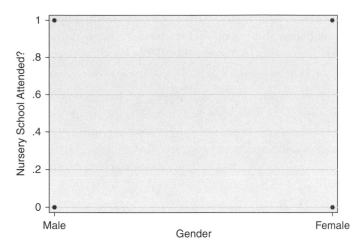

Figure 5.10 Scatterplot of nursery school attendance by gender for students in the South.

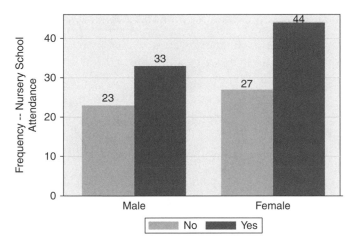

Figure 5.11 Clustered bar graph of nursery school attendance and gender for students in the South.

If there were a relationship between gender and nursery school attendance, then the pattern of frequencies of the four cells, represented by the four points in Figure 5.10, would vary in a systematic way. That is, a relationship would be suggested if, for example, the relative frequency of girls who attended nursery school were different from the relative frequency of boys who attended nursery school. Said differently, if the likelihood of attending nursery school varied as a function of gender, then a relationship between the two variables would be said to exist. To obtain information on the frequencies, an alternative graphic is the clustered bar graph.

MORE Stata: To obtain a clustered bar graph (as shown in Figure 5.11)

graph bar (count) if region == 3, over (nursery) over(gender) asyvars blabel(total) ytitle("Frequency – Nursery School Attendance")

Note: **asyvars** informs Stata that nursery, the variable named in the first **over()** option, is to be assigned to the y-axis. **blabel(total)** instructs Stata to label the top of each bar with the total number of cases represented by each bar (see Figure 5.11).

Notice that each bar represents one of the four points of the scatterplot depicted in Figure 5.10 and that the heights of the bars represent the corresponding frequencies. The relative difference in bar heights between those who have attended nursery school and those who have not is similar for males and females in both direction and magnitude. This similarity in profiles suggests little or no relationship between nursery school attendance and gender for these students in the South.

MORE Stata: To obtain a crosstab (as given in Figure 5.12)

To obtain a crosstab table, instead of a clustered bar graph, of the frequencies of each of the four cells represented by nursery attended and gender, we type:

tabulate nursery gender if region == 3

To understand whether nursery school attendance varies as a function of gender, we may compare the pattern of the total counts either for gender or for nursery school to the pattern of cell counts by either row or column. The total counts are called *marginals* since they appear in the margins of the crosstabs table. The nursery school (or row) marginals are 50 and 77 while the gender (or column) marginals are 56 and 71.

The proportion of males who did attend nursery school relative to the total number of individuals who did attend nursery school is $33/77 = .43$. That is, 43 percent of the individuals who did attend nursery school are males. Analogously, the proportion of males who did not attend nursery relative to the total number of individuals who did not attend nursery school is $23/50 = .46$. That is, 46 percent of the individuals who did not attend nursery school are males. Because these proportions are nearly equal, we may conclude that there is little or no relationship between gender and nursery school attendance. An analysis based on a comparison between those who did and did not attend nursery school for males and females separately would have led to the same result.

An alternative analysis of the relationship may be based on a comparison of the ratio of frequencies that appears in the column marginals (e.g., 56 to 71) to the ratio of frequencies that appears in the columns within each row of the table. That is, we would expect the same ratio of column marginals between males and females (e.g., 56 to 71) to be replicated in each row if there were no relationship. The ratio of males to females overall is 56 to 71 (equivalently, 1 to 1.27); the ratio of males to females for those who attended nursery school is 33 to 44 (equivalently, 1 to 1.33); and, the ratio of males to females for those who did not attend nursery school is 23 to 27 (equivalently, 1 to 1.17). These ratios are not identical, but they are close in value, suggesting, once again, little or no relationship between gender and nursery school attendance.

We may measure the magnitude of this relationship by computing the Phi Coefficient. To do so, we calculate the Pearson Correlation Coefficient as before, since the Phi Coefficient is a special case of the Pearson. The result of this calculation is that $r = .031$, suggesting that, as expected, little or no relationship exists between these variables. Based on our earlier

Figure 5.12 Crosstabulation of nursery school attended by gender for students in the South.

Nursery School Attended?	Gender		Total
	Male	Female	
No	23	27	50
Yes	33	44	77
Total	56	71	127

interpretation of the results of the Crosstabs, you should be able to justify the positive sign associated with this correlation value.

☞ **Remark.** The crosstabulation of Figure 5.12 also is called a *contingency table* because the entries in each cell are contingent upon the row and column of each cell.

☞ **Remark.** The Phi Coefficient may be expressed as a special case of the Pearson Correlation Coefficient that relates to the entries in the contingency table. In particular, if we label the cells

A	B
C	D

then the phi coefficient is given by Equation 5.6,

$$\phi = \frac{AD - BC}{\sqrt{(A+B)(C+D)(A+C)(B+D)}} \tag{5.6}$$

In the case of the data of Figure 5.9, we obtain the following result:

$$\phi = \frac{44 \times 23 - 33 \times 27}{\sqrt{77 \times 50 \times 56 \times 71}} = \frac{121}{3,912.5} = 0.031$$

which agrees with our earlier result when using the Pearson Correlation Coefficient.

We now return to solving the second part of Example 5.6.

Solution.

2)

MORE Stata: To plot a clustered bar graph (Figure 5.13) and a crosstab (Figure 5.14) between computer and gender for those in the West

graph bar (count) if region == 4, over(computer) over(nursery) asyvars blabel(total) ytitle("Frequency – Computer Ownership in 8th Grade")

tabulate computer nursery if region == 4

The bar graph of Figure 5.13 suggests a relationship between eighth grade computer ownership and past nursery school attendance. The relative difference in bar heights

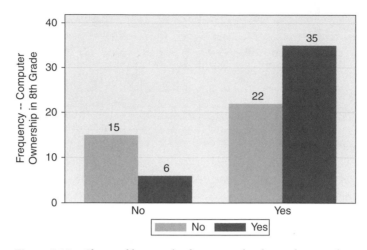

Figure 5.13   Clustered bar graph of nursery school attendance and computer ownership for students in the West.

Computer Owned by Family in 8th Grade?	Nursery School Attended?		
	No	Yes	Total
No	15	22	37
Yes	6	35	41
Total	21	57	78

Figure 5.14   Crosstabulation of computer ownership by nursery school attendance for students in the West.

between those who owned computers in eighth grade and those who did not is strikingly different in both magnitude and direction for those who attended nursery school and those who did not. In particular, those who attended nursery school were more likely to own a computer in eighth grade whereas those who did not attend nursery school were more likely not to own a computer in eighth grade.

As one would expect, Figure 5.14 also suggests a relationship between these two variables. Among students who had attended nursery school, 39 percent did not own a computer while among students who had not attended nursery school, 71 percent did not own a computer.

Alternatively, the ratio of noncomputer ownership to computer ownership for those who attended nursery school is 22 to 35 (equivalently, 1 to 1.59) while the ratio for those who did not attend nursery school is 15 to 6 (equivalently, 1 to 0.4). Because the individual row ratios differ from the marginal ratio of 1 to 1.11 (and from each other), a systematic relationship appears to exist between these two dichotomous variables for region == 4. In particular, the likelihood of computer ownership is greater for those families who sent their children to nursery school (1.59 versus 1.11) than did not (0.4 versus 1.11).

To measure the magnitude of this relationship using a single summary statistic, we compute the Pearson Correlation Coefficient using Stata and find the correlation for region

== 4 to be moderate in size ($r = .292$). The positive direction of the correlation tells us that low values on computer ownership (no's) associate with low values on attended nursery school (no's) and vice versa, thus corroborating our conclusions based on either the clustered bar graph of Figure 5.13 or contingency table of Figure 5.14.

OTHER VISUAL DISPLAYS OF BIVARIATE RELATIONSHIPS

In the foregoing sections of this chapter, we discussed the quantification of linear relationships between two variables in the case where (1) both variables are at least interval, (2) both are dichotomous, (3) one is at least interval and the other is dichotomous, and (4) both are ranked. We also discussed ways to visually represent the relationships contained within these four cases. In this section we revisit the boxplot and clustered bar graph and show their versatility in representing relationships that arise from (2) and (3) and variations of (2) and (3) that involve nominal- and ordinal-leveled variables that are not necessarily dichotomous. We present these graphics without corresponding indices for quantifying the nature and magnitude of the relationships represented.

EXAMPLE 5.7. Use a boxplot to depict for students in the West the relationships between (1) gender and achievement in science in 12th grade and (2) gender and achievement in reading in 12th grade. This question was addressed earlier in Example 5.5.

Solution.
Notice that the boxplot in Figure 5.15 resembles closely the scatterplot of Figure 5.8 and offers the same interpretation – males tend to score higher than females on science achievement in twelfth grade for students in the West.

The boxplot depicting reading achievement in twelfth grade by gender appears in Figure 5.16 and also resembles closely the scatterplot of Figure 5.9.

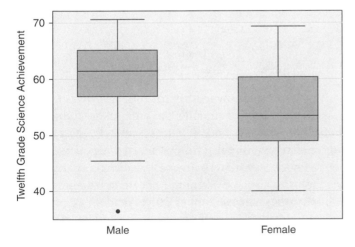

Figure 5.15 Boxplot of science achievement in 12th grade by gender for students in the West.

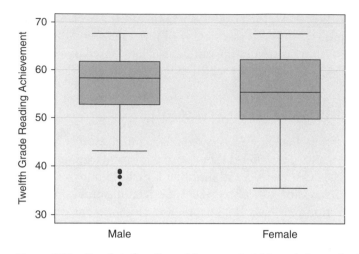

Figure 5.16   Boxplot of reading achievement in 12th grade by gender for students in the West.

Although we have used the boxplot to compare the distributions of a continuous measure for two groups, we may also use boxplots to compare the distributions of a continuous measure for any (reasonably small) number of groups, and in so doing, look for a relationship between group membership and the continuous measure.

☞ **Remark.** Because group membership typically is nominal-leveled, with more than two groups, the relationship between group membership and a continuous measure cannot be described meaningfully as linear. From this it follows that one would not want to compute a Pearson Correlation Coefficient on nominal data with more than two categories because its interpretation, as a measure of linear relationship, would be meaningless. The type of relationship that can be explored with such data is simply whether the groups, on average, differ from one another on the continuous measure. An index for measuring the strength of this type of relationship will be discussed in a later chapter.

• •
EXAMPLE 5.8. Construct a boxplot of twelfth grade math achievement by region and use it to determine whether there appears to be a relationship between the two variables.

Solution. Because region is a nominal-leveled variable, the order of the four region categories (Northeast, North Central, South, and West) on the X-axis is arbitrary. As a result, it would not be meaningful to attempt to interpret the relationship between region and mathematics achievement in twelfth grade as linear (Figure 5.17). The best we can do is to define relationship between these two variables in terms of the extent to which the four regions, on average, differ from one another on mathematics achievement in twelfth grade.

Given that the medians for the four groups are different from one another, we say that there appears to be a relationship between region and twelfth grade math achievement for the students in our *NELS* data set. The highest level of math achievement is in the West, while the lowest is in the South, with the other regions being intermediate.

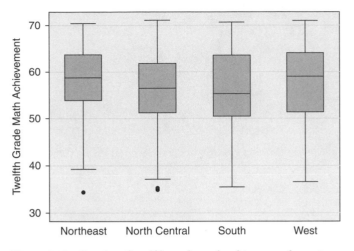

Figure 5.17   Boxplot of twelfth grade math achievement by region.

As we have seen, when both variables are dichotomous, an appropriate visual display is the *clustered bar graph* and an appropriate statistical indicator of the relationship is the contingency table and the associated percentages. The clustered bar graph, the contingency table, and percentages may be used also when one or both variables have more than two, yet a reasonably small number of categories.

• •

EXAMPLE 5.9. Do families in the *NELS* data set differ on computer ownership by the region of the country in which they reside?

Solution. The contingency table generated using the command **tabulate computer region** is reproduced below:

Computer Owned by Family in 8th Grade?	Geographic Region of School				
	Northeast	North Cen	South	West	Total
No	46	89	86	42	263
Yes	60	62	64	51	237
Total	106	151	150	93	500

The results in the contingency table indicate that there is a relationship between computer ownership and region. Students in the Northeast and West were more likely to own a computer than not, with 56.6 percent and 54.8 percent, respectively, owning a computer. Students in the North Central and South were less likely to own a computer than not, with 41.1 percent and 42.7 percent, respectively, owning a computer.

The clustered bar graph is given below using the command:

graph bar (count), over(computer) over(region) asyvars blabel(total) ytitle("Frequency –
    Computer Ownership in 8th Grade")

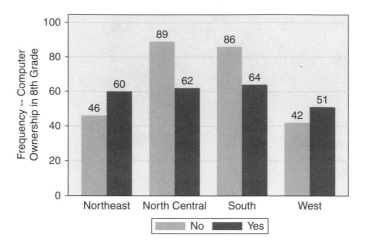

SELECTION OF APPROPRIATE STATISTIC/GRAPH TO SUMMARIZE A RELATIONSHIP

The table provides guidelines for selecting appropriate graphs and statistics for describing bivariate relationships. Other choices may also be correct.

Levels of measurement	Nominal with two categories	Nominal with more than two categories or ordinal with more than two categories but not more than five categories	Ordinal with five or more categories	Scale
Normal with two categories	Pearson correlation or percentages from crosstabulation and clustered bar graph	Percentages from crosstabulation and clustered bar graph	Spearman correlation and interactive scatterplot or boxplot	Pearson correlation and interactive scatterplot or boxplot
Nominal with more than two categories or ordinal with more than two categories but not more than five categories	Percentages from crosstabulation and clustered bar graph	Percentages from crosstabulation and clustered bar graph	Spearman correlation (if both ordinal) or medians and interactive scatterplot or boxplot	Means or medians (depending on skew) and interactive scatterplot or boxplot
Ordinal with five or more categories	Spearman correlation and interactive scatterplot or boxplot	Spearman correlation (if both ordinal) or medians and interactive scatterplot or boxplot	Spearman correlation and scatterplot	Spearman correlation and scatterplot
Scale	Pearson correlation and interactive scatterplot or boxplot	Means or medians (depending on skew) and interactive scatterplot or boxplot	Spearman correlation and scatterplot	Pearson correlation and scatterplot. Correlation should not be used if scatterplot is well fit by a simple curve

SUMMARY OF STATA COMMANDS IN CHAPTER 5

For a complete listing of all Stata commands associated with this chapter, you may access the Do-file for Chapter 5 located on the text website.

Create	Command Lines
Scatterplot (Figure 5.1)	**twoway (scatter calories fat)**
Scatterplot with values restricted on an axis (Figure 5.4)	**twoway (scatter marij year) if (year >=1987) & (year <=1996)**
Scatterplot with title added	**twoway (scatter marij year) if (year >=1987) & (year <=1996), title (marijuana use across years, size(medlarge) color(red))**
Scatterplot with customized points	**twoway (scatter marij year if (year >=1987) & (year <=1996), title(Marijuana Usage Across Years, size(medlarge) color(red)) msymbol(D) mcolor(blue) msize(large))**
Scatterplot with fit line added (Figures 5.5)	**graph twoway (scatter ay ax) (lfit ay ax)**
Scatterplot with value labels on one axis (Figure 5.7)	**twoway scatter calories cheese, xlabel(0 1, valuelabel)**
Scatterplot with points adjusted slightly to avoid clumping	**twoway scatter achsci12 gender if region == 4, xlabel(0 1, valuelabel) jitter(5)**
Scatterplot with points identified by name of value of another variable (Exercise 5.4)	**scatter teachpay educexpe, mlabel(state)**
Scatterplot with points identified by color by another variable (Exercise 5.25)	**twoway (scatter supportc conserva if vote1 == 0, mcolor(blue)) (scatter supportc conserva if vote1 == 1, mcolor(red))**
Pearson correlation	**correlate calories fat**
	OR
	pwcorr calories fat, obs
Pearson correlation on a subsample (Example 5.5)	**correlate achsci12 gender if region == 4**
Spearman correlation	**spearman calories fat**
Crosstabulation or contingency table	**tabulate nursery gender**

EXERCISES

*Create a.do file for each Exercise that requires the use of Stata. Run the commands from the. do file by highlighting them and hitting **Control+d**. Save each.do file using a name associated with the Exercise for which it was created. It is recommended that you review the Do-file for* Chapter 5 *located on the textbook's website before completing these exercises. To facilitate doing each exercise, it may be helpful to copy and paste relevant commands from the Do-file for* Chapter 5 *into your own Do-file and modify them as needed.*

Exercises 5.1–5.5 involve scatterplots.

5.1. Use the *States* data set to create a scatterplot to depict the relationship between the percentage of students taking the SAT (pertak) and the average SAT Writing score (satw). Use it to explain why a correlation will capture one aspect of the relationship, but that it is probably not the most appropriate technique to use for measuring this relationship.

5.2. Use the *States* data set to create a scatterplot to depict the relationship between the average teacher salary (teachpay) and the average SAT Math (satm). Use it to determine whether states that pay their teachers better tend to have higher SAT Math scores, on average.

5.3. Use the *States* data set and scatterplots to investigate the relationships between the average SAT Critical Reading score for the state (satcr) and the following three variables: Average SAT Math score for the state (satm), percentage of eligible students taking the SAT for the state (pertak), and the average student teacher ratio for the state (stuteach). You may create separate bivariate graphs, or create a matrix scatterplot which gives pairwise scatterplots between all involved variables by using the Stata command **graph matrix satcr satm pertak stuteach**. Use the graphs that you create to answer the following questions.

a) Rank these linear relationships from strongest to weakest.
b) Describe the nature of the linear relationship, or indicate that little or no linear relationship exists, between the average Critical Reasoning SAT for the state and the average Math SAT for the state.
c) Describe the nature of the linear relationship, or indicate that little or no linear relationship exists, between the average Critical Reasoning SAT for the state and the percentage of eligible students taking the SAT for the state.
d) Describe the nature of the linear relationship, or indicate that little or no linear relationship exists, between the average Critical Reasoning SAT for the state and the average student teacher ratio for the state.

5.4. Use the *States* data set to create a scatterplot to depict the relationship between the average teacher's salary (teachpay) and the expenditure per pupil (educexpe). Label the points by state. Use your scatterplot to answer the following questions.

To create and label the scatterplot by each State's name using Stata, use the following command in Stata. Type the following into your.do file.

scatter teachpay educexpe, mlabel(state)

Run the syntax from the.do file and the graph will appear in a new window.

---

a) Describe the nature of the linear relationship, or indicate that little or no linear relationship exists, between the expenditure per pupil and the average annual salary for public school teachers.
b) Name a state that appears to be unusual relative to this trend. How can you tell? In what way is this state unusual?
c) Do the middle Atlantic states (New York, New Jersey, Connecticut) appear to cluster together? Why do you suppose such geographical clusters exist?

5.5. In Example 5.5, using the *NELS* data set, we selected cases to investigate students from the West and identified the outlier for the relationship between achsci12 and gender as id number 194. This exercise takes you through the steps that enabled that determination and then asks you to perform a similar analysis using the *Framingham* data set.

In order to select cases from the West, make sure always to add **"if region == 4"** at the end of each command that you run in this section.

Label the scatterplot by ID by adapting the instructions given in Exercise 5.4.
  a) Where is case number 194?
  b) For the *Framingham* data set, report and interpret the correlation between the initial body mass index (BMI1) and the initial total cholesterol (TOTCHOL1).
  c) Create the scatterplot between these two variables. Which person is most unusual in terms of this trend? What is his or her ID number? Is this person a male or a female? How old was this person when the study began?
  d) Calculate the correlation between these two variables without this person in the data set. Does the correlation value change as a result of omitting this person from the data set?

In addition to labeling points on scatterplots by an identifying variable, as in Exercise 5.5, points on scatterplots can also be labeled to differentiate between subgroups. This option is illustrated in Exercise 5.26.

Exercises 5.6–5.8 involve Pearson Correlation between two scale variables.

5.6. Conduct a correlation analysis using the *States* data set to determine whether various factors are associated with educexpe, the average educational expenditure per pupil. These factors are stuteach, student teacher ratio, satcr, average verbal SAT score for the state, and teachpay, the average salary of public school teachers in the state.
  a) Create a matrix scatterplot of the variables and determine whether a linear model is an appropriate representation of the relationships between all pairs of these variables.
  b) Calculate the correlation matrix between all pairs of these variables.
  c) Do states in which expenditures per pupil are higher tend to pay their teachers more?
  d) Do states in which expenditures per pupil are higher tend to have higher verbal SAT scores, on average?
  e) Do states in which expenditures per pupil are higher tend to have lower pupil per teacher ratios?
  f) Of the three variables, pupils per teacher, average SAT verbal scores, and teacher salary, which is most strongly correlated with expenditure per pupil?

5.7. For each of the following variables in the *NELS* data set, indicate whether you think their correlations with mathematics achievement in grade 12 (achmat12) is positive, negative, or near zero. Use Stata to determine if your thinking is correct.
  a) Socioeconomic status (ses).
  b) The extent to which students agree with the statement "My teachers are interested in their students" (tcherint), Where 1 represents "Strongly Agree" and 4 represents "Strongly Disagree".
  c) Family size (famsiz).

5.8. The following questions, using the *NELS* data set, show how both linear and nonlinear transformations can affect the value of a correlation coefficient.

a) Find and interpret the correlation between schattrt, the average daily school attendance rate (as a percentage) of the school the student attends, and slfcnc08, the student's eighth grade self-concept score.

b) In Exercise 4.4 b), the variable schattpp was created to give the average daily school attendance rate as a proportion (rather than as a percentage) for the school that the student attends. Based only on your answer to 5.8 (a), and without using Stata, what is the correlation between schattpp and slfcnc08?

c) In general, do children who have higher socioeconomic status expect to have greater incomes by age 30? Construct the scatterplot and determine the correlation coefficient between expin30 and ses. Interpret the results.

d) Rather than simply eliminating the most extreme value in the scatterplot, we reduce its undue influence on the value of the correlation by following the methods in Chapter 4, and creating a new variable that represents the square root of expinc30. Label this new variable expincsq. Construct the scatterplot and determine the correlation coefficient between expincsq and ses. Do children who have higher ses expect to have higher incomes by age 30?

e) What is the correlation between expincsq and expinc30? Under what circumstance would the correlation be equal to 1.00?

f) For students in the Northeast, find the Pearson Correlation Coefficient between slfcnc12 and expinc30.

g) Using the procedures described in Chapter 4, create new variables which are the square root of expected income and the logarithm of the reflection of the self-esteem variable. For students in the Northeast, find the Pearson Correlation Coefficient between the transformed versions of esteem and expected income.

h) Which is stronger, the correlation between the original or reflected variables?

i) Why are the signs of the correlations between the transformed and untransformed variables different?

j) Has the general interpretation of the relationship changed now that the sign is negative?

Exercises 5.9–5.14 involve using the Pearson Correlation when at least one of the variables is dichotomous.

5.9. In this exercise, we use the *NELS* data set to look at the relationship of socioeconomic status with eighth grade computer ownership (computer), a dichotomous variable. Do students whose families owned a computer when they were in eighth grade tend to have higher socioeconomic statuses than those whose families did not own a computer when they were in eighth grade?

a) Create a scatterplot between computer and ses. Use it to describe whether students whose families owned a computer when they were in eighth grade tend to have higher socioeconomic statuses than those whose families did not own a computer when they were in eighth grade.

b) Calculate the correlation between these variables to determine the extent to which there is a relationship as described.

5.10. Use the *Learndis* data set to investigate whether different variables are associated with reading achievement. Determine the correlations between all pairs of the following variables: reading achievement (readcomp), grade level (grade), Intellectual ability (iq) and whether the student was placed in the resource room for part of the day or in a full-time self-contained classroom (placemen, where 0 = resource room and 1 = self-contained classroom).

a) Interpret the correlation between reading comprehension and intellectual ability.

b) Based on the correlation table, which group, on average, has higher reading comprehension, those in the resource room or those in a self-contained classroom? Explain.

c) Interpret the correlation between type of placement and grade level.

d) Interpret the correlation between grade level and reading comprehension for these students.

5.11. In this exercise, you are asked about the relationship between pairs of variables in the *Framingham* data set.

a) Compute the correlation (r) between the initial diastolic blood pressure at time 1 (DIABP1) and whether or not the person was taking anti-hypertensive (blood pressure) medication at time 1 (BPMEDS1). Interpret your result.

b) What is another name for the special case of the Pearson Correlation Coefficient calculated between DIABP1 and BPMEDS1?

c) In part (a), a positive, yet weak, correlation was noted between the taking of blood pressure medication and blood pressure level. That is, that those who take blood pressure medication have higher blood pressure levels, on average, than those who don't. What is a likely explanation for this relationship?

d) Which gender (SEX) is more likely to have developed coronary heart disease (CHD) by the end of the study (ANYCHD4)? Explain and support your answer with appropriate statistic(s).

e) What is another name for the special case of the Pearson Correlation Coefficient calculated between SEX and ANYCHD4?

f) Explain why correlation is not the most appropriate way to statistically describe the relationship between the initial casual glucose level (GLUCOSE1) and the initial number of cigarettes smoked per day (CIGPDAY1).

5.12. According to the data in the *Framingham* data set, what evidence is there in these data to suggest that HDL is "good" cholesterol and LDL is "bad" cholesterol? [HINT: Compute the correlation between HDL3 and ANYCHD4 and between LDL3 and ANYCHD4.]

5.13. In the *NELS* data set, the variable computer indicates whether the student's family owned a computer when the student was in eighth grade. In this question we will look at the effect that the coding of this variable has on the correlation.

a) Compute and interpret the correlation between ses and computer.

b) Recode the variable computer into comp1 so that 1 = No and 2 = Yes. Write the equation representing this linear transformation. Does this transformation include a reflection of the original variable computer? Recall that the original coding is: 0 = No and 1 = Yes.

c) What is the correlation between computer and comp1?

d) Recode the variable computer into comp2 so that 0 = Yes and 1 = No. Write the equation representing this linear transformation. Does this transformation include a reflection of the original variable computer?

e) What is the correlation between computer and comp2?

f) Without using Stata, what is the correlation between ses and comp1? Between ses and comp2?

5.14. The median split, discussed in Chapter 4, is a type of nonlinear transformation that serves to symmetrize the distribution of a continuous variable into two equal halves. The resulting variable is dichotomous since all values below the median are assigned one code and all values above the median are assigned a different code. Depending upon the nature of the underlying distribution of the continuous variable, the correlation between the newly-formed dichotomous variable (via the median split transformation) and another variable may be stronger or weaker in magnitude than the correlation based on the original continuous variable and that other variable. This example illustrates the case, using the *NELS* data set, in which the resulting correlation becomes weaker in magnitude.

a) Find and interpret the correlation between ses and slfcnc12.

b) Create new variables sesdi and slfcnc12 that are the median splits of ses and slfcnc12, respectively. Find and interpret the correlation between sesdi and slfcnc12.

c) Comment on the effect of using the median split transformation in this case given that one of the continuous variables (slfcnc12) is skewed negatively.

Exercise 5.15 involves Spearman Correlation.

5.15. In this exercise, we investigate the relationship of two variables with excurr12, participation in extracurricular activities in twelfth grade in the *NELS* data set. Note that this variable is measured using an ordinal level of measurement.

a) Is there a correlation between smoking cigarettes (cigarett) and participation in extracurricular activities in twelfth grade (excurr12)? If so, describe the nature of the correlation. Provide statistical support for your answer.

b) Is there a correlation between missing school in twelfth grade (absent12) and participation in extracurricular activities in twelfth grade (excurr12)? If so, describe the nature of the correlation. Provide statistical support for your answer.

c) Is there a correlation between socioeconomic status (ses) and participation in extracurricular activities in twelfth grade (excurr12)? If so, describe the nature of the correlation. Provide statistical support for your answer.

Exercises 5.16–5.18 involve contingency tables (crosstabulation).

5.16. Use Crosstabs applied to two variables from the *NELS* data set (advmath8 and urban) to obtain a summary of who took advanced math in eighth grade by type of environment. Use the resulting summary to answer the following, related questions.

a) What proportion of students took advanced math in eighth grade from each of the three environments: urban, suburban, and rural?

b) What proportion of students took advanced math in eighth grade over all environments?

c) Which environment has the largest proportion of advanced math takers, urban, suburban, or rural?

d) Is there a relationship between urbanicity and enrollment in advanced math in eighth grade? Explain.

5.17. In this exercise, we make use of the *Framingham* data set to explore the relationship between gender and cigarette use at time 1 and at time 3.

    a) Create a contingency table of cigarette use at time 1 (CURSMOKE1) by sex and use it to determine whether the two variables are related.

    b) Create a contingency table on cigarette use at time 3 (12 years into the study) (CURSMOKE3) by sex and use it to determine whether the two variables are related.

    c) Calculate the correlation between cigarette use at time 1 (CURSMOKE1) and sex and use it to confirm that the two variables are not related.

    d) Calculate the correlation between cigarette use 12 years into the study (CURSMOKE3) and sex and use it to determine whether the two are related.

5.18. The Body Mass Index is a tool for indicating weight status in adults. It is a measure of weight for height; and for adults over 20 years old, the BMI index falls into one of three weight status categories: Below 18.5 – Underweight; 18.5 to 24.9 – Normal; 25.0 to 29.9 – Overweight; Above 30.0 – Obese. In this exercise, we make use of these categories. HINT: To create this new categorical variable, BMIindex, use the following Stata code:

(NOTE: In Stata, the assignment of value labels to a variable is a two-step process. We first need to define the labels and their associated values using the **label define** command as shown below and then we need to attach these value labels to the variable of interest, in this case, BMIindex. For the attachment step, we use the command **label values**, as shown below. The variable that contains the value labels can be called anything other than the name of the new variable you are creating. We have called it BMIcateg.)

```
capture gen BMIindex = 0
replace BMIindex = 1 if (BMI1 <= 18.5)
replace BMIindex = 2 if (BMI1 >= 18.5 & BMI1 <= 24.9)
replace BMIindex = 3 if (BMI1 >= 24.9 & BMI1 <= 29.9)
replace BMIindex = 4 if (BMI1 >= 29.9)
replace BMIindex =. if BMI1 ==.
```
***This is the two-step process for giving variables value labels. In the first step
***we associate values (1, 2, 3, 4) with labels ("underweight", "normal weight",
    ***"overweight", "obese") and give the associated values a variable name
*** (BMIcateg). In the second step, we attach those value labels (in BMIcateg)
*** to the variable BMIindex.
label define BMIcateg 1 "underweight" 2 "normal weight" 3 "overweight" 4 "obese"
label values BMIindex BMIcateg

    a) Initially, at time 1, what is the distribution of men and women in this sample across these categories? [HINT: Use Crosstabs]. According to this distribution, what percentage of men is categorized as overweight or obese versus women?

    b) Are there differences in weight category by gender? Explain.

    c) Compare the relative proportions of those who did not experience a coronary heart disease (CHD) event over the course of this study versus those who did (ANYCHD4) for men and for women. Use the obtained ratio of proportions within sex as the basis for comparison.

    d) How are these ratios affected if we restrict the samples of men and women only to those who are obese?

Exercise 5.19 requires you to select an appropriate statistic for answering the question asked and to analyze the NELS data set using that statistic.

5.19. Select an appropriate statistic that conveys the magnitude and nature of the relationship that exists between pairs of variables in the *NELS* data set. When describing that relationship, use terms that someone who has not taken statistics could understand (for example, positive correlation is not sufficient).

   a) Is there a relationship between years of math taken in high school (unitmath) and math achievement in twelfth grade (achmat12)? If so, describe that relationship.

   b) Is there a relationship, between the number of times the student is late to school in twelfth grade (late12) and the number of times the student skipped/cut classes in twelfth grade (cuts12)? If so, describe that relationship.

   c) Is there a relationship between the school type attended in eighth grade (schtyp8) and whether or not the student took any Advanced Placement classes in high school (approg)? If so, describe that relationship

   d) Is there a relationship between family size (famsize) and self-concept in twelfth grade (slfcnc12)? If so, describe that relationship.

   e) Is there a relationship between socioeconomic status (ses) and science achievement in twelfth grade (achsci12)? If so, describe that relationship.

   f) Is there a relationship between region of the country (region) and whether or not a student took advanced math in eighth grade (advmath8)? If so, describe that relationship.

   g) Is there a relationship between number of classes cut in twelfth grade (cuts12) and whether or not the student took advanced math in eighth grade (advmath8)? If so, describe that relationship.

   h) Is there a relationship between cigarette use (cigarett) and urbanicity (urban)? If so, describe that relationship.

   i) Is there a relationship between whether or not students took advanced math in eighth grade (advmath8) and whether or not they took an AP class (approg) in high school? If so, describe that relationship.

   j) Is there a relationship between the frequency of cutting class in twelfth grade (cuts12) and being absent from school in twelfth grade (absent12)? If so, describe that relationship.

   k) Is there a relationship between twelfth grade self-esteem (slfcnc12) and socioeconomic status (ses)? If so, describe that relationship.

   l) Is there a relationship, between socioeconomic status (ses) and nursery school attendance (nursery)? If so, describe that relationship.

   m) Is there a relationship between socioeconomic status (ses) and urbanicity (urban)? If so, describe that relationship.

Exercises 5.20–5.25 include a variety of topics. The exercises are based on the Impeach data set, created by Professor Alan Reifman of Texas Tech University in response to a U.S. Senate vote taken on February 12, 1999 on whether to remove a president from office, based on impeachment articles passed by the U.S. House of Representatives. This was only the second time in U.S. history that such a vote took place. The data contain descriptions of each senator as a way to try to understand each senator's voting behavior.

5.20. The questions in this exercise relate to a correlation analysis carried out between all pairs of the following variables: the vote on perjury (vote1), the degree of conservatism of the senator (conserva), the state voter support for Clinton (supportc), and whether or not the senator was first-term (newbie).

    a) Was it appropriate to compute a correlation between conserva and supportc? Why or why not?

    b) Describe the magnitude and nature of the linear relationship between these two variables, the degree of conservatism of the senator and the state voter support for Clinton.

    c) Based on the results of the correlation analysis, can you determine whether conservative senators are more likely to vote guilty or not guilty on perjury? Explain.

    d) Based on the results of the correlation analysis, can you determine whether senators from states that supported Clinton in 1996 were more likely to vote guilty or not guilty on perjury? Explain.

    e) Based on the results of the correlation analysis, can you determine whether first term senators were more likely to vote guilty or not guilty on perjury? Explain.

    f) If you were looking for one variable to statistically discriminate between those senators who voted guilty and those who voted not guilty on perjury, which variable (conserva, supportc, newbie) would you choose? Explain.

    g) Explain why it would not be appropriate to calculate the correlation between the region of the country that the senator is from (region, where 1 = Northeast, 2 = Midwest, 3 = South, and 4 = West) and the vote on perjury. Give the name of an alternative analysis that could be used to analyze the relationship between the two variables.

5.21. Create two scatterplots, one to depict the relationship between conservatism and the vote on perjury and the other to depict the relationship between conservatism and the vote on obstruction of justice. Use them to answer the following questions.

    a) Describe the nature of the relationship between the vote on obstruction of justice and conservatism. Use language that someone who has never taken statistics could understand.

    b) Based on your political knowledge, explain why your answer to part (a) makes sense.

    c) According to the scatterplots, which pair of variables has the stronger correlation? Explain.

5.22. Create a contingency table that gives the breakdown of the vote on perjury by region. Use it to answer the following questions.

    a) How many senators voted not guilty on perjury?

    b) What percentage of senators voted not guilty on perjury?

    c) Of all not guilty votes, what percentage (or proportion) came from the south?

    d) Of all votes from the south, what percentage (or proportion) were not guilty votes?

    e) According to the contingency table, are there differences in the vote on perjury depending on the region from which the senator comes? Explain in a way that someone with no background in statistics could understand and support your answer with the values of relevant statistics.

    f) What type of graph is best used to display the relationship between the vote on perjury and region? Create this graph.

g) Explain why a contingency table should not be used to analyze the relationship between region and conservatism.

5.23. Create a clustered bar graph that gives the number of guilty and not guilty votes on perjury (vote1) for both first-term and more senior senators (newbie). Use it to answer the following questions.

    a) Is there a relationship between the vote on perjury and whether or not the senator is first-term? Explain.

    b) Without calculating, what is the sign of the Pearson correlation between vote1 and newbie? Explain.

5.24. Create two clustered bar graphs that depict the relationships between whether or not the senator was first term (newbie) and how the senator voted on obstruction of justice (vote2). Let one graph represent those senators who were up for re-election in 2000 and the other graph represent those who were up for re-election in 2002. Use them to answer the following questions.

    a) For those senators up for re-election in 2000, describe the nature of the relationship between seniority status as a senator (whether the senator was first-term or not) and voting behavior on the issue of obstruction of justice. Explain.

    b) Is the Pearson Correlation Coefficient that may be calculated to describe the relationship noted in part a) positive, negative, or near zero? Explain.

    c) According to these clustered bar graphs, is the correlation between whether or not the senator was first-term and his or her vote on obstruction of justice stronger for senators up for re-election in 2000 or in 2002? Explain.

5.25. In order to determine whether the relationship between state voter support for Clinton (supportc) and conservatism (conserva) varies as a function of how the senator voted on perjury (vote1), create a scatterplot of supportc by conserva and differentiate the points by vote1.

The Stata command to create a scatterplot where the points are differentiated by another variable is

twoway (scatter supportc conserva if vote1 == 0, mcolor(blue)) (scatter supportc conserva if vote1 == 1, mcolor(red))

Use your scatterplot to answer the following questions. Follow up by splitting the file, calculating the correlation coefficients, and using them to corroborate the answers based on the scatterplot.

    a) Describe the nature of the relationship, or indicate that there is not one, between state voter support for Clinton and conservatism for those senators who voted guilty on perjury.

    b) Describe the nature of the relationship, or indicate that there is not one, between state voter support for Clinton and conservatism for those senators who voted not guilty on perjury.

Exercises 5.26–5.35 test conceptual understanding and do not require the use of Stata.

5.26. The correlation between manual dexterity (X) and Age from 2 years to 80 years (Y) is $r = 0.08$. Nevertheless, the investigator was able to make reasonably accurate predictions of a person's manual dexterity score on the basis of his or her age. Explain how this could be possible.

5.27. What (if anything) is wrong with the following statement? "A Pearson Correlation Coefficient value of $r = 0.8$ between two variables represents twice the linear relationship that a Pearson Correlation Coefficient value of $r = 0.4$ represents."

5.28. Read the following excerpt from the article "TV, video games at night may cause sleep problems in kids," by Amanda Gardner on June 27th, 2011. You do not need to read the entire article to answer the related questions, but it may be found online at: http://healthland.time.com/2011/06/27/tv-video-games-at-night-may-cause-sleep-problems-in-kids/. Use it to answer the related questions.

Watching television or playing video games close to bedtime can act like a jolt of caffeine to young children, making them more likely to experience difficulty falling asleep, nightmares, and daytime fatigue, a new study in the journal *Pediatrics* suggests.

In the study, 28% of preschoolers who watched TV or played video games for at least 30 minutes after 7 p.m. had sleep problems most nights of the week, versus 19% of children whose TV and video-game use took place only before 7 p.m.

The study included 612 children ages 3 to 5. Garrison and her colleagues asked the parents to keep a detailed diary of their child's media consumption over the course of one week, including the title, timing, and duration of each show or game. (To determine the level of violence, researchers consulted parental guidance ratings and actually analyzed specific shows and games.)

On average, the kids spent 73 minutes per day in front of a TV or computer. The more time they spent watching TV or playing video games in the evening, the more likely they were to experience a sleep problem.

a) *According to the results of this study*, if you had a much younger brother or sister, should you limit television and video game time after 7 pm in order to ensure a good night's sleep? Explain. Be as detailed as you can.

b) Create the clustered bar graph depicting the relationship between whether or not the child watched television or played video games for at least 30 minutes after 7 pm and whether or not the child had sleep problems most nights of the week as described in the article. Make sure to label your axes and the bars.

c) Based on the information in the excerpt from the article, is it fair to conclude that the number of children who watch TV after 7 p.m. and have sleep problems is more than the number of children who don't watch TV after 7 p.m. and have sleep problems? Why or why not?

5.29. Read the following excerpt of the article, "Pain pills add cost and delays to job injuries" by Barry Meier from the New York Times on June 2, 2012. Use the excerpt to answer the following questions.

Workers who received high doses of opioid painkillers to treat injuries like back strain stayed out of work three times longer than those with similar injuries who took lower doses, a 2008 study of claims by the California Workers Compensation Institute found.

When medical care and disability payments are combined, the cost of a workplace injury is nine times higher when a strong narcotic like OxyContin is used than when a narcotic is not used, according to a 2010 analysis by Accident Fund Holdings, an insurer that operates in 18 states.

    a) What is the sign (positive or negative) of the correlation between dose of opiod painkillers and number of days out of work?

    b) According to the results of this article, should doctors stop prescribing painkillers to people with workplace injuries? Explain.

5.30. What (if anything) is wrong with the following statement? "A Pearson Correlation Coefficient value of $r = 1.05$ was found between two variables X and Y. This represents a very strong linear relationship between the two variables."

5.31. What (if anything) is wrong with the following statement about the *NELS* data? "The correlation between region and the number of Advanced Placement classes offered is $r = .11$ indicating that the higher the region, the more Advanced Placement courses offered, on average."

5.32. What (if anything) is wrong with the following statement: "If the correlation between X and Y is $r = .50$, then you can perform any linear transformation on the variable X and the correlation between the transformed X and Y will still be $r = .50$."

5.33. What (if anything) is wrong with the following statement? "If the correlation between average math SAT and average verbal SAT for all 50 states is $r = .97$, that implies that the scores on the verbal portion are higher than the scores on the math portion."

5.34. Draw a scatterplot for which the Pearson Product Moment correlation would not capture the true magnitude and nature of the relationship between the two variables.

5.35. The following questions relate to the scatterplot below, which shows the relationship between X and Y for four different subgroups. For each subgroup, select the Pearson Correlation Coefficient, r, from the column at right, that best represents the relationship between X and Y for the subgroup. You may select a value more than once.

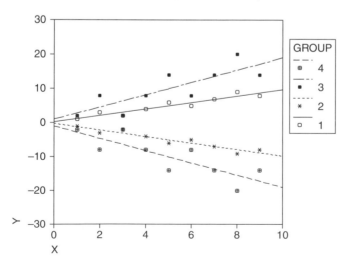

For each subgroup, select the Pearson correlation Coefficient, r, from the column at right, that best represents the relationship between X and Y for the subgroup. You may select a value more than once.

Group 1: _____   a) $r = 1.25$

                       b) $r = -1.25$

Group 2: _____   c) $r = .95$

                       d) $r = -.95$

Group 3: _____   e) $r = .82$

                       f) $r = -.82$

Group 4: _____   g) $r = 0$

CHAPTER SIX

Simple Linear Regression

In the previous chapter, we remarked that even when a strong linear correlation exists between two variables, X and Y, it may not be possible to talk about either one of them as the cause of the other. Even so, there is nothing to keep us from using one of the variables to *predict* the other. In making predictions from one variable to another, the variable being predicted is called the *dependent variable* and the variable predicting the dependent variable is called the *independent variable*. The dependent variable may also be referred to as the *criterion* or *outcome* while the independent variable may also be referred to as the *predictor* or *regressor*. One way of facilitating such predictions is to obtain a linear equation that somehow fits, or represents, the available data. This equation can then be used to predict the variable Y from the variable X. It can also be used to *explain* the relationship between Y and X in more detail than correlation alone provides. In particular, the equation can be used to study how a change in one variable, X, relates to a change in the other variable, Y.

In this chapter, we introduce a technique for finding such a linear equation, called the *regression equation*, and measuring the extent to which it describes the data. As we will see, the stronger the correlation between X and Y, the more accurately Y can be predicted from X; and the weaker the correlation, the less accurately Y can be predicted from X.

THE "BEST-FITTING" LINEAR EQUATION

If the linear relationship between X and Y were perfect so that all points of the data set fell along a single straight line, the task of finding a linear equation that fits the given data exactly would be quite straightforward. With the help of some coordinate geometry, we could find the equation of the single straight line passing through all the points.

In behavioral and social research, however, it is extremely unlikely to encounter data that are perfectly linearly related. The question we would like to investigate in this section is: "How do we find the best-fitting line to predict one variable from another when the two variables are not perfectly linearly related?" Let us return to the data from our McDonald's example reproduced here as Table 6.1. Recall that the Pearson Correlation Coefficient between fat and calories for these is .996.

Although $r = 0.996$ implies an extremely strong positive linear relationship between fat and calories, the fact that it is not a perfect linear relationship means that no one line passes exactly through all five points of the scatterplot. However, because such a strong correlation value implies that the relationship between fat (X) and calories (Y) is *almost* perfectly linear, there should be many lines that almost work. Three such lines are illustrated in Figure 6.1 with the scatterplot of our data.

TABLE 6.1. Fat grams and calories by type of McDonald's hamburgers

Type of McDonald's Hamburger	Grams of fat (X)	Calories (Y)
Hamburger	10	270
Cheeseburger	14	320
Quarter Pounder	21	430
Quarter Pounder w/ cheese	30	530
Big Mac	28	530

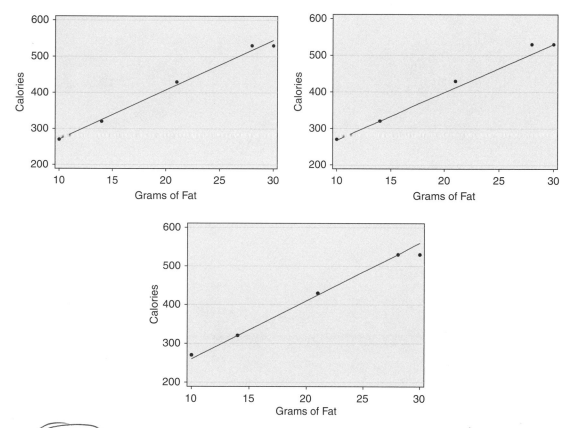

Figure 6.1 Three lines that almost fit the data of Table 6.1.

Because all three lines in Figure 6.1 (as well as many others) almost fit the data of Table 6.1, they would all seem reasonable to use for prediction purposes. But which one is the best-fitting line, and how do we find its equation? The question of which line is best fitting is subjective and depends to a large extent on what we mean by "best." We might, for example, select the line that actually goes through as many of the points of the scatterplot as possible. But if we do this, the line might turn out to be very far from the points it does not pass through. The usual way of choosing a best-fitting line, and the one we will use, is to take one that, on the average, comes "closest" in terms of squared deviations to *all* the points of the scatterplot. Such a line is called a (least squares) *regression line* or

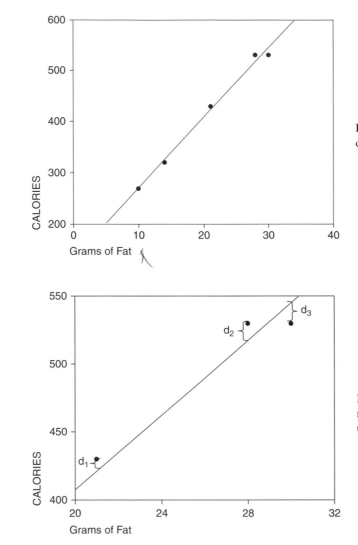

Figure 6.2   The regression line for the data of Table 6.1.

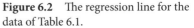

Figure 6.3   Residuals from the regression line: A magnified view using three points.

(least squares) *prediction line*, and its equation is called a (least squares) *linear regression equation*. Let us now see what is meant by a *deviation* and how we find the equation of the best-fitting line.

Suppose we have a line L that we think of using to predict calories (Y) from fat (X) for the data of Table 6.1 (see Figure 6.2). For each of our given X_i values ($i = 1, 2, 3, 4, 5$), let $\hat{Y}_i$ be the Y value that the equation of line L predicts from X_i (i.e., the value that is obtained when X_i is substituted into the equation of line L; or, equivalently, the value that when paired with X_i gives a point X_i, Y_i on line L). Then, because Y_i is the actual Y value paired with X_i, and $\hat{Y}_i$ is the Y value predicted by L to pair with X_i, their difference (or deviation) $d_i = Y_i - \hat{Y}_i$ is just the error of prediction (or error of estimate) at X_i when using L. While we have been referring to errors of prediction as deviations, they are also, more commonly, referred to as *residuals*, since they represent that part of the actual Y score that is *left over* after taking into account the predicted Y score. Figure 6.3 zooms in on three pairs of X,Y values to provide a magnified view of their residuals.

Note that for the three points of Figure 6.3, two residuals (d$_i$'s) are positive, whereas one is negative. Positive residuals indicate that the predicted Y value, $\hat{y}$, is less than the actual Y value, whereas negative residuals indicate that the predicted Y value, $\hat{y}$, is greater than the actual Y value. If we obtained the sum of the residuals for all five pairs of values in our data set based on the regression line, the negative residuals would cancel out the positive residuals, resulting in a false impression that there is no error of prediction. To obtain a valid measure of error of prediction (one that avoids cancellation of positive with negative error terms), we could either take the absolute value of each term before summing, or we could square each error term before summing. These are exactly the two alternatives we faced in Chapter 3 when defining a measure of variability. As before, we choose to square each of the individual error terms d$_i$ to obtain d$_i^2$ before summing. To make this squared index of error independent of the number of pairs of data values, we divide the sum of the d$_i^2$'s by N to obtain what is called the *average squared deviation* (or *average squared* error) D^2. Finally, to bring the measure back to the original units of the data, we take the square root of D^2, and obtain D, the *standard error of estimate* or *prediction*:

$$D = \sqrt{\frac{\sum d_i^2}{N}} \tag{6.1}$$

We see that D is approximately the average vertical distance to the regression line in the same way that the standard deviation is approximately the average distance to the mean. We will use D as our index of error of prediction for a given prediction line on a given set of data.

We now can define what we mean by the best-fitting line for a given set of data. The best-fitting line is the line that minimizes (or gives the smallest possible number for) the value of D for the given data. It is called the (least squares) *regression line* or (least squares) *prediction line*. The equation of the regression line is called the *linear regression equation*, and the criterion we use to define it (that of minimizing the value of D) is called the *least squares criterion*. Although the actual derivation of the equation for the regression line is beyond the scope of this book, the equation itself is really quite simple. Given a set of paired data X,Y with N pairs, the equation of the regression line (the linear regression equation) for predicting Y from X is

$$\hat{Y} = bX + a \tag{6.2}$$

where

$$b = r \frac{S_Y}{S_X} \tag{6.3}$$

$$a = \overline{Y} - b\overline{X} \tag{6.4}$$

In Equation 6.2, $\hat{y}$ represents the predicted value for Y. The value of b for use in the linear regression equation to predict Y from X is called the *regression coefficient*. In Equation 6.2 the regression coefficient, b, represents the slope of the linear regression equation, and the constant, a, represents the Y-intercept.

While the regression equation, Equation 6.2, can be used to find the predicted Y for a given value of X, the values of b and a can be used to explain the relationship between X and Y.

Equation 6.3 shows the relationship between the slope, b, of the regression equation and the value of the Pearson Correlation Coefficient, r. Because standard deviation is always positive, we see that b and r always have the same sign. That is, if b is positive, then Y will increase with an increase in X, whereas if b is negative, then Y will decrease with an increase in X. Moreover, b can always be interpreted as the amount of change in $\hat{Y}$, on average, for each unit increase in X.

Equation 6.4 shows the relationship between the Y intercept of the regression line, a, and the means of both X and Y. In particular, a is defined so that an X value equal to the mean of X would be predicted to have a Y value equal to the mean of Y. That is, so that $(\overline{X}, \overline{Y})$ lies on the regression line. The value of a can be interpreted as the predicted Y for the value $X = 0$. Such an interpretation makes sense only when 0 is a reasonable value for the variable X and when data close to $X = 0$ have been collected.

☞ **Remark.** According to Equation 6.3, when $r = 0$, that is, the two variables are not linearly associated, $b = 0$. In this case, we see that $\hat{Y}$ is just the constant, $\overline{Y}$. Said differently, if X and Y are not linearly related, then given any X value, the predicted Y value is simply the mean of Y.

☞ **Remark.** Suppose you were told that the mean height of ten-year-old girls is 4 feet 1 inch and that the mean weight for ten-year-old girls is 82 pounds. Alice is a ten-year-old girl who is 4 feet 1 inch tall. Based on this information alone, what would you predict Alice's weight to be? If you said 82 pounds, the mean weight for ten-year-old girls, you would agree with the prediction that would be obtained from the linear regression equation for predicting weight from height for ten-year-old girls.

Regression to the Mean: How Regression Got Its Name. In the previous Remark it was noted that a least squares regression equation will predict the weight of a ten-year-old girl who is at the mean height of all ten-year-old girls in that sample (4 feet 1 inch tall) to be equal to 82 pounds, the mean weight of all ten-year-old girls in that sample. That is, given the correlation between height and weight for these ten-year-old girls, the regression equation will predict the weight of a girl whose height equals the mean height for that sample to be equal to the mean weight for that sample.

It is also true that if we select a subsample of ten-year-old girls from that sample who are extremely tall (whose height is much greater than the overall mean height of 4 feet 1 inch) then that subsample's predicted mean weight will tend to be less extreme on weight than it was on height. The same can be said for a subsample selected from that sample to be extremely short (whose height is much lower than the overall mean height for the overall sample); namely, its predicted mean weight will tend to be less extreme on weight than it was on height. That is, in both cases, their predicted means on weight will tend to *regress toward the mean* weight of the total sample.

This phenomenon was first noticed by Sir Francis Galton (1886) in the late nineteenth century in his use of linear modeling to study the heights of a large sample of fathers and their adult sons. He called the phenomenon *regression to the mean*, and the linear models that produced these results, *regression models*.

In particular, Galton found that the fathers who were above average in height tended to have sons who were shorter than they; and, the fathers who were below average in height tended to have sons who were taller than they. But, he also found the reverse to be true. Most of the tallest sons had fathers shorter than they, and most of the shortest sons had fathers taller than they. Furthermore, because Galton found that, overall, the standard deviation of the sons' heights were just about equal to the standard deviation of their fathers' heights, he realized that the heights of the younger generation of sons were not becoming more homogeneous in height.

In its most general form, when there is an imperfect correlation between X and Y (as there is between height and weight), subsamples that are more extreme on X will tend to be less extreme on Y; i.e., their means will be regressed to the mean of the overall sample, and we will have regression to the mean.

As will be noted in Chapter 12, because regression to the mean can impact the interpretation of research results, it must be considered in the design of research studies. The reader who is interested in learning more about the history of this phenomenon is referred to Stigler (1997), and in learning more about the phenomenon itself is referred to Darlington (1990)

* *

EXAMPLE 6.1. Given the data of Table 6.1, use Stata to obtain the linear regression equation for predicting calories (Y) from fat content (X) in two ways. (1) Derive the regression equation from Equations 6.2 through 6.4 using Stata to obtain the required values. (2) Derive the equation directly using Stata. (3) Interpret the slope, and if meaningful, the intercept of the regression equation. (4) Create a scatterplot and edit it in Stata to include the regression line. (5) Use the regression line found in parts (1) and (2) and the graph of the regression line found in part (4) to find the predicted number of calories for a McDonald's hamburger with fat content of 28 grams.

Solution.

1) Using the Stata commands: **summarize calories fat** and **correlate calories fat** (or **pwcorr calories fat**), we find that $\bar{Y}$ = 416 calories, S_Y = 119.08 calories, $\bar{X}$ = 20.6 fat grams, S_X = 8.65 fat grams, and r_{XY} = .996. We need to use these values to find a and b.

Using Equation 6.3, we find that $b = r\dfrac{S_Y}{S_X} = .996\dfrac{119.08}{8.65} = 13.71$

Using Equation 6.4, we find that $a = \bar{Y} - b\bar{X} = 416 - (13.71)(20.6) = 133.57$
Equation 6.2 gives the general form of the regression equation:

$\hat{Y} = bX + a.$

Substituting for a and b, we have $\hat{Y} = 13.71X + 133.57$ or

$\hat{Y} = 13.71(\text{fat}) + 133.57.$

2)

MORE Stata: To obtain a regression analysis using calories and fat

regress calories fat

calories	Coef.	Std. Err.	t	P>|t|	[95% Conf.	Interval]
fat	13.70989	.7328086	18.71	0.000	11.37777	16.04202
_cons	133.5762	16.12512	8.28	0.004	82.25888	184.8935

Figure 6.4 Coefficient information for the simple linear regression equation

The above command only will output the unstandardized regression coefficients. In order to obtain the standardized regression coefficients (the beta weights) as well, we add the option **beta.**

regress calories fat, beta

That part of the output relevant to finding the unstandardized regression equation is reproduced below in Figure 6.4.

In this output, "Coef." refers to the unstandardized regression coefficients. Note that the regression coefficient b, for FAT, equals approximately 13.71. The value of the constant, a, also appears under the column labeled Coef., in the row labeled _cons. The constant equals approximately 133.58. These values agree, within rounding, with the values obtained in part (1).

As before, we write the regression equation using Equation 6.2.

$$\hat{Y} = 13.71X + 133.58 \text{ or } \hat{Y} = 13.71(\text{fat}) + 133.58.$$

3) The slope of 13.71 tells us that each additional gram of fat is associated with 13.71 additional calories, on average. The intercept of 133.57 is not meaningful because none of the hamburgers in the data set had close to 0 grams of fat, so that the value $X = 0$ is beyond the range of the data.

4)

MORE Stata: To obtain the scatterplot with the regression line superimposed.

graph twoway (scatter calories fat) (lfit calories fat)

Note that the syntax within the first set of parentheses will produce the scatterplot for these variables with calories on the y-axis. The syntax within the second set of parentheses will superimpose the fitted regression line (lfit) onto the scatterplot.

The regression line should appear as it does in Figure 6.2.

5) To find the predicted calorie content of a hamburger with 28 grams of fat using the regression equation, we substitute the value $X = 28$ into $13.71X + 133.57$.

$$\hat{Y} = (13.71)(28) + 133.57 = 517.45.$$

Thus, we predict that a hamburger with 28 grams of fat will have approximately 517 calories.

To estimate the predicted calorie content of a hamburger with 28 grams of fat using the scatterplot of the regression equation, we approximate the location of $X = 28$ on the horizontal axis, read up to the regression line, and then read across to the predicted number of calories. We get the less accurate estimate of approximately 520 calories.

Note in Table 6.1 that there actually *was* a hamburger in our original data set for which the fat content was 28 grams, and for that amount of fat, there is 530 calories. According to Example 6.1, however, we would predict the number of calories to be approximately 517. Because of this discrepancy between actual and predicted Y values, a question arises. In which of these two values (517 or 530) can we place more confidence when making predictions about different types of hamburger at McDonald's for which the fat content is 28 grams?

Recall that our interest was in developing a *general* prediction model based on the available data – a model that could then be used to make predictions in similar situations occurring in the future. By making the simplifying assumption that our prediction model should be linear and by *making use of all the available data*, we were able to develop the linear regression equation that is just such a general prediction model. Clearly, predictions made using the linear regression equation (which is based on *all* the available data) can be made with more confidence than predictions made using other prediction systems that are *not* based on all the available data. It follows, therefore, that we can place more confidence in the prediction based on the linear regression equation than on a prediction based on a single observation.

THE ACCURACY OF PREDICTION USING THE LINEAR REGRESSION MODEL

Our goal in this section is to show the relationship between the Pearson Correlation Coefficient r and the standard error of estimate or prediction, D.

Recall that r was introduced in Chapter 5 as a measure of the linear relationship between two variables and that the more the points of the scatterplot conform to a straight line, the closer the value of r will be to a perfect correlation of either -1 or $+1$. Recall further that D was introduced as a measure of how well a given linear equation fits a set of data and that the linear regression equation was then defined as the particular linear equation that minimized D. From now on we will reserve the symbol D to indicate the standard error of estimate based on the linear regression equation, not on just any linear equation. Because the linear regression equation is the best-fitting line for the points of the scatterplot and D is the measure of error of fit for this best-fitting line, it is clear that when r is close to a perfect correlation value of $+1$ or -1, the regression line should fit the scatterplot almost perfectly and consequently the value of D should be close to zero. Thus, an inverse relationship between D and the magnitude of r is suggested. Namely, when the magnitude of r is small (r near 0), D should be large; and when the magnitude of r is large (r near $+1$ or -1.00), D should be small. Because it is the magnitude (not the sign) of r that is apparently inversely related to D, we might obtain a better indication of this relationship by comparing D with r^2 rather than with r. There is, in fact, a simple equation that relates the values of D and r^2 for a given set of X, Y data pairs. It is

$$D = \sqrt{S_Y^2 (1 - r_{XY}^2)} \qquad (6.5)$$

where S_Y^2 is the variance of the given Y values.

From Equation 6.5, it should now be clear that, in general, the closer r is to a perfect correlation, the more accurate the prediction equation will be for the data on which it is based. It is tempting to infer that the more accurate the prediction equation is for the data on which it is based (the closer r is to a perfect correlation), the more accurate we can expect it to be when we are using it to make predictions in the future under similar circumstances. Although this inference is usually a valid one, many factors (such as the number of pairs of data values on which the linear regression equation is based) influence the relationship between the magnitude of r and the accuracy of prediction in the future. These factors involve an understanding that we have not as yet acquired of the basic concepts of inferential statistics. We must therefore postpone a more complete discussion of linear regression analysis until Chapter 14.

THE STANDARDIZED REGRESSION EQUATION

When the regression analysis is computed on the standardized variables (the z-score transformations of X and Y) z_X and z_Y, the resulting equation takes the form:

$$\hat{z}_Y = rz_X \tag{6.6}$$

Equation 6.6 is a simplification of Equation 6.2 because for standard scores, $\overline{z}_X = \overline{z}_Y$ $z = 0$ and $S_{z_X} = S_{z_X} = 1$. The slope of the standardized regression equation is denoted as β.

As shown in Equation 6.6, $\beta + r$ in the case where there is only one independent variable (simple linear regression). Not surprisingly, therefore, the value Beta, or β, is given as .996 in Figure 6.4. The value of r between X and Y is also .996.

The standard score regression equation is not particularly useful for making predictions, because generally scores are given in raw form. When we study multiple regression in Chapter 15, we will see how β may be used to assess the relative importance of the independent variables in the equation.

R AS A MEASURE OF THE OVERALL FIT OF THE LINEAR REGRESSION MODEL

As part of the regression output, Stata provides a model summary, including R-squared. For now, we will limit our discussion of that summary to the value of R, which is the correlation between the actual and predicted values of Y, and may be obtained as the positive square root of R-squared. For the McDonald's example, the summary is provided in Figure 6.5, from which we may compute R to equal sqrt(.9915) = .996.

In the McDonald's example, $R = r$. That is, in this example, the correlation between Y and $\hat{Y}$ is the same as the correlation between Y and X. We will see that this is also the case in Example 6.4. However, as we shall see in Example 6.3, it is not true in general in simple linear regression that $R = r$. Because R is always positive, $R = r$ only when r is positive. When r is negative, then $R = -r$. In general, we may say that $R = |r|$, the absolute value of r.

. . . .

EXAMPLE 6.2. (1) Use Stata to find the predicted values, $\hat{y}$, for the McDonald's example. (2) Find the correlation between predicted calories ($\hat{y}$) and calories (Y) and compare this

Source	SS	df	MS
Model	56237.9813	1	56237.9813
Residual	482.018717	3	160.672906
Total	56720	4	14180

Number of obs	=		5
F(1,3)	=		350.02
Prob > F	=		0.0003
R-squared	=		0.9915
Adj R-squared	=		0.9887
Root MSE	=		12.676

Figure 6.5 Model summary for simple linear regression

TABLE 6.2. Predicted Values for the McDonald's example.

Type	Fat	Calories	yhat
Hamburger	10	270	270.68
Cheeseburger	14	320	325.52
Quarter Pounder™	21	430	421.48
Quarter Pounder with Cheese™	30	530	544.87
Big Mac™	28	530	517.45

value to the correlation between fat content (X) and calories (Y). (3) Construct a scatterplot of Y and $\hat{y}$ and of X and $\hat{y}$.

Solution.

1)

MORE Stata: To obtain the predicted values, $\hat{y}$ (Yhat)

regress calories fat, beta
predict yhat

Note: The **predict** command is an example of what Stata refers to as a post-estimation command (as opposed to a post-estimation statistic). That is, once the regression equation is estimated, we can derive other estimates based on that equation. Predicting yhat is the default option for the **predict** command, the option being defined by **xb**.

To predict the residual values (y-yhat) we would use the **predict** command with the option **residual** (which may be shortened to **res**).

predict yminusyhat, residual

The predicted yhat values are provided in Table 6.2.

2) Using the Stata commands **correlate calories fat** and **correlate calories yhat**, we find that the correlation between fat and calories $r_{XY} = .996$ and that the correlation between predicted calories and calories $r_{Y\hat{Y}} = .996$.

☞ **Remark.** In the McDonald's example, the correlation between fat content (X) and calories (Y) is equal to the correlation between predicted calories ($\hat{y}$) and calories (Y). In general, that is not true. Because, in simple linear regression, $R = |r|$, R and r will have the same magnitude, but they may not have the same sign.

3) The scatterplot between Y and $\hat{Y}$ is given below.

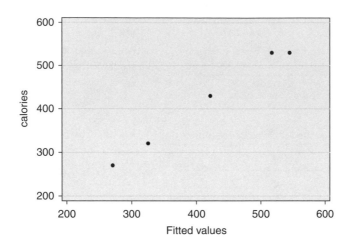

Conceptually, it makes sense that the correlation between the actual and predicted values of Y is always positive. It is desirable for high actual values to be associated with high predicted values and for low actual values to be associated with low predicted values. Hence, the correlation between Y and $\hat{y}$ will always be positive.

The scatterplot of X *(grams of fat)* and $\hat{y}$ is given below.

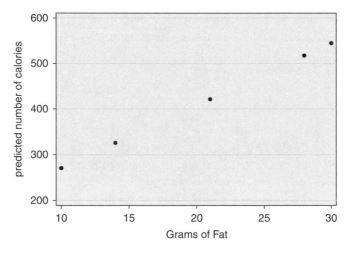

Notice that the points fall along a perfect straight line with positive slope, indicating that the correlation between X and $\hat{y}$ is +1. This is because $\hat{y}$ is defined as a linear transformation of X $(bX + a)$ for which b is positive. If b were negative, the line would have a negative slope and the correlation would be –1.

R does not enhance our understanding of the overall fit of our regression equation to our data over and above r in the case of simple regression. The situation is different in multiple regression as we shall see in Chapter 15.

● ●

EXAMPLE 6.3. In Chapter 5, using the file states.dta, we performed a correlation analysis to determine that in the United States, the average SAT Critical Reading score of a state (satcr) is inversely related to the percentage of students who have taken the SAT in that state (pertak). In this example, we perform a regression analysis to predict the average SAT Critical Reading score for these states, and use it to answer the following questions.

1) Why is a regression analysis appropriate for these data?
2) Write down the regression equation for predicting the SAT Critical Reading score from the percentage of students who have taken the SAT in the state.
3) What is the value of the intercept of this regression equation and what is its interpretation within the context of this problem?
4) What is the value of the slope of this regression equation and what is its interpretation within the context of this problem?
5) Use the regression equation to predict the average SAT Critical Reading score for a state with 25 percent of the students taking the SAT.
6) Construct a scatterplot of Y and $\hat{Y}$ and compare that scatterplot to the scatterplot constructed in part (1). What does this comparison imply about the relationship between R and r?

Solution.

1) To determine whether regression analysis is appropriate, we construct the scatterplot, add the fit line, and note that the pattern of the points is linear, confirming that regression analysis is appropriate for these data. The scatterplot is produced below. We also note that both variables are measured at the scale or ratio level, which is appropriate for regression.

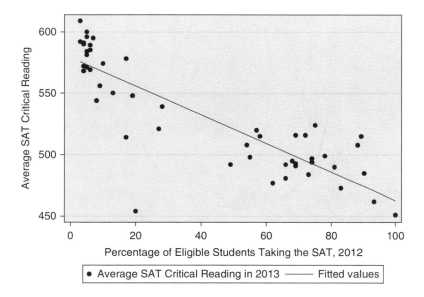

2) We use the Stata regression procedure. We see from the coefficients table, reproduced below, that the regression equation is

$$\hat{Y} = -1.163(\text{PERTAK}) + 578.975, \text{where } \hat{Y} = \text{predicted SATVCR.}$$

satcr	Coef.	Std. Err.	t	P > |t|	Beta
pertak	−1.162872	.0993575	−11.70	0.000	−.8582151
_cons	578.9746	5.188854	111.58	0.000	.

3) The value of the intercept is 578.98. The intercept indicates the predicted average SATCR score when a state has no students taking the SAT. In this case, it is impossible for a state to have an average of no students take the SAT, so the value of the intercept is not meaningful to interpret.

4) The value of the slope is −1.16. The slope indicates that every additional 1 point increase in the percentage of students taking the SAT in the state is associated with a 1.16 point decrease in the average SATCR score for the state.

5) $\hat{y} = -1.163(25) + 578.976 = 549.90$

6) The scatterplot of Y and $\hat{y}$ is given below. It suggests a positive relationship between Y and $\hat{y}$ in contrast to the scatterplot given in part (1), which suggests a negative relationship between X and Y. Hence, while R, a measure of the relationship between Y and $\hat{y}$ is positive, r, a measure of the relationship between X and Y is negative in this case. Because we know from the Coefficients Table in part (2) that $\beta = -.86$ and we know that $\beta = r$, we know that $r = -.86$. Because $R = |r|$, we know that $R = .86$, as expected from the positive linear shape of the scatterplot.

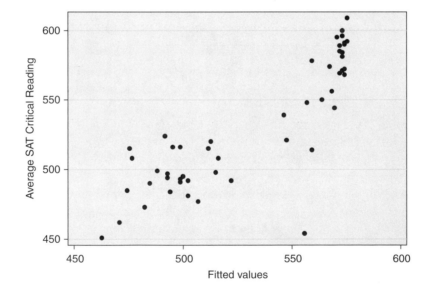

SIMPLE LINEAR REGRESSION WHEN THE INDEPENDENT VARIABLE IS DICHOTOMOUS

In this section we present an example of simple linear regression when the independent variable is dichotomous and highlight the connection between the strength of a correlation and the difference between the means on the continuous variable of the two groups represented by the dichotomy.

TABLE 6.3. Calories and cheese content by type of McDonald's hamburgers

Type of McDonald's Hamburger	Cheese? (X)	Calories (Y)
Hamburger	0	270
Cheeseburger	1	320
Quarter Pounder	0	430
Quarter Pounder w/ cheese	1	530
Big Mac	1	530

● ●

EXAMPLE 6.4. In Example 6.1 we were concerned with obtaining a regression equation that predicts calories from fat content. In this example, we wish to predict calories from whether or not the hamburger contains cheese. Table 6.3 contains the data for our example. Notice that variable X, representing the presence of cheese, equals 1 when cheese is present and 0 otherwise. Variable X is therefore a dichotomous variable.

A regression analysis is performed to predict the number of calories based on whether or not the hamburger contains cheese. The Coefficients Table from the Stata output is provided below. Use it to respond to the following items.

calories	Coef.	Std. Err.	t	P > |t|	Beta
cheese	110.	108.2692	1.02	0.384	.5059589
_cons	350	83.86497	4.17	0.025	.

[handwritten annotation: → correlation]

[handwritten annotation: ↓ slope → is having 110 extra cheese.]

1) What is the correlation between calories and cheese?
2) Write down the regression equation for predicting the calories from the presence of cheese. How well does the model fit the data?
3) What is the value of the intercept of this regression equation and what is its interpretation within the context of this problem?
4) What is the value of the slope of this regression equation and what is its interpretation within the context of this problem?
5) Compute the mean number of calories for hamburgers with cheese.
6) Use the regression equation to predict the calorie content of a burger with cheese.
7) Compute the mean number of calories for hamburgers without cheese.
8) Use the regression equation to predict the calorie content of a burger without cheese.
9) What is the difference in calorie content between a burger with cheese and one without cheese? How is this reflected in the regression equation?
10) Construct a scatterplot with the names of the different hamburgers as case labels and superimpose the regression fit line on the total plot.
11) Use the graph you constructed in part 10 to determine the sign of the residual for the cheeseburger.

Solution.
1) $r = .506$.
2) $\hat{Y} = 110(\text{cheese}) + 350$, where $\hat{Y}$ = predicted calories. Note that cheese takes on the values 0 and 1. The correlation of $r = .506$ is strong, indicating that the model fits the data well.

3) The value of the intercept is 350. The intercept indicates the predicted Y value when $X = 0$. In this case, it indicates that when CHEESE = 0, that is, the burger does not have cheese, the predicted number of calories is 350.

4) The value of the slope is 110. The slope indicates the change in the predicted Y value for a unit increase in the X value. In this case, it indicates that a unit increase in the value of CHEESE is associated with a 110 calorie increase, that is, a burger with cheese is predicted to have 110 more calories than a burger without cheese.

5) The mean number of calories for hamburgers with cheese (320+530+530)/3 = 460.

6) Using the regression equation we may find the predicted number of calories for hamburgers with cheese (cheese = 1) as $\hat{y} = 110(1) + 350 = 460$, which equals the mean number of calories for hamburgers with cheese. The predicted value is the mean or expected value for the number of calories in a burger with cheese.

7) The mean number of calories for hamburgers without cheese is (270+430)/2 = 350.

8) The predicted number of calories for hamburgers without cheese may be found using the regression equation with cheese = 0 as $\hat{y} = 110(0) + 350 = 350$. This is the mean or expected value of the number of calories for hamburgers without cheese.

9) The difference in calories between a burger with cheese and one without is 460 − 350 = 110. This is the value of the slope of the regression equation as explained in part (4).

10)

MORE Stata: To obtain the scatterplot with the regression line and points labeled by the values of a variable

twoway (scatter calories cheese, mlabel(name)xlabel(0 1, valuelabel)) (lfit calories cheese), ytitle("calories")

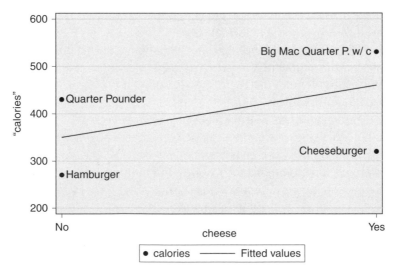

11) The actual number of calories for a cheeseburger is lower than the value that is predicted by the model, so the residual (Y − Yhat) is negative.

☞ **Remark.** We should point out that as reflected by the equation for the Point Biserial Correlation Coefficient (Equation 5.5), the stronger the correlation between the dichotomous variable (cheese, in this case) and the dependent variable (calories, in this case), the greater the separation between the means on the dependent variable for the two groups represented by the dichotomous variable (relative to the spread). Here the means of the two groups are 460 and 350. If the spread of the calories in each group stayed the same, but the mean of 460 was now 500, the correlation between cheese and calories would be even stronger than what it is now.

USING r AND R AS MEASURES OF EFFECT SIZE

The *effect size* of the simple linear regression model refers to the strength of the linear relationship between the two variables. As we have seen, one measure of effect size for the linear relationship is r, the Pearson Correlation Coefficient between the variables, and we have used Cohen's scale to evaluate the size of the effect. We also have noted that when the independent variable is dichotomous, the difference between means on the continuous dependent variable relative to the spread may be expressed as a correlation coefficient. Accordingly, the correlation coefficient is a good measure of effect size for simple linear regression, whether it is used to assess the strength of a linear relationship between two variables or the difference between the means of two groups relative to spread. Because r and R always have the same magnitude, either may be used to express the size of the effect.

EMPHASIZING THE IMPORTANCE OF THE SCATTERPLOT

Throughout this book we have made the point that summary statistics may be misleading if the data they are purported to characterize are anomalous (if, for example, they contain outliers or are skewed in other ways). The linear regression model is no exception. Because the regression model serves to characterize, in summary form, the linear relationship between two variables as a line with intercept and slope, it too may be misleading, or in some way, fail to capture the salient features of the data. The use of graphical displays is critical in the process of assessing how appropriate a given model is for describing a set of data.

To illustrate, we consider the four panels of X,Y pairs located in Table 6.4 (Anscombe, 1973). For all panels, the respective X and Y means, X and Y standard deviations, and correlations, slopes, intercepts, and standard errors of estimate are equal. In particular, for each of the four panels, using Stata, $\overline{X} = 9.0$, $\overline{Y} = 7.5$, $S_X = 3.32$, $S_Y = 2.03$, the equation of regression line is $\hat{Y} = 0.5X + 3$, and $r_{XY} = .82$. Accordingly, without a visual representation of these four panels, one might assume that the statistics from all four panels summarize the same data set. Yet, if we look at the four scatterplots of Figures 6.6(a) through (d), we see to what extent these data sets are different from one another.

In only one case, that of panel (a), is the linear model a good characterization of the underlying data. In panel (b) nonlinearity is a salient feature, yet that feature is not captured by the linear regression model. In panel (c), the presence of the outlier, perhaps due to an error in data entry, unduly influences the result of the analysis, and in so doing, compromises what otherwise would have been a perfectly fitting model. Finally, the regression model in panel (d) exists only because of the single outlier. Without this outlier, we would have been unable to fit a nonvertical line to these data at all.

TABLE 6.4. Anscombe's data in four panels

I		II		III		IV	
X	Y	X	Y	X	Y	X	Y
10.0	8.04	10.0	9.14	10.0	7.46	8.0	6.58
8.0	6.95	8.0	8.14	8.0	6.77	8.0	5.76
13.0	7.58	13.0	8.74	13.0	12.74	8.0	7.71
9.0	8.81	9.0	8.77	9.0	7.11	8.0	8.84
11.0	8.33	11.0	9.26	11.0	7.81	8.0	8.47
14.0	9.96	14.0	8.10	14.0	8.84	8.0	7.04
6.0	7.24	6.0	6.13	6.0	6.08	8.0	5.25
4.0	4.26	4.0	3.10	4.0	5.39	19.0	12.50
12.0	10.84	12.0	9.13	12.0	8.15	8.0	5.56
7.0	4.82	7.0	7.26	7.0	6.42	8.0	7.91
5.0	5.68	5.0	4.74	5.0	5.73	8.0	6.89

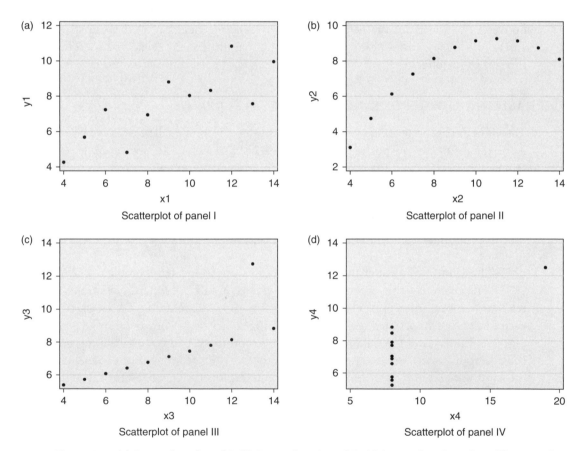

Figure 6.6   (a) Scatterplot of panel I. (b) Scatterplot of panel II. (c) Scatterplot of panel III. (d) Scatterplot of panel IV.

Although the correlation coefficient in all four panels is $r = 0.82$, which, by itself, suggests a strong linear relationship between the X and Y pairs, and a good-fitting linear model, our visual displays tell us otherwise. The moral of this story is to beware of summary statistics without accompanying visual representations!

SUMMARY OF STATA COMMANDS IN CHAPTER 6

For a complete listing of all Stata commands associated with this chapter, you may access the Do-file for Chapter 6 located on the text website.

Create	Command Lines
Regression analysis	**regress calories fat**
Regression analysis with standardized coefficients	**regress calories fat, beta**
Regression analysis with creation of predicted and residual values for each observation	**regress calories fat, beta**
	predict predicted
	predict residual, res
Scatterplot with regression line	**graph twoway (scatter calories fat)**
	(lfit calories fat)
Scatterplot with regression line with points labeled by a variable and a title on the vertical axis	**twoway (scatter calories cheese,**
	mlabel(name)) (lfit calories
	cheese), ytitle("calories")

EXERCISES

*Create a .do file for each exercise that requires the use of Stata. Run the commands from the .do file by highlighting them and hitting **Control+d**. Save each .do file using a name associated with the Exercise for which it was created. It is recommended that you review the Do-file for* Chapter 6 *located on the textbook's website before completing these exercises. To facilitate doing each exercise, it may be helpful to copy and paste relevant commands from the Do-file for* Chapter 6 *into your own Do-file and modify them as needed.*

Exercises 6.1–6.7 involve simple linear regression models between variables that are interval or ratio.

6.1. In Exercise 5.6, we used the *States* data set to determine that there was a positive linear relationship between educexpe, the average educational expenditure per pupil and teachpay, the average salary of public school teachers in the state. In this exercise, we expand on that relationship to create and interpret a model to predict educexpe from teachpay.
   a) Verify that regression is appropriate in this case.
   b) Find the regression equation for predicting educexpe from teachpay.
   c) Interpret the value of the slope of the regression equation in the context of this exercise using language that someone who hasn't taken statistics would understand.
   d) Interpret the value of the intercept in the context of this exercise using language that someone who hasn't taken statistics would understand or indicate why it is not meaningful.
   e) What is the predicted educational expenditure for a state with teacher pay of $40,000?

f) Is it appropriate to use the regression equation to find the predicted educational expenditure for a state with teacher pay of $80,000?

g) Report the value of R and interpret it in the context of this analysis.

6.2. In this exercise, we use the States data set to find the variables that are the best predictors, in a linear sense, of the variable teachpay, which gives the average salary of public school teachers in the state. The possible independent variables are pupils per teacher (stuteach), average SAT critical reading (satcr), and expenditure per pupil (educexpe).

a) Is linear regression appropriate for these three models? Explain.

b) Of the three variables, pupils per teacher, average SAT verbal, and expenditure per pupil, which would be the best predictor of teacher salary using the technique of simple linear regression?

c) Explain why it would not be appropriate to use region as an independent variable for the prediction of teachpay.

6.3. Using the *NELS* data set, can twelfth grade math achievement (achmat12) be predicted by eighth grade socioeconomic status (ses) for students in the *NELS* data set? Perform a regression analysis using Stata and use the results to answer the questions that follow.

a) Create a scatterplot of achmat12 by ses. Edit the graph to include the regression line. Determine that regression is an appropriate technique to use for predicting achmat12 from ses.

b) What is the regression equation for predicting achmat12 from ses?

c) Is there a way to interpret the slope that is meaningful in the context of this analysis? If so, explain what additional information it provides.

d) Is there a way to interpret the y-intercept that is meaningful in the context of this analysis? If so, explain what additional information it provides.

e) What is the predicted twelfth grade math achievement score of a student with ses = 20?

f) For the first student in the *NELS* data set (id = 1), what is the value of the actual twelfth grade math achievement score?

g) For the first student in the *NELS* data set (id = 1), what is the value of the predicted twelfth grade math achievement score?

6.4. Use the *Impeach* data set to perform a simple linear regression analysis to predict the conservatism of the senator (conserva) based on his or her state's voter support for Clinton (cupportc). Use it to answer the following questions.

a) Create a scatterplot and use it to verify that the data have an approximately linear shape.

b) What is the correlation, r, between conservatism and state voter support for Clinton?

c) What is the value of R, a measure of the goodness of fit of the regression model to the data? Describe the goodness of fit for this example.

d) Write down the linear regression equation for predicting conservatism (Y) from the state voter support for Clinton (X).

e) What is the interpretation of the slope of the regression equation in the context of this analysis?

f) Interpret the Y-intercept or constant within the context of this analysis, or explain why it is not meaningful.

g) Use the regression equation to predict the conservatism score for a senator with voter support (the percent of the vote Clinton received in the 1996 presidential election in the senator's state) of 50.

6.5. The following scatterplot, created using variables from the *Framingham* data set, shows the relationship between initial body mass index (BMI1) and initial diastolic blood pressure (DIABP1). The points are labeled by the ID number of the person. Use the scatterplot to answer the following questions.

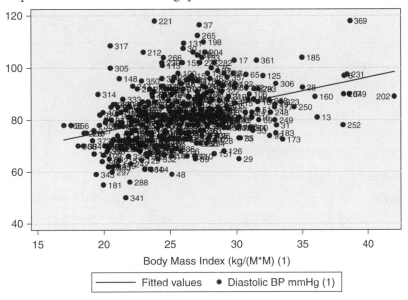

a) Is linear regression appropriate to analyze the relationship between these variables? Explain.

b) Is the slope of the regression line positive, negative, or near 0? What does that tell you about the relationship between the variables involved?

c) Use the regression line in the scatterplot to estimate the initial diastolic blood pressure of a person with an initial body mass index of 19.

d) Explain why the regression model should not be used to estimate the initial diastolic blood pressure of a person with an initial body mass index of 50.

6.6. In this exercise, we use scatterplots created using the *Framingham* data set to compare the relationship between initial body mass index (BMI1) with initial diastolic blood pressure (DIABP1) to the relationship between initial body mass index (BMI1) with initial heart rate (HEARTRTE1)

a) Create two scatterplots, one depicting the relationship between BMI and DIABP1 and the other depicting the relationship between BMI1 and HEARTRTE1. Add the regression line to both scatterplots.

b) Based on the scatterplots, which relationship with BMI has the stronger Pearsons r value, diastolic blood pressure or heart rate? Explain.

c) On average, is a one unit increase in BMI associated with a greater increase in diastolic blood pressure or heart rate?

6.7. Select those in the *Framingham* data set who are not on blood pressure medication at period 1(BPMEDS1 = 0).

    a) Construct a scatterplot of SYSBP1 by AGE1 and label points by SEX. Super-impose fit lines for each sex. The Stata commands to create the scatterplot are

---

MORE Stata: To obtain a customized scatterplot varying color and pattern

twoway (scatter SYSBP1 AGE1 if SEX==1, mcolor(blue)) (scatter SYSBP1 AGE1 if SEX==2, mcolor(red)) (lfit SYSBP1 AGE1 if SEX == 1, lpattern(dash))(lfit SYSBP1 AGE1 if SEX == 2, lpattern(solid)), legend(label(1)label(2 Men) label(3 Women)) ytitle("Systolic Blood Pressure at Time 1"), if BPMEDS1 == 0

---

    b) Construct, for each sex, a regression equation to predict systolic blood pressure (SYSBP1) from age (AGE1).

    c) Interpret results.

    d) Comment on the goodness of fit of each regression line.

    e) Use the respective regression lines to predict the systolic blood pressure for a man and a woman who are each 50 years old.

Exercises 6.8–6.9 involve residual analysis for simple linear regression.

6.8. In Exercise 6.1, we used the *States* data set to create and interpret a model to predict educexpe from teachpay. In this exercise, we examine and interpret some of the residuals.

MORE Stata: To run the regression analysis and generate predicted and residual values for each observation (state).

regress educexpe teachpay
predict predicted
predict residual, res

---

    a) For Alabama, the first state in the data set, what is the predicted average educational expenditure for the state?

    b) For Alabama, the first state in the data set, what is the actual average educational expenditure for the state?

    c) For Alabama, the first state in the data set, what is the value of the residual?

    d) Does the model over- or under- predict the value of educexpe for Alabama?

    e) What state deviates the most from the model?

    f) What is the value of the largest positive residual in the data set? To what state does it correspond? Does the model over- or under- predict the value of educexpe for this state?

    g) Was there a larger residual (in magnitude) for the first state in the data set, or for the second?

6.9. In this exercise, we use the *Framingham* data set to create and interpret the residuals from a scatterplot of the linear regression equation to predict the initial the initial total cholesterol (TOTCHOL1) from the initial body mass index (BMI1).

a) Create the scatterplot between these two variables. Label the scatterplot by ID number and superimpose the regression line.

b) Would you say that linear regression is appropriate in this case? Explain.

c) Based on the scatterplot, approximate the predicted serum cholesterol for the person with ID = 165. (the point in the bottom left of the graph).

d) Based on the scatterplot, approximate the actual serum cholesterol for the person with ID = 165.

e) Based on the scatterplot, approximate the residual serum cholesterol for the person with ID = 165.

f) According to the scatterplot, which person is most unusual in terms of the linear trend between serum cholesterol and BMI? What is his or her ID number? Looking at the data set, is this person a male or a female? How old was this person when the study began?

g) With all people included in the data set, what is the slope of the regression line?

h) With the bivariate outlier, identified in part f) omitted, what is the slope of the regression line? Does the b-value change as a result of omitting this person from the data set?

Exercises 6.10–6.11 involve the use of linear transformations.

6.10. Perform a simple linear regression analysis using the *Learndis* data set with reading comprehension score (readcomp) as the dependent variable and grade level (grade) as the independent variable.

a) What is the regression equation to predict the reading comprehension score from the grade level of the student?

b) Recall that in Exercise 4.18 (b) you created a linear transformation to convert grade to age. Use the variable age that you created to find the regression equation to predict the reading comprehension score from the age of the student.

c) Why do you suppose that the slope of the regression line does not change, in this case?

d) Why do you suppose that the intercept is 16.725 points larger for the model with age as the independent variable?

6.11. The variable schattrt in the *NELS* data set gives the average daily attendance percentage for the school that the student attends.

a) Find the regression equation to predict slfcnc08 from schattrt. Find also the means and standard deviations of slfcnc08 and schattrt.

b) If we were to transform schattrt by dividing its values by 100 we would create a variable schattpp that gives the average daily attendance proportion for the school that the student attends. Using the information obtained in part (a), find the regression equation to predict slfcnc08 from schattpp.

Exercise 6.12 involves the use of nonlinear transformations in simple linear regression.

6.12. In this exercise, we create a model to predict socioeconomic status (SES) from expected income at age 30 (expinc30).

a) Conduct initial univariate and bivariate analyses of the variables involved in the multiple regression model.

b) Use the square root and log transformations to diminish the severe negative skew in the variable expinc30. Which, if any, are effective?

c) Perform a correlation analysis to determine the variable that is most highly correlated with socioeconomic status, the untransformed expected income or the log or square root transformation of the variable.

d) Of the three expected income variables correlated with socioeconomic status in part (c), select the one that will give the best-fitting regression model for predicting socioeconomic status and construct that model.

e) Use your regression equation to predict the socioeconomic status of a student who predicted that he or she would earn $75,000 a year at age 30.

Exercises 6.13–6.14 involve simple linear regression when the independent variable is dichotomous.

6.13. In this exercise, we use the *NELS* data set to create a model to predict socioeconomic status (ses) from eighth grade computer ownership (computer), a dichotomous variable.

a) Create the scatterplot between ses and computer, using an Interactive scatterplot so the computer axis is nicely labeled.

b) What is the regression equation for predicting ses from computer ownership?

c) Interpret the slope of the regression equation in the context of this analysis.

d) Interpret the intercept of the regression equation in the context of this analysis or indicate why it would not be meaningful to do so.

e) Use the regression equation to predict the ses of those who owned a computer in eighth grade.

f) Use the regression equation to predict the ses of those who did not own a computer in eighth grade.

g) Use Stata to find the mean ses of those who did and those who did not own a computer in eighth grade.

h) If the coding of computer had been changed into the variable comp1, with 1 representing those that did not own and 2 representing those that did, what would be the regression equation for predicting ses from comp1?

i) If the coding of computer had been changed into the variable comp2, with 1 representing those that did not own and 0 representing those that did, what would be the regression equation for predicting ses from comp2?

j) Is it ever not meaningful to interpret the intercept of the regression equation in the case of an independent dichotomous variable?

6.14. Students in an introductory college statistics course took the SATS (Survey of Attitudes Toward Statistics (Schau, Stevens, Dauphinee, Del Vecchio; 1995), a regression model was conducted to predict VALUE (Attitudes about the usefulness, relevance, and worth of statistics in personal and professional life. Rated on the average of several 1–7 Likert scale items) from GENDER (Coded with 1 representing male and 2 representing female). The regression equation is $\hat{Y} = .573(\text{GENDER}) + 4.059$. You do not have this data set, so you must use the given regression equation and the coding to answer the following questions.

a) What is the sign of the correlation between GENDER and VALUE?

b) Which gender tended to give a higher rating to the value of the course?

c) What is the predicted VALUE score for females?

d) What is the average VALUE score for males?

Exercises 6.15–6.25 are on a variety of regression topics. For each question, select the most appropriate answer from among the response alternatives.

6.15. If r is 0, and one were asked to predict Y for a given value of X, the best prediction of Y, in a least squares sense, would be:

a) The mean of all the X values

b) The mean of all the Y values

c) The given X value

d) None of the above

6.16. If there is a positive linear correlation between X and Y, then we know that the regression equation for predicting Y from X will have a

a) positive slope

b) negative slope

c) positive y-intercept

d) negative y-intercept

6.17. The degree to which the points of a scatterplot cluster about the regression line predicting Y from X is reflected by:

a) The correlation between X and Y

b) The standard error of prediction

c) The slope of the regression equation, b

d) Both (a) and (b)

e) Both (a) and (c)

f) Both (b) and (c)

g) (a), (b), and (c)

6.18. A regression line for predicting Y from X always:

a) Passes through the origin (0,0)

b) Passes through $(\bar{X}, \bar{Y})$

c) Has a positive slope, b

d) Has a positive Y intercept, a

6.19. If the correlation coefficient between X and Y is $r = 0.60$, and the standard deviations of the Y scores and the X scores are 8 and 4, respectively, then the slope of the regression line for predicting Y from X must be

a) 1.20

b) 0.60

c) 0.30

d) 1.00

e) One cannot determine from the data

6.20. During the semester, the students in a statistics class provided their average weekly study time and their course grade (on a scale from 0.0 to 4.0) for purposes of analysis. The regression equation for predicting grade from the number of hours studied was found to be $\hat{Y} = 1.2X + 0.3$. If a student studies 3 hours per week on average, what is her predicted numerical grade in the course?

a) 2.25
b) 3.90
c) 3.60
d) One cannot determine from the data

6.21. Given the scenario in Exercise 6.16, which of the following conclusions is warranted?
a) For each additional hour of study per week, the predicted grade increases by 1.2 on average
b) For each additional hour of study per week, the predicted grade increases by 0.3 on average
c) For each additional hour of study per week, the predicted grade decreases by 1.2 on average
d) For each additional hour of study per week, the predicted grade decreases by 0.3 on average

6.22. The correlation between exhaustion level and performance on an essay exam was found to be $r = -.90$. If Alejandro scores below the mean on exhaustion level, it is likely that he will score
a) above the mean on the essay exam
b) below the mean on the essay exam
c) on the mean on the essay exam
d) in an unpredictable way on the essay exam

6.23. We know that unless certain restrictions are placed on a regression model, such models may not be used to make causative claims. Give a concrete example to illustrate a situation in which prediction makes sense, but causation does not

6.24. The following questions relate to the scatterplot below, which shows the relationship between X and Y for four different subgroups.

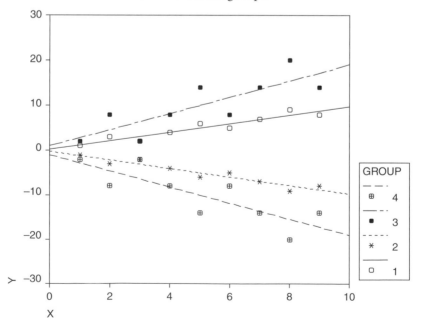

For each subgroup, select the slope of the regression line, b, from the column at right, that best represents the relationship between X and Y for the subgroup. You may select a value more than once.

Group 1: _____   a) $b = .95$

                        b) $b = -.95$

Group 2: _____   c) $b = 1.80$

                        d) $b = -1.80$

Group 3: _____   e) $b = 0$

Group 4: _____

6.25. It is known that the correlation between X and Y is $r = -.46$.
   a) Find the correlation between X and X
   b) Find the correlation between Y and $\hat{Y}$
   c) Find the correlation between X and $\hat{Y}$

Exercises 6.26–6.29 involve the use of formulas to enhance understanding of regression analysis.

6.26. Use Equations 6.2 and 6.4 to show that the regression line always passes through the point $(\overline{X}, \overline{Y})$.

6.27. Use Equations 6.3 and 5.5 to show that in the case where one variable is dichotomous and one is continuous that $b = \overline{Y}_0 - \overline{Y}_1$. Hint: you will need to use the fact that $S_X = \sqrt{pq}$, assuming that X is the dichotomous variable.

6.28. Use Equation 6.2 to show that the mean of the predicted values is $\overline{Y}$.

6.29. Use the regression equation to show that $R = |r|$.

Exercise 6.30 relates to different ways of obtaining D, the standard error of the estimate.

6.30. Given the data in Table 6.1, the *Hamburg* data set, use Stata to obtain D, the standard error of the estimate in three ways.
   a) Calculate D from Equation 6.1 using Stata to obtain the values required by this equation.
   b) Calculate D from Equation 6.5 using Stata to obtain the values required by this equation.
   c) Use Stata to obtain D directly from the regression output.
   d) Compare these three values of D to one another.

CHAPTER SEVEN

Probability Fundamentals

In Chapter 1, we made a distinction between descriptive and inferential statistics. We said that when the purpose of the research is to describe the data that have been (or will be) collected, we are in the realm of descriptive statistics. In descriptive statistics, because the data are collected on *all* the individuals about whom a conclusion is to be drawn, conclusions can be drawn with 100 percent certainty. In inferential statistics, by contrast, the purpose of the research is not to describe the set of data that have been collected, but to generalize or make inferences based on them to a larger group called the *population*. Because data are not available on the entire population, however, we cannot draw conclusions about the population with 100 percent certainty. One of the questions that confronts us in inferential statistics is therefore: "What degree of certainty do we have that our inferred conclusions about the population are correct, and how can we quantify this degree of certainty?" The quantification of degree of certainty is defined in terms of basic probability.

While the concepts of probability apply to variables that are either discrete or continuous, for ease of understanding, in this chapter we illustrate our discussion of probability with examples based on variables that are discrete. In the next chapter, we introduce the continuous case and describe how the fundamentals introduced in this chapter are modified for the continuous case.

THE DISCRETE CASE

We begin the topic of basic probability with the definition of a (*simple*) *experiment*. A (*simple*) *experiment* is defined as any action (such as tossing a coin or answering an item on a test) that leads to an observable outcome. The observable outcomes of any experiment, or any combinations of observable outcomes, are called *events*. If our experiment is to take a die and roll it once, we can observe six possible outcomes {1, 2, 3, 4, 5, 6}, and any one or any combination of these six outcomes can be classified as an event. For example, "The die comes up 6" is an event; "The die comes up 4 or 6" is also an event; and "The die comes up odd" is a third example of an event.

. . . .

EXAMPLE 7.1. Take a fair coin and toss it once.

a. List all the possible outcomes of this simple experiment.
b. State some examples of events for this simple experiment.

Solution.

a. The outcomes of this simple experiment are: {Head (H), Tail (T)}
b. Some examples of events for this simple experiments are:

"The coin comes up heads" "The coin comes up tails"

• •
EXAMPLE 7.2. Take a fair coin and toss it twice.

a. List all the possible outcomes of this simple experiment.
b. State some examples of events for this simple experiment.

Solution.
a. The possible outcomes of this experiment are: {HH, HT, TH, TT}.
b. Some examples of events for this experiment are:
    "The coin comes up first H and then T"   "The coin comes up HH"
    "The coin comes up with an H and a T in any order"   "The coin comes up TT"

How can we determine the *probability*, or degree of certainty, that a particular event will occur when an experiment is actually carried out. *If we assume that all outcomes of an experiment are equally likely* (that they all have the same chance of occurring), then we can define the probability of an event E, P(E), as the number of outcomes that satisfy the event E divided by the total number of outcomes of the experiment.

$$P(E) = \frac{\text{Number of Outcomes Satisfying E}}{\text{Total Number of Outcomes of the Experiment}} \qquad (7.1)$$

For example, in terms of the die experiment mentioned at the beginning of this section, we obtain the probability of the event E: "The die comes up 6" as $P(E) = \frac{1}{6}$, because only one outcome of the six possible outcomes (the outcome "6") satisfies the event E.

• •
EXAMPLE 7.3. In the experiment of taking a fair coin and tossing it twice, what is the probability of the event E: "HH"? (Said differently, "What is the probability of obtaining two heads?")

Solution. Because there are four possible equally likely outcomes for this experiment {HH, HT, TH, TT} and only of them, HH, satisfies the event E, Equation 7.1 gives $P(E) = \frac{1}{4}$.

• •
EXAMPLE 7.4. In the *NELS* data set, there are 227 males and 273 females. If the experiment consists of selecting one individual from this data set at random,

a. What is the probability that the individual is a female?
b. What is the probability that the individual is a male?
c. What is the probability that the individual is a toddler?
d. What is the probability that the individual is either a female or a male?

Solution. There are 500 possible outcomes for this experiment, 227 outcomes are male and 273 outcomes are female. Because we are selecting one of these individuals at random, we can assume that all 500 possible outcomes are equally likely. Therefore, we use Equation 7.1.

a. $P(\text{individual is a female}) = \dfrac{273}{500} = 0.546$

b. $P(\text{individual is a male}) = \dfrac{227}{500} = 0.454$

c. $P(\text{individual is a toddler}) = \dfrac{0}{500} = 0.00$, because there are no toddlers in the *NELS* data set.

d. $P(\text{individual is either a female or a male}) = \dfrac{500}{500} = 1.00$, because all 500 individuals are either female or male.

☞ **Remark.** From part (c) of Example 7.4, we note that the probability of an event that has no chance of occurring in the given experiment is 0, whereas, from part (d), we note that the probability of an event that occurs with certainty in the given experiment is 1.00. In general, the probability of an event is a number between 0 and 1 inclusive. We may also note from parts (a) and (b) that events that are more likely to occur have higher probabilities. If you were asked to bet on whether a randomly sampled individual from the *NELS* data set were male or female, the better choice would be female since there is a greater probability of selecting a female from this data set than a male. Keep in mind that only within the context of a well-defined experiment are events and their probabilities of occurrence defined.

☞ **Remark.** Notice that the probability of an event is its relative frequency. As such, probability values are often reported as percentages.

THE COMPLEMENT RULE OF PROBABILITY

Let us take another look at parts (a) and (b) of Example 7.4. Because males and females have no possible outcomes in common (in other words, a female individual cannot also be male and vice versa), we call these two events *mutually exclusive* or *disjoint*. In addition, because there are only two categories, the event, "The individual selected is male" may be described as well as "The individual selected is *not* female." Accordingly, we say that the event, "The individual selected is male," is the *complement* of the event, "The individual selected is female."

Complement rule of probability: If two events E1 and E2 are complements of each other, then

$$P(E_1) = 1 - P(E_2) \tag{7.2}$$

Given that the probability is 0.546 that the individual selected is a female, we could have obtained the answer to part (b) of Example 7.4 as $1 - 0.546 = 0.454$.

THE ADDITIVE RULES OF PROBABILITY

In part (d) of Example 7.4, we sought the probability of occurrence for the event: "The individual selected is *either* male *or* female," which, in this case, equals 1.00 because all individuals in our sample are either male or female. We can approach the solution to this problem in a slightly different way. Because this event consists of a combination of two types of outcome (selecting a male, selecting a female), we can consider each of these types of outcome as separate events and recast the problem as *finding the compound probability of the two events*, E1: "The person selected is a male" and E2: "The person selected is a female." We are now seeking the probability of the combined event "E1 *or* E2," labeled, P(E1 *or* E2). Because E1 and E2 have no possible outcomes in common (in other words, the outcomes that satisfy E1 do not also satisfy E2, and vice versa, because a male cannot also be a female), we call these two events *mutually exclusive* or *disjoint*. In this case, we can find P(E1 *or* E2) by simply adding together the simple probabilities, P(E1) and P(E2). Using this new approach, we find that for Example 7.4 (d) that P(individual is female) + P(individual is male) = P(individual is either a female or a male) = $\dfrac{273}{500} + \dfrac{227}{500} = \dfrac{500}{500} = 1.00$.

We may state this more formally as the *First Additive Rule of Probability*.

FIRST ADDITIVE RULE OF PROBABILITY

First Additive Rule of Probability. When two events E1 and E2 of the same experiment are mutually exclusive (or disjoint) and we seek to find the probability of the event "E1 or E2," we can do so by adding P(E1) and P(E2) together. In other words,

$$P(E_1 \text{ or } E_2) = P(E_1) + P(E_2) \qquad\qquad (7.3)$$

This rule also holds for more than two events if they are all *pairwise disjoint*, which means that no two of them can occur at the same time.

• •
EXAMPLE 7.5. The number of students in the *NELS* data set by region is given below based on having used the command, **tabulate region**. If a student is selected at random from this data set, find the probability that:

Geographic Region of School	Freq.	Percent	Cum.
Northeast	106	21.20	21.20
North Central	151	30.20	51.40
South	150	30.00	81.40
West	93	18.60	100.00
Total	500	100.00	

a. The student is from the Northeast.
b. The student is from the South.
c. The student is from either the Northeast or South.
d. The student is not from the South.

Solution. Because we are selecting randomly one of the students from the data set, we can reasonably assume that all 500 students are equally likely to be chosen.

a. $P(\text{Northeast}) = \dfrac{106}{500} = .21$

b. $P(\text{South}) = \dfrac{150}{500} = .30$

c. If we define the events, E1 and E2 as

> E1: "The student is from the Northeast"
> E2: "The student is from the South"

then, E1 and E2 are mutually exclusive events: they cannot both occur at the same time. Therefore, we can use the First Additive Rule of Probability. Accordingly, $P(\text{Northeast or South}) = P(E_1 \text{ or } E_2) = P(E_1) + P(E_2) = .21 + .30 = .51$.

d. We may calculate the probability of the event E: "The student is not from the South," in two ways, either through the First Additive Rule or through the Complement Rule. Using the First Additive Rule,

> $P(E) = P(\text{Northeast or North Central or West}) = P(\text{Northeast}) + P(\text{North Central}) + P(\text{West}) = .21 + .30 + .19 = .70$.

Using the Complement Rule, $P(E) = 1 - P(\text{South}) = 1 - .30 = .70$.

In part (c) of Example 7.5, we were able to determine the probability of the event "The student is from the Northeast *or* South" as the sum of the probabilities of the two mutually disjoint events "The student is from the Northeast" and "The student is from the South." If, however, the two were *not* mutually exclusive, we would not have been able to use the First Additive Rule of Probability to find the answer. A more general rule is the *Second Additive Rule of Probability* which applies to whether the events are either mutually exclusive or not.

SECOND ADDITIVE RULE OF PROBABILITY

Second Additive Rule of Probability. Given two events E1 and E2 of the same experiment, if we seek to find the probability of the event "E1 *or* E2," we can do so by using the equation:

$$P(E_1 \text{ or } E_2) = P(E_1) + P(E_2) - P(E_1 \text{ and } E_2) \tag{7.4}$$

where P(E1 *and* E2) represents the probability of the outcomes that E1 and E2 have in common.

☞ **Remark.** If, in the Second Additive Rule of Probability, the events E1 and E2 are disjoint, then they have no outcomes in common and P(E1 and E2) = 0. Consequently, when the events are mutually disjoint, the Second Additive Rule gives the same answer as the First Additive Rule. The Second Additive Rule may, therefore, be considered the more general of the two, and may be used in either case.

••

EXAMPLE 7.6. A cross-tabulation of the number of students in the *NELS* data set by region and whether or not the family owned a computer when the student was in eighth grade is given below based on having used the command, **tabulate computer region**. If a student is selected at random from this data set, determine the probability of selecting a student who is from the South or whose family owned a computer.

Computer Owned by Family in 8th Grade?	Geographic Region of School				Total
	Northeast	North Cen	South	West	Total
No	46	89	86	42	263
Yes	60	62	64	51	237
Total	106	151	150	93	500

Solution. The events "Student is from the South" and "Student's family owned a computer" are not mutually exclusive because they have 64 outcomes in common, students who are from the South and who attended nursery school. Therefore, we use the more general Second Additive Rule with E1 = "Student is from the South" and E2 = "Student's family owned a computer" to find:

$$P(E_1 \text{ or } E_2) = P(E_1) + P(E_2) - P(E_1 \text{ and } E_2) = \frac{150}{500} + \frac{237}{500} - \frac{64}{500} = \frac{323}{500} = .65.$$

THE MULTIPLICATIVE RULE OF PROBABILITY

Suppose, in an experiment involving the toss of single fair coin twice, we are interested in finding the probability of obtaining a head on the first toss and a head on the second toss. That is, we want the probability that the events E1: "Head on first toss" and E2: "Head on second toss" will both occur. This is denoted by P(E1 *and* E2). One way of proceeding is simply to enumerate all possible outcomes of the experiment and then find the desired probability by inspection. The possible outcomes of this experiment are: {HH, HT, TH, TT}.

The only outcome of this experiment that satisfies *both* E_1 and E_2 is {HH}. Accordingly,

$$P(E_1 \text{ and } E_2) = P(HH) = \frac{1}{4} = .25.$$

In more complex situations, the job of enumerating such probabilities becomes rather tedious. In some problems, it may actually be impossible to enumerate a set of equally likely outcomes. In such cases, the following rule, called the *Multiplicative Rule of Probability*, can sometimes be used.

Multiplicative Rule of Probability. Suppose E1 and E2 are independent events of the same experiment. (E1 and E2 are said to be *independent* events if they have no effect on each other; that is, the occurrence of E1 has no effect on the probability of E2.) Then,

$$P(E_1 \text{ and } E_2) = P(E_1) \bullet P(E_2) \tag{7.5}$$

This result also holds for more than two events if they are mutually independent.

We can use the Multiplicative Rule of Probability to obtain the answer to our last problem of finding $P(E_1 \text{ and } E_2)$ where E_1: "Head on first toss" and E_2: "Head on second toss" because, in this case, E_1 and E_2 are independent events. Simply,

$$P(E_1 \text{ and } E_2) = P(E_1) \bullet P(E_2) = P(\text{Head on first toss}) \bullet P(\text{Head on second toss}) = \frac{1}{2} \bullet \frac{1}{2} = \frac{1}{4} = .25$$

EXAMPLE 7.7. We select, at random, a student from the entire *NELS* data set and note whether that student ever smoked marijuana. Then, we select again, at random, from the entire *NELS* data set and note again whether the newly selected student (which, according to our sampling scheme, may be the same student that was selected first) ever smoked marijuana. What is the probability that neither student smoked marijuana?

☞ **Remark.** The type of sampling scheme used in Example 7.7 is called *sampling with replacement* because the student selected on the first draw was replaced before the second draw was made. When sampling with replacement, the entire data set is available for selection at each draw and, therefore, the probability of drawing any student from the data set (e.g., one who has ever smoked marijuana) remains constant from one draw to the next. The topic of sampling will be covered in more detail later in this chapter.

Solution. We first obtain the frequency distribution for marijuana use by students in the *NELS* data set using the command, **tabulate marijuan**.

Smoked Marijuana Ever?	Freq.	Percent	Cum.
Never	408	81.60	81.60
Yes	92	18.40	100.00
Total	500	100.00	

We define E1 as: "The first student selected never smoked marijuana" and E2 as: "The second student selected never smoked marijuana." We want the probability of the event E1 and E2. At each stage of the selection process, the probability of selecting a student who never smoked is $\frac{408}{500} = .816$. In addition, because we used sampling with replacement, E1 and E2 are independent of each other. Therefore, we can use the Multiplicative Rule of Probability.

P(neither student ever smoked marijuana) = P(first student never smoked marijuana and the second student never smoked marijuana) = $P(E_1 \text{ and } E_2) = P(E_1) \bullet P(E_2) = .816 \bullet .816 = .67$.

EXAMPLE 7.8. Three students are randomly selected with replacement from the *NELS* data set. What is the probability that

a. the first two students never smoked marijuana while the third student did?
b. the first and third students never smoked marijuana while the second student did?
c. the second and third students never smoked marijuana while the first student did?
d. exactly two of the three students never smoked marijuana?

Solution.
a. Letting the events E1, E2, and E3 be defined as
   E1: "The first student never smoked marijuana"
   E2: "The second student never smoked marijuana"
   E3: "The third student smoked marijuana"

We are looking for the probability of the event "E1 *and* E2 *and* E3." For each student selected, the probability that the student never smoked marijuana is .816, and the probability that the student smoked marijuana is .184. Furthermore, because E1, E2, and E3 all refer to a different stage of the selection process and because sampling is with replacement, the student selected at any one stage will not affect who is selected at any other stage, these three events are independent of each other. Therefore, we can use the Multiplicative Rule of Probability.

$$P(E_1 \text{ and } E_2 \text{ and } E_3) = P(E_1) \bullet P(E_2) \bullet P(E_3) = .816 \bullet .816 \bullet .184 = .1225$$

b. Letting the events E1, E2, and E3 be defined as
    E1: "The first student never smoked marijuana"
    E2: "The second student smoked marijuana"
    E3: "The third student never smoked marijuana"

Once again, we are looking for the probability of the event "E1 *and* E2 *and* E3" and we can use the Multiplicative Rule of Probability.

$$P(E_1 \text{ and } E_2 \text{ and } E_3) = P(E_1) \bullet P(E_2) \bullet P(E_3) = .816 \bullet .184 \bullet .816 = .1225$$

c. Letting the events E1, E2, and E3 be defined as
    E1: "The first student smoked marijuana"
    E2: "The second student never smoked marijuana"
    E3: "The third student never smoked marijuana"

Once again, we are looking for the probability of the event "E1 *and* E2 *and* E3" and we can use the Multiplicative Rule of Probability.

$$P(E_1 \text{ and } E_2 \text{ and } E_3) = P(E_1) \bullet P(E_2) \bullet P(E_3) = .184 \bullet .816 \bullet .816 = .1225$$

d. If we define the events F, G, and H as
    F:"The first two students never smoked marijuana while the third student did"
    G:"The first and third students never smoked marijuana while the second student did"
    H:"The second and third students never smoked marijuana while the first student did"

Then, we can think of the event "Exactly two of the three students never smoked marijuana" as F *or* G *or* H because these three combinations are the only ways in which the event "Exactly two of the three students never smoked marijuana" can occur. As we have seen in parts (a), (b), and (c), of this example, P(F) = .1225, P(G) = .1225, and P(H) = .1225. The three events, F, G, and H, are mutually disjoint, because no two of them can occur at the same time. Therefore, we can use the First Additive Rule of Probability.

P(Exactly two of the three students never smoked marijuana)

$$= P(F \text{ or } G \text{ or } H)$$
$$= P(F) + P(G) + P(H)$$
$$= .1225 + .1225 + .1225$$
$$= .3675$$

THE RELATIONSHIP BETWEEN INDEPENDENCE AND MUTUAL EXCLUSIVITY

The Multiplicative Rule of Probability can be used only when the two events, E1 and E2, are independent of one another, whereas the First Additive Rule of Probability can be used only when the two events, E1 and E2, are mutually exclusive, or disjoint from one another. Because confusion often arises over the distinction between independence and mutual exclusivity, we include the following statement to clarify the relationship between these two concepts:

Given two events, E1 and E2, of the same experiment, E1 and E2 cannot be both independent of one another and mutually exclusive of one another. However, they can be (1) independent and not mutually exclusive, (2) not independent and mutually exclusive, or (3) not independent and not mutually exclusive. We return to this point in Exercises 7.9–7.11.

CONDITIONAL PROBABILITY

As we have mentioned already, when two events E1 and E2 are independent, they have no effect on each other, and the probability of each event does not depend upon whether or not the other event has occurred. When two events are not independent, however, the probability of one event does depend upon whether or not the other has occurred. To denote the probability of an event E1 given that an event E2 has occurred, we write $P(E_1|E_2)$.

· ·

EXAMPLE 7.9. We know from Example 7.7 that the probability that a randomly selected student from the *NELS* data set has never smoked marijuana is .816 $\left(\dfrac{408}{500}\right)$. Is this probability the same for males and females? That is, is the probability of never having smoked marijuana *given* that the student is male equal to the probability of never having smoked marijuana *given* that the student is female?

Solution. We obtain, as shown in table below, the cross-tabulation of gender by marijuana use for the *NELS* data set based on having used the command, **tabulate gender marijuan**.

Gender	Smoked Marijuana Ever?		Total
	Never	Yes	
Male	185	42	227
Female	223	50	273
Total	408	92	500

a. To find the probability that a randomly selected student from the *NELS* data set never smoked marijuana *given that the student is male*, we need only consult the first row of the table because that row contains all the information we need to solve this problem. From the first row, we find that

P(student never smoked marijuana | student is male) = $\dfrac{185}{227}$ = .815.

b. To find the probability that a randomly selected student from the *NELS* data set never smoked marijuana *given that the student is female*, we need only consult the second row of the table because that row contains all the information we need to solve this problem. From the second row, we find that

$$P(\text{student never smoked marijuana} \mid \text{student is female}) = \frac{223}{273} = .817.$$

According to these results, the probability of never smoking marijuana is effectively the same for males and females.

. . . .

EXAMPLE 7.10. Find the probability that a randomly selected student is male given that the student never smoked marijuana.

Solution. Using the table associated with Example 7.9, we refer to column one to find that

$$P(\text{student is male} \mid \text{student never smoked marijuana}) = \frac{185}{408} = .453.$$

☞ **Remark.** Because P(student never smoked marijuana | student is male) does not equal P(student is male | student never smoked marijuana), we may note that $P(E_1|E_2)$ and $P(E_2|E_1)$ do not have to be equal to each other. In fact, they will be equal to each other only when $P(E_1) = P(E_2)$.

To find a conditional probability, as we have done in Examples 7.9 and 7.10, we may use Equation 7.6 as an alternative approach.

$$P(E_1|E_2) = P\frac{(E_1 \text{ and } E_2)}{P(E_2)} \tag{7.6}$$

In applying Equation 7.6 to the problem of Example 7.9 (a), we let E_1 = "The student never smoked marijuana" and E_2 = "The student is male." Then, $P(E_1 \text{ and } E_2) = \frac{185}{500} = .370$, $P(E_2) = \frac{227}{500} = .454$. Substituting these values into Equation 7.6, we obtain

$$P(E_1|E_2) = P\frac{(E_1 \text{ and } E_2)}{P(E_2)} = \frac{.370}{.454} = .815,$$

the same result as before.

☞ **Remark.** By the Multiplicative Rule of Probability, if events E_1 and E_2 are independent, then $P(E_1 \text{ and } E_2) = P(E_1) \bullet P(E_2)$. Consequently, by Equation 7.6,

$$P(E_1|E_2) = P\frac{(E_1 \text{ and } E_2)}{P(E_2)} = \frac{P(E_1) \bullet P(E_2)}{P(E_2)} = P(E_1)$$

In other words, if E_1 and E_2 are independent, the probability of E_1 is the same whether or not we know that E_2 has occurred, which goes back to the definition of independence.

THE LAW OF LARGE NUMBERS

So far we have been interested in probabilities simply as a way of determining the likelihood of events when an experiment is performed once. The theory of probability is even more useful, however, when an experiment is repeated several times. This fact is illustrated by the following law, which provides the basic link between the theoretical notion of probability and the applied, empirical one. It is known as the *Law of Large Numbers*.

Law of Large Numbers. Suppose E is an event in an experiment and the probability of E is p ($P(E) = p$). If the experiment is repeated n independent and identical times (each repetition may be called a trial), then the relative frequency of E occurring in these n trials will be approximately equal to p. In general, the larger the number of trials, the better p is as an approximation of the relative frequency of E actually obtained.

☞ **Remark.** We can therefore think of p, the probability of event E, as the relative frequency with which E will occur "in the long run" (i.e., for an infinite number of trials). A value of $p = .75$ would then mean that in the long run, event E will occur 75 percent of the time. Because we never actually do any of our experiments an infinite number of times, all we can expect, as stated in the Law of Large Numbers, is for p to approximate the relative frequency of E, with the approximation generally becoming better as the number n of trials increases.

EXERCISES

Exercises 7.1–7.5 relate to the NELS data set.

7.1. Create a frequency and percent distribution table of the variable edexpect, which indicates the highest level of education the students in eighth grade expect to achieve eventually. If one student is selected at random from the *NELS* data set, what is the probability that:
   a) The student anticipates earning a bachelor's degree?
   b) The student anticipates earning a master's degree?
   c) The student anticipates earning either a bachelor's or master's degree?
   d) The student anticipates earning something other than a bachelor's degree?

7.2. Create a crosstabulation of edexpect by gender. Use it to find the following probabilities if one student is selected at random from the *NELS* data set.
   a) the student expects to earn less than a college degree.
   b) the student is female.
   c) the student expects to earn less than a college degree and is female.
   d) the student expects to earn less than a college degree or is female.
   e) the student does not expect to earn less than a college degree.
   f) the student is female given that the student expects to earn less than a college degree.
   g) the student expects to earn less than a college degree given that the student is female.
   h) the student is female given that the student does not expect to earn less than a college degree.

7.3. Use the frequency and percent distribution table you created in Exercise 7.1 to find the following probabilities. One student is selected at random from those in the *NELS* data set. This student is then replaced and a second student is selected at random. What is the probability that:

    a) The first student anticipates earning a bachelor's degree?

    b) The second student anticipates earning a master's degree?

    c) The first student anticipates earning a bachelor's degree and the second student anticipates earning a master's degree?

    d) Can you use the Multiplicative Rule of Probability to answer part c) of this exercise? Explain why or why not.

7.4. Use the frequency and percent distribution table you created in Exercise 7.1 to find the following probabilities. One student is selected at random from those in the *NELS* data set. Without replacement, a second student is selected at random. What is the probability that:

    a) The first student anticipates earning a bachelor's degree?

    b) The first student anticipates earning a bachelor's degree and the second student anticipates earning a master's degree?

    c) Can you use the Multiplicative Rule of Probability to answer part b) of this exercise? Explain why or why not.

7.5. Use the frequency and percent distribution table you created in Exercise 7.1 to find the following probabilities. One student is selected at random from those in the *NELS* data set. If this experiment is repeated 1000 times, approximately how many times of the 1000 do you expect to select:

    a) A student who anticipates earning a bachelor's degree?

    b) A student who anticipates earning a master's degree?

    c) A student who anticipates earning either a bachelor's or master's degree?

    d) A student who anticipates earning something other than a bachelor's degree?

7.6. The numbers 1–10 inclusive are written on pieces of paper and the pieces of paper are put in a bowl. If one of them is drawn at random, what is the probability that the number selected is

    a) even?

    b) odd?

    c) either even or odd?

    d) either less than 5 or even?

    e) either greater than 2 or odd?

7.7. What (if anything) is wrong with the following statement? Consider the events

E1: "Before finishing this book you will inherit $1 million"

E2: "Before finishing this book you will not inherit $1 million"

Because these two events are mutually exclusive and exhaustive (one of them must occur and both of them cannot occur at the same time),

7.8. What (if anything) is wrong with the following statement? "We are given an urn containing white and black marbles in equal numbers. It is impossible to determine the probability that one marble selected at random from this urn is white, because we do not know how many marbles there are in the urn to begin with."

7.9. In this exercise, we see that two events of the same experiment, E1 and E2, can be independent and not mutually exclusive. Suppose we toss a fair coin twice. Let E1 and E2 be defined as

E1: "The first toss is a head"

E2: "The second toss is a head"

     a) Show that E1 and E2 are *not* mutually exclusive.

     b) Show that E1 and E2 are independent of each other.

Hint for part (b): To show that E2 is independent of E1, show that the probability of E2 occurring is not influenced by whether or not E1 occurs. This can be done in three steps. First, find the probability of E2 assuming we have no information about whether E1 occurred. Second, determine the probability of E2 assuming we know that E1 has occurred. Third, determine the probability of E2 assuming we know that E1 has not occurred. Because these three values are equal, we may conclude that the occurrence or nonoccurrence of E1 has no effect on the probability of E2 and thus that E2 is independent of E1.

7.10. In this exercise, we see that two events of the same experiment, E1 and E2, can be dependent and mutually exclusive. Suppose we toss a fair coin once. If it comes up heads, we stop. If it comes up tails, we toss it again. Let E1 and E2 be defined as

E1: "The first toss is a head"

E2: "The second toss is a head"

     a) Show that E1 and E2 are mutually exclusive.

     b) Show that E1 and E2 are dependent.

7.11. In this exercise, we see that two events of the same experiment, E1 and E2, can be dependent and not mutually exclusive. Suppose we toss a fair coin once. If it comes up heads, we stop. If it comes up tails, we toss it again. Let E1 and E2 be defined as

E1: "The first toss is a tail"

E2: "The second toss is a tail"

     a) Show that E1 and E2 are not mutually exclusive.

     b) Show that E1 and E2 are dependent.

CHAPTER EIGHT

Theoretical Probability Models

A theoretical probability model is a mathematical representation of a class of experiments having certain specified characteristics in common, and from which we may derive the probabilities of outcomes of any experiment in the class. The extent to which the probabilities derived from the theoretical model are correct for a particular experiment depends on the extent to which the particular experiment possesses the characteristics required by the model. In most cases, the match between the theoretical model and a specific experiment will not be perfect, and the answer we obtain using the model will be only an approximation of the true answer. The advantage of using a theoretical model, however, is that it enables us to answer questions about all the experiments that have the specified characteristics of the model without having to treat each experiment as a completely new and unique situation. Theoretical probability models are applicable when all possible outcomes of an experiment, taken together, follow a pattern of regularity that may be described by the model. As a result, they enable us to obtain the probability of any single outcome or combination of outcomes for that experiment.

In this chapter we present two theoretical probability models that have widespread applicability; the binomial probability model and the normal probability model. The binomial probability model answers questions about a particular type of discrete variable, whereas the normal probability model answers questions about a particular type of continuous model. Of the two models, the normal is more widely used. In fact, the normal is perhaps the most widely used of all theoretical probability models.

THE BINOMIAL PROBABILITY MODEL AND DISTRIBUTION

In general, the binomial probability model applies to experiments that consist of *independent* and *identical* trials, the outcomes of which on any one trial may be thought of as *dichotomous* (as either success or failure). This dichotomy is the reason for the name *binomial*; there are two outcomes (such as head/tail, pass/fail, or absent/present).

Recall Example 7.8 (d) in which we sought the probability that exactly two of three students selected randomly with replacement from the NELS data set never smoked marijuana. Using the language of the binomial model, we define a trial as the selection of one student from the data set, and recognize that, for this example, there are three trials. As we shall see, the three trials satisfy the assumptions of the binomial probability model in that they are independent and identical and their outcomes are each dichotomous.

The trials are *independent* because each student is selected at random with replacement; knowing who is selected at one trial tells us nothing about who will be selected as subsequent trials. The trials are *identical* because each and every trial consists of selecting one student at random from the 500 students of the NELS data set. And finally, because the outcome of each trial may be categorized as either "student has smoked marijuana" or "student has never smoked marijuana," each outcome is *dichotomous*.

In Example 7.8 (d), we are interested in the probability that two of the three students never smoked marijuana. In the language of the binomial model, we may say that we are interested in the probability of obtaining two "successes" in three trials. A *success*, in this case, therefore means, *the student never smoked marijuana*.

Of course, given that there are three trials in this example, a *complete* description of the probabilities associated with each possible result would include knowing the probabilities of observing 0 successes, 1 success, 2 successes, and 3 successes in the three trials. These probabilities, obtained "by hand" using the approach of Example 7.8 (d), are given in Table 8.1 and displayed as a bar graph in Figure 8.1. Taken together, these probabilities define what is called the *binomial probability distribution* for this case. That is, the number of trials (denoted by *n*) equals 3, the probability of a success on any one trial (denoted by *p*) equals .816, and the number of successes (denoted by *k*) takes on the values 0, 1, 2, and 3, in turn. Then, the binomial probability distribution consists of the probabilities associated with each possible number of successes and is given numerically in Table 8.1 and graphically in Figure 8.1.

TABLE 8.1. Binomial probability distribution for n = 3 and p = .816

k	Probability of k successes
0	.006
1	.083
2	.368
3	.543

Notice that the probabilities associated with obtaining either 2 or 3 successes are much greater than the probabilities associated with obtaining either 0 or 1 success. In other words, this discrete distribution is skewed negatively. Can you explain why this distribution is skewed negatively? (HINT: Recall that it is quite likely [with probability .816] that a randomly selected student never smoked marijuana.)

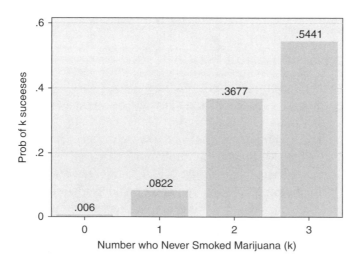

Figure 8.1   Bar graph of binomial probability distribution for n = 3 and p = .816

☞ **Remark.** In defining a complete binomial probability distribution, we need to specify the values of n and p and allow k, the number of successes, to vary from 0 (no successes) to n (all successes). If we do this, we can evaluate the probability for each possible value of k individually and construct a corresponding probability distribution and probability bar graph for the given experiment.

☞ **Remark.** Two interesting observations may be made concerning the bars in the binomial distribution bar graph of Figure 8.1. First, the probability of each of the individual events (0 students never smoked marijuana, 1 student never smoked marijuana, 2 students never smoked marijuana, 3 students never smoked marijuana) is just the height of the corresponding bar in the bar graph. Therefore, we can obtain any desired probability by summing the heights of the appropriate bars in the bar graph. But moreover, because each bar has the same width, and the sum of the areas of all the bars is 1, we can also obtain any desired probability by summing the areas of the appropriate bars in the bar graph. In general, whenever we are using a probability distribution in which the total area of the graph is 1, we can obtain the probability of any event by finding the proportion of the area under the graph corresponding to that event. Thinking of probabilities as proportions of area under the relevant probability graph (or curve) will be extremely useful in solving problems for situations in which only areas are available, such as those involving continuous, as opposed to discrete variables.

While we computed the probabilities in Table 8.1 by hand, using the approach of Example 7.8 (d), there are three other approaches we can take. Given a binomial distribution, we can use Stata's binomial probability distribution function, **binomialp(n,k,p)** to obtain the probability of obtaining k success in n trials where p equals the probability of a success on each trial, or we can use Table 3 in Appendix C, provided in the online text resources, www.cambridge.org/Stats-Stata, which summarizes the binomial probability distribution to approximate this particular binomial distribution, or we can solve Equation 8.2 directly with help from Stata. We illustrate all three approaches in Example 8.1.

● ●

EXAMPLE 8.1. Obtain the probability that exactly 2 students out of 3, who are randomly selected from the NELS data set, never smoked marijuana.

Solution Using Stata. Using the language of the binomial probability model we may rephrase this problem in terms of the probability of obtaining $k = 2$ successes in $n = 3$ trials, where a success is defined as the "student never smoked marijuana" and $p = .816$, the probability of a success on any one trial and run the command:

display binomialp(3, 2, 0.816)

The Output Window will contain the value .368, which is the probability of obtaining $k = 2$ students who smoked marijuana out of n=3 students randomly selected from the NELS dataset. This is the value we calculated by hand.

───────────────────────────────

MORE Stata: The built-in calculator: the **display** command

The **display** command, used here to calculate and display (in the Output Window) the answer to this binomial probability distribution problem, and used previously to calculate and display the standard error of the skewness statistic in Chapter 3, can be used more generally to calculate any numeric expression.

For example, if we were interested in calculating 5 x 6 + 3, we could simply type **display 5*6 + 3** in the Command Window, and the answer, 33, would appear in the Output Window. The asterisk represents multiplication in Stata, and ^ represents exponentiation. To find $(5 + 2)^2$, for example, we would type **display (5 + 2)^2** in the Command Window and the value 49 would appear in the Output Window.

MORE Stata: Finding probabilities in the binomial model and graphing them

To create list of probabilities given in Table 8.1 and the bar graph of Figure 8.1, we use the following series of Stata commands that are in the Do-file associated with Chapter 8.

```
set obs 4
gen n = _n
gen k = n-1
list n k
generate prob = binomialp(3,k,.816)
list n k prob
histogram k [fweight=int(prob*1000)], discrete ytitle("Prob of k suceeses") color(gs12)
    barwidth(.75) addlabels xtitle("Number who Never Smoked Marijuana (k)")
```

Solution Using Table 3 **in Appendix C online**, www.cambridge.org/Stats-Stata. To obtain this distribution using Table 3, we have $n = 3$, and $p = .816$. The box associated with $n = 3$ contains many columns, each representing the binomial distribution for fixed values of p. Note that the highest value of p given is $p = .5$. In our case, we have defined "success" to be "the student never smoked marijuana," and for a single randomly selected student the probability of "success" is .816. However, because the table is made to approximate distributions with $p \le .5$, we redefine "success" as "the student smoked marijuana at least once." Because the probability is .816 that the student never smoked marijuana, then 1-.816, or .184 is the probability that the student smoked marijuana at least once. Also, because $n = 3$, the event "0 students never smoked marijuana" is equivalent to the event "3 students smoked marijuana at least once."

Because there is no value of p equal to .184 exactly, we use the closest tabled value, which is $p = .20$. From the table, we see that the probability that 0 students smoked marijuana is approximately .512, that 1 student smoked marijuana is approximately .384, that 2 students smoked marijuana is approximately .096 and that 3 students smoked marijuana is approximately .008. Accordingly, the probability that 0 students never smoked marijuana is approximately .008, the probability that 1 student never smoked marijuana is .096, and so on. These values are close to the ones provided by Stata in Table 1 based on the more precise $p = .816$.

Alternatively, the individual probability also may be estimated using Table 3 in Appendix C online, www.cambridge.org/Stats-Stata, by looking up $n = 3$, $k = 1$, and $p = .20$. We use $k = 1$ because the probability that 2 students of 3 never smoked marijuana is the same as the probability that 1 student of 3 smoked marijuana at least once. The individual value is .384.

Solution Using Equation 8.2. The binomial formula, which gives the probability of obtaining k successes in n trials, where p is the probability of success and q is the probability of failure, involves notation that we have not used before. Before presenting the binomial equation itself, we provide a discussion of factorial notation and combinations.

We introduce the new notation, *factorial notation*, to help us more conveniently denote the operation of sequential multiplication. The mathematical symbol $n!$ (read "n factorial") is defined, for the positive integer n, as the ordered product of all the positive integers from 1 up to and including n: $n! = 1 \times 2 \times 3 \times \ldots \times (n-1) \times (n)$

For example, $5! = 1 \times 2 \times 3 \times 4 \times 5 = 120$.

☞ **Remark.** It would be meaningless to try to use the equation $n! = 1 \times 2 \times 3 \times \ldots \times (n-1) \times (n)$ to evaluate $0!$ Because we could not start at 1 and multiply "up to" 0, because 0 is less than 1. Because there are formulas involving factorial notation in which we may want to use this notation for all the nonnegative integers including 0, we now define the symbol $0!$ As $0! = 1$.

We also introduce combination notation. Given n objects, the number of ways in which k of these objects (k between 0 and n inclusive) can be combined, or selected, without regard to order of selection is denoted by the symbol $_nC_k$ or the symbol $\binom{n}{k}$ and is given by Equation 8.1

$$\binom{n}{k} = \frac{n!}{k!(n-k)!} \tag{8.1}$$

We can now express the binomial equation that gives the probability of obtaining k successes in n trials, where p is the probability of success and q is the probability of failure.

$$\Pr(k \text{ successes in n trials}) = \binom{n}{k} p^k q^{n-k} \tag{8.2}$$

Applying Equation 8.2 to the example at hand, we have $n = 3$, $p = .816$ and $q = 1 - .816 = .184$.

For k = 0, $\Pr(0 \text{ students ever smoked marijuana}) = \binom{3}{0}.816^0.184^3 = .006$.

For k = 1, $\Pr(1 \text{ student ever smoked marijuana}) = \binom{3}{1}.816^1.184^2 = .083$.

For k = 2, $\Pr(2 \text{ students ever smoked marijuana}) = \binom{3}{2}.816^2.184^1 = .368$.

For k = 3, $\Pr(3 \text{ students ever smoked marijuana}) = \binom{3}{3}.816^3.184^0 = .543$.

☞ **Remark.** Of course, we did not need to generate the complete distribution to answer the particular question of Example 8.1. We did so to describe how to generate an entire binomial distribution. With that knowledge in hand, we can suggest a more simple and straightforward solution to Example 8.1.

☞ **Remark.** The complete binomial distribution may be described in summary statistic form like any other distribution. Fairly simple equations are available for both the mean and the standard deviation. For the case of the binomial, these summary statistics are in terms of number of successes. The equations, presented without derivation, are:

$$Mean = np; \quad Standard\ deviation = \sqrt{npq} \tag{8.3}$$

where n = number of trials, p = probability of success on any one trial, and q = probability of failure on any one trial. Note that for Example 8.1, the mean and standard deviation of the binomial distribution equal $(3)(.816) = 2.45$ and $\sqrt{(3)(.816)(.184)} = .67$, respectively. Both Table 8.1 and Figure 8.1 indicate that these values are reasonable for this distribution. Notice that this binomial distribution is negatively skewed. Because the probability of a success, p, on any one trial is large ($p = .816$), it is unlikely that we would observe a relatively small number (near zero) of successes and likely that we would observe a relatively large number of successes. In general, when $p > .5$ the binomial distribution is skewed negatively, when $p < .5$ it is skewed positively, and when $p = .5$, it is symmetric.

THE APPLICABILITY OF THE BINOMIAL PROBABILITY MODEL

We were able to use the binomial probability model to solve the problem of Example 8.1 because, as we noted, this problem satisfied the assumptions of this model. In this section we seek to clarify the criteria an experiment must meet to be considered a binomial experiment by examining situations to which the model does and does not apply.

To review, the criteria an experiment must meet to be considered a binomial experiment are:

1. The experiment consists of n identical trials ($n \geq 1$).
2. The trials are independent of each other.
3. On each trial, the outcomes can be thought of in a dichotomous manner as Success and Failure, so that the two events Success and Failure are mutually exclusive (cannot both happen at the same time) and exhaustive (each trial must result in either a Success or a Failure).
4. If Pr(Success) = p and Pr(Failure) = q, then p and q do not change their values from trial to trial, and (by criterion 3) $p + q = 1$ on each trial.

EXAMPLE 8.2. Does the binomial model apply to the following situation: In randomly sampling with replacement ten students from the NELS data set, what is the probability that 5 are from the Northeast, 3 from the South, 1 from the West, and 1 from the North Central regions?

Solution. No, the binomial model does not apply to this situation because the outcomes of the experiment on any one trial are not dichotomous. In particular, four events are specified on each trial: obtaining a student from the Northeast, obtaining a student from the South, obtaining a student from the West, and obtaining a student from the North Central region.

EXAMPLE 8.3. Does the binomial model apply to the following situation: In randomly sampling with replacement ten students from the NELS data set, what is the probability that 5 are from the Northeast, and 5 from the South?

Solution. No, the binomial model does not apply to this situation. Although only two events are specified on each trial, the sum of the probabilities, p and q, for these two events does not equal 1.00. The probability, p, of obtaining a student from the Northeast is $106/500 = .21$ and the probability, q, of obtaining a student from the South is $150/500 = .30$. Therefore, $p + q = .51$, not 1.00. The reason $p + q$ is not equal to 1 in this example is that the events "the student is from the Northeast" and "the student is from the South" are not exhaustive. That is, it is possible for an outcome of a trial to be neither a student from the Northeast nor a student from the South; for example, the student could be from the West.

• •

EXAMPLE 8.4. Does the binomial model apply to the following situation: Ten students are randomly selected from the NELS data set *without* replacement. What is the probability that exactly ten students are from the South?

Solution. No. The binomial model does not apply to this situation because by sampling without replacement, we caused the values of p and q to change from one trial to the next. On the first trial, the probability, p, that the student is from the South is $150/500$ or $.30$ and the probability, q, that the student is not from the South is $350/500$ or $.70$. On the second trial, however, the probabilities of p and q depend on the outcome of the first trial. If, on the first trial, the student selected is from the South, then on the second trial, the probability of selecting a student from the South is $149/499$ or $.299$. On the other hand, if, on the first trial, the student selected is not from the South, then on the second trial, the probability of selecting a student from the South is $150/499$ or $.301$. In either case, the values of p and q will have changed from the first trial to the second (and will continue to change in each subsequent trial). Because p and q change from one trial to the next, these trials may not be considered to be either identical or independent.

• •

EXAMPLE 8.5. Does the binomial model apply to the following situation: Ten students are randomly selected from the NELS data set *with* replacement. What is the probability that exactly five students are from the South?

Solution. Yes! The binomial model does apply to this situation. Because we are explicitly interested in obtaining students from the South, we can define Success as "selecting a student from the South" and Failure as "not selecting a student from the South." In each trial, the probability of Success is $.30$, whereas the probability of Failure is $.70$ and p and q do not change from trial to trial. Because the events defined as Success and Failure are mutually exclusive and exhaustive, $p + q = 1.00$.

Given that this example satisfies the binomial probability model, let's find the answer to the question posed using Stata, approximate it using Table 3 in Appendix C online, www.cambridge.org/Stats-Stata, and calculate it using Equation 8.2.

MORE Stata: The binomial probability distribution function, **binomialp**

We use the following to obtain the binomial probability when n = 10, k = 5, and p = .30.

display binomialp(10, 5, .30)

We obtain as our answer, prob = .103.

Using Table 3, we look up $n = 10$, $k = 5$, and $p = .30$. We find that the probability is .1029 or .103 when rounded to three decimal places.

Computing the probability directly from Equation 8.2, by solving,

$$\Pr(5 \text{ successes in 10 trials}) = \binom{10}{5}.30^5.70^5,$$

with the help of Stata's built-in calculator, **display.** In particular, we multiply $(.30^5) * (.70)^5$ by the number of combinations of taking n = 10 things k = 5 at a time, $(1*2*3*4*5*6*7*8*9*10)/(1*2*3*4*5*1*2*3*4*5)$ as follows:
display ((1*2*3*4*5*6*7*8*9*10)/ (1*2*3*4*5*1*2*3*4*5))* (.30^5)*(.70)^5

MORE Stata: The combinations routine **comb(n,k)**

To find the number of combinations of *n* =10 things taken *k* = 5 at a time, we can, more simply, make use of the combinations routine, **comb(n,k).**

display comb(10,5) * (.30^5)*(.70)^5

As before, the probability of obtaining five students from the South in a sample of ten students randomly selected with replacement from the NELS data set is found to be .103.

By the Law of Large Numbers we may interpret this result to mean that if we repeated this experiment 1,000 times, then our sample of ten will contain exactly five students from the South approximately 103 times.

Following are some other examples to which the binomial model applies that do not rely on the *NELS* data set.

• •
EXAMPLE 8.6. Jill is taking a 10-question multiple-choice examination on which there are four possible answers to each question. Assuming that Jill just *guesses* the answer to each question, what is the probability of her getting exactly four of the questions correct?

Solution. Let Success on each question (or trial) be "getting the correct answer" and Failure be "getting an incorrect answer." Because these two events are mutually exclusive and exhaustive on each trial, and because Jill is *guessing* on each question, so that $p = 1/4$ and $q = 3/4$ (there are four possible answers to each question and only one of them is correct), the binomial model is applicable to this situation ($k = 4$, $n = 10$, $p = .25$).

Using Stata's **binomialp(n,k,p)** function, we obtain Pr(4 successes in 10 trials) = .1460.
    display binomialp(10,4,.25)
    Using Table 3 in Appendix C online, www.cambridge.org/Stats-Stata, we find also that the probability is .1460.
    Computing the probability directly from Equation 8.2,

$$\Pr(4 \text{ successes in 10 trials}) = \binom{10}{4}.25^4.75^6,$$

using **display comb(10,4)*(.25^4)*(.75^6),** we obtain prob = .1460.
    By the Law of Large Numbers, we can interpret this result in the following way: If a large number of people take this 10-question exam and guess on each of the questions,

we can expect approximately 15 percent of them to get exactly 4 of the 10 questions correct.

● ●

EXAMPLE 8.7. Erie Pharmaceutical Company manufactures a drug for treatment of a specific type of ear infection. They claim that the drug has probability .40 of curing people who suffer from this ailment. Assuming their claim to be true, if the treatment is applied to 50 people suffering from this ailment, what is the probability that exactly 25 of these 50 people will be cured?

Solution. If we consider the treatment of each person with this ailment to be a trial, we can define Success and Failure on each trial as "the person's ailment is cured" and "the person's ailment is not cured," respectively. These two events are mutually exclusive and exhaustive for each trial (each person being treated). Because the claim is that the long-run probability of this treatment working is .40 (and we are accepting this claim as true), we can take this value as the probability of success on each trial. Therefore, the binomial probability model is applicable to this situation ($k = 25$, $n = 50$, $p = .40$).

Using Stata, we run the command **display binomialp(50,25,.40)** to find that Pr(25 successes in 50 trials) = .0405.

Because the maximum value of n given in Table 3 is 20, we cannot use Table 3 to find a solution to this problem. For those interested, an alternative approach is discussed in Exercise 8.27 using the normal distribution to approximate the binomial.

Computing the probability directly from Equation 8.2,

$$\text{Pr(25 successes in 50 trials)} = \binom{50}{25}.4^{25}.6^{25} = .0405.$$

using **display comb(50, 25)*(.4^25)*(.6^25),** we obtain prob = .0405.

By the Law of Large Numbers, we may say that if the Company's claim is true, and a large number of groups of 50 people are each treated with this drug, then we should expect to see exactly 25 people cured in approximately 4 percent of these groups.

● ●

EXAMPLE 8.8. Using the same situation as in Example 8.7, what is the probability of obtaining:

(a) at most 15 Successes (cures)?
(b) at least 20 Successes (cures)?

Solution. As we saw in Example 8.7, the binomial model is applicable to this situation with $n = 50$, and $p = .40$.

a. "At most 15 Successes" is the same as "15 or fewer Successes" and can be expressed as $k \leq 15$. The answer may be obtained directly using the cumulative binomial probability distribution function available in Stata.

MORE Stata: The cumulative binomial probability function

Given the binomial probability distribution, we may find the probability that the number of successes *is less than or equal to* some value, say k by using Stata's cumulative binomial probability function:

display binomial(n, k, p)

replacing **n** with the value equal to the number of trials, **k** with the value equal to the number of successes, and **p** with the value equal to the probability of a success on each trial.

For this problem, we use the command **display binomial(50, 15, .40)**, to obtain Prob = .0955.

By the Law of Large Numbers, we may say that if a large number of groups of 50 people each are treated with this drug, we should expect to see at most 15 people cured in approximately 10 percent of these groups.

b. "At least 20 Successes" is the same as "20 or more Successes" and can be expressed as $k \geq 20$.

MORE Stata: The complement of the cumulative binomial probability function

Given the binomial probability distribution, we may find the probability that the number of successes *is greater than or equal to* some value, say *k*, by using **binomialtail**.

display binomialtail(n, k, p)

where n = the number of trials; k = the number of successes; and p = the probability of a success on each trial.

To find the probability that *at least* 20 of the 50 people will be cured we use the following command:

display binomialtail (50, 20,.40)

and obtain the value .5535.

By the Law of Large Numbers, we may say that if a large number of groups of 50 people are each treated with this drug, then we should expect to see at least 20 people cured in approximately 55 percent of these groups.

In summary, in a binomial experiment with n trials, where p equals the probability of a success on each trial,

To find the probability of exactly k successes, we use the command **display** along with Stata's **binomialp** function: **display binomialp(n,k,p)**

To find the probability of at most k successes (which equals the probability of k or fewer successes), we use the command **display** along with Stata's cumulative binomial function, **binomial**: **display binomial(n, k, p)**

To find the probability of at least k successes (which equals the probability of k or more successes), we use the command **display** along with Stata's **binomialtail** function:

display binomialtail(n, k, p)

THE NORMAL PROBABILITY MODEL AND DISTRIBUTION

The importance of the normal probability model lies in the fact that in the real world many traits – such as height, weight, IQ scores, and the like – have relative frequency curves that are closely approximated by this model. Moreover, as we shall see, throughout the course of this book, many problems in mathematical statistics either are solved, or can be solved, by using the normal probability model or a probability model based on the normal.

The normal probability model was developed by one of the greatest mathematicians of all time, Johann Friedrich Carl Gauss (1777–1855). Most mathematicians of Gauss' period were interested in applying mathematics to real-world problems, such as astronomy and navigation. Knowing that data obtained through observation and measurement contained errors due to the imprecision of the measuring instruments employed, Gauss studied many different sets of such data and noticed that they all possessed certain common characteristics. In general, each set of observations was symmetric about some central value and the farther from this central value, the fewer and fewer such observations there were. Based on such studies, Gauss was able to develop a mathematical model that could be used to describe the distribution of errors contained in these sets of data. Gauss called the mathematical model *the normal probability model*, and the distribution of errors the normal probability distribution.

We will use the normal probability model descriptively, to describe real variables. Further, we will use it when we introduce inferential statistics, to describe the sampling distribution of the mean when the standard deviation of the population is known.

Although the normal probability model is given by a mathematical equation, we will not present that equation here. Instead, we will list three characteristics of the distributions described by the normal probability model. The model is used to find the probabilities of certain score ranges by finding the corresponding areas under the normal curve.

1. A normal distribution is symmetric about its mean, $\overline{X}$.
2. A normal distribution extends indefinitely to the right and to the left of the mean, always getting closer and closer to the horizontal axis but never quite reaching it. (That is, observations that are farther from the mean have smaller relative frequencies than observations that are closer to the mean.)
3. The total area under the normal distribution is 1. By symmetry, this means that one-half of the area is to the right of the mean and one-half is to the left.

In general, all normal distributions have the same bell-shape appearance, and differ from each other only in their particular mean and standard deviation values. The mean indicates where the distribution is located on the horizontal axis, whereas the standard deviation indicates the extent to which the scores tend to cluster about the mean. Figure 8.2 shows a general normal distribution curve with mean $\overline{X}$ and standard deviation S, and indicates what proportion of the distribution can be expected to lie within one and two standard deviations of the mean.

MORE Stata: To create the graph of the standard normal distribution of Figure 8.2:

twoway function y=normalden(x), range(-4.0 4.0) xtitle("{it: z-scores}") ytitle("Density") title("Standard Normal Distribution")

More details about this command may be found in the Do-file associated with Chapter 8.

The normal probability model describes the entire family of normal probability distributions, each with its own mean and standard deviation. The particular normal distribution with mean 0 and standard deviation 1 is called the *standard normal distribution*.

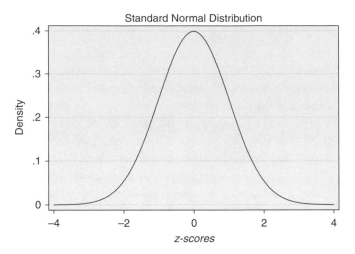

Figure 8.2   The Standard Normal Distribution

The family of normal probability distributions may be used to answer probability questions about sets of data that are either known, or assumed, to be normally distributed. In general probabilities can be obtained as proportions of area under the appropriate normal curve.

Because the probabilities are found as areas, all probability values in the continuous case are between 0 and 1 inclusive.

The probability that a single randomly selected score will be lower than a particular score, x, is found by calculating the area under the normal distribution curve to the left of x. The probability that a single randomly selected score will be higher than a particular score, x, is found by calculating the area under the normal distribution curve to the right of x.

Alternatively, by the Complement Rule, the probability that a single score selected at random from a normal distribution is higher than the score x may be calculated as 1 – the probability that the score selected is lower than the score x.

Because the normal distribution is symmetric, with area under the curve equal to 1, the probability that a single randomly selected score is above the mean equals .5 and the probability that the score is below the mean equals .5.

Because the distribution is continuous rather than discrete, the probability that a randomly selected score will have a particular value is 0. As a result, the probability that a single randomly selected score is greater than a particular value, x, is the same as the probability that the single randomly selected score is greater than or equal to x.

We illustrate finding probabilities under the normal curve using Stata and Table 8.1 which contains areas under the standard normal curve.

Recall the histogram of the ses distribution from the *NELS* dataset illustrated in Chapter 2 as Figure 2.6 and reproduced here as Figure 8.3. You will note that in Figure 8.3 a normal curve is superimposed on the histogram.

MORE Stata: To create the ses histogram of Figure 8.3 with normal curve overlay:

histogram ses, normal color(gs10) ytitle("Density")

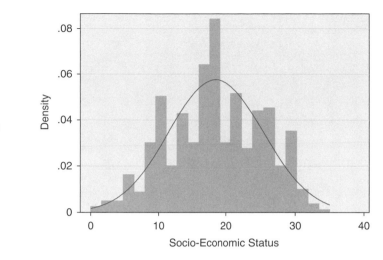

Figure 8.3 Ses distribution with normal curve overlay

While the ses distribution is not normally distributed, it may be considered to be approximately so with mean 18.40 and standard deviation 6.92 and we may use the normal probability distribution to estimate areas under the ses curve.

. . . .

EXAMPLE 8.9. Use the normal distribution with mean 18.40 and standard deviation 6.92 to approximate the proportion of students in the NELS data set with SES values *less than or equal to* 26.

Solution Using Stata. To find the area under the normal curve to the left of $X = 26$ (see Figure 8.4), we use the following cumulative distribution function command:

display normal(*z*)

where z is replaced with either the z-score value itself or the expression for computing the z-score value given by Equation 4.2,

$$z = \frac{X - \bar{X}}{S_X}.$$

For this problem, we simply would use the following command,

display normal((26 − 18.40)/6.92)

to obtain the result .86 in the Output Window:

This result means that the area under this normal curve to the left of the value of 26 equals .86, or that, if you were to randomly select a score from a normal distribution with mean 18.4 and standard deviation 6.92, the probability is .86 that it would fall below the value of 26.

In the context of our example, this means that approximately 86 percent of the individuals in our *NELS* data set have ses scores at or below the value 26.

Of course, rather than include the expression for the calculation of the z-score within the parentheses following the word normal, as we have done in this example, we first could have calculated the z-score using the following command,

display (26 − 18.40)/6.92

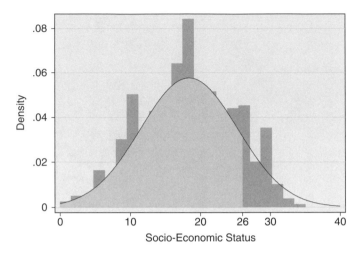

Figure 8.4 The area under the normal curve with $\overline{X} = 18.40$ and $s = 6.92$ to the left of 26.

to obtain the result that $z = 1.10$ and then used:

display normal(1.10)

MORE Stata: To plot a histogram with a shaded normal curve overlay as in Figure 8.4

graph twoway histogram ses, color(gs10) || function y=normalden(x,18.40,6.92), range (040) || functiony=normalden(x,18.40,6.92),range(026)recast(area)color(gs12)xlabel (0 10 20 26 30 40) legend(off) xtitle("Socio-Economic Status") ytitle("Density")

Solution Using Table 1 **in Appendix C** online, www.cambridge.org/Stats-Stata. To use Table 1 to find the proportion of students in the *NELS* data set with SES values less than or equal to 26 in a distribution with mean 18.40 and standard deviation 6.92, we also would first need to convert the value 26 to a z-score using Equation 4.3. We need to do so because Table 1 only gives areas under the standard normal curve with mean 0 and standard deviation 1.

$$z = \frac{X - \overline{X}}{S_X} = \frac{26 - 18.40}{6.92} = 1.10$$

This z-score may be decomposed as 1.1 + .00. According to Table 1, the area to the right of this z-score is .1357. To find the area to the left of the z-score, we use the complement rule and compute 1 – .1357 = .8643, which is the proportion we seek.

We may see how far this estimate departs from the actual percentage of cases at or below an SES score of 26 to assess the accuracy of our approximation. To do so, we may use Stata to find the percentile rank of the value 26, estimated from the cumulative percent column (labeled Cum.), the cumulative percent of scores at or below a score of 26 is 85.6, suggesting that the approximation using the normal curve is a good one in this case.

☞ **Remark.** Because ses is a continuous variable, when we ask about the proportion of cases at or below an ses value of 26, it is equivalent to ask about the proportion of cases

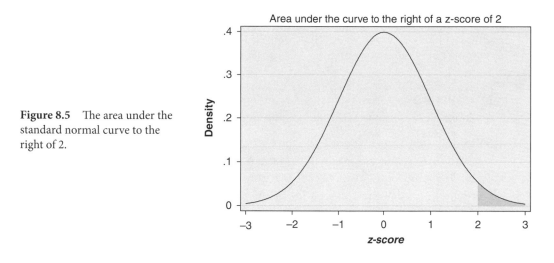

Figure 8.5 The area under the standard normal curve to the right of 2.

below an ses value of 26. This is because, for truly continuous variables, the value of exactly 26 has zero probability of occurring.

In inferential statistics, for reasons that will become clear in the next chapter, we focus on the upper and lower tails of a probability distribution, as opposed to its mid area. Hence, the next example has as its focus the area in the right tail of a normal distribution.

• •

EXAMPLE 8.10. Determine how likely it is to select a value at random from a set of scores known to be normally distributed that is 2 or more standard deviations above the mean.

Solution Using Stata. This is equivalent to finding the area under the normal curve to the right of a z-score of 2. This area is shaded in Figure 8.5. Although we will use the same Stata cumulative distribution function (**normal()**) as before, because we now want the area to the *right* of the z-score and the **normal** function gives us areas to the left, we use the Complement Rule to find the area we want. We run the following command:

display normal(2)

to obtain the probability value .977

And, then, subtract this probability value from 1 using the following command

display 1 − .977

to obtain the probability value we seek. The area to the right of a z-score of 2 is .023.

MORE Stata: To plot a normal curve with shading as in Figure 8.5:

twoway function y = normalden(x, 0, 1), range(2 3) recast(area) color(gs12) | | function y = normalden(x, 0, 1), range(−3 3) lcolor(black) xtitle("{it: z-score}") ytitle("Density") title("Area under the curve to the right of a z-score of 2") legend(off) xlabel(−3 −2 −1 0 1 2 3)

Solution Using Table 1 **in Appendix C online**, www.cambridge.org/Stats-Stata**.** To use Table 1 to find the area under the standard normal curve to the right of z = 2.00, we decompose 2.00 as 2.0 plus .00 and find the area under the curve to the right of this value to be .0228.

That is, the probability is only .023 of randomly selecting a score from a normal distribution that is 2 or more standard deviations above the mean. Said differently, only 2.3 percent of scores fall in this range.

• •

EXAMPLE 8.11. Assuming that SES has a normal distribution with mean 18.4 and standard deviation 6.92, find the SES value that has an area of .025 to its right.

Solution Using Stata. In contrast to the two earlier problems wherein we sought an area corresponding to a given score, in this problem we seek a score corresponding to a given area. To do so, we make use of Stata's inverse normal probability function as shown below. In this command, *p* represents the area under the curve to the left and the output from this command provides the z-score corresponding to this area.

display invnormal(*p*)

In our example, we want the score that marks off .025 of the area to its right, which is equivalent to the score that marks off .975 of the area to its left. Accordingly, we run this command with p = .975, as follows:

display invnormal(.975)

to obtain the following result in the Output Window: 1.96

We see from this result that the z-score that marks off .975 of the area under a normal curve to its left (or equivalently .025 of the area to its right) is approximately 1.96.

To convert the z-score of 1.96 into a value within the SES metric, we use Equation 4.4 ($X = Sz + \overline{X}$) and the built-in Stata calculator and type the following:

display 6.92*1.96+ 18.40

The SES score we obtain in the Output Window is 31.96:

This result tells us that under the normally distributed SES curve, .025 of the area falls to the right of an SES value equal to 31.96.

Solution Using Table 1 **in Appendix C online**, www.cambridge.org/Stats-Stata. To use Table 1 to find the z-score that has an area of .025 to its right under the standard normal curve, we look for .0250 in the body of the table and see what its corresponding z-score is. We find .0250 in the row labeled 1.9 and column labeled .06. Accordingly, the z-score we seek is 1.9 plus .06 = 1.96, and convert to a score within the SES metric as before.

• •

EXAMPLE 8.12. Find the left-tailed area corresponding to a z-score of −2.45.

Solution Using Stata. We use the following **display normal(−2.45)** and obtain .0071 as the result.

Solution Using Table 1 **in Appendix C online**, www.cambridge.org/Stats-Stata. To use Table 1 to find the area to the left of z= −2.45, we use symmetry to see that it is the same as the right-tailed area for z = 2.45. The right-tailed area corresponding to z = 2.45 is .0071. Thus, the left-tailed area corresponding to z = −2.45 equals .0071.

USING THE NORMAL DISTRIBUTION TO APPROXIMATE THE BINOMIAL DISTRIBUTION

As n, the number of trials in a binomial experiment increases, the binomial distribution more closely resembles, or approaches, the normal distribution. In fact, as long as both products np and nq are greater than or equal to 5, the approximation of the binomial by the normal is quite good. The values p and q, in addition to n, are important as conditions for this approximation because a larger value of n is needed to compensate for the skewness introduced whenever $p \neq q$. Exercise 8.28 illustrates how to compute an approximation of a binomial probability using the normal distribution.

SUMMARY OF CHAPTER 8 STATA COMMANDS

For a complete listing of all Stata commands associated with this chapter, you may access the Do-file for Chapter 8 located on the text website.

Create	Command Lines
Calculate the probability of obtaining $k = 2$ successes in $n = 3$ trials, with the probability of success, $p = .816$ (Example 8.1)	**display binomialp(3, 2, 0.816)**
Calculate the probabilities of obtaining all possible number of in $n = 3$ trials, with the probability of success, $p = .816$ and create the associated bar graph (Table 8.1 and Figure 8.1)	**set obs 4** **gen n = _n** **gen k = n−1** **list n k** **generate prob = binomialp(3,k,.816)** **list n k prob** **histogram k [fweight=int(prob*1000)], discrete ytitle("Prob of k suceeses") color(gs12) barwidth(.75) addlabels xtitle("Number who Never Smoked Marijuana (k)")**
Calculate the number of combinations of $n = 10$ things taken $k = 5$ at a time (Example 8.5)	**display comb(10,5) * (.30^5)*(.70)^5**
Calculate the probability of at most $k = 15$ successes in $n = 50$ trials, with the probability of success, $p = .40$ (Example 8.8)	**display binomial(50, 15, .40),**
Plot the graph of the standard normal distribution (Figure 8.2)	**twoway function y=normalden(x), range(−4.0 4.0) xtitle("{it: z-scores}") ytitle("Density") title("Standard Normal Distribution")**
Create the histogram of ses with normal curve overlay (Figure 8.3)	**histogram ses, normal color(gs10) ytitle("Density")**

Create	Command Lines
Calculate the area under the normal curve with mean 18.40 and standard deviation 6.92 to the left of 26 (Example 8.9)	**display normal((26 − 18.40)/6.92)**
Plot the histogram of ses with shaded normal curve overlay (Figure 8.4)	**graph twoway histogram ses, color(gs10) ∥function y=normalden(x,18.40,6.92), range(0 40) ∥ function y=normalden(x,18.40,6.92), range(0 26) recast(area) color(gs12) xlabel(0 10 20 26 30 40) legend(off) xtitle("Socio-Economic Status") ytitle("Density")**
Plot a normal curve with shading to the right of $z = 2$ (Figure 8.5)	**twoway function y=normalden(x, 0, 1), range(2 3) recast(area) color(gs12) ∥ function y=normalden (x, 0, 1), range(−3 3) lcolor(black) xtitle("{it: z-score}") ytitle("Density") title("Area under the curve to the right of a z-score of 2") legend(off) xlabel(−3 −2 −1 0 1 2 3)**
Calculate the area under the standard normal curve to the left of $z = 2$ (Example 8.10)	**display normal(2)**
Calculate the z-score with area .975 below it (Example 8.11)	**display invnormal(.975)**

EXERCISES

*Create a .do file for each exercise that requires the use of Stata. Run the commands from the. do file by highlighting them and hitting **Control+d**. Save each .do file using a name associated with the Exercise for which it was created. It is recommended that you review the Do-file for* Chapter 8 *located on the textbook's website before completing these exercises. To facilitate doing each exercise, it may be helpful to copy and paste relevant commands from the Do-file for* Chapter 8 *into your own Do-file and modify them as needed.*

Exercises 8.1–8.13 involve the binomial probability model. In Exercises 8.1–8.8 inclusive, decide whether the given problem satisfies the conditions of a binomial experiment. Only if it does, solve the exercise.

8.1. A person taking a 15-item true/false examination has studied the material to be covered on the exam. What is the probability that this person will get exactly 10 of the 15 items correct?

8.2. A new drug is being tested, and the results of treatment with this drug are being categorized as full recovery, partial recovery, and additional treatment required. The probabilities of these three possible outcomes are 1/3, 1/3, and 1/3, respectively. If this drug is used on 100 patients, what is the probability that exactly 40 of the patients will have full recovery, 20 will have partial recovery, and 40 will need further treatment?

8.3. It is known that the toys produced by a certain toy manufacturer have a 1-in-10 chance of containing imperfections. What is the probability that in a day's production of 500 of these toys, exactly 50 will have imperfections?

8.4. Suppose giving birth to a girl and giving birth to a boy are equally likely, and Mrs. Fecund is due to give birth to triplets. What is the probability that exactly one of the three children born will be a girl?

8.5. A 10-item multiple-choice test is given with four possible answers on each item. If a student guesses on each item, what is the probability that she will get
  a) none of the 10 items correct?
  b) exactly 3 of the 10 items correct?
  c) all of the 10 items correct?
  d) at least 8 of the 10 items correct?
  e) at most 4 of the 10 items correct?
  f) between 2 and 5 of the 10 items (inclusive) correct?

8.6. Use the frequency and percent distribution table provided in Exercise 7.1 to find the probability that if 10 schools are selected at random from this data set with replacement that exactly 5 are from the Northeast.

8.7. Suppose that a certain automobile manufacturing company has a problem installing airbags. Usually, these are installed correctly 95% of the time. However, on Friday afternoons, these are installed correctly only 90% of the time. Assuming that the company manufactures 1,000 cars per week, what is the probability that exactly 950 of these will have correctly installed airbags?

8.8. Women over 50 are advised to get a mammogram every year, so there is a need to be aware of the prevalence of false positive results. A false-positive is defined as a mammogram that is interpreted as indicative of cancer, indeterminate, or prompts recommendations for additional tests in a woman who is not diagnosed with breast cancer within a year. Assuming that the risk of a false positive result is constant from year to year, the probability of a false positive result from a single mammogram is $p = .0653$. Given that, find the probability of at least one false positive result in 10 mammograms. The information in this exercise is based on Elmore (1998).

*Exercise 8.9 requires the use of Stata, the NELS data set and the binomial distribution. As in previous chapters, create a.do file for each Exercise that requires the use of Stata. Run the commands from the.do file by highlighting them and hitting **Control+d**. Save each.do file using a name associated with the Exercise for which it was created.*

8.9. If one student is selected at random from the NELS data set, use the variable URBAN to determine the probability that:
  a) The student is from an urban environment.
  b) The student is from a suburban environment.
  c) The student is not from a rural environment.
  d) The student is from a rural or a suburban environment.

If five students are selected at random with replacement from the NELS data set, determine the probability that:
  e) At most 3 of them are from urban environments.

   f) Exactly 3 of them are from urban environments.
   g) At least 3 of them are from urban environments.
   h) No more than 3 of them are from urban environments.

8.10. An individual tosses a fair coin 10 times. Find the probability of getting:
   a) Heads on the first five tosses and tails on the second five tosses.
   b) Five heads and five tails in any order.

8.11. Suppose you are going to toss a fair coin three times and want to determine the probability of obtaining exactly two heads in the three tosses. Why do the following two methods of solving this problem give different answers?

Solution 1. In terms of numbers of heads obtained, the possible outcomes of the experiment are

    0 heads   1 head   2 heads   3 heads

Because only one of the four outcomes listed satisfies the given condition (2 heads), the probability of this even is $1/4 = .25$.

Solution 2. In terms of the way each toss comes out, the possible outcomes of the experiment are

    HHH   HTH   HTT   TTH
    HHT   THH   THT   TTT

Because three of the eight outcomes listed satisfy the given condition (HHT, HTH, THH), the probability of this event is $3/8 = .375$.

8.12. Is the following statement true or false? "By the Law of Large Numbers, you are much more likely to obtain 5 heads in 10 tosses of a fair coin than to obtain 2 heads in 4 tosses of a fair coin."

8.13. Given a binomial experiment with $n = 6$ and $p = .5$:
   a) Determine the probability distribution for this experiment
   b) Construct the corresponding probability bar graph and describe the shape of the distribution.
   c) Use Equation 8.3 to find the mean and the standard deviation of the binomial distribution.

Exercises 8.14–8.18 involve the standard normal probability model.

8.14. If a single score is selected at random from a standard normal distribution, find the probability that:
   a) The score is above $z = 1.36$.
   b) The score is above $z = -2.08$.
   c) The score is below $z = 1.36$.
   d) The score is below $z = -2.08$.
   e) The score is between $z = -2.08$ and $z = 1.36$.
   f) The score is between $z = .40$ and $z = 1.36$.
   g) The score is between $z = -.40$ and $z = -1.36$.
   h) The score is less than $z = -.40$ or greater than $z = .40$.

8.15. If a single score is selected at random from a standard normal distribution,

a) What is the value of the score, z, such that the probability of selecting a score greater than or equal to z is approximately 30 percent?

b) What is the value of the score, z, such that the probability of selecting a score greater than or equal to z is approximately 65 percent?

c) What is the value of the score, z, such that the probability of selecting a score less than or equal to z is approximately 30 percent?

d) What is the value of the score, z, such that the probability of selecting a score less than or equal to z is approximately 65 percent?

8.16. If a distribution is normally distributed, what proportion of the scores fall:

a) at least two standard deviations below the mean?

b) at least two standard deviations above the mean?

c) at least two standard deviations away from the mean?

d) Between $z = -2$ and $z = 2$?

8.17. Find the area under the standard normal curve and

a) to the right of $z = 2.15$

b) more extreme than $z - \perp.85$, that is, more than .85 standard deviations away from the mean

c) to the left of $z = -1.63$

d) to the left of $z = 1.3$

8.18. Find the following z-scores.

a) What z-score on the standard normal curve has an area of .1151 to its right?

b) What z-score on the standard normal curve has an area of .6446 to its right?

c) What z-score on the standard normal curve has an area of .3372 to its left?

Exercises 8.19–8.31 involve the use of the normal probability model. In some cases, we assume a normal distribution and find probabilities related to that distribution. In other cases, we look to see the extent to which the normal distribution gives a good approximation to the distribution of the observed data

8.19. If a single score is selected at random from a normal distribution with mean 50 and standard deviation 10, find the probability that:

a) The score is above 70.

b) The score is above 40.

c) The score is below 70.

d) The score is below 40.

e) The score is between 40 and 70.

f) The score is between 60 and 70.

g) The score is between 30 and 40.

h) The score is 10 or more points away from the mean.

8.20. If a single score is selected at random from a normal distribution with mean 50 and standard deviation 10,

a) What is the value of the score, X, such that the probability of selecting a score greater than or equal to X is 10 percent?

b) What is the value of the score, X, such that the probability of selecting a score greater than or equal to X is 90 percent?

     c) What is the value of the score, X, such that the probability of selecting a score less than or equal to X is 90 percent?

     d) What is the value of the score, X, such that the probability of selecting a score less than or equal to X is 10 percent?

8.21. Suppose a distribution is normally distributed with mean 75 and standard deviation 10.

     a) What is the value of the score, X, such that the probability of selecting a score less than or equal to X is 5 percent?

     b) What is the value of the score, X, such that the probability of selecting a score greater than or equal to X is 5 percent?

     c) If a single score is selected at random from the distribution, what is the probability that the score falls above 90?

     d) If a single score is selected at random from the distribution, what is the probability that the score falls at 90 or above?

     e) If a single score is selected at random from the distribution, what is the probability that the score falls between 70 and 80?

     f) If a single score is selected at random from the distribution, what is the probability that the score falls below 50?

     g) If a single score is selected at random from the distribution, what is the probability that the score falls between 70 and 90?

8.22. Find the z-score that has the following percentages of area under the standard normal curve contained between $-z$ and z.

     a) 90 percent

     b) 95 percent

     c) 99 percent

8.23. Given a set of scores that is normally distributed with mean 90 and standard deviation 8, what proportion of individuals will score:

     a) Between 92 and 96 inclusive?

     b) At least 94?

     c) At most 98?

8.24. One way to qualify to join Mensa, a high IQ society, is to score in the top 2 percent on a standardized IQ test such as the Wechsler Adult Intelligence Scales Full Scale IQ Test. The scores on the Full Scale IQ test are normally distributed and standardized to have a mean of 100 and a standard deviation of 15. What score is necessary on this test to qualify for Mensa?

8.25. Suppose the distribution of maximum daily temperatures for a 1,000-day period in a certain tropical area is normal in shape with a mean of 87 degrees Fahrenheit and a standard deviation of 3 degrees Fahrenheit.

     a) How many of these days had maximum daily temperatures above 80 degrees Fahrenheit?

     b) What would be the percentile rank in this distribution for a day that had a maximum temperature of 80 degrees Fahrenheit?

8.26. Suppose you are told that 1,000 scores from a nationally administered achievement test are normally distributed with mean 50 and standard deviation 5.

     a) How many people would you expect to score greater than 57?

b) What is the percentile rank of a score of 52?

c) What raw score would you expect 10 percent of the scores to fall above?

8.27. Suppose you are told that the distribution of weights for all 12-month-old males in the United States is normally distributed with a mean of 18 pounds and a standard deviation of 3 pounds. If your son is 12 months old and weighs 22.5 pounds:

a) What proportion of the 12-month-old male population weighs less than your son?

b) What is your son's percentile rank relative to this population?

Exercises 8.28–8.30 involve the NELS data set and require the use of Stata.

8.28. Use the normal distribution to approximate the percentage of students in the NELS data set with eighth grade math achievement scores less than or equal to 72. Then, find the actual percentile rank of 72. How do these two values compare and what does this comparison suggest about the appropriateness of using the normal curve to approximate the distribution of eighth grade math achievement scores?

8.29. Use the normal distribution to approximate the number of students in the NELS data set with eighth grade math achievement scores (ACHMAT08) that are within one standard deviation of the mean. How does the estimate based on the normal probability model compare to the actual number of scores in the NELS data set that are so extreme?

8.30. While some distributions of observed data, especially those based on the sum or average of many items, are approximately normal, others are not. In this exercise, we look at an instance where the normal distribution does not give a good approximation of a distribution. Use the normal distribution to approximate the number of students in the NELS coming from a school in which 6 or more AP classes are offered (apoffer). Compare the estimate based on normal distribution to the actual number of students coming from a school in which 6 or more AP classes are offered. Speculate on the reason for the discrepancy.

Exercise 8.31 involves the Impeach data set and requires the use of Stata.

8.31. Consider the variable supportc which gives the distribution of the percentages of the voter support for Clinton. Unless otherwise specified, use the *normal curve* to approximate the distribution of supportc in order to answer the following questions.

a) Create a histogram with a normal curve overlay of the variable supportc. Describe the shape of the distribution.

b) What supportc score has $z = 1.3$?

c) If supportc = 35 percent what is z?

d) Use the normal curve to estimate the proportion of states with voter support for Clinton at or below 35 percent.

e) Use a frequency distribution table to find the actual proportion of states with voter support for Clinton at or below 35 percent.

f) What is the approximate percentile rank of a score of 35 percent in supportc?

g) What proportion or percent of senators score above supportc = 55 percent for their states?

h) What proportion or percent of senators score below supportc = 55 percent for their states?

i) What proportion or percent of senators score between supportc = 35 percent and supportc = 55 percent for their states?

j) What supportc score cuts off the bottom 30 percent of supportc values?

k) What supportc score would place you in the top 5 percent of scores?

l) Use the normal curve to estimate the state voter support for Clinton percentage that would place a state at the 50th percentile for these states.

Exercise 8.28 involves normal approximations to the binomial.

8.32. Given a binomial experiment with number of trials n, probability of success p, and probability of failure q, if both the products np and nq are greater than or equal to 5, we may use a normal curve with mean $\overline{X} = np$ and standard deviation SD $= \sqrt{npq}$ to approximate the binomial distribution. This exercise demonstrates how.

a) We take a fair coin and toss it 20 times. What is the probability of obtaining between 10 and 15 heads inclusive? Answer this question using the binomial distribution.

b) Demonstrate that the criterion for a normal approximation to the binomial is satisfied.

c) What are the mean and standard deviation of the normal distribution that we will use to approximate this binomial distribution?

d) It is not quite so simple as to approximate the area under this normal curve between 10 and 15 because the normal distribution is continuous and the binomial distribution is discrete. We need to use a continuity correction. We accomplish this by thinking of the binomial distribution as if it were really continuous with all scores being reported to the nearest integer value. Therefore, the event "between 10 and 15 successes inclusive" should be thought of as if it were really "between 9.5 and 15.5 inclusive." Note that all we have done is to extend the original interval (10 to 15 inclusive) by 0.5 in each direction. This extension of the real interval by 0.5 in each direction is called a correction for continuity and is employed whenever a (continuous) normal distribution is used to approximate a (discrete) binomial distribution for calculating binomial probabilities. Find the area under the normal curve with mean and standard deviation specified in part (c) between 9.5 and 15.5 inclusive. This number is the normal approximation to the answer you obtained in part (a).

CHAPTER NINE

The Role of Sampling in Inferential Statistics

As noted at the beginning of Chapter 7, a distinction exists between descriptive and inferential statistics. Whereas descriptive statistics are used to describe the data at hand, inferential statistics are used to draw inferences from results based on the data at hand to a larger *population* from which the data at hand have been selected. The data at hand form what is called a *sample*. In this chapter we discuss some fundamental components of inferential statistics, including sampling, sampling distributions, and characteristics of estimators.

SAMPLES AND POPULATIONS

Why, you may ask, should we study a sample at all if what we are really interested in is the population? Why not just study the population itself and be done with it? The answer to this question is that in actual research situations, it is often not possible, in terms of both time and resources, to obtain the desired data from the entire population.

For example, suppose we wanted to know, in a particular election year, how people were going to vote in the upcoming presidential election. The population, in this case, consists of all the people eligible to vote in the general election. Clearly, it would be enormously expensive and time-consuming to gather and tabulate data from each person in the population. Instead, we would select a sample that is somehow representative of the entire population, poll the sample on how they will vote, and then draw conclusions about the population from the sample. Though we are studying the sample, our real interest in inferential statistics is the population, and the conclusions we will draw are always about it.

We can describe measures taken on populations of things in the same ways that we can describe measures taken on samples of things. For example, if we could get data from the entire population, we could compute all measures of location, variability, and relationship (e.g., the mean, standard deviation, and correlation) just as we can on a sample taken from that population. When computed for populations, the values of such descriptive measures are called *parameters*; when computed for samples, they are called *statistics*. In inferential statistics, we use statistics computed on a sample to draw conclusions about unknown parameters in the population. In order to make it clear whether we are talking about a measure taken on a sample or on a population, we denote statistics by Roman letters and parameters by Greek letters. Table 9.1 contains examples of these symbols.

As another example, consider that we want to find the mean (average) number of hours eighth graders in the United States spend watching television per week. In order to find exactly what we want, the population mean, μ, we would somehow have to obtain the number of hours of television viewing for each member of the population. This is obviously impractical. Instead we might pick a sample of, say, 1,000 eighth graders in the New York

---

TABLE 9.1. Symbols for common statistics and parameters.

Statistics	Parameters
$\overline{X}$ = M = Sample Mean	μ = Population Mean
S^2 = Sample Variance	σ^2 = Population Variance
S = Sample Standard Deviation	σ = Population Standard Deviation
r = Sample Correlation	ρ = Population Correlation

---

metropolitan area, find the mean number of hours of television watched in the sample, and then use our calculated value of the sample mean, $\overline{X}$, as an estimate of the unknown population mean μ.

Do you think the procedure we have just outlined is a good one for estimating the mean number of hours of television viewing, μ, of the population described? Actually, there are several things wrong with it. First, we have not explained how our sample is to be picked or why we want it to be of size $N = 1,000$. Do we just walk into the nearest middle school and pick the first 1,000 eighth graders we see? If we are going to draw valid conclusions about the population from calculations made on the sample, we want the sample to be representative of the population. Second, can we expect the sample mean $\overline{X}$ to be a good estimator of the population mean μ? Analogously, can we expect the sample mode to be a good estimator of the population mode and the sample variance to be good estimator of the population variance? After all, the sample size N is not a good estimator of the population size, is it? Considerations like these are crucial for the correct use and understanding of inferential statistics. Before proceeding, let us take a closer look at them.

RANDOM SAMPLES

In order for conclusions about our population to be accurate, the sample we use must be a subset of the population. For example, if we were interested in estimating the median income for all practicing attorneys in the United States (the population), it would make no sense to select a sample of medical doctors on which to base the estimate. Obviously, our sample should be comprised of attorneys from the population. That is, we would, in some way, select a sample of attorneys from our population of all practicing attorneys in the United States and compute the median income of the sample. We might then be able to use this sample median as an estimator of the median of the population. Many samples could be picked from this population; however, each sample would differ somewhat from all the other samples, even though they all come from the same population. The accuracy of our estimate will therefore depend, among other things, on how representative our sample is of the population. If our sample is truly representative of the population, we can expect our estimate of the population median to be accurate. On the other hand, if our sample deviates to some extent from being truly representative of the population, we would expect our estimate to be inaccurate to some extent.

The question that naturally arises in this connection is whether it is possible to determine just how representative a particular sample is, and therefore how accurate the corresponding estimate is. The answer to this question is that in most cases we cannot make such a determination with a particular sample, but that we can do so in the long run if we use specific sampling procedures in selecting our sample, called *probability sampling*. If we follow the procedure known as *simple random sampling* (or just *random sampling)* to select our sample, we can often determine probabilistically just how representative or nonrepresentative our sample can be expected to be. This is not possible or feasible with many other types of sampling procedures, which is why much of inferential statistics is based on the assumptions of random sampling from populations.

Suppose, for example, we wish to estimate the proportion of students enrolled in fifth grade throughout the state of Idaho who are female. Suppose too that somehow we are able to determine that if we use simple random sampling to select a sample of size $N = 25$, the probability of selecting a representative sample is high. We then go ahead and select a random sample of 25 fifth graders in Idaho and find that our sample consists of 25 males and no females. Our estimate of the proportion of students enrolled in the fifth grade who are female would therefore be 0/25, or 0.

In this example, we know enough about the characteristics of the population under study (all fifth graders in Idaho) to realize that the sample we have selected, by virtue of the fact that it contains no females, is not representative of the population. In most cases, however, we will simply not know enough about the characteristics of the population to determine whether the sample actually selected is representative. (If we knew so much about the population, we probably would not be using inferential statistics on it in the first place.) *Before selecting our sample*, we will know only what the *chances* are of obtaining a sample with a given degree of representativeness. All we can do is set up our sampling procedures so as to ensure that the probabilities of obtaining representative samples are large and the probabilities of obtaining nonrepresentative samples are small. And we must be aware that either type of sample *could* occur. We will then be able to answer such questions as: "What is the probability that a random sample of 200 practicing lawyers in the United States will have a median income that differs from the median income of all practicing lawyers in the United States by less than $1,000?" If that probability is high and the sample median turns out to be $25,000, we can be reasonably sure that the population median is somewhere between $24,000 ($25,000 − $1,000) and $26,000 ($25,000 + $1,000). With this introduction, we turn to a discussion of simple random sampling.

OBTAINING A SIMPLE RANDOM SAMPLE

Once we have decided we want to use random sampling, the question becomes: "What is a random sample and how do we get one?" Simply stated, a simple *random sample* is a sample chosen from a given population in such a way as to ensure that each person or thing in the population has an equal and independent chance of being picked for the sample. To understand what we mean by the words *equal and independent*, think of the selection of a sample as picking a first object from the population to be in the sample, then picking a second object from those remaining in the population, and so on. *Equal* means that at each stage of the selection process, all the objects remaining in the population are equally likely to be picked for the sample. *Independent* means that no pick has any effect on any other pick. Violating either one of these conditions results in a nonrandom sample.

Let us illustrate what can go wrong in selecting a random sample. Suppose you are the president of the local Democratic Club and you want to get some indication of how the registered Democrats in your district feel about a certain bill. You plan to select a random sample of size 20 from the population of registered Democrats in your district and ask the people in the sample their opinion of the bill. After randomly selecting 19 registered Democrats, you suddenly notice that all 19 are female, so you decide to pick your 20th member of the sample from among the male registered Democrats only. Is your sample a random one? It is not, because at the last stage (the 20th selection), all the people remaining in the population *did not have an equal chance of being picked*. In fact, the women remaining at the last stage had no chance of being picked.

As another example, suppose you want some information about all the students in the local high school. To save time, you are going to select a random sample of 25 students from this population, find out from the sample what you want to know, and then infer from the sample to the population. You also decide, however, that you do not want more than one student from any one family in the sample. Is this a random sample of your population? It is not if the population contains any brother-brother, sister-sister, or brother-sister pairs. If such pairs exist, the different stages of the selection process *might not be independent of each other*. In other words, each selection of a member of the sample disqualifies all that student's brothers and sisters from selection in later stages of the selection process.

The actual selection of a random sample can be accomplished through the use of a uniform random-number generator available in most statistical software packages, including Stata. The important properties of a uniform random-number generator are: (1) each digit generated is independent of all other digits; and (2) in the long run, each digit occurs with equal frequency. For example, one million digits generated by a uniform random-number generator should contain approximately one hundred thousand 0's, one hundred thousand 1's, …, and one hundred thousand 9's.

Suppose you have 5,000 cases in your population from which you would like to select a simple random sample of size 50 and collect data on these 50. Number the objects in your population from 1 to 5,000. We may perform the selection using Stata by opening a new data file and by defining, for example, a variable id that has values, ordered consecutively, from 1 to 75, the size of the desired sample plus 25 to take into account the generation of possible duplicate values. The 75 values may be entered manually or, by using the following syntax typed into your Do-file:

set obs 75
gen id = _n

Highlight both lines of syntax and press **Control + d** to execute these commands. The first line of syntax sets the number of observations in the new dataset to be 75, and the second line generates a new variable called id that will contain the values from 1 to 75, in successive order. If you open your Data Editor Window (by typing **edit** in the Command Window or by adding the command **edit** to your Do-file and executing it by highlighting it and pressing **Control+d**) you will see the variable id, with its values from 1 to 75.

Once the variable id is defined with all 75 values, to obtain a simple random sample of 75 observations from a population of 5,000, we use Stata's uniform random number generator, **runiform**. We do so because a uniform random generator, by definition, will select each of our 5,000 values, numbered from 1 to 5,000, in a uniform way; that is, in a way that gives each value from 1 to 5,000 an equal and independent chance of being selected. Accordingly, we add the following as our next line of syntax to our Do-file (open the Do-file associated with this chapter).

generate random = floor((*5000–1+1*)*runiform() + 1)

This particular command generates integer random numbers from a uniform random distribution with maximum value 5000 and minimum value 1. The general form of this command is:

generate random = floor((*b–a+1*)*runiform() + *a*)

where b and a represent, respectively, the maximum and minimum values to be generated.

If you open the Data Editor, you will note that the variable, random, has now been added to the dataset and that it contains seventy-five random integers ranging in value from 1 to 5,000. You will notice also that the variable random has duplicate values. Accordingly, to select your sample of 50 cases, open the Data Editor and read down the list of random variables, one number at a time. Select each case from your population that corresponds to the next random number in the list. If the random number in the list duplicates an earlier number, discard it and move on to the next random number. By having a list of 75 random numbers, there should be at least 50 unique entries to obtain your desired random sample of 50 cases.

If instead, for reasons other than wanting to select a sample of cases from a large, numbered population of cases, you wanted to generate a random variable that has a decimal component, and a range in values from **a** to **b**, you would use the following Stata command:

generate double random = (b – a) *runiform() + a

SAMPLING WITH AND WITHOUT REPLACEMENT

Simple random sampling is an example of what is called *sampling without replacement*. That is, once an object from the population has been selected to be included in the sample, it is removed from consideration in all remaining stages of the selection process. (Although the same number may be *picked* more than once, it is never *used more* than once in obtaining the sample.) In *sampling with replacement*, *every* object in the population is available for selection to the sample at every stage of the selection process, regardless of whether it has already been selected. Note that one consequence of sampling with replacement is that the same object may be picked more than once. Because simple random sampling is sampling without replacement, this cannot happen in our sampling procedure. The following example illustrates some of the differences between these two sampling procedures.

EXAMPLE 9.1. We have a deck of 52 playing cards (consisting of 4 suits, clubs, diamonds, hearts, spades, with 13 cards per suit, Ace, 2, 3, 4, 5, 6, 7, 8, 9, 10, Jack, Queen, and King), and we want to select a sample of size 2 from this population. Describe both sampling with and without replacement in this context and the probabilities of selection associated with each.

Solution

1. *With replacement.* One of the 52 cards is selected to be in the sample. Then this card is replaced in the deck and a second card is selected to complete the sample. Because the

TABLE 9.2. Probabilities of selecting the second card (Population size = 52; Sample size = 2)

	With replacement	Without replacement
Probability of Ace of hearts	$\frac{1}{52} = .0192307$	$\frac{0}{52} = .0$
Probability of all other cards	$\frac{1}{52} = .0192307$	$\frac{1}{51} = .0196078$

card that is picked first is replaced before the second card is selected, the same card can be selected both times, and the probability of any particular card being picked does not change from the first selection to the second. (The probability of any particular card being picked is 1/52 on the first selection and 1/52 on the second selection.)

2. *Without replacement.* One of the 52 cards is selected to be in the sample. Then, without this card being replaced, a second card is selected from the remaining 51 to complete the sample. In this case, the same card *cannot* be selected both times, and the probability of any particular card being picked *does* change from the first selection to the second. (For the first selection, each card has a probability of 1/52 of being picked. For the second selection, the card that was picked the first time has a probability of 0 of being picked, while all the other cards have a probability of 1/51 of being picked.)

Why have we gone to the trouble of discussing and comparing these two types of sampling? Although random sampling is sampling *without* replacement, many of the techniques we will want to use in inferential statistics hold only when sampling with replacement is being used. Somehow we must reconcile this apparent conflict of interest. We can do this by introducing the concept of an infinite population.

A population is said to be *infinite* if it has at least as many objects in it as there are positive integers 1, 2, 3, … If we draw a finite sample from an infinite population, then sampling with and without replacement are essentially the same because discarding a few objects will not appreciably alter the relative occurrence of objects in the population. Most realistic applications of inferential statistics involve very large, but still finite, populations. When our population size is very large relative to the sample size N, then *for all practical purposes* it can be thought of as an infinite population, in which case sampling with and without replacement are essentially the same. For most statistical purposes, this is the case when the population size *is at least 100 times* as large as the sample size. To illustrate, let us return to the example of selecting a sample of size 2 from a deck of playing cards. If the first card selected were the ace of hearts, the probabilities for selecting the second card are as given in Table 9.2.

Note how different the probabilities are with and without replacement. This is because the population is only 26 times as large as the sample being drawn from it (52 compared to 2). If, on the other hand, we take one hundred decks of cards as our population, the proportions are still the same (each type of card makes up 100/5,200 or 1/52 of the population), but now the population is 2,600 times as large as the sample (5,200 compared to 2). If we again assume that the first card selected was an ace of hearts, the probabilities for selecting the second card are as given in Table 9.3.

The probabilities for sampling with and without replacement are much closer to each other in Table 9.3 than in Table 9.2. In other words, when the population is at least 100

TABLE 9.3. Probabilities of selecting the second card (Population size = 5,200; Sample size = 2)

	With replacement	Without replacement
Probability of Ace of hearts	$\dfrac{100}{5,200} = .0192307$	$\dfrac{99}{5,199} = .0190421$
Probability of all other cards	$\dfrac{100}{5,200} = .0192307$	$\dfrac{100}{5,199} = .0192344$

times as large as the sample being drawn from it, we can assume that, for all practical purposes, sampling with and without replacement are essentially the same.

☞ **Remark.** The inferential statistical techniques we will present from this point on are really appropriate only for sampling with replacement. However, by assuming that all populations are at least 100 times as large as the samples being drawn from them, we will be able to use sampling without replacement and obtain quite accurate results.

SAMPLING DISTRIBUTIONS

Now that we are somewhat more familiar with what a random sample is and how one is selected, we will turn to the question of how it is used in inferential statistics.

As mentioned previously, the basic idea in inferential statistics is to use a statistic calculated on a sample in order to estimate a parameter of a population. This procedure is made difficult by the unavoidable fact that in most cases, the value we get for any statistic will vary somewhat from sample to sample, even when all the samples are randomly selected from the same "parent" population.

DESCRIBING THE SAMPLING DISTRIBUTION OF MEANS EMPIRICALLY

Imagine the process of deciding on a particular sample size *N* to use, randomly choosing and listing all possible samples of size *N* from the parent population, and for each sample, recording the value of the statistic we are interested in. (Of course, each *sample* of size *N* is replaced in the population before the next sample of size *N* is selected.) If we then take all the values we have obtained for this statistic, we can construct a frequency distribution of them just as we can construct a frequency distribution of any collection of numbers. Such a distribution is called an *empirical* (or observed) *sampling distribution* for the given statistic.

EXAMPLE 9.2. Use the following population of 10 scores and compute by hand the *sampling distribution of means* for samples of size N = 2 drawn from it. Use the sampling distribution of means to determine the probability that when a single sample of size N = 2 is selected from the population that its mean will be within 2 points of the actual population mean.

(We really should not use a population that is only five times as large as the sample being drawn from it, but doing so makes the sampling distribution easier to enumerate.)

Population: 0 1 3 3 5 7 7 7 8 10
Note that the population mean is 5.1 and the population standard deviation is 3.25.

Solution. In the following table, we list all possible random samples of size N = 2 that could possibly be drawn from this population and for each one calculate its sample mean $\bar{X}$.

Sample	Mean	Sample	Mean	Sample	Mean	Sample	Mean	Sample	Mean
0,0	0.0	3,0	1.5	5,0	2.5	7,0	3.5	8,0	4.0
0,1	0.5	3,1	2.0	5,1	3.0	7,1	4.0	8,1	4.5
0,3	1.5	3,3	3.0	5,3	4.0	7,3	5.0	8,3	5.5
0,3	1.5	3,3	3.0	5,3	4.0	7,3	5.0	8,3	5.5
0,5	2.5	3,5	4.0	5,5	5.0	7,5	6.0	8,5	6.5
0,7	3.5	3,7	5.0	5,7	6.0	7,7	7.0	8,7	7.5
0,7	3.5	3,7	5.0	5,7	6.0	7,7	7.0	8,7	7.5
0,7	3.5	3,7	5.0	5,7	6.0	7,7	7.0	8,7	7.5
0,8	4.0	3,8	5.5	5,8	6.5	7,8	7.5	8,8	8.0
0,10	5.0	3,10	6.5	5,10	7.5	7,10	8.5	8,10	9.0
1,0	0.5	3,0	1.5	7,0	3.5	7,0	3.5	10,0	5.0
1,1	1.0	3,1	2.0	7,1	4.0	7,1	4.0	10,1	5.5
1,3	2.0	3,3	3.0	7,3	5.0	7,3	5.0	10,3	6.5
1,3	2.0	3,3	3.0	7,3	5.0	7,3	5.0	10,3	6.5
1,5	3.0	3,5	4.0	7,5	6.0	7,5	6.0	10,5	7.5
1,7	4.0	3,7	5.0	7,7	7.0	7,7	7.0	10,7	8.5
1,7	4.0	3,7	5.0	7,7	7.0	7,7	7.0	10,7	8.5
1,7	4.0	3,7	5.0	7,7	7.0	7,7	7.0	10,7	8.5
1,8	4.5	3,8	5.5	7,8	7.5	7,8	7.5	10,8	9.0
1,10	5.5	3,10	6.5	7,10	8.5	7,10	8.5	10,10	10.0

For example, the first pair listed in the table (0,0) represents the sample of size 2 containing the values 0 and 0. Its corresponding sample mean is (0 + 0)/2 = 0.0.

We can now enter these sample mean values into Stata (in the Data Editor Window) and create a frequency distribution table (using the **tabulate** command) and a corresponding frequency histogram (using the **histogram command**) as shown in Table 9.4 and Figure 9.1, respectively.

The histogram depicts the way in which the process of sampling at random from a population produces a distribution of mean values. It is an example of what we have called an empirical sampling distribution – in this case, a sampling distribution of means from samples of size N = 2.

To use the sampling distribution of means to determine the probability that a sample mean selected at random will be within 2 points of the actual population mean, we find the proportion of sample means that are between 3.5 and 7 inclusive. According to the frequency distribution table, 62 of the 100 equally likely sample means fall within that range, so that we conclude that the probability that a randomly selected sample mean will be within 2 points of the actual population mean is .62.

• •
EXAMPLE 9.3. Compare the graph of Figure 9.2, the sampling distribution of means from the population {0, 1, 3, 3, 5, 7, 7, 7, 8, 10} based on 10,000 samples of size 8 randomly selected with replacement from this population of 10 scores, with that of Figure 9.1.

Table 9.4. Frequency and percent distribution table for the sampling distribution of means for samples of size N = 2.

means	Freq.	Percent	Cum.
0	1	1.00	1.00
0.5	2	2.00	3.00
1	1	1.00	4.00
1.5	4	4.00	8.00
2	4	4.00	12.00
2.5	2	2.00	14.00
3	6	6.00	20.00
3.5	6	6.00	26.00
4	12	12.00	38.00
4.5	2	2.00	40.00
5	15	15.00	55.00
5.5	6	6.00	61.00
6	6	6.00	67.00
6.5	6	6.00	73.00
7	9	9.00	82.00
7.5	8	8.00	90.00
8	1	1.00	91.00
8.5	6	6.00	97.00
9	2	2.00	99.00
10	1	1.00	100.00
Total	100	100.00	

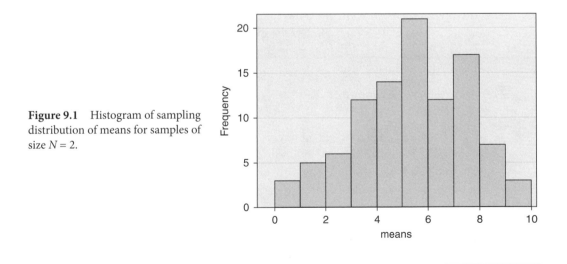

Figure 9.1 Histogram of sampling distribution of means for samples of size N = 2.

MORE Stata: Using the **bootstrap** command to generate the sampling distribution of means of Figure 9.2 with N = 8.

We begin by creating a data set that contains these ten values. So that we start with a clean slate, the first command we type in our Do-file is the command **clear**. This syntax may be found in the Do-file associated with this chapter.

```
clear
set obs 10
input x
0
1
3
3
5
7
7
7
8
10
```

To run the Do-file, highlight all lines and press **Control + d** as usual.

Next, you will need to create a data set that contains the 10,000 samples of size 8 randomly selected with replacement from this population of ten scores. But before doing so, for simplicity, we change our working directory to the one in which we would like to save our data set of 10,000 means. To do so we enter and run the command **cd**, which stands for, change directory. One good place for storing these results is on the Desktop of our C: drives. To do so, we would use a variation of the following command that is tailored to our specific computer environment.

```
cd "C:\...\Desktop"
```

We now create the dataset of 10,000 means by typing the following bootstrap command into your.do file, but we include the command **capture erase bootstrap.dta** beforehand as shown below. We do so to erase the **bootstrap.dta** file if it already exists. If the file does not already exist, including the word **capture** will prevent us from getting an error message that we are trying to erase a file that does not exist. Such an error message would cause our program to stop.

```
capture erase bootstrap.dta
bootstrap, reps(10000) size(8) saving(bootstrap.dta): mean x
```

The bootstrap command will randomly sample with replacement a sample of size 8 from our data set of size 10, compute the mean of these 8 randomly selected values and save that mean to the file "bootstrap.dta" located within our working directory. It will then repeat this 10,000 times. Understandably, the procedure is likely to take a few minutes to complete.

To construct a histogram of these data, open the file boostrap.dta dataset from the directory in which you saved the file (presumably your working directory). The one variable in this data set is named (by Stata), "**_b_x**". This variable contains the 10,000 means based on the samples of size 8 that were randomly selected from your data set of ten values. We include the option for creating 62 bins in the **histogram** command to allow the distribution of means room to take shape.

```
histogram _b_x, bin(62)
```

Because the mean values plotted in Figure 9.2 are based on sets of eight values that have been randomly selected from the ten values in our data set, each time we run this Do-file, a different set of mean values will be generated. Accordingly, the histogram based on the means generated from your execution of the Do-file will be similar, but not necessary identically equal to Figure 9.2.

☞ **Remark.** If you would like the same random values to be selected each time you run the bootstrap procedure (in case you would like to reproduce your results in the future), you should insert the command **set seed #** directly before the bootstrap command, where # may be any integer you choose from 0 to some very large number. The seed value arbitrarily set in the Do-file associated with this chapter is 56732. To learn more about the **set seed** command, run the command **help seed** either from the Command Window or the Do-file.

As noted earlier in this text, once the … are each filled in with the appropriate path depending upon your specific computer environment, the entire Do-file can be run in one step by highlighting all of the lines in it and pressing **Control+d**.

```
clear
set obs 10
input x
0
1
3
3
5
7
7
7
8
10
cd "C:\...\Desktop"
capture erase bootstrap.dta
set more off
set seed 1234
bootstrap, reps(10000) size(8) saving(bootstrap.dta): mean x
save "C:\...\Desktop\bootstrap.dta"
use "C:\...\Desktop\bootstrap.dta", clear
edit
histogram _b_x, bin(62)
```

Solution. We can use Figures 9.1 and 9.2 to compare how much we can expect our sample statistic value to vary from sample to sample depending upon the size of the sample. For example, the Figure 9.1 reveals that if we were to select at random a sample of size $N = 2$ with replacement from the given population, the mean value for this sample would most likely fall somewhere between 3 and 8. Notice that sample mean values down to 0.0 and up to 10 would also be possible but less likely. Figure 9.2 reveals that if we were to select at random, and with replacement, a sample of size $N = 8$ from the given population, the mean value for this sample would most likely fall somewhere between the narrower interval of 4.0 to 6.5. Sample mean values below 2 and above 8 would also be possible, but far less likely.

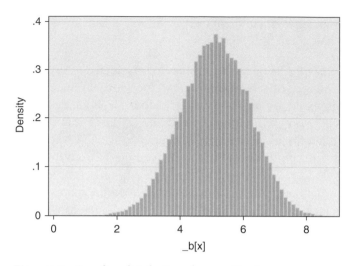

Figure 9.2 Sampling distribution of means, N = 8.

Based on this comparison, we find that the range of mean values *most likely* to be obtained decreases as the sample size increases. We also note that the population mean for our 10 scores is $\mu = 5.1$, which falls within both intervals, 3 and 8, and 4.5 and 6.0, the sample mean values most likely to be obtained, in the two cases, respectively. Thus, we find that as we increase the size of our sample, we can expect to obtain a more accurate estimate of the population mean. As a general rule, when we are Using sample statistics to estimate population parameters, the larger the sample we use, the more accurate we can expect the estimate to be.

Figures 9.1 and 9.2 not only illustrate that the larger the sample size the more accurately we may estimate the population parameter, but they also illustrate that the larger the sample size, the more the shape of the sampling distribution resembles the normal distribution. Notice that Figure 9.2 looks much more like a normal distribution than Figure 9.1. The population we used in these examples (9.2 and 9.3) consists of a particular set of ten scores with a particular distribution. It can be shown, however, that if we had begun with a different population of scores with a different distribution (and, of course, there are an infinite number of distributions that we could have chosen), we would have obtained a similar result. That is, regardless of the population distribution of scores, as the sample size increases, the estimate of the population mean becomes more accurate and the shape of the sampling distribution of means becomes much more like that of a normal distribution. This is what is called the *Central Limit Theorem (CLT)*, which is more formally stated in the next section.

DESCRIBING THE SAMPLING DISTRIBUTION OF MEANS THEORETICALLY: THE CENTRAL LIMIT THEOREM

Using the methods of mathematical statistics, it is often possible to determine *theoretically* what the sampling distribution of a particular sample statistic should look like. While the previous example was concerned with the mean, theoretical sampling distributions may be obtained for other common sample statistics as well, including, for example, the variance and correlation coefficient. As noted in the previous section, the sampling distribution of means becomes more normal in shape as the sample size increases. As we will see in later chapters, the theoretical sampling distributions of many of the other common statistics covered in this book (e.g., the variance) approach a different set of shapes as the sample size increases. Regardless of their eventual shape, however, these theoretical sampling distributions provide the foundation for drawing inferences about the population by making explicit the relationship that exists between the parameters of that population and those of the sampling distribution.

We now present a more formal statement of the *Central Limit Theorem*, which specifies the shape, mean, and standard deviation of a sampling distribution of means in terms of the parameters, μ and σ, of the population from which these samples have been derived.

CENTRAL LIMIT THEOREM (CLT)

Given a population of values with no specified distribution, and a sample size N that is sufficiently large, the *sampling distribution of means* for samples drawn from this population with replacement can be described as follows:

1. Its shape is *approximately* normally distributed.
2. Its mean, $\mu_{\bar{X}}$, is equal to μ.
3. Its standard deviation, $\sigma\bar{x}$, is equal to $\sigma/\sqrt{N}$.

☞ **Remark.** Notice that we denote the mean of the sampling distribution of means as $\mu_{\bar{x}}$ because it is the mean of means. Furthermore, we denote the standard deviation of the sampling distribution of means as $\sigma\bar{x}$ because it is the standard deviation of means. The standard deviation of the sampling distribution of means, $\sigma\bar{x}$, is also referred to as the *standard error of the mean*.

Note that the CLT requires that the samples be drawn from the population with replacement. However, as long as the population being considered is relatively large compared to the sample being drawn from it (for our purposes, at least 100 times as large), sampling with and without replacement will give approximately equivalent results, so the CLT will hold approximately. One of the statements in the CLT is that if the sample size N being used is sufficiently large, then certain results will be true. Just what is meant here by "sufficiently large"? This is a subjective question. The answer will vary from one situation to another and from one researcher to another. In general, the larger the sample size N being used, the closer the approximation will be, and it is up to the researcher to decide just how good an approximation is desired. By empirical observation, for our purposes in this book, we will consider that the distribution of means based on samples of N greater than or equal to 30 ($N \geq 30$) gives a good enough approximation to a normal distribution.

☞ **Remark.** Notice that Figure 9.2 looks quite normal in shape despite the fact that the conditions of the CLT are not met. That is, the parent population is not normally distributed and $N = 8$. It is likely that Figure 9.2 looks quite normal in shape because the distribution of the population from which the samples have been randomly selected is approximately symmetric. When distributions are known to be symmetric or approximately so, a minimum

N value of 30 is rather conservative. When distributions are known to be nearly normal, sample sizes as low as 10 or even 8 may be appropriate, and when distributions are known to be exactly normal, any size sample will yield a normally-distributed sampling distribution.

The Central Limit Theorem was first proved by Abraham de Moivre in connection with his interest in developing techniques for the calculation of gamblers' odds that emerged from his frequent visits to London coffeehouses. The proof, along with the techniques he developed, was first published in 1716 in his book, The Doctrine of Chances (Salsburg, 2001; Stigler, 1986).

The CLT is a powerful and extremely useful statement of probability theory that underlies why the normal distribution commonly is used to model (or approximate the distribution of) observed data.

Let us look at some examples of how to use the CLT to determine, for given populations and sample sizes, what sampling distributions of means should look like.

• •

EXAMPLE 9.4. Suppose we are given a normally distributed population of 5,000 scores with mean equal to 15 and standard deviation equal to 3. (a) What will the corresponding sampling distribution of means for samples of size $N = 16$ (with replacement) look like? (b) If we were to select a single sample of size $N = 16$ at random from this population of scores, what is the probability that the mean for this sample will fall between 13 and 17?

Solution.
1. Because the parent population is normally distributed, the sampling distribution of means will also be normally distributed; that its mean, $\mu_{\bar{x}}$, will be equal to the mean of the population, 15, and that its standard deviation $\sigma\bar{x}$ will be given by $\sigma\bar{x} = \sigma/\sqrt{N} = 3/4 = .75$. The parent population and the corresponding sampling distribution of means based on 1,000 samples, each of size 16, randomly drawn from the population with replacement are shown in Figures 9.3 and 9.4, respectively. Notice that while the means are the same in both figures, the range of scores on the horizontal axis in Figure 9.3 is from 6 to 24, while in Figure 9.4 it is only from 12 to 18.
2. Because we are making a statement about the sampling distribution of means, which is known to be normally distributed with mean 15 and standard deviation .75, we use the following Stata syntax:

display (normal((17 − 15)/.75)) − (normal((13 − 15)/.75))

The value obtained is .99, indicating that almost all such sample means fall within the specified range.

• •

EXAMPLE 9.5. Suppose we are given an arbitrarily distributed (say, positively skewed as in the distribution given in Figure 9.5) population of 1,000 scores with mean equal to 8 and standard deviation equal to 4. What will the corresponding sampling distribution of means for samples of size $N = 100$ (with replacement) look like?

Solution. Because the sample size ($N = 100$) is sufficiently large, we know from the CLT that the sampling distribution of means will be approximately normally distributed; that its standard deviation will be equal to $\sigma\bar{x} = \sigma/\sqrt{N} = 4/10 = 0.4$; and that its mean $\mu_{\bar{x}}$ will be equal to the mean of the parent population, 8. Figure 9.5 shows what the parent population might

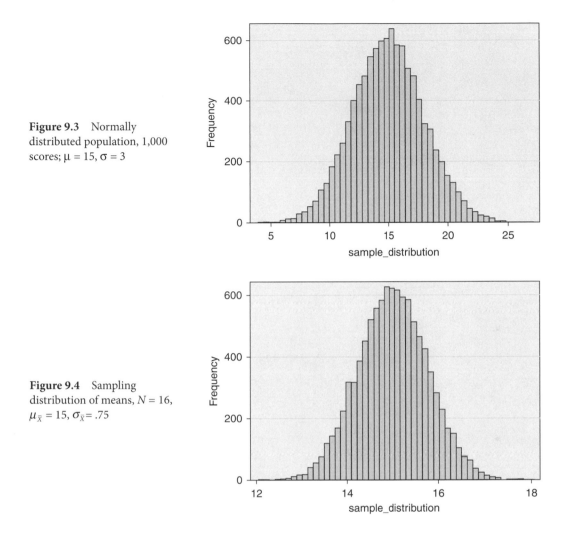

Figure 9.3 Normally distributed population, 1,000 scores; μ = 15, σ = 3

Figure 9.4 Sampling distribution of means, $N = 16$, $\mu_{\bar{X}} = 15$, $\sigma_{\bar{X}} = .75$

look like and Figure 9.6 shows what the corresponding sampling distribution of means based on 10,000 samples, each of size 100, randomly selected from the positively skewed parent population with replacement will look like.

Recall that because the means are generated by this program through a random process, one that relies on randomly selecting samples from the positively skewed parent population, the histogram you obtain on re-running this program will be similar, but not necessarily identical to the histogram of Figure 9.6. To obtain the identical graphic, use the command **set seed 1234**, that appears in the Do-file associated with this chapter.

MORE Stata: Using the CLT to generate and plot the sampling distribution of means of Figure 9.6

To generate the 10,000 normally distributed values with mean 8 and standard deviation 0.4 and to plot Figure 9.6 we use the following commands based on the Central Limit Theorem (see the Do-file associated with this chapter):

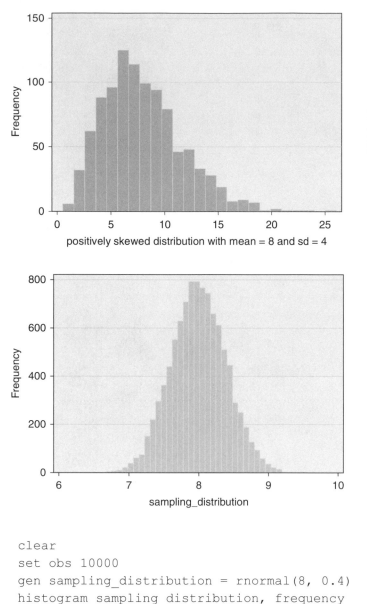

Figure 9.5 Positively skewed population of 1,000 scores; $\mu = 8, \sigma = 4$

Figure 9.6 Sampling distribution of 10,000 means, each of size 100; $\mu_{\bar{X}} = 8$, $\sigma_{\bar{X}} = 0.4$.

```
clear
set obs 10000
gen sampling_distribution = rnormal(8, 0.4)
histogram sampling_distribution, frequency
```

One of the things the CLT tells us is that as long as sampling with replacement is used and the other conditions specified are satisfied, the sampling distribution of means will have its mean equal to the mean of the parent population. As a matter of fact, this result is exactly true even if sampling is without replacement, even if the sample size is not sufficiently large, and even if the population is not at least 100 times as large as the sample being drawn from it. In other words, given any size population and any sample size N, and whether we are sampling with or without replacement, the sampling distribution of means of size N from this population will have its mean equal to the mean of the parent population. We will use this fact in the next section on estimators and bias.

Another immediate consequence of the CLT is that whenever its conditions are satisfied, we can, by increasing the sample size N, make the sampling distribution of means cluster as closely as we want around its mean μ. (Look again at the formula for the standard deviation of the sampling distribution given in the CLT. Because the denominator is just the square root of N, we can make $\sigma_{\bar{x}}$ as small as we like by making N sufficiently large, and a small standard deviation implies that the scores are all clustered about the distribution's mean.) Because the mean of the sampling distribution is also the mean of the parent population, we can conclude once again, that as the sample size we are using increases, we can expect our sample means $\bar{X}$ to become more and more accurate as estimators of the population mean μ.

ESTIMATORS AND BIAS

Suppose that we have a population with an unknown mean μ and that we want to use a random sample to estimate μ. It seems reasonable to expect that the sample mean $\bar{X}$ should be a better estimator of μ than either the sample mode or sample median. But just what is it that makes an estimator good or bad? One important property, and the one we will discuss in this section, is what is called "unbiasedness."

A sample statistic is said to be an *unbiased estimator* for a population parameter if the sampling distribution for this statistic has mean value equal to the parameter being estimated. In other words, the statistic is an unbiased estimator if the values of the statistic obtained from sampling are, on average, equal to the parameter.

As we mentioned earlier, the sample mean $\bar{X}$ has exactly this property as an estimator of the population mean μ. Therefore, we can say that $\bar{X}$ is an unbiased estimator of μ. The sample variance, however, when computed Using the usual variance formula, $S_2 = \dfrac{\sum(X_i - \bar{X})^2}{N}$, will *not* be an unbiased estimator of the population variance σ^2. It will be a biased estimator. In particular, the mean of all the S^2 for a given sample size will always be smaller than the value of σ^2. If the N in the denominator of the variance formula were replaced by an $N - 1$, however, it can be shown mathematically that the resulting formula would be an unbiased estimator of σ^2. For the purpose of estimating the variance of the population, we will therefore define a new sample statistic $\hat{\sigma}^2$ that will be called the *variance estimator*, given by Equation 7.8.

$$\hat{\sigma}^2 = \frac{\sum(X_i - \bar{X})^2}{N-1} \tag{9.1}$$

Recall that Stata calls this variance estimator, the variance. When our aim is to describe the "spread" of scores in the sample for its own sake and not estimate the variance of the population, we seek the sample variance and therefore need to adjust the variance value that Stata provides by multiplying that value by $(N - 1)/N$. When the purpose is to estimate the population variance σ^2, however, we seek the variance estimator provided directly by Stata.

If we take the positive square root of the variance estimator, we obtain $\hat{\sigma}$ which is referred to as the *square root* of the variance estimator. We do not call $\hat{\sigma}$ the standard deviation estimator because, even though $\hat{\sigma}^2$ is an unbiased estimator of σ^2, $\hat{\sigma}^2$, is *not* an unbiased estimator of σ.

SUMMARY OF CHAPTER 9 STATA COMMANDS

For a complete listing of all Stata commands associated with this chapter, you may access the Do-file for Chapter 9 located on the text website.

Create	Command Lines
Define a variable id that has values, ordered consecutively, from 1 to 75	**set obs 75** **gen id = _n**
Generate integer random numbers from a uniform random distribution with maximum value 5000 and minimum value 1 (Need to create data set with id variable first)	**generate random = floor((*5000–1+1*)* runiform() + *1*)**
Enter a data set (Example 9.3)	**clear** **set obs 10** **input x** **0** **1** **3** **3** **5** **7** **7** **7** **8** **10**
Create distribution of 10,000 means of size 8 from data set (Example 9.3)	**capture erase bootstrap.dta** **set more off** **set seed 1234** **bootstrap, reps(10000) size(8) saving(bootstrap.dta): mean x**
Create histogram of representation of sampling distribution of means (Figure 9.2)	**histogram _b_x, bin(62)**
Given a sampling distribution of the mean with population mean 15 and standard error .75, find the probability of extracting a single sample mean between 13 and 17 (Example 9.4)	**display (normal((17 – 15)/.75)) – (normal((13 – 15)/.75))**
Create and graph a positively skewed distribution with mean 8 and standard deviation 4 (Figure 9.5)	**clear** **set seed 12468** **set obs 1000** **generate x = rchi2(8)**

Create	Command Lines
	histogram x, bin(25) frequency xtitle("positively skewed distribution with mean=8 and sd = 4")
	summarize x
Create the set of 10,000 normally distributed values with mean 8 and standard deviation 0.4 (Figure 9.6) along with a histogram of these sample mean values	**clear**
	set obs 10000
	gen sampling_distribution = rnormal(8, 0.4)
	histogram sampling_distribution, frequency

EXERCISES

*Create a.do file for each exercise that requires the use of Stata. Run the commands from the. do file by highlighting them and hitting **Control+d**. Save each.do file using a name associated with the Exercise for which it was created. It is recommended that you review the.do-file for* Chapter 9 *located on the textbook's website before completing these exercises. To facilitate doing each exercise, it may be helpful to copy and paste relevant commands from the.do-file for* Chapter 9 *into your own.do-file and modify them as needed.*

9.1. Given the following population of values: {0, 1, 2, 3, 4, 5, 6, 7, 8, 9}.
   a) Describe the shape of the distribution of the population scores.
   b) Make a list of all the samples of size $N = 2$ that could be selected with replacement from this population.
   c) Enter the list of the means of these samples into a new Stata data set. Create a frequency and percent distribution table.
   d) Construct a histogram for the distribution of sample means found in part (b). This graph depicts the sampling distribution of means for samples of size $N = 2$ from our population. Describe the shape of this distribution.
   e) Find the mean and standard deviation of both the population and the sampling distribution of means. How do they compare?
   f) If we were to use the mean of a randomly selected sample of size $N = 2$ to estimate the population mean in this exercise, what would be the probability of getting an estimate within two points of the exact answer?

9.2. Adapt the Stata instructions for Example 9.3 to generate an approximation to the sampling distributions of means from the population {0, 1, 2, 3, 4, 5, 6, 7, 8, 9}, based on 10,000 samples of size 9. Construct a histogram of the distribution. Compare the actual mean and standard deviation for the sampling distribution of means to those based on the Central Limit Theorem.

9.3.
   a) Describe how one obtains the sampling distribution of means for samples of size $N = 8$.
   b) If a certain population is normally distributed with mean 70 and standard deviation of 2.5, give the mean and the standard deviation of the sampling distribution of means of size $N = 8$.

c) Describe the effect on your answer to part (b) of increasing the sample size.

d) If we were to select a single sample of size $N = 8$, what is the probability that the mean of this sample will be two or more points higher than the actual population mean?

9.4. Suppose we are given a normally distributed population of scores with mean equal to 500 and standard deviation equal to 100.

a) Describe the shape of the sampling distribution of means of size $N = 30$ (with replacement).

b) What is the mean of the sampling distribution of means of size $N = 30$ (with replacement)?

c) What is the standard deviation of the sampling distribution of means of size $N = 30$ (with replacement), also called the standard error of the mean?

d) If we were to select a single sample of size $N = 30$ at random from this population of scores, what is the probability that the mean for this sample will be more than two standard errors away from the actual population mean?

e) What will the sampling distribution of means of size $N = 9$ (with replacement) look like?

9.5. Suppose we are given a uniformly distributed population of scores with mean equal to 500 and standard deviation equal to 100.

a) Describe the shape of the sampling distribution of means of size $N = 50$ (with replacement).

b) What is the mean of the sampling distribution of means of size $N = 50$ (with replacement)?

c) What is the standard deviation of the sampling distribution of means of size $N = 50$ (with replacement), also called the standard error of the mean?

d) If we were to select a single sample of size $N = 50$ at random from this population of scores, what is the probability that the mean for this sample will be more than two standard errors away from the actual population mean?

e) What will the sampling distribution of means of size $N = 9$ (with replacement) look like?

9.6. Suppose we are given a negatively skewed population with mean 100 and standard deviation 10.

a) Describe or give the value of the following characteristics of the sampling distribution of means of size N = 64 (with replacement): Shape, mean, and standard error.

b) What proportion of sample means falls below 98?

9.7. Suppose that a certain population is normally distributed with $\mu = 500$ and $\sigma = 100$. Indicate whether each statement is true (T) or false (F).

a) The standard deviation of the population is also called the standard error.

b) The mean of a sample of size 16 is the same as the population mean.

c) An increase in sample size from N = 16 to N = 25 will produce a sampling distribution with a smaller standard deviation.

d) The mean of a sampling distribution of means is equal to the population mean divided by the square root of the sample size.

e) The larger the sample size, the more the sample resembles the shape of the population.

    f) The larger the sample size, the more the sampling distribution of means resembles the shape of the population.

    g) The sampling distribution of means is a normal distribution.

    h) The mean of the sampling distribution of means for samples of size N = 15 will be the same as the mean of the sampling distribution for samples of size N = 100.

9.8. Use the uniform random number generator in Stata to select 10 random numbers between 1 and 50 inclusive.

9.9. In order to get some idea of what television programs people in New York City watch, we hand out a questionnaire to the members of all statistics classes at New York University and then tabulate the answers we receive. Is this a random sample of the population in which we are interested? Why or why not?

9.10. What (if anything) is wrong with the following statement: "A sampling distribution of means is always normally distributed."

9.11. What (if anything) is wrong with the following statement: "In order to obtain a sampling distribution of means for use in inferential statistics, one must empirically draw many samples of size *N* from the population of interest and record the corresponding sample mean values obtained."

9.12. Suppose researchers want to estimate the IQ of children who have a twin brother or twin sister. Assume that 100 children (50 pairs of twins) constitute the available population and that the researchers can administer intelligence tests to 30 children. Each time the researchers choose a child at random, they also select that child's twin. Using this procedure, will the researchers obtain a simple random sample of children who have a twin brother or twin sister? Why or why not?

9.13. Given the population of 5,000 scores with $\mu = 8$ and $\sigma = 4$ as shown below:

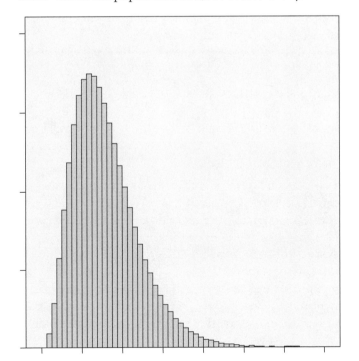

c) If a researcher randomly draws a single sample of 300 values from this population, what is the likely shape of the distribution of sample scores, negatively skewed, positively skewed, approximately normal, or exactly normal?

d) If a researcher randomly draws 200 samples, each containing 300 values, from this population and computes the sample mean for each of the 200 samples, what is the likely shape of the distribution of sample means, negatively skewed, positively skewed, approximately normal, or exactly normal?

e) What is an appropriate label for the horizontal axis of the distribution described in part a)?

f) What is an appropriate label for the horizontal axis of the distribution described in part b)?

CHAPTER TEN

Inferences Involving the Mean of a Single Population When σ Is Known

One population parameter that is of particular interest to the behavioral scientist is the mean μ of a population. In this chapter, we will discuss two approaches to statistical inference involving the mean of a population: interval estimation and hypothesis testing. Although these approaches are both carried out using samples and they give essentially equivalent results, there is a basic difference between them and it is important to know what this difference is.

In interval estimation of the population mean μ, we begin with no a priori belief about the value of μ. We select at random a sample from the population of interest, compute its sample mean $\overline{X}$, and then use this sample value $\overline{X}$ to construct an interval centered at $\overline{X}$ that will contain μ with a known degree of confidence. In hypothesis testing, we start with an a priori belief about the value of the population mean μ. We select at random a sample from the population of interest, compute its sample mean $\overline{X}$, and then use this sample value $\overline{X}$ to decide whether this belief about the value of μ is plausible.

For example, inference concerning the average amount of some trait possessed by the people or objects of a particular population, where "average" is generally construed to be the arithmetic mean, could be concerned with the mean height of all American males, the mean number of cavities of all children aged 7–8 years in Los Angeles in a particular year, or the mean annual rainfall in inches in Chicago for each year since 1925. Although our discussion of statistical inference in this chapter will be confined to examples concerning the mean μ, it applies equally well to many of the other parameters we will encounter later in the book.

ESTIMATING THE POPULATION MEAN, μ, WHEN THE POPULATION STANDARD DEVIATION, σ, IS KNOWN

The use of a single sample value such as $\overline{X}$ to estimate a population value is known as *point estimation*, because the single value $\overline{X}$ represents one point (or one number) on the real-number line. Referring to the task of trying to estimate the mean height of all American males, we might select a random sample of 25 American males, calculate the sample mean height $\overline{X}$, and then use this sample-mean value as our *point estimate* of the population mean μ.

Although the technique of point estimation is often employed in inferential statistics, it has some serious drawbacks that we should know. One of the drawbacks is illustrated by Example 9.1 in the previous chapter in the section on sampling distributions. In this example, we were given the following population of 10 values: {0, 1, 3, 3, 5, 7, 7, 7, 8, 10}.

From this population, we constructed the sampling distribution of means for all possible samples of size $N = 2$. If we look at the list of all possible sample means that could occur from samples of this size taken from this population, we see that the only values $\overline{X}$ could take on are the following:

Sample Means That Could Be Observed

0.0	0.5	1.0	1.5	2.0	2.5	3.0	3.5	4.0	4.5
5.0	5.5	6.0	6.5	7.0	7.5	8.0	8.5	9.0	10.0

But the real mean of this population is $\mu = 5.1$, and none of the sample means listed is exactly equal to 5.1. In other words, in this example it would have been impossible, using point estimation with samples of size 2, to obtain a perfectly accurate estimate of μ.

Suppose, however, that around each sample mean $\overline{X}$ on the list we had constructed an interval of length 6 centered at the sample mean. Considering the intervals rather than just the sample points themselves, we find from Table 10.1 that 79 of the 100 intervals (or 79 percent) actually contain the population mean 5.1.

This result leads us to consider using intervals centered at the sample statistic, rather than just the sample statistic points themselves, to estimate the population parameter. While for this example we chose an interval length of 6, as we shall see later in this chapter, it is always possible to choose an interval length for which some nonzero percent of intervals contain ("capture") the population mean μ. Furthermore, in most cases it is possible to determine just what length interval should be used to give exactly any desired percent of intervals that "work" (capture μ).

TABLE 10.1. Intervals of length 6 constructed about sample means

Sample mean value $\overline{X}$	Frequency of $\overline{X}$	Interval of length 6 centered around $\overline{X}$	Contains $\mu = 5.1$?
0.0	1	(−3.0, 3.0)	No
0.5	2	(−2.5, 3.5)	No
1.0	1	(−2.0, 4.0)	No
1.5	4	(−1.5, 4.5)	No
2.0	4	(−1.0, 5.0)	No
2.5	2	(−0.5, 5.5)	Yes
3.0	6	(0.0, 6.0)	Yes
3.5	6	(0.5, 6.5)	Yes
4.0	12	(1.0, 7.0)	Yes
4.5	2	(1.5, 7.5)	Yes
5.0	15	(2.0, 8.0)	Yes
5.5	6	(2.5, 8.5)	Yes
6.0	6	(3.0, 9.0)	Yes
6.5	6	(3.5, 9.5)	Yes
7.0	9	(4.0, 10.0)	Yes
7.5	8	(4.5, 10.5)	Yes
8.0	1	(5.0, 11.0)	Yes
8.5	6	(5.5, 11.5)	No
9.0	2	(6.0, 12.0)	No
10.0	1	(7.0, 13.0)	No

INTERVAL ESTIMATION

Interval estimation involves the estimation of a population parameter by means of a line segment (or interval) on the real-number line within which the value of the parameter is thought to fall. For example, we might estimate the mean height (to the nearest inch) of all American males by using the interval 65–71 inches centered at the sample-mean value $\overline{X} = 68$ inches rather than by using the sample-mean value, $\overline{X} = 68$ inches itself. We could then say we believe μ to be one of the numbers within the interval 65–71 or, equivalently, that we believe the interval 65–71 contains μ. Of course, this is not as precise a statement as saying that we believe $\mu = 68$ inches exactly. But because both statements are statements of belief, we may ask: "In which of the two statements (the interval statement or the point statement) do we have more confidence that our belief is true?"

In general, we can place more confidence in interval estimations than in point estimations and, by extension, more confidence in interval estimation using longer intervals than in interval estimation using shorter intervals. There is a trade-off between the precision of an estimate and our confidence that the estimate is true.

If we develop a procedure for constructing intervals of estimation that has a prescribed probability of giving an interval that contains μ, then we can use this probability as our measure of confidence that the population mean falls within the interval. Such procedure is based on the Central Limit Theorem.

Recall that under the conditions of the Central Limit Theorem, the sampling distribution of means calculated on samples of size N drawn at random from a population with mean μ and standard deviation σ, is either exactly or approximately normally distributed, with mean μ and standard error $\sigma_{\overline{x}} = \sigma/\sqrt{N}$. Also recall from Example 8.11 that 95 percent of the area under any normal curve lies within 1.96 standard deviations of its mean (within $z = \pm 1.96$ of its mean). Using these two pieces of information, as Figure 10.1 illustrates, 95 percent of the sample means fall within 1.96 standard errors of the population mean; that is, from $\mu - 1.96\sigma_{\overline{x}}$ to $\mu + 1.96\sigma_{\overline{x}}$. Said differently, the probability of selecting at random a sample of size N whose mean $\overline{X}$ lies between $\mu - 1.96\sigma_{\overline{x}}$ and $\mu + 1.96\sigma_{\overline{x}}$ is .95, or the probability that $\overline{X}$ lies within a distance of $1.96\sigma_{\overline{x}}$ from μ is .95.

But, if $\overline{X}$ lies within a distance of $1.96\sigma_x$ from μ, then μ must lie within a distance of $1.96\sigma_{\overline{x}}$ from $\overline{X}$, and μ must lie within the interval $\overline{X} - 1.96\sigma_{\overline{x}}$ to $\overline{X} + 1.96\sigma_{\overline{x}}$. Because 95 percent of all sample means *will* fall within a distance $1.96\sigma_{\overline{x}}$ from μ, it follows that 95 percent of all intervals $\overline{X} - 1.96\sigma_{\overline{x}}$ to $\overline{X} + 1.96 \sigma_{\overline{x}}$ will capture μ.

Stata syntax for creating many of the figures in the chapter are available in the Do-file associated with this chapter and in summary form in a table at the end of the chapter.

Figure 10.2 shows graphically that when $\overline{X}$ is within $1.96\sigma_{\overline{x}}$ of μ (and it will be 95 percent of the time), the resulting interval around $\overline{X}$ will capture μ. Figure 10.3 shows graphically that when $\overline{X}$ is farther than $1.96\sigma_{\overline{x}}$ from μ (and it will be 5 percent of the time), the resulting interval around $\overline{X}$ will not capture μ.

The interval $(\overline{X} - 1.96\sigma_{\overline{x}}, \overline{X} + 1.96\sigma_{\overline{x}})$ is called a *confidence interval (CI) for μ*, and its confidence level is defined as the proportion of such intervals that can be expected to capture μ, in this case .95, or 95 percent. Although any level of confidence may be used, three that are most commonly employed are 90 percent, 95 percent, and 99 percent.

A general equation for the confidence interval for estimating μ is:

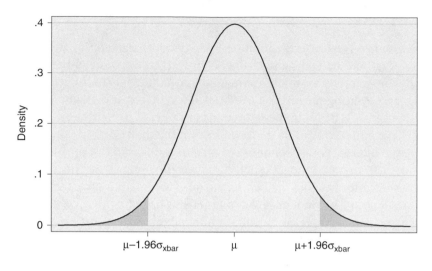

Figure 10.1   Sampling distribution of means: 95 percent of the sample means falls between the points $\mu - 1.96\,\sigma_{\bar{x}}$ and $\mu + 1.96\sigma_{\bar{x}}$.

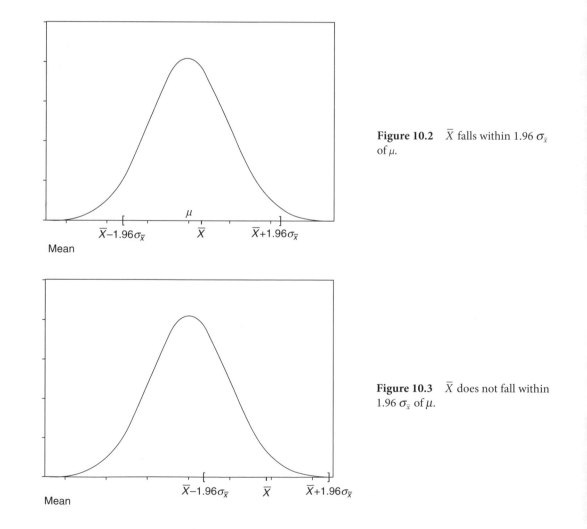

Figure 10.2 $\bar{X}$ falls within 1.96 $\sigma_{\bar{x}}$ of μ.

Figure 10.3 $\bar{X}$ does not fall within 1.96 $\sigma_{\bar{x}}$ of μ.

$$\text{Upper Limit} = \bar{X} + z_c \sigma_{\bar{X}} = \bar{X} + z_c \frac{\sigma}{\sqrt{N}} \qquad (10.1)$$

$$\text{Lower Limit} = \bar{X} - z_c \sigma_{\bar{X}} = \bar{X} - z_c \frac{\sigma}{\sqrt{N}}$$

Or, equivalently, $\bar{X} - z_c \dfrac{\sigma}{\sqrt{N}} \le \mu \le \bar{X} + z_c \dfrac{\sigma}{\sqrt{N}}$

Or, equivalently, $\bar{X} \pm z_c (\text{s.e.})$

where

z_c = 1.645 for a 90 percent CI
  1.960 for a 95 percent CI
  2.576 for a 99 percent CI

☞ **Remark.** Because these confidence intervals require the value of $\sigma/\sqrt{N}$ in their construction, they are based on the assumption that σ, the population standard deviation is known; that it does not need to be estimated. In practice, this assumption is not tenable and one would normally need to estimate σ. We make this assumption here for heuristic reasons and will present a more realistic approach in the next chapter.

• •

EXAMPLE 10.1. Never Ready Flashlight Company has just invented a new, longer-lasting flashlight. Company analysts believe the life expectancy of this new model to have the same variance as the old model, $\sigma^2 = 16$, but they do not know the mean life expectancy, μ. (Keep in mind that μ represents the *population* mean, and in this example, the population consists of *all* these new flashlights.) To estimate μ, they take a random sample of size $N = 100$ flashlights and run them until they die out. If the sample mean turns out to be $\bar{X} = 150$ hours, find a 95 percent CI for μ.

Solution. Because $N = 100$ is large enough to permit us to use the Central Limit Theorem and we know that $\sigma = \sqrt{16} = 4$, we can use Equation 10.1 with $\bar{X} = 150$, $\sigma_{\bar{x}} = \sigma/\sqrt{N} = 4/10 = .4$, and $z_c = 1.960$.

Thus, our 95 percent CI for μ is (149.216, 150.784) hours.

☞ **Remark.** Keep in mind that the procedure and equation given in this chapter for the construction of confidence intervals rests on the assumption that the sampling distribution of means is normally or approximately normally distributed. If this were not true, the z-values provided in Equation 10.1 would not be accurate. Thus, either the population must be known to be normally distributed or the sample must be large enough ($N \ge 30$) to invoke the Central Limit Theorem to be sure that the sampling distribution of means is normally or approximately normally distributed.

☞ **Remark.** Contrary to what you might believe, the CI constructed in Example 10.1 does not have a 95 percent chance of containing the true average lifetime of these new flashlights, μ. Said differently, we are not 95 percent confident or certain that the true average lifetime of these new flashlights is between 149 and 151 hours. Once we have selected our sample, calculated $\overline{X}$, and found the corresponding confidence interval, either μ, the true average lifetime of these new flashlights, is in this interval or it is not, and the probability that the interval contains that true mean is either 1 (if it contains μ) or 0 (if it does not contain μ), not .95. What we can say about Example 10.1 is that if we repeated the *process* of sampling 100 flashlights randomly and computing their average lifetimes, then 95 percent of all the intervals we would construct about these sample means would contain μ. The particular interval that we have constructed (149, 151) may be either one of the 95 percent that do contain the true average lifetime of these new flashlights or one of the 5 percent that do not. Because such a large proportion of all the intervals would contain μ, the true average lifetime of these new flashlights, however, we cannot help but believe that this particular interval is one of those that does.

☞ **Remark.** Based on the above discussion, the reader should convince himself or herself that the 95 percent confidence interval (149, 151) also does NOT imply, for example, that 95 percent of all of such new flashlights will last between from 149 to 151 hours, nor that 95 percent of the particular new flashlights in our sample of 100 flashlights will last between from 149 to 151 hours, nor that there is a 95 percent probability that each of the flashlights in our sample of 100 will last between from 149 to 151 hours. Said simply, the level of confidence (in this case 95 percent) is a statement about the likely true average lifetime of such flashlights, and not about the lifetime of individual flashlights themselves.

☞ **Remark.** The notion of the confidence interval was first introduced by Jerzy Neyman, another giant in the development of the history of modern statistics, in 1934 in a talk before the Royal Statistical Society, entitled "On the Two Different Aspects of the Representative Method" (Salsburg, 2001, p. 120).

RELATING THE LENGTH OF A CONFIDENCE INTERVAL, THE LEVEL OF CONFIDENCE, AND THE SAMPLE SIZE

Based on Equation 10.1, we may note that:

1. If we increase the confidence level, say from 90 percent to 95 percent, and keep the sample size the same, the resulting confidence interval will be longer. Our estimate of μ will then be less precise, but we will be more confident that it is accurate.
2. If we increase the sample size N and keep the confidence level the same, the resulting confidence interval will be shorter.
3. If we decrease the length of the confidence interval and keep the sample size N the same then the confidence level will decrease.

In actual research situations employing interval estimation, it is often possible to specify a desired precision of estimation (i.e., a desired confidence interval length). Because a direct relationship exists between the precision of estimation and the sample size N, as we will discuss in a later section on power, it should be possible to obtain any desired precision of estimation by simply selecting an appropriate sample size N.

HYPOTHESIS TESTING

By contrast to interval estimation where we do not need to begin with an a priori belief about the population parameter of interest (e.g., μ), in hypothesis testing we do. We usually make hypotheses based on our own past experiences and any other available information and then act on these hypotheses. To take an example from everyday life, we take aspirin when we have a headache because we hypothesize, from what we read, from what other people say and from our own experiences that aspirin helps to relieve headaches. But, if the headache gets better some of the time and other times it gets worse, then these experiences are inconsistent with our original hypothesis, and so we may decide that our original hypothesis is not plausible. As another example, we pay for the privilege of using certain credit cards because we hypothesize, from their advertisements, that using them will make our shopping and traveling easier. If it turns out, however, that many of the stores in which we shop do not honor these credit cards, then these experiences are inconsistent with our original hypothesis, and so we may decide that our hypothesis is not plausible. How then, do we decide whether data we have obtained are consistent or inconsistent with our hypothesis; that is, whether a hypothesis we have made is plausible? One way is to use the method of hypothesis testing.

Suppose, based on past observation and theory, you believe that the average mathematics aptitude of first-year college students in California is better than that of the country at large and you would like to test your belief. You decide to use the Scholastic Aptitude Test in Mathematics (SAT-M) to measure mathematics aptitude. You know that the mean score for the national population on which the test was standardized is known to be 500, but you believe that the mean score for California students is higher. Because you have limited funds, you are able to collect data on only a sample of students from the population of 160,000 first-year college students in California and you randomly select a sample of 1,600 from this population. For the time being, assume that you do not have any reason to believe that the variability of the population of California students is different from that of the national standardization population for which the standard deviation is known to be 100.

When stated formally, your belief (that, on average, California students perform better than the country at large on the SAT-M) is called a *hypothesis*. Because your hypothesis challenges conventional wisdom, that California students do not score higher than the country at large in terms of mathematics aptitude, your hypothesis is called the *alternative hypothesis*, denoted in this book by the symbol H_1. The hypothesis that represents current thinking and that will be believed true until you demonstrate that it is implausible (or nullifies it), is called the *null hypothesis*, denoted in this book by the symbol H_0. By contrast, the alternative hypothesis is the statement we would switch to if, through your experiment or study, H_0 were shown to be implausible and H_1 plausible; that is, if the observed results were inconsistent with H_0.

The null hypothesis, in this case, states that the mean of the population of California first-year college students is 500 and may be expressed symbolically as:

$H_0: \mu = 500$

The alternative hypothesis, in this case, states that the mean of the population of California first-year college students is *greater than* 500 and may be expressed symbolically as:

$H_1: \mu > 500$

In sum, the null hypothesis is the hypothesis of no effect (that, in this case, California is no different from the rest of the country in its SAT-M performance); it is also the hypothesis we would like to nullify, or cast doubt on. The alternative hypothesis, on the other hand, is the hypothesis of an effect; it is the hypothesis that we would like to support. H0 and H1 represent two different statements about the state of the California population in this case. The purpose of hypothesis testing is to determine which one of the two is the more plausible.

The outcome of the hypothesis test will be determined by the data you obtain on your random sample of size $N = 1,600$. In particular, if your data are consistent with H_0 (i.e., if $\overline{X}$ is close to 500), then you should conclude that H_0 is a plausible hypothesis. If, on the other hand, your data are not consistent with H_0 (i.e., if $\overline{X}$ is far larger than 500) then you should conclude that H_0 is an implausible hypothesis and H_1 is a plausible one. Notice, that as constructed, the focus of the hypothesis test is on H_0, the null hypothesis, because this is the hypothesis that represents what is believed currently and what will be believed in the future unless something or someone casts doubt upon it through some experiment or study.

In determining which sample outcomes are likely and which are not we assume that H0 is true (that $\mu = 500$) and use the CLT to provide us with information concerning the distribution of all possible sample means that could be obtained. In this example, we know from the CLT that the sampling distribution of means is approximately normally distributed with mean $\mu_{\overline{X}} = 500$, and standard deviation $\sigma_{\overline{x}} = \sigma/\sqrt{N} = 100/\sqrt{1,600} = 100/40 = 2.5$. From this information we can assess, given H_0 is true, the probabilities of obtaining all possible sample means. Let's consider two possible sample means, $\overline{X} = 505$ and $\overline{X} = 502$, and find the probabilities associated with them given that H_0 is true. The shaded areas of Figures 10.4 and 10.5 represent these respective probabilities. As noted earlier, the Do-file associated with this chapter, as well as the summary table at the end of this chapter, contain the syntax for creating these and many of the remaining figures in this chapter.

The shaded area in both cases represents the probability of obtaining a result (e.g., sample mean) that is as or more extreme than the actual result (e.g., sample mean) observed, given that the null hypothesis is true. This probability is called the *p-value* of the test.

First we consider the case where $\overline{X} = 505$. To obtain the *p*-value, or probability of obtaining a mean of 505 or more, we may use either Stata or Table 1 in Appendix C online, www.cambridge.org/Stats-Stata.

To use Stata, you may simply input and execute the following command in your Do-file.

display "p = " 1– normal((505 – 500)/2.5)

The *p*-value returned in the Output Window is **.0228**

To use Table 1, we need to first convert the mean of 505 to a *z*-score to find the number of standard errors $\overline{X} = 505$ is away from $\mu = 500$. To do so we adapt Equation 4.3, the *z*-score formula as Equation 10.2. Equation 10.2 gives the number of standard errors $(\sigma_{\overline{x}})$ the observed mean $(\overline{X})$ is away from the null hypothesized mean (μ) under the sampling distribution of means.

$$z = \frac{\overline{X} - \mu}{\sigma_{\overline{X}}} \qquad (10.2)$$

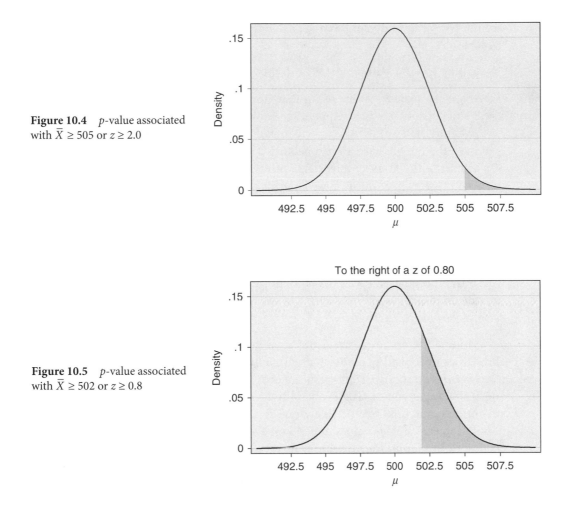

Figure 10.4 *p*-value associated with $\overline{X} \geq 505$ or $z \geq 2.0$

Figure 10.5 *p*-value associated with $\overline{X} \geq 502$ or $z \geq 0.8$

According to Equation 10.2, the obtained *z*-score is $z = \dfrac{505 - 500}{2.5} = 2.0$, which also may be obtained using Stata's built-in calculator (**display (505 − 500)/2.5**). We may then consult Table 1 to find the area under the curve to the right of $z = 2.0$. Whether we use Stata or Table 1, we find that the *p*-value associated with $\overline{X} \geq 505$ is .023.

Given that this probability of occurrence is so small, if the null hypothesis were true, we could hardly expect to obtain a sample of 1600 first-year college students with a mean mathematics aptitude score that would be so much greater than 500. Accordingly, we would have to question the truth of the null hypothesis. In fact, if we were to obtain a sample with such a large mean value, we would have evidence to support our belief in the alternative hypothesis. Based on this evidence we would decide to reject the null hypothesis in favor of the alternative.

☞ **Remark.** Because this test is based on a variation of the *z*-score formula (Equation 10.2), in general, a hypothesis test of the parameter μ when σ is known is called a *z-test*.

Now we consider the case where $\overline{X} = 502$. To obtain the *p*-value, or probability of obtaining a mean of 502 or more, we may, once again, use either Stata or Table 1 in Appendix C online, www.cambridge.org/Stats-Stata. Either we input and execute the following Stata syntax:

display "*p* = " 1 − normal((502 − 500)/2.5)

Or we calculate a *z*-value using Equation 10.2 and Stata's built-in calculator to obtain *z* = .8 and consult Table 1 in Appendix C online, www.cambridge.org/Stats-Stata. In either case, we find the *p*-value to be approximately .21.

Given that, in this case, the probability is large (there is a one chance in five of obtaining 502 or more), the result is consistent with the null hypothesis, casting doubt on our belief in the alternative hypothesis. Based on this result we would decide not to reject the null as implausible.

☞ **Remark.** The *p*-value may be viewed as the degree to which the observed result is consistent with the null hypothesis. The less consistent the observed result is with the null hypothesis, the lower the *p*-value. In our example, a result of 505 or more is less consistent with a true population mean of 500 than is a result of 502 or more. Accordingly, *p*-values provide an indication of the strength of evidence to reject or not to reject the null hypothesis in favor of the alternative.

While we have categorized .023 as a probability associated with an unlikely event and .21 as a probability associated with a likely one, it is up to the researcher to decide, *when setting up the hypothesis test*, the probability level that distinguishes between likely and unlikely outcomes. The probability level that the researcher chooses to distinguish an unlikely outcome from a likely one is called the *significance level* of the test, and is denoted by α. While *p*-values depend on the particular result observed, significance levels do not. A significance level may be considered a standard or criterion from which to judge the strength of evidence against the null hypothesis. Commonly used significance levels are $\alpha = .10$, $\alpha = .05$, and $\alpha = .01$. When a significance level is set at .01, for example, stronger evidence is required to reject the null hypothesis than when either .05 or .10 is used. Accordingly, $\alpha = .01$ is considered to be a more stringent criterion than $\alpha = .05$ or .10.

While the commonly used significance levels in the behavioral and social sciences are .10, .05, and .01, a range of reasonable values should be considered before one is chosen. Significance levels greater than .10, however, are generally not used because they allow too great a chance of incorrectly rejecting H_0. Significance levels less than .01 are also generally not used because they tend to make the test so conservative that we run a large risk of retaining H_0 when we should not have done so (we will talk more about this type of error later in this chapter). The significance level α is set as the largest risk of incorrectly rejecting the null hypothesis that the researcher is willing to make in a particular situation. According to Fisher (1959), the individual who introduced the hypothesis testing procedure in the 1920s, "no scientific worker has a fixed level of significance at which, from year to year, and in all circumstances, he rejects [null] hypotheses; he rather gives his mind to each particular case in the light of his evidence and his ideas" (p. 42).

In our example, we implicitly used .05 as our significance level, and as a result, judged the *p*-value of .023 as providing sufficiently strong evidence to reject the null hypothesis in favor of the alternative. In the first case, therefore, we concluded that, on average, first-year college students in California score statistically significantly higher on the SAT-M than the country as a whole ($\overline{X} = 505$, $\sigma = 100$, $p = .023$). Analogously, using a .05 significance level, or even a .10 significance level, a p-value of .21 does not provide sufficiently strong evidence to reject the null hypothesis in favor of the alternative. In the second case, therefore, we concluded that, on average, first-year college students in California do not score statistically significantly higher on the SAT-M than the country as a whole ($\overline{X} = 502$, $\sigma = 100$, $p = .21$).

In general, if the p-value is less than α we reject the null hypothesis as implausible in favor of the alternative and say that the result is statistically significant. Alternatively, if the p-value is greater than α we retain the null hypothesis as plausible and say that the result is not statistically significant.

We remarked at the beginning of Chapter 9 that when we work in the area of inferential statistics, we can never be 100 percent certain of our conclusions. We should note here that whenever a hypothesis is tested, the decision to reject or not to reject H_0 is always made with some degree of uncertainty. In other words, the possibility always exists that the decision made is, in fact, the wrong decision.

Suppose that, with respect to our example, we did observe a mean of 505. While the p-value of .023 associated with a mean of 505 or greater renders this event *unlikely* if H_0 is true, it does not render this event *impossible*. There is still a possibility, albeit small ($p = .023$), that we would have observed a mean of 505 or greater in a sample selected randomly from a population whose true mean is 500.

Analogously, suppose we did observe a mean of 502. While the p-value of .21 associated with a mean of 502 or greater renders this event likely if H_0 is true, this p-value does not prove that H_0 is true. There is still an unknown possibility that we would have observed a mean of 502 or greater in a sample selected randomly from a population whose true mean is greater than 500.

Thus, while rejection of a null hypothesis does not, by itself, say a lot about the truth of that null hypothesis, neither does non-rejection. By failing to reject a null hypothesis, one cannot conclude that the null hypothesis is true; all that one can conclude is that one cannot conclude that the null hypothesis is false (Cohen, 1990). However, the null hypothesis testing procedure provides a way to make sense of the observed result in terms of whether it is real or merely apparent (due to sampling error).

☞ **Remark.** As mentioned earlier, Sir Ronald A. Fisher introduced the null hypothesis testing procedure in the 1920s. In his approach, one states a hypothesis that describes in null form the state of affairs in a population with regard to the value of some parameter, such as a mean. Through the collection of data, randomly sampled from that population, one then seeks to nullify that hypothesis with some degree of probability, and in so doing, engage in a scientific process of proof through disproof. Jerzy Neyman and Egon Pearson, Karl Pearson's son, later expanded Fisher's approach by incorporating an alternative hypothesis and by forcing a choice between the null and its alternate. In the Neyman and Pearson approach, which is the one currently used today, one does not simply reject the null hypothesis, but, rather, rejects the null *in favor of the alternative*.

The Neyman and Pearson null hypothesis testing procedure is further illustrated in Example 10.2.

EXAMPLE 10.2. Suppose Write-On Pen Company manufactures a pen that has a mean and a standard deviation, measured in hours of continuous writing, of $\mu = 100$ and $\sigma = 9$, respectively. To increase its sales, the company has slightly modified the manufacturing process to produce a pen that it claims will last longer than the old pens. It has no reason to believe, however, that the new process alters the variability of these pens in terms of hours of continuous writing. To test this claim, the company selects at random $N = 400$ pens manufactured under the new process and uses them continuously until they no longer work. If the sample mean in terms of hours of continuous writing turns out to be $\overline{X} = 101$ and the significance level selected is $\alpha = .05$, what conclusion can the company draw about this new pen?

Solution. The company would like to claim that its new pen is an improvement (in terms of hours of continuous writing) over its old pen, that the mean writing time of the new pen is greater than that of the old pen. However, until evidence is provided to the contrary, the company must assume that the mean writing time of the new pen is 100 hours, the same as the mean writing time of the old pen. These hypotheses may be stated symbolically as:

$$H_0: \quad \mu = 100$$
$$H_1: \quad \mu > 100$$

where μ represents the mean continuous writing time (in hours) of the population of all pens manufactured using the new process.

☞ **Remark.** While expressed as $H_0: \mu = 100$ versus $H_1: \mu > 100$, there are two reasons why a more logical rendition of these hypotheses would be $H_0: \mu \leq 100$ versus $H_1: \mu > 100$. First, it would be in the company's best interests to nullify the hypothesis that the mean writing time of its new pen is *at most* 100 hours (not simply *equals* 100 hours), in favor of the hypothesis that the mean writing time of its new pen is greater than 100 hours. Second, the hypotheses, $H_0: \mu \leq 100$ versus $H_1: \mu > 100$, account for *all* possible values of μ, not just those equal to or greater than 100. Why then do we express the hypotheses as $H_0: \mu = 100$ versus $H_1: \mu > 100$? Simply stated, the CLT requires a single-valued null hypothesis (e.g., $H_0: \mu = 100$) to describe the sampling distribution of means upon which the hypothesis test rests; the single value used (100 in this case) is most reasonable because any sample result that would cause us to reject $H_0: \mu = 100$ in favor of $H_1: \mu > 100$ would also cause us to reject any other single value of μ less than 100.

Because the null hypothesis specifies a particular (single) value for μ (i.e., 100), we can use the CLT to describe the sampling distribution of means. If we assume H0 true, the sampling distribution of means for samples of size $N = 400$ from this population should be approximately normal with mean $\mu_{\overline{x}} = \mu = 100$, and standard deviation $\sigma_{\overline{x}} = \sigma/\sqrt{N} = 100/\sqrt{400} = 9/20 = 0.45$. Using the **display 1- normal((101 − 100)/.45)** command in Stata or Table 1 in Appendix C online, we determine the p-value, the probability of observing a mean of 101 hours or greater given the null hypothesis is true, to be $p = .013$ (see Figure 10.6).

Figure 10.6. p-value associated with $\overline{X} \geq 101$

Because the significance level for this test has been set at $\alpha = .05$, and because p is less than α in this case, we reject the null hypothesis as implausible in favor of the alternative. That is, the new pen lasts statistically significantly longer than the old pen ($\overline{X} = 101$, $\sigma = 9$, $p = .013$).

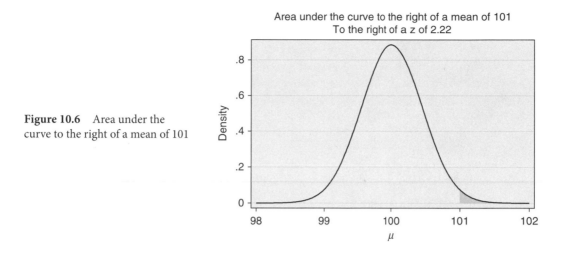

Figure 10.6 Area under the curve to the right of a mean of 101

☞ **Remark.** In our example, we were able to reject the null in favor of the alternative that the new pen lasts longer than the old pen because the observed sample mean was sufficiently *greater than* 100. Had the sample mean been *less than* 100, no matter how much less, logically, we would not have been able to reject the null hypothesis in favor of the alternative because under this circumstance, the alternative would have been even less plausible than the null. Because the alternative hypothesis stipulates a direction of difference from the null, as illustrated in Figure 10.6, only one-tail under the normal curve would yield an appropriate *p*-value. As illustrated in Figure 10.6, for this example, the one tail that will yield an appropriate *p*-value is the right tail. Had the alternative hypothesis been of the form $H_1: \mu < 100$, the left tail would have been the one to yield an appropriate *p*-value. Directional alternative hypotheses always give rise to *one-tailed tests*.

The alternative hypotheses in both the SAT-M and Write-On Pen situations were directional and hence required one-tailed tests. In the next example we present an example where the alternative hypothesis is non-directional and the hypothesis test is *two-tailed*.

EXAMPLE 10.3. P. Ahjay, a well-known researcher in learning theory, would like to determine whether a particular type of preconditioning affects the time it takes individuals to solve a given set of anagram problems. In the past, individuals without such preconditioning have solved the set of problems in an average of 280 seconds with a standard deviation of 20 seconds. For her study, Ms. Ahjay selects a random sample of $N = 100$ individuals, gives them the preconditioning, and then computes the time it takes them to solve the set of problems. While she expects the preconditioning to affect mean performance, she has no reason to believe that it will affect performance variability. Accordingly, she assumes that the standard deviation of the population with preconditioning is the same as the standard deviation of the population without preconditioning, $\sigma = 20$ seconds. (In the next chapter, we will discuss more fully the reasonableness of this assumption about the standard deviation, but for the time being we need to make such an assumption to use the Central Limit Theorem.) If she finds the mean time for solving this set of problems for her sample to be $\overline{X} = 276$ seconds, determine, using the null hypothesis testing procedure and $\alpha = .05$, whether preconditioning affects the mean time for solving this set of problems.

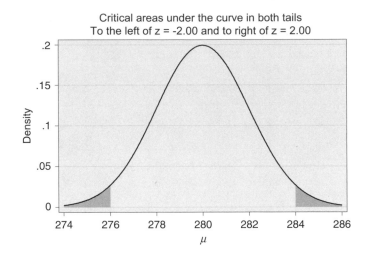

Figure 10.7   Shaded areas for a non-directional two-tailed test

Solution. Because preconditioning may have the effect of increasing or decreasing the time it takes to solve the set of anagram problems, P. Ahjay would like to support the hypothesis that mean time to complete the set of anagrams is *different* (either more or less) with pre-conditioning than without. However, until evidence is provided to the contrary, she must assume that the mean time to solve this set of problems is 280 seconds, the same as without preconditioning. Therefore, our null and alternative hypotheses are:

H_0: $\mu = 280$
H_1: $\mu \neq 280$

where μ represents the mean time (in seconds) for the population to solve the anagram task with pre-conditioning.

Because the null hypothesis specifies a particular value for μ (i.e., 280), we can use the CLT to describe the sampling distribution of means. If we assume H_0 true, the sampling distribution of means for samples of size $N = 100$ from this population should be approximately normal with mean $\mu_{\bar{x}} = \mu = 280$, and standard deviation $\sigma_{\bar{x}} = \sigma/\sqrt{N} = 20/\sqrt{100} = 20/10 = 2$.

☞ **Remark.** Recall that when the alternative hypothesis is directional and we are using a one-tailed test, we find the *p*-value by finding the probability of obtaining the observed result or one that is more extreme in the direction of the tail that will allow us to reject the null in favor of the alternative. If the alternative hypothesis is of the form: $H_1: \mu >$ some value, then the appropriate tail is on the right. On the other hand, if the alternative hypothesis is of the form: $H_1: \mu <$ some value, then the appropriate tail is on the left. In the case of a non-directional alternative hypothesis, we find the *p*-value by finding the probability of obtaining the observed result or one that is more extreme in the direction of *both tails* because an extreme value in either tail would logically allow us to reject the null hypothesis in favor of the alternative. See Figure 10.7.

Because the observed result in our example is 276 seconds, a difference of 4 from the hypothesized population mean μ of 280 seconds, a result more extreme than 276 seconds is defined as 276 or fewer seconds *or* 284 or more seconds. Figure 10.7 illustrates the two areas under the normal curve that when combined yield the p-value we seek; that is, the probability of observing a mean result of 276 seconds or fewer, or 284 seconds or more given the null hypothesis is true. Using the display normal((276–280)/2)*2 command in Stata we determine this p-value to be .046.

Alternatively, we could have found the p-value associated with $\overline{X} \leq 276$ or $\overline{X} \geq 284$ relative to a mean of 280 and a standard error of 2 as the area associated with $z \leq -2$ or $z \geq 2$ relative to a mean of 0 and a standard deviation of 1 using Table 1 in Appendix C online, www.cambridge.org/Stats-Stata.

(Note that from Equation 10.3, $z = \dfrac{276 - 280}{2} = -2$, and that $z = \dfrac{284 - 280}{2} = 2$). In this case, as well, the p-value equals .046.

Because the significance level for this test has been set at $\alpha = .05$, and because p is less than α in this case, we reject the null hypothesis as implausible in favor of the alternative. That is, the pre-conditioning statistically significantly affects the time it takes to complete the anagram task. Furthermore, because the observed result of 276 seconds is below 280 seconds, we may conclude that pre-conditioning statistically significantly decreases the amount of time it takes to complete the anagram task ($X = 276, \sigma = 20, p = .046$).

THE RELATIONSHIP BETWEEN HYPOTHESIS TESTING AND INTERVAL ESTIMATION

In the introduction to this chapter, we noted that interval estimation and hypothesis testing of the mean μ give essentially equivalent results. We explore this more closely in relation to Example 10.3.

Recall that in Example 10.3, P. Ahjay hypothesized that a certain type of preconditioning affects the time it takes individuals to solve a given set of anagram problems. In particular, she hypothesized that with preconditioning the population mean time to complete the anagram task would be different from 280 seconds, the known time to complete this task without preconditioning. Using a random sample of $N = 100$ individuals, she found the mean time, with preconditioning, to be $\overline{X} = 276$ seconds. She set $\alpha = .05$ and found the probability to be only $p = .046$ of observing this mean, or one more extreme in either direction, in a random sample selected from a population whose true mean is $\mu = 280$. Accordingly, she concluded that, preconditioning statistically significantly affects the mean time for solving this set of problems, and, in fact, decreases it.

Suppose, that instead of running a hypothesis test of H_0: $\mu = 280$ versus H_1: $\mu \neq 280$, P. Ahjay decided to use her sample result to construct a 95 percent CI for μ. Using Equation 10.1, the 95 percent CI she would have constructed is $(276 - 1.96(2), 276 + 1.96(2))$, or equivalently, $(272.08, 279.92)$. Given this interval, she would have confidence that μ is equal to one of the values within the interval 272.08 to 279.92, and that μ is *not* equal to any of the values outside the interval 272.08 to 279.92.

Because $\mu = 280$ is *not* within the confidence interval, she would conclude that it is unlikely that 280 is a plausible value of μ. In hypothesis test terms this would imply a rejection of H_0: $\mu = 280$ in favor of H_1: $\mu \neq 280$. Because in this case $\mu = 280$ falls above the upper limit of the CI, she would conclude that preconditioning statistically significantly decreases the mean time for solving this set of problems, which is exactly the conclusion she reached on the basis of her earlier hypothesis test.

In general, given a (1 − α) × 100 percent CI estimate of μ,

1. *the values that fall within the confidence interval are exactly those values of μ that would be retained as plausible in a nondirectional hypothesis test at significance level α.*
2. *the values that fall outside the confidence interval are exactly those values of μ that would be rejected as implausible in a nondirectional hypothesis test at significance level α.*

Constructing a $(1 − \alpha) \times 100$ percent confidence interval estimate of μ may be viewed as the equivalent of running nondirectional hypothesis tests at significance level α simultaneously on all possible values of μ from negative infinity to positive infinity.

Because confidence intervals capture the magnitude of the difference between the observed and null hypothesized values, they provide more meaningful information as to the magnitude of the treatment effect than just whether the difference is likely to be zero in the population.

EFFECT SIZE

From Equation 10.2, we may note that the size of the z-value, representing the degree to which the observed mean deviates from the null hypothesized mean, depends not only on $\overline{X}$, μ, and σ, but also on the sample size, N. When N is large, even when the difference between $\overline{X}$ and μ is small, z will be large because the standard error of the mean, $\sigma_{\overline{x}} = \sigma/\sqrt{N}$, the denominator of the z-ratio, will be small. As a result, even trivially small deviations from the null hypothesized mean can be statistically significant. While the hypothesis test tells us how likely the observed sample result is given the null hypothesis is true, it tells us nothing about *the degree to which* the null hypothesis is false; that is, the degree to which the observed result departs from the value of the null hypothesis. To be useful in helping us discover truths about phenomena of interest, the null hypothesis test must be supplemented by other forms of analysis that are independent of sample size to determine the nature and magnitude of the result obtained. Knowing the magnitude of the result obtained, called the *effect size*, allows us to determine whether our statistically significant result is also *practically significant*.

In Example 10.3, the test result was statistically significant, indicating that H_1: $\mu \neq 280$ was a more plausible statement about the true value of the population mean μ than H_0: $\mu = 280$. Taking this result literally, all we have shown is that there is reason to believe that μ differs from 280. The amount by which μ differs from 280 is not specified by our conclusion. That is, our conclusion could imply that μ differs from 280 by a great deal or by a trivially small amount. If trivially small, the difference is likely not to have practical significance or importance, and would render inconsequential the fact of having achieved statistical significance.

In our example, preconditioning resulted in a 4-second reduction in the solution time for the sample. Whether this reduction is deemed to be trivially small must rely on the content area experience and best judgment of the researcher carrying out this study. Of course, the researcher may gain insight into the importance of her finding by constructing a confidence interval to consider the range of plausible values for μ, so that she can determine how close the boundaries of the interval are to the null hypothesized value of 280, in this case. That the upper limit to the CI in this case is 279.92 suggests a potential population mean difference of only .08 seconds (from 280), which one could assume is small. She may also gain insight by computing Cohen's (1988) d, one of many possible measures of effect size that are independent of sample size.

In this situation, d is computed by taking the difference between the observed mean and null hypothesized mean, μ, and dividing that difference by the population standard deviation, σ, assumed to be known. An algebraic expression for Cohen's d is given by Equation 10.3,

$$d = \frac{\bar{X} - \mu}{\sigma} \tag{10.3}$$

For Example 10.2, $d = \dfrac{276 - 280}{20} = \dfrac{-4}{20} = -.20$. The sign indicates the direction of the effect (it is negative in this example because the observed mean falls below the null hypothesized mean), while the absolute value indicates the magnitude of the effect (.20 standard deviations). Thus, Cohen's d tells our researcher that the observed result falls only .20 standard deviations below the null hypothesized mean of 280. This finding would appear to corroborate the CI estimate of a small effect and suggest that preconditioning has limited utility in altering the time to solve such anagram problems. In the final analysis, however, judgments about the magnitude of effect size are subjective and must be based ultimately on the content area knowledge of the researcher. In the absence of such knowledge, Cohen (1988) offers the following guidelines for evaluating effect sizes in terms of d:

> $d = .20$ represents a "small" effect size
> $d = .50$ represents a "medium" effect size
> $d = .80$ represents a "large" effect size.

These guidelines suggest the effect of preconditioning to be small in the case of these anagrams.

TYPE II ERROR AND THE CONCEPT OF POWER

When a decision is made based on a hypothesis test, four different situations can result:

1. H_0 is true but we reject it.
2. H_0 is true and we retain it.
3. H_0 is false and we reject it.
4. H_0 is false but we retain it.

These outcomes and their probabilities of occurrence are displayed in Figure 10.8. Notice that while situations 1 and 4 represent incorrect decisions, situations 2 and 3 represent correct decisions.

	Reject H_0	Retain H_0
H_0 is true	Incorrect decision: Type I error Probability $= \alpha$	Correct decision Probability $= 1 - \alpha$
H_0 is false	Correct decision Probability $= 1 - \beta$	Incorrect decision: Type II error Probability $= \beta$

Figure 10.8   The four possible outcomes of a hypothesis test.

The incorrect decision of situation 1 is what we have called a Type I error. The risk of committing a Type I error equals the α level of the test, the level at which we would regard an observation to be unlikely to occur by chance. The incorrect decision of situation 4 is what is called a Type II error. The risk of committing a Type II error equals the β (beta) level of the test.

When we conduct a hypothesis test, we want to minimize the probability of making either a Type I error or a Type II error. Unfortunately, these two types of errors are, in a sense, inversely related. The typical research situation of concern in this book is one in which H_0 represents some established procedure and H_1 represents a deviation from it. A decision to reject H_0 in favor of H_1 might therefore result in further expenditures, further testing, and possibly even in some basic changes in the established procedure.

Accordingly, if we are to reject H_0, we certainly do not want to reject it falsely (commit a Type I error), so we generally try to set our test so that the significance level α is the one that is kept small at the possible expense of having a relatively large β.

The correct decision of situation 2 arises when the test does not detect a difference from the null hypothesis when the null hypothesis is in fact true. The probability of this correct decision is represented by the complement of α, $1 - \alpha$. Finally, the correct decision of situation 3 arises when the test does detect a difference from the null hypothesis when the null hypothesis is in fact false (when the alternative hypothesis is true). The probability of this correct decision is represented by the complement of β, $1 - \beta$, and because of its importance within the null hypothesis test procedure, this probability is called the *power* of the test.

The power of a hypothesis test may be likened to the power of magnification used to view a cell under a microscope (Hays, 1973). Suppose, for example, a particular cell in which we are interested has a break in its cell wall that we cannot observe with the naked eye. If we place the cell under the microscope and use a low power setting, we still do not detect the break in the cell wall. In this case, we say that the microscope lacks sufficient power to detect the difference or break in the cell wall that exists. When we increase the microscope power setting to high we detect the difference in the cell wall. In this case, the power of the microscope is sufficiently high to detect the break in the cell wall.

Without sufficient power in the microscope, we are not likely to detect the difference that exists in the cell wall. So, it is the same for the hypothesis test. Without sufficient power in the hypothesis test, we are not likely to detect a difference from the null hypothesis even when such a difference exists. Hence, when we set up a hypothesis test, we want to maximize the power of the test, $1 - \beta$. We also want to minimize the risk of making a Type I error, α. As noted earlier, an α level greater than .10 is seldom used. Likewise, a power level less than .80 is also seldom used. When conducting a hypothesis test, researchers like to have a probability of at least .80 of detecting a difference where one exists. In that case, if no difference were detected, and the null hypothesis were retained, the researcher would

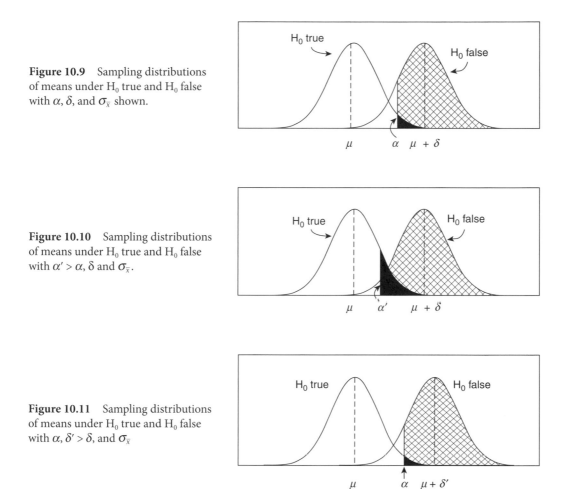

Figure 10.9 Sampling distributions of means under H_0 true and H_0 false with α, δ, and $\sigma_{\bar{x}}$ shown.

Figure 10.10 Sampling distributions of means under H_0 true and H_0 false with $\alpha' > \alpha$, δ and $\sigma_{\bar{x}}$.

Figure 10.11 Sampling distributions of means under H_0 true and H_0 false with α, $\delta' > \delta$, and $\sigma_{\bar{x}}$

be reasonably confident that a difference did *not* exist rather than that a difference did exist and that the test had insufficient power to detect it.

A good way to understand power is through its graphic representation as shown in Figure 10.9. In Figure 10.9, the curve labeled "H_0 true" represents the sampling distribution of means given that H0 is true. Note that variations of these figures may be obtained using the Stata code in the do-file associated with Chapter 10.

We know by the Central Limit Theorem that this curve is normal in shape. We also know by the Central Limit Theorem that the mean of the means, $\mu_{\bar{x}}$, under this distribution equals μ and that the standard deviation of the means, $\sigma_{\bar{x}}$, under this distribution equals $\sigma/\sqrt{N}$, where N equals the size of the sample randomly selected from the population of interest. The shaded area under the curve in the right tail depicts α; that is, if $\alpha = .05$, for example, then the shaded area represents 5 percent of the area under that curve. The z-value that marks off this shaded area to its right is labeled z_c. Whenever the observed sample mean $\bar{X}$ exceeds z_c, our decision is to reject H_0 as implausible. Hence, the shaded area (to the right of z_c) represents the probability of rejecting H_0 as implausible when in fact H_0 is true.

The curve labeled "H_0 false (H_1 true)" represents the sampling distribution of means given that H_0 is false by a difference of δ units. Once again, we know by the Central Limit

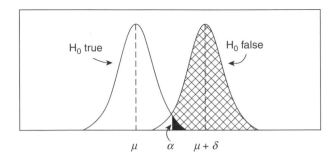

Figure 10.12 Sampling distributions of means under H_0 true and H_0 false with α, δ, and $\sigma'_{\bar{x}} < \sigma_{\bar{x}}$.

Theorem that this curve is normal in shape. We also know by the Central Limit Theorem and the rules of transformation, that the mean of the means, $\mu_{\bar{x}}$, under this distribution equals $\mu + \delta$ and that the standard deviation of the means, $\sigma_{\bar{x}}$, under this distribution equals $\sigma/\sqrt{N}$, where N equals the size of the sample randomly selected from the population of interest. (We assume that the curves differ only in their means, by an amount δ, that their standard deviations are the same.) The cross-hatched area under this curve depicts $1 - \beta$, the power of the test, because in this area H_0 is false and our decision is to reject H_0 as implausible since in this area, the observed $\bar{X}$ exceeds z_c. If $1 - \beta = .80$, for example, then the shaded area represents 80 percent of the area under that curve.

☞ **Remark.** By separating the two curves by an amount equal to δ units, we are indicating that we wish to find the power associated with this hypothesis test for detecting a difference of δ units from the null hypothesized mean μ. When units are expressed in terms of standard deviation units, the difference of δ units is the effect size. In practice if the effect size is set equal to the minimum-sized difference that the researcher would like to detect as meaningful, and if the power of the hypothesis test is adjusted to detect that effect size as statistically significant, then only meaningful or important effects, as judged by the researcher, should be declared statistically significant. In general, such practice will avoid the problem of detecting trivially important effects to be statistically significant. Effects that are trivially important are just that, even in the face of statistical significance. Hence, effects that are statistically significant but trivially important should not be declared significant in the broad sense of the term. To be truly significant, an effect should be both statistically and practically significant.

If we wish to adjust power to detect differences that are deemed to be important, we must understand the factors that influence power. Using Figures 10.10 through 10.12 in conjunction with Figure 10.9 we shall illustrate that the size of the cross-hatched area, the area that represents the power of the test, will vary as a function of α, δ, and $\sigma_{\bar{x}}$. That is, we shall illustrate that, all things being equal, if the value of any one of the parameters, α, δ, or $\sigma_{\bar{x}}$, changes, the result will be a change in the proportion of the cross-hatched area under the curve; that is, the power of the test.

INCREASING THE LEVEL OF SIGNIFICANCE, α

If we hold δ and $\sigma_{\bar{x}}$ to be the same as in Figure 10.9, but we increase α, the level of significance, to α', then the shaded area associated with the level of significance in Figure 10.10 exceeds that of Figure 10.9. If we compare Figure 10.9 with 10.10, we may note that an increase in the level of significance, while keeping δ and $\sigma_{\bar{x}}$ the same, increases the proportion of cross-hatched area under the H_0 false curve. Said differently, *an increase in the level of significance of a hypothesis test, with δ and $\sigma_{\bar{x}}$ held constant, will increase the power of that test.* Because, as noted earlier, however, levels of significance greater than 0.10 are seldom used, an increase in α to achieve greater power is self-limiting.

INCREASING THE EFFECT SIZE, δ

If we hold α and $\sigma_{\bar{x}}$ to be the same as in Figure 10.9, but we increase δ, the effect size to δ', then in Figure 10.11, the cross-hatched area associated with the power of the test will increase. Said differently, *an increase in the minimum effect size, the minimum difference in population means that we would like to detect by a hypothesis test, with α and $\sigma_{\bar{x}}$ held constant, will increase the power of that test.* Because there are specific, minimum-sized differences in population means that a researcher would like to detect as meaningful, the effect size, like the level of significance, cannot be set to be arbitrarily large for the sake of increasing power.

DECREASING THE STANDARD ERROR OF THE MEAN, $\sigma_{\bar{x}}$

If we hold α and δ to be the same as in Figure 10.9, but decrease $\sigma_{\bar{x}}$, the standard error of the means, to $\sigma'_{\bar{x}}$ then in Figure 10.12, the cross-hatched area associated with the power of the test will increase. Said differently, *an increase in the standard error of the means, $\sigma_{\bar{x}}$, with α and δ held constant, will decrease the power of the test.* Furthermore, because $\sigma_{\bar{x}} = \sigma/\sqrt{N}$, a simple way to decrease $\sigma_{\bar{x}}$ is by increasing the sample size, N. Thus, *an increase in sample size N, with α and δ held constant, will increase the power of the test.*

Of the three factors shown to affect the power of a test, the level of significance α, the effect size δ, and the standard error of the means, $\sigma_{\bar{x}} = \sigma/\sqrt{N}$, an increase in sample size, N, is usually the most viable in producing an increase in power.

In practice, given a specified α-value, one should set the power of the test to detect a difference from the null hypothesis that is of practical importance. As noted earlier, this approach can avoid detecting trivially small departures from the null hypothesis as statistically significant. The usual procedure is to set α, to decide on the appropriate effect size worth detecting, and to find the sample size N that will decrease the standard error of the means sufficiently to achieve the desired power. A number of computer programs are available both commercially and from the internet that are designed to help researchers find the sample size required to achieve a desired power with specified α and δ. Alternatively, one may use a book of power tables, such as the one by Cohen (1988), to make this determination.

To give some perspective on the sample size required to obtain a power of .80 to detect a small, medium, and large effect given α = .05, two-tailed, we present Table 10.2.

TABLE 10.2. Approximate sample sizes required to obtain a power of .80 for different effect sizes when α = .05.

Effect Size (Cohen's d)	Sample Size (N)
.20	196
.50	31
.80	12

☞ **Remark.** For other values of Cohen's *d*, when $\alpha = .05$ and the alternative hypothesis is non-directional, we may use the following equation to find N to achieve a power of .80.

$$\sqrt{N} = \frac{2.80}{d} \quad (10.4)$$

CLOSING REMARKS

This chapter has been concerned with inferences involving the population mean based on interval estimation and the null hypothesis testing procedure. For some time now, and with greater frequency more recently, the null hypothesis testing procedure has been the subject of much scrutiny and public debate (Bakan, 1966; Carver, 1978; Cohen, 1990, 1994; Falk & Greenbaum, 1995; Hagen, 1997; Harlow, Mulaik, & Steiger, 1997; Kaplan, 1964; Kirk, 1996; Lykken, 1968; Meehl, 1967; Rosnow & Rosenthal, 1989; Rozeboom, 1960; Thompson, 1994, 1996).

Intended as a method of ruling out chance as an explanation of observed results, the null hypothesis testing procedure has become, since its introduction by Fisher in the 1920s, a ubiquitous technique in the behavioral sciences. Not only is it "identified with 'scientific method,' but it is so mechanically applied that it undermines the very spirit of scientific inquiry" (Kaplan, 1964, p. 29). For this reason, in this chapter we have taken care to point out some of the pitfalls associated with using the null hypothesis testing procedure in so purely a mechanical way.

We reiterate that statistical significance without practical significance does not advance our knowledge regarding the truths concerning phenomena of interest, and that practical significance may be established only through an interplay of strong theories, critical thinking, and subjective judgment. To have greatest impact on a field of inquiry, the research process must be a process in the true sense of the word. It must rely on scientific principles and formulations, but it must also engage the researcher with all his good judgment, creative energies, and content area expertise. As Kaplan (1964) suggests, "Electronic computers, game-theoretic models, and statistical formulas are but instruments after all; it is not *they* (italics in original) that produce scientific results but the investigator who uses them scientifically" (p. 29).

In the remainder of this book we present some of the instruments of scientific inquiry and rely upon you, our reader, to provide your own good judgment, creative energies, and content area expertise to use these instruments scientifically.

SUMMARY OF CHAPTER 10 STATA COMMANDS

For a complete listing of all Stata commands associated with this chapter, you may access the Do-file for Chapter 10 located on the text website.

Create	Command Lines
Figure 10.1	**twoway function y=normalden(x), range(-4 − 1.96) recast(area) color(gs12) ‖ function y=normalden(x), range(1.96 4) recast(area) color(gs12) ‖ function**

Create	Command Lines
	y=normalden(x), range(-4 4) lcolor(black) xtitle("{it: Mean ") ytitle("Density") title("Critical Values for the Standard Normal Distribution") subtitle("95% of the area falls between -1.96 and +1.96 se's of the population mean") legend(off) xlabel(-1.96 0 1.96)
Figure 10.4	twoway function y=normalden(x, 500, 2.50), range(505 510) recast(area) color(gs12)|| function y=normalden(x, 500, 2.50), range(490 510) lcolor(black) xtitle("{it: Mean}") ytitle("Density") title("Area under the curve to the right of a mean of 505") subtitle("To the right of a z of 2.0") legend(off) xlabel(492.5 495.0 497.5 500 502.5 505.0 507.5)
Figure 10.5	twoway function y=normalden(x, 500, 2.50), range(502 510) recast(area) color(gs12)|| function y=normalden(x, 500, 2.50), range(490 510) lcolor(black) xtitle("{it: Mean}") ytitle("Density") title("Area under the curve to the right of a mean of 502") subtitle("To the right of a z of 0.80") legend(off) xlabel(492.5 495.0 497.5 500 502.5 505.0 507.5)
Figure 10.6	twoway function y=normalden(x, 100, .45), range(101 102) recast(area) color(gs12) || function y=normalden(x, 100, .45), range(98 102) lcolor(black) xtitle("{it: Mean}") ytitle("Density") title("Area under the curve to the right of a mean of 101") subtitle("To the right of a z of 2.22") legend(off) xlabel(98 99 100 101 102)
Figure 10.7	twoway function y=normalden(x, 280, 2), range(284 286) recast(area) color(gs12)|| function y=normalden(x, 280, 2), range(274 276) recast(area) color(gs12) || function y=normalden(x, 280, 2), range(274 286) lcolor(black) xtitle("{it: Mean}") ytitle("Density") title("Critical areas under the curve in both tails") subtitle("To the left of z = -2.00 and to right of z = 2.00") legend(off) xlabel(274 276 278 280 282 284 286)
Calculate the one tailed p-value associated with sample mean 505 in a distribution with $\mu = 500$ and standard error = 2.5	display (1 – (normal((505 – 500)/2.5)))

Create	Command Lines
Calculate the two tailed p-value associated with sample mean 276 in a distribution with $\mu = 280$ and standard error = 2 (Example 10.3)	**display normal((276–280)/2)*2**

EXERCISES

*Create a Do-file for each exercise that requires the use of Stata. Run the commands from the Do-file by highlighting them and hitting **Control+d**. Save each Do-file using a name associated with the Exercise for which it was created. It is recommended that you review the Do-file for* Chapter 10 *located on the textbook's website before completing these exercises. To facilitate doing each exercise, it may be helpful to copy and paste relevant commands from the Do-file for* Chapter 10 *into your own Do-file and modify them as needed.*

10.1. Suppose we want to estimate the mean height μ for American males and we know that the standard deviation σ, for the entire population is 3 inches. We take a random sample of American males of sample size $N = 100$ from this population and find that its sample mean is $\bar{X} = 68$.
- a) Explain why the normal curve gives a good approximation of the sampling distribution of means.
- b) Use this information to construct a 90 percent CI for μ.
- c) To what does the 90 percent refer?
- d) Can we conclude that 90 percent of the males from this population have heights within the interval of values obtained in part b)?
- e) Would the 95 percent CI be longer or shorter?

10.2. Suppose we know that the standard deviation for the IQ of all Americans is $\sigma = 15$ but we do not know the mean IQ score μ. To estimate μ we select a random sample of size $N = 225$ and find that the sample has mean $\bar{X} = 105$.
- a) Use this information to construct a 99 percent CI for μ.
- b) To what does the 99 percent refer?
- c) Can we conclude that 99 percent of the 225 individuals from this sample have IQ's within the interval of values obtained in part b)?
- d) Can we conclude that we are 99 percent certain that each individual from this population of Americans has an IQ within the interval of values obtained in part b)?

10.3. Given that $N = 100$, $\sigma = 15$, and $\bar{X} = 92$ for a random sample selected from a given population of values,
- a) Construct a 90 percent CI for the population mean μ.
- b) Using the result of part (a), what would your decision be if you were to run the following hypothesis test at $\alpha = .10$?
  $H_0: \mu = 96$
  $H_1: \mu \neq 96$
- c) Using the result of part (a), what would your decision be if you were to run the following hypothesis test at $\alpha = .10$?

$H_0: \mu = 91.5$
$H_1: \mu \neq 91.5$

10.4. In order to estimate the mean air-pollution index μ for Pittsburgh, Pennsylvania, over the past five years, we randomly select a sample of $N = 64$ of those days and compute the mean air-pollution index for this sample. Assuming that the sample mean is found to be $\bar{X} = 15$ and the population is known to have a standard deviation of $\sigma = 4$, find a 95 percent CI for μ. Use the confidence interval to determine whether the air-pollution index for the past five years is statistically significantly different from 14.

10.5. The Weston, Massachusetts Postal Service is thinking of introducing a training program for their employees on how to sort mail by zip code number in order to increase sorting speed. They know that without any such training their employees sort an average of 600 letters per hour with a standard deviation of 20. A random sample of $N = 400$ postal employees is selected and given the training program. Their average mail-sorting speed at the end of training is recorded as 603. Assume that the standard deviation is no different with training from without training.

a) State the null and alternative hypotheses in terms of specific values for the population mean for determining whether the training program increases the sorting speed.
b) Explain why the z-distribution may be used as a basis of the hypothesis test, in this instance, by explaining why the sampling distribution of means is normally or approximately normally distributed.
c) Calculate the observed z-statistic.
d) Is the test one- or two-tailed?
e) Find the p value for conducting a hypothesis test at significance level .10 on whether training increases mail-sorting speed.
f) What can you conclude based on your results in part (e)?
g) If the result of the hypothesis test is statistically significant, find and interpret an appropriate effect size.
h) Would you recommend that the town endorse such training? Why or why not?
i) Could a 90 percent confidence interval have been used to determine whether training increases mail-sorting speed?

10.6. Children graduating from a particular high school district in a disadvantaged area of New York City have on the average scored 55 on a standard college-readiness test with a standard deviation of 12. A random sample of 36 students from this district is selected to participate in Project Advance, a special program to help high school students prepare for college. At the end of the project, the 36 students are given the college-readiness test. They obtain a sample mean of $\bar{X} = 56$. Assume that the standard deviation for the population of all students in this district who might participate in Project Advance is no different from that for all those who would not participate ($\sigma = 12$). Conduct a hypothesis test at significance level $\alpha = .05$ to determine whether students in this district who participate in Project Advance in general score *higher* on the college-readiness test than those who do not participate. State your conclusions clearly in the context of the problem.

10.7. The average cholesterol level for adults in the United States is known to be 200mg per dl. A group of 50 randomly selected adults in the United States participated in a study on the efficacy of diet in reducing cholesterol. They ate a low-fat diet (less than 30 percent of their total daily calories came from fat) for 6 months. After 6 months their average serum cholesterol level in mg per dl was 185. Assume that the standard deviation for the population of cholesterol levels for adults in the United States following the diet is the same as it is for all adults in the United States, $\sigma = 50$, and that the distribution of cholesterol levels for the population of adults in the United States following the diet is normally distributed.

    a) Conduct a hypothesis test at significance level $\alpha = .05$ to determine whether adults following the diet have significantly *lower* cholesterol levels than 200mg per dl, on average. State your conclusions clearly in the context of the problem.

    b) If the result in part (a) is statistically significant, find and interpret the effect size, classifying its magnitude according to Cohen's scale. Does the effect size indicate that the result is practically significant?

10.8. You are dean of a college that has just admitted 1,000 first-year students, and you want to know whether these students have a scholastic aptitude (as measured on a standard scholastic aptitude test) *different* from that of previous first-year classes. You pick a random sample of size $N = 81$ from the new class and give them the scholastic aptitude test on which previous first-year classes scored a mean of 100. Assume that this entire first-year class would have a standard deviation of $\sigma = 9$ on this test if they all took it.

    a) Construct a 95 percent CI for the mean scholastic aptitude for all 1,000 current first-year students if the sample mean is 101.5.

    b) Use the confidence interval to determine whether the current first-year students, on average, have a scholastic aptitude *different* from that of previous first-year classes. If their average is statistically significantly different from that of previous first-year classes, determine whether it is statistically significantly higher or lower.

    c) If the result is statistically significant, approximate and describe the effect size.

    d) The 90 percent confidence interval for the mean scholastic aptitude for all 1,000 current first-year students would be:

      (1)   longer (wider) than the 95 percent confidence interval

      (2)   shorter (narrower) than the 95 percent confidence interval

      (3)   the same as the 95 percent confidence interval

    e) If the sample selected had been smaller, but with the same mean and standard deviation as in the original analysis, the 95 percent confidence interval for the mean scholastic aptitude for all 1,000 current first-year students would be:

      (1)   longer

      (2)   shorter

      (3)   the same

    f) If everything had been the same as in the original analysis, except that the standard deviation had been 10 instead of 9, then the 95 percent confidence interval for the mean scholastic aptitude for all 1,000 current first-year students would have been:

      (1)   longer

      (2)   shorter

      (3)   the same

10.9. A test of general intelligence is known to have a mean of 100 and a standard deviation of 15 for the population at large. You believe that students at the university where you teach have a *different* mean on this test. To test this belief, you randomly select a sample of 36 students at your university and give them this test of general intelligence. Assume that the standard deviation of your university's students is no different from that of the population at large and that your sample result is $\overline{X} = 106$? Construct a 90 percent confidence interval and use it to test your belief. State your conclusions clearly in the context of the problem. If the result is statistically significant, calculate and interpret the effect size.

10.10. Curriculum planners decided to determine whether a curriculum change should be instituted to increase the reading comprehension of eighth graders in Seattle, Washington. The mean reading-comprehension score under the old curriculum was 92 on the Stanford Secondary School Comprehension Test. After the new curriculum was used for one term, the mean of a sample of 400 students was 95. Assume that the standard deviation for the entire population of eighth graders in Seattle is the same under the new curriculum as under the old ($\sigma = 10$). Test at significance level .01 whether there would be an *improvement* in reading comprehension in general if the entire population of eighth graders in Seattle were taught using the new curriculum. State your conclusions clearly in the context of the problem. If the result is statistically significant, calculate and interpret the effect size. Could a confidence interval have been used to answer the research question? Explain.

10.11. A publishing company has just published a new college textbook. Before the company decides to charge $79 for the textbook, it wants to know the average price of all such textbooks in the market, to determine whether it is statistically significantly different from $79. The research department at the company takes a random sample of 40 such textbooks and collects information on their prices. This information produced a mean price of $76.40 for the sample. Assume that the standard deviation of the prices of all such textbooks is $7.50. Test at a significance level of .05 whether the mean price of all such textbooks is different from $79. State your conclusions clearly in the context of the problem. If the result is statistically significant, calculate and interpret the effect size.

10.12. Explain why $z_c = 1.96$ for a 95 percent CI.

10.13. Given the scenario of problem 10.9, assume that the students at the university where you teach have a higher mean on this test. Would the *power* of the test have been less, the same, or greater had you wanted to determine whether the students had a higher mean on this test, instead of whether the students had a different mean on this test? Explain.

Inferences Involving the Mean When σ Is Not Known: One- and Two-Sample Designs

In the previous chapter we presented a statistical model for answering questions about a single population mean μ when σ was known. Because σ usually is not known in practice, we present in this chapter a statistical model that is appropriate for answering questions about a single population mean when σ is not known. We also present two other statistical models that are appropriate for answering questions about the equality of two population means. In one model the groups representing the two populations are related and in the other they are not. In later chapters we consider different research questions that involve different designs and different parameters of interest (including the mean, variance, correlation, and so on) and we present statistical models appropriate to each situation. In general, you will find that by knowing the features of a particular design as well as the parameter of interest you will be able to make sense of the array of statistical models presented and choose one or more that are appropriate to a given situation.

SINGLE SAMPLE DESIGNS WHEN THE PARAMETER OF INTEREST IS THE MEAN AND σ IS NOT KNOWN

As you should have noted in Chapter 10, which, in part, dealt with questions about the mean of a single population, a wide range of questions may be addressed by studies that are carried out to estimate or test the value of a single population mean. While the type of questions we will address in this section are like those addressed in Chapter 10, different, and more realistic, assumptions are made in this section about the nature of our data. These different assumptions change the procedures for estimating or testing the value of the single population mean.

In Chapter 10 we assumed that σ, the standard deviation of the population, was known so that we could use the Central Limit Theorem to justify the use of the normal distribution of the sampling distribution of means and to compute the standard error, $\sigma_{\bar{X}} = \dfrac{\sigma}{\sqrt{N}}$. We used the z-test, $z = \dfrac{\bar{X} - \mu}{\dfrac{\sigma}{\sqrt{N}}}$ provided in Equation 10.2 of Chapter 10 to determine how deviant a particular sample mean $\bar{X}$ is from the population mean μ. Because, in most cases, however, the value of σ is not known, in this chapter we introduce another way to describe the sampling distribution of means, one that does not rely on knowledge of σ. As we shall see, when the parent population is normally distributed, but when σ is not known, we can use what is called *Student's t-*(or just *t-*) *distribution* to describe the sampling distribution of means.

In this section we will use the *t*-distribution to determine whether adult African American males, on average, have a systolic blood pressure that is different from the general population of adult American males; whether college bound females from the South who have always been at grade level take three years of mathematics in high school on average; and, whether college-bound males from the South who have always been at grade level take more than three years of mathematics in high school on average.

For all questions regarding a single population mean, we can represent the null and alternative hypotheses as follows:

$H_0: \mu = c$
$H_1: \mu \neq c$ or $H_1: \mu < c$ or $H_1: \mu > c$

where c is a specified number.

THE *t* DISTRIBUTION

From Chapter 9 we know that $\hat{\sigma}^2$ calculated from sample data is an unbiased estimator of σ^2. If we substitute $\hat{\sigma}$ for σ in the z-test equation, we obtain a new statistic called Student's t, or simply t, as our measure of sample mean deviation from μ. Equation 11.1 displays the equation for the t statistic for the one sample *t*-test.

$$t = \frac{\overline{X} - \mu}{\dfrac{\hat{\sigma}}{\sqrt{N}}} = \frac{\overline{X} - \mu}{\hat{\sigma}_{\overline{X}}}$$

(11.1)

Although the t statistic resembles the z statistic in form, there is an important difference between them. In the z statistic, the numerator $\overline{X} - \mu$ depends on the particular sample selected, because $\overline{X}$ is the sample mean. Hence, the value of $\overline{X} - \mu$ will in general vary from one sample to another. The denominator $\dfrac{\sigma}{\sqrt{N}}$ of the z-statistic, however, depends only on the population parameter σ and the sample size N and, therefore, will stay constant from sample to sample. By contrast, both numerator $\overline{X} - \mu$ *and* denominator $\dfrac{\hat{\sigma}}{\sqrt{N}}$ of the t statistic depend on the particular sample selected, and therefore, in general, both will vary from sample to sample.

Because the *t*-statistic appears to be a reasonable measure of sample-mean deviation that may be used in place of the *z*-statistic when σ is not known, we should be interested in knowing the shape of the *t*-distribution. Because of the differences between the *z* and *t*-statistics, we should not expect the *t*-distribution to have exactly the same shape as the *z*. In fact, as discovered by a young chemist named William Sealy Gossett in the early twentieth century, they do not. His results appeared in a short paper entitled "The Probable Error of the Mean," published in the journal, *Biometrika* in 1908 (Salsburg, 2001). Because the company he worked for, the Guiness Brewing Company of Dublin, Ireland, prohibited its employees from publishing, Gossett published under the pseudonym Student. He chose that pseudonym because he considered himself to be a student of statistics; hence the name given to this distribution.

Gossett set up a normal parent population, empirically selected random samples of size N from this population, and computed a *t*-statistic as given in Equation 11.1 for each sample selected. He then constructed a distribution of these t-statistics and found it to be generally similar in shape to the standard normal curve distribution but flatter at its center and taller in its tails. When different sample sizes N were used, he obtained distributions with slightly different shapes, indicating that there are really many t-distributions, one for each sample size N. He also found that the family of t-distributions varies not by their sample size N but, rather, as a function of their sample size, called their degrees of freedom, symbolized by df or by the Greek letter v (*nu*).

DEGREES OF FREEDOM FOR THE ONE SAMPLE t-TEST

The number of degrees of freedom of a statistic not only depends on the number of observations in the sample (N), but also considers other factors that tend to affect the sampling distribution.

The number of degrees of freedom of a statistic is the number of *independent pieces* of data used in computing that statistic.

The t statistic, as given in Equation 11.1, relies on the square root of the variance estimator, $\hat{\sigma}$, which may be computed from Equation 9.1 in Chapter 9, and reproduced here as Equation 11.2.

$$\hat{\sigma} = \sqrt{\frac{\sum \left(X_i - \bar{X} \right)^2}{N - 1}} \tag{11.2}$$

From Equation 11.2 it appears at first glance that the value of $\hat{\sigma}$ depends on N independent pieces of data: $d_1 = X_1 - \bar{X}, d_2 = X_2 - \bar{X}, d_3 = X_3 - \bar{X}, \ldots, d_N = X_N - \bar{X}$. Recall, however, that the sum of all deviations about the mean must equal 0 ($\sum d_i = 0$), so that if we know $N - 1$ of the d_i's, then the Nth, or last one, must be completely determined by them.

For example, suppose you are told to make up a set of five scores using any numbers you desire, provided that the scores have a mean of 3. Suppose that as your first four numbers you freely and arbitrarily select the numbers 4, 2, 7, and 1. Accordingly, $d_1 = X_1 - \bar{X} = 4 - 3 = 1, d_2 = -1, d_3 = 4, d_4 = -2$. Do you now have the same freedom of choice in selecting the fifth score to complete the set? Clearly you do not. The only score that will be consistent with $\sum d_i = 0$, is $X_5 = 1$, making $d_5 = -2$. In short, you had no freedom in selecting the fifth or last score; the choice was determined by the fact that the mean had been specified. Thus, with a specified mean, required for the estimation of the variance, there are only four degrees of freedom for selecting a set of five scores. In general, with a specified mean, there are only $N-1$ degrees of freedom for selecting a set of N scores.

When σ is not known, the number of degrees of freedom associated with the one-sample t-statistic for μ is $df = N - 1$ when either constructing a confidence interval or carrying out a hypothesis test.

☞ **Remark.** In general, t-distribution curves resemble the standard normal curve in that they are symmetric and unimodal, but they are flatter at the middle and taller in the tails. The mean of a t-distribution with any number of degrees of freedom df is 0, the same mean as in the standard normal curve. The variance of t-distribution, however, is not always 1, as it is in the standard normal curve. For a t-distribution with more than two degrees of freedom ($df > 2$), the variance is $\dfrac{df}{df - 2}$. The smaller the value of df, the larger the variance;

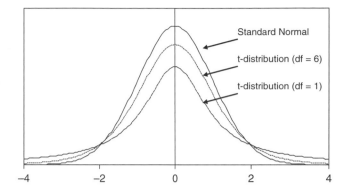

Figure 11.1 Comparison of two *t*-curves with the standard normal curve.

and as *df* becomes large, the variance of the *t*-distribution approaches 1, the variance of the standard normal curve. As a matter of fact, as the number of degrees of freedom *df* increases, the *t*-distribution itself approaches the standard normal curve; that is, the *t*-distribution has the standard normal curve as a limiting curve (see Figure 11.1).

In addition to Stata, we may use Table 2 in Appendix C online, www.cambridge.org/Stats-Stata, to obtain *t*-distribution values for right-tail areas. That is, the *t*-value that has .05 of the area to its right under a distribution with 10 degrees of freedom, for example, may be found in Table 2 at the intersection of the row labeled *df* = 10 and column labeled .05. This *t*-value is 1.812. With an infinite number of *df*, the *t*-value with .05 of the area to its right is 1.645, which, as you will recall, equals the *z*-value with .05 of the area to its right under the standard normal distribution, thus confirming that as the degrees of freedom increase, the *t*-distribution approaches the standard normal distribution. Table 2 may also be used to find approximate *p*-values corresponding to approximate *t*-values.

VIOLATING THE ASSUMPTION OF A NORMALLY DISTRIBUTED PARENT POPULATION IN THE ONE SAMPLE *t*-TEST

The *t*-distribution defines a sampling distribution of means when the parent population is normally distributed and when σ needs to be estimated from sample data. If Gossett had not placed a restriction of normality on the parent population, however, he would not have been able to determine the distribution of *t*-statistics in a simple form. Although the requirement of normality in the parent population may seem too limiting to be useful in practice, it is often actually a reasonable assumption to make. As we mentioned in our discussion of normal curves, many natural occurrences due to chance give rise to normally distributed probability curves. In addition, even when the parent population is not normally distributed, it can be shown mathematically that for a sufficiently large sample size *N*, the *t*-distribution will not be affected appreciably by violations of the normality assumption.

In general, the more the parent population deviates from normality, the larger the sample size must be to apply the *t*-distribution to determine sample-mean deviation. For this reason, there is no specific sample size above which deviation from normality in the parent population can always be ignored. It has been found, however, that unless the parent population deviates radically from normality, a sample of size 30 or larger will be sufficient to compensate for lack of normality in the parent population. It is therefore a good idea in general to use samples of size 30 or larger. In practice, however, this is not a real restriction because the sample size necessary to obtain reasonably high power when using the null hypothesis test procedure almost always exceeds 30 as does the sample size necessary to obtain reasonably high precision when constructing a confidence interval.

CONFIDENCE INTERVALS FOR THE ONE SAMPLE t-TEST

We may construct confidence intervals about μ using the t-distribution when the parent population is known to be normally distributed (or the sample size is sufficiently large) and when σ needs to be estimated using sample data. We could use Equation 11.3 to find the confidence intervals by hand.

☞ **Remark.** The confidence interval based on the t-distribution is obtained by hand using Equation 11.3 instead of Equation 10.1. You will note that by contrast to Equation 10.1, Equation 11.3 uses t_c instead of z_c and $\hat{\sigma}_{\bar{X}}$ instead of $\sigma_{\bar{X}}$.

$$\text{Upper Limit} = \bar{X} + t_c\,\hat{\sigma}_{\bar{X}} \tag{11.3}$$

$$\text{Lower Limit} = \bar{X} - t_c\,\hat{\sigma}_{\bar{X}}$$

To find the value of tc using Stata we can use the functions called **t, ttail** and **invttail**. As shown in Example 11.1, by specifying the degrees of freedom and the p-value, we may use **invttail** to obtain the critical t value of interest.

· ·

EXAMPLE 11.1. Construct a 95 percent confidence interval using the data given below to determine whether adult African American males, on average, have a systolic blood pressure that is different from the general population of adult American males, which is known to be 120. The data are based on a sample of 21 African American adult males selected randomly from the population of African American adult males. These data come from the Data and Story Library (DASL) website and are available in the text's website saved under the filename *Blood*.

Systolic blood pressure (mm per Hg)

107 110 123 129 112 111 107 112 135 102 123 109 112 102
98 114 119 112 110 117 130

Solution. If we knew σ, the standard deviation of the parent population, we would use the Central Limit Theorem and proceed as we did in Chapter 10, using Equation 10.1, to construct the desired 95 percent confidence interval. Because we do not know σ, however, we estimate it as $\hat{\sigma}$ using Equation 11.2. We then construct the 95 percent confidence interval based on the t-distribution using Equation 11.3.

For these data,

$$\bar{X} = (107+110+123+129+112+111+107+112+135+102+123+109+112+$$
$$102+98+114+119+112+110+117+130)/21=114$$

$$\hat{\sigma}^2 = [(107-114)^2+(110-114)^2+(123-114)^2+(129-114)^2+\ldots+(112-114)^2+$$
$$(110-114)^2 + (117-114)^2 + (130-114)^2]/(21-1) = 92.16$$

$$\hat{\sigma} = \sqrt{92.16} = 9.60; \ \hat{\sigma}_{\bar{x}} = \frac{\hat{\sigma}}{\sqrt{N}} = \frac{9.60}{\sqrt{21}} = 2.10$$

To find the critical t-value, t_c, we make use of either Stata or Table 2 from Appendix C online, www.cambridge.org/Stats-Stata.

To use Stata, we use the **invttail(df,p)** function. where p is the proportion of area to the right of the t-value. Because we want the 95 percent CI, we need the t values that mark off .025 area in each of the two tails.

MORE Stata: To calculate the t-value with .025 area to its right

Type the following syntax into your Do-file, highlight, and press **Control+d**:

display invttail(20, .025)

The Output Window will list the t-value with .975 area to its left (or .025 of its area to the right) as 2.086.

To use Table 2 in Appendix C online, www.cambridge.org/Stats-Stata, to find the critical t-value, we refer to the value at the intersection of the row labeled $df = 20$ and the column labeled .025. Like the **invttail** function in Stata, the p-value in Table 2 marks off that proportion of area under the t-distribution to its right. The t-value from Table 2 that marks off .025 area to its right is 2.086, which agrees with the value obtained from Stata. Because of symmetry we know that the t-value that marks off .025 of the area under the t-distribution to its left is −2.086. To calculate Upper and Lower Limits we use only the positive t-value.

Lower Limit $= \bar{X} - t_c \hat{\sigma}_{\bar{x}} = 114 - t_c(2.10) = 114 - (2.086)(2.10) = 114 - 4.38 = 109.62$

Upper Limit $= \bar{X} + t_c \hat{\sigma}_{\bar{x}} = 114 + t_c(2.10) = 114 + (2.086)(2.10) = 114 + 4.38 = 118.38$

Accordingly, the 95 percent confidence interval for μ in this case is (109.62, 118.38). Because $\mu = 120$ does not fall within this interval, it is not a plausible value of the population mean systolic blood pressure for adult African American males. Based on the interval, plausible population mean values fall in the range from 109.62 to 118.38, and suggest that the mean systolic blood pressure for adult African American males is statistically significantly lower than 120.

Alternatively, we may use Stata to obtain the confidence interval directly. These data may be found in the *Blood* data set.

First, we run the following syntax to examine the descriptive statistics for the variable systolc1, including its skewness ratio. To keep a record of the steps we are taking for this analysis, and to facilitate being able to run those steps again in the future, we continue to input the syntax into our Do-file, highlight the code we want to run, and press **Control+d** to run.

summarize systolc1, detail
summskew systolc1

The output for this analysis is as follows:

Initial blood pressure

	Percentiles	Smallest		
1%	98	98		
5%	102	102		
10%	102	102	Obs	21
25%	109	107	Sum of Wgt.	21
50%	112		Mean	114
		Largest	Std. Dev.	9.596874
75%	119	123		
90%	129	129	Variance	92.1
95%	130	130	Skewness	.5676055
99%	135	135	Kurtosis	2.708193

skewness = .56760552; seskew = .50119474; skewness ratio = 1.1325049

As expected, the mean and standard deviation values are the same as calculated by hand.

The skewness is less than 1 in magnitude and the skewness ratio is less than 2 in magnitude, suggesting that the normality assumption is tenable. To examine, more specifically, the extent to which the systolc1 distribution departs from that of a normal curve, we use graphical methods, and, in particular, the **qnorm** and **histogram** commands.

Running the syntax **qnorm systolc1** from our Do-file, we obtain a plot of the quantiles (percentiles) of **systolc1** against the quantiles of the normal distribution (q-q plot) (see Figure 11.2). In general, if our variable of interest is normally distributed, the quantiles of that variable will equal the quantiles of a normal distribution and the points of the plot will fall along a straight line. By examining the nature of the departure of points from a straight line will allow us to identify the source of our variable's non-normality (e.g., whether it is due to a few or many outliers).

And adding **histogram systolc1, freq normal** to our Do-file, and running this command, we obtain Figure 11.3.

The slight concave (u-shape) form of the q-q plot and the appearance of the histogram both suggest the slight positive skew of systolc1 as measured by its skewness of .57 and skewness ratio of 1.13.

More Stata: To customize the histogram of Figure 11.3

We may, for example, choose the labels we wish to appear on the x-axis, choose where to locate the tick marks on the x- and y-axes, choose the width of each bin, and add a title among other options. A histogram with the x-axis labelled from 95 to 140 in increments of 5, with tick marks on the x-axis from 95 to 140 in increments of 5, with bin width 10, and with the title, "Customized histogram of systolc1" is obtained using the following command and given as Figure 11.4. The three slashes at the end of the first line of the command informs Stata that the command is continued onto the next line. These slashes are used in the do-files, but not as part of the Stata command lines.

histogram systolc1, freq normal xlabel(95(5)140) xtick(95(5)140) width(10) ///
title("Customized histogram of systolc1")

For additional customizing options, type **help histogram**

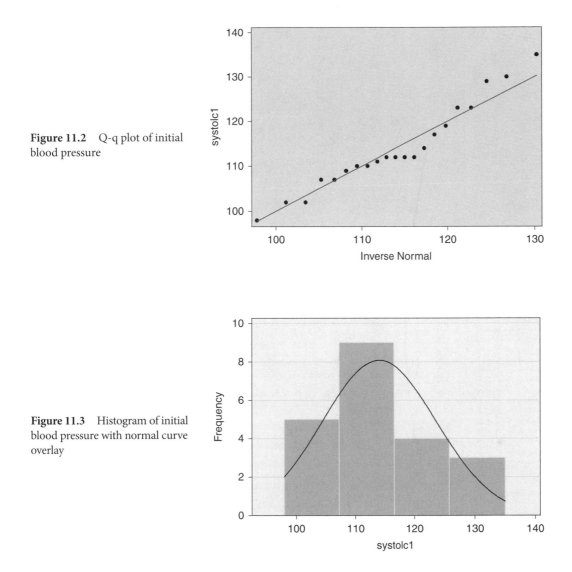

Figure 11.2 Q-q plot of initial blood pressure

Figure 11.3 Histogram of initial blood pressure with normal curve overlay

Based on these graphical and statistical analyses, we conclude that the assumption of the normality of systolc1 underlying the one-sample *t*-test is tenable, and we continue to construct the desired confidence interval using Stata.

MORE Stata: Constructing the 95% Confidence Interval

To obtain the 95 percent CI for μ when σ is not known for a one-sample design, we type the following syntax into our do-file, highlight it, and hit **Control+d** to run.

ttest systolc1 == 0

The use of the one-sample test is dictated by the fact that our design contains only one sample in this case. We obtain the Stata output in the Output Window:

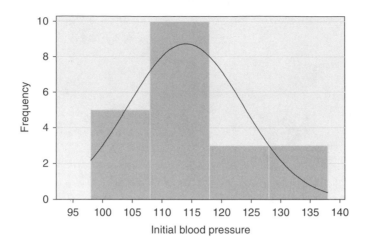

Figure 11.4 Customized histogram of systolc1

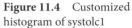

One-sample t test

Variable	Obs	Mean	Std. Err.	Std. Dev.	[95% Conf.	Interval]
systolc1	21	114	2.09421	9.596874	109.6316	118.3684

```
         mean = mean (systolc1)                                        t = 54.4358
Ho:  mean = 0                                            degrees of freedom = 20

   Ha: mean < 0                    Ha: mean ! = 0                    Ha: mean > 0
   Pr (T < t) = 1.0000         Pr (|T| > |t|) = 0.0000         Pr (T > t) = 0.0000
```

The 95 percent confidence interval from Stata (109.63, 118.37) agrees within rounding error with the interval we obtained by hand.

- -

EXAMPLE 11.2. Use Stata to construct a 95 percent CI to estimate the population mean number of units (years) of mathematics taken in high school by females who live in the South. Recall that the population of such students is defined as those who responded to all four administrations of the *NELS* survey, who were always at grade level, and who pursued some form of post-secondary education. Assume that σ is not known and that it needs to be estimated from the sample data. Note that the data on math units taken were collected originally by the National Assessment of Educational Progress (NAEP) and then incorporated into the *NELS* data set.

Solution. If we knew σ, the standard deviation of the parent population, we would use the Central Limit Theorem and proceed as we did in Chapter 10, using Equation 10.1, to construct the desired 95 percent confidence interval. Because we do not know σ, however, we construct the 95 percent confidence interval based on the *t*-distribution. This construction is readily performed using Stata.

To get a sense of our data, and to check on the tenability of the underlying normality assumption, we obtain descriptives for our variable, unitmath, using the command

summarize unitmath, detail

To obtain the descriptive statistics only for girls in the South, we include the syntax **",if gender == 1 & region == 3"** at the end of the **summarize** command as follows:

summarize unitmath, if gender == 1 & region == 3, detail.

MORE Stata: To calculate skewness statistics for a continuous variable on a subset of cases defined by the values of two categorical variables, we use a new command, **summskewcell**.

Like the **summskew** command, the **summskewcell** command is, by default, not part of Stata, and so it first needs to be installed before we can use it. Because the instructions to install **summskewcell** are exactly the same as those for installing **summskew**, if you already have installed **summskew** there is nothing further to do. If, on the other hand, you have not already installed **summskew**, then please return to page 94 to follow the instructions for installing **summskew**.

Once these programs are installed, the **summskewcell** syntax for this example is:

summskewcell unitmath gender region

The output will include the skewness statistics for all eight (2x4) combinations of gender and region.

Note: The general form of **summskewcell** is **summskewcell y x1 x2**, where y is a continuous variable and **x1** and **x2** are two categorical variables.

Units in Mathematics (NAEP)				
	Percentiles	Smallest		
1%	2	2		
5%	3	2		
10%	3	2	Obs	84
25%	3	2.5	Sum of Wgt.	84
50%	4		Mean	3.664048
		Largest	Std. Dev.	.7225592
75%	4	5		
90%	4.29	5	Variance	.5220919
95%	5	5	Skewness	.1198044
99%	6	6	Kurtosis	3.478051

The following are the skewness statistics for gender==1 & region==3:

skewness = .11980437; seskew = .26265054; skewness ratio = .45613602

Recall that the standard deviation given in the Stata output is actually $\hat{\sigma}$. Thus, we know that $N = 84$, $\overline{X} = 3.66$, $\hat{\sigma} = 0.72$, and skewness = .12. The skewness statistic as well as the q-q plot in Figure 11.5 (using the command **qnorm unitmat if gender == 1 & region == 3**) suggest that our normality assumption for this sample of unitmath scores is tenable. Furthermore, the sample of size 84 is sufficiently large to warrant the use of the t-distribution in this case.

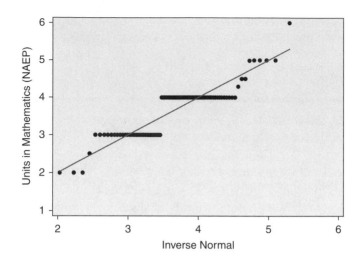

Figure 11.5 Q-Q plot (using the command qnorm) of unitmat

The q-q plot looks the way it does in Figure 11.5 because unitmath is a ratio-level variable consisting only of integers.

We use Stata to construct the 95 percent confidence interval as before. Once again, the use of the one-sample t-test is dictated by the fact that our design contains only one sample in this case. We obtain the following output from the command **ttest unitmath == 0 if (gender == 1 & region == 3)**:

One-sample t test						
Variable	Obs	Mean	Std. Err.	Std. Dev.	[95% Conf.	Interval]
unitmath	84	3.664048	.0788377	.7225592	3.507243	3.820853

mean = mean (unitmath)   t =   46.4758
Ho: mean = 0   degrees of freedom =   83

Ha: mean < 0   Ha: mean ! = 0   Ha: mean > 0
Pr (T < t) = 1.0000   Pr (|T| > |t|) = 0.0000   Pr (T > t) = 0.0000

Of interest in this example is the 95 percent CI, (3.51, 3.82). In other words, it is plausible that the mean number of years of math taken in high school for the population of Southern girls represented by our sample falls between 3.51 and 3.82. Said differently, this result means that if we were to construct an interval estimate of μ for all possible random samples of size 84 from this population, exactly 95 percent of all these interval estimates would in fact contain μ and only 5 percent would not. Does this estimate surprise you? Would you have expected college-bound females from the South to take fewer or more years of math in high school?

EXAMPLE 11.3. Use the same data as in Example 11.2 to construct a 99 percent CI about μ.

MORE Stata: To obtain the 99% Confidence Interval about μ for the variable unitmath
Type the following syntax into your Do-file, highlight it, and press **Control + d** to run.

ttest unitmath == 0, level(99), if gender == 1 & region == 3

In so doing, we obtain the following results.

One-sample t test

Variable	Obs	Mean	Std. Err.	Std. Dev.	[99% Conf.	Interval]
unitmath	84	3.664048	.0788377	.7225592	3.456202	3.871893

mean = mean (unitmath)   t = 46.4758
Ho: mean = 0   degrees of freedom = 83

Ha : mean < 0   Ha: mean ! = 0   Ha: mean > 0
Pr (T < t) = 1.0000   Pr (|T| > |t|) = 0.0000   Pr (T > t) = 0.0000

Notice that the 99 percent CI (3.46, 3.87) is longer than the 95 percent CI. As noted in the previous chapter, if we increase the confidence level, say from 95 percent to 99 percent, and keep the sample size the same, the resulting CI will be longer. Our estimate of μ will then be less precise, but we will be more confident that it is accurate.

HYPOTHESIS TESTS: THE ONE SAMPLE t-TEST

When the parent population is known to be normally distributed (or the sample size is sufficiently large) and when σ is not known and needs to be estimated using sample data we may conduct hypothesis tests of μ by carrying out a t-test (as opposed to a z-test). A t-test is based on the t-distribution while the z-test is based on the normal distribution. We may ask, as we have done previously, whether adult African American males, on average, have a systolic blood pressure that is different from the general population of adult American males, which is known to be 120. In reference to our *NELS* data, we may ask, for example, whether college-bound females from the South who have always been at grade level take an average of three years of math in high school. We may also ask, among other questions, whether college-bound males from the South who have always been at grade level take an average of more than three years of math in high school. We use Stata to carry out these tests, but we also carry out the systolic analysis by hand.

• •
EXAMPLE 11.4. Use the same data as in Example 11.1 to test, using a one sample t-test, whether adult African American males, on average, have a systolic blood pressure that is different from the general population of adult American males, which is known to be 120. Use μ .05. Carry out the analysis by hand and also by Stata.

Solution. If we knew σ, the standard deviation of the parent population, we would use the Central Limit Theorem and proceed as we did in Chapter 10 to test these hypotheses. Because we do not know σ, however, we use the t-distribution as the basis for the null hypothesis testing procedure in this case. We are warranted to do so because from Example 11.1, we know that our sample is sufficiently symmetric to make the assumption of normality a reasonable one.

The null and alternative hypotheses are: H_0: $\mu = 120$ versus H_1: $\mu \neq 120$.

Based on our earlier calculations in connection with Example 11.1, we know that

$$\bar{X} = 114; \hat{\sigma}^2 = 92.16; \hat{\sigma} = \sqrt{9216} = 9.60; \hat{\sigma}_{\bar{X}} = \frac{\hat{\sigma}}{\sqrt{N}} = \frac{9.60}{\sqrt{21}} = 2.10.$$

Using the t-ratio of Equation 11.1, we may determine the number of standard errors the observed sample mean of 114 is from the population mean of 120 as follows:

$$t = \frac{\bar{X} - \mu}{\dfrac{\hat{\sigma}}{\sqrt{N}}} = \frac{\bar{X} - \mu}{\hat{\sigma}_{\bar{X}}} = \frac{114 - 120}{2.10} = -2.86.$$

The t-ratio tells us that the observed mean of 114 is 2.86 standard errors below the hypothesized mean of 120.

To find the p-value associated with this t-ratio, we use Stata and Table 2 in Appendix C online, www.cambridge.org/Stats-Stata. In both cases we need the value of the t-ratio and its associated degrees of freedom. We have $t = -2.86$. Given this is a one-sample t-test, $df = N - 1 = 21 - 1 = 20$.

MORE Stata: To obtain the area to the left of an observed t-value

Type t(df,t), with appropriate values substituted for df and t. This function returns the cumulative (lower or left tail) Student's t distribution with df degrees of freedom.

Because, for this problem, the degrees of freedom are 20 and the observed t-value is -2.86, we input and run the following command:

```
display t(20, -2.86)
```

The p-value, listed in the Output Window as .0048, is a one-tailed value because it represents the area in the left tail only. To find the two-tailed p-value we multiply .0048 by 2 to obtain .0096.

To use Table 2 in Appendix C online, www.cambridge.org/Stats-Stata, to find this p-value, we make use of the symmetry of the t-distribution. Because the t-distribution is symmetric, we may ignore the negative sign and look for the printed value closest to 2.86 in Table 2 to approximate the obtained p-value. We scan the row labeled $df = 20$ in Table 2 and find that the closest printed t-value to 2.86 is 2.845. This value has .005 of the area under the t-distribution to its right. Because the alternative hypothesis is non-directional (H_1: $\mu \neq 120$), we multiply this value by 2 to obtain the approximate two-tailed p-value which is p = .005 x 2 = .010.

That is, the probability that we have observed a mean as, or more, extreme than 114 that comes from a population with mean equal to 120 is only .01. Because this probability is so small (it is smaller than .05), we conclude that it is likely that the population mean is not equal to 120 and we reject the null hypothesis in favor of the alternative. Because the sample mean of 114 is smaller than the null hypothesized value of 120, we conclude that the systolic blood pressure of African-American males ($M = 114$, $SD = 9.6$) is statistically significantly lower than 120, the mean for the general population of adult American males, $t(20) = -2.86$, $p = .01$.

We now carry out the analysis for this example using Stata.

MORE Stata: To find the p-value associated with a one-sample t-test
Type and highlight the command in the do-file and press **Conrol+d**.
ttest systolc1 == 120

We obtain the following results.

One–sample t test						
Variable	Obs	Mean	Std. Err.	Std. Dev.	[95 % Conf.	Interval]
systolc1	21	114	2.09421	9.596874	109.6316	118.3684

mean = mean (systolc1)   t   =   –2.8650
Ho: mean = 120   degrees of freedom   =   20

Ha: mean < 120   Ha: mean ! = 120   Ha: mean > 120
Pr (T < t) = 0.0048   Pr (|T| > |t|) = 0.0096   Pr (T > t) = 0.9952

The observed t-value of -2.87 matches the one we obtained by hand within rounding error and the two-tailed p-value of 0.0096 associated with the non-directional alternative hypothesis H_1: μ != 120 also agrees with our earlier result. Recall that != stands for "not equal to". Notice that Stata refers to the alternative hypothesis as H_a rather than as we do in the text as H_1.

☞ **Remark.** The 95% CI does not include the null hypothesis test value of 120. Because the CI contains all values of the null hypothesis that would not be rejected at the 0.05 two-tailed level of significance, the fact that the value of 120 falls outside this CI, we should not be surprised that the hypothesis test, H_0: μ=120 was rejected in favor of the alternative that H_1: μ≠120.

MORE Stata: To obtain the area to the right of an observed t-value
If our alternative hypothesis were H_1: $\mu \geq 120$ to find the area to the right of the observed t-value, we would use Stata's **ttail(df,t)** function, which returns the reverse cumulative (upper or right tail) Student's t distribution with df degrees of freedom, and input the observed t-value and its associated degrees of freedom.

☞ **Remark.** As indicated by Equation 11.1, a *t*-value is simply the ratio of a statistic divided by the standard error of that statistic. In Equation 11.1, that statistic is the mean, however, it need not be. In the case of skewness, by dividing the skewness statistic by its standard error, we are forming a t-ratio as well. The skewness ratio (*t*-value)in this case is 1.13, which is not considered to be large given that we typically consider t-ratios greater than 2 to be large.

EFFECT SIZE FOR THE ONE SAMPLE *t*-TEST

In terms of *d*, the effect size for a one-sample *t*-test equals

$$d = \frac{\bar{X} - \mu}{\hat{\sigma}} \tag{11.4}$$

The effect size for the result in Example 11.4 is $d = \frac{114 - 120}{9.60} = -.625$, which indicates that the mean systolic blood pressure of adult African-American males is .625 standard deviations below 120. This is a moderate to large effect in this case according to Cohen's rule of thumb guidelines.

• •

EXAMPLE 11.5. Suppose that a recent survey conducted in the southern region of the United States indicates that college-bound females who have always been at grade level take an average of three years of math in high school. Based on your own personal knowledge and what you have read in the literature, you believe that this is not the case, although you do not know whether the number of years is more or less than 3. Accordingly, you wish to carry out a test to nullify the hypothesis that $H_0:\mu = 3$ in favor of the alternative hypothesis that $H_1:\mu \neq 3$. Use the *NELS* data set and set $\alpha = .05$.

Solution. If we knew σ, the standard deviation of the parent population, we would use the Central Limit Theorem and proceed as we did in Chapter 10 to test these hypotheses. Because we do not know σ, however, we use the *t*-distribution as the basis for the null hypothesis testing procedure in this case. We are warranted to do so because of the size of our sample ($N = 84$) and the fact that, from Example 11.2, we know that our sample is sufficiently symmetric to make the assumption of normality a reasonable one.

We select cases as in Example 11.2. Because the data set is large, we do not carry out the computations by hand; rather we use Stata.

MORE Stata: To find the *p*-value associated with the *t*-test for a subset of cases
For this problem, type and run the following syntax in our Do-file:

ttest unitmath == 3 if gender == 1 & region == 3

We obtain the following results.

One-sample t test						
Variable	Obs	Mean	Std. Err.	Std. Dev.	[95 % Conf.	Interval]
unitmath	84	3.664048	.0788377	.7225592	3.507243	3.820853

mean = mean (unitmath)   t   =   8.4230
Ho: mean = 3   degrees of freedom   =   83

Ha: mean < 3	Ha: mean ! = 3	Ha: mean > 3
Pr (T < t) = 1.0000	Pr (|T| > |t|) = 0.0000	Pr (T > t) = 0.0000

The *t*-value is 8.42 with 83 degrees of freedom ($df = N - 1 = 84 - 1 = 83$, in this case) and the *p*-value (for a two-tailed test) is given in the output as "Ha: mean!=3." Although *p*-values for both one-tailed tests also are given in this output, for our example, the two-tailed test is most appropriate because our alternative hypothesis is non-directional. Our conclusion then is to reject the null hypothesis in favor of the alternative that the mean number of units of math taken in high school by southern females is indeed different from 3. Furthermore, because the obtained sample mean is $\overline{X} = 3.66$, we may conclude that the mean number of units of math taken in high school is statistically significantly *higher* than 3.

In terms of *d*, the effect size equals $d = \dfrac{\overline{X} - \mu}{\hat{\sigma}} = \dfrac{3.66 - 3}{.72} = .92$, which indicates that the mean number of years of math taken by college-bound females from the South who have always stayed on grade level is .92 standard deviations larger than 3 and which suggests a large effect in this case according to Cohen's rule of thumb guidelines.

☞ **Remark.** Note that we should not interpret $p = .0000$ as if p were identically equal to zero. The reason that p is reported as .0000 is because Stata reports results to four significant digits. Our result is highly unlikely given that the null hypothesis is true, but not impossible, which would be the case if p were truly identically equal to zero. To indicate that p is not identically equal to zero, we write $p < .0005$ when reporting such results.

☞ **Remark.** If we had used the 95% CI that we constructed in Example 11.2 to test $H_0:\mu=3$ versus $H_1:\mu\neq3$, we would have arrived at the same conclusion to reject H_0 in favor of H_1 that we did in Example 11.5. That 95% CI so constructed in Example 11.2 equals (3.51, 3.82). By the definition of a CI we know that the values falling within the CI (from 3.51 to 3.82) are exactly those values of μ that would *not* be rejected as implausible in a non-directional hypothesis test at significance level .05. We also know that the values of μ falling outside the CI are the ones that would be rejected in a non-directional hypothesis test at significance level .05. Because the null-hypothesized value of 3 does not fall within the CI, it is not considered to be a plausible value of μ and so must be rejected in the context of a hypothesis test.

· ·

EXAMPLE 11.6. Suppose that a recent survey conducted in the southern region of the United States indicates that college-bound males who have always been at grade level take an average of three years of math in high school. Based on your own personal knowledge and what you have read in the literature, you believe that this is not the case, that, in fact, they take more than 3 years of math in high school. Accordingly, you wish to carry out a test to nullify the hypothesis that $H_0 : \mu = 3$ in favor of the alternative hypothesis that $H_1 : \mu > 3$. You use the NELS data set and set $\alpha = .05$.

Solution. The descriptive statistics given below on *NELS* data set males from the South show that $N = 66$, the skewness is .148, and the skewness ratio = 0.49 and suggest that the data set is sufficiently large and symmetric to justify our use of the *t*-distribution in this case to test the null hypothesis of interest.

			Units in Mathematics (NAEP)	
	Percentiles	Smallest		
1%	2	2		
5%	3	3		
10%	3	3	Obs	66
25%	3	3	Sum of Wgt.	66
50%	4		Mean	3.916667
		Largest	Std. Dev.	.7368505
75%	4	5		
90%	5	5	Variance	.5429487
95%	5	5	Skewness	.1447716
99%	6	6	Kurtosis	3.124289

skewness = .14477164; seskew = .29495267; skewness ratio = .49083007

We do not use the *z*-test because σ is not known and needs to be estimated from the data. We carry out the test to determine whether the amount by which 3.9 exceeds 3 is significant of a real difference or is due only to sampling error. Had the obtained value been less than 3, there would have no reason to carry out the hypothesis test at all because the null hypothesis would be more plausible than the alternative.

We proceed as in Example 11.5 to find the *p*-value associated with the *t*-test (syntax is **ttest unitmath == 3 if gender == 0 & region == 3**) and obtain the following results:

One-sample t test

Variable	Obs	Mean	Std. Err.	Std. Dev.	[95 % Conf.	Interval]
unitmath	66	3.916667	.0907	.7368505	3.735526	4.097807

mean = mean (unitmath)		t = 10.1066
Ho: mean = 3		degrees of freedom = 65

Ha: mean < 3	Ha: mean ! = 3	Ha: mean > 3
Pr (T < t) = 1.0000	Pr (|T| > |t|) = 0.0000	Pr (T > t) = 0.0000

For this example, we expect the degrees of freedom to be $N - 1 = 66 - 1 = 65$, which is the value reported in the output. The *t*-value of 10.11 with 65 degrees of freedom has an associated two-tailed p-value of .000 ($p < .0005$). Because, in this case, the alternative hypothesis is directional, a one-tailed p-value is most appropriate. As such, we can use the p value associated with the output "Ha: mean > 3" for this analysis. Given that the p-value is less than 0.0005, we know that our result is statistically significant, that the population of college-bound males in the southern region of the United States take more than three years of math in high school on average.

We could not have used a confidence interval to determine whether college-bound males from the South take more than three years of high school math, because as formulated in this text, confidence intervals can be used only in the case of non-directional research questions.

Given that the results of the one-sample t-test are statistically significant, they should be further analyzed for practical significance, using a measure of the magnitude of the effect.

In terms of d, the effect size is $\dfrac{\overline{X} - \mu}{\hat{\sigma}} = \dfrac{3.92 - 3}{.74} = 1.24$, which indicates that the mean number of years of math taken by college-bound males from the South who have always stayed on grade level is approximately 1.24 standard deviations larger than 3, a very large effect, according to Cohen's rule of thumb guidelines, in this case.

TWO SAMPLE DESIGNS WHEN THE PARAMETER OF INTEREST IS μ, AND σ IS NOT KNOWN

In this section we expand the number of groups in the design from one to two, and in so doing allow for the possibility of answering a whole different set of questions. As related to the various populations represented by the *NELS* data set, we may ask, for example, whether

1. on average, college-bound males from the South who have always been on grade level differ in the number of years of math in high school from females from the South?
2. on average, college-bound females from the Northeast who have always been on grade level who own a computer score higher in twelfth grade math achievement than those who do not own a computer?
3. on average, college-bound females from the South who have always been on grade level change in self-esteem from eighth grade to twelfth grade?

Each of these questions is concerned with estimating the means of two populations, μ_1 and μ_2, for the purpose of comparing them to each other. In question 1, we may define μ_1 as the mean number of years of math taken in high school by females from the South and μ_2 as the mean number of years of math taken in high school by males from the South. In question 2, we may define μ_1 as the mean math achievement score in 12th grade for those who own a computer and μ_2 as the mean math achievement score in 12th grade for those who do not own a computer. Finally, in question 3, we may define μ_1 as the mean self-esteem score of females in 8th grade and μ_2 as the mean self-esteem scores of the same females, now in 12th grade. In each case, we are concerned with knowing whether a difference between the two population means exists; that is, whether it is plausible that the difference between population means is zero. If the difference is not zero, then we would be interested in knowing the magnitude of the difference that exists.

To test whether in fact the two population means μ_1 and μ_2 differ from each other, we begin by estimating μ_1 and μ_2 by $\bar{X}_1$ and $\bar{X}_2$, respectively, where we calculate each sample mean on a sample randomly selected from the appropriate population. We then compute the difference between $\bar{X}_1$ and $\bar{X}_2$. Because our interest is not with the sample mean difference per se, but rather with the population mean difference, we need a procedure for judging whether the sample mean difference is real or merely apparent (due to sampling error). In the last section, when the design involved only one sample and σ was unknown, we used the one-sample t-distribution, the sampling distribution of means when σ is unknown, to determine whether the observed sample mean was statistically significantly different from the hypothesized value, μ. In the present case, our design involves two samples and we assume that $\sigma_1 = \sigma_2 = \sigma$ and that σ is not known. By analogy, we turn to the sampling distribution of differences between means $\bar{X}_1$ and $\bar{X}_2$ calculated on samples of size N_1 and N_2, respectively, to determine whether the observed difference between sample means is statistically significantly different from the hypothesized difference $\mu_1 - \mu_2$.

INDEPENDENT (OR UNRELATED) AND DEPENDENT (OR RELATED) SAMPLES

To determine whether an observed difference in sample means is large enough to cause us to infer a difference in population means we need first to consider another aspect of study design, the degree to which factors extraneous to the main variable of interest are controlled. We may think of the observed difference in sample means as comprised of two components: a *signal* component that reflects the true difference between sample means in terms of the variable under study (e.g., the number of years of math taken during high school) and a *noise* component that reflects the difference between sample means due to extraneous and random factors (e.g., educational aspirations, academic interests, and career goals). By analogy, we may think of the signal as a radio broadcast and the noise as static in the airwaves. Just as our ability to detect a particular radio signal will depend upon the amount of static present, so our ability to detect a statistical difference will depend upon the degree to which extraneous and random factors have not been controlled.

In question 1 above, if all variables that might impact on the number of years of math taken in high school were the same for males and females (e.g., educational aspirations, academic interests, career goals, and so on), we would say that the system contained little or no noise. In this case, we would have little difficulty detecting the signal, the true difference, no matter how small. On the other hand, if none of the variables that might impact on number of years of math taken in high school were controlled, we would say that the system contained a great deal of noise. In this case, we might have great difficulty detecting the signal, the true difference, no matter how large. In general, the more control we exercise over extraneous factors, the smaller the difference between $\bar{X}_1$ and $\bar{X}_2$ that we will be able to detect as statistically significant; i.e., as significant of a difference between population means.

If, with respect to question 1, a random sample of males were selected and a random sample of females were selected *independently*, extraneous factors such as educational aspirations, academic interests, career goals and the like would not be controlled for explicitly. Any or all of these factors would be considered as noise in the system and they could contribute to the observed difference between $\bar{X}_1$ and $\bar{X}_2$. Explicit control over extraneous factors may be achieved if a random sample of males were selected and a sample of females were then selected in such a way that each female *matched* each male on a one-to-one, pair-wise basis with respect to as many of the extraneous factors as possible. A result of such control is a reduction in the noise component and a consequent expectation of smaller differences between means. Accordingly, decisions as to whether a statistical difference is real or apparent (merely due to sampling error) must depend, at least, in part, upon whether the design of the study controls for extraneous factors or not.

When the selection of subjects for one sample has no effect whatsoever on the selection of subjects for the second sample (as when the females were selected independently of the males), the two samples are said to be *independent, or unrelated*. When the samples are selected in such a way as to allow individual matching into pairs on extraneous factors across samples (as when individuals are matched on educational aspirations, academic interests, career goals, etc.), the two samples are said to be *dependent, paired, or related*.

A particular case of related samples arises when *the same individuals* are tested twice with an intervening treatment or interval of time (as in question 3 at the beginning of the chapter). Because measures are taken repeatedly on the same individuals, this type of design is often called a *repeated measures design*. Although repeated-measures designs do, in general, afford more control than unrelated-samples designs, repeated-measures designs are usually employed to comply with the theoretical framework of the research problem rather than for explicit control.

Because the size of sample mean differences $\overline{X}_1 - \overline{X}_2$ depends in part on whether the design controls for extraneous factors or not (i.e., whether it is based on related or unrelated samples), we must treat the cases of related and unrelated samples separately in our discussion of sampling distributions. We first consider designs that use independent samples.

INDEPENDENT SAMPLES *t*-TEST AND CONFIDENCE INTERVAL

In the previous section on the one-sample *t*-test, we determined that southern U.S. college-bound males and females who have always been at grade level each take an average of more than three years of math in high school. But, does the population of males differ from the population of females in terms of the number of years of math taken in high school? Questions like these imply a comparison of one group mean to the other, rather than a separate comparison of each group mean to a specified value, three in this case. Furthermore, because the males and females are each selected independently of each other, the appropriate test to answer this question is the independent samples *t*-test.

The sample means and standard deviations of the number of years of high school mathematics taken by both males and females from the South obtained using the compare means procedure are given in Table 11.1. The results were obtained using a Stata command that was not used previously in this text, but is useful for producing tables in a concise format especially when only few statistics are requested. The maximum number of statistics that can be requested for this command is five. The Stata command is: **table gender if region == 3, contents(n unitmath mean unitmath sd unitmath min unitmath max unitmath)**.

As with the one group *t*-test, our question concerns whether the observed mean difference between males and females (3.92 − 3.66 = .26) is large enough to conclude that a real difference exists between males and females in the population. To determine whether

Table 11.1. Descriptive statistics for units of math taken by males and females in the southern region.

Gender	N(unitmath)	mean(unit~h)	sd(unitmath)	min(unitm~h)	max(unitm~h)
Male	66	3.9166667	.7368505	2	6
Female	84	3.6640476	.7225592	2	6

it is large enough, we need to extend the procedure we used in relation to the one-sample t-test to incorporate the fact that we are now interested in making judgments about differences between means rather than about means alone. Recall that the one-sample t-ratio is described by Equation 11.1, as

$$t = \frac{(\bar{X} - \mu)}{\hat{\sigma}_{\bar{X}}}.$$

In extending this ratio to the case of mean differences, we simply substitute a mean difference quantity for every instance of a mean. We thus obtain Equation 11.5 as the t-ratio that is used to test hypotheses about mean differences on independent samples:

$$t = \frac{(\bar{X}_1 - \bar{X}_2) - (\mu_1 - \mu_2)}{\hat{\sigma}_{\bar{X}_1 - \bar{X}_2}} \tag{11.5}$$

While the computation of the numerator of this ratio contains no new notation, the denominator requires some explanation. In short, $\hat{\sigma}_{\bar{X}_1 - \bar{X}_2}$ is the standard deviation of the sampling distribution of sample mean differences, also called the *standard error of mean differences*. The equation for determining $\hat{\sigma}_{\bar{X}_1 - \bar{X}_2}$ when the variances for the two populations from which the samples are drawn are equal is given as

$$\hat{\sigma}_{\bar{X}_1 - \bar{X}_2} = \sqrt{\frac{(N_1 - 1)\hat{\sigma}_1^2 + (N_2 - 1)\hat{\sigma}_2^2}{N_1 + N_2 - 2}\left(\frac{1}{N_1} + \frac{1}{N_2}\right)} \tag{11.6}$$

Equation 11.6 is based on a weighted average of the two variance estimators, $\hat{\sigma}_1^2$ and $\hat{\sigma}_2^2$. Notice that $\hat{\sigma}_1^2$ is weighted by the degrees of freedom of sample one, $N_1 - 1$, and $\hat{\sigma}_2^2$ is weighted by the degrees of freedom of sample two, $N_2 - 1$. The degrees of freedom, $N_1 - 1$ and $N_2 - 1$, for each group respectively is a function of its size. Because, in general estimators from larger samples are more accurate, Equation 11.6 weights more heavily the estimate that comes from the larger sample.

Substituting Equation 11.6 into Equation 11.5, we present an alternate version of the t statistic for the two-population, unrelated-samples case with homogeneous variances as

$$t = \frac{(\bar{X}_1 - \bar{X}_2) - (\mu_1 - \mu_2)}{\sqrt{\frac{(N_1 - 1)\hat{\sigma}_1^2 + (N_2 - 1)\hat{\sigma}_2^2}{N_1 + N_2 - 2}\left(\frac{1}{N_1} + \frac{1}{N_2}\right)}} \tag{11.7}$$

The number of degrees of freedom for this t statistic may be determined by recalling that we are using both sample variance estimators $\hat{\sigma}_1^2$ and $\hat{\sigma}_2^2$ to obtain the denominator of this statistic and that $\hat{\sigma}_1^2$ has $N_1 - 1$ degrees of freedom associated with it, whereas $\hat{\sigma}_2^2$ has $N_2 - 1$ degrees of freedom associated with it. Because $\hat{\sigma}_1^2$ and $\hat{\sigma}_2^2$ come from independent samples, the total number of independent pieces of information contained in the data, and therefore the number of degrees of freedom for this t statistic, is

$$v = v_1 + v_2 = (N_1 - 1) + (N_2 - 1) = N_1 + N_2 - 2 \tag{11.8}$$

To estimate the mean difference between populations, we construct a confidence interval using Equation 11.9.

$$\text{Upper Limit} = (\bar{X}_1 - \bar{X}_2) + (t_{crit})(\hat{\sigma}_{\bar{X}_1 - \bar{X}_2}) \tag{11.9}$$

$$\text{Lower Limit} = (\bar{X}_1 - \bar{X}_2) - (t_{crit})(\hat{\sigma}_{\bar{X}_1 - \bar{X}_2})$$

Where $\hat{\sigma}_{\bar{X}_1 - \bar{X}_2}$, the standard error of the mean difference is given in Equation 11.6 and t_{crit} is found as before using **invttail** with *df* equal to $N_1 + N_2 - 2$.

Notice that Equation 11.9 is an extension of Equation 11.3 for constructing confidence intervals in the one-sample design when σ is not known.

THE ASSUMPTIONS OF THE INDEPENDENT SAMPLES *t*-TEST

Although the *t*-test procedure just outlined results in a sample statistic, there is in general no guarantee that this procedure will yield a *t-statistic* with a corresponding *t-distribution*. If certain conditions are satisfied by our two populations, however, then the statistic will be a *t*-statistic. These conditions are as follows:

1. The null hypothesis is true.
2. Both parent populations are normally distributed.
3. The two populations have equal variances (this is called homogeneity of variance).

If any of these three conditions is not met, then the statistic obtained may not be distributed as a *t*-distribution with hypothesized mean difference $\mu_1 - \mu_2$ and estimated variance $\hat{\sigma}^2 \bar{X}_1 - \bar{X}_2$, so that the *p*-values calculated based on this distribution would be invalid.

In testing the difference between population means, if conditions 2 and 3 are known to be satisfied and an unusual sample outcome is observed, then the plausibility of the remaining condition, condition 1, becomes questionable and one would decide to reject H_0 as implausible.

Thus, it appears that conditions 2 and 3 need to be satisfied in order to test condition 1 using the *t*-statistic provided in Equation 11.7 that H_0 is true. For this reason, conditions 2 and 3 are usually referred to as the underlying assumptions of this *t*-test.

In actual research situations, we cannot always be certain that either or both conditions 2 and 3 hold and we must expend some effort to investigate the tenability of these assumptions.

Violations of the first underlying assumption, normality of the two parent populations, may be assessed qualitatively by constructing either boxplots or histograms and quantitatively by the skewness ratio. Sometimes violations of the normality assumption may be corrected using nonlinear transformations as discussed in Chapter 4. Violations of the second underlying assumption, equality of the two parent population variances, may be assessed by Levene's test. As we shall see, results from this test are not provided in Stata in the output of an independent samples t-test, but we may obtain results from this test as well as those from other robust tests for the equality of variances using the command **robvar**.

For now, it is enough to know that the null hypothesis tested by Levene's test is that the two population variances are equal (H_0: $\sigma_1^2 = \sigma_2^2$) and the alternative hypothesis is that the two population variances are not equal (H_1: $\sigma_1^2 \neq \sigma_2^2$). If the p-value associated with Levene's test is less than α, following usual procedure, we reject H_0 in favor of H_1 that the two population variances are not equal and conclude that the third assumption is not tenable. On the other hand, if the p-value associated with Levene's test is greater than α, we conclude that the homogeneity of variance assumption is tenable.

Because the t-distribution is based on the assumptions of normality and homogeneity of variance, there has been much research on the effect of violations of these assumptions on the t-test. Based on the results of such research, we know that, under certain conditions, the t-test can withstand a great deal of deviation from its underlying assumptions. In statistical terms, we say that the t-test is *robust*. For an extensive review of research related to the consequences of violating the assumptions of the t-test on the probability statements of the t-test, the interested reader is referred to Glass, Peckham, and Sanders (1972).

Violations of the normality assumption may be essentially ignored if the sample from the non-normal parent population is sufficiently large (30 or larger will usually suffice, as in the statement of the Central Limit Theorem). Or, if the sample cannot be large, then if the distribution of the non-normal parent population is approximately symmetric.

Violations of the homogeneity of variance assumption may be essentially ignored as long as the samples being used have equal or approximately equal sizes. If, however, Levene's test indicates that the assumption of equal population variances is not tenable, and the samples are of unequal size, it would be incorrect to pool the two variance estimates using Equation (11.5). The assumption of equal variances can be avoided by using an estimate of variance proposed by Satterthwaite (1946),

$$\hat{\sigma}_s^2 = \frac{\hat{\sigma}_1^2}{N_1} + \frac{\hat{\sigma}_2^2}{N_2} \tag{11.10}$$

The degrees of freedom associated with Equation 11.10 are not $N_1 + N_2 - 2$, but are given by the following, much more complicated, expression that does not necessarily result in an integer value.

$$df = v = \frac{\left(\dfrac{\hat{\sigma}_1^2}{N_1} + \dfrac{\hat{\sigma}_2^2}{N_2}\right)^2}{\left(\dfrac{1}{N_1 - 1}\right)\left(\dfrac{\hat{\sigma}_1^2}{N_1}\right)^2 + \left(\dfrac{1}{N_2 - 1}\right)\left(\dfrac{\hat{\sigma}_2^2}{N_2}\right)^2} \tag{11.11}$$

A good rule of thumb, therefore, is that if both sample sizes are large and equal (or approximately equal), then violations of either or both underlying assumptions, normality and homogeneity of variance, will not seriously affect the applicability of the t-test for unrelated samples. If the samples are not equal, then Levene's test should be used to test for the assumption of homogeneity of variance. If according to Levene's test we find that the homogeneity of variance assumption is not tenable, we should use the t-statistic based on separate sample variances to estimate the two different population variances with degrees of freedom given by Equation 11.11.

For heuristic reasons, we begin by illustrating by hand the tests of inference described in this section using an extended data set from Example 11.1 that incorporates another feature of this study.

• •

EXAMPLE 11.7. To determine whether an increase in calcium intake reduces blood pressure, 10 of the 21 men in Example 11.1 were randomly assigned to a treatment condition that required them to take a calcium supplement for 12 weeks. The remaining 11 men received a placebo for the 12 weeks. Conduct an analysis to determine whether there is a mean difference in the initial systolic blood pressure readings between the men assigned to the treatment and placebo conditions before they begin the experimental protocol. The data are provided below and are also available online, www.cambridge.org/Stats-Stata, under the filename *Blood*. Those in the treatment condition are coded 1; those in the placebo condition are coded 0. Systolic has been renamed systolc1 to underscore the fact that these data are *initial*, pretreatment measures of systolic blood pressure. Use $\alpha = .05$.

Treatment Condition	Systolic blood pressure (mm per Hg)
1	107
1	110
1	123
1	129
1	112
1	111
1	107
1	112
1	136
1	102
0	123
0	109
0	112
0	102
0	98
0	114
0	119
0	112
0	110
0	117
0	130

Solution. In statistical terms, the null and alternative hypotheses for this test are:

$H_0 : \mu_T = \mu_P,$ or equivalently, $H_0 : \mu_T - \mu_P = 0$
$H_1 : \mu_T \neq \mu_P,$ or equivalently, $H_1 : \mu_T - \mu_P \neq 0.$

As usual, we begin the analysis by reviewing the descriptive statistics for each group.

To obtain the table of descriptive statistics for both groups simultaneously, as we have done previously, we could run the **summarize** command twice, the first time modified by **if** group == 1 and the second time modified by if group == 0.

Alternatively, we also could use a **by statement** as shown below to run the analysis separately for each group. In using the by statement, we first need to sort the data set in terms of the grouping variable so that all records pertaining to the first group come first in the data set, followed by all records pertaining to the second group. The specific commands for this example are the following:

MORE Stata: To obtain summary statistics by treatment group (treatmen)
Type and run the following syntax:

by treatmen, sort: summarize systolc1, detail

Descriptive statistics requested for systolc1 will be printed for each of the separate treatment groups.

```
-> treatmen = Placebo

                          Initial blood pressure

            Percentiles      Smallest
     1%         98               98
     5%         98              102
    10%        102              109        Obs              11
    25%        109              110        Sum of Wgt.      11

    50%        112                         Mean         113.2727
                                Largest    Std. Dev.    9.023202
    75%        119              117
    90%        123              119        Variance     81.41818
    95%        130              123        Skewness     .1040208
    99%        130              130        Kurtosis     2.647079


-> treatmen = Calcium

                          Initial blood pressure

            Percentiles      Smallest
     1%        102              102
     5%        102              107
    10%       104.5             107        Obs              10
    25%        107              110        Sum of Wgt.      10

    50%       111.5                        Mean           114.8
                                Largest    Std. Dev.    10.62283
    75%        123              112
    90%        132              123        Variance     112.8444
    95%        135              129        Skewness     .8208611
    99%        135              135        Kurtosis     2.392622
```

Further, we run the following commands to generate the skewness ratios for both groups:

summskew systolc1, by(treatmen)

```
For treatmen = 0: skewness = .10402079; seskew =.66068745; skewness ratio = .1
> 5744327
For treatmen = 1: skewness = .82086116; seskew = .68704289; skewness ratio = 1.
> 1947743
```

We use these descriptive statistics to provide an initial review of t-test assumptions. The skewness value for each group is lower than 1.00 (and the skewness ratios of both groups are less than 2 in magnitude), suggesting that the normality assumption is reasonable. The sample standard deviations, however, are not equal, leaving open the possibility that the population variances are not equal either and that the assumption of homogeneity of variances is not met for these data. For now we assume that this assumption is met and continue with the independent samples t-test by hand to determine whether initial systolic blood pressure differs, on average, between those assigned to the calcium condition and those assigned to the placebo condition. We will use Stata in a later analysis to formally test the homogeneity of variance assumption and we shall see that it is a reasonable assumption for these data.

While we already know the descriptive statistics for each group from our Stata results, for instructional purposes we determine them by hand. We arbitrarily label the Calcium Group, Group 1 and the Placebo Group, Group 2.

For the Calcium Condition (Group 1):

$$N_1 = 10$$

$$\bar{X}_1 = (107+110+123+129+112+111+107+112+136+102)/10 = 114.8$$

$$\hat{\sigma}_1^2 = \left[\begin{array}{c} (107-114.8)^2 + (110-114.8)^2 + (123-114.8)^2 + \cdots \\ +(112-114.8)^2 + (136-114.8)^2 + (102-114.8)^2 \end{array} \right] / (10-1) = 112.78$$

$$\hat{\sigma}_1 = \sqrt{112.78} = 10.62$$

For the Placebo Condition (Group 2):

$$N_2 = 11$$

$$\bar{X}_2 = (123+109+112+102+98+114+119+112+110 \\ +117+130)/11 = 113.27$$

$$\hat{\sigma}_2^2 = \left[\begin{array}{c} (123-113.27)^2 + (109-113.27)^2 + (112-113.27)^2 + \cdots \\ +(110-113.27)^2 + (117-113.27)^2 + (130-113.27)^2 \end{array} \right] / (11-1) = 81.36$$

$$\hat{\sigma}_2 = \sqrt{81.36} = 9.02$$

Substituting these values into Equation 11.7, we obtain the following result:

$$t = \frac{(\bar{X}_1 - \bar{X}_2) - (\mu_1 - \mu_2)}{\sqrt{\dfrac{(N_1-1)\hat{\sigma}_1^2 + (N_2-1)\hat{\sigma}_2^2}{N_1+N_2-2} \left(\dfrac{1}{N_1} + \dfrac{1}{N_2} \right)}}$$

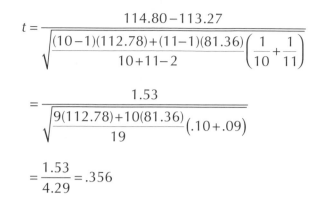

$$t = \frac{114.80 - 113.27}{\sqrt{\frac{(10-1)(112.78) + (11-1)(81.36)}{10+11-2}\left(\frac{1}{10} + \frac{1}{11}\right)}}$$

$$= \frac{1.53}{\sqrt{\frac{9(112.78) + 10(81.36)}{19}(.10 + .09)}}$$

$$= \frac{1.53}{4.29} = .356$$

To find the *p*-value associated with this *t*-ratio, we use Stata and Table 2 in Appendix C online, www.cambridge.org/Stats-Stata. In both cases we need the value of the *t*-ratio and its associated degrees of freedom. We have *t* = .356 and given that this t-value is from an independent samples *t*-test, *df* = $N_1 + N_2 - 2$ = 10+11–2 = 19.

To obtain the one-tailed *p*-value using Stata, we run the following command:

display ttail(19, .356). The resulting one-tailed p-value is .363.

The two-tailed *p*-value is obtained by multiplying .363 by 2, yielding *p* = .726.

We may use Table 2 to approximate the obtained *p*-value. In this case, we scan the row labeled *df* = 19 to find that the closest printed *t*-value to .356 is .688. From this poor approximation, we can say that the area to the right of .356 is greater than .25. We multiply .25 by 2 because the null hypothesis is non-directional, and obtain the result that *p* > .5. The large discrepancy between *p* = .726 and p > .5 is due to the fact that Table 2 provides only a limited set of *p*-values relative to the t-distribution. The *p*-values provided are only those associated with the commonly used definitions of statistical significance. The *t*-distribution given by Stata, however, is complete, and may be relied upon to provide accurate estimates of *p*-values for associated *t*-values.

From the more accurate Stata *p*-value we know that the probability of observing a mean difference as, or more, extreme than 1.53 coming from two populations with a mean difference of zero is .726. Because this probability is so large, we conclude that the obtained result is consistent with the statement of the null hypothesis that $\mu_P = \mu_C$. We therefore do not reject the null hypothesis in favor of the alternative hypothesis and conclude, based on this *p*-value, that those assigned to the Calcium Condition are no different, on average, from those assigned to the Placebo Condition in terms of their initial, pre-treatment systolic blood pressure.

To estimate the population mean difference in initial systolic blood pressure between Groups 1 and 2, we may construct a 95% CI for $\mu_P - \mu_C$. To do so we substitute the earlier values we calculated by hand for this example into Equation 11.9.

To find the t_c value we may use either Stata or Table 2 in Appendix C online, www.cambridge.org/Stats-Stata.

To find t_c using Stata, we use the syntax **display invttail(19, .025)** and obtain t_c = 2.09.

To find t_c using Table 2, we find the value at the intersection of the row labeled *df* = 19 and the column labeled .025. The *t*-value that has area .025 to its right is 2.09.

$$\text{Upper Limit} = (\bar{X}_1 - \bar{X}_2) + (t_c)(\hat{\sigma}_{\bar{x}_1 - \bar{x}_2}) = (114.80 - 113.27) + t_c \tag{4.29}$$
$$= 1.53 + 2.09(4.29) = 1.53 + 8.97 = 10.50$$

$$\text{Lower Limit } = (\bar{X}_1 - \bar{X}_2) + (t_c)(\hat{\sigma}_{\bar{x}_1 - \bar{x}_2}) = (114.80 - 113.27) - t_c \quad (4.29)$$
$$= 1.53 - 2.09(4.29) = 1.53 - 8.97 = 10.50$$

Accordingly, we estimate the mean difference in systolic blood pressure between the Calcium and Placebo populations to be between –7.45 and 10.50. Because 0 falls within this interval it is plausible that the mean difference between populations is 0; that the null hypothesis of a zero population mean difference is true, which is the conclusion we reached from the earlier t-test.

We now carry out the analysis for this example using Stata.

MORE Stata: To perform an independent samples t-test, followed by Levene's test

Type and run the following two commands:

ttest systolc1, by(treatmen)
robvar systolc1, by(treatmen)

This syntax assumes a 95% confidence interval. The command in the first line runs the independent samples t-test. The command in the second line runs a Levene's test for Equality of Variances.

We obtain the results shown below.

Two-sample t test with equal variances

Group	Obs	Mean	Std. Err.	Std. Dev.	[95% Conf.	Interval]
Placebo	11	113.2727	2.720598	9.023202	107.2109	119.3346
Calcium	10	114.8	3.359233	10.62283	107.2009	122.3991
combined	21	114	2.09421	9.596874	109.6316	118.3684
diff		−1.527273	4.287816		−10.50178	7.44723

diff = mean (Placebo) − mean (Calcium)   t   =   −0.3562
Ho: diff = 0   degrees of freedom   =   19

Ha: diff < 0   Ha: diff ! = 0   Ha: diff > 0
Pr (T < t) = 0.3628   Pr (|T| > |t|) = 0.7256   Pr (T > t) = 0.6372

Treatment	Summary of Initial blood pressure		
	Mean	Std. Dev.	Freq.
Placebo	113.27273	9.0232024	11
Calcium	114.8	10.622827	10
Total	114	9.5968745	21

W0 = 0.55843812   df (1, 19)   Pr > F = 0.46403885

W50 = 0.07751167   df (1, 19)   Pr > F = 0.78370563

W10 = 0.32679039   df (1, 19)   Pr > F = 0.57425644

Levene's Test for Equality of Variances is provided by the W0 estimate in the output associated with the **robvar** command. Because $p = .464$ and $\alpha = .05$ for this example, we conclude that the population variances are not different and that the assumption of homogeneity of variance is met for these data.

According to the independent groups t-test results, $t(19) = .356$, $p = .726$, suggesting that there is no difference in mean initial systolic blood pressure between the calcium and placebo groups. These are the hypothesis tests results we obtained in our hand calculation. The mean difference and standard error of the mean difference (1.53 and 4.29, respectively) are given as well. These also agree with our hand calculations as does the 95% CI of the population mean difference given as -10.50 to 7.45.

· ·

EXAMPLE 11.8. Does the population of college-bound males from the southern United States who have always been on grade level differ from the corresponding population of females in terms of the number of years of math in high school? Conduct the significance test at $\alpha = .05$.

Solution. In statistical terms, the null hypothesis for this test is $H_0{:}\mu_M = \mu_F$, or equivalently, $H_0{:}\mu_M - \mu_F = 0$ and the alternative hypothesis is $H_1{:}\mu_M \neq \mu_F$, or equivalently, $H_1{:}\mu_M - \mu_F \neq 0$. As before, we begin with an evaluation of the underlying assumptions of this t-test. From the earlier descriptive statistics given for females and males, in Examples 11.2 and 11.3, respectively, we know that both assumptions, normality and homogeneity of variance, appear to be met. Boxplots of the variable, number of years in math in high school, for males and females from the south visually confirm these impressions. Note that the boxplots suggest a trivially small difference between the two groups.

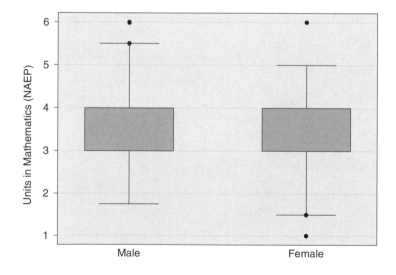

The output of the t-test and Levene's test are as follows.

Two-sample t test with equal variances

Group	Obs	Mean	Std. Err.	Std. Dev.	[95% Conf.	Interval]
Male	66	3.916667	.0907	.7368505	3.735526	4.097807
Female	84	3.664048	.0788377	.7225592	3.507243	3.820853
combined	150	3.7752	.060195	.7372356	3.656254	3.894146
diff		.252619	.1198904		.015701	.4895371

diff = mean (Male) – mean (Female)   t   =   2.1071
Ho : diff = 0   degrees of freedom   =   148

Ha : diff < 0   Ha : diff ! = 0   Ha : diff > 0
Pr (T < t) = 0.9816   Pr (|T| > |t|) = 0.0368   Pr (T > t) = 0.0184

	Summary of Units In Mathematics (NAEP)		
Gender	Mean	Std. Dev.	Freq.
Male	3.9166667	.73685054	66
Female	3.6640476	.72255924	84
Total	3.7752	.73723565	150

W0 = 1.10870013   df (1,148)   Pr > F = 0.29408074

W50 = 0.18583937   df (1,148)   Pr > F = 0.66702951

W10 = 1.55063528   df (1,148)   Pr > F = 0.21500965

Because $p = .294$ is greater than $\alpha = .05$, the results of Levene's test corroborate our visual impressions that the two samples are from populations with equal variances. Hence the results from the t-test with equal variances are relevant ($t(148) = 2.107$, $p = .04$.

☞ **Remark.** If Levene's test were statistically significant, suggesting that the homogeneity of variance assumption is not met for these data, we would add the option, **unequal** to the **ttest** command to obtain the results for the two-sample t-test with unequal variances. In particular, the command we would type is:

ttest unitmath if region == 3, by(gender) unequal

Because $p < .05$, we reject the null hypothesis in favor of the alternative and conclude that there is a statistically significant difference in terms of the mean number of years of math taken in high school between college-bound males and females from the South who have always stayed on track. Based on the means given in the group statistics output, we may further conclude that this population of males appears to take statistically significantly more years in math in high school than this population of females.

We could have calculated the t-value by substituting the descriptive statistics given in the Stata output into Equation 11.6 as follows:

$$t = \frac{(\bar{X}_1 - \bar{X}_2) - (\mu_1 - \mu_2)}{\hat{\sigma}_{\bar{X}_1 - \bar{X}_2}} = \frac{\text{Mean Difference}}{\text{Standard Error of the Difference}} = \frac{.253}{.120} = 2.107.$$

with $df = N_M + N_F - 2 = 66 + 84 - 2 = 148$ and then used Stata syntax,

display ttail(148, 2.107), or Table 2 to find the p-value of .0184, which we multiply by 2 to obtain the two-tailed p-value of .037.

The 95 percent confidence interval can also be used to determine whether the population of college-bound males from the southern United States who have always been on grade level differ from the corresponding population of females in terms of the number of years of math in high school. Because 0 is not contained in the 95 percent confidence interval, (.02, .49), we may conclude that the difference $\mu_M - \mu_F$ is not likely to be 0, and may be as great as one-half year. That is, as observed in connection with the null hypothesis test, the two group means are statistically significantly different from each other. Based on the means given in the group statistics output, we may further conclude that this population of males appears to take statistically significantly more years in math in high school than this population of females.

Note that in the case of a non-directional alternative hypothesis, we can base our conclusion on either a p-value or a confidence interval.

EFFECT SIZE FOR THE INDEPENDENT SAMPLES t-TEST

In addition to the confidence interval, we may extend Cohen's index of effect size, d, to the present case to obtain another estimate of the magnitude of the difference between population means.

Assuming the null hypothesis to be $H_0: \mu_1 = \mu_2$, Cohen's d, expressed as the difference between the two group means relative to the common standard deviation, is given by Equation 11.12.

$$d = \frac{\bar{X}_1 - \bar{X}_2}{\sqrt{\dfrac{(N_1 - 1)\hat{\sigma}_1^2 + (N_2 - 1)\hat{\sigma}_2^2}{N_1 + N_2 - 2}}} \tag{11.12}$$

The effect size, d, for the case of Example 11.8, which may be obtained using Stata's built-in calculator, **display**, is equal to

$$d = \frac{3.917 - 3.664}{\sqrt{\dfrac{(65)(.737)^2 + (83)(.723)^2}{66 + 84 - 2}}} = \frac{.253}{.729} = 0.35$$

That is, the number of years of math, on average, taken by college-bound southern males exceeds that for college-bound southern females by .35 standard deviations, a small to moderate effect size, further corroborating the results supported by the confidence interval.

Finally, we present the point biserial correlation coefficient as another measure of effect size that may be used in connection with the independent samples t-test. The point biserial correlation coefficient may be obtained as the correlation between group membership (males or females, in this case) and the variable of interest (years of math taken in high school, in this case). The greater the magnitude of the correlation, the greater the difference between group means relative to the common standard deviation. For example, if the difference in means between the two groups is zero, the point biserial correlation coefficient also is zero. Likewise, the larger the difference between group means relative to the common standard deviation, the closer the magnitude of the point biserial correlation coefficient is to one.

The scatterplot depicting differences in number of years of math taken in high school for males (gender = 0) and females (gender = 1) is given below.

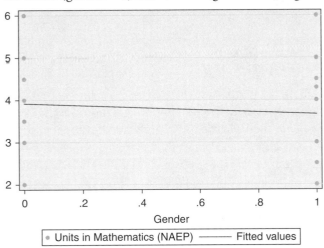

Notice that the best fitting line, which passes through the means of the two groups, is nearly horizontal, indicating, once again, that the difference between the two group means is small. Based on what we have learned about correlation and regression, the nearly horizontal orientation of the line suggests a near zero correlation between gender and unitmath. In fact, using Stata, we find the correlation between gender and unitmath to be r = −0.171 (syntax: **correlate gender unitmath if region == 3**), a small to moderate effect that further supports the results of the confidence interval and hypothesis test that there is a difference between the gender groups.

☞ **Remark.** The independent samples t-test of whether the population mean difference equals 0 is mathematically equivalent to the test of whether the population point biserial correlation coefficient equals 0. In a later chapter, we discuss inferential tests involving correlation coefficients.

• •

EXAMPLE 11.9. Among college-bound students in the northeastern United States who have always been on grade level, do those who own a computer score higher in math achievement in twelfth grade than those who do not? Conduct the significance test at $\alpha = .05$.

Solution. For this question, the null and alternative hypotheses are, respectively: $H_0: \mu_C = \mu_{NC}$ and $H_1: \mu_C > \mu_{NC}$. To inspect visually the math achievement distributions for both groups, we obtain the following boxplot. We also obtain the corresponding descriptive statistics for each group separately.

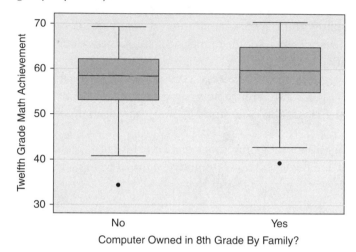

Both distributions have outliers, suggesting some negative skew for each; however, the samples are large enough to ignore the normality assumption. According to the boxplot, the variances appear to be homogeneous. Because the two samples are not equal in size, $n_C = 60$ and $n_{NC} = 46$, we will rely on Levene's test to evaluate the tenability of this assumption.

–> computer = No

Twelfth Grade Math Achievement

	Percentiles	Smallest		
1%	34.36	34.36		
5%	44.24	40.78		
10%	49.38	44.24	Obs	46
25%	53.09	47.73	Sum of Wgt.	46
50%	58.4		Mean	57.33457
		Largest	Std. Dev.	7.156028
75%	62.14	66.72		
90%	66.62	66.87	Variance	51.20873
95%	66.87	68.25	Skewness	–.8652418
99%	69.37	69.37	Kurtosis	4.121939

–> computer = Yes

Twelfth Grade Math Achievement

	Percentiles	Smallest
1%	39.28	39.28
5%	42.83	42.74

10%	46.65	42.76	Obs		60
25%	54.91	42.9	Sum of Wgt.		60
50%	59.675		Mean		58.944
		Largest	Std. Dev.		7.798042
75%	64.84	68.38			
90%	67.865	69.38	Variance		60.80945
95%	68.88	70.24	Skewness		−.7050442
99%	70.42	70.42	Kurtosis		2.779993

The descriptive statistics for both groups corroborate our visual impressions regarding skewness and homogeneity of variance. We may note also that the students in the *NELS* data set who own a computer score higher on the math achievement test than the students who do not. Because the direction of difference is as hypothesized, we proceed with the *t*-test on means to determine whether the observed difference is significant of a difference in the population.

The syntax to run this analysis is.

ttest achmat12 if region == 1, by(computer)
robvar achmat12 if region == 1, by(computer)

Two-sample t test with equal variances

Group	Obs	Mean	Std. Err.	Std. Dev.	[95% Conf.	Interval]
No	46	57.33457	1.055099	7.156028	55.20949	59.45964
Yes	60	58.944	1.006723	7.798042	56.92955	60.95845
combined	106	58.24557	.7317468	7.533794	56.79465	59.69648
diff		−1.609435	1.47509		−4.534594	1.315725

diff = mean (No) − mean (Yes) t = −1.0911
Ho: diff = 0 degrees of freedom = 104

Ha: diff < 0	Ha: diff ! = 0	Ha: diff > 0
Pr (T < t) = 0.1389	Pr (|T| > |t|) = 0.2778	Pr (T > t) = 0.8611

Computer Owned by Family in 8th Grade?	Summary of Twelfth Grade Math Achievement		
	Mean	Std. Dev.	Freq.
No	57.334565	7.1560277	46
Yes	58.944	7.7980417	60
Total	58.245566	7.5337942	106

W0 = 0.77581135 df (1, 104) Pr > F = 0.38045621

W50 = 0.81281478 df (1, 104) Pr > F = 0.36937254

W10 = 0.80387855 df (1, 104) Pr > F = 0.372007

Because Levene's test is not statistically significant ($p = .38$), the homogeneity of variance assumption is met for these data. The t-test results suggest that the observed difference in means is not statistically significant (note that we adjust the p-value by dividing by 2 to obtain the one-tailed test result: $p = .278/2 = .14$). Hence, we conclude that students who own a computer do not score statistically significantly higher in 12th grade math than those who do not, $t(104) = -1.09$, $p = .14$.

PAIRED SAMPLES t-TEST AND CONFIDENCE INTERVAL

Earlier in this chapter we posed three questions, each involving a comparison of two means. We asked whether, on average, males and females from the South differ in the number of math courses taken in college, whether, on average, those who own computers from the Northeast show greater achievement in twelfth grade math than those who do not, and whether, on average, college-bound females from the South change in self-esteem from eighth grade to twelfth grade. While the first two questions make use of an independent or unrelated samples design, the third question makes use of a dependent or related groups design because the same individuals are measured twice, in eighth grade and again in twelfth. Because the same individuals are measured twice, this design controls for several factors including socioeconomic status, peer group, physical appearance, and so on that may be related to self-concept.

The name *repeated measures* or *longitudinal* is used to describe this type of design in which observations are taken on the same objects across time. With only two sets of observations, one at time 1 and the other at time 2, we have, in this case, what is also called a *pre-post* design. Had we chosen, instead, to answer the third question using a *cross-sectional* design, we would have studied simultaneously a sample of females from eighth grade and an independently selected sample of females from twelfth grade, and we would have used the independent samples t-test to analyze our data. Because the scores in our two groups of data are matched pairwise, we select a method of analysis that exploits the particular paired or dependent structure of the data: the paired samples t-test.

The paired samples t-test capitalizes on the dependent structure of the data by basing its calculations on the difference scores computed for each matched pair. As such, the paired samples t-test may be viewed simply as a one-sample t-test on the difference scores, D, calculated on each matched pair and may be expressed as Equation 11.13, which is an adaptation of Equation 11.1, the one-sample t-test.

$$t = \frac{\bar{D} - \mu_D}{\hat{\sigma}_{\bar{D}}} \tag{11.13}$$

$df = N - 1 =$ Number of pairs $- 1$

The standard error of the mean difference, $\hat{\sigma}_{\bar{D}}$, is given by Equation 11.14.

$$\hat{\sigma}_{\bar{D}} = \frac{\hat{\sigma}_D}{\sqrt{N}} \tag{11.14}$$

Because difference scores form the basis of the paired samples t-test, the null hypothesis for this test is expressed as H_0: $\mu_D = 0$ which is equivalent to H_0: $\mu_1 - \mu_2 = 0$ because the difference of the sample means, $\bar{X}_1 - \bar{X}_2$, equals the mean of the paired differences, $\bar{D}$.

To estimate the mean difference between populations in a paired samples design, we construct a confidence interval using Equation 11.15:

$$\text{Upper Limit} = \bar{D} + (t_c)(\hat{\sigma}_{\bar{D}}) \tag{11.15}$$

$$\text{Lower Limit} = \bar{D} - (t_c)(\hat{\sigma}_{\bar{D}})$$

where $\hat{\sigma}_{\bar{D}}$, the standard error of the mean difference is given by Equation 11.14 and t_c is found as before using the Stata syntax for **display invttail(df, p)** or by using Table 2 in Appendix C online, www.cambridge.org/Stats-Stata, both with *df* equal to $N - 1$.

THE ASSUMPTIONS OF THE PAIRED SAMPLES *t*-TEST

The underlying assumptions of the paired samples *t*-test and confidence interval are the same as those for the independent samples *t*-test: normality and homogeneity of variance of the two parent populations. While the normality assumption requires some investigation in the case of the paired samples *t*-test, the homogeneity of variance assumption does not. The two groups are, by design, equal in size, and as noted earlier with respect to the independent samples *t*-test, violations of the homogeneity of variance assumption may be ignored when this is the case. Hence, Levene's test of homogeneity of variance is unnecessary.

For heuristic reasons, we extend the situation described in Example 11.7 to illustrate how a paired samples *t*-test may be carried out by hand. Recall that these data may be found in the file *Blood* on the text's website.

• •

EXAMPLE 11.10. The ten men in the Calcium Condition are given calcium supplements for the next 12 weeks, while the eleven men in the Placebo Condition are given a placebo for the next 12 weeks. At the end of this time period, systolic blood pressure readings of all men are recorded. Use the paired samples *t*-test to test whether there is a mean reduction in blood pressure from pretest to posttest based on the entire group of 21 men. Use $\alpha = .05$. The data occupy the first three columns of the table provided below. systolc2 contains the posttest measures of systolic blood pressure.

Treatment Condition	systolc1 (mm per Hg)	sysolc2 (mm per Hg)	d = systolc1-systolc2
1	107	100	7
1	110	114	−4
1	123	105	18
1	129	112	17
1	112	115	−3
1	111	116	−5
1	107	106	1
1	112	102	10
1	135	125	10
1	102	104	−2

(continued)

Treatment Condition	systolc1 (mm per Hg)	sysolc2 (mm per Hg)	d = systolc1-systolc2
0	123	124	−1
0	109	97	12
0	112	113	−1
0	102	105	−3
0	98	95	3
0	114	119	−5
0	119	114	5
0	112	114	−2
0	110	121	−11
0	117	118	−1
0	130	133	−3

Solution. The null and alternative hypotheses for this test are

$$H_0: \mu_{\bar{D}} = 0 \text{ and } H_1: \mu_{\bar{D}} > 0.$$

Because we wish to test whether there is a reduction in blood pressure, we expect the mean of the difference scores, assuming we subtract SYSTOLC2 from SYSTOLC1, to be positive. Hence this test is a directional, one-tailed paired samples t-test.

We compute the difference scores using the Stata command **gen d = systolc1-systolc2**. These appear in the fourth column of the previous table. The descriptive statistics for D, SYSTOLC1 and SYSTOLC2 are provided below.

		d		
	Percentiles	Smallest		
1%	−11	−11		
5%	−5	−5		
10%	−5	−5	Obs	21
25%	−3	−4	Sum of Wgt.	21
50%	−1		Mean	2
		Largest	Std. Dev.	7.687652
75%	7	10		
90%	12	12	Variance	59.1
95%	17	17	Skewness	.6725446
99%	18	18	Kurtosis	2.590572
		Initial blood pressure		
	Percentiles	Smallest		
1%	98	98		
5%	102	102		
10%	102	102	Obs	21
25%	109	107	Sum of Wgt.	21
50%	112		Mean	114
		Largest	Std. Dev.	9.596874

75%	119	123		
90%	129	129	Variance	92.1
95%	130	130	Skewness	.5676055
99%	135	135	Kurtosis	2.708193

Final blood pressure				
	Percentiles	Smallest		
1%	95	95		
5%	97	97		
10%	100	100	Obs	21
25%	105	102	Sum of Wgt.	21
50%	114		Mean	112
		Largest	Std. Dev.	9.782638
75%	118	121		
90%	124	124	Variance	95.7
95%	125	125	Skewness	.118209
99%	133	133	Kurtosis	2.462048

Because the skewness values are low, we may assume that the normality assumption is tenable for these data. Notice from the table, that the difference of blood pressure means (114–112) equals the mean of the difference (2). Notice also that the standard deviation of the difference, d, is lower than the standard deviation of either systolc1 or systolc2. This is because the two samples are paired and systolc1 and systolc2 are positively related. The paired samples design, in this case, provides a more powerful hypothesis test than would an independent samples test carried out on the same data. Can you figure out why?

Given the D values, which are, incidentally, easily computed by hand, we now compute $\bar{D}$ and $\hat{\sigma}_{\bar{D}}$.

$$\bar{D} = \left(\begin{array}{l} 7-4+18+17-3-5+1+10+10-2-1 \\ +12-1-3+3-5+5-2+11-1-3 \end{array}\right)/21 = 42/21 = 2$$

$$\hat{\sigma}_D = \sqrt{\frac{(7-2)^2+(-4-2)^2+(18-2)^2+\ldots+(11-2)^2+(-1-2)^2+(-3-2)^2}{21-1}}$$

$$= \sqrt{\frac{1182}{20}} = \sqrt{59.1} = 7.69$$

$$\hat{\sigma}_{\bar{D}} = \frac{\hat{\sigma}_D}{\sqrt{N}} = \frac{7.69}{\sqrt{21}} = \frac{7.69}{4.58} = 1.68$$

Substituting these values into Equation 11.13, we obtain:

$$t = \frac{\bar{D}-\mu_{\bar{D}}}{\hat{\sigma}_{\bar{D}}} = \frac{2-0}{1.68} = 1.19$$

and $df = N - 1 =$ Number of pairs $- 1 = 21 - 1 = 20$.

We find p either by using Stata or by using Table 2 in Appendix C online, www.cambridge .org/Stats-Stata. To use Stata, we use the syntax **display ttail(20, 1.19)** and obtain $p = .12$. To use Table 2, we look at the row with $df = 20$ and find that the closest t value is 1.064. The associated p value, located at the top of the column, is p = .15, which we use as our estimate.

We conclude that there is not a mean reduction in blood pressure from pretest to posttest, $t(20) = 1.19$, $p = .12$.

While ordinarily we would not compute a 95 percent CI for this one-tailed test, we do so here for heuristic purposes. Substituting the values calculated by hand into Equation 11.15, we obtain:

$$\text{Upper Limit} = \bar{D} + (t_c)(\hat{\sigma}_{\bar{D}}) = 2 + t_c(1.68) = 2 + 2.086(1.68) = 2 + 3.47 = 5.47$$
$$\text{Lower Limit} = \bar{D} - (t_c)(\hat{\sigma}_{\bar{D}}) = 2 - t_c(1.68) = 2 - 2.086(1.68) = 2 - 3.47 = -1.47$$

The critical t value ($t_c = 2.086$) was obtained either by computing **invttail** (20,.025) or from Table 2 in row labeled $df = 20$ and column labeled .025.

Accordingly, the 95 percent CI ranges from –1.47 to 5.47. We obtain the same results using the paired samples t-test in Stata (within rounding error).

MORE Stata: To perform a paired samples

Type the following syntax into your Do-file, highlight it, and hit **Control + d** to run:

ttest systolc1 == systolc2

By default, this test computes a 95% confidence interval.

The output will appear as such:

Paired t test						
Variable	Obs	Mean	Std. Err.	Std. Dev.	[95% Conf.	Interval]
systolc1	21	114	2.09421	9.596874	109.6316	118.3684
systolc2	21	112	2.134747	9.782638	107.547	116.453
diff	21	2	1.677583	7.687652	–1.499377	5.499377

mean (diff) = mean (systolcl – systolc2)   t = 1.1922
Ho: mean (diff) = 0   degrees of freedom = 20

Ha: mean (diff) < 0   Ha: mean (diff) ! = 0   Ha: mean (diff) > 0
Pr (T < t) = 0.8764   Pr (|T| > |t|) = 0.2471   Pr (T > t) = 0.1236

We employ the paired samples t-test in Example 11.11 to answer the third question posed in this section related to self-esteem.

• •

EXAMPLE 11.11. Do college-bound females from the South who have always been on grade level change in self-esteem from eighth grade to twelfth grade on average? Conduct the significance test at $\alpha = .05$.

Solution. In statistical terms, the null hypothesis for this test is H_0: $\mu_D = 0$ and the alternative hypothesis is H_1: $\mu_D \neq 0$. We begin with an evaluation of the underlying assumption of normality using the boxplot (**graph box slfcnc08 slfcnc12 if gender == 1 & region == 3**) and accompanying descriptive statistics (**summarize slfcnc08 slfcnc12 if gender == 1 &**

region == 3), and then conduct the paired ttest (**ttest slfcnc08 == slfcnc12 if gender ==1 & region == 3**).

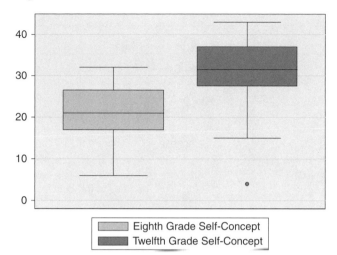

Eighth Grade Self-Concept
Twelfth Grade Self-Concept

Eighth Grade Self-Concept				
	Percentiles	Smallest		
1%	6	6		
5%	12	8		
10%	13	8	Obs	84
25%	17	9	Sum of Wgt.	84
50%	21		Mean	21.29762
		Largest	Std. Dev.	6.557953
75%	26.5	32		
90%	30	32	Variance	43.00674
95%	32	32	Skewness	−.0722981
99%	32	32	Kurtosis	2.244179

Twelfth Grade Self Concept				
	Percentiles	Smallest		
1%	4	4		
5%	19	15		
10%	25	16	Obs	84
25%	27.5	16	Sum of Wgt.	84
50%	31.5		Mean	31.80952
		Largest	Std. Dev.	7.193498
75%	37	43		
90%	41	43	Variance	51.74641
95%	41	43	Skewness	−.8317844
99%	43	43	Kurtosis	4.604554

While the eighth grade distribution of self-concept is approximately symmetric, the twelfth grade distribution is negatively skewed. Because the sample size of $N = 84$ for each sample is large, however, we are not concerned about the possible deviation of the population distributions from normality. We may note also the large increase in female self-concept from eighth to twelfth grade among the students in the data set.

Results of this *t*-test are given below.

Paired t test						
Variable	Obs	Mean	Std. Err.	Std. Dev.	[95 % Conf.	Interval]
slfcnc08	84	21.29762	.7155313	6.557953	19.87446	22.72078
slfcnc12	84	31.80952	.784875	7.193498	30.24844	33.37061
diff	84	−10.5119	.7206674	6.605026	−11.94528	−9.078526

mean (diff) = mean (slfcnc08 − slfcnc12)
Ho: mean (diff) = 0

t = −14.5863
degrees of freedom = 83

Ha: mean (diff) < 0	Ha: mean (diff) ! = 0	Ha: mean (diff) > 0
Pr (T < t) = 0.0000	Pr (|T| > |t|) = 0.0000	Pr (T > t) = 1.0000

From the first of the three tables we learn that descriptively, in eighth grade, females from the South have, on average, a self-concept score of 21.30 with standard deviation 6.56, and that in twelfth grade they have, on average, a self-concept score of 31.81 with standard deviation 7.19. These descriptive statistics indicate higher self-concept for the sample in twelfth grade.

The third table contains the results of the hypothesis test. From these, we see that the difference of 10.51 points in self-concept may not be attributable to chance, that it indicates a statistically significant increase in self-concept in the population ($t = -14.59$, $p < .0005$).

Alternatively, the third table also contains the confidence interval. It informs us that it is likely that the self-concept mean difference between grades 8 and 12 falls between −11.95 and −9.08. Because 0 is not contained in this interval, it is indicative of a statistically significant increase in self-concept in the population.

EFFECT SIZE FOR THE PAIRED SAMPLES *t*-TEST

In the situation of the paired samples *t*-test, the effect size is measured relative to the standard deviation of the paired differences, $\hat{\sigma}_D$, and is given by Equation 11.16.

$$d = \frac{\bar{D}}{\hat{\sigma}_D} \tag{11.16}$$

$\hat{\sigma}_D$ is provided by Stata in the paired samples *t*-test output. In this example, $\hat{\sigma}_D$ equals 6.61.

For the situation of Example 11.11, $d = \dfrac{31.81 - 21.30}{6.61} = \dfrac{10.51}{6.61} = 1.59$, suggesting that twelfth grade self-concept among females in the south is 1.59 standard deviations (of the paired differences) higher than it was in eighth grade, a large effect.

Given the paired nature of the data, we may compute the correlation between self-concept scores measured in eighth and twelfth grades to determine to what extent those who score low on self-concept in eighth grade tend to score low on self-concept in twelfth grade, and so forth. In an independent groups design we would expect this correlation to be 0. If, by matching, one or more sources of variability have been controlled, as intended, then we would expect a positive correlation between pairs. The positive correlation represents the degree to which the matched pairs design improves the power of the analysis. By contrast, a negative correlation implies that we have compromised the power of our analysis by matching on the particular values we have. While negative correlations typically do not arise in the context of repeated measures designs, they sometimes do arise when subjects are sampled in pairs (e.g., husbands and wives, fathers and sons) or when subjects are matched by pairs on some basis by the researcher (e.g., on age and education level).

The correlation value of .542 given in the second of the three tables of output is positive and moderately strong. It suggests that by utilizing before-after matching we have removed one or more sources of variability related to self-concept and thereby improved the power of our analysis relative to a cross-sectional, independent samples design.

THE BOOTSTRAP

As discussed earlier in this chapter, certain assumptions need to be met for the obtained t- statistic to be distributed as a t-distribution. In the case of the one-sample t test, the assumptions are that the null hypothesis is true, and that the parent population from which the sample has been selected is normally distributed. In the case of both the independent and paired samples t-tests, in addition to the two assumptions required by the one-sample t-test, there is also the assumption of homogeneity of variance. When it is questionable whether these parametric assumptions have been met, and we are uncertain as to whether the theoretically-derived t-distribution provides the correct sampling distribution of means or mean differences, we may use the type of simulation technique we demonstrated in Chapter 9 to illustrate the Central Limit Theorem, which required that the population distribution was known and that we had access to it,. As you may recall, in Chapter 9 we repeatedly drew random samples from our known and accessible population to generate an empirically-derived sampling distribution of means.

If, however, the population is *not* known, we may use a different technique, called *the bootstrap*, introduced in 1979 by Bradley Efron (1979, 1982), to derive empirically the sampling distribution of means or mean differences and use that empirically-derived sampling distribution to test our hypotheses or construct confidence intervals.[1] Unlike the simulation method we used in Chapter 9, which requires us to know and have access to the full population of values, the bootstrap technique considers our sample to be the population and draws repeated samples in a specific way from that original sample (aka, 'the population').

In particular, it draws repeated samples (called *bootstrap samples*) *randomly with replacement* from our original sample so that each bootstrap sample is equal in size to that of the original sample. Accordingly, if the size of our original sample is 100, for example, then the size of each bootstrap sample is also 100.

---

[1] In addition to offering a robust way to estimate standard errors and confidence intervals when the usual parametric assumptions (on which tests of inference are based) are questionable, the bootstrap also may be used when analytic procedures are too complex to derive the theoretical standard errors mathematically, as in the paper by Weinberg, Carroll, and Cohen (1984) on three-way multidimensional scaling.

To emphasize the notion of sampling with replacement, consider a hypothetical situation in which our original sample contained only five values, 1, 2, 3, 4, and 5. A single bootstrap sample drawn with replacement from this original sample could contain the five values 1, 1, 4, 5, and 4. That is, values from the original sample could appear more than once in the bootstrap sample, other values could appear not at all. Sampling with replacement is what allows our bootstrap samples to be equal in size to our original sample.

The process of drawing repeated bootstrap samples is called *resampling*, and to obtain accurate bootstrap estimates, the resampling process typically is repeated a large number of times (e.g., 1,000 times). For each bootstrap sample, our statistic of interest (e.g., a sample mean) is calculated, providing us with a large number (say, 1000) of sample means, one from each of the say, 1,000 bootstrap samples. Our sampling distribution of means is then obtained from the frequency distribution and histogram of these 1,000 bootstrap sample means. The standard deviation of this sampling distribution of means would be our *bootstrap estimate* of the standard error of the mean, which we could then use to test a hypothesis about μ or compute a confidence interval to estimate μ with high probability.

This entire process may be implemented using Stata, as the following examples demonstrate.

● ●

EXAMPLE 11.12. Consider Example 11.2 in which we constructed a 95% confidence interval about the population mean, μ, of the number of units of math taken in high school by females who live in the South.

MORE Stata: To implement the bootstrap technique for this one sample *t*-test using the 95% confidence interval

We would follow the same procedure used in connection with Example 11.2, but would include the word **bootstrap** as a *prefix command* and specify the statistic of interest (in this case, **mean**) that we would like calculated on each bootstrap sample. As noted earlier, the bootstrap estimate of the standard error of the mean will be obtained as the standard deviation of the specified number (e.g., 1,000) of bootstrap sample means. In this example, the prefix command includes the command **bootstrap** followed by the name of the variable we choose to assign (by way of the = sign) to the returned bootstrap mean estimates (labelled **r(mu_1)** by Stata). For this example, we assign the name **mean** to the returned bootstrap estimates **r(mu_1),** by including, **mean=r(mu_1)**, in our syntax. Finally we specify as an option the number of replications or bootstrap samples on which we would like the 95% bootstrap confidence interval to be based, **reps(1000).** The default number of replications for this command is 50. Because 95% is Stata's default confidence level value for this command, we do not need to add the option **level(95)** after **reps(1000)**. The syntax following the colon is the same as what it was in the original *t*-test command for this example.

bootstrap mean = r(mu_1), reps(1000): ttest unitmath == 0 if region == 3 & gender == 1

The output for this command is as follows:

```
Bootstrap replications (1000)
----+--- 1 ---+--- 2 ---+--- 3 ---+--- 4 ---+--- 5
.......................................................  50
.......................................................  100
.......................................................  150
.......................................................  200
.......................................................  250
.......................................................  300
.......................................................  350
.......................................................  400
.......................................................  450
.......................................................  500
.......................................................  550
.......................................................  600
.......................................................  650
.......................................................  700
.......................................................  750
.......................................................  800
.......................................................  850
.......................................................  900
.......................................................  950
.......................................................  1000


Bootstrap results                    Number of obs    =      84
                                     Replications     =    1000

     command: ttest unitmath == 0
       mean: r(mu_1)


-------------------------------------------------------------
          |  Observed  Bootstrap                Normal-based
          |   Coef.    Std. Err.    z    P>|z|  [95% Conf. Interval]
-------------------------------------------------------------
  mean  |  3.664048  .0787647  46.52  0.000  3.509672  3.818424
-------------------------------------------------------------
```

The bootstrap estimate of the 95% confidence interval is given as (3.510, 3.818), which, rounded to two decimal places, equals the result given in Example 11.2.

● ●

EXAMPLE 11.13. Consider Example 11.5 in which a one-sample t-test was conducted to test the hypothesis that the mean number of units of math taken in high school by females who live in the South is 3 versus not 3 (i.e., H_0: $\mu = 3$ versus H_1: $\mu \neq 3$).

MORE Stata: To implement the bootstrap technique for this one sample *t*-test using the *p*-value

We would follow the same procedure used in connection with Example 11.5, but would include the bootstrap as a prefix command, and once again, specify that we would like a bootstrap estimate of the population mean. In this case, we include the option **nodots** to avoid having a listing of the replications printed in the Output Window, and we include the option **seed(12345)** to set the seed of the random number generator equal to some value (chosen arbitrarily to be 12345 in this case)so that we may replicate these exact bootstrap results if we were to run this command again in the future.

bootstrap mean = r(mu_1), reps(1000) nodots seed(12345): ttest unitmath == 3 if region == 3 & gender == 1

The bootstrap results are given as follows:

Bootstrap results					Number of obs = 84	
command: ttest unitmath == 3 mean: r(mu_1)					Replications = 1000	
	Observed Coef.	Bootstrap Std. Err.	z	P>|z|	Normal–based [95% Conf.	Interval]
mean	3.664048	.0781598	46.88	0.000	3.510857	3.817238

These results are equal, after rounding to two decimal places, to those of Example 11.5.

• •

EXAMPLE 11.14. Consider Example 11.8 in which a two-group independent *t*-test was conducted to test the hypothesis that the mean number of units of math taken in high school by males who live in the South differs from that of females who live in the South (i.e., $H_0: \mu_M = \mu_F$ versus $H_1: \mu_M \neq \mu_F$).

MORE Stata: To implement the bootstrap technique in the case of a two-group independent *t*-test

We would follow the same procedure used in connection with Example 11.8, but would include the bootstrap as a prefix command and specify that we would like a bootstrap estimate of the difference in population means of the two groups, specified as **r(mu_1) – r(mu_2)**. The name we have chosen to be assigned to this difference in population mean estimates is **meanmale_minus_meanfem**. Once again we include the **nodots** and **seed** options.

bootstrap meanmale_minus_meanfem = (r(mu_1) – r(mu_2)), reps(1000)nodots seed(1765): ttest unitmath if region == 3, by (gender)

The bootstrap results given below are, once again, highly consistent with the theoretically-driven results given earlier for this problem in Example 11.8:

	Observed Coef.	Bootstrap Std. Err.	z	P>|z|	Normal–based [95% Conf. Interval]	

Bootstrap results

Number of obs = 150
Replications = 1000

command: ttest unitmath, by (gender)
meanmale_mi~m: r(mu_1) − r(mu_2)

	Observed Coef.	Bootstrap Std. Err.	z	P>|z|	Normal–based [95% Conf.	Interval]
meanmale_minus_mean~m	.252619	.1201358	2.10	0.035	.0171572	.4880809

EXAMPLE 11.15. Consider Example 11.11 in which a paired samples t-test was conducted to test the hypothesis that the self-esteem of females who live in the South changes from eighth to twelfth grade (i.e., H_0: $\mu_D = 0$ versus H_1: $\mu_D \neq 0$).

MORE Stata: To implement the bootstrap technique for this paired samples t-test

We would follow the same procedure used in connection with Example 11.11, but would include the bootstrap as a prefix command and specify that we would like a bootstrap estimate of the difference in population means of the two groups, specified as **r(mu_1) − r(mu_2)**. To suggest that we are dealing with a paired groups mean comparison (as stipulated by the **ttest** command itself), we have chosen as our variable name **meandiff** to be assigned to the returned difference in population mean estimates. Once again we use the **nodots** and **seed** options.

bootstrap meandiff = (r(mu_1) − r(mu_2)), reps(1000) nodots seed(1765): ttest slfcnc08 == slfcnc12 if gender ==1 & region == 3

The bootstrap results given below are, once again, highly consistent with the theoretically-driven results given earlier for this problem in Example 11.11:

Bootstrap results

Number of obs = 84
Replications = 1000

command: ttest slfcnc08 == slfcnc12
meandiff: r(mu_1) − r(mu_2)

	Observed Coef.	Bootstrap Std. Err.	z	P>|z|	Normal–based [95% Conf.	Interval]
meandiff	−10.5119	.723736	−14.52	0.000	−11.9304	−9.093408

☞ **Remark.** The substantial agreement that we have observed in these four examples between the empirically-derived estimates of the standard errors and confidence intervals based on the bootstrap and the corresponding theoretically-derived estimates based on the t-distribution reflects the fact that the underlying t-test assumptions did not appear to be violated to any great extent, but also because, as noted in this chapter, the t-test is quite robust to violations of its underlying assumptions.

TABLE 11.2. Equations for obtaining observed *t*-test values.

Test	Obtained Statistic using the notation in the book	Obtained Statistic using the notation from the Stata output
One-Sample *t*-test	$t = \dfrac{\bar{X} - \mu}{\dfrac{\hat{\sigma}}{\sqrt{N}}} = \dfrac{\bar{X} - \mu}{\hat{\sigma}_{\bar{x}}}$ $df = N - 1$	$t = \dfrac{\text{Mean} - \text{Test Value}}{\text{Std. Error Mean}}$ $df = N - 1$ The test value is the null hypothesized value for the population mean
Independent Samples *t*-test	$t = \dfrac{(\bar{X}_1 - \bar{X}_2) - (\mu_1 - \mu_2)}{\sqrt{\dfrac{(N_1 - 1)\hat{\sigma}_1^2 + (N_2 - 1)\hat{\sigma}_2^2}{N_1 + N_2 - 2}\left(\dfrac{1}{N_1} + \dfrac{1}{N_2}\right)}}$ $df = N_1 + N_2 - 2$	$t = \dfrac{\text{Mean Difference}}{\text{Std. Error Difference}}$ $df = N_1 + N_2 - 2$
Paired Samples *t*-test	$d = \dfrac{\bar{D} - \mu_D}{\hat{\sigma}_{\bar{D}}}$ $df = N - 1$	$t = \dfrac{\text{Paired Differences Mean}}{\text{Paired Differences Std. Error Mean}}$ $df = N - 1$

TABLE 11.3. Equations for obtaining confidence intervals based on the *t* distribution. To find t_c, use the equations for the degrees of freedom found in Table 11.2.

Test	Confidence Interval using the notation in the book	Confidence Interval using the notation from the Stata output
One-Sample *t*-test	Upper Limit $= \bar{X} + t_c\hat{\sigma}_{\bar{X}}$ Lower Limit $= \bar{X} - t_c\hat{\sigma}_{\bar{X}}$	U.L. $=$ Mean $+ (t_c)(\text{Std. Error Mean})$ L.L. $=$ Mean $- (t_c)(\text{Std. Error Mean})$
Independent Samples *t*-test	Upper Limit $= (\bar{X}_1 - \bar{X}_2) + t_c \bullet \hat{\sigma}_{\bar{X}_1 - \bar{X}_2}$ Lower Limit $= (\bar{X}_1 - \bar{X}_2) - t_c \bullet \hat{\sigma}_{\bar{X}_1 - \bar{X}_2}$	U.L. = Mean Difference + $(t_c)(\text{Std. Error Difference})$ L.L. = Mean Difference − $(t_c)(\text{Std. Error Difference})$
Paired Samples *t*-test	Upper Limit $= \bar{D} + t_c \bullet \hat{\sigma}_{\bar{D}}$ Lower Limit $= \bar{D} - t_c \bullet \hat{\sigma}_{\bar{D}}$	U.L. = Paired Differences Mean + $(t_c)(\text{Paired Differences Std. Error Mean})$ L.L. = Paired Differences Mean − $(t_c)(\text{Paired Differences Std. Error Mean})$

SUMMARY

Table 11.2 below contains a summary of the equations for the different hypothesis tests based on the *t*-distribution given in this chapter. Table 11.3 contains a summary of the equations for the confidence intervals based on the *t*-distribution given in this chapter. Table 11.4 contains a summary of the equations for the effect sizes for the different hypothesis tests given in this chapter. Tables 11.5 through 11.7 contain flow charts for the one sample, independent samples, and paired samples *t*- tests, respectively.

TABLE 11.4. Effect size equations associated with t-tests.

Test	Approximate Effect Size using the notation in the book	Approximate Effect Size using the notation from the Stata output
One-Sample t-test	$d = \dfrac{\bar{X} - \mu}{\hat{\sigma}}$	$d = \dfrac{\text{Mean} - \text{Test Value}}{\text{Std. Deviation}}$
Independent Samples t-test	$d = \dfrac{(\bar{X}_1 - \bar{X}_2)}{\sqrt{\dfrac{(N_1 - 1)\hat{\sigma}_1^2 + (N_2 - 1)\hat{\sigma}_2^2}{N_1 + N_2 - 2}}}$	$d = \dfrac{\text{Mean Difference}}{\sqrt{\dfrac{(N_1 - 1)SD_1^2 + (N_2 - 1)SD_2^2}{N_1 + N_2 - 2}}}$
Paired Samples t-test	$d = \dfrac{\bar{D}}{\hat{\sigma}_D}$	$t = \dfrac{\text{Paired Differences Mean}}{\text{Paired Differences Std. Deviation}}$

TABLE 11.5. Flow chart for one sample t-test

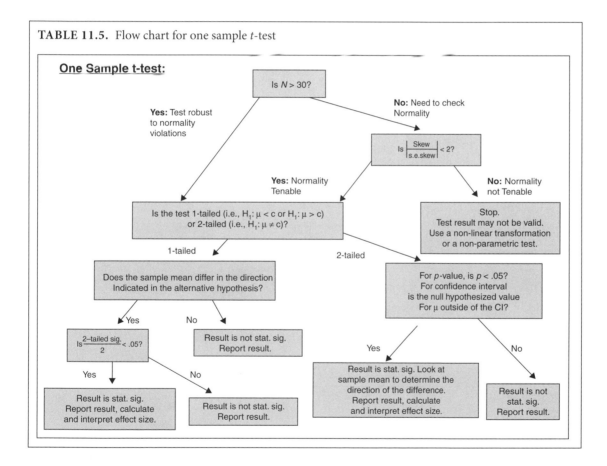

SUMMARY OF CHAPTER 11 STATA COMMANDS

For a complete listing of all Stata commands associated with this chapter, you may access the Do-file for Chapter 11 located on the text website.

TABLE 11.6. Flow chart for independent samples *t*-test

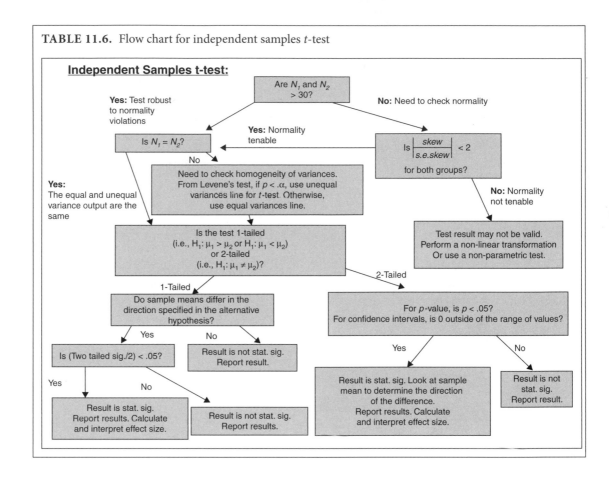

COMMANDS INVOLVING THE *t*-DISTRIBUTION

Create	Command Lines
To calculate the *t*-value with *df* = 20 and .025 area to its right (Example 11.1)	**display invttail(20, .025)**
To calculate the *p*-value associated with the two tailed test with *t*-value −2.86 with *df* = 20 (Example 11.4)	**display 2*t(20, −2.86)** **OR** **display 2*ttail(20,2.86)**

ONE SAMPLE *T*-TEST COMMANDS

Create	Command Lines
Summarize the variable systolc1 including the skewness ratio (Example 11.1)	**summarize systolc1, detail** **summskew systolc1**
Create a q-q plot of the variable systolc1 (Example 11.1)	**qnorm systolc1**
Compute the 95 percent confidence interval for systolc1 (Example 11.1)	**ttest systolc1 == 0**

TABLE 11.7. Flow chart for paired samples *t*-test

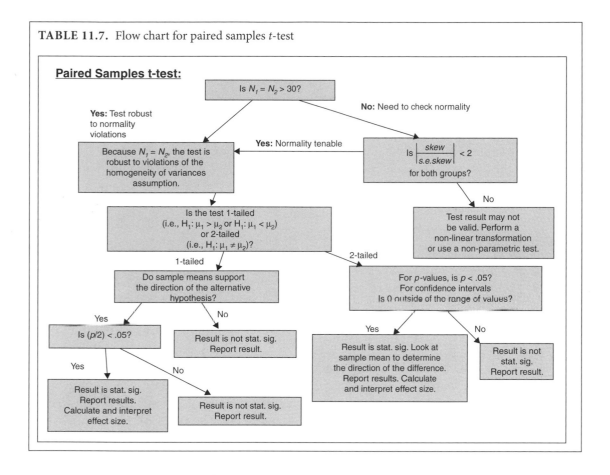

Paired Samples t-test:

Create	Command Lines
Summarize the variable unitmath for a subset of the *NELS* data set, in this case for women from the south (Example 11.2)	**summarize unitmath, detail, if gender == 1 & region == 3** **summskewcell unitmath gender region**
Compute the 95 percent confidence interval for unitmath for a subset of the *NELS* data set, in this case for women from the south (Example 11.2)	**ttest unitmath == 0 if (gender == 1 & region == 3):**
Compute the 99 percent confidence interval for unitmath for a subset of the *NELS* data set, in this case for women from the south (Example 11.3)	**ttest unitmath == 0, level(99), if gender == 1 & region == 3**
Perform the one sample t-test to determine whether the average initial systolic blood pressure in the population is 120 (Example 11.4)	**ttest systolc1 == 120**

(continued)

Create	Command Lines
Use the bootstrap technique to construct a 95% confidence interval about the population mean of the number of units of math taken in high school by females who live in the South (Example 11.12)	**bootstrap mean = r(mu_1), reps(1000): ttest unitmath == 0 if region == 3 & gender == 1**
Use the bootstrap technique to conduct a one-sample t-test using the p-value to test the hypothesis that the mean number of units of math taken in high school by females who live in the South is 3 (Example 11.13)	**bootstrap mean = r(mu_1), reps(1000) nodots seed(12345): ttest unitmath == 3 if region == 3 & gender == 1**

INDEPENDENT SAMPLES t-TEST COMMANDS

Create	Command Lines
Generate descriptive statistics for units of math taken by males and females in the southern region (Table 11.1)	**table gender if region == 3, contents (n unitmath mean unitmath sd unitmath min unitmath max unitmath)**
Obtain summary statistics by treatment group (treatmen) (Example 11.7)	**by treatmen, sort: summarize systolc1, detail** **summskew systolc1, by(treatmen)**
Perform the independent samples t-test of systolc1 by treatmen (Example 11.7)	**ttest systolc1, by(treatmen)** **robvar systolc1, by(treatmen)**
Perform the independent samples t-test of unitmath by gender for students in the south when the homogeneity of variances assumption is not tenable (Example 11.8)	**ttest unitmath if region == 3, by(gender) unequal**
Use the bootstrap technique to conduct an independent samples t-test to test the hypothesis that the mean number of units of math taken in high school by males who live in the South differs from that of females who live in the South (Example 11.14)	**bootstrap meanmale_minus_ meanfem = (r(mu_1) − r(mu_2)), reps(1000)nodots seed(1765): ttest unitmath if region == 3, by (gender)**

PAIRED SAMPLES t-TEST COMMANDS

Create	Command Lines
Perform the paired samples t-test of systolc1 and systolc2 (Example 11.10)	**ttest systolc1 == systolc2**
Use the bootstrap technique to conduct a paired samples t-test to test the hypothesis that the self-esteem of females who live in the South changes from eighth to twelfth grade (Example 11.15)	**bootstrap meandiff = (r(mu_1) − r(mu_2)), reps(1000) nodots seed(1765): ttest slfcnc08 == slfcnc12 if gender ==1 & region == 3**

EXERCISES

*Create a Do-file for each exercise that requires the use of Stata. Run the commands from the Do-file by highlighting them and hitting **Control+d**. Save each Do-file using a name associated with the Exercise for which it was created. It is recommended that you review the Do-file associated with* Chapter 11 *located on the textbook's website before completing these exercises. To facilitate doing each exercise, it may be helpful to copy and paste relevant commands from the Do-file for* Chapter 11 *into your own Do-file and modify them as needed.*

Exercises 11.1–11.2 involve one sample t-tests using variables from the Learndis data set. For inferential purposes, we consider the children in the data set to be a random sample of all children attending public elementary school in a certain city who have been diagnosed with learning disabilities. Use α = .05 for all significance tests.

11.1. The mean intellectual ability (iq) score for all children attending public elementary school in the city is 100 with standard deviation, $\sigma = 15$. The children in our sample are a random subset of the population of all children attending public elementary school in this city who are diagnosed with learning disabilities. Use Stata to construct a 95 percent confidence interval to estimate the mean iq score for this population. We do not want to assume that the standard deviation of the population of learning disabled children is the same as for all children attending public elementary school in this city, but instead want to use the sample to obtain an estimate of the standard deviation. Answer the related questions.

   a) Address the reason for choosing a *t*-test over a *z*-test, in this case.
   b) Evaluate the tenability of the normality assumption or indicate why the assumption is not an issue for this analysis, that the results of the *t*-test would not be compromised by a failure to meet this assumption.
   c) What is the 95 percent confidence interval for the mean iq score of all children attending public elementary school in this city who have been diagnosed with learning disabilities?
   d) State the null and alternative hypotheses for determining whether or not children attending public elementary school in this city who are diagnosed with learning disabilities have a mean iq score of 100.
   e) Using the results of the 95 percent CI, can the null hypothesis be rejected? Why or why not?
   f) State the results of the hypothesis test in context.

11.2. Find the *p*-value associated with the one-sample *t*-test to determine whether the mean reading comprehension score (readcomp) of children attending public elementary school in this city who are diagnosed with learning disabilities is 75. Answer the related questions.

   a) Evaluate the tenability of the normality assumption or indicate why the assumption is not an issue for this analysis, that the results of the *t*-test would not be compromised by a failure to meet this assumption.
   b) What are the null and alternative hypotheses?
   c) What is the *p*-value associated with the one sample *t*-test for testing these null and alternative hypotheses?
   d) Use the *p*-value to determine whether or not the null hypothesis can be rejected in favor of the alternative.

e) State the results of the hypothesis test in context.

f) What is the 95 percent confidence interval for the mean reading comprehension score of children attending public elementary school in this city who are diagnosed with learning disabilities?

g) Using the results of the 95 percent CI, can the null hypothesis be rejected? Why or why not?

h) Would the test have been more or less powerful if the sample size had been larger than 76, say 300? Explain.

Exercises 11.3–11.4 involve one sample t-tests using variables from the Framingham data set. For inferential purposes, we consider the people in the Framingham data set to be a random sample of the population of all non-institutionalized adults. Use $\alpha = .05$ for all significance tests.

11.3. A person with body mass index higher than 25 is classified as overweight. In this exercise, we will determine whether the mean body mass index of the population of non-institutionalized adults as measured during the first examination (BMI1) is greater than 25.

a) Evaluate the tenability of the normality assumption or indicate why the assumption is not an issue for this analysis, that the results of the test would not be compromised by a failure to meet this assumption.

b) State the null and alternative hypotheses for determining whether the mean body mass index of the population of non-institutionalized adults as measured during the first examination is greater than 25.

c) Conduct the one-sample t-test and determine, based on the resulting p-value whether the mean body mass index of the population of non-institutionalized adults as measured during the first examination is greater than 25?

d) Calculate and interpret Cohen's d as a measure of effect size for the analysis.

e) Why is the confidence interval provided in the one-sample t-test output not appropriate for determining whether the mean body mass index of non-institutionalized adults at first examination is greater than 25?

11.4. Normal systolic blood pressure is less than 120 mmHg. In this exercise we will determine whether the mean systolic blood pressure of non-institutionalized adults at first examination (SYSBP1) is less than 120 mmHg.

a) State the null and alternative hypotheses for determining whether the mean systolic blood pressure of the population of non-institutionalized adults as measured during the first examination is less than 120 mmHg.

b) Explain why it is not necessary to carry out a test of these hypotheses in this case.

Exercises 11.5–11.11 involve one sample t-tests using variables from the NELS data set. For inferential purposes, we consider the students in the data set to be a random sample of the population of all college-bound students who have always been at grade level. Use $\alpha = .05$ for all significance tests.

11.5. Use the variable famsize, which gives the number of people in a household, to construct a 95% CI to determine whether the average family size is 4.5 (two parents and 2.5 kids) for college-bound high school students who are always at grade level. After opening the NELS, create a do- file that includes all the commands you used to carry out this set of analyses.

a) Evaluate the tenability of the normality assumption or indicate why the assumption is not an issue for this analysis, that the results of the t-test would not be compromised by a failure to meet this assumption.

b) What is the 95% confidence interval for the average family size?

c) Use the confidence interval to determine whether the average family size for this population is 4.5. If it is not 4.5, indicate whether it is higher or lower than 4.5.

d) Calculate and interpret the value of Cohen's d as a measure of the effect size.

e) Use the bootstrap approach to calculate the 95% CI. What is the result? Use your bootstrapped CI to determine whether the average family size for this population is 4.5. Are the results consistent with those found using the theoretically-derived parametric approach in part c)? Why do you suppose that is?

11.6. Use a 95 percent confidence interval to estimate the average twelfth grade self-concept score (slfcnc12) of the population of college-bound students who have always been at grade level. Use this interval to determine whether the average twelfth grade self-concept score is different from 32 for the population of college-bound students who have always been at grade level.

11.7 Use the p-value derived from an appropriate test of inference to determine whether the average twelfth grade self-concept score (slfcnc12) is different from 32 for the population of college-bound students who have always been at grade level. Create a do- file to provide a record of your analyses and report its contents. After using the one sample t-test, repeat the procedure using the bootstrap approach. Are the results of the two approaches consistent?

11.8. Use the p-value derived from an appropriate test of inference to determine whether the population of college-bound students who have always been at grade level on average take more than 3.6 units of mathematics in high school (unitmath).

11.9. For the population of college-bound students from the Northeast (region = 1) who have always been at grade level, use a 95 percent confidence interval to estimate the average number of years of English taken in high school (unitengl).

a) Restrict the sample to students from the Northeast.

b) Evaluate the tenability of the normality assumption or indicate why the assumption is not an issue for this analysis, that the results of the t-test would not be compromised by a failure to meet this assumption.

c) What is the 95 percent confidence interval for the average number of years of English taken in high school?

d) According to the 95 percent confidence interval, is the estimate for the average number of years of English taken in high school by this population of college-bound students from the Northeast three?

e) Calculate and interpret the value of Cohen's d as a measure of the effect size.

11.10. Does the population of college-bound twelfth graders who have always been at grade level and who attend rigorous academic schools (hsprog = 1) have a mean social studies achievement score (achsls12) larger than 55?

a) Evaluate the tenability of the normality assumption or indicate why the assumption is not an issue for this analysis, that the results of the test would not be compromised by a failure to meet this assumption.

b) State the null and alternative hypotheses.

c) Verify that the sample mean supports the hypothesized direction of the difference.

d) Find the *p*-value associated with the appropriate test of inference for determining whether the mean social studies achievement score for this population is greater than 55.

e) Is this result statistically significant?

f) State the conclusion in context.

g) Calculate and interpret the value of Cohen's *d* as a measure of the effect size.

h) Conceptually, not computationally, what is the difference between what the standard deviation value of 8.56 represents and what the standard error of the mean value of .70 represents?

i) If the standard deviation had been 20 instead of 8.56, and the mean and sample size remained the same, would the *p*-value have been smaller or larger? Explain.

11.11. For the population of college-bound students who were always at grade level and whose parents were divorced when they were in eighth grade (parmarl8 = 1), use a 95 percent confidence interval to estimate the mean twelfth grade self-concept score (slfcnc12).

a) Evaluate the tenability of the normality assumption or indicate why the assumption is not an issue for this analysis, that the results of the test would not be compromised by a failure to meet this assumption.

b) What is the 95 percent confidence interval for the mean twelfth grade self-concept score for college-bound students who were always at grade level and whose parents were divorced when they were in eighth grade?

Exercises 11.12–11.13 involve independent samples t-tests using variables from the Learndis data set. For inferential purposes, we consider the children in the data set to be a random sample of all children attending public elementary school in a certain city who have been diagnosed with learning disabilities. Unless otherwise specified, use α = .05 for all significance tests.

11.12. Conduct an independent samples *t*-test to determine whether there are gender (gender) differences in average math comprehension (mathcomp) among children attending public elementary school in a certain city who have been diagnosed with learning disabilities. Answer the following related questions.

a) Evaluate the tenability of the normality assumption or indicate why the assumption is not an issue for this analysis, that the results of the test would not be compromised by a failure to meet this assumption.

b) According to Levene's test of equality of variances, should the *t*-ratio be calculated using equal or unequal variances, in this case?

c) State the null and alternative hypotheses.

d) According to the *p*-value associated with this test, are there statistically significant gender differences in average math comprehension for this type of student? If so, describe the nature of the differences.

e) Calculate and interpret the value of Cohen's *d* as a measure of the effect size.

11.13. Conduct an independent samples *t*-test to determine whether there are differences in mean intellectual ability (iq) by the type of placement (placemen, self-contained classroom or resource room) among children attending public elementary school in a certain city who have been diagnosed with learning disabilities Answer the following related questions. Create a do- file that includes the complete set of complete set of commands used in carrying out this set of analyses beginning with the **use** command.

a) Evaluate the tenability of the normality assumption or indicate why the assumption is not an issue for this analysis, that the results of the test would not be compromised by a failure to meet this assumption.

b) According to Levene's test of equality of variances, should the t-ratio be calculated using equal or unequal variances, in this case?

c) According to the 95 percent confidence interval, are there statistically significant differences in mean intellectual ability by type of placement? If so, describe the nature of the differences.

d) Calculate and interpret the value of Cohen's d as a measure of the effect size.

e) Use the bootstrap approach to calculate the 95% CI. What is the result? Use your bootstrapped CI to determine whether there are statistically significant differences in mean intellectual ability by type of placement. Are the results consistent with those found based on the theoretically-derived t-distribution used in part c)? Why do you suppose that is?

f) Print out your do-file containing the commands you used to run this set of analyses.

Exercises 11.14–11.18 involve independent samples t-tests using variables from the Framingham data set. For inferential purposes, we consider the people in the Framingham data set to be a random sample of the population of all non-institutionalized adults. Use $\alpha = .05$ for all significance tests.

11.14. Use the independent samples t-test to investigate whether on average there are initial differences in age (AGE1) between the sexes (SEX) for the population of non-institutionalized adults represented in the Framingham data set?

a) Based on the boxplots, do the assumptions underlying the independent samples t-test appear tenable? What do you anticipate the result of the independent samples t-test to be? Explain.

b) Evaluate further the tenability of the normality assumption or indicate why the assumption is not an issue for this analysis, that the results of the test would not be compromised by a failure to meet this assumption.

c) According to Levene's test of equality of variances, should the t-ratio be calculated using equal or unequal variances, in this case?

d) According to the p-value, are there initial differences in age on average between the sexes of all non-institutionalized adults? If so, describe the nature of the differences.

e) Use the 95 percent CI to estimate the average difference in age between males and females at initial examination, which we know from the hypothesis is not statistically significant.

f) Under what circumstances can we expect the results of the independent samples t-test based on the p-value to be consistent with those based on the confidence interval, as they relate to this hypothesis test?

11.15. Is the mean body mass index (BMI3) of smokers (CURSMOKE3) lower than that for non-smokers as measured at the third and final examination time 3 (1968) among the population of non-institutionalized adults? Assume that both the normality and equality of variance assumptions are tenable.

a) What is the p-value derived from the independent samples t-test for determining whether, on average, the body mass index of smokers is lower than that for non-smokers among the population represented by the Framingham data and what does it convey?

b) If the question had been whether among the population of non-institutionalized adults the mean BMI of smokers is different (instead of lower) than it is for non-smokers, would the independent samples *t*-test have been more or less powerful?

11.16. While one can expect initial differences in body mass index (BMI1) between males and females, we may question whether there are differences between males and females in their changes in BMI from 1956 to 1968 (BMI3 – BMI1). In this exercise, we will investigate the change in body mass index for both males and females. You will need to compute a new variable that captures these change values.

a) Create a new variable BMIDIFF that captures the change in body mass index. Report and interpret BMIDIFF for the first person in the data set (ID = 1).

b) Create an associated boxplot, one for males and one females on the same axes. Describe the nature of this new variable for the two groups.

c) Evaluate the tenability of the normality assumption or indicate why the assumption is not an issue for this analysis, that the results of the test would not be compromised by a failure to meet this assumption.

d) According to Levene's test of equality of variances, should the *t*-ratio be calculated using equal or unequal variances, in this case?

e) According to the *p*-value derived from the appropriate test of inference, are there differences, on average, in the change in body mass index between males and females for this population of non-institutionalized adults? If so, describe the nature of the differences.

f) Calculate and interpret the value of Cohen's *d* as a measure of the effect size.

11.17. In this exercise, we use a non-linear transformation in conjunction with the independent samples *t*-test in order to determine, using the *Framingham* data set, whether there are differences in average systolic blood pressure (SYSBP3) between those who were and those who were not taking antihypertensive (blood pressure) medication at time 3 (BPMEDS3).

a) Evaluate the tenability of the normality assumption or indicate why the assumption is not an issue for this analysis, that the results of the test would not be compromised by a failure to meet this assumption.

b) Demonstrate that the log transformation is effective in normalizing the distribution of SYSBP3 for both groups.

c) Conduct an independent samples *t*-test on the log transformed systolic blood pressure at time 3 between those who did and did not take anti-hypertensive medication at time 3. Report and interpret the results.

d) Is it fair to conclude that taking anti-hypertensive medication appears to increase systolic blood pressure? Explain.

11.18. Use an independent samples *t*-test to determine whether, among the population of non-institutionalized adults, there are differences in total serum cholesterol (TOTCHOL3) by sex (SEX). Be sure to address the underlying assumptions. Interpret the results using either a *p*-value (with $\alpha = .05$) or a 95% confidence interval. If the result is statistically significant, report and interpret a measure of effect size.

Exercises 11.19–11.20 involve independent samples t-tests using variables from the NELS data set. For inferential purposes, we consider the students in the data set to be a random sample of the population of all college-bound students who have always been at grade level. Use $\alpha = .05$ for all significance tests.

11.19. Among the population of college-bound students who have always been at grade level, do students whose families owned a computer in eighth grade (computer) score differently in twelfth grade math achievement (achmat12), on average, than those whose families did not own a computer?

    a) Explain why an independent samples *t*-test is more appropriate than a one-sample or paired samples test to answer this question.

    b) Evaluate the tenability of the normality assumption or indicate why the assumption is not an issue for this analysis, that the results of the test would not be compromised by a failure to meet this assumption.

    c) According to Levene's test of equality of variances, is there reason to believe that a violation of the homogeneity of variances assumption would compromise the validity of the *t*-test results?

    d) State the null and alternative hypotheses regarding whether among this population, students whose families owned a computer in eighth grade score, on average differently in twelfth grade math achievement than those whose families did not own a computer.

    e) Find the *p*-value for determining whether among the population of college-bound students who have always been at grade level, students whose families owned a computer in eighth grade score differently in twelfth grade math achievement, on average, than those whose families did not own a computer.

    f) Interpret the results of the hypothesis test using the context of the problem.

    g) Find the 95 percent confidence interval for the mean difference in twelfth grade math achievement between those whose families owned a computer in eighth grade and those whose families did not.

    h) According to the 95 percent confidence interval, among the population of college-bound students who have always been at grade level, do students whose families owned a computer in eighth grade score differently in twelfth grade math achievement, on average, than those whose families did not own a computer?

    i) Calculate and interpret the value of Cohen's *d* as a measure of the effect size.

    j) Which is longer, the 99 percent CI of the difference or the 95 percent CI of the difference? Use Stata to confirm your answer.

11.20. Use an independent samples *t*-test to answer the following questions or indicate why it is not appropriate to do so. In each case, the population is comprised of college-bound students who have always been at grade level and the data are from the *NELS* data set. Be sure to address the underlying assumptions. Interpret the results using either a hypothesis test with $\alpha = .05$ or a 95 percent confidence interval. If the result is statistically significant, report and interpret a measure of effect size.

    a) Among college-bound students who are always at grade level, is the average twelfth grade self-concept score (slfcnc12) different for smokers and non-smokers (cigarett)?

b) Among college bound students who are always at grade level, do students who take advanced math in eighth grade (advmath8) have different expectations for future income (expinc30) than students who do not?

c) Among college bound students who are always at grade level, do students who take advanced math in eighth grade (advmath8) have better eighth grade self-concepts (slfcnc08) than students who do not?

d) Among college bound students who are always at grade level, do females (gender) have a better self-concept (slfcnc12) than males in twelfth grade?

e) Among college bound students who are always at grade level, do females (gender) do better on twelfth grade reading achievement tests (achrdg12) than males?

f) Among college bound students who are always at grade level, do those who attended nursery school (nursery) tend to have smaller families (famsiz) than those who did not?

g) Among college bound students who are always at grade level, do those who live in the Northeast (region = 1) have mean ses that is higher than that of those who live in the West (region = 4)?

Exercise 11.21 relates to the Blood data set. The creation of a new variable is necessary to perform the independent samples t-test in this example.

11.21. Ten randomly selected African American males are given calcium supplements for 12 weeks, while eleven randomly selected African American males are given a placebo for 12 weeks. At both the beginning and the end of this time period, systolic blood pressure readings of all men were recorded. Create a new variable, reduct; that is, systolc1–systolc2. This variable represents the reduction in blood pressure over the 12 weeks. Conduct an independent samples *t*-test to determine whether there is a difference in the average blood pressure reduction between the calcium and the placebo groups. Use $\alpha = .05$.

Exercise 11.22 involves paired samples t-tests using variables from the Learndis data set. For inferential purposes, we consider the children in the data set to be a random sample of all children attending public elementary school in a certain city who have been diagnosed with learning disabilities. Use $\alpha = .05$ for all significance tests.

11.22. Answer the following questions about using a paired samples *t*-test to determine whether public school elementary school children in a certain city diagnosed with learning disabilities perform better in math comprehension (mathcomp) or in reading comprehension (readcomp).

a) Evaluate the tenability of the normality assumption or indicate why the assumption is not an issue for this analysis, that the results of the test would not be compromised by a failure to meet this assumption.

b) Explain why failure to meet the homogeneity of variances assumption for the paired samples *t*-test would not compromise the results of this test.

c) State the null and alternative hypotheses when determining whether public elementary school children in the city diagnosed with learning disabilities perform better in math comprehension or in reading comprehension.

d) Use the results of the paired samples hypothesis test to determine whether public elementary school children in the city diagnosed with learning disabilities perform better in math comprehension or in reading comprehension.

e) Use the results of the 95 percent confidence interval to determine whether public elementary school children in the city diagnosed with learning disabilities perform better in math comprehension or in reading comprehension.

f) Report and interpret Cohen's *d* as a measure of effect size as a way to measure the practical significance of the test result.

Exercises 11.23–11.24 involve paired samples t-tests using variables from the Framingham data set. For inferential purposes, we consider the people in the Framingham data set to be a random sample of the population of all non-institutionalized adults. Use α = .05 for all significance tests.

11.23. Answer the following questions about using a paired samples *t*-test to determine whether systolic blood pressure (SYSBP1, SYSBP3) increases over time, on average, in non-institutionalized adults. Assume that the normality and equality of variance assumptions are tenable. Create a Syntax file that includes all the commands used in carrying out this set of analyses.

a) What is the *p*-value associated with the paired *t*-test for determining whether among the population of non-institutionalized adults, systolic blood pressure, on average, increases over time?

b) According to the *p*-value, does systolic blood pressure increase, on average, over time among non-institutionalized adults?

c) Report and interpret Cohen's *d* as a measure of effect size, a measure of the magnitude of practical significance.

d) Conduct the analysis again using a bootstrap approach. What is the associated *p*-value? When using the bootstrap p-value to test the hypotheses, are the results consistent with those in part b)? Why do you suppose that is?

11.24. In this exercise, we investigate whether diastolic blood pressure decreases over time (DIABP1, DIABP3). What is the best way to demonstrate that among non-institutionalized adults, the diastolic blood pressure does not does decrease significantly, on average, from time 1 (1956) to time 3 (1968)?

11.25. In this exercise, we investigate whether non-institutionalized adults smoke fewer cigarettes over time (CIGPDAY1, CIGPDAY3).

a) What is the best way to demonstrate that among non-institutionalized adults, the number of cigarettes smoked per day, on average, does decrease significantly from time 1 (1956) to time 3 (1968)?

b) What explanations can be offered to support the average decline in cigarette smoking over this time period, for the sample of non-institutionalized adults in the Framingham data set?

Exercises 11.26–11.27 involve paired samples t-tests using variables from the NELS data set. For inferential purposes, we consider the students in the data set to be a random sample of the population of all college-bound students who have always been at grade level. Use α = .05 for all significance tests.

11.26. Among the population of college-bound students who have always been at grade level, does the level of science achievement, on average, change from eighth (achsci08) to twelfth grade (achsci12) relative to all students in the grade?

a) Explain why a paired samples *t*-test is more appropriate than a one-sample or independent samples test to determine whether the level of science achievement, relative to all students in the grade, changes from eighth to twelfth grade.

b) Evaluate the tenability of the normality assumption or indicate why the assumption is not an issue for this analysis, that the results of the test would not be compromised by a failure to meet this assumption.

c) State the null and alternative hypotheses.

d) Find the *p*-value associated with the paired samples *t*-test to determine whether the level of science achievement changes, on average, from eighth to twelfth grade achievement among the population of college-bound students who have always been at grade level.

e) According to this *p*-value, does the level of science achievement change from eighth to twelfth grade among this population of college-bound students?

f) Find the 95 percent confidence interval for the mean difference in science achievement between eighth and twelfth grade.

g) According to the 95 percent confidence interval, does the level of science achievement change from eighth to twelfth grade for this population?

11.27. Use a paired samples *t*-test to determine whether among the population of college-bound students who have always been at grade level, the level of self concept, relative to all students in the grade, increases from eighth (slfcnc08) to twelfth grade (slfcnc12). Be sure to address the underlying assumptions. Interpret the results using either a hypothesis test with $\alpha = .05$ or a 95 percent confidence interval. If the result is statistically significant, report and interpret a measure of effect size.

Exercises 11.28–11.32 involve selection of appropriate tests.

11.28. A study was undertaken to determine different sources of stress among college students. A sample of 1,000 college students was asked to rate their level of agreement to experiencing stress from different potential sources, such as parents, roommates, partners, and final exams on a 5 point Likert scale. They were also asked to provide demographic information including number of enrolled credits and gender. For each of the following questions relative to this data set, select an appropriate statistical procedure from the list below for answering this question. Assume for now that the underlying assumptions for these tests have been met.

Procedures:
(1) One-tailed, one sample *t*-test
(2) Two-tailed, one sample *t*-test
(3) One-tailed, independent samples *t*-test
(4) Two-tailed, independent samples *t*-test
(5) One-tailed, paired samples *t*-test
(6) Two-tailed, paired samples *t*-test

Questions:
a) Are undergraduates at large urban universities more stressed by their parents or their roommates?

b) Are undergraduates at large urban universities more stressed by their parents than their roommates?

c) Do undergraduates at large urban universities in the Northeast typically take 15 credits per semester?

d) Are there gender differences in the stress level due to final exams among undergraduates at large urban universities?

e) Among undergraduates at large urban universities, are males more stressed than females by their partners?

11.29. For each of the following questions based on the *NELS* data set, select an appropriate statistical procedure to use to answer it from the list below. Then, use Stata to conduct the appropriate hypothesis test in cases where the underlying assumptions are tenable. If the result of a hypothesis test is statistically significant, report and interpret an appropriate measure of effect size.

Procedures:
(1) One-tailed, one sample *t*-test
(2) Two-tailed, one sample *t*-test
(3) One-tailed, independent samples *t*-test
(4) Two-tailed, independent samples *t*-test
(5) One-tailed, paired samples *t*-test
(6) Two-tailed, paired samples *t*-test

Questions:
a) Among college-bound students who are always at grade level, do those who attended nursery school (nursery) tend to have higher ses than those who did not?

b) Among college-bound students who are always at grade level, does self-concept differ in eighth (slfcnc08) and tenth (slfcnc10) grades?

c) Among college-bound students who are always at grade level, do those who attend public school (schtyp8) perform differently in twelfth grade math achievement (achmat12) from those who attend private school? (Note that to answer this question, the variable schtyp8 will have to be *recoded* to be dichotomous as described in Chapter 4).

d) Among college-bound students who are always at grade level, do families typically have four members (famsize)?

e) Among college-bound students who are always at grade level, do students tend to take more years of English (unitengl) than Math (unitmath)?

11.30. In this exercise we demonstrate, by example using the *NELS* data set, that the paired samples *t*-test is equivalent to a one sample *t*-test of the difference scores. For college-bound students who are always at grade level, does relative math achievement change from eighth (achmat08) to twelfth grades (achmat12)? Follow the steps below to use both a paired samples and a one-sample *t*-test to answer the question.

a) Use a graphical display of your choice to anticipate the answer to the question posed.

b) Answer the question by using a paired samples *t*-test. Use $\alpha = .05$.

   c) Use Stata to verify that the paired samples t-test results are the same as those from a one-sample t-test on the difference scores. First use Stata to create a new variable that represents the difference between eighth and twelfth grade math achievement. You can do this with the command **capture gen math_diff = achmat12 − achmat08** Then use a one-sample t-test on this new variable to answer the question. Use $\alpha = .05$.

   d) How do your answers to parts (b) and (c) compare?

   e) Would the results have been the same as the paired t-test had we ignored the pairing of scores and conducted an independent samples t-test on the eighth and twelfth grade math achievement scores? Explain.

11.31. Explain why a one-sample t-test should not be used with the *NELS* data set to determine whether the average number of times late for school in twelfth grade (late12) is 4 times (late12 = 4).

11.32. In this exercise, based on the *NELS* data set, we contrast a descriptive and inferential approach for determining the relationship, if any, between high school cigarette use and twelfth grade math achievement

   a) For the students in the *NELS* data set, is there a difference in twelfth grade math achievement (achmat12) between those who do and do not smoke cigarettes (cigarett)?

   b) For college-bound students who are always at grade level, is there a difference in twelfth grade math achievement (achmat12) between those who do and do not smoke cigarettes (cigarett)? Use $\alpha = .05$.

Exercises 11.33–11.43 include calculations by hand and small data sets.

11.33. Given $t = 2.364$ and $df = 100$ for a one-sample t-test, calculate p or indicate that the result is not statistically significant, under the following conditions:

   a) $H_0: \mu = 30$ vs. $H_1: \mu \neq 30$

   b) $H_0: \mu = 30$ and $H_1: \mu < 30$

   c) $H_0: \mu = 30$ and $H_1: \mu > 30$

11.34. Given $t = 1.283$ and $df = 500$ for an independent samples t-test, calculate p or indicate that the result is not statistically significant, under the following conditions:

   a) $H_0: \mu = 30$ and $H_1: \mu \neq 30$

   b) $H_0: \mu = 30$ and $H_1: \mu < 30$

   c) $H_0: \mu = 30$ and $H_1: \mu > 30$

11.35. Given $t = -1.23$ and $df = 100$ for a paired samples t-test, calculate p or indicate that the result is not statistically significant, under the following conditions:

   a) $H_0: \mu = 30$ and $H_1: \mu \neq 30$

   b) $H_0: \mu = 30$ and $H_1: \mu < 30$

   c) $H_0: \mu = 30$ and $H_1: \mu > 30$

11.36. Given $t = 1.8$ and $df = 800$ for a one-sample t-test, calculate p or indicate that the result is not statistically significant, under the following conditions:

   a) $H_0: \mu = 30$ and $H_1: \mu \neq 30$

   b) $H_0: \mu = 30$ and $H_1: \mu < 30$

   c) $H_0: \mu = 30$ and $H_1: \mu > 30$

11.37. A one-sample *t*-test, based on the *Learndis* data set, was conducted to determine whether the mean intellectual ability score for all children attending public elementary school in the city who have been diagnosed with learning disabilities is 85. Partial results, with test value equal 85, are reproduced below. Use the available information and Stata or Table 2 to find the mean difference, *t*, *df*, and *p*. Then, indicate whether the mean intellectual ability score for all children attending public elementary school in the city who have been diagnosed with learning disabilities differs from 85.

Variable	Obs	Mean	Std. Dev.	Min	Max
iq	105	81.49524	10.94051	51	105

One-Sample Test

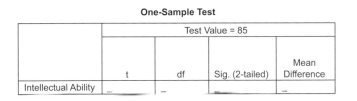

	Test Value = 85			
	t	df	Sig. (2-tailed)	Mean Difference
Intellectual Ability	_	_		_

11.38. A one-sample *t*-test, based on the *Learndis* data set, was conducted to determine whether the mean intellectual ability score for all children attending public elementary school in the city who are diagnosed with learning disabilities is 85. Partial results, with test value equal 0, are reproduced below. Use the available information and Stata or Table 2 to find the 95 percent confidence interval for the mean IQ. Then, indicate whether the mean intellectual ability score for all children attending public elementary school in the city who are diagnosed with learning disabilities differs from 85.

Variable	Obs	Mean	Std. Dev.	Min	Max
iq	105	81.49524	10.94051	51	105

One-Sample Test

	Test Value = 0	
	95% Confidence Interval of the Difference	
	Lower	Upper
Intellectual Ability	_	_

11.39. An independent samples *t*-test, based on the *Learndis* data set, was conducted to determine whether there are gender differences in average math comprehension among children attending public elementary school in a certain city who have been diagnosed with learning disabilities. Partial results are reproduced below. Use the available information and Stata or Table 2 to obtain the mean difference, *t*, *df*, and *p*, and the 95 percent confidence interval. Then, indicate whether there are gender differences in average math comprehension among children attending public elementary school in a certain city who have been diagnosed with learning disabilities.

–> gender = Male

Variable	Obs	Mean	Std. Dev.	Min	Max
mathcomp	60	84.05	12.95811	61	121

–> gender = Female

Variable	Obs	Mean	Std. Dev.	Min	Max
mathcomp	34	90.20588	14.42174	66	118

Independent Samples Test

		t-test for Equality of Means					95% Confidence Interval of the Difference	
		t	df	Sig. (2-tailed)	Mean Difference	Std. Error Difference	Lower	Upper
Math Comprehension	Equal variances assumed	–	–	–	–	2.898	–	–

11.40. A paired samples t-test, based on the *Learndis* data set, was conducted to determine whether public school elementary school children in a certain city diagnosed with learning disabilities score differently, on average, in math and reading comprehension. Partial results are reproduced below. Use the available information and Stata or Table 2 to obtain the mean difference, t, df, p and the 95 percent confidence interval to answer the question posed.

Variable	Obs	Mean	Std. Err.	Std. Dev.	[95% Conf.	Interval]
readcomp	74	77.78378	1.527275	13.13812	74.73993	80.82764
mathcomp	74	86.40541	1.696297	14.5921	83.02469	89.78612

Paired Samples Test

		Paired Differences							
		Mean	Std. Error Mean	95% Confidence Interval of the Difference		t	df	Sig. (2-tailed)
				Lower	Upper			
Pair 1	Math Comprehension - Reading Comprehension	–	1.627	–	–	–	–	–

11.41. From a normally distributed population, the following sample is randomly selected:

25 27 22 20 27 26 24 25 20 30 27 25 29 26 22 25

    a) Use this sample to construct a 95 percent confidence interval for μ. Use your confidence interval to estimate μ and to see whether 27 is one of the plausible values for μ.

    b) Find and interpret the p-value associated with a one-sample t-test on $H_0: \mu = 27$ versus $H_1: \mu \neq 27$ at the significance level $\alpha = .05$.

11.42. In order to test whether a new drug for individuals who suffer from high blood pressure affects mental alertness, a random sample of 12 patients suffering from high blood pressure is selected from a large number of such patients who regularly visit an outpatient clinic. Tests of mental alertness are administered to these patients both before and after they receive the drug. Their scores are shown in the following table. Is there evidence of a decrease in mental alertness, on average, after receipt of the drug for the population of all such patients at this outpatient clinic? Assume that the mental alertness scores are normally distributed, both before and after treatment, in the population of all such patients at this outpatient clinic and that the variances are equal in the populations. Use $\alpha = .05$.

Before	10	14	5	6	9	15	1	20	10	2	7	10
After	5	9	7	3	10	15	4	16	12	5	3	6

11.43. Eight one-year olds and eight two-year olds took the same test. Scores were compared (on the average, not on an individual paired basis) to determine whether there is an age difference on the skill measured for the populations from which these two samples were randomly selected, at a significance level of $\alpha = .05$. Assume that the test scores are normally distributed for both age groups in the population and that the variances are equal in the populations. Complete the analysis using the following data and draw your conclusion:

One-year olds	7	7	0	1	9	3	8	5
Two-year olds	13	13	9	9	13	5	5	5

Exercises 11.44–11.49 are conceptual and do not require the use of Stata.

11.44. Explain why it is impossible for p to be identically equal to zero for any hypothesis test using the t-distribution.

11.45. As the sample size increases, what happens to the magnitude of tc in a one-sample t-test?

11.46. As the sample size increases, what happens to the standard error of the mean in a one-sample t-test?

11.47. A researcher conducted a one-tailed, one-sample t-test for which the results were not statistically significant. Should she then conduct a two-tailed test? Explain.

11.48. A researcher conducted a two-tailed independent samples t-test, the results of which were statistically significant. Should she then conduct two one-tailed tests to determine the nature of the mean difference? Explain.

CHAPTER TWELVE

Research Design: Introduction and Overview

By this time, no doubt, you will have begun to appreciate the important role that analytic methods play in the research process by their ability to enable us to uncover the story contained in our data. The overall research process, however, begins not with the analysis of data but, rather, with the posing of questions that interest us. It is the questions we ask that motivate us to conduct research, and it is the nature of these questions, from most simple to most challenging, that gives rise to how we design a research study, how we define and measure relevant variables, and how we collect and analyze our data to answer these questions. In this chapter we will explore many of the different types of questions that we may pose, the related types of research designs that they engender, and the conclusions that they do and do not foster.

QUESTIONS AND THEIR LINK TO DESCRIPTIVE, RELATIONAL, AND CAUSAL RESEARCH STUDIES

We begin by considering a question that is so simple in its nature that, by itself, it hardly constitutes what we think of when we envision a research study: "To what extent do two individuals possess a certain trait?" A more concrete version of this type of question is, "How much do college freshmen John and Mary weigh?"

THE NEED FOR A GOOD MEASURE OF OUR CONSTRUCT, WEIGHT

In thinking through the elements needed to answer this question, we realize that in addition to our two freshmen, Mary and John, we would need a good measure of their respective weights, one that we can rely on to produce accurate weight values.

In the language of tests and measurement (psychometrics), we would want our measures of weight to have both *validity* and *reliability*.[1] The validity of a measure is the extent to which the measure assesses what it purports to measure (Cohen, Swerdlik, & Sturman, 2012). The reliability of a measure is the extent to which the measure is free from chance factors (random error) that occur at the time of measurement (e.g., John doesn't stand in the middle of the scale; the needle on the scale wavers from John's unsteady stance, etc.) that would cause John's recorded weight value to vary from one measurement occasion to the next, if in fact, John were weighed more than once on this scale at the same time on each occasion (e.g., at early morning rising). Because reliable measures are free of error, they are expected to yield consistent results from one measurement occasion to the next.

---

[1] Covering issues in measurement in greater detail is beyond the scope of this book. The interested reader is referred to Cohen, Swerdlik, and Sturman (2012) for further study.

From a more mathematical perspective, in terms of what is known as Classical Test Theory, an observed value, X, contains both a true weight value component and an error component, expressed by Equation (12.1) as:

$$X = T + E \tag{12.1}$$

Using Equation (12.1), we may express the reliability of John's observed weight, X, in terms of Equation (12.2); namely, as the variance of John's observed weight ($\text{Var}(X)$) minus the variance of the error component ($\text{Var}(E)$) contained in his observed weight divided by the variance of his observed weight, $\text{Var}(X)$. This expression may, in turn, be expressed as the ratio of the true variance of X ($\text{Var}(T)$) to the observed variance of X ($\text{Var}(X)$) as shown in Equation (12.2).

$$\text{Reliability}(X) = [\text{Var}(X) - \text{Var}(E)]/\text{Var}(X) = \text{Var}(T)/\text{Var}(X) \tag{12.2}$$

As a ratio or proportion, the reliability of a measure will range from 0 to 1. At the extremes, if the measure is error free so that $\text{Var}(E) = 0$, its reliability will equal 1; if the measure is nothing but error so that $\text{Var}(X) = \text{Var}(E)$, its reliability will equal 0.

Measures may have no validity, yet be highly reliable as in a situation in which hair length is used to measure a person's weight from one day to the next. One would be hard-pressed to consider hair length as a measure of weight, yet from one day to the next, one's hair length would remain reasonably consistent or stable (i.e., it would be a reliable, but not a valid measure of weight). In assessing the reliability of a measure of say, one's mood, one must not confuse the reliability of a measure of mood with the natural day to day variation that occurs in one's mood. The attempt to assess the reliability of a measure of a trait as distinguished from that trait's natural time to time variation makes the assessment of reliability, in general, a challenging task and has given rise to the multiple ways in which reliability is assessed. For traits that do not naturally change from time to time, test-retest reliability may be used, but for traits that do change naturally from time to time (like mood), assessing the reliability of a measure at a single point in time is more appropriate. One of the most popular approaches to assessing the reliability of a measure at a single point in time is Cronbach's alpha internal consistency reliability coefficient (Cohen, Swerdlik, & Sturman, 2012).

THE DESCRIPTIVE STUDY

Assuming that our measure of weight has both validity and reliability, we may use our two observed weight values to describe or characterize John and Mary's weight, respectively. As such, this type of question leads to what may be called a *descriptive study*. It is descriptive because our aim simply is to describe the *status quo*, or the ways things are rather than to explain *why* things are the way they are. In a more realistic example of a descriptive study, we may be interested in the question, "How much do male and female college freshmen weigh?" In this case, we are seeking to describe the respective weights of two populations of college freshmen, one male and one female. These two populations may be described as our *target populations* because these are the groups in which we are interested; those about which we would like to draw conclusions (Shadish, Cook, & Campbell, 2002).

In addition to defining or operationalizing our construct of interest (e.g., weight) and identifying or developing a way to measure that construct well, we also would need to determine the sampling methods[2] by which to select our males and females from their respective populations (assuming it is not possible to obtain information about everyone from both populations), and to determine the statistical methods that would enable us to make an appropriate inference from our respective samples to our respective target populations. Based on our discussion of sampling in Chapter 9, we could obtain a random sample of the male population and another of the female population using, for example, simple random sampling. We could then use the material in Chapter 11 related to estimating a single population mean, μ, to construct two confidence intervals, one based on the unbiased sample mean estimator, $\overset{G}{X}$, of μ for males and the other for females, to estimate their corresponding population means. The respective confidence intervals could then be constructed to contain with high probability the true population mean weight for each of the male and female populations.

FROM DESCRIPTIVE TO RELATIONAL STUDIES

If the aim of the previous question were extended from wanting simply to describe the status quo of male and female college freshmen weight, to wanting to explain why things are the way they are; and, in particular, perhaps, to determine if there is an association between a college freshman's weight and his/her sex, or even between a college freshman's weight and his/her sex and height, we are in the realm of what may be called a *relational study*. To determine whether there is a relationship between sex and weight considering the population of male and female college freshmen, one could use the independent groups t-test discussed in Chapter 11 to test whether such a relationship exists. If the null hypothesis of no difference is not rejected, we would have reason to believe that there is no association between college freshmen weight and sex in the population of college freshmen, and if rejected, we would have reason to believe otherwise. More generally, in relational studies, the use of correlation and regression techniques in the inferential setting are useful in making inferences from sample results to the target populations of interest. Although you already are familiar with correlation and regression techniques in the descriptive setting, these methods will be covered again later in this text in Chapters 15 and 16 within the inferential setting. In Chapter 15, you will see that, in fact, the independent group t-test is equivalent to having computed and tested the correlation in the population between the continuous variable weight and the dichotomous variable, sex.

FROM RELATIONAL TO CAUSAL STUDIES

Recalling one of the tenets of correlation analysis, covered in Chapter 5, that correlation does not imply causation, one cannot simply use a correlation to answer whether a change in one variable actually causes a change in another variable, called an outcome variable. There are many examples of variables that are correlated but where changing one does not cause the other to change in a predictable way. When we want to determine whether variables are causally related, we conduct a *causal study*. Within the context of our ongoing example about weight, one would need a causal study to address the question, "What is the

---

[2] The method of simple random sampling was discussed in Chapter 9. A more complete discussion of different sampling methods is beyond the scope of this book. The interested reader is referred to Groves, Fowler, Couper, Lepkowski, Singer, and Tourangeau (2009).

causal effect of a particular college freshman diet provided by a university on weight gain/ loss from September to June?"

If the goal of a study is to make claims that are causal in nature, certain restrictive conditions must hold. In particular, for a study to claim that X causes Y, not only must X be correlated with Y, but X must also precede Y in time, and there must be no alternative plausible explanation for the observed X-Y relationship; that is, the X-Y relationship must not be attributable to any other variable not included in the study. (Shadish, Campbell, & Cook, 2002).

Often a causal claim is made between X and Y, bolstered by the facts that X and Y are correlated and X precedes Y in time, yet alternative plausible explanations exist to offset the validity of the claim. One such example is a study, *Justice at Work and Reduced Risk of Coronary Heart Disease Among Employees,* (Kivimaki, Ferrie, Brunner, Head, Shipley, Vahtera, & Marmot), published in the *Archives of Internal Medicine* (October 24, 2005) and reported in the *New York Times* column "Vital Signs" (Nagourney, November 1, 2005), under the heading, *Injustices at Work May Harm Men's Hearts.* For the study, approximately 6,500 men between the ages of 35 to 55 completed questionnaires about justice at work, job strain, and effort-reward imbalance during the time period from 1985 to 1990. From 1990 through 1999, the men were tracked for incidence of coronary heart disease (CHD). Given that the authors found that those who perceived a high level of justice at work showed evidence of CHD at 70 percent of the rate of those who did not, can they conclude with authority that "justice at work may protect against CHD," or said differently, that being treated unfairly at work may cause heart problems? Are there variables, other than a perception of being unfairly treated at work, that may be the true cause of the reduction in heart problems? The authors report that men who perceived higher levels of justice were more likely to be older and that "[a]fter adjustment for age, men who perceived higher levels of justice were more likely to be married and have a higher education level, higher employment grade, and lower BMI [Body Mass Index] compared to those with perceived lower levels of justice" (p. 2247).

Because these factors are clearly potential alternative explanations for the causal claim that a perception of injustice increases the evidence of CHD, the authors controlled for these factors, and still found the relationship to exist. It remains doubtful, however, that the list of variables included in their analysis exhausts all possible variables that may explain the causal relationship noted. In acknowledgement of this situation, Nagourney, the author of the Vital Signs column, extends a note of caution in accepting the causal claim as true by noting that "the results were based on observational data rather than a controlled experiment."

Observational studies are those in which individuals merely are observed and data are collected on an outcome (or outcomes) of interest. In this study, individuals were given a questionnaire to obtain data on their perceptions of job strain and effort-reward imbalance. Other data were then collected over time on indicators of these men's coronary heart problems. There was no attempt made by the investigators to affect the outcome (coronary heart problems) through the administration of a treatment, and, the formation at the outset of the study, of a treatment and control group. Instead, the individuals in this study formed themselves into different comparison groups by their scores on the questionnaire, so that the researcher was working with intact groups. In the context of a two-group design, one may say that, in this case, the "treatment" group was comprised of those who were observed to perceive a high level of justice at work, and the "comparison" or "control" group were those who were observed to perceive a low or moderate level of justice at work. The problem with studies that are based on intact groups is that they may differ on other important variables in addition to the grouping variable. In this example, the group that perceived higher levels of justice was also more likely to be older, married, and more educated.

In other situations, the investigator decides at the outset who is to be in the treatment group and who is to be in the no-treatment, or control group. When the investigator assigns individuals to the groups randomly, we have what is called a *controlled randomized study* or *true experiment*. This is the type of study that Nagourney, the Vital Signs column author of the job strain study, makes reference to in his word of caution. When, by contrast, the investigator assigns individuals to treatment and control groups using other than random assignment, we have what is called a *nonrandomized controlled study*, which is a type of observational study, also called a *quasi-experimental study*.

THE GOLD STANDARD OF CAUSAL STUDIES: THE TRUE EXPERIMENT AND RANDOM ASSIGNMENT

In short, in order for causal claims to be valid, a true experiment, rather than a nonrandomized controlled study should be used. The defining feature of a true experiment is that units (e.g., individuals) are *randomly assigned* to treatment and control groups. Those in the treatment group receive the intervention or treatment, those in the control group do not.

In the study described earlier that a perception of unjust behavior in the workplace causes an increase in the evidence of CHD, the authors acknowledged that men who perceived higher levels of justice were more likely to be older and that "[a]fter adjustment for age, men who perceived higher levels of justice were more likely to be married and have a higher education level, higher employment grade, and lower BMI compared to those with perceived lower levels of justice" (p. 2247). The two groups being compared differed in ways that could explain the observed difference in the outcome measure and confound the interpretation of results. Accordingly, such variables are called *confounders*. The presence of confounders goes counter to having groups that are *balanced* at the outset of a study.

Although the authors controlled for these confounders, in this study the possibility exists that there still could be other variables on which the two groups differ, and these variables could be the ones that are the real reasons for the observed increase in coronary heart problems by those who perceived the workplace to be unfair. Random assignment to treatment and control groups, however, guarantees that with samples of large enough size, the two groups will be balanced (not different) on all variables. As such, neither the experimental nor the control group will be more endowed on a variable or set of variables that might positively affect the outcome, leaving the treatment itself as the only possible cause of the obtained outcome result.

To repeat, groups that are balanced on all variables that might potentially affect the outcome rules out the possibility that some other variable (or variables) lurking in the background (even variables unobserved or unmeasured) is the real reason for having observed the difference on the outcome variable between the two groups. If there is a difference on the outcome variable between the two groups, it must, therefore, be because one group was given the treatment and the other group was not; through randomization, with large enough sized groups, the groups are otherwise equivalent at the outset.

It should be noted that with small sample sizes, the two groups could be statistically significantly different at the outset on some variables. Accordingly, although not a perfect even foolproof way of achieving balanced groups in the case of small samples, random assignment "is nonetheless the only way of doing so, and the essential way" (Cook & Campbell, 1979: p. 15). In this sense, then, a true experiment, defined by random assignment of treatment and control groups, provides the gold standard for reaching causal conclusions.

Of course, random assignment may not always be possible for ethical or practical reasons (Shadish, Campbell, & Cook, 2002). For example, if one were interested in testing the impact of smoking on the incidence of lung cancer, for ethical reasons, one could not randomly assign individuals to a smoking condition as opposed to a nonsmoking condition. Or, if one were studying different approaches to teaching statistics in a college setting, under ordinary circumstances, for practical reasons, the researcher would not be able to randomly assign students to a treatment or control class because college students tend to choose the particular classes they take during a semester based on their own schedules and class availability. Or, in the unjust behavior in the workplace example, intact groups were used as defined by responses to a questionnaire. One could imagine how difficult, for both ethical and practical reasons, it would have been to assign individuals randomly to either "unjust" or "just" supervisors at work. In the next section, we illustrate the extent to which the absence of random assignment to treatment and control groups, for whatever the reason, can result in the wrong causal conclusion regarding the magnitude and even the sign (direction) of the treatment effect.

COMPARING TWO KIDNEY STONE TREATMENTS USING A NON-RANDOMIZED CONTROLLED STUDY

In this study, the success rates of two Treatments, A and B, for kidney stones are compared.[3] Patients with kidney stones were not randomly assigned to one of the two treatments. The table below gives the overall success rates and numbers of cases treated for both Treatments, A and B. A comparison of these overall success rates would appear to show quite clearly that overall Treatment B is more effective than Treatment A, since for Treatment B the success rate is 83 percent, while for Treatment A it is only 78 percent.

success rates (successes/total)	
Treatment A	**Treatment B**
78% (273/350)	83% (289/350)

However, because individuals were not assigned randomly to Treatments A and B, it may be that those assigned to Treatment A differ from those assigned to Treatment B on

---

[3] C. R. Charig, D. R. Webb, S. R. Payne, & O. E. Wickham (March 1986). Comparison of treatment of renal calculi by operative surgery, percutaneous nephrolithotomy, and extracorporeal shock wave lithotripsy. *Br Med J (Clin Res Ed)* 292 (6524): 879–882; Steven A. Julious and Mark A. Mullee (December 1994). Confounding and Simpson's paradox. *BMJ* 309 (6967): 1480–1481.

variables that could affect the outcome of the study (the success rate of the treatment). One such variable, for example, that is likely to affect the success rate of a treatment, and on which the two groups may differ, is kidney stone size (an indicator of the severity of one's kidney stone problem). As a result, kidney stone size may be a confounding variable lurking in the background of this study, and may be the real reason why Treatment A appears overall to be superior to Treatment B in the analysis above.

As the next table indicates, when kidney stone size is included in the analysis as a control, the same set of treatments suggests a wholly different result. Treatment A now appears to be more effective than Treatment B under both severity scenarios:

Success rates accounting for kidney stone size			
small stones		large stones	
Treatment A	Treatment B	Treatment A	Treatment B
Group 1	Group 2	Group 3	Group 4
93% (81/87)	87% (234/270)	73% (192/263)	69% (55/80)

The inequality between the two successes/total ratios is now reversed from what it was before. This reversal (or sign change) in the inequality between the two ratios, which creates what is called *Simpson's Paradox*, happens because two effects occur together, or are *confounded*. In particular, the sizes of the groups which are combined when the lurking variable (kidney stone size) is ignored are very different. Doctors tend to give the severe cases the better treatment (Group 3 in the table), and the milder cases the inferior treatment (Group 2). Therefore, the overall totals are dominated by these two groups, and not by the much smaller Groups 1 and 4. The lurking variable has a large effect on the ratios, that is, the success rate is more strongly influenced by the severity of the case than by the choice of treatment. Therefore, Group 3 does worse than Group 2.

This example illustrates a problem that could rise in the computation of a weighted mean (recall that Chapter 3 includes a discussion of the weighted mean) and points to the importance of taking into account variables in an analysis that may confound results, and thereby produce estimates of a treatment effect that are simply wrong (or *biased*) to a great extent. Without including and controlling for the confounder, kidney stone size, Treatment A is deemed to be better than Treatment B, yet with it, the bias is so substantial that the reverse conclusion is reached. In addition to controlling for potentially confounding variables, like kidney stone size, at the analysis stage, one may also control for them in the design itself, as the next section describes.

INCLUDING BLOCKING IN A RESEARCH DESIGN

Without including kidney stone size in the analysis, the bias that emerged in estimating the treatment effect was due to the fact that doctors tended to give the severe cases the better treatment and the milder cases the inferior treatment. That is, the severity of the case, as reflected in the size of the kidney stone, was disproportionately represented in the two treatments. If each treatment condition, Treatment A and Treatment B, had an equal probability of being assigned subjects with small and large kidney stones, we would not expect the groups to differ on this important variable that is highly correlated with the outcome of the study; and there would be no bias in the estimate of the treatment effect. If we formed two homogeneous pools of subjects, one with small kidney stones and the other with large kidney stones, and then assigned subjects from each pool randomly to the different treatment conditions, "we would feel quite confident that the groups were nearly equivalent at the outset" (Keppel, 1991: p. 298), not only in terms of the severity of their kidney stone problem but also in terms of other relevant characteristics as well.

This type of design is called a *blocking design* or a *randomized block design* because the homogeneous pools of subjects are known as *blocks*. If the blocking factor is highly correlated with the outcome (in the kidney stone example, stone size is highly correlated with the outcome, treatment success rate), a blocking design has the additional advantage of having more power than an unblocked design because each of the groups defined by a particular block and treatment condition is more homogeneous relative to the outcome variable. As noted by Keppel, a blocking design is constructed in "two steps: first an initial grouping of subjects into blocks and then the random assignment of subjects within each block to the different conditions" (p. 300). In the next chapter, we will present an analysis, called the one-way analysis of variance, appropriate for analyzing data from a single factor nonblocked design, where individuals are randomly assigned to treatments, and in Chapter 14, we will present an analysis, called a two-way analysis of variance, appropriate for analyzing data from a two-factor (called a *factorial*) design, where one factor may be a treatment factor and the other may be a blocking factor. As will be discussed in Chapter 14, blocking designs can provide greater statistical power, and, as such, may be described as being more statistically valid than nonblocking counterparts.

UNDERSCORING THE IMPORTANCE OF HAVING A TRUE CONTROL GROUP USING RANDOMIZATION

The randomized block design makes use of randomization to assign individuals within each block to a treatment condition so that the treatment groups to be compared will be equivalent or balanced from the outset.[4] In this section, we take a closer look at estimating a treatment effect when random assignment to treatment and control conditions is difficult or even impossible, and return to the question posed in an earlier section of this chapter when the notion of a causal study was first introduced, "What is the causal effect of a particular college freshman diet provided by a university on weight gain/loss from September to June?"

If in the study designed to answer this question, college freshmen were not assigned randomly either to the particular diet under study (the treatment condition) or to a different diet (the control condition), can the researcher ever conclude with certainty that it was the particular diet itself that caused the weight gain/loss, rather than something else, if indeed there was a weight change. If the two groups are not balanced at the outset of the study (in September) on all potential variables that might affect weight gain/loss freshman year (e.g., the stress of college, the amount of increased exercise from walking greater distances from class to class, the late nights partying), such variables could be the real reasons for any observed average weight gain/loss, rather than the diet itself. In such instances, the

---

[4] Based on Lord, F.M. (1967). A paradox in the interpretation of group comparisons. *Psychological Bulletin*, 68, 304–305; and Holland, P. W., & Rubin, D. B. (1982). *On Lord's Paradox*. ETS RR-82-36, Princeton, NJ.

average estimate of weight loss caused by the diet itself (called, the *average treatment effect*) would not solely reflect the treatment; it would be biased.

In this particular situation, however, the university has only one diet for its freshmen class. Accordingly, the entire freshman class is assigned this diet, which means that there is no control diet and only a treatment group. We shall designate the treatment group as Group 1. If there were a control group, we would designate that group as Group 0. As one would expect, in order to measure weight gain/loss of its college freshmen from September to June, the university measures the weight of each freshman twice, once in September and then again in June. This type of design is known as a *repeated measures design*, or a *panel design*. The September weight may be viewed as a pretest and the June weight as a posttest, and as such, this particular type of repeated measures design with only two measurement occasions, one before and one after, also is referred to as a *one-group pretest-posttest design* (Shadish, Campbell, & Cook, 2002). Recall that we analyzed data from this type of design using a paired groups *t*-test in the previous chapter.

Let us depart from this situation for a moment and consider for now a different scenario in which we do not have simply a treatment group, but also a control group, and that, as before, each of these groups is measured twice, once in September and then again in June. Let us also assume that individuals are assigned randomly to one of these two groups; the treatment group is assigned the particular college freshman diet, the control group is assigned a diet other than the particular college freshman diet. If we let X, in general, represent the students' observed September weights, student *i* in the treatment group (Group 1) would have his/her September weight represented by X_{1i} and student *i* in the control group (Group 0) would have his/her September weight represented by $X_{0i.}$ Analogously, if Y represents, in general, the students' observed June weights, then student *i* in the treatment group would be represented by Y_{1i} and student *i* in the control group would have his/her June weight represented by Y_{0i}.

Because in this situation individuals *are* randomly assigned to treatment and control groups, with large enough sized groups we can expect the two groups to be equal, on average, with respect to their September weights. We also can expect the two groups to be balanced on the host of measured and unmeasured variables that might affect their June weights (e.g., activity level, metabolism, stress level, etc.). Accordingly, in this situation, to obtain an estimate of the average treatment effect of the university diet, we simply would need to compare the average June weight of the college freshmen in the treatment group, denoted $E(Y_1)$, to the average June weight of the college freshmen in the true control group (those randomly not exposed to the university diet), denoted $E(Y_0)$.[5] This comparison may be expressed simply as Equation (12.3), which defines the average treatment effect in equation form.

$$E(Y_1) - E(Y_0). \tag{12.3}$$

But, unfortunately, the situation defined by our university diet problem differs from this one in that *all* college freshmen are assigned the university diet, and as such, they are

---

[5] Through random assignment, we are trying to achieve a situation in which the college freshmen who were not exposed to the university diet (the control group) are basically clones of those who were exposed to the university diet (the treatment group) so that the difference between the average June weights of the two groups is an unbiased estimate of the average treatment effect, due wholly to the treatment itself and to no other lurking variables.

all in the treatment group. There is no control group to which students have been randomly assigned. As a result, we will not have a direct estimate of $E(Y_0)$, namely, the average effect of the diet for a true control group as measured in June.

Without a direct estimate of $E(Y_0)$, it is sensible to ask: How can we solve for Equation (12.3) and obtain the university diet's average treatment effect on weight gain/loss? Said differently, we may ask: How can we assess the university diet's average treatment effect if we do not know *the amount by which the college freshmen's weight would have changed from September to June if they were NOT exposed to the particular diet provided by the university*?

Because, in this example, there is no one in the freshman class who was not exposed to this particular university diet, what we need is information related to a situation that is literally contrary to fact. Such situations are called *counterfactuals*.[6] Some examples of *counterfactuals* are:

- If I had taken three Advil instead of only one, my headache would be gone by now.
- If I were you, I would have applied for the job, eaten more spinach, run the marathon, etc.

The term counterfactual is often used as a synonym for control group or comparison. What is the counterfactual? This question just usually means, "To what is the treatment being compared?" When causative claims are made in a research study, it is always sensible to ask, "What is the counterfactual?"

The question before us is: Can we make a causal claim about the effect of the university diet on college freshmen's weight gain/loss without such a counterfactual or true control group?

Without a counterfactual or true control group, we may obtain the average weight change for all college freshmen from September to June by computing each individual student's weight change from September to June as $Y_{1i} - X_{1i}$, and then taking the mean or average of these differences to obtain what is called the *expected value*[7] of these differences, denoted as $E(Y_{1i} - X_{1i})$. Notice in this expression, we use the subscript 1 to convey the fact that everyone is in the treatment group (Group 1) since all are assigned the university diet. There is no one in a control group (Group 0).

If the distribution of weight in September, X_1, is no different from the distribution of weight in June, Y_1, and the mean of the distribution of weight differences calculated between September and June equals zero, we may conclude that the difference in mean weight for college freshmen from September to June is zero as shown by Equation (12.4),

$$E(Y_{1i} - X_{1i}) = E(Y_1) - E(X_1) = 0 \tag{12.4}$$

The right-hand side of Equation (12.4) equals the left-hand side because the difference of means equals the mean of differences.

Given the result shown in Equation (12.4), can we conclude also that the diet did not cause a mean change in student weight over the academic year?

Although, at first glance, we might want to agree with this causal claim, on more careful analysis we recall that in order for this causal claim to be valid, according to Equation (12.3), we need to compare $E(Y_1)$, the average weight of college freshmen in June, not to $E(X_1)$, the average weight of college freshmen in September, but, rather to $E(Y_0)$, the average weight of college freshmen in June assigned to a true control group diet.

---

[6] See Wainer, H. (2011). *Uneducated Guesses: Using evidence to uncover misguided education policies.* Princeton, NJ: Princeton University Press. (See pp. 123–126.)

[7] Note: The expected value of X, denoted $E(X)$, is simply the mean of the X distribution.

If we can assume that $E(X_1) = E(Y_0)$, then we can assume that Equations (12.3) and (12.4) are equivalent, and, if they are equivalent, the causal claim may be deemed to be correct. But, what does it mean to assume that the average weight of college freshmen in September, $E(X_1)$ equals what the average weight of a true control group of college freshmen would have been in June, $E(Y_0)$? It means simply to assume that under some control diet, each student's weight remains constant from September to June, and that the response to that control diet, whatever it might be, is given by the student's weight in September. If this assumption is true, it makes sense to substitute $E(X_1)$ for $E(Y_0)$ in Equation (12.3). On what basis, however, can we decide that this assumption is true?

Without randomization to treatment and control diets, a test of the validity of the assumption that $E(X_1) = E(Y_0)$ would require us to have weight data from September and June on the *same* students exposed to a true control group condition to see if their weights actually did stay the same over this time period. But the same students cannot be exposed to the control diet given they were exposed to the treatment diet and so our belief in the truth of this assumption must be based only on intuition and/or subject-matter expertise. Unfortunately, this assumption is untestable.

The *fundamental problem of causal inference*[8] is that only either Y_1 or Y_0, but *not* both, can be observed on any one subject. We can never observe both situations. And as such, one or more assumptions must be made about what would have happened had that person been in the other group or taken the other path.

In sum, it is *not* the difference $E(Y_1) - E(X_1)$ that measures a treatment effect, but rather the difference $E(Y_1) - E(Y_0)$, and so the extent to which the average difference $E(Y_1) - E(X_1)$ will have causal significance will depend upon the extent to which X_1 can serve as a substitute for the counterfactual Y_0. But, as in the university diet example, assumptions regarding counterfactual outcomes tend to be untestable with the data that are available, and this is what gives causal inference in observational settings an air of uncertainty.

By contrast, as we have discussed in this chapter, random assignment with large enough numbers of individuals allows us to assume that, on average, the experimental and control groups are the same on any number of traits (both observable and unobservable) relevant to the outcome, and is what allows us to have confidence in making causal inference in such situations. Without random assignment, one must find a control group that is as close to those in the treatment group as possible so as to reduce bias in the estimate of the treatment effect. Controlling for variables that are known, through literature review and other means, to relate to the outcome variable is important for obtaining an unbiased estimate of the treatment effect. Such control variables, at the individual level, may be socioeconomic status, gender, ability, work status, and include variables at the community or school level (so-called contextual variables), and so on, depending on the outcome to be measured. Because it is not possible to think of all such variables (observed and unobserved) that need to be controlled so as to isolate the effects of the treatment effect, important variables may often be omitted in error, as was the case in analyzing the overall relative effectiveness of the two kidney stone treatments, resulting in a biased estimate of the treatment effects.

---

[8] For a more complete, yet accessible discussion of causal inference, the interested reader is referred to chapter 9 in Gelman, A., & Hill, J. (2007). *Data analysis using regression and multilevel/hierarchical models.* New York, NY: Cambridge University Press.

ANALYTIC METHODS FOR BOLSTERING CLAIMS OF CAUSALITY FROM OBSERVATIONAL DATA (OPTIONAL READING)

Because of the abundance of observational data, and a general desire to draw causal conclusions based on the analysis of such data, as in the example presented earlier in this chapter on perceived job strain and incidence of coronary heart problems, a number of advanced analytic approaches recently have been developed that seek to bolster a researcher's claim of causality by helping to reduce or even eliminate bias in the estimation of a treatment effect or other variable in which one is interested. Although a full discussion of these cutting edge analytical techniques is beyond the scope of this book, a few of them will be listed here with brief descriptions so as to make the reader aware of what is possible analytically in this emerging field. References for further study for the interested reader are included as well.

Propensity Score Matching. This is an approach used in observational studies to attempt to make the treatment and control groups balanced, in a way that mimics what would have been the case had there been random assignment to groups. In particular, this approach estimates (usually via logistic regression) the probability (called a propensity score) that an individual (or other unit of analysis) is assigned to the treatment or control groups based on all observed covariates thought to affect the assignment to treatment. Based on the propensity score values, individuals from the treatment group are matched as closely as possible to one or more individuals in the control group using a variety of matching algorithms. The approach is useful in reducing the imbalance between groups to the extent that a substantial overlap in observables can be created between treatment and control groups after matching, and that there are no lurking, unobservable, latent variables that have not been accounted for that affect assignment to treatment groups. This approach was introduced by Rosenbaum and Rubin (1983).[9]

Instrumental Variables. This is another such approach used in observational studies to help make the treatment and control groups more balanced so as to reduce bias in estimating the effect of a variable in which one is interested. The use of instrumental variables is used particularly to reduce what is called *endogeneity*, a problem that arises when there is a correlation between the error term in a regression model with one of the independent variables of interest in that regression model. As will be discussed in more detail in Chapter 16 of this book, this type of correlation violates one of the assumptions underlying regression in the inferential context and leads to a biased estimate of the effect of that variable of interest. To reduce or even eliminate this type of correlation, a researcher may attempt to identify new variables, called *instruments*, which correlate directly with the variable of interest, and indirectly with the dependent variable through this variable of interest. The following example is based on one used by Card (1995) to illustrate this approach.

Suppose one were interested in estimating the effect of years of schooling on earnings. In this case our variable of interest is years of schooling and our dependent variable is earnings. Assume that we do not have information available on an individual's academic ability in the data set containing the individual's years of schooling and earnings and that therefore our regression model does not include academic ability. Because those with higher

[9] Rosenbaum, Paul R., & Rubin, Donald B. (1983). The Central Role of the Propensity Score in Observational Studies for Causal Effects. *Biometrika* 70 (1): 41–55.

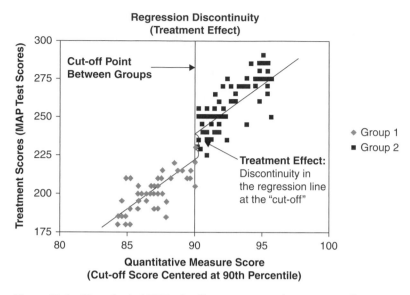

Figure 12.1   Hypothetical RDD plot illustrating a simple treatment effect

academic ability will tend to have more years of schooling and also greater earnings, the error term of the regression model with only years of schooling as a sole regressor will correlate with the unobserved ability. In the instrumental variable approach one tries to identify a variable that will be an instrument for ability. As an instrument for ability, this variable will not correlate directly with ability, or directly with earnings, yet will correlate directly with years of schooling and will correlate only indirectly with earnings through years of schooling. Such a variable is proximity to a college/university because of the fact that individuals who live far from a college/university will be less likely to attend college/university and, therefore, will tend to have a reduced number of years of schooling compared to those who live near a college/university. It should be noted that instrumental variables are difficult to identify as they must satisfy a number of strong assumptions in order for them to fulfill their role as instruments in reducing bias in the estimation of the effect of a variable of interest, like years of schooling.

Regression Discontinuity Designs (RDD). As illustrated in Figure 12.1, regression discontinuity analyses are well-suited to situations in which individuals (e.g., children) are placed in a treatment group (e.g., a special program for the gifted and talented) if they score at or just above some cut point (e.g., the 90th percentile) on a standardized assessment, and are placed in the control group if they score immediately below that cut point, but close enough (87th to 89th percentile, for example) to be cognitively on par with those who did meet the criteria. The treatment and control groups thus created will not only be quite similar on a cognitive dimension related to the outcome of achievement, but also on a motivation to achieve dimension because all children in both groups had chosen to take the assessment, deemed a prerequisite for acceptance into the special program. If the assumptions in RDDs hold, the difference between treatment and control groups "close" to the threshold should provide an accurate estimate of the treatment effect (Shadish, Galindo, Wong, Steiner, & Cook, 2011). For a more comprehensive review of RDD, the reader is referred to Bloom (2009) and Imbens and Lemieux (2008).

In addition to analytic approaches to help reduce bias in the estimation of a treatment effect, so as to make the causal claims more compelling, one needs to be aware of how elements in the design of a study also can contribute to reducing bias in the estimation of a treatment effect. Accordingly, some of these design elements are considered in the following sections.

QUASI-EXPERIMENTAL DESIGNS

When randomization to treatment and control groups is not possible, yet when one can introduce other aspects of an experimental design into a research study, including the selection of research participants, the use of a control group, the repeated observations before and after the intervention (e.g., a university diet) to gauge the effect of the intervention, and so on, we have what is called a quasi-experimental design (Campbell & Stanley, 1963), as opposed to a true experimental design. What distinguishes a true experimental design from a quasi-experimental design is that a true experimental design includes also the randomization of participants to treatment and control groups.

As discussed earlier in this chapter, we know that without randomization it is likely that the treatment and control groups may not be balanced at the outset, that the two groups may differ systematically on some important variables that might explain the observed effect other than the treatment itself. In carrying out a quasi-experimental design, it is therefore important to consider in a systematic way the alternative plausible explanations for the observed effect other than the intervention itself. As noted by Shadish, Cook, and Campbell (2002):

In quasi-experiments, the researcher has to enumerate alternative explanations one by one, decide which are plausible, and then use logic, design, and measurement to assess whether each one is operating in a way that might explain any observed effect. The difficulties are that these alternative explanations are never completely enumerable in advance, that some of them are particular to the context being studied, and that the methods needed to eliminate them from contention will vary from alternative to alternative and from study to study. (Shadish, Cook, & Campbell, 2002, p. 14)

In the next section, we enumerate some of these factors, referred to by Shadish, Cook, and Campbell (2002), which may create bias in the estimation of an average treatment effect. Collectively, these factors are known as threats to the *internal validity* of a quasi-experimental study. In the following section, we describe briefly another type of threat, one that does not potentially compromise the validity of the causal claim itself, but does impact the ability of the researcher to generalize that causal claim to other "populations, settings, treatment variables, and measurement variables" (Campbell & Stanley, 1963: p. 5). This type of validity is called a study's *external validity*. The interested reader is referred to Shadish, Campbell, and Cook (2002) for a full, detailed discussion of these topics, as well as others related to experimental and quasi-experimental design methodology.

THREATS TO THE INTERNAL VALIDITY OF A QUASI-EXPERIMENTAL DESIGN

Threats to the internal validity of a study (Cook & Campbell, 1979; Shadish, Cook, & Campbell, 2002) are those that provide alternative plausible reasons for the observed result rather than the treatment itself. Accordingly, they can compromise the validity of causal claims made about the treatment's effectiveness by producing a biased (either too low or too high) estimate of the average treatment effect.

History. In addition to the treatment, an event external to the study that could produce a differential change in the outcome variable for one of the groups, and, in turn, a biased estimate of a treatment effect.

Maturation. Changes in the participants that occur over time within the course of the study that could differentially affect the outcome variable for the groups, such as growing older, more tired, more aware of being in an experiment, and so on, and result in a biased estimate of the treatment effect.

Testing. Taking the pretest may have a differential practice or other type effect (e.g., sensitization effect) on how one scores on the posttest, resulting in a biased estimate of a treatment effect.

Instrumentation. Changing the means by which measures are taken (different tests, different raters or interviewers, etc.) from pretest to posttest may have a differential impact for the two groups on the posttest measure.

Statistical Regression. The effect produced when one of the groups is selected for being extremely high or low on the pretest measure. On second testing, these extreme scores will regress toward the mean even without an intervention resulting in a biased estimate of the treatment effect. Regression toward the mean is a topic that was covered in Chapter 6 of this book.

Selection Bias. When there is differential selection of subjects for groups, and subjects in the treatment group compared to the control group have, on average, different endowments on the pretest and other relevant covariates that are known to affect the outcome variable, the estimate of the treatment effect will be biased. This is called *selection bias*, for short. This source of invalidity is probably the most common and is the one that may be a problem in our job strain example. The extent to which this source of invalidity can adversely affect one's estimate of a treatment effect is given by example in the next section.

Experimental Mortality. When there is differential attrition of subjects from the treatment and control groups, the estimate of the treatment effect might be biased. For example, if a physical fitness course were so demanding in the type of physical exercise imposed on participants in the treatment group that it caused those who were physically weaker to drop out, and yet in the absence of such a demanding protocol of exercise, all participants in the control group continued in their course until the end of the study, the resulting estimate of the treatment effect, the impact of the course on one's physical fitness, would be biased and invalid.

THREATS TO THE EXTERNAL VALIDITY OF A QUASI-EXPERIMENTAL DESIGN

In addition to sources of internal invalidity, which impact the estimate of a treatment effect itself, sources of external invalidity do not impact the estimate of a treatment effect, but do impact the generalizability of a result to other populations, settings, treatment variables, and measurement variables. Although we will not enumerate the possible threats to a study's external validity, these sources typically involve an interaction between some aspect of the design and the treatment group. For example, given a study designed to test whether a film on sexual harassment in the workplace is effective in making individuals more aware of the issues and problems related to such harassment, if, in that study, a pretest were administered before the film was shown to measure an individual's baseline knowledge of sexual harassment issues, the pretest could have the result of sensitizing the individuals in that study to the topic of sexual harassment, in general, and, in turn, amplify the effects of the film for those individuals in the study. This source of external invalidity would be due to what is called a *testing by treatment interaction*, which would limit the generalizability of the amplified effect of the film to pretested populations only, rather than to an intended target population of workers who are not given a pretest before viewing the film.

THREATS TO THE VALIDITY OF A STUDY: SOME CLARIFICATIONS AND CAVEATS

It should be noted that the use of randomization in the design of a study does not guarantee the validity of the resulting causal claim as other factors may intervene after randomization takes place, and experimental and control groups are established, that can compromise the validity of the findings. For example, consider the physical fitness study described earlier under the heading, experimental mortality as a threat to a study's internal validity. In that example, even if the treatment and control groups had been randomly assigned to individuals and balance had been achieved between the two groups at the outset of the study, the fact that the participants with less physical stamina dropped out of the treatment group because it was too physically demanding, while all those in the control group remained until the end of the study, renders questionable the validity of the resulting causal claim regarding the impact of the physical fitness course. Accordingly, even in the context of a true experiment, one should consider the range of alternative plausible factors or threats that could contribute to an invalid causal conclusion. In helping one to consider the role and influence of a threat in a particular study, Shadish, Campbell, and Cook (2002) suggest that the following three questions are critical: "(1) How would the threat apply in this case? (2) Is there evidence that the threat is plausible rather than just possible? (3) Does the threat operate in the same direction as the observed effect, so that it could partially or totally explain the observed findings?" (Shadish, Campbell, & Cook, 2002: p. 40)

The goals of achieving internal and external validity are often at odds with each other. For example, by choosing a more homogenous set of study participants and randomly assigning them to either the treatment or control group, as one would do in a blocking design, the statistical power is increased as is the internal validity of the design, but with more homogeneous groups, the external validity is compromised. This makes it more difficult to generalize results to other populations, etc. A case in point is the "Justice at Work" article referenced earlier in this chapter. In this article, analyses were carried out on a male sample that was overwhelmingly White. Accordingly, in one of their concluding comments, the authors write, "Finally, as our evidence was based on [an overwhelmingly White sample of] male civil servants, further research is needed to determine whether the effect of justice on heart health is generalizable to women, in other contexts, and across ethnic groups" (p. 2250).

Given a choice between bolstering the internal versus the external validity of a design, one should give clear priority to bolstering the internal validity and to including elements in the design that do so. After all, and simply stated, only valid causal conclusions are worthy of being generalized.

THREATS TO THE VALIDITY OF A STUDY: SOME EXAMPLES

EXAMPLE 12.1. An approach for teaching early readers how to decode words was developed using a deck of flashcards wherein each flashcard contains a single word. The approach requires the teacher to show each flashcard in turn to students, pronounce each word on a card, and pass through the deck a number of times, repeating the process with each card. To test the efficacy of this approach, students were given a pretest to determine how many words they could decode at baseline, and then given a posttest that required each student to read each word off the deck of cards that the teacher had practiced with them. As anticipated by the researchers, students scored higher on the posttest than on the pretest as they were able to say more words printed on the cards after the treatment than before. The researchers concluded that this approach is highly effective for teaching decoding skills.

Plausible alternative explanation for the causal claim: As it turns out, the students had not learned to decode the words; instead, they had memorized extraneous features of the words and cards. For instance, a thumb print, dog-eared corner, or smeared ink enabled them to remember which card contained which word. Rather than the approach to teaching decoding as the cause of the students' impressive performance on the posttest, the students' skills in memorizing the cards' appearances was likely the cause of their success with the task. (From Gough, P. [1996]. How children learn to read and why they fail. *Annals of Dyslexia*, *46*(1), 1–20.

EXAMPLE 12.2. To determine whether the socioeconomic status of undergraduate college students directly impacts their success at obtaining offers for and securing summer internships, an observational study was carried out at a large, private urban university. In particular, after controlling for a number of personal (age and gender) and academic (major, course year, and GPA) characteristics, it was found that summer internships were held predominantly by those students with higher socioeconomic status, and therefore it was concluded that having a higher socioeconomic status caused students to be more successful in gaining offers for and securing a summer internship.

Plausible alternative explanation for the causal claim: This study does not consider the extent to which students from higher socioeconomic levels may self-select into the pool of summer internship applicants and therefore receive more internship offers than students of lower socioeconomic levels. Because jobs classified as "internships" typically are unpaid, those from lower socioeconomic backgrounds are less likely to be able to afford, via both actual and opportunity costs, to work in internships, and may therefore decide not to apply for internships, but instead to apply for part-time or full-time jobs that come with a salary.

EXAMPLE 12.3. An observational study was conducted to determine if a particular type of therapy for stroke patients improves swallow function to a greater extent for those in the acute phase of recovery (within the first six months post onset) compared to those in the chronic phase of recovery (greater than one year post onset). After controlling for a number of relevant factors, including patient age, gender, socioeconomic status, etiology and severity of the swallowing disorder, and frequency of treatment, it was found that patients in the acute phase of recovery demonstrated greater improvement in swallow function (as evidenced by a decrease in the frequency of overt signs/symptoms of choking/aspiration) following this treatment than patients in the chronic phase of recovery. It was concluded that the treatment was the cause of this difference.

Plausible alternative explanation for the causal claim: Because it is well known that brain tissue heals naturally during the first six months following a stroke, causing spontaneous recovery, it may be that rather than the treatment itself, the observed greater improvement in swallow function may be due wholly or in part to this natural healing process that occurs during the first six months and does not extend beyond the first year following a stroke,. As such, the natural healing process that occurs during the first six months following a stroke, acts as a confounder in this study to bias the estimate of the treatment effect. To correct for this problem, patients within the same time period following a stroke should have been compared.

EXERCISES

In Exercises 12.1.–12.7., identify one or more plausible alternative explanations that call into question the validity of the causal claim made.

12.1. To determine if residents of China who have a higher level of education spend more time on the Internet than those with a lower level of education, an observational study was conducted. After controlling for a number of relevant variables, such as gender, race/ ethnicity, employment status, occupation, and so on, it was found that those who have a higher level of education did, in fact, spend more time on the Internet than those with a lower level of education. The researchers concluded that having a higher education causes an individual to spend a greater amount of time on the Internet.

12.2. A study at a small Midwestern university was carried out to determine whether a semester-long remedial reading course improves the reading skills of freshmen, who by virtue of their extremely low performance on a test of reading skills, are deemed to be in need of remedial instruction in reading. At the conclusion of the course, the same test that was administered initially to assess these students' reading skills was administered again as a posttest. Based on the average positive gain between the two administrations of this test, the researchers of this study concluded that the remedial reading course caused an improvement in reading skills.

12.3. A study was conducted to determine whether dental students' clinical skills improve more when their lectures are supplemented by instructional videos. Students were randomly assigned to one of two groups. One group was given lectures only and the other group was given both lectures and video instruction. Because the classroom equipped with video equipment was available only in the morning, the group that had both lectures and video instruction met in the morning, whereas the other group met after lunch in the afternoon. Because the group exposed to both lectures and video instruction performed better in the clinical setting than the group with lectures only, it was concluded that video instruction as a supplement to lectures causes an improvement in clinical skills.

12.4. A skateboarding video game was developed to determine whether one's balance could improve after forty-five minutes of play. Individuals were invited to participate on a voluntary basis. Using a pretest-posttest design, those who volunteered were administered a balance assessment before and after exposure to the video game. It was found that, on average, the balancing abilities of players were no better after playing the game than before, leading the researchers to conclude that their skateboarding game was not effective in enhancing one's balancing skills.

12.5. To determine if young children of non-working mothers have better communication skills than children of mothers who work full-time, an observational study was carried out. After controlling for a number of relevant variables, including the age, sex, race/ethnicity, and number of siblings of the child, and age of the mother, it was found that the children of nonworking mothers did, in fact, have higher communication skills than the children of mothers who work full-time. The researchers concluded that mother's working outside the home causes a delayed development in a child's communication skills.

12.6. A study was conducted to determine whether a reading intervention could improve the reading ability of the lowest achieving students at a certain school. Those who scored in the bottom 5 percent of all students on the standard reading test at the start of the year were selected for the intervention. At the end of the year, the students' scores on the standard reading test had improved, on average. The researchers concluded that the intervention was effective.

12.7. To determine whether caffeine use increases short term memory, an experimental study was carried out. Students were randomly assigned to drink either Coca-Cola, Caffeine Free Diet Coca-Cola, or Water. They then studied a set of figures in order. After five minutes, the figures were taken away and the students were asked to recreate the sequence. For each student the number of shapes listed in the correct order was recorded as the measure of short term memory. It was found that students assigned to drink Coca-Cola correctly were able to place statistically significantly more shapes in order than students assigned to the other conditions. The researchers concluded that caffeine use does increase short term memory.

12.8. Read the article "Effects of Zinc Supplementation in Occurrence and Duration of Common Cold in School Aged Children during Cold Season: a Double Blind Placebo Controlled Trial" located in the web resources associated with this text. Answer the following related questions:
    a) What was the purpose of the study?
    b) Is the study observational or experimental?
    c) Why was it important to have a placebo group?
    d) What does it mean for the experiment to be double blind and why was it important for the experiment to be double blind?
    e) Why was it important to include both males and females in the study?
    f) How many females were in the placebo group?
    g) What was the average number of family members for children in the zinc group?
    h) Why was it important to determine that there were no statistically significant differences in the average number of family members between children in the zinc-supplemented and placebo groups?

    i) Which of the three tests in Chapter 11 could have been conducted to determine that that there were no statistically significant differences in the average number of family members between children in the zinc-supplemented and placebo groups?

    j) What was the statistical support provided for the finding that the occurrence of the common cold differed for the zinc-supplemented and placebo groups?

12.9. Read the following excerpt from the Vital Signs column from the *New York Times* on February 4, 2011, by Roni Caryn Rabin, "Childhood: Obesity and School Lunches." Use it to answer the related questions.

Researchers say they have identified another risk factor for childhood obesity: school lunch.

A study of more than 1,000 sixth graders in several schools in southeastern Michigan found that those who regularly had the school lunch were 29 percent more likely to be obese than those who brought lunch from home.

Spending two or more hours a day watching television or playing video games also increased the risk of obesity, but by only 19 percent.

Of the 142 obese children in the study for whom dietary information was known, almost half were school-lunch regulars, compared with only one-third of the 787 who were not obese.

"Most school lunches rely heavily on high-energy, low-nutrient-value food, because it's cheaper," said Dr. Kim A. Eagle, director of the University of Michigan Cardiovascular Center, and senior author of the paper, published in the December issue of American Heart Journal. In some schools where the study was done, lunch programs offered specials like "Tater Tot Day," he said.

    a) Is this study observational or experimental?

    b) Based on the results of this study, if your cousin attended school in southeastern Michigan, would you ask her parents to pack a lunch in order to prevent her from becoming obese?

12.10. In 1999 there was an article published in the journal *Nature* (http://www.nature.com/news/1999/990513/full/news990513-1.html) the results of which indicated that infants who slept in a room with a nightlight were more likely to be nearsighted as adults. Based on the results of this study, should nightlights be removed from infants' rooms?

12.11. Sarah wants to design a study to determine whether students taking statistics who have access to their computers during class do worse than those who don't. She is teaching two sections of statistics and would allow one section to use their computers during class and the other would not be allowed to. What are three important design considerations?

12.12. Josh wants to design a study to determine whether brushing your teeth in an up and down or circular pattern is more effective at eliminating plaque. What are three important design considerations?

12.13. Read the article by Susan Dynarski, available at http://www.nytimes.com/2014/08/07/upshot/study-on-parental-longevity-is-short-on-causation.html?_r=0, about the use of natural experiments as an alternative to randomized controlled experiments. Answer the following related questions:

a) In the article, Dynarski takes issue with the causal conclusions reached by two sociologists in their study of a child's college attendance and his/her parents' longevity. What is her criticism of that finding?

b) Read the article and propose a question that may be or already has been addressed using a natural experiment.

CHAPTER THIRTEEN

One-Way Analysis of Variance

In the previous chapter we presented statistical models for answering questions about population means when the design involves either one or two groups and when the population standard deviation is not known. In the case of two groups, we distinguished between paired and independent group designs and presented statistical models tailored to each. In this chapter we extend the two independent groups model to handle questions about population means of three or more groups.

When there are more than two groups in our design, we will test the null hypothesis that *all* populations have the same mean versus the nondirectional alternative that not all populations have the same mean. For example, using the *NELS* data set, we may be interested in comparing (1) the mean number of years of math taken in high school for the populations of students from the Northeast, North Central, South, and West, or (2) twelfth grade self-concept by type of high school program (rigorous academic, academic, vocational and other), or (3) school attendance rate by region.

If there are K populations, we can represent these hypotheses as follows:

$H_0: \mu_1 = \mu_2 = \mu_3 = \ldots = \mu_K$
$H_1:$ not H_0

The null hypothesis is true only if *all* the population means are equal to one another, and false if any two are not equal to each other.

THE DISADVANTAGE OF MULTIPLE *t*-TESTS

A question that you might be thinking at this point is why must we introduce a new model for testing H_0 against H_1? Why can't we simply use the independent groups *t*-test introduced in the last chapter to test H_0 against H_1 by making all possible pairwise comparisons of means?

For example, if $K = 3$ and the null and alternative hypotheses are:

$H_0: \mu_1 = \mu_2 = \mu_3$
$H_1:$ not H_0,

a set of t-tests, one on each pair of samples, would produce the following three hypothesis tests:

$H_0: \mu_1 = \mu_2$	$H_0: \mu_1 = \mu_3$	$H_0: \mu_2 = \mu_3$
versus	versus	versus
$H_1: \mu_1 \neq \mu_2$	$H_1: \mu_1 \neq \mu_3$	$H_1: \mu_2 \neq \mu_3$

Following this approach, we would reject H_0: $\mu_1 = \mu_2 = \mu_3$ if at least one of the three pairwise tests in the set is statistically significant at $\alpha = .05$.

While intuitively appealing, there is a problem that arises in connection with this approach: the probability of making a Type I error and falsely rejecting the null hypothesis (H_0: $\mu_1 = \mu_2 = \mu_3$) will *exceed* the chosen level of significance, .05.

Two definitions of Type I error rate are implied here. A Type I error rate attached to each pairwise test (called a *per-comparison error rate* (α)) and a Type I error rate attached to the *complete set* of pairwise tests related to the original null hypothesis (called a *family-wise error rate* (α_{FW})). A "family" of comparisons is a set of comparisons that are logically and conceptually linked.

A family may consist of multiple comparisons conducted on a single dependent variable in a design consisting of more than two groups, or of multiple comparisons conducted on separate dependent variables in a design consisting of two or more groups. A series of three pairwise t-tests for testing H_0: $\mu_1 = \mu_2 = \mu_3$ in terms of say, twelfth grade math achievement, is an example of the first type of family. A series of four t-tests that compares males and females in terms of twelfth grade math achievement, reading achievement, science achievement, and social studies achievement is an example of the second type of family.

As implied, when several logically linked comparisons are conducted, each at α, the overall family-wise error rate, α_{FW}, will exceed α. The amount by which α_{FW} exceeds α may be obtained from Equation 13.1 that expresses the relationship between these two Type I errors.

α_{FW}, *the probability of making at least one Type I errors in conducting a set of K conceptually linked tests is approximated by:*

$$\alpha_{FW} = 1 - (1 - \alpha)^K \tag{13.1}$$

If the number of tests carried out to test H_0: $\mu_1 = \mu_2 = \mu_3$ is $K = 3$, then α_{FW} will equal approximately $1 - (.95)(.95)(.95) = 1 - .95^3 = 1 - .8574 = .1426$.

That is, for every 100 times we tested H_0: $\mu_1 = \mu_2 = \mu_3$ using a set of $K = 3$ mutually independent tests (e.g., a combination of pairwise and more complex comparisons), we would make a Type I error, or reject the H_0 falsely, approximately 14 times on average, instead of 5.

A simpler expression of the relationship between α_{FW} and α is given by Equation 13.2.

$$\alpha_{FW} \leq K\alpha \tag{13.2}$$

This relationship, proven by Bonferroni, an Italian mathematician, states that the family-wise Type I error rate will always be less than or equal to the per comparison Type I error rate times the number of comparisons conducted.

When $K = 3$ and $\alpha = .05$, as in the current illustration, Equation 13.2 suggests that

$$\alpha_{FW} \leq (3)(.05) = .15,$$

which is consistent with our result from Equation (13.1) that $\alpha_{FW} = .1426$.

Equations 13.1 and 13.2 make amply clear the fact that as the number of comparisons in a set increases so does the family-wise error rate relative to α.

To control the family-wise Type I error at the chosen level α regardless of how many comparisons are conducted, we present two possible approaches: the one-way analysis of variance, abbreviated by the acronym ANOVA and the Bonferroni adjustment.

THE ONE-WAY ANALYSIS OF VARIANCE

One-way ANOVA is a nondirectional procedure that tests the equality among two or more population means using independent groups while controlling the family-wise Type I error rate at the chosen level α regardless of the number of groups in the design. When applied to only two groups, the one-way ANOVA is exactly identical to the nondirectional t-test for independent groups. Simply stated, one-way ANOVA may be thought of as an extension of the independent two-group t-test to two or more groups.

☞ **Remark.** The name, analysis of variance, given to a procedure to test the equality of population means may seem like a misnomer. Actually, the name comes from the method that is used to test for the equality of means. As we shall see, not unlike the two independent groups t-test, ANOVA tests hypotheses about the equality of means by analyzing variances defined in different ways relative to the groups in the design.

☞ **Remark.** The method of analysis of variance was developed by Ronald Aylmer Fisher, one of the giants in the history of the development of modern statistics, as a way to evaluate the separate effects of various treatments (e.g., fertilizer, soil type, weather, crop variety) on crop production. Hired in 1919 to work at the Rothamsted Agricultural Experimental Station in Harpenden, a rural area north of London, to examine and make sense of the enormous body of data collected in connection with the agricultural experiments that had been conducted to date at that time, R.A. Fisher introduced the analysis of variance in an article published in 1923; it was the second in a series of six papers entitled "Studies in Crop Variation" (Salsburg, 2001). As written by Salsburg (2001) "[t]hese papers show a brilliant originality and are filled with fascinating implications that kept theoreticians busy for the rest of the twentieth century, and will probably continue to inspire more work in the years that follow" (p. 43).

A GRAPHICAL ILLUSTRATION OF THE ROLE OF VARIANCE IN TESTS ON MEANS

Suppose the director of a drug rehabilitation center is interested in comparing the effects of three methods of therapeutic treatment on manual dexterity. Accordingly, she selects at random a sample of individuals from the population of applicants to her program and randomly assigns each to one of the three treatments, labeled Treatment 1, Treatment 2, and Treatment 3. After five weeks in the treatment programs, the participants are administered the Stanford Test of Manual Dexterity.

Suppose the three score distributions on this test, for Treatments 1, 2, and 3, are given in Figure 13.1 with means, $\bar{X}_1 = -3, \bar{X}_2 = 0, \bar{X}_3 = 3$, respectively. Based on the differences in these means, can the director conclude that the three treatments differ in their effects on the mean levels of manual dexterity for the population of potential participants from whom the sample was drawn? The answer will depend upon whether the score distributions are separate enough to suggest that each resulted from a different treatment. Because there is no observed overlap among the different group score distributions in Figure 13.1, the groups may be separate enough to suggest that the treatments have an effect on manual dexterity for the population of participants from whom the sample was drawn.

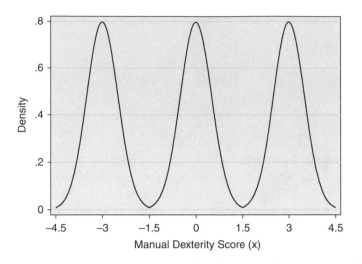

Figure 13.1 Nonoverlapping score distributions with means –3, 0, and 3, respectively

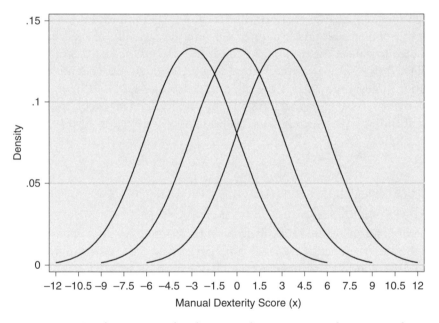

Figure 13.2 Overlapping score distributions with means –3, 0, and 3, respectively

Figure 13.2 offers a contrasting scenario to Figure 13.1. While the three means remain the same as in Figure 13.1 ($\overline{X}_1 = -3, \overline{X}_2 = 0, \overline{X}_3 = 3$) in Figure 13.2, considerable overlap exists among the score distributions. Accordingly, in contrast to Figure 13.1, the groups may not be separate enough to suggest that the treatments have a differential effect on manual dexterity for this population. While an individual in Figure 13.1 with a manual dexterity score of 1.00 clearly received Treatment II, there is a good chance that an individual with the same score in Figure 13.2 received Treatment II, or to a lesser extent, Treatment III. There is even a small chance that the individual received Treatment I.

Clearly, because Figures 13.1 and 13.2 display the same group means, more than mean differences determine the degree of overlap, or separation, between groups. As we shall make more explicit in the next section, we have already measured group separation as more than merely a difference between means in our use of the independent group t-test.

ANOVA AS AN EXTENSION OF THE INDEPENDENT SAMPLES t-TEST

In the two, independent groups t-test, the t-ratio of the hypotheses H_0: $\mu_1=\mu_2$ versus H_1: $\mu_1 \neq \mu_2$ is given as:

$$t = \frac{\left(\bar{X}_1 - \bar{X}_2\right) - \left(\mu_1 - \mu_2\right)}{\sqrt{\dfrac{\left(N_1-1\right)\hat{\sigma}_1^2 + \left(N_2-1\right)\hat{\sigma}_2^2}{N_1 + N_2 - 2}\left(\dfrac{1}{N_1} + \dfrac{1}{N_2}\right)}}$$

We may note that with H_0: $\mu_1 - \mu_2 = 0$, the numerator of this ratio equals the difference between groups as represented by the respective group means $\left(\bar{X}_1 - \bar{X}_2\right)$, and the denominator of this ratio equals (a function of) the weighted average of the two variance estimators, $\hat{\sigma}_1^2$ and $\hat{\sigma}_2^2$, computed respectively within each group.

More generally, we may say, that the t-ratio describes the *variability between groups*, expressed as a difference between means, relative to the *variability within groups*, expressed as a weighted average of within group variances. When there are only two groups, the variability between groups may be expressed simply as a difference between means; however, when there are more than two groups, the variability between groups may not be expressed so simply. To express the variability between groups in the case of more than two groups, we compute, instead, the *variance* (or variance estimator) of the group means. That is, we compute a variance on a set of mean values. If the group means are all equal, the variance of the means will be zero. On the other hand, if the group means are quite distinct, the variance of the means will be correspondingly large.

Thus, we may conceptualize the t-test as a test of the relative size of two different variances, a between group variance and a within group variance, for the purpose of judging hypotheses about two independent group means. Like the t-test, the one-way analysis of variance, as discussed in this book, is, by extension, a test of the relative size of a between group variance and a within group variance for the purpose of judging hypotheses about *more than two independent* group means.

☞ **Remark.** A form of analysis of variance, called repeated measures analysis of variance, may be used to test hypotheses about more than two *paired* group means. This procedure is beyond the scope of this book.

DEVELOPING AN INDEX OF SEPARATION FOR THE ANALYSIS OF VARIANCE

To determine whether, in fact, the groups displayed in Figures 13.1 and 13.2 are separate enough to suggest differential treatment effects, we use a single measure of group separation based on the between and within group variances. The *between group variance*, or spread of the means between groups, represents the degree to which the different treatments separate or pull apart individuals (on the test of manual dexterity) by virtue of their exposure to different treatments. The *within group variance*, or spread of scores within each group, represents the naturally occurring variability that exists (in manual dexterity) among individuals who have received the same treatment and may be due to such factors as natural ability, skill, motivation, age, gender, and so on. Such naturally occurring variability among individuals who have received the same treatment is said to be due to *individual differences*. These are differences that are left unexplained by treatment effects and for this reason are referred to not only as within group variance, but also *residual variance*.

In Figure 13.1 we may note that the between group variance, as measured by the distance of each group mean from another, is quite large relative to the within group variance, as measured by the spread of scores within each group. In Figure 13.2, however, the between group variance is quite small relative to the within group variance. The ratio of these two measures of variance (between to within) may be used to reflect the degree of separation among groups. As in the *t*-test, this ratio will help to determine whether the observed separation among score distributions is sufficiently large to suggest a real difference in the respective population means.

CARRYING OUT THE ANOVA COMPUTATION

Suppose the director of the drug rehabilitation center had selected 30 individuals from the population of applicants to her program and randomly assigned 10 to Treatment 1, 10 to Treatment 2 and 10 to Treatment 3. After five weeks of treatment, a manual dexterity test is administered for which a higher score indicates greater manual dexterity. Suppose the scores on the manual dexterity test are as follows: These data can be found in the file *ManDext.dta* . The variable that contains the scores is called ManualDex and the treatment variable is called Treatment.

Treatment 1	Treatment 2	Treatment 3
6	4	6
10	2	2
8	3	2
6	5	6
9	1	4
8	3	5
7	2	3
5	2	5
6	4	3
5	4	4
$\bar{X}_1 = 7$	$\bar{X}_2 = 3$	$\bar{X}_3 = 4$

Does the variation in treatment group means suggest a real difference in treatment means for the population, using $\alpha = .05$? We compute the ratio of between group variance to within group variance to find out.

Because both between and within group variances are variance estimators, we define each as the sum of squared deviations about its respective mean divided by the appropriate degrees of freedom (SS/df). In the context of ANOVA, variance estimators are called *mean squares*, short for mean or average sum of squares, and are denoted by the letters MS. Thus, we say $MS = SS/df$.

To form the ratio of between group variance to within group variance we compute both the mean square between (MS_B) and the mean square within (MS_W). This ratio, (MS_B/MS_W) is our index of separation in the one-way ANOVA.

☞ **Remark.** We may recall that with one group of N values, the degrees of freedom of a variance estimator are $N - 1$. With two groups of N values ($N = N_1 + N_2$), the degrees of freedom are $N_1 + N_2 - 2 = N - 2$ (as in the independent groups t-test). And, therefore, with K groups of N values ($N = N_1 + N_2 + N_3 + \ldots + N_K$), the degrees of freedom are $N - K$. We use this information in presenting the equations for MS_B and MS_W.

The Between Group Variance (MS_B)

The MS_B is computed as a variance on the group means. It is given by Equation 13.3.

$$MS_B = \frac{SS_B}{df} = \frac{\sum_{j=1}^{K} N_j (\bar{X}_j - \bar{\bar{X}})^2}{K - 1} \tag{13.3}$$

where N_j equals the number of values in group j, X_j equals the mean of the values in group j, $\bar{\bar{X}}$ equals the overall or grand mean of all values in all groups (equivalently, the mean of the group means), and K = the total number of groups in the design.

☞ **Remark.** The between group variance is based on a collection of K mean values. Its degrees of freedom, therefore, are $K - 1$. Because each of the means represents a different group of values, and not all groups are of the same size, we include a weighting factor, N_j, in Equation 13.3. N_j weights each squared deviation from the grand mean by the size of the corresponding group j so that deviations of large-sized groups are weighted more heavily than deviations of small-sized groups.

Using Equation 13.3, we compute the MS_B for the data from our example.

$$N_1 = N_2 = N_3 = 10; \bar{X}_1 = 7, \bar{X}_2 = 3, \bar{X}_3 = 4; \bar{\bar{X}} = 4.67; K = 3$$
$$SS_B = 10(7 - 4.67)^2 + 10(3 - 4.67)^2 + 10(4 - 4.67)^2 = 54.29 + 27.89 + 4.49 = 86.67$$
$$MS_B = 86.67/(3 - 1) = 86.67/2 = 43.34$$

The Within Group Variance (MS_W)

The MS_W is computed as the sum of the separate sums of squares computed on each group divided by the appropriate degrees of freedom. It is given by Equation 13.4.

$$MS_W = \frac{SS_W}{df} = \frac{\sum_{i,j} (X_{i,j} - \bar{X}_j)^2}{N - K} \tag{13.4}$$

where $X_{i,j}$ represents the score of individual i in group j (e.g., $X_{1,3}$ represents the score of individual 1 in group 3; $X_{3,1}$ represents the score of individual 3 in group 1).

☞ **Remark.** The within group variance is based on K groups of N values total. Its degrees of freedom are, therefore, $N - K$.

Using Equation 13.4, we compute the MSW for the data from our example.

$$SS_W = [(6-7)^2 + (10-7)^2 + (8-7)^2 + (6-7)^2 + (9-7)^2 + (8-7)^2 + (7-7)^2 + (5-7)^2 +$$
$$(6-7)^2 + (5-7)^2] + [(4-3)^2 + (2-3)^2 + (3-3)^2 + (5-3)^2 + (1-3)^2 + (3-3)^2 +$$
$$(2-3)^2 + (2-3)^2 + (4-3)^2 + (4-4)^2] + [(6-4)^2 + (2-4)^2 + (2-4)^2 + (6-4)^2 +$$
$$(4-4)^2 + (5-4)^2 + (3-4)^2 + (5-4)^2 + (3-4)^2 + (4-4)^2]$$

$$= 1+9+1+1+4+1+0+4+1+4+1+1+0+4+4+0+1+1+1+0+4+4+4+4+0+1+1+1+$$
$$1+1+0$$

$$= 60$$

$$MS_W = 60/(30-3) = 60/27 = 2.22$$

The index of separation, MSB/MSW is called the F-ratio. If certain assumptions are satisfied by our K populations, then the distribution of all possible F-ratios, called an F-distribution, will have a particular shape. We use the F-distribution in much the same way we used the t-distribution, to judge whether our observed statistic, in this case, the observed F-ratio, may be attributable to chance.

THE ASSUMPTIONS OF THE ONE-WAY ANOVA

We make the following assumptions in the one-way ANOVA:

1. The null hypothesis is true.
2. The scores are independent of each other.
3. The parent populations are normally distributed for all groups under study.
4. The parent populations have equal variances (this is called homogeneity of variance) for all groups under study.

Scores are independent if they are randomly selected from their respective parent population so that the selection of scores from one population has no bearing on the selection of scores from any other population. Independence may be achieved if each score is from a separate individual who has been randomly assigned to one of the treatment conditions of the design.

If any of these four conditions is not met, then the statistic obtained may not be distributed as an F-distribution with hypothesized mean difference zero.

In testing the equality of population means, if conditions 2, 3, and 4 are known to be satisfied and an unusual sample outcome is observed, then the plausibility of the remaining condition, condition 1, becomes questionable and one would decide to reject H_0 as implausible.

Thus, it appears that conditions 2, 3, and 4 need to be satisfied in order to test condition 1 using the F-ratio. For this reason, conditions 2, 3, and 4 are usually referred to as the underlying assumptions of the one-way ANOVA.

In actual research situations, we cannot always be certain whether either or both conditions 3 and 4 hold and we must expend some effort to investigate the tenability of these assumptions.

Violations of the assumption of normality do not affect, or only minimally affect, the validity of the ANOVA. That is, ANOVA has been shown to produce correct results even when the data are not normally distributed in the population as long as there are at least 30 subjects in each cell. In statistical terms, we say that ANOVA is *robust* to violations of the assumption of normality (see Glass, Peckham, & Sanders, 1972, for a review of studies on the empirical consequences of failing to meet ANOVA assumptions). In the case of a small data set, however, we recommend checking within cell distributions for outliers and other evidence of nonnormality to ensure that a small set of values does not unduly influence the results of the analysis.

Violations of the assumption of homogeneity of variance do not affect, or only minimally affect, the validity of the ANOVA when cell sizes are large and equal. When sample sizes are unequal and small, however, and when populations have heterogeneous variances, the Type I error rate associated with the F-test will actually be greater than what is reported. For example, under such conditions, a reported p-value of .05 may actually be .10. When samples are larger, yet still unequal in size, and when variances are unequal, there is less distortion in Type I error. That is, reported Type I error levels come closer to actual levels and the effect of unequal variances is reduced when samples are larger.

In the face of heterogeneity of variance, when sample sizes are neither equal nor large, we recommend that the researcher transform scores nonlinearly to reduce heterogeneity. We recommend also that a more stringent Type I error rate (e.g., 0.01 instead of 0.05) be employed under conditions of heterogeneity to compensate for the tendency of the F-test to report p-values in excess of what they truly are.

TESTING THE EQUALITY OF POPULATION MEANS: THE F-RATIO

If the underlying assumptions are satisfied, then the distribution of all possible ratios MS_B/MS_W that could be observed from these populations will form what is called an *F distribution with $K - 1$, $N - K$ degrees of freedom*. The $K - 1$ degrees of freedom are associated with MS_B, in the numerator, and the $N - K$ degrees of freedom are associated with MS_W, in the denominator.

$$F(K - 1, N - K) = MS_B/MS_W \tag{13.5}$$

We use Equation 13.5 to determine whether the ratio MS_B/MS_W based on our sample data is likely to be observed when the null hypothesis of equal population means is true. Because we would reject the null hypothesis in favor of the alternative only when MS_B exceeds MS_W (as in Figure 13.1), we are only interested in situations in which MS_B exceeds MS_W, and consider areas only in the right tail of the F distribution. Whenever the observed F ratio is large enough to be considered unlikely to have occurred by chance (when p is small, say, less than 0.05), we would reject the null hypothesis that all population means are equal in favor of the alternative hypothesis that not all population means are equal.

Like the t-distribution, the F-distribution consists of a family of curves. Unlike the t-distribution, however, the F is defined by two degrees of freedom, one related to the numerator and the other related to the denominator. Equation 13.5 refers to the particular F-distribution that has $K - 1$ degrees of freedom in its numerator and $N - K$ degrees of freedom in its denominator. Figures 13.3(a) to 13.3(d) illustrate four F-distributions each with 27 degrees of freedom in the denominator (as in our example) but with different numbers of degrees of freedom in the numerator; namely, 1, 2, 4, and 16, respectively. The lowest tick on the vertical axis of all four figures represents the probability value of zero.

☞ **Remark.** Notice that as the numerator degrees of freedom increase, the shape of the F-distribution changes considerably and becomes more symmetric. We may note without

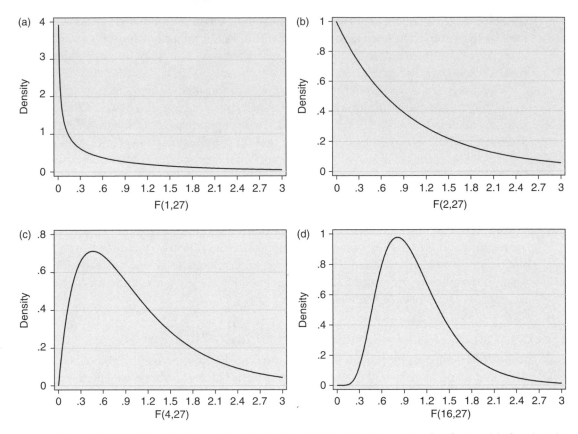

Figure 13.3 (a) The $F(1, 27)$ sampling distribution. (b) The $F(2, 27)$ sampling distribution. (c) The $F(4, 27)$ sampling distribution. (d) The $F(16, 27)$ sampling distribution.

illustration that the shape of the F-distribution remains relatively constant if we change the denominator degrees of freedom but keep the numerator degrees of freedom the same.

HOW TO READ THE TABLES AND USE STATA FUNCTIONS FOR THE F-DISTRIBUTION

Table 3, located in Appendix C online, www.cambridge.org/Stats-Stata, contains an F-distribution summary table that can be used to estimate p-values and F-values that cut off a given area. Two sets of degrees of freedom are associated with the F statistic, one set for the numerator, or variance due to the effect, and one set for the denominator, or within variance. In the case of one-way ANOVA, the numerator degrees of freedom is given by $K - 1$ and the denominator degrees of freedom is given by $N - K$. In Table 3, the top row has the numerator degrees of freedom, whereas the leftmost column has the denominator degrees of freedom. For each pair of numerator and denominator degrees of freedom, there are 6 F-values listed that have area α to their right. For example, we see from the first entry in the table that with 1 degree of freedom in both the numerator and the denominator, $F = 5.83$ has area .25 to its right.

So, the F-value associated with 2 degrees of freedom in the numerator and 3 degrees of freedom in the denominator that has area .05 to its right is 9.55. We may express the

F-value 9.55 associated with 2 degrees of freedom in the numerator and 3 degrees of freedom in the denominator as $F(2, 3) = 9.55$.

• •

EXAMPLE 13.1. Use Table 3 to estimate the p-value associated with the following F-values.

a) $F(2, 3) = 8.66$
b) $F(2, 3) = 1.56$
c) $F(2, 50) = 3.5$

Solution.

a) The table below contains the F-values and corresponding α's or areas to the right associated with 2 degrees of freedom in the numerator and 3 degrees of freedom in the denominator.

F	α
2.28	.25
5.46	.10
9.55	.05
16.04	.03
30.82	.01
148.49	.001

We find that the F-values that are closest to $F = 8.66$ are $F = 5.46$ and $F = 9.55$. The area to the right of $F = 5.46$ is .10 and the area to the right of $F = 9.55$ is .05. The p-value, or the area to the right of $F = 8.66$, is less than .10 but larger than .05. We have the estimate $.05 < p < .10$.

b) We find that the F-value that is closest to $F = 1.56$ is $F = 2.28$. The area to the right of $F = 2.28$ is .25. The p-value, or the area to the right of $F = 1.56$, is greater than .25. We have the estimate $p > .25$.

c) Because the table contains no entry for 50 degrees of freedom in the denominator, we take a conservative approach and use the closest value that is smaller than 50, or $df = 40$. We find the estimate $.03 < p < .05$. We may also get a better estimate of these areas by using the Stata syntax. **Ftail(df1, df2, f)** returns the area to the right of the value F=f. **F(df1, df2, f)** returns the area to the left of the value F=f. In order for us to see the results in the Output Window, as in previous chapters, we use the **display** command as follows to find the area to the right of F = 2.28: **display Ftail(2,3, 2.28)**

Returning to the data of our example, $F(2, 27) = MS_B/MS_W = 43.34/2.22 = 19.52$, which from Figure 13.3(b) appears to fall far into the right tail of the distribution. We will estimate the p-value "by hand" in two ways. First, we will estimate the p-value using Table 3. Then, we will get a better estimate using Stata's **display** command along with its Ftail probability distribution function.

To find the proportion of area to the right of 19.52 (that is, the p-value associated with this $F(2, 27)$) using Table 3, we estimate the denominator degrees of freedom by 26 and see that the closest F-value with 2 degrees of freedom in the numerator and 26 degrees of freedom in the denominator is $F = 9.12$, which has area .001. Because our observed F-value, 19.52, has less area to its right, we obtain the estimate $p < .001$.

MORE Stata: To find the *p*-value associated with an F value with df1, df2

We type the command, **display Ftail(df1, df2, f)**, substituting 19.52 for *f*, 2 for df_1, and 27 for df_2:

display Ftail(2, 27, 19.52)

The value that is returned is given in scientific notation and is equivalent to $p = .0000057$, which equals the area under the curve to right of 19.52. The *p*-value suggests that the probability of observing an *F*-ratio of 19.52 by chance given that the null hypothesis is true (that all population means are equal) is quite small. The α value adopted in this instance is $\alpha = .05$. Accordingly, we reject the null hypothesis in favor of the alternative that not all population means are equal.

Our conclusion is that there are differences in average manual dexterity scores between at least two of the treatments.

For heuristic reasons, we carried out the computations associated with this example by hand. We now show how to use Stata to provide these same results. We assume these data have been input into a data file with two variables, Treatment that signifies the treatment group to which an individual has been assigned and ManualDex that signifies an individual's score on the manual dexterity test.

MORE Stata: To carry out a one-way ANOVA

We type the following syntax into a Do-file or into the Command window based on the *ManDext* data set.

oneway ManualDex Treatment, tabulate

The first variable following the command **oneway** is the dependent variable, and the second variable is the factor, or group, variable. Including **tabulate** as an option computes summary statistics for the treatment groups.

We obtain the following results, including descriptive statistics, the ANOVA summary table, and Bartlett's test for the equality of variances. We turn attention to the last two sets of results.

Recall that when we introduced the *F*-ratio, we assumed that all parent populations under study were normally distributed and had equal variances. However, like the independent groups *t*-test, the ANOVA test has been found to be quite insensitive to violations of normality and to violations of the assumption of equal variances as long as relatively large and equal or approximately equal sample sizes are used.

Because these sample sizes are not large, we evaluate the normality assumption by examining skewness for each group. We do so by running from our Do-file the **tabstat** command that includes the **by(Treatment)** option. Alternatively, as shown in the Do-file associated with this chapter, we could have run the **by Treatment, sort: summarize ManualDex** command with the **detail** option to obtain descriptive statistics, including skewness. The second set of commands will generate the skewness ratio, if desired.

treatmen	Summary of Manual Dexterity		
	Mean	Std. Dev.	Freq.
1	7	1.6996732	10
2	3	1.2472191	10
3	4	1.490712	10
Total	4.6666667	2.2488822	30

	Analysis of Variance				
Source	SS	df	MS	F	Prob > F
Between groups	86.6666667	2	43.3333333	19.50	0.0000
Within groups	60	27	2.22222222		
Total	146.666667	29	5.05747126		

Bartlett's test for equal variances: chi2 (2) = 0.8089   Prob > chi2 = 0.667

MORE Stata: To obtain a table of means, sd's, etc. by a grouping variable

tabstat ManualDex, by (Treatment) statistics(n mean sd min max skewness)

OR

by Treatment, sort: summarize ManualDex, detail

To obtain the skewness ratio, if desired

summskew ManualDex, by(Treatment)

Treatment	N	mean	sd	min	max	skewness
1	10	7	1.699673	5	10	.429351
2	10	3	1.247219	1	5	0
3	10	4	1.490712	2	6	0
Total	30	4.666667	2.248882	1	10	.5173661

For Treatment = 1: skewness = .429351; seskew = .68704289; skewness ratio = .62492603
For Treatment = 2: skewness = 0; seskew = .68704289; skewness ratio = 0
For Treatment = 3: skewness = 0; seskew = .68704289; skewness ratio = 0

We see that all of the skewness values are less than 1 (and all skewness ratios less than 2) so that the normality assumption is tenable.

The ANOVA output includes a test of the underlying assumption of equal (or homogeneous) variances in all cases, even when samples are equal in size. Bartlett's test relies on the F distribution to provide a p-value noted under the column labeled Sig., to test the null hypothesis that all populations have equal variances. Because $p = .518$ ($p > .05$) in this case, we may conclude that the homogeneity of variance assumption is met for these data. In the event that Bartlett's test is statistically significant, we should take this as a warning to check our data for possible outliers and skewness and to think through why one or more group variances would be so different from the others. Of course, as we have argued throughout this text, one should explore the distributional properties of one's sample data before placing confidence in one's summary statistics and using them in tests of inference. In fact, Bartlett's test is less robust to violations of its assumptions than another test, called the Levene's test for the equality of variances, introduced in Chapter 11. To obtain Levene's test in connection with the oneway ANOVA, we use the following Stata command **robvar**, which stands for robust variance tests. Levene's test results are given as a W0 test statistic as shown below.

MORE Stata: To obtain Levene's test for homogeneity of variance

robvar ManualDex, by(Treatment)

And we obtain the following p-value, which corroborates with that of Bartlett's test.

W0 = 0.67500000 df(2, 27) Pr > F = 0.51754064

ANOVA SUMMARY TABLE

The ANOVA summary table provides, in a neatly organized way, the results we obtained by hand. Notice that the F-ratio of 19.5 is reported to have a p-value of .0000. Of course, the p-value is not identically equal to zero, but rather, equals 0 to four decimal places. From our previous computation, we know that the p-value is more closely equal to .000006.

We may note the addition of a row labeled Total in the summary table that contains the sum of SS_B (Between Groups) and SS_W (Within Groups) as well as the sum of their respective degrees of freedom. The total of these sums of squares, denoted SS_T (Total), has its own meaning. It is simply the total variability contained in the entire set of scores when one ignores group membership. As such, it reflects the distance of each individual score from the overall mean and may be calculated using Equation 13.6. If there are N scores total in the data set, then the degrees of freedom associated with SS_T are simply $N - 1$.

$$SS_T = \sum \left(X_{i,j} - \overline{\overline{X}} \right)^2 \tag{13.6}$$

Using some elementary algebra, it can be shown that the sum of squares total is in fact equal to the sum of the sum of squares between and the sum of squares within,

$$SS(\text{Total}) = SS(\text{Between Groups}) + SS(\text{Within Groups}) \tag{13.7}$$

Our earlier ANOVA summary table result (namely that, 146.67 = 60 + 86.67) exemplifies Equation (13.7).

MEASURING THE EFFECT SIZE

Equation 13.7 offers additional insight into ANOVA. Beginning with a data set that contains total variability SS_T, Equation 13.6 implies that ANOVA divides or partitions SS_T into two separate components, SS_B and SS_W. SS_B is that part of SS_T that is accounted for, or explained by, group differences; SS_W is that part of SS_T that is left over, or unexplained, after accounting for such group differences.

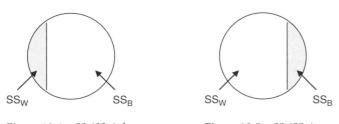

Figure 13.4 SS_B/SS_T is large   **Figure 13.5** SS_B/SS_T is small.

Figures 13.4 and 13.5 illustrate the partitioning of SS_T into these two components under two scenarios. Figure 13.4 corresponds to the scenario depicted in Figure 13.1 in which between group variance is large relative to within group variance, implying that SSB accounts for a large proportion of the variability represented by SS_T. Figure 13.5, on the other hand, corresponds to the scenario depicted in Figure 13.2 in which between group variance is small relative to within group variance, implying that SS_B accounts for a small proportion of the variability represented by SS_T. In Figure 13.5 there is much left over, or *residual*, variability yet to be explained. We shall see in the next chapter that in an attempt to account for or explain this residual variability, one may include another factor (variable) in the design, in addition to, say, treatment group and analyze the degree to which it does account for the residual variance.

Because the ratio SS_B/SS_T reflects the magnitude of the effect of the between groups factor (e.g., treatment group), it is useful as a descriptive measure of effect size, expressed as the degree of association between the dependent variable and grouping variable in the sample. Because the measure is independent of sample size and, as a proportion, ranges from 0 to 1, it provides a useful adjunct to the F-test for statistical significance. It should be noted that SS_B/SS_T provides an overestimate of the proportion of dependent variable variance accounted for by the grouping variable in the population.

Applying this ratio to the data from our example, we find that the proportion of manual dexterity variance explained by treatment is $SS_B/SS_T = 86.67/146.67 = .59$. This proportion may also be expressed as a percentage: 59 percent of the variance in manual dexterity is explained by treatment.

☞ **Remark.** From here on we shall refer to SS_B/SS_T as R^2. Following effect size conventions set forth by Cohen (1988), we offer the following scale for evaluating R^2.

$R^2 = .01$ represents a "small" effect
$R^2 = .09$ represents a "medium" effect
$R^2 = .25$ represents a "large" effect

∙∙∙

EXAMPLE 13.2. Determine whether there are differences in the mean number of years of mathematics studied in high school (unitmath) among the four regions (region)of the country, Northeast, North Central, South, and West, using the *NELS* data. Let $\alpha = 0.01$.

Solution. Because we have *one* grouping variable, or factor, and a dependent variable that is ratio-leveled, we will use one-way ANOVA to find a solution to this problem. Prior to carrying out the ANOVA, we explore our data using the boxplot (see the Do-file associated with this chapter for the exact form of the Stata command we used). Despite the presence of some outliers, these distributions appear to be relatively homogeneous in their variances.

Furthermore, given the large number of cases per category, departures for normality, resulting from the outliers, would not pose a problem to the validity of the *F*-statistic.

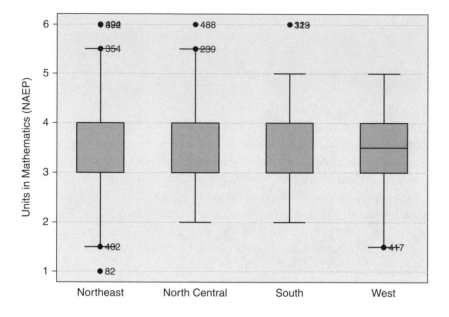

Following the procedure outlined earlier, we run the oneway ANOVA in Stata by using the following syntax:

oneway unitmath region, tabulate

We obtain the following results, which includes a table of means, standard deviations, and frequencies by virtue of having included the option, tabulate in the command:

Geographic Region of School	Summary of Units in Mathematics (NAEP)		
	Mean	Std. Dev.	Freq.
Northeast	3.7920755	.88756995	106
North Cen	3.5322517	.80778889	151
South	3.7752	.73723565	150
West	3.4094624	.75234469	93
Total	3.63738	.80770224	500

	Analysis of Variance				
Source	SS	df	MS	F	Prob > F
Between groups	11. 8856728	3	3.96189095	6.27	0.0004
Within groups	313. 653395	496	.632365716		
Total	325. 539068	499	.652382901		

Bartlett's test for equal variances: chi2 (3) = 4.9584 Prob > chi2 = 0.175

From the table of descriptives, we note that some variation in sample means appears to exist, especially when the Northeast and South are compared to the North Central and West. Students in the West appear to enroll in the fewest number of years of math in high school. We also note that the standard deviations of this variable appear rather homogeneous for all four regions of the country. Bartlett's test corroborates this impression regarding homogeneity of variance as $p = .175$ for this test. Given the large sample size, very small deviations from equality would have been detected. Hence, we can place confidence in Bartlett's test that for these data, the assumption of homogeneity of variance is met.

According to the ANOVA summary table, we note that the obtained $F(3, 496) = 6.27$ with $p < .0005$, suggesting that it is highly unlikely that the null hypothesis (H_0: $\mu_1 = \mu_2 = \mu_3 = \mu_4 = 0$) is true. Our data are more consistent with the alternative hypothesis that a difference among means exists. Hence, we reject the null in favor of the alternative.

We note, however, that $SS_B/SS_T = 11.89/325.54 = 3.7$ percent, suggesting that region by itself accounts for a very small proportion of unitmath variance. Clearly, other factors need to be considered in addition to region to explain the residual variance in number of years taken in high school (that is, the variance that remains after region has been accounted for).

Even though Bartlett's test was not significant, suggesting that the homogeneity of variance assumption is met for these data, we apply the bootstrap technique to obtain a robust bootstrap estimate of the standard error of the F-statistic, one that does not rely on homogeneity of variance across groups, to see if the F-statistic, using this nonparametric resampling approach, continues to be statistically significant. The F-statistic is deemed to be statistically significant if the p-value associated with the z-test given in the output is less than 0.05.

We use the following command to find 1,000 bootstrap-derived F-statistics, which we have named, F_bs, for this oneway ANOVA. r(F) is the name given by Stata to the variable that contains the value of the F-statistic computed as part of the ANOVA procedure; it is included in the list of such statistics when we type the command, **return list**, following the ANOVA command. Using the expression F_bs = r(F), we are assigning the name F_bs to r(F) so as to label it more clearly as an F-statistic estimated in connection with the bootstrap procedure.

MORE Stata: To obtain bootstrap-derived F-statistics and related confidence intervals for our oneway ANOVA

bootstrap F_bs=r(F),reps(1000)nodots seed(999):oneway unitmath region, tabulate
estat bootstrap, all

This syntax will provide 1,000 bootstrap estimates for the *F*-statistic generated by the oneway ANOVA, one on each of the 1,000 replications specified by **reps(1000)**. The bootstrap standard error of the *F*-statistic that is given in the output is derived from the variation in F-statistics obtained on the 1,000 empirically-derived samples drawn randomly with replacement. The standard error of the *F*-statistic is not derived theoretically, and is therefore not based on the tenability of underlying assumptions.

The output for this analysis appears as such:

Bootstrap results
Number of obs   =   500
Replications   =   1000

command : oneway unitmath region, tabulate
F_bs : r(F)

	Observed Coef.	Bootstrap Std. Err.	z	P>|z|	Normal-based [95% Conf. Interval]	
F_bs	6.265189	3.116969	2.01	0.044	.1560427	12.37434

. estat bootstrap, all / *prints the estimated F-value with confidence intervals based on the bootstrap method*/

Bootstrap results
Number of obs   =   500
Replications   =   1000

command: oneway unitmath region, tabulate
F_bs: r(F)

	Observed Coef.	Bias	Bootstrap Std. Err.	[95% Conf.	Interval]	
F_bs	6.2651894	1.253704	3.1169688	.1560427	12.37434	(N)
				2.454842	14.328	(P)
				1.777729	12.06727	(BC)

(N)   normal confidence interval
(P)   percentile confidence interval
(BC)   bias-corrected confidence interval

We may note that the z-test of the F_bs statistic has $p = 0.044$, which is less than 0.05, and therefore statistically significant. Accordingly, these results corroborate the finding from our original ANOVA, which found the F-statistic to be statistically significant and allowed us to reject the null hypothesis of equal population means.

☞ **Remark.** The command **estat bootstrap, all** instructs Stata to print three estimates of the confidence interval for the estimated F-statistic value. The first is based on normal theory (*normal confidence interval*), the second on a straightforward calculation of the 2.5th and 97.5th percentiles of the distribution of estimated F-statistic values (*percentile confidence interval*), and the third is based on a bias-corrected version of the percentile confidence interval (*bias-corrected confidence interval*). Because the F-statistic is a ratio of variances, it is always positive and so we cannot use our usual method for judging whether a statistic is statistically significant by whether the value of 0 is contained in the confidence interval or not. Nonetheless, printing the percentile and bias-corrected confidence intervals, which are based on the empirically-derived standard error, gives us an idea of the estimated range of values for the F-statistic, and, in particular, its lower bound.

Now that we know that we can reject the null hypothesis that the unitmath means across regions are different in the population, a natural question that arises is which specific region means are different from which others?

Unfortunately, the *F*-test tells us nothing about which means are different, only that not all of them are equal. To find out where specific mean differences exist based on our observation of the data, we use, what are called, *post-hoc* tests. Post-hoc refers to the fact that we are using the data to decide which comparisons to make; that our decisions are made *after the fact* of obtaining a statistically significant result from the ANOVA and knowing, therefore, that not all population means are equal.

POST-HOC MULTIPLE COMPARISON TESTS

Our goal in conducting post-hoc tests is to extract as much meaningful information from our data as possible while still maintaining the family-wise error rate at a reasonable level. A large number of post-hoc tests exist and recommendations for choosing among them are plentiful. In this book we present two post-hoc tests that are appropriate when one is interested in making only pairwise comparisons between means. We do so because we believe that most applied research that employs an ANOVA-type design is concerned ultimately with ordering the means of the *K* groups on the dependent variable and a series of pairwise comparisons is useful for this purpose.

Tukey's Honestly Significant Difference (HSD), developed in 1953, directly maintains the family-wise error rate at the chosen level regardless of how many pairwise comparisons are made. The sampling distribution for the HSD is called the *Studentized range distribution*. This distribution is based on the expectation that: (1) for random samples drawn from a normal population, the larger the size of the sample, the larger the difference should be between the extreme values in the sample (i.e., the range of the sample); and (2) when *K* samples are selected from a normal population, the larger *K* is, the larger the difference should be between the extreme sample means.

Accordingly, when *K* is greater than two (which it is in an ANOVA-type design), we would expect a larger difference between the two extreme means than if *K* were only two. The HSD takes this into account by increasing the size of the critical values (or equivalently, by reducing the size of the critical regions, α) associated with statistical significance. In so doing, the HSD makes it more difficult to obtain statistical significance for each comparison and maintains the overall family-wise error rate at the chosen value, say .05.

The formula for the Tukey test for comparing the means of treatment groups *j* and *k* is given by Equation 13.8 where *q*, called the *Studentized range statistic*, represents a value in the Studentized range distribution and the sample sizes for groups *j* and *k* are equal:

$$q = \frac{\overline{X}_j - \overline{X}_k}{\sqrt{\dfrac{MS_w}{n}}} \tag{13.8}$$

where $\overline{X}_j$ and $\overline{X}_k$ are the sample means from treatment groups *j* and *k*, respectively and $\overline{X}_j > \overline{X}_k$. MS_w is the value of the mean square within from the original ANOVA; and *n* is the common sample size for all treatment groups.

When the treatment groups do not all have a common sample size, an approximate Tukey HSD test statistic can be computed by substituting n' for *n*, where n' is the harmonic mean of the sample sizes of all the treatment groups. The equation for computing the harmonic mean is:

$$n' = \frac{K}{\left[\dfrac{1}{n_1} + \dfrac{1}{n_2} + ... + \dfrac{1}{n_K}\right]} \tag{13.9}$$

Critical values of the Studentized range statistic are provided in Table 6 of Appendix C online, www.cambridge.org/Stats-Stata. Like the F-test associated with the original ANOVA, the Tukey HSD is a test of a nondirectional alternative hypothesis, but uses only the right tail of the sampling distribution for the rejection region. To use Table 6, one needs both the degrees of freedom associated with the number of treatment groups in the original ANOVA design, K, and the MS_w term from the original ANOVA, df_w.

Another test, Fisher's Least Significant Difference (LSD), known also as the protected t-test, developed in 1935, is not as effective in maintaining the overall family-wise error at the chosen value. The sampling distribution for the LSD is the t-distribution. That is, given a statistically significant F-test associated with the original ANOVA (called the *omnibus F-test*), the LSD follows with a series of t-tests to compare means pairwise. If the original F-test is not statistically significant and the original null hypothesis is not rejected, no further testing would be performed.

The difference between the LSD and a series of t-tests is the requirement of a rejection of the original null hypothesis at the chosen level α. Because the risk of a Type I error in conjunction with the omnibus test is maintained at α, the series of t-tests following a statistically significant ANOVA will be carried out mistakenly (when all population means are truly equal) only 5 times in 100 (if $\alpha = .05$). In this way, a statistically significant omnibus ANOVA protects the t-tests carried out subsequently. However, statisticians have pointed out that under certain circumstances, such protection is not enough; the LSD family-wise Type I error may exceed α by some unknown extent that depends, in part, upon the number of pairwise comparisons made.

The choice between the HSD and LSD must depend upon the philosophies and beliefs of the researcher. As we shall demonstrate in our examples, the LSD is generally more powerful than the HSD because for each pairwise comparison, the LSD uses α whereas the HSD uses a reduced α so as to maintain the overall family-wise error rate. Thus, the LSD is able to detect true differences with greater power. On the other hand, the LSD runs a greater risk of committing a Type I error, of declaring a difference between means where there truly is none. Thus, as a researcher, one must consider the number of pairwise comparisons to be made and weigh the risks of both types of error, Type I and Type II, in deciding which procedure makes sense in a particular case.

Alternatively, one could use both procedures and draw conclusions based on the results of both. If results are consistent for the two approaches, then the conclusions to be drawn are clear. If they do not agree, then careful thinking must be done to balance the relative risks of Type I and Type II errors, taking into account the number of comparisons made and other relevant factors particular to the issue being studied. Such thinking should be made public in say, a report of final results, so that a reader or listener can understand the researcher's process in reaching the reported conclusions. With this information, the reader can then decide whether to agree or disagree with these conclusions and to suggest others of his own.

In addition to these two tests, other multiple comparison tests covered in this text are the Scheffe and Bonferroni tests. Both of these tests are provided along with the output from Stata's **oneway** ANOVA procedure.

· ·

EXAMPLE 13.3. Use the Bonferroni, Scheffe, LSD, and Tukey HSD post-hoc tests to determine which methods of therapeutic treatment on manual dexterity for the drug rehabilitation center population are different from which others. Let $\alpha = 0.05$.

Solution. We recall that a statistically significant omnibus F-test was obtained in connection with this example, indicating that not all three population means are equal. From the table of summary statistics, we note that the three treatment group means are: $\bar{X}_1 = 7, \bar{X}_2 = 3, \bar{X}_3 = 4$. Accordingly, the mean difference between groups 1 and 2 is 4; between groups 1 and 3 is 3; and between groups 2 and 3 is –1.

To carry out the Tukey HSD test by hand, we compute Equation 13.8 for each pair of treatment means because in this case, $n_1 = n_2 = n_3 = 10$. From the original ANOVA, we note that $MS_w = 2.22$ and $df_w = 27$ and $K = 3$.

(1) Comparing μ_1 and μ_2:

$$q = \frac{7-3}{\sqrt{\dfrac{2.22}{10}}} = \frac{4}{0.47} = 8.49$$

Table 6 in Appendix C online, www.cambridge.org/Stats-Stata does not list $df_w = 27$ exactly, and so we will use the more conservative values associated with $df_w = 30$. In doing so, we find that 8.49 exceeds 3.49, the critical value associated with $p = .05$ when $K = 3$. Hence, we conclude that $\mu_1 \neq \mu_2$ and $p < .05$.

(2) Comparing μ_1 and μ_3:

$$q = \frac{7-4}{\sqrt{\dfrac{2.22}{10}}} = \frac{3}{0.47} = 6.38$$

As in the previous case, 6.38 exceeds 3.49, the critical value associated with $p = .05$ when $K = 3$ and $df_w = 28$. Hence, we conclude that $\mu_1 \neq \mu_3$ and $p < .05$.

(3) Comparing μ_2 and μ_3:

$$q = \frac{4-3}{\sqrt{\dfrac{2.22}{10}}} = \frac{1}{0.47} = 2.13$$

The value of 2.13 is less than 3.49, the critical value associated with $p = .05$ when $K = 3$ and $df_w = 28$. Hence, we conclude that $\mu_2 = \mu_3$ and $p > .05$.

Because we already have computed the independent groups t-test by hand, we do not carry out the LSD post-hoc test by hand. Rather, we rely solely on Stata to carry out this protected t-test.

MORE Stata: To obtain Bonferroni and Scheffe test results

We simply add the following syntax to the end of the **oneway** command:

oneway ManualDex Treatment, bonferroni scheffe

Alternatively, we may use the **pwmean** command as follows:

pwmean ManualDex, over(Treatment) mcompare(bonferroni) effects
pwmean ManualDex, over(Treatment) mcompare(scheffe) effects

To compute the Tukey and LSD (unadjusted) tests, we use the **pwmean** command:

pwmean ManualDex, over(Treatment) mcompare(tukey) effects
pwmean ManualDex, over(Treatment) mcompare(noadj) effects

The output from the Bonferroni and Scheffe post-hoc comparisons is as follows:

Analysis of Variance

Source	SS	df	MS	F	Prob > F
Between groups	86.6666667	2	43.3333333	19.50	0.0000
Within groups	60	27	2.22222222		
Total	146.666667	29	5.05747126		

Bartlett's test for equal variances: chi2 (2) = 0.8089 Prob > chi2 = 0.667

Comparison of Manual Dexterity by Treatment (Bonferroni)

Row Mean–Col Mean	1	2
2	−4 0.000	
3	−3 0.001	1 0.436

Comparison of Manual Dexterity by Treatment (Scheffe)

Row Mean–Col Mean	1	2
2	−4 0.000	
3	−3 0.001	1 0.339

And, the output from the LSD and Tukey post-hoc comparison tests is as follows:

Pairwise comparisons of means with equal variances

over   :   Treatment

ManualDex	Contrast	Std. Err.	Undjusted t	P > |t|	Unadjusted [95% Conf.	Interval]
Treatment						
2 vs 1	−4	.6666667	−6.00	0.000	−5.367887	−2.632113
3 vs 1	−3	.6666667	−4.50	0.000	−4.367887	−1.632113
3 vs 2	1	.6666667	1.50	0.145	−.367887	2.367887

.pwmean ManualDex, over (Treatment) mcompare (tukey) effects

Pairwise comparisons of means with equal variances

over   :   Treatment

	Numberof Comparisons
Treatment	3

ManualDex	Contrast	Std. Err.	Tukey t	P > |t|	Tukey [95% Conf.	Interval]
Treatment						
2 vs 1	−4	.6666667	−6.00	0.000	−5.652945	−2.347055
3 vs 1	−3	.6666667	−4.50	0.000	−4.652945	−1.347055
3 vs 2	1	.6666667	1.50	0.307	−.6529451	2.652945

Although the specific p-values do not duplicate each other across methods, the results from all methods inform us that the mean difference between groups 1 and 2 is statistically significant ($p < .0005$) as is the mean difference between groups 1 and 3 ($p < .0005$). (The p-values are found in the column labeled Sig. and have been written as "< .0005" instead of "= .000" to reflect that they are not exactly equal to zero.) However, the mean difference between groups 2 and 3 is not statistically significant ($p > .140$).

EXAMPLE 13.4. Use the Bonferroni, Scheffe, LSD, and HSD post-hoc tests to determine which specific regions of the country are different from which others in terms of the mean numbers of years of math taken in high school. Let $\alpha = 0.05$.

Solution. We recall that a statistically significant omnibus F-test was obtained in connection with this example, indicating that the observed sample mean differences are not attributable to random sampling error. From the table of descriptive statistics, we note that the four treatment group means are: $\overline{X}_{NE} = 3.79, \overline{X}_{NC} = 3.53, \overline{X}_S = 3.78, \overline{X}_W = 3.41$. The mean differences between groups, along with their respective statistical significance values, are given in the Multiple Comparisons table obtained from Stata using the procedure detailed above and in the Do-file associated with this chapter.

The output from the Bonferroni and Scheffe post-hoc comparisons is below:

		Analysis of Variance				
Source	SS		df	MS	F	Prob > F
Between groups	11.8856728		3	3.96189095	6.27	0.0004
Within groups	313.653395		496	.632365716		
Total	325.539068		499	.652382901		

Bartlett's test for equal variances: chi2(3) = 4.9584 Prob > chi2 = 0.175

Comparison of Units in Mathematics (NAEP) by Geographic Region of School
(Bonferroni)

Row Mean-Col Mean	Northeas	North Ce	South
North Ce	−.259824 0.061		
South	−.016875 1.000	.242948 0.050	
West	−.382613 0.005	−.122789 1.000	−.365738 0.003

Comparison of Units in Mathematics (NAEP) by Geographic Region of School
(Scheffe)

Row Mean-Col Mean	Northeas	North Ce	South
North Ce	−.259824 0.085		
South	−.016875 0.999	.242948 0.072	
West	−.382613 0.010	−.122789 0.712	−.365738 0.007

The output from the LSD and Tukey tests is as follows:

According to the Bonferroni post-hoc comparison, there are statistically significant differences in the units of math taken between the Northeast and West, the Northeast and North Central and the Northeast and South, and between the South and West. The difference

Pairwise comparisons of means with equal variances

over   : region

unitmath	Contrast	Std. Err.	Unadjusted t	P > |t|	Unadjusted [95% Conf.	Interval]
region						
North Central vs Northeast	−.2598238	.1007649	−2.58	0.010	−.4578025	−.0618451
South vs Northeast	−.0168755	.1009033	−0.17	0.867	−.2151262	.1813752
West vs Northeast	−.3826131	.1129838	−3.39	0.001	−.604599	−.1606272
South vs North Central	.2429483	.0916713	2.65	0.008	.0628364	.4230603
West vs North Central	−.1227893	.1048212	−1.17	0.242	−.3287376	.083159
West vs South	−.3657376	.1049543	−3.48	0.001	−.5719474	−.1595278

. pwmean unitmath, over (region) mcompare (tukey) effects

Pairwise comparisons of means with equal variances

over   : region

	Number of Comparisons
region	6

unitmath	Contrast	Std. Err.	Tukey t	P > |t|	Tukey [95% Conf.	Interval]
region						
North Central vs Northeast	−.2598238	.1007649	−2.58	0.050	−.5195717	−.0000759
South vs Northeast	−.0168755	.1009033	−0.17	0.998	−.2769802	.2432293
West vs Northeast	−.3826131	.1129838	−3.39	0.004	−.6738585	−.0913678
South vs North Central	.2429483	.0916713	2.65	0.041	.0066417	.479255
West vs North Central	−.1227893	.1048212	−1.17	0.645	−.3929933	.1474147
West vs South	−.3657376	.1049543	−3.48	0.003	−.6362847	−.0951905

between the Northeast and North Central is close to being significant, but the significance level exceeds 05.

The Scheffe post-hoc comparison is the most conservative of all of these, and so the p-values are, in general, larger for this procedure than for the others. For the results of this test, only the South and West and the Northeast and West are statistically significantly different in terms of the variable, units of math taken.

By contrast to the Scheffe, the LSD is the most powerful procedure, and results in the smallest *p*-values and the greatest number of significant differences.

The HSD is intermediate in power between the Scheffe and the LSD. For the HSD, the Northeast differs statistically significantly from the North Central and West, the North Central differs from the Northeast and South, the South differs from the North Central and West, and the West differs from the Northeast and South.

EXAMPLE 13.5. Does twelfth grade self-concept vary as a function of one of three types of high school program (rigorous academic, academic, vocational and other)? Notice that for this example, the variable HSPROG was recoded so that the categories Some Vocational and Other form a single category. The Stata syntax for doing this recoding is given in the Do-file associated with this chapter. Use the *NELS* data set and let $\alpha = 0.01$.

Solution. Given that type of high school program represents groups or categories and the dependent variable, twelfth grade self-concept, may be considered to be interval-leveled, we use one-way ANOVA to find a solution to the question. To check assumptions and get a sense of what our data look like, we obtain the following boxplots.

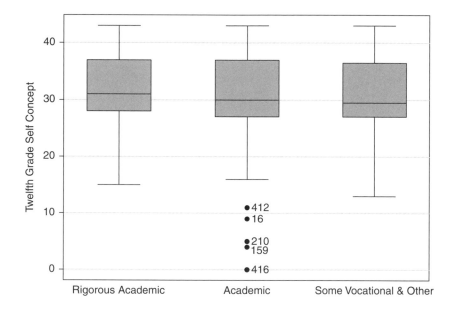

According to the boxplots, aside from the five cases of relatively low self-concept in the academic program category, the distributions appear relatively homogeneous in their variances. Furthermore, given the large number of cases per category, departures from normality resulting, for example, from the five cases of low self-concept in the academic category, would not pose a problem to the validity of the *F*-statistic. We may also note that based on the boxplots alone twelfth grade self-concept does not appear to vary as a function of high school program type.

We turn to the one-way ANOVA to see whether these sample results are upheld in the population using the following commands. Recall that the robvar command computes Levene's test.

oneway slfcnc12 hsprog3, tabulate
robvar slfcnc12, by(hsprog3)

The output is as follows:
And, like Bartlett's test, Levene's test is not statistically significant:

W0 = 1.3708216 df(2, 497) Pr > F = 0.25485655

Type of High School Program	Summary of Twelfth Grade Self Concept		
	Mean	Std. Dev.	Freq.
Rigorous	31.973154	6.4377962	149
Academic	31.326165	7.5568157	279
Some Voca	31.055556	7.5318832	72
Total	31.48	7.2311949	500

Analysis of Variance

Source	SS	df	MS	F	Prob > F
Between groups	55.8106084	2	27.9053042	0.53	0.5874
Within groups	26036.9894	497	52.3883086		
Total	26092.8	499	52.2901804		

Bartlett's test for equal variances: chi2 (2) = 5.0390 Prob> chi2 = 0.081

Like the boxplot medians, the means are quite homogeneous suggesting that it is unlikely that self-concept varies with type of high school program. We may note that, as expected, both Bartlett's and Levene's test are nonsignificant, and the homogeneity of variance assumption is met for these data. The obtained $F = .533$ for the oneway ANOVA is nonsignificant ($p = .587$), confirming the impression that the means are not statistically significantly different from each other.

Because there are no differences among self-concept means ($p = .587$), no further testing is warranted. Our conclusion is simply that a student's self-concept does not appear to be linked to the type of high school program in which that student is enrolled. While self-concept does vary from individual to individual ($SS_{TOT} = 26093$ units), the amount of that variability due to the type high school program in which that individual is enrolled is quite low ($SS_B = 56$ units). Other factors need to be considered if we are to understand why there is variability among students in self-concept. Ways to consider these other factors analytically are discussed in the next chapter.

EXAMPLE 13.6. Is there a relationship between school attendance rate and region? Said differently, does school attendance rate depend upon the location of the school, whether it is in the Northeast, North Central, South, or West? Let $\alpha = 0.05$.

Solution. Given that there is one grouping variable, region, and that the dependent variable, school attendance rate, is ratio-leveled, a one-way ANOVA is appropriate for answering this question. Following a logical sequence of steps in the analysis, we first examine the data using the boxplot.

While there are a number of extreme values per region to suggest skewness, there are two cases of particular concern: ID #64 and ID #396. From the *NELS* data set itself, we see that

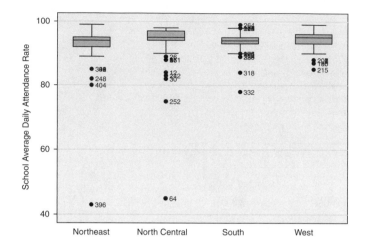

the schools that these students attended had average daily attendance rates of 45 and 43, respectively.

We have discussed two ways of handling such outliers. First, if the values are suspicious, it may make sense to eliminate them and report results based on two analyses, one with outliers excluded and another with outliers included. Second, a nonlinear transformation may be applied to reduce the influence of the outliers while using all of the available data in the analysis. Because secondary school attendance rates of 45 percent and 43 percent are suspiciously low, we have chosen here to conduct the analysis without these two cases. The Do-file associated with this chapter contains the commands used to generate the analyses, both with and without the two outliers.

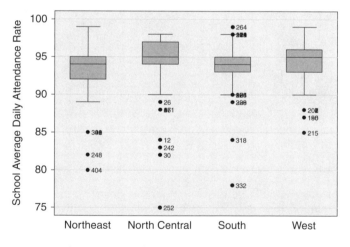

Once these two outliers are eliminated, as depicted by boxplots, the variances of the four regions appear to be more reasonably homogeneous. Furthermore, the number of cases per region is sufficiently high for us not to be concerned about violations of the normality assumption. We note that although the vast majority of schools have a daily attendance rate in excess of 90 percent, there does appear to be some waiver in the actual levels of attendance by region. We turn to the ANOVA to determine whether this observed waiver is significant of differences among the respective population means, or whether it may be attributable to random sampling error.

Geographic Region of School	Summary of School Average Daily Attendance Rate		
	Mean	Std. Dev.	Freq.
Northeast	92.954545	3.3284185	88
North Cen	94.403101	3.3715709	129
South	93.913386	2.8256861	127
West	94.070423	3.067451	71
Total	93.889157	3.1839351	415

	Analysis of Variance				
Source	SS	df	MS	F	Prob > F
Between groups	113.349132	3	37.783044	3.80	0.0104
Within groups	4083.55207	411	9.93564981		
Total	4196.9012	414	10.1374425		

Bartlett's test for equal variances: chi2 (3) = 4.6336 Prob > chi2 = 0.201

And, the results of Levene's test are:

$W0 = 1.66309909$ $df(3, 413)$ $Pr > F = 0.17434885$

Results based on both Bartlett's and Levene's test suggest that, as expected, population variances are homogeneous, and there is a statistically significant difference among school mean daily attendance rates ($F(3,411) = 3.80$, $p = .01$). We note that while the result is statistically significant, $R^2 = 113/4197 = .027$, indicating that only 3 percent of the variance in average daily attendance rate can be explained by region, a reasonably small effect.

Because the omnibus F-test is statistically significant, however, we seek to continue our analysis to determine which specific means are statistically significantly different from which others. That is, starting with a global analysis of all four means considered simultaneously, we proceed to a local analysis that deals with comparisons between specific means taken pairwise. The results of the Bonferroni, Sheffe, LSD, and Tukey HSD *post-hoc* comparisons are provided below.

Comparison of School Average Daily Attendance Rate by Geographic Region of School (Bonferroni)			
Row Mean-Col Mean	Northeas	North Ce	South
North Ce	1.44856 0.006		
South	.95884 0.173	−.489715 1.000	
West	1.11588 0.162	−.332678 1.000	.157037 1.000

(continued)

Comparison of School Average Daily Attendance Rate by Geographic Region of School (Scheffe)			
Row Mean-Col Mean	Northeas	North Ce	South
North Ce	1.44856 0.012		
South	.95884 0.188	−.489715 0.672	
West	1.11588 0.179	−.332678 0.917	.157037 0.990

Pairwise comparisons of means with equal variances

over   : region

schattrt	Contrast	Std. Err.	Unadjusted t	Unadjusted P > |t|	Unadjusted [95% Conf.	Interval]
region						
North Central vs Northeast	1.629818	.6412773	2.54	0.011	.369244	2.890393
South vs Northeast	1.520127	.644348	2.36	0.019	.2535167	2.786738
West vs Northeast	1.677164	.7416966	2.26	0.024	.2191929	3.135135
South vs North Central	−.1096911	.5815452	−0.19	0.850	−1.252849	1.033467
West vs North Central	.0473456	.6878403	0.07	0.945	−1.304759	1.39945
West vs South	.1570367	.6907041	0.23	0.820	−1.200697	1.514771

. pwmean schattrt, over (region) mcompare (tukey) effects

Pairwise comparisons of mean swith equal variances

over   : region

	Number of Comparisons
region	6

schattrt	Contrast	Std. Err.	Tukey t	Tukey P > |t|	Tukey [95% Conf.	Interval]
region						
North Central vs Northeast	1.629818	.6412773	2.54	0.055	−.0243697	3.284007
South vs Northeast	1.520127	.644348	2.36	0.087	−.1419818	3.182237
West vs Northeast	1.677164	.7416966	2.26	0.109	−.2360578	3.590386
South vs North Central	−.1096911	.5815452	−0.19	0.998	−1.609799	1.390417
West vs North Central	.0473456	.6878403	0.07	1.000	−1.726953	1.821644
West vs South	.1570367	.6907041	0.23	0.996	−1.624649	1.938722

Results of the Bonferroni and Scheffe *post-hoc* tests suggest that the daily attendance rate in the Northeast is significantly different (and larger) than the daily attendance rate in the North central region. That comparison, however, is the only statistically significant difference.

Likewise, the HSD suggests that differences in school mean daily attendance rate are limited to the Northeast and North Central ($p=.055$), and that the North Central, South, and West are not different from each other in this respect nor are the Northeast, South and West. In the HSD analysis, the Northeast stands apart from only the North Central.

By contrast, the LSD procedure suggests that the Northeast region is different from all others in terms of school daily attendance rate.

It seems plausible to conclude that the school daily attendance rate in the Northeast is different from that in the North Central. Notice that these two regions occupy the extremes in a ranking of regions based on mean school daily attendance rates and that the difference between them equals a little bit more than one percentage point.

Even though the LSD test suggests that the Northeast region differs from all others in terms of school daily attendance rate, we recommend following the results of the more conservative tests that there are no differences between other pairs of regions, but for the Northeast and North Central. Whether this result represents the actual truth or not, our recommendation is based on a decision to be more conservative rather than less in our risk of committing a Type I error. It also takes into account the size of the effect, on how meaningful such differences are in substantive terms.

We note only small, nonsubstantive differences between the ANOVA results based on all values, including the two outliers that were eliminated from this analysis and on the set of values without the two outliers. By eliminating these outliers, we gained in variance stability without compromising the substantive conclusions of our findings.

☞ **Remark.** It sometimes happens that although the omnibus *F*-test is statistically significant, none of the *post-hoc* pairwise comparisons is statistically significant. Such contradictory results are due to the fact that our inferential estimates are subject to sampling error and that the omnibus *F*-test is more powerful than the multiple comparison tests that follow. Results based on the *F*-distribution, the sampling distribution of means for testing the null hypothesis that all K population means are equal, may not agree with results based on an appropriate, yet different, sampling distribution of means based on particular pairwise comparisons. To reduce the probability of such logically contradictory results, we need to reduce the effects of sampling error so that our estimates are more precise and our tests are more powerful. A natural way to do so is through the use of larger samples.

☞ **Remark.** Other logical inconsistencies arise from the presence of random sampling error, which would not arise if we were able to compute the population parameters directly from the entire population, rather than from a random sample of that population. For example, we may observe, based on our sample data, that $\overline{X}_1 \neq \overline{X}_2 \neq \overline{X}_3$. After taking into account sampling error through the inferential process, we may conclude that $\mu_1 = \mu_2$ and that $\mu_2 = \mu_3$, but that $\mu_1 \neq \mu_3$. That is, the observed differences between $\overline{X}_1$ and $\overline{X}_2$, and between $\overline{X}_2$ and $\overline{X}_3$ are close enough to be attributable to random sampling error, while the observed difference between $\overline{X}_1$ and $\overline{X}_3$ is not. We may note that the inferred pattern of population mean differences appears to contradict the rule of transitivity, that things equal to the same thing are equal to each other. While μ_1 and μ_3 are both equal to μ_2, μ_1 and μ_3 are not equal to each other. The point simply is that in the presence of sampling error, such logical inconsistencies are possible!

THE BONFERRONI ADJUSTMENT: TESTING PLANNED COMPARISONS

In each of the examples presented in this chapter, an analysis of variance was used to test a *global hypothesis* about the equality of means. Following a significant omnibus F-test, and a review of the data obtained, post-hoc multiple comparison tests were then conducted to investigate whether any of the observed mean differences were statistically significant. Sometimes, however, *specific hypotheses* motivate a researcher to plan and conduct a particular study. As we shall discuss in this section, the Bonferroni test may be used for planned comparisons as well.

In our drug rehabilitation example, Treatments I, II, and III were described merely as different types of treatment that were suspected of having a differential effect on manual dexterity. Accordingly, the purpose of the study was to test a general hypothesis about the equality of population means associated with Treatments I, II, and III. If, on the other hand, however, Treatment III had been designed as a control or placebo condition, our interest might naturally have focused on conducting only two specific comparisons – that of Treatments I and II against the control Treatment III. In fact, in the initial planning of the design for this study, we might have designated Treatment III as the control or placebo so as to draw conclusions about these specific and presumably meaningful comparisons.

Specific comparisons that derive directly from the questions that motivate a researcher to plan a study in the first place are called *planned comparisons*. The use of planned comparisons is an alternative to the analysis of variance that is made without regard to an omnibus F-test. While the method of planned comparisons offers a direct method for testing the specific questions posed, its limitation is that it does not allow for other un-anticipated questions to be addressed. For that, one requires the more general approach of the one-way analysis of variance.

To carry out a test of planned comparisons, we must recognize the fact that planned comparisons are another form of multiple comparisons, and as such, give rise to an inflated family-wise Type I error rate. Without adjustment, α_{FW} for these two planned comparisons (Treatment I versus Treatment III and Treatment II versus Treatment III) approximately equals $1-(1 - .05)^2 = .0975$. A similar result is obtained from Equation 13.2, which states that α_{FW} will approximately be equal to, albeit less than, $K\alpha$, where K is the number of planned comparisons. In this example, $K\alpha = 2(.05) = .10$.

Thus, we may use Equation 13.2 to adjust the overall family-wise Type I error to be equal to the desired level, say .05, by dividing .05 by K. We would then conduct each of the K planned comparisons at the new per-comparison error rate, α_{FW}/K, so as to maintain the overall α_{FW} at .05. For a comparison to be called statistically significant, the obtained p-value associated with this comparison must be less than α_{FW}/K. If $K = 3$ and we wish to maintain α_{FW} at .05, then each per-comparison α level must be set at $.05/3 = .017$. This adjustment to the per-comparison α level is called the *Bonferroni adjustment* as it is based on the equation developed by Bonferroni.

Clearly, the greater the number of planned comparisons, the smaller each per comparison α must be to maintain α_{FW} at .05. Because the smaller the per-comparison α, the lower the power of each test, Bonferroni adjustments should be reserved for situations in which K is relatively small.

● ●

EXAMPLE 13.7. Suppose that a series of recent publications in demography indicated that rural areas have lower socioeconomic status than either suburban or urban areas. Use planned comparisons to test whether this result is replicated in the *NELS* data set. Control the family-wise Type I error rate at 0.05.

Solution. To answer this question, we need to draw comparisons: rural SES with suburban SES, and rural SES with urban SES. These comparisons form a family of comparisons and each comparison may be tested using an independent group t-test. To control αFW at 0.05, we use the Bonferroni adjustment and divide .05 by 2. Each pairwise comparison is conducted at 0.025. The results of the two t-tests are given below. The specific commands that were used in carrying out these analyses are provided in the Do-file associated with this chapter.

Urban versus Rural

Urban Versus Rural

Two-sample t test with equal variances

Group	Obs	Mean	Std. Err.	Std. Dev.	[95% Conf.	Interval]
Urban	123	20.3252	.6240008	6.920504	19.08993	21.56048
Rural	162	15.94444	.5110729	6.504895	14.93517	16.95372
combined	285	17.83509	.4158529	7.020405	17.01654	18.65363
diff		4.380759	.7997581		2.806529	5.954988

diff = mean (Urban) - mean (Rural)   t =   5.4776
Ho: diff = 0   degrees of freedom =   283

Ha: diff < 0   Ha: diff ! = 0   Ha: diff > 0
Pr (T < t) = 1.0000   Pr (|T| > |t|) = 0.0000   Pr (T > t) = 0.0000

Suburban versus Rural

Suburban Versus Rural

Two-sample t test with equal variances

Group	Obs	Mean	Std. Err.	Std. Dev.	[95% Conf.	Interval]
Suburban	215	19.22791	.4589148	6.729011	18.32333	20.13248
Rural	162	15.94444	.5110729	6.504895	14.93517	16.95372
combined	377	17.81698	.3513454	6.821893	17.12613	18.50782
diff		3.283463	.6901619		1.92639	4.640535

diff = mean (Suburban) – mean (Rural)   t =   4.7575
Ho: diff = 0   degrees of freedom =   375

Ha: diff < 0   Ha: diff ! = 0   Ha: diff > 0
Pr (T < t) = 1.0000   Pr (|T| > |t|) = 0.0000   Pr (T > t) = 0.0000

Because both two-tailed p-values are $p < .0005$, the two corresponding one-tailed p-values will be $p < .00025$. Because both observed p-values are less than $\frac{a}{2} = \frac{.05}{2} = .025$, the results reported in the literature are replicated using our *NELS* data set.

THE BONFERRONI TESTS ON MULTIPLE MEASURES

Another situation that calls for a Bonferroni adjustment to control the family-wise Type I error rate at a chosen value, say 0.05, arises when groups are compared on multiple measures. The following example illustrates the use of the Bonferroni adjustment in such contexts.

EXAMPLE 13.8. Do males and females differ in twelfth grade achievement in any of the four core areas, math, science, reading, and social studies? Use $\alpha = .05$.

Solution. Because the intent of this example is to compare males and females on these four core measures considered separately, a series of four independent group t-tests is appropriate. To avoid an inflated Type I error rate that would result if we were to conduct each of these multiple t-tests at $\alpha = 0.05$, we consider the four tests to be a family of tests and use a Bonferroni adjustment to maintain the family-wise error rate at 0.05. In particular, we conduct each of the four tests at $\alpha = \alpha_{FW}/4 = .05 / 4 = .0125$. See the Do-file associated with this chapter for the Stata commands that were used.

To check assumptions and get a sense of what our data look like, we obtain the following boxplots.

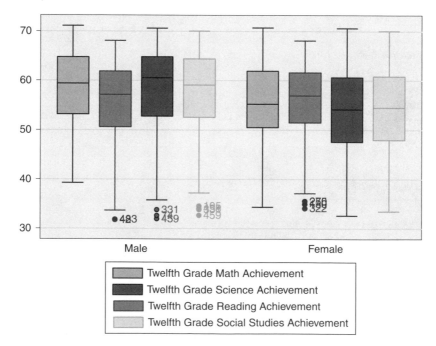

According to the boxplots, there are a few extremely low achievement scores. Given the large number of cases per group, however, such apparent departures from normality cannot be expected to compromise the validity of the *t* statistic. The distributions also appear relatively homogeneous in their variances, despite the presence of extreme values in some of the groups. According to these boxplots, in general males score higher than females. The sample means and results are provided in the following table:

Summary statistics: N, mean, sd, min, max, skewness
by categories of: gender (Gender)

gender	achmat12	achrdg12	achsci12	achsls12
Male	227	227	226	225
	58.63326	55.31035	58.42031	57.746
	7.427049	8.560149	8.086407	8.347075
	39.28	31.76	31.95	32.64
	71.12	68.09	70.6	70.04
	−.465718	−.7428548	−.8018522	−.776225
Female	273	273	272	272
	55.47092	55.84429	53.56048	53.94831
	7.97766	7.480366	8.336535	8.396877
	34.36	34.11	32.59	33.51
	70.69	68.09	70.6	70.04
	−.3660618	−.5711548	−.2110744	−.2345016
Total	500	500	498	497
	56.90662	55.60188	55.76594	55.66759
	7.884027	7.984924	8.56529	8.577259
	34.36	31.76	31.95	32.64
	71.12	68.09	70.6	70.04
	−.422077	−.6832322	−.430817	−.4447249

According to results, males perform statistically significantly better than females in math ($t(498) = 4.55$, $p < .0005$), science ($t(496) = 6.57$, $p < .0005$), and social studies ($t(495) = 5.03$, $p < .0005$). Statistically significant gender differences were not detected in reading achievement ($t(498) = .351$, $p = .73$).

Table 13.1 contains a flow chart for the oneway analysis of variance.

SUMMARY OF STATA COMMANDS IN CHAPTER 13

For a complete listing of all Stata commands associated with this chapter, you may access the Do-file for Chapter 13 located on the text website.

Create	Command Lines
Calculate the *p*-value associated with an *F* value of 19. and 2 and 27 degrees of freedom	**display Ftail(2, 27, 19.52)**

(continued)

TABLE 13.1. Flow chart for one-way ANOVA

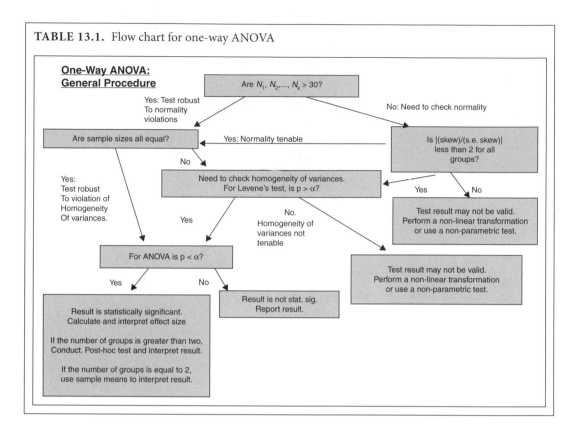

Create	Command Lines
Carry out a one way ANOVA investigating mean differences in ManualDex by Treatment	**oneway ManualDex Treatment, tabulate**
Generate descriptive statistics associated with the ANOVA for detecting mean differences in ManualDex by Treatment To find the skewness ratio	**tabstat ManualDex, by (Treatment) statistics(n mean sd min max skewness)** **OR** **by Treatment, sort: summarize ManualDex, detail** **summskew ManualDex, by(Treatment)**
To obtain the results of Levene's test associated with the ANOVA for detecting mean differences in ManualDex by Treatment	**robvar ManualDex, by(Treatment)**
Perform the bootstrap version of one way ANOVA for unitmath by region (Example 13.2)	**bootstrap F_bs=r(F),reps(1000) nodots seed(999):oneway unitmath region, tabulate** **estat bootstrap, all**

Create	Command Lines
Perform post hoc testing for the ANOVA for detecting mean differences in ManualDex by Treatment. The first line gives the Bonferroni and Scheffe test results. The second and third give the unadjusted (LSD) and Tukey tests, respectively (Example 13.3)	**oneway ManualDex Treatment, bonferroni scheffe** **pwmean ManualDex, over(Treatment) mcompare(noadj) effects** **pwmean ManualDex, over(Treatment) mcompare(tukey) effects**

EXERCISES

*Create a Do-file for each exercise that requires the use of Stata. Run the commands from the Do-file by highlighting them and hitting **Control+d**. Save each Do-file using a name associated with the Exercise for which it was created. It is recommended that you review the Do-file for* Chapter 13 *located on the textbook's website before completing these exercises. To facilitate doing each exercise, it may be helpful to copy and paste relevant commands from the Do-file for* Chapter 13 *into your own Do-file and modify them as needed.*

Exercises 13.1–13.7 involve one-way ANOVA using variables from the NELS data set. For inferential purposes, we consider the students in the data set to be a random sample of the population of all college-bound students who have always been at grade level. Use $\alpha = .05$ for all significance tests.

13.1. Does the average math achievement in eighth grade (achmat08) of college-bound students who have always been at grade level vary as a function of whether they are enrolled in a rigorous academic, academic, some vocational, or other high school program (hsprog)? Use the following questions to guide your analysis.

a) Why is a one-way ANOVA appropriate to use to answer the question posed?

b) Based on the boxplots, do the assumptions underlying the one-way ANOVA appear tenable? What do you anticipate the results of the one-way ANOVA to be? Explain.

c) Evaluate the tenability of the normality assumption or indicate why the assumption is not an issue for this analysis, that the results of the test would not be compromised by a failure to meet this assumption.

d) Use Levene's test to evaluate the tenability of the homogeneity of variance assumption or indicate why the assumption is not an issue for this analysis, that the results of the ANOVA would not be compromised by a failure to meet this assumption.

e) State the null and alternative hypotheses for determining whether or not the average math achievement in eighth grade of college-bound students who always have been at grade level varies as a function of whether they are enrolled in a rigorous academic, academic, or vocational and other high school program.

f) What is the *p*-value associated with the one-way ANOVA for testing these null and alternative hypotheses?

g) Use the *p*-value to determine whether or not the null hypothesis can be rejected in favor of the alternative.

h) State the results of the analysis of variance in context. That is, do the ANOVA results suggest that for this population, math achievement in eighth grade varies as a function of high school program type?

i) Calculate and interpret R^2 as a measure of effect size for the analysis.

j) Is it necessary to conduct a post hoc-test in this case? If so, report and interpret the results of the Least Significant Differences or unadjusted and Tukey post hocests. If not, explain why. In this exercise we have included two of the four tests we have learned about in this chapter. Because the method of interpretation is the same, we will rely on the Tukey test only for the rest of the exercises. As you do analyses on your own, you will need to decide, based on a review of your discipline specific literature and your level of conservativeness desired, the most appropriate test to select.

13.2. Does eighth grade self-concept (slfcnc08) of college-bound students who have always been at grade level vary as a function of whether they live in an urban, suburban, or rural setting (urban)? Use the following questions to guide your analysis.

a) Address the reason for choosing a one-way ANOVA over an independent samples *t*-test, in this case.

b) Based on the boxplots, do the assumptions underlying the one-way ANOVA appear tenable? What do you anticipate the results of the one-way ANOVA to be? Explain.

c) Evaluate the tenability of the normality and homogeneity of variance assumption or indicate why these assumptions are not an issue for this analysis, that the results of the test would not be compromised by a failure to meet these assumptions.

d) Conduct the ANOVA and interpret your results in context.

e) Calculate and interpret R^2 as a measure of effect size for the analysis.

f) Is it necessary to conduct a post hoc-test in this case? If so, report and interpret the results of the Tukey Test. If not, explain why.

g) Conduct the analysis based on a series of *t*-tests using the Bonferroni adjustment. Is the result obtained different from the one obtained through post-hoc testing?

13.3. Does the twelfth grade math achievement (achmat12) of college-bound students who have always been at grade level vary as a function of whether or not they ever tried cigarettes (cigarett)? Use the following questions to guide your analysis.

a) Based on the boxplots, do the assumptions underlying the one-way ANOVA appear tenable? What do you anticipate the results of the one-way ANOVA to be? Explain.

b) Evaluate the tenability of the underlying assumptions or indicate why these assumptions are not an issue for this analysis, that the results of the test would not be compromised by a failure to meet these assumptions.

c) Conduct the ANOVA and interpret your results in context.

d) Calculate and interpret R^2 as a measure of effect size for the analysis.

e) Is it necessary to conduct a post-hoc test in this case? If so, report and interpret the results of the Tukey Test. If not, explain why.

f) Compare the results of the ANOVA to those of an independent samples *t*-test. Are they consistent? Is that what you would expect?

g) Could the one-way ANOVA have been used to determine whether among college-bound students who are always at grade level those who never smoked cigarettes perform *better* in twelfth grade math achievement than those who smoked cigarettes at least once? Explain.

13.4. Perform a one-way ANOVA to determine whether for college-bound students who have always been at grade level the number of units of mathematics taken (unitmath) varies as a function of the highest degree the student anticipates earning (edexpect).

a) Based on the boxplots, do the assumptions underlying the one-way ANOVA appear tenable? What do you anticipate the results of the one-way ANOVA to be? Explain.

b) Evaluate the tenability of the underlying assumptions or indicate why these assumptions are not an issue for this analysis, that the results of the test would not be compromised by a failure to meet these assumptions.

c) Conduct the ANOVA and interpret your results in context.

d) Calculate and interpret R^2 as a measure of effect size for the analysis.

e) Is it necessary to conduct a post hoc-test in this case? If so, report and interpret the results of the Tukey Test. If not, explain why.

f) Use the bootstrap approach to conduct the ANOVA. What is the result? Are the results consistent with those found using the theoretically-derived parametric approach in part c)? Why do you suppose that is?

13.5. Perform a one-way ANOVA to determine whether for college-bound students who have always been at grade level there are differences in the average daily attendance rates (schattrt) of the schools that smokers attended and those that nonsmokers attended (cigarett).

a) Based on the boxplots, do the assumptions underlying the one-way ANOVA appear tenable? What do you anticipate the results of the one-way ANOVA to be? Explain.

b) Evaluate the tenability of the underlying assumptions or indicate why these assumptions are not an issue for this analysis, that the results of the test would not be compromised by a failure to meet these assumptions.

c) Conduct the ANOVA and interpret your results in context.

d) Is it necessary to conduct a post hoc-test in this case? If so, report and interpret the results of the Tukey Test. If not, explain why.

e) If a *t*-test had been carried out instead with a directional alternative hypothesis (that smokers have a lower school attendance rate than nonsmokers), would results have been statistically significant?

13.6. For each of the following questions based on the *NELS* data set, conduct a one-way ANOVA or explain why a different analysis should be used to answer the research question posed.

a) Among college-bound students who are always at grade level, do those who owned a computer (computer) tend to have higher socio economic status (ses), on average, than those who did not?

b) Among college-bound students who are always at grade level, does twelfth grade reading achievement (achrdg12) vary by home language background (homelang), on average?

c) Among college-bound students who are always at grade level, do students tend to take more years of English (unitengl) or Math (unitmath), on average?

d) Among college-bound students who are always at grade level, does computer ownership (computer) vary by home language background (homelang), on average?

e) Among college-bound students who are always at grade level, do those who take advanced math in eighth grade (advmat08) tend to have better attendance in twelfth grade (absent12) than those who do not, on average?

f) Among college-bound students who are always at grade level, are there regional differences (region) in the size of the family (famsize), on average?

g) Does the average twelfth grade self-concept (slfcnc12) of college-bound students who have always been at grade level vary as a function of the population density of their environment (urban), on average?

13.7. At the end of Chapter 3, a descriptive analysis was performed to determine the extent to which eighth grade males expect larger incomes at age 30 (expinc30) than eighth grade females. Explain why an inferential analysis based on the one-way ANOVA would not be appropriate to answer this question, by indicating which underlying assumptions are violated. Use the bootstrap approach to conduct the ANOVA. What is the result?

Exercise 13.8 involves selection of appropriate tests of means.

13.8. For each of the following questions based on the *Learndis* data set, select a statistical procedure from the list below that would be appropriate for answering that question. For inferential purposes, we consider the children in the data set to be a random sample of all children attending public elementary school in a certain city who have been diagnosed with learning disabilities.

(1) One-tailed, one sample *t*-test
(2) Two-tailed, one sample *t*-test
(3) One-tailed, independent samples *t*-test
(4) Two-tailed, independent samples *t*-test
(5) One-tailed, paired samples *t*-test
(6) Two-tailed, paired samples *t*-test
(7) One-way ANOVA

a) Do public-school elementary school females diagnosed with learning disabilities in New York City perform better in reading comprehension than males drawn from the same population of children with learning disabilities?

b) Is the average IQ of public-school children with learning disabilities in New York City equal to 100?

c) Do public-school children with learning disabilities in New York City have higher math comprehension scores or reading comprehension scores?

d) Are there differences in math comprehension by grade?

e) Do public-school children with learning disabilities in New York City have higher math comprehension scores than reading comprehension scores?

Exercises 13.9–13.10 may be used to practice calculations by hand.

13.9. A recent study was conducted on levels of tryptophan, a naturally occurring amino acid that is used by the body to produce serotonin, a mood and appetite-regulating chemical in the brain. The study sought to determine whether bulimics, recovering bulimics, and a control group of people without bulimia differed in their levels of this amino acid. Suppose that 40 individuals from each of the three populations were randomly selected and that the observed group means were 20, 28, and 30, respectively. Complete the ANOVA summary table. Interpret results as best as can be expected with the information available.

ANOVA

	Sum of Squares	df	Mean Square	F	Sig.
Between Groups	2,240				
Within Groups	26,208				
Total					

13.10. In an effort to improve their program for teaching students how to speak French, Western Ohio University language instructors conducted the following experiment. They randomly selected 20 students from all those who registered to take first-term spoken French and randomly divided them into four groups of five students each. Group 1 is taught French the traditional, lecture-recitation way; Group 2 is taught French from a pro-grammed text; Group 3 is taught French from tape-recorded lessons; and Group 4 is taught French from films of people and life in France. At the end of the semester, all 20 students are given the same oral final examination on ability to speak French. The following scores are recorded.

Group 1	Group 2	Group 3	Group 4
75	68	80	87
70	73	65	90
90	70	70	85
80	60	68	75
75	65	72	80

a) Use these data to perform a test at $\alpha = .05$ to determine whether, in general, these four teaching methods have differential mean effects on ability to speak French.

b) Is it appropriate now to perform a Tukey test to determine specific differences between means? If so, perform the Tukey test and describe the results.

CHAPTER FOURTEEN

Two-Way Analysis of Variance

In Chapter 13 we introduced a method for analyzing mean differences on a single dependent variable between two or more independent groups while controlling the risk of making a Type I error at some specified α level. We explained the connection between the method and its name, analysis of variance, and showed how the method was a generalization of the independent group t-test.

The examples presented were concerned with determining whether the observed variance of the dependent variable (e.g., manual dexterity variance or self-concept variance) was related to a single grouping variable (e.g., gender or type of high school program). The examples were also concerned with determining the proportion of the dependent variable variance that was explained by that grouping variable.

Because, in practice, a single grouping variable is not sufficient to explain all dependent variable variance, we can expect some unexplained portion of dependent variable variance to remain after taking into account the grouping variable. A second grouping variable is often included in a design in an attempt to explain additional residual dependent variable variance and to gain further insight into the nature of the dependent variable.

In this chapter we introduce a method called two-way analysis of variance that is an extension of one-way analysis of variance to designs that contain two grouping or independent variables. The two-way analysis of variance is used to assess mean differences through an analysis of dependent variable variance explained by the two grouping variables. The method also assesses the amount of variance explained by each of the two grouping variables and by something called the interaction between the two grouping variables. The concept of interaction is an important one and will be explained in some detail in this chapter.

THE TWO-FACTOR DESIGN

In the introductory example of Chapter 13, we were interested in comparing the effects of three methods of therapeutic treatment on manual dexterity for a specified population. Thirty individuals were selected randomly from the specified population. Each was then assigned randomly to one of the three treatments resulting in 10 individuals per treatment. After five weeks in the treatment, all 30 were administered the Stanford Test of Manual Dexterity. The scores obtained on this measure are reproduced in Table 14.1 and available in the data file, ManDext.

Under the assumption that all three populations were normally distributed and had equal variances, we used a one-way ANOVA to test the equality of all three population

TABLE 14.1. Scores on the Stanford Test of Manual Dexterity by Treatment Group

Treatment I	Treatment II	Treatment III
6	4	6
10	2	2
8	3	2
6	5	6
9	1	4
8	3	5
7	2	3
5	2	5
6	4	3
5	4	4

	Treatment I	Treatment II	Treatment III
Male			
Female			

Figure 14.1 A schematic of a 2 X 3 factorial design

means and obtained $F(2,27) = 19.5$, $p < .0005$. Given this result we concluded that not all population means were equal. We also described the effect size for treatment. Treatment accounted for 59 percent of manual dexterity variance. While treatment accounted for an extremely large proportion of manual dexterity variance, it left unexplained 41 percent of this variance.

In this chapter we consider the importance of a second variable, gender, in explaining additional residual manual dexterity variance. Accordingly, we note which of the 30 individuals in our data set are male and which are female and re-organize the thirty scores into a two-dimensional table (gender by treatment) as shown in Figure 14.1.

Figure 14.1 has two rows and three columns. The row dimension represents the grouping variable, or *factor*, gender, and the column dimension represents the grouping variable, or factor, treatment. Each row represents a category, or *level*, of gender and each column represents a category, or level, of treatment. Each of the six cells in the design represents a unique combination of a level of the gender factor and a level of the treatment factor. For example, the upper left-hand cell represents all subjects in the sample who are male and who received Treatment I.

Because all unique combinations of factor levels are represented in this design (males receive all levels of treatment, I, II, and III as do all females), we call such designs *crossed*. In crossed designs, we may multiply the number of levels of one factor by the number of levels of the second factor to determine the total number of cells in the design. In this example, we multiply 2 by 3 to obtain 6 cells. Because each dimension in the design is defined by a separate factor, such designs also are referred to as *factorial designs*. Taken together, we may say that Figure 14.1 represents a 2 x 3 (read as '2 by 3') *crossed factorial design*, where 2 refers to the number of levels of the row factor (gender) and 3 refers to the number of levels of the column factor (treatment). We may say also that Figure 14.1 represents a *two-way analysis of variance design*.

We assume for simplicity that each treatment group of 10 individuals contains 5 males and 5 females and that the re-organized raw scores and means are shown in Table 14.2.

☞ **Remark.** We have assumed for simplicity that there are equal numbers of males and females in each treatment. In reality, however, if we were interested in using Sex as a second factor, we would design the study so that equal numbers of males and females would be assigned to each treatment. In particular, we would randomly select equal numbers of males and females from their respective populations and then randomly assign equal numbers of each to each treatment condition. Such designs are called *randomized blocks designs*. In this

TABLE 14.2. A 2 X 3 crossed factorial design using the data of Table 14.1.

	Treatment I	Treatment II	Treatment III	
Male	10, 9, 8, 8, 7 $\overline{X}_{11} = 8.4$	5, 4, 3, 2, 1 $\overline{X}_{12} = 3$	4, 3, 3, 2, 2 $\overline{X}_{13} = 2.8$	Row 1 Mean = 4.73
Female	6, 6, 6, 5, 5 $\overline{X}_{21} = 5.6$	4, 4, 3, 2, 2 $\overline{X}_{22} = 3$	6, 6, 5, 5, 4 $\overline{X}_{23} = 5.2$	Row 2 Mean = 4.60
	Col. 1 Mean = 7.0	Col. 2 Mean = 3.0	Col. 3 Mean = 4.0	Overall Mean = 4.67

TABLE 14.3. Stata representation of the data set of Table 14.2. For Sex, 1 represents male and 2 represents female.

Treatment	Sex	ManualDex
1	1	10
1	1	9
1	1	8
1	1	8
1	1	7
1	2	6
1	2	6
1	2	6
1	2	5
1	2	5
2	1	5
2	1	4
2	1	3
2	1	2
2	1	1
2	2	4
2	2	4
2	2	3
2	2	2
2	2	2
3	1	4
3	1	3
3	1	3
3	1	2
3	1	2
3	2	6
3	2	6
3	2	5
3	2	5
3	2	4

case, each category of Sex defines a block. For additional information on such designs, the interested reader is referred to Keppel (1991).

In order to enter the data into Stata, we require 3 variables, or columns: one for treatment, one for gender, and one for score. The data as they are displayed by Stata are given in Table 14.3. We call the treatment variable Treatment. For the variable Sex, 1 represents male and 2 represents female.

MORE Stata: To calculate individual cell means, marginal row and column means, and the overall mean

table Sex Treatment, contents(n ManualDex mean ManualDex sd ManualDex) row col format(%6.2f)

OR

tabulate Sex Treatment, summarize(ManualDex)

The resulting output is reproduced as Table 14.4.

There are six individual cell means in Table 14.2 (8.4, 3.0, 2.8, 5.6, 3.0, and 5.2). There are also two row means (4.73 and 4.60), three column means (7.0, 3.0, and 4.0), and an overall or *grand mean* (4.67).

Each of the six individual cell means equals the mean on the manual dexterity test of the five subjects in that particular cell. For example, 8.4 equals the manual dexterity mean of the five male subjects who received Treatment I.

Each row mean, also called a *row marginal mean* because it appears in the row margin of the table, equals the mean on the manual dexterity test of those subjects in that particular row. For example, the row marginal mean of 4.73 equals the manual dexterity mean of the 15 male subjects. Alternatively, it equals the mean of the three cell means for males. In computing the row mean, we ignore the treatment the subjects received and consider only the row they are in.

Analogously, each column marginal mean equals the mean on the manual dexterity test of those subjects in that particular column. For example, the column marginal mean of 7.0 equals the manual dexterity mean of the ten subjects who received Treatment I. In computing the column mean, we ignore the sex of the subject and consider only the column they are in.

Table 14.4. Cell Frequencies, Means, and Standard Deviations of Manual Dexterity of Table 14.2 data.

Sex	Treatment 1	2	3	Total
Male	5	5	5	15
	8.40	3.00	2.80	4.73
	1.14	1.58	0.84	2.91
Female	5	5	5	15
	5.60	3.00	5.20	4.60
	0.55	1.00	0.84	1.40
Total	10	10	10	30
	7.00	3.00	4.00	4.67
	1.70	1.25	1.49	2.25

Finally, the overall or grand mean equals the mean on the manual dexterity test of all subjects in the study. In this example, it is the manual dexterity mean based on the 30 subjects.

If we ignore row distinctions, and consider only the columns, we have all the information necessary to conduct a one-way ANOVA on manual dexterity to evaluate the effect due to treatment. Analogously, if we ignore column distinctions, and consider only the rows, we have all the information necessary to conduct a one-way ANOVA on Gender to evaluate the effect due to gender. In the context of two-way ANOVA, the effects due to treatment and gender are called *main effects* as each is evaluated "in the main," ignoring the effect of the other factor. Thus, a two-factor design contains all the information necessary to conduct two separate one-way ANOVAS on the two different factors, respectively. It also contains additional information that tells how the two factors interact with each other in terms of the dependent variable.

THE CONCEPT OF INTERACTION

We note that the row marginal mean for males is 4.7 and the row marginal mean for females is 4.6. A comparison of these two values suggests that the mean manual dexterity score for males is similar to the mean manual dexterity score for females; that is, there is no main effect for gender. Because row marginal means represent averaged effects, averaged over all columns in that row, they do not reflect the variation in means contained in that row. By extension, a comparison of row marginal means does not reflect the variation in male-female mean comparisons by treatment. While on average males and females may be quite similar in terms of manual dexterity, it may be that males do better than females under some treatments and worse under others or it may be that their relative performance is constant for all treatments. Only by making such treatment by treatment comparisons

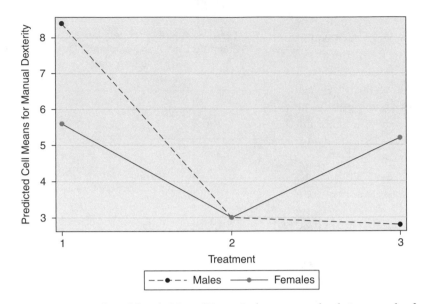

Figure 14.2   Male and female Manual Dexterity by treatment level: An example of a disordinal interaction

between males and females can we gain access to this important information that is carried by the individual cells of the table.

Based on the cell means of Table 14.2, we observe that for Treatment 1, males have a substantially higher mean than females (8.4 versus 5.6), for Treatment 2, males and females have the same mean (3.0 versus 3.0), and for Treatment 3, males have a substantially lower mean than females (2.8 versus 5.2). To show the situation more clearly, we present a line graph of these six means in Figure 14.2. The vertical axis of the graph contains a scale of manual dexterity means, the horizontal axis represents the levels of treatment and each line represents a gender type.

MORE Stata: To create a line graph of means to illustrate the two-way ANOVA

anova ManualDex Sex Treatment Sex#Treatment
predict yhat
twoway (line yhat Treatment if Sex == 1, lpattern(dash)) (line yhat Treatment if Sex == 2, lpattern(solid)), legend(label(1 "Males") label(2 "Females")) ytitle("Predicted Cell Means for Manual Dexterity") xlabel(1 2 3)

Note: This syntax will run the two way ANOVA with main effects for Sex and Treatment, as well as for the interaction of Sex and Treatment, represented by the **Sex#Treatment** term. The predicted cell values based on the ANOVA are the cell means used for plotting the graph. You may access these data and run this syntax from the Do-file associated with this chapter.

From Figure 14.2 it is clear that *treatments do not have a constant effect on manual dexterity performance for males and females.* If an individual were to be assigned to a particular treatment (I, II, or III) for optimal manual dexterity, one would want to know the gender of the individual before making that assignment. Said differently, *if one were to ask, "To which*

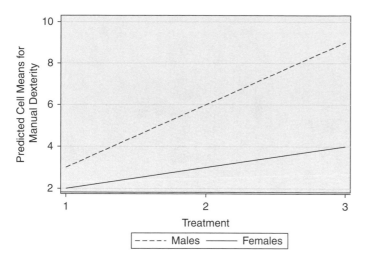

Figure 14.3 Male and female Manual Dexterity by treatment level: An example of an ordinal interaction

treatment should we assign an individual?" the answer would be "It depends on whether the individual is male or female." If male, the individual would be assigned to Treatment I, if female, the individual would be assigned to Treatment I or, perhaps, Treatment III.

Whenever the relative effects of one factor (e.g., Treatment) change across the levels of the other factor (e.g., males and females), we have what is called an <u>interaction</u> between the two factors. The particular type of interaction illustrated in Figure 14.2 is called a *disordinal interaction* because the lines actually cross in the graph. That is, relative to females, males do better under Treatment I, they do the same under Treatment II, and they do worse under Treatment III. If we computed the difference between the male and female manual dexterity means for each treatment, we would find that these differences change from positive (8.4 − 5.6 = 2.8) to zero (3.0–3.0=0), to negative (2.8 − 5.2 = −2.4). Mean differences between levels of one factor computed at each level of the second factor will always change sign when interactions are disordinal.

Not all interactions are disordinal, however. Figure 14.3 depicts a different set of sample means that illustrates what is called an *ordinal* interaction. In this case, while the relative effects of one factor change across the levels of the other factor, the lines maintain their ordinality; that is, one line remains higher than the other line across all levels of the second factor. The lines do not cross in the graph. As shown in Figure 14.3, males perform better than females under all treatments and their relative superiority on the manual dexterity test increases as treatments change from Treatment 1 to 2 to 3.

☞ **Remark.** In describing the interactions of Figures 14.2 and 14.3 we may say that *there is an interaction between gender and treatment on manual dexterity.* In so doing, we recognize the role of three variables in defining a two-way interaction, the two independent variables or factors (e.g., gender and treatment) and the dependent variable (e.g., manual dexterity).

If, on the other hand, the relative effects of one factor are constant across the levels of the other factor, then we say that there is no interaction between the two factors. Figures 14.4(a) through (d) illustrate four possible scenarios of no interaction in the context of our 2 x 3 factorial design. Assume that these scenarios represent population means,

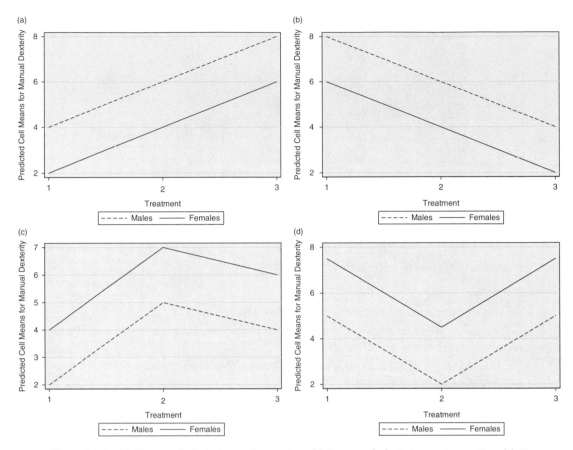

Figure 14.4   (a) Line graph depicting no interaction. (b) Line graph depicting no interaction. (c) Line graph depicting no interaction. (d) Line graph depicting no interaction.

that are, therefore, not subject to sampling error. We may observe that Figures 14.4(a) through (d) share a common feature: all line segments are equidistant from each other; that is, they are parallel.

Notice that in the absence of an interaction, we would *not* need to take into account gender before assigning an individual to a particular treatment because the pattern of manual dexterity performance remains the same for males and females across all treatments. Figure 14.4(a) illustrates the situation in which males perform better than females across all treatments. Also, males and females have the same pattern of performance across all levels of treatment. Figures 14.4(b) through (d) illustrate other possible outcomes. The point is that in the absence of an interaction, we do not need to qualify the relative effectiveness of treatments by gender or qualify the relative performance of males and females by the treatment they received. Effects are constant in both directions.

The distances between line segments may be expressed as mean differences in terms of manual dexterity between males and females at Treatment I as $\bar{X}_{11} - \bar{X}_{21}$, at Treatment II as $\bar{X}_{12} - \bar{X}_{22}$, and at Treatment III as $\bar{X}_{13} - \bar{X}_{23}$. When these differences are all equal, all line segments are parallel and there is no interaction. When any two are not equal, all line segments are not parallel and there is an interaction. Thus, a two-way interaction may be observed when the mean differences computed between the levels of one factor for

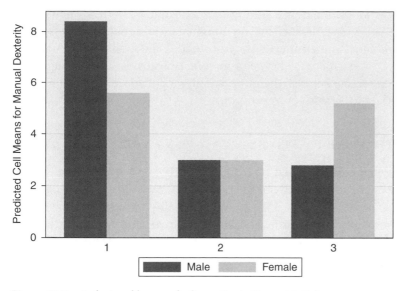

Figure 14.5 A clustered bar graph alternative to Figure 14.4(a).

each level of the second factor are not all equal. Alternatively, when there is an interaction between factors, differences between the mean differences are different!

☞ **Remark.** We have used line graphs to depict interaction effects. While this is standard practice, because the horizontal axis reflects a nominal-leveled variable (i.e., Treatment), one should be cautioned against reading a trend into the result. That is, in Figure 14.4(a), for example, one might be tempted to conclude that manual dexterity increases at a constant rate across treatments for males and females because of the use of line segments in the graph. To avoid possible misinterpretations of this kind, researchers sometimes use clustered bar graphs to display interaction effects involving nominal-leveled variables. Figure 14.5 displays a clustered bar graph as an alternative to Figure 14.4(a). (The syntax to produce these clustered bar graphs is provided in the Do-file associated with this chapter as well as below.) The equal distances between line segments in Figure 14.4(a), characteristic of no interaction, are represented as equal differences between bar heights within clusters in Figure 14.5.

MORE Stata: To generate the clustered bar graph of Figure 14.5

graph bar yhat, over(Sex) over(Treatment) asyvars
ytitle("Predicted Cell Means for Manual Dexterity")

By analogy, when an interaction is present, a bar graph would show unequal differences between bar heights within clusters. The decision to use line graphs or clustered bar graphs to display interactions is entirely up to the researcher.

Our discussion thus far has assumed no sampling variability and, in particular, that for example, a difference in sample means implies a difference in population means as well. When sampling variability is present, however, lines do not need to be perfectly parallel to imply no interaction and marginal means do not need to be perfectly equal to imply no main effects. Deviation from parallelism and marginal mean equality due to sampling variability may be present. To determine in practice whether an observed interaction between factors, or an observed difference between marginal means, is large enough to rule out sampling variability and to suggest, therefore, an interaction, or main effect, in the population, we rely on the two-way ANOVA procedure.

THE HYPOTHESES THAT ARE TESTED BY A TWO-WAY ANALYSIS OF VARIANCE

Three separate hypotheses are tested by a two-way ANOVA: a row main effect, a column main effect, and an interaction between the two factors, each at significance level α.

The test of the row main effect is a test of the equality of row marginal means in the population. In our example, it is a test of whether the mean manual dexterity score for males equals that for females in the population. The null and alternative hypotheses for this example are:

$$H_0: {}_R\mu_1 = {}_R\mu_2$$
$$H_1: {}_R\mu_1 \neq {}_R\mu_2$$

where R represents row and ${}_R\mu_1$ represents the row marginal mean for row 1 (males) and ${}_R\mu_2$ represents the row marginal mean for row 2 (females).

The test of the column main effect is a test of the equality of column marginal means in the population. In our example, it is a test of whether the mean manual dexterity score for Treatment I equals that for Treatment II, which in turn, equals that for Treatment III. The null and alternative hypotheses are:

$$H_0: {}_C\mu_1 = {}_C\mu_2 = {}_C\mu_3$$
$$H_1: \text{not } H_0$$

where C represents column and ${}_C\mu_1$ represents the column marginal mean for column 1 (Treatment I), and so on.

The null and alternative hypotheses for the test of the 2 X 3 (Gender X Treatment) interaction may be expressed simply as:

H_0: There is no interaction in the population between the effects of Gender and Treatment on manual dexterity.

H_1: There is an interaction in the population between the effects of Gender and Treatment on manual dexterity.

ASSUMPTIONS OF THE TWO-WAY ANALYSIS OF VARIANCE

As in the one-way ANOVA model of Chapter 13, the two-way ANOVA model in this chapter is based on the assumption that the scores are independent. Scores are independent, if, for example, each score is from a separate individual who has been randomly assigned to one of the treatment conditions of the design. In addition, like the one-way ANOVA, the two-way ANOVA model makes distributional assumptions about the scores within each group. In a one-way ANOVA, within-group distributions consist of the sample of scores within each level of the single factor (e.g., scores within Treatment I, scores within Treatment II, and scores within Treatment III). By extension, in a two-way ANOVA, within group distributions consist of the sample of scores within each combination of factors (i.e., within each cell of the two-way design). The six within-cell distributions in our working example are the distributions of male scores within Treatment I, male scores within Treatment II, male scores within Treatment III, female scores within Treatment I, female scores within Treatment II, and female scores within Treatment III. In the two-way ANOVA, all within-cell samples of scores are assumed to come from populations that are normally distributed with equal variances. Considerations that deal with violations of these assumptions are discussed in Chapter 13 and apply to the two-way ANOVA as well.

Prior to conducting a two-way analysis of variance on the data in Table 14.2, we evaluate the underlying assumptions of the analysis.

The scores are independent because each score is from a separate individual who has been randomly assigned to one of the treatment conditions of the design.

Because we have fewer than 30 subjects in each cell, we evaluate the viability of the assumption that the within-cell samples of scores come from populations that are normally distributed.

MORE Stata: To examine the within-cell normality assumption using Stata

We examine the skewness for Manual Dexterity scores by Treatment status and Sex and obtain a compact Sex by Treatment table of skewness values using the **statsby** and **tabdisp** commands:

statsby skew=r(skewness), by(Treatment Sex): summarize ManualDex, detail
tabdisp Sex Treatment, cell(skew)

To obtain a more complete set of summary statistics:

by Sex Treatment, sort: summarize ManualDex, detail

MORE Stata: To obtain the standard error of skewness and the skewness ratio when, as in the case of two-way anova, there are two grouping variables, we use **summskewcell**

Like the **summskew** command, the **summskewcell** command is, by default, not part of Stata, and so it first needs to be installed before we can use it. Because the instructions to install **summskewcell** are exactly the same as those for installing **summskew**, if you already have installed **summskew** there is nothing further to do. If, on the other hand, you have not already installed **summskew**, then please return to page 94 to follow the instructions for installing **summskew**.

Once these programs are installed, the **summskewcell** syntax for this example is:

summskewcell ManualDex Treatment Sex

Note: As noted in Chapter 11, the general form of the **summskewcell** command is **summskewcell y x1 x2**, where **y** is a continuous variable and **x1** and **x2** are two categorical variables. In the context of a two-way anova, **y** is a dependent variable, and **x1** and **x2** are two independent variables.

The **statsby** and **tabdisp** output is follows:

	Treatment		
Sex	1	2	3
Male	.2715454	0	.3436216
Female	−.4082483	0	−.3436216

Looking at the skewness values for each of the cells, we see that all six are less than 1 in magnitude, indicating that the normality assumption is tenable.

And, the **summskewcell** output is as follows:

```
For Sex = 1 and Treatment = 1: N = 5; skewness = .27154541; seskew = .91287094;
> skewness ratio = .29746309
For Sex = 1 and Treatment = 2: N = 5; skewness = 0; seskew = .91287094; skewnes
> s ratio = 0
For Sex = 1 and Treatment = 3: N = 5; skewness = .34362161; seskew = .91287094;
> skewness ratio = .37641862
For Sex = 2 and Treatment = 1: N = 5; skewness = −.40824831; seskew = .91287094
>; skewness ratio = −.44721359
For Sex = 2 and Treatment = 2: N = 5; skewness = 0; seskew = .91287094; skewnes
> s ratio = 0
For Sex = 2 and Treatment = 3: N = 5; skewness = −.34362161; seskew = .91287094
>;skewness ratio = −.37641862
```

Looking at the skewness ratios for each of the cells, we see that all six are less than 2 in magnitude, indicating that the normality assumption is tenable.

Because the cell sizes are equal, there are 5 research participants in each cell, the two-way ANOVA is robust to violations of the homogeneity of variance assumption, so the assumption is not evaluated.

BALANCED VERSUS UNBALANCED FACTORIAL DESIGNS

In the one-way ANOVA, no restriction was placed on the relative sizes of the samples that comprised each level of the factor studied. The model, as described, allowed for either equal or unequal cell sizes. The model presented in this chapter for two-way ANOVA is based on the assumption that the number of subjects in each cell is equal. This is to ensure that the design is *balanced* (or *orthogonal*). An advantage of balanced designs is that they allow us to consider the two main effects as separate entities, which may be tested without regard to each other. For example, the results pertaining to one main effect may be interpreted without regard to the results pertaining to the other main effect. Said differently, the sum of squares due to each main effect in a two-way balanced design equals the sum of squares due to each main effect if each main effect were analyzed separately in a one-way design.

Analytical approaches different from those presented in this chapter are required when applying the two-way ANOVA to nonorthogonal or unbalanced designs. We shall touch on some of the more complicated issues that arise in connection with unbalanced designs in Chapter 15 on multiple regression.

PARTITIONING THE TOTAL SUM OF SQUARES

In Chapter 13, we pointed out that one-way ANOVA partitions the total variability (SS_T) of our dependent variable into two unrelated (orthogonal) components: variability due to the between groups effect (SS_B) and variability that remains unexplained within group after the between groups effect is accounted for (SS_W). Equation 14.1 uses the context of our working example to express the partitioning of the total manual dexterity sum of squares in a one-way design into a sum of squares due to Treatment and a sum of squares due to what remains within group once Treatment is accounted for:

$$SS_{TOT} = SS_{TREAT} + SS_{WITHIN\text{-}GROUP} \tag{14.1}$$
$$146.67 = 86.67 + 60.00$$

In an analogous way, two-way ANOVA also partitions the total sum of squares into unrelated (orthogonal) component parts. In the case of the two-way design of our working example, these components of variability are due to Treatment, Gender, the Gender by Treatment interaction, and what remains unexplained within cell after all these sources of variation are accounted for. Equation 14.2 expresses this breakdown of variability for the two-way design.

$$SS_{TOT} = SS_{TREAT} + SS_{GENDER} + SS_{INTER} + SS_{WITHIN\text{-}CELL} \tag{14.2}$$
$$146.67 = 86.67 + 60$$

Notice, that because in both models, the SS_{TOT} is equal to the sum of squares based on the whole set of 30 manual dexterity scores without regard to any grouping variable, the value of SS_{TOT} remains the same in both models (146.67). Analogously, because SS_{TREAT} in the two-way ANOVA continues to equal the sum of squared deviations of the three treatment means about the grand mean without regard to gender, it also has the same value in the two-way ANOVA as in the one-way ANOVA (86.67).

In the two-way design, the addition of the second factor, gender, allows for the opportunity to explain more of the 60 units of residual variability that is left unexplained in the one-way design. According to Equation 14.2, the sum of SS_{GENDER}, SS_{INTER} and $SS_{WITHIN\text{-}CELL}$ equals 60. If neither Gender nor the interaction between Gender and Treatment accounts for any additional residual variability, then SS_W will remain at 60, and there will be nothing gained by using the two-way design. In general, the degree to which we gain in explanatory power from using the two-way design relates to the amount by which the residual variability left unexplained in the one-way design can be reduced by the additional sources of variation, Gender and Gender by Treatment, in the two-way design.

USING THE *F*-RATIO TO TEST THE EFFECTS IN TWO-WAY ANOVA

To test whether each of the three sources of variation (main effect due to Treatment, main effect due to Gender, and interaction effect due to Gender and Treatment) explains a statistically significant proportion of total variance (that is, a proportion that is not attributable to chance), we carry out a series of three F-tests as shown in Table 14.5, each at a specified α level. As in the one-way ANOVA, the denominator of each *F*-test is based on the left-over, residual variance, denoted MS_W, and the numerator of each *F*-test is based on one of the

TABLE 14.5. Forming F-ratios in a two-way ANOVA design with a Row and a Column Factor

Source of Variation	SS	df	MS	F-ratio
Factor R	SS_R	$R-1$	$MS_R = SS_R/(R-1)$	MS_R/MS_W
Factor C	SS_C	$C-1$	$MS_C = SS_C/(C-1)$	MS_C/MS_W
R×C Interaction	SS_{RxC}	$(R-1)(C-1)$	$MS_{R\times C}=SS_{R\times C}/(R-1)(C-1)$	$MS_{R\times C}/MS_W$
Within cells	SS_W	$N-RC$		
Total	SS_T	$N-1$		

TABLE 14.6. A 2×3 crossed factorial design using the data of Table 14.2.

	Treatment I	Treatment II	Treatment III	
Male	10, 9, 8, 8, 7	5, 4, 3, 2, 1	4, 3, 3, 2, 2	$_R\overline{X}_1 = 4.73$
	$\overline{X}_{11} = 8.4$	$\overline{X}_{12} = 3$	$\overline{X}_{13} = 2.8$	
Female	6, 6, 6, 5, 5	4, 4, 3, 2, 2	6, 6, 5, 5, 4	$_R\overline{X}_2 = 4.60$
	$\overline{X}_{21} = 5.6$	$\overline{X}_{22} = 3$	$\overline{X}_{23} = 5.2$	
	$_C\overline{X}_1 = 7.0$	$_C\overline{X}_2 = 3.0$	$_C\overline{X}_2 = 4.0$	Overall Mean = 4.67

three between group variances defined by its respective source of variation. As before, the degrees of freedom for a main effect equals one less than the number of groups for that main effect (e.g., $R-1$ for the row main effect). The degrees of freedom for the interaction effect equals the product of $R-1$ and $C-1$. The degrees of freedom for the error or within cells effect equals $N - RC$, the total sample size less the total number of cells in the design represented as the product of the number of rows by the number of columns (RC). Finally, the total degrees of freedom equals $N-1$. We may note that the degrees of freedom for the separate effects in the design sum to the total degrees of freedom for the design (that is, $R-1 + C-1 + (R-1)(C-1) + N-RC = N-1$).

Table 14.5 shows how the F-ratios are formed to construct the respective F-tests beginning with the SS terms. In the next section, we describe within a conceptual framework how these SS terms are generated and we carry out the two-way ANOVA by hand using our manual dexterity example.

CARRYING OUT THE TWO-WAY ANOVA COMPUTATION BY HAND

The manual dexterity scores of the 30 individuals, organized by the two factors of the two-way design, are given again as Table 14.6.

The Sum of Squares associated with the row effect, SS_R, is given by Equation 14.3.

$$SS_R = \sum_{i=1}^{r} {}_R N_i ({}_R\overline{X}_i - \overline{\overline{X}})^2 \tag{14.3}$$

where r represents the number of levels of the row factor, $_R N_i$ equals the number of values in row i, $_R\overline{X}_i$ equals the mean of the values in row i, and $\overline{\overline{X}}$ equals the overall or grand mean of all values in the sample.

Using Equation 14.3, we compute SS_R for the manual dexterity example.

$$_RN_1 = {_R}N_2 = 15; \, _R\overline{X}_1 = 4.73, \, _R\overline{X}_2 = 4.60; \overline{\overline{X}} = 4.67; r = 2.$$

$$SS_R = 15(4.6-4.67)^2 + 15(4.7 - 4.67)^2 = 0.13.$$

The Sum of Squares associated with the column effect, SS_C, is given by Equation 14.4.

$$SS_C = \sum_{j=1}^{c} {_C}N_j({_C}\overline{X}_j - \overline{\overline{X}})^2 \tag{14.4}$$

where c represents the number of levels of the column factor, $_CN_j$ equals the number of values in column j, $_C\overline{X}_j$ equals the mean of the values in column j, and $\overline{\overline{X}}$ equals the overall or grand mean of all values in the sample.

Using Equation 14.4, we compute SS_C for the manual dexterity example.

$$_CN_1 = {_C}N_2 = {_C}N_3 = 10; \, _C\overline{X}_1 = 7.0, \, _C\overline{X}_2 = 3.0, \, _C\overline{X}_3 = 4.0; \overline{\overline{X}} = 4.67; c = 3.$$

$$SS_C = 10(7 - 4.67)^2 + 10(3-4.67)^2 + 10(4-4.67)^2 = 86.67.$$

The Sum of Squares associated with the interaction effect, $SS_{R \times C}$, is given by Equation 14.5.

$$SS_{R \times C} = \sum_{i=1}^{r} \sum_{j=1}^{c} N_{i,j}(\overline{X}_{i,j} - {_R}\overline{X}_i - {_C}\overline{X}_j + \overline{\overline{X}})^2 \tag{14.5}$$

where $N_{i,j}$ equals the number of values in cell i,j, $\overline{X}_{i,j}$ equals the mean of the values in cell i,j, $_R\overline{X}_i$ equals the mean of the values in row i, $_C\overline{X}_j$ equals the mean of the values in column j, and $\overline{\overline{X}}$ equals the overall or grand mean of all values in the sample.

Using Equation 14.5, we compute $SS_{R \times C}$ for the manual dexterity example.

$$N_{11} = N_{12} = N_{13} = N_{21} = N_{22} = N_{23} = 5;$$

$$\overline{X}_{11} = 8.4, \overline{X}_{12} = 3.0, \overline{X}_{13} = 2.8, \overline{X}_{21} = 5.6, \overline{X}_{22} = 3.0, \overline{X}_{23} = 5.2;$$

$$_R\overline{X}_1 = 4.73, \, _R\overline{X}_2 = 4.60; \, _C\overline{X}_1 = 7.0, \, _C\overline{X}_2 = 3.0, \, _C\overline{X}_3 = 4.0; \overline{\overline{X}} = 4.67.$$

$$\begin{aligned} SS_{RxC} = \, &5(8.4 - 4.73 - 7.0 + 4.67)^2 + 5(3.0 - 4.73 - 3.0 + 4.67)^2 + \\ &5(2.8 - 4.73 - 4.0 + 4.67)^2 + 5(5.6 - 4.60 - 7.0 + 4.67)^2 + 5(3.0 - 4.60 - 3.0 + 4.67)^2 + \\ &5(5.2 - 4.60 - 4.0 + 4.67)^2 \\ = \, &33.87. \end{aligned}$$

The Sum of Squares associated with the remaining within-cell variation, SS_W, is given by Equation 14.6.

$$SS_W = \sum_{i,j,k} (X_{i,j,k} - \overline{X}_{i,j})^2 \tag{14.6}$$

where $X_{i,j,k}$ represents the kth score in row i and column j, and $\overline{X}_{i,j}$ represents the mean of the scores in row i and column j.

Using Equation 14.6, we compute SS_W for the manual dexterity example.

$$SS_W = (10 - 8.4)^2 + (9 - 8.4)^2 + (8 - 8.4)^2 + (8 - 8.4)^2 + (7 - 8.4)^2 + (5 - 3)^2 + (4 - 3)^2$$
$$+ (3 - 3)^2 + (2 - 3)^2 + (1 - 3)^2 + (4 - 2.8)^2 + (3 - 2.8)^2 + (3 - 2.8)^2 + (2 - 2.8)^2$$
$$+ (2 - 2.8)^2 + (6 - 5.6)^2 + (6 - 5.6)^2 + (6 - 5.6)^2 + (5 - 5.6)^2 + (5 - 5.6)^2$$
$$+ (4 - 3)^2 + (4 - 3)^2 + (3 - 3)^2 + (2 - 3)^2 + (2 - 3)^2 + (6 - 5.2)^2 + (6 - 5.2)^2$$
$$+ (5 - 5.2)^2 + (5 - 5.2)^2 + (4 - 5.2)^2 = 2.56 + .36 + .16 + .16 + 1.96 + 4 + 1 + 0$$
$$+ 1 + 4 + 1.44 + .04 + .04 + .64 + .64 + .16 + .16 + .16 + .36 + .36 + 1 + 1 + 0$$
$$+ 1 + 1 + .64 + .64 + .04 + .04 + 1.44 = 26.00.$$

Finally, the Sum of Squares associated with the Total variability, SS_{TOT}, is given by Equation 14.7.

$$SS_{TOT} = \sum \left(X_{ijk} - \overline{\overline{X}} \right)^2 \tag{14.7}$$

Using Equation 14.7, we compute SS_{TOT} for the manual dexterity example.

$$SS_{TOT} = (10 - 4.67)^2 + (9 - 4.67)^2 + (8 - 4.67)^2 + (8 - 4.67)^2 + (7 - 4.67)^2$$
$$+ (5 - 4.67)^2 + (4 - 4.67)^2 + (3 - 4.67)^2 + (2 - 4.67)^2 + (1 - 4.67)^2 + (4 - 4.67)^2$$
$$+ (3 - 4.67)^2 + (3 - 4.67)^2 + (2 - 4.67)^2 + (2 - 4.67)^2 + (6 - 4.67)^2$$
$$+ (6 - 4.67)^2 + (6 - 4.67)^2 + (5 - 4.67)^2 + (5 - 4.67)^2 + (4 - 4.67)^2 + (4 - 4.67)^2$$
$$+ (3 - 4.67)^2 + (2 - 4.67)^2 + (2 - 4.67)^2 + (6 - 4.67)^2 + (6 - 4.67)^2 + (5 - 4.67)^2$$
$$+ (5 - 4.67)^2 + (4 - 4.67)^2 = 146.67.$$

Substituting these values for their respective SS, we obtain the second column of Table 14.5.

We then calculate the values of df, MS and F, following the formulas given in the ANOVA summary in Table 14.3.

We first find these values for the within cells:

$$Df_W = N - RC = 30 - 6 = 24, MS_W = SS_W/df_W = 26/24 = 1.08$$

For the main effect of gender, we obtain the following values:

$$df_R = R - 1 = 2 - 1 = 1, MS_R = SS_R/df_R = 0.13/1 = 0.13.$$
$$F = MS_R/MS_W = 0.13/1.08 = 0.12$$

For the main effect of treatment, we obtain the following values:

$$Df_C = C - 1 = 3 - 1 = 2, MS_C = SS_C/df_C = 86.76/2 = 43.34.$$
$$F = MS_C/MS_W = 43.34/1.08 = 40.13$$

For the interaction effect, we obtain the following values:

$$df_{R \times C} = (R - 1)(C - 1) = 1 \times 2 = 2, MS_{R \times C} = SS_{R \times C}/df_{R \times C} = 33.87/2 = 16.93.$$
$$F = MS_{R \times C}/MS_W = 16.93/1.08 = 15.69$$

The three Sig. values, or significance values, or p-values, are obtained either by using Table 3 in Appendix C online, www.cambridge.org/Stats-Stata, which may be obtained online, or by using the Stata probability distribution functions. Both approaches are described.

Table 3 in Appendix C online, www.cambridge.org/Stats-Stata, may be used to approximate the associated p-values.

TABLE 14.7. Summary table of results of the two-way ANOVA on manual dexterity.

Source of Variation	SS	df	MS	F-ratio	Sig.
Gender	0.13	1	0.14	0.12	.72
Treatment	86.67	2	43.34	40.13	.00
Gender X Treatment	33.87	2	16.93	15.69	.00
Within cells	26.00	24	1.08		
Total	146.67	29			

To find the p-value for the main effect of gender, we want an estimate of the area to the right of $F = .12$ with numerator degrees of freedom 1 and denominator degrees of freedom 24. To do so, we find all of the α values associated with df for numerator = 1 and df for denominator = 24. We see that the F-value 1.39 cuts off area .25 to its right, that 2.93 cuts off area .10 to its right, etc. Because $F = .12$ is less than 1.39, we conclude that the area to the right of $F = .12$ is greater than .25, that is, that $p > .25$.

To find the p-value for the main effect of treatment, we want an estimate of the area to the right of $F = 40.13$ with numerator degrees of freedom 2 and denominator degrees of freedom 24. To do so, we find all of the α values associated with df for numerator = 2 and df for denominator = 24. We find the closest value that is smaller than 40.13. In this case, the F-value 9.34 cuts off area .001 to its right. Because $F = 40.13$ is greater than 9.24, it must cut off even less area, so that we conclude that the area to the right of $F = 40.13$ is less than .001, that is, that $p < .001$.

To find the p-value for the interaction effect, we want an estimate of the area to the right of $F = 15.69$ with numerator degrees of freedom 2 and denominator degrees of freedom 24. As with the main effect of treatment, because $F = 15.69$ is greater than 9.24, $p < .001$.

The Stata F probability distribution function **Ftail** may be used to find the associated p-values in the right tail of the F-distribution. In particular, we use

display Ftail(1, 24, .12) to find the p-value associated with the main effect due to Sex;
    display Ftail(2, 24, 40.13) to find the p-value associated with the main effect for Treatment; and,
display Ftail(2, 24, 15.69) to find the p-value associated with the Sex by Treatment interaction.

The results are summarized in Table 14.7. Note that the values for Sig. are those obtained using Stata and are rounded to two decimal places.

When interpreting the results of the two-way ANOVA, we compare each of the p-values (found in the Sig. column) to the α level, which in this case is $\alpha = .05$. The results of the two-way ANOVA indicate that there is a statistically significant main effect of treatment, $F(2, 24) = 40.13$, $p < .005$ and a statistically significant interaction effect $F(2, 24) = 40.13$, $p < .005$. Because the presence of a statistically significant interaction indicates that the best treatment depends on the gender, we focus on the interaction instead of the main effect of treatment. In order to understand the nature of the interaction effect, that is, the way in which the best treatment depends on the gender, we conduct post-hoc multiple comparison tests. These are discussed in a later section.

Several comparisons with the one-way ANOVA results are worthwhile. First, we notice that, as expected, the SS_{TOT} and $SS_{TREATMENT}$ remain the same at 146.67 and 86.67, respectively. Second, we notice that $SS_{GENDER} + SS_{INTER} + SS_W = 0.13 + 33.87 + 26.0 = 60$, as we also had expected. Third, we notice that $SS_{TOT} = SS_{TREATMENT} + SS_{GENDER} + SS_{INTER} + SS_W$, suggesting that this two-way ANOVA does partition the total variability of manual dexterity values into these four independent (orthogonal) components.

Finally, we notice that the denominator of the F-ratios, the MSW term, is smaller in the two-way ANOVA than in the one-way ANOVA, suggesting that we have explained additional residual variance by the inclusion of Gender and the interaction between Gender and Treatment in the design. Because the denominator of the F-ratio in the two-way design is smaller than in the one-way design, we say that the two-way design is more *precise* than the one-way ANOVA in that it exacts greater control over variation due to individual differences. In the one-way ANOVA, the F-ratio for testing the Treatment effect is only 19.52, while in the two-way design, because of the smaller denominator, the F-ratio for testing the Treatment effect is 40.13. More precise designs give rise to larger F-ratios and, therefore, provide a greater chance of detecting significant differences where they exist. Accordingly, more precise designs are also known as more powerful designs.

Thus, we include additional variables in a design not only because we may be interested in testing the relationships between these variables and the dependent variable, but also because we are interested in enhancing the power of our design by controlling the effects of these other variables. In our example, we have reduced the within-group variance by controlling for individual differences in manual dexterity due to the interaction between Gender and Treatment.

Suppose, instead, we had added a different variable other than Gender, say, preference for ice cream or yogurt, which has nothing to do with manual dexterity, as either a main or interaction effect. In this case, the variable preference would not have helped to control for additional individual differences in manual dexterity and the design would not have been more precise than the one-way design. Accordingly, the power of the two-way ANOVA in testing the Treatment effect would not have improved. In fact, by adding a variable to a design that is not related to the dependent variable, either individually or through interaction, the power of the test will diminish as Example 14.1 illustrates.

• •

EXAMPLE 14.1. Show that the two-way design including Preference for ice cream or yogurt, which is unrelated to the dependent variable of manual dexterity, and Treatment has lower power for testing the Treatment effect than the one-way design with only Treatment.

Solution. Because we believe that preference for ice cream or yogurt has nothing (zero) to do with manual dexterity as a main or interaction effect, we set SS_{PREF} and $SS_{PREFxTREAT}$ to zero in Table 14.3. We leave the degrees of freedom as they are because like Gender, Preference has only two levels: Ice cream and Yogurt. We compute a new, revised SS_W and obtain the following results.

Source of Variation	SS	df	MS	F-ratio
Preference	0	1	0/1 = 0	0/2.5 = 0
Treatment	86.67	2	86.76/2 = 43.34	43.34/2.5 = 17.34
Preference X Treatment	0	2	0/2 = 0	0/2.5 = 0
Within cells	60	24	60/24 = 2.5	
Total	146.67	29		

Notice that the *F*-ratio for Treatment decreases from a value of 19.52 in the one-way design to a value of 17.34 in the two-way design. Simply stated, adding the variable Preference to our one-way design compromises the power of our test of the Treatment effect. Preference used up one degree of freedom as a main effect and another degree of freedom as an interaction effect without explaining additional residual variance. Variables, such as these, which cannot be expected to "pull their own weight" in a design context are best excluded. Alternatively, variables that are theoretically or otherwise known to relate strongly to the dependent variable as a main or interaction effect ought to be included.

DECOMPOSING SCORE DEVIATIONS ABOUT THE GRAND MEAN

Each of the *SS* terms used to test for the main and interaction effects in a two-way design derives from a simple mathematical identity that expresses a score's total deviation from the grand mean $\left(X_{ijk} - \overline{\overline{X}} \right)$ as a sum of its component parts. In particular, we may express this identity as Equation 14.8.

$$X_{ijk} - \overline{\overline{X}} = \left({}_R\overline{X}_i - \overline{\overline{X}} \right) + \left({}_C\overline{X}_j - \overline{\overline{X}} \right) + \left(\overline{X}_{ij} - {}_R\overline{X}_i - {}_C\overline{X}_j + \overline{\overline{X}} \right) + \left(X_{ijk} - \overline{X}_{ij} \right) \qquad (14.8)$$

Equation 14.8 makes explicit the notion that each score deviation about the grand mean is represented in two-way ANOVA as a sum of (1) the row deviation about the grand mean, (2) the column deviation about the grand mean, (3) the interaction between the row and column factors, and (4) an individual difference, called error, measured as the difference between an individual's score and the mean of the group for that individual.

☞ **Remark.** What makes Equation 14.8 a mathematical identity is the fact that after simplifying the expression by removing parentheses and rearranging terms, we find, as shown in (14.9), that the value to the left of the equal sign is identical to the value to the right of the equal sign.

$$X_{ijk} - \overline{\overline{X}} = \left({}_R\overline{X}_i - \overline{\overline{X}} \right) + \left({}_C\overline{X}_j - \overline{\overline{X}} \right) + \left(\overline{X}_{ij} - {}_R\overline{X}_i - {}_C\overline{X}_j + \overline{\overline{X}} \right) + \left(X_{ijk} - \overline{X}_{ij} \right)$$

$$= X_{ijk} + {}_R\overline{X}_i + {}_C\overline{X}_j - {}_R\overline{X}_i - {}_C\overline{X}_j - \overline{\overline{X}} - \overline{\overline{X}} + \overline{\overline{X}} + \overline{X}_{ij} - \overline{X}_{ij} \qquad (14.9)$$

$$= X_{ijk} - \overline{\overline{X}}.$$

The importance of breaking down $X_{ijk} - \overline{\overline{X}}$ into its component parts is that it facilitates our understanding of where the SS terms used for testing the main and interaction effects come from. In short, Equation 14.8 makes explicit the connection between the breakdown of the total score deviation into its component parts and the partition of the total SS into its component parts. The total *SS* associated with the score deviation about the grand mean is also called the *corrected total SS*.

In particular, each score deviation in Equation 14.8 corresponds to a different *SS* term in Equation 14.2. In particular, the score deviation about the grand mean gives rise to the SS_{TOT}, the row deviation about the grand mean gives rise to the SS_{ROW}; the column deviation about the grand mean gives rise to the SS_{COL}; the interaction term gives rise to the SS_{INTER}; and the error term gives rise to SS_W.

MODELING EACH SCORE AS A SUM OF COMPONENT PARTS

If we add $\bar{\bar{X}}$ to both sides of Equation 14.8, we obtain Equation 14.10 which suggests that each score in ANOVA is comprised of a sum of five parts: (1) the grand mean, (2) the effect due to the row factor, (3) the effect due to the column factor, (4) the effect due to the interaction between row and column factors, and (5) the within-cell deviations that represent the left over, unexplained individual differences (the error). The grand mean may be thought of as a baseline value to which the value of each effect (row, column, interaction, and error) is added to obtain the score itself.

$$X_{ijk} = \bar{\bar{X}} + \left({}_R\bar{X}_i - \bar{\bar{X}} \right) + \left({}_C\bar{X}_j - \bar{\bar{X}} \right) + \left(\bar{X}_{ij} - {}_R\bar{X}_i - {}_C\bar{X}_j + \bar{\bar{X}} \right) + \left(X_{ijk} - \bar{X}_{ij} \right) \qquad (14.10)$$

In the context of our working example, Equation 14.10 suggests that two-way ANOVA models the manual dexterity score of each individual as the sum of the grand mean (which may be viewed as a baseline value), plus the effect of the individual's gender, plus the effect of which treatment the individual received, plus the joint effect of the individual's gender and treatment, plus an unexplained amount, called error. The SS associated with the original raw scores are called *raw total SS*.

EXPLAINING THE INTERACTION AS A JOINT (OR MULTIPLICATIVE) EFFECT

We have referred to the interaction between the row and column factors as a joint effect. A joint effect appropriately suggests that the combination of factors produces an effect that is more than the sum of its parts (that is, more than the sum of the effects of the two separate factors). Hays (1973) likened an interaction to what happens when two parts of hydrogen combine with one part of oxygen to produce water. Clearly that combination of hydrogen and oxygen produces an effect that is more than the sum of its parts.

We use a subset of Equation 14.8 to show that, in fact, the interaction effect is more than the sum of its parts. Equation 14.8 describes the total score deviation as a sum of its component parts. These parts may be classified broadly as the between group effects and the within group effect. In this section we consider only between group effects which are based on the difference between each group mean $\left(\bar{X}_{ij} \right)$ and the grand mean $\left(\bar{\bar{X}} \right)$. This difference is defined in Equation 14.11 as the sum of the component score deviations representing the two main effects and the interaction.

$$\bar{X}_{ij} - \bar{\bar{X}} = \left({}_R\bar{X}_i - \bar{\bar{X}} \right) + \left({}_C\bar{X}_j - \bar{\bar{X}} \right) + \left(\bar{X}_{ij} - {}_R\bar{X}_i - {}_C\bar{X}_j + \bar{\bar{X}} \right) \qquad (14.11)$$

By rearranging the terms we may show that Equation 14.11, like Equation 14.8, is a mathematical identity that simplifies to $\bar{X}_{ij} - \bar{\bar{X}} = \bar{X}_{ij} - \bar{\bar{X}}$. We may isolate the term representing the interaction effect on the right hand side of the equation by subtracting from the row and column effects from both sides of the equation. In so doing, we obtain Equation 14.12.

$$\left(\bar{X}_{ij} - \bar{\bar{X}} \right) - \left({}_R\bar{X}_i - \bar{\bar{X}} \right) - \left({}_C\bar{X}_j - \bar{\bar{X}} \right) = \left(\bar{X}_{ij} - {}_R\bar{X}_i - {}_C\bar{X}_j + \bar{\bar{X}} \right) \qquad (14.12)$$

According to Equation 14.12, the interaction is that part of the between groups effect that remains after subtracting out the sum of the separate row and column effects. Said differently, the interaction is what remains after the additive effects of the row and column factors are removed. As such, the interaction effect may be thought of as representing the joint or multiplicative effect of both row and column factors.

MEASURING EFFECT SIZE

In Chapter 13 we measured the size of an effect (e.g., Treatment) as the ratio of the SS due to that effect divided by the SS_{TOT}. As such, this ratio represents the proportion of total variance explained by or accounted for by that effect. We extend this notion to the case of two-way ANOVA where interest is in measuring the magnitude of not one, but rather three effects, the two main effects and the interaction.

By extension, the proportion of total variance explained by the row main effect, denoted as R^2_{ROW} is given by Equation 14.13.

$$R^2_{ROW} = \frac{SS_{ROW}}{SS_{TOT}} \tag{14.13}$$

The proportion of total variance explained by the column main effect, denoted as R^2_{COL}, is given by Equation 14.14.

$$R^2_{COL} = \frac{SS_{COL}}{SS_{TOT}} \tag{14.14}$$

The proportion of total variance explained by the interaction effect, denoted as R^2_{INTER}, is given by Equation 14.15.

$$R^2_{INTER} = \frac{SS_{INTER}}{SS_{TOT}} \tag{14.15}$$

Applying these ratios to the data from our manual dexterity example, we find that the proportion of manual dexterity variance due to Gender is $0.13/146.67 = .0009 = .09\%$, due to Treatment is $86.67/146.67 = .59 = 59\%$, and due to the Gender by Treatment interaction is $33.87/146.67 = .23 = 23\%$. Based on the guidelines given in Chapter 10, both the main effect due to Treatment and the Gender by Treatment interaction are very large while the main effect due to Gender is miniscule. The variable Gender contributes to this analysis not as a main effect, but in combination with Treatment as an interaction. Collectively, the three effects account for approximately 82% of the total manual dexterity variance, leaving approximately 18% unexplained.

An alternative measure of effect size is the ratio of SS due to that effect divided by the sum of the SS due to that effect plus the SS due to unexplained error after controlling for all other effects. As such, this measure of effect size may be thought of as the proportion of variance due to an effect after controlling for all other effects in the design. These measures of effect size *are* called *partial eta squared* terms because they are based on controlling for or partialling out the other effects in the design. The expressions of partial eta squared, denoted η^2, for the row and column main effects and the interaction effect are given in Equations 14.6 through 14.18, respectively. In general, for any given effect, η^2 will be larger than the corresponding R^2 for that effect.

$$\eta_{ROW}^2 = \frac{SS_{ROW}}{SS_{ROW} + SS_W} \qquad\qquad (14.16)$$

$$\eta_{COL}^2 = \frac{SS_{COL}}{SS_{COL} + SS_W} \qquad\qquad (14.17)$$

$$\eta_{INTER}^2 = \frac{SS_{INTER}}{SS_{INTER} + SS_W} \qquad\qquad (14.18)$$

• •

EXAMPLE 14.2. Use Stata to conduct a two-way ANOVA on the manual dexterity data. Verify that the answers from Stata are the same as those we obtained by hand computation.

Solution. We open the ManDext data set, which contains the data we used to conduct the one-way ANOVA consisted of two variables, treatment and score. Treatment contains the value of the treatment group (1, 2, or 3) to which an individual has been assigned, and score contains an individual's score on the manual dexterity test. In this analysis, we add another variable, Sex, that represents the gender of an individual.

MORE Stata: To carry out a two-way ANOVA with interaction

anova ManualDex Sex Treatment Sex#Treatment

Note: This syntax is similar to the syntax for the oneway ANOVA but includes the interaction between Sex and Treatment, which, as noted earlier, is represented by the term Sex#Treatment.

We obtain the following results:

	Number of obs = 30	R-squared = 0.8227			
	Root MSE = 1.04083	Adj R-squared = 0.7858			
Source	Partial SS	df	MS	F	Prob > F
Model	120.666667	5	24.1333333	22.28	0.0000
Sex	.133333333	1	.133333333	0.12	0.7288
Treatment	86.6666667	2	43.3333333	40.00	0.0000
Sex#Treatment	33.8666667	2	16.9333333	15.63	0.0000
Residual	26	24	1.08333333		
Total	146.666667	29	5.05747126		

We notice, as expected, that the model for the two-way design contains a Sex effect, a Treatment effect and an interaction effect denoted by the term Sex#Treatment. The Sex#Treatment term actually represents the product between the Sex and Treatment variables, and, as such, aligns with the fact that the interaction term represents a joint, multiplicative effect over and above the additive effects of Sex and Treatment.

The values in the two-way anova summary table for each of the effects, including the Residual (aka the within-cell or left-over variability after accounting for main and interaction effects) agree with those we obtained through our hand computation.

The SS for the term labeled Model is simply the sum of the SS terms associated with the three model effects: Sex, Treatment, and the Sex by Treatment interaction. If we divide SS_{MODEL} by SS_{TOTAL} we obtain an overall measure of the proportion of total variance explained by the model. As this measure is analogous to the measures presented in Equations 14.13 through 14.15, it too is denoted by R^2. For our working example, we have

$$R^2_{MODEL} = \frac{SS_{MODEL}}{SS_{TOTAL}}$$
$$= \frac{120.667}{146.667} \tag{14.19}$$
$$= .823$$

which is the same value we obtained from our hand computation. Because 82.3% of the total manual dexterity variance is accounted for by all three model effects taken collectively, we know that approximately 18% of this total variance remains unexplained variance. What other variables might we include in the model to account for some of this additional unexplained residual variance?

MORE Stata: To test for homogeneity of variance using Levene's test

We first need to use **egen** to arrange the cells currently organized by rows and columns into an array consisting of a single row with the number of cells equal to the product of the number of rows and columns. We then can use the **robvar** command as we did for the oneway anova.

egen cell = group(Treatment Sex)
robvar ManualDex, by(cell)

FIXED VERSUS RANDOM FACTORS

In setting up the two-way ANOVA in Stata, we treated Sex and Treatment as fixed factors. There is also the possibility to consider these variables as random factors.

A *fixed factor* is a factor whose levels have been fixed or specified by the researcher because he or she has interest in those particular levels. Because these are the levels about which the researcher would like to draw conclusions, if a replication were planned, these same levels would be present in the replication as well. Analysis of variance models appropriate for analyzing designs containing only fixed factors are called *fixed-effects models*. In the last analysis we were interested in drawing conclusions specifically about the particular Treatment I, II, and III and about Males and Females.

If, on the other hand, the researcher was not interested in the particular Treatments I, II, and III, but only in these treatments as a random sampling from the whole population of possible drug rehabilitation treatments, we could consider Treatment a *random factor*.

A *random factor* is a factor whose levels have been selected randomly from the population of all possible levels. If a replication were planned, the levels used in the first study would not necessarily be present in the replication study because in each study the levels are based on a random selection from the population of all possible levels. Analysis of variance models appropriate for analyzing designs containing only random factors are called *random-effects models*. Analysis of variance models appropriate for analyzing designs containing both fixed and random factors are called *mixed-effects models*.

In this book we restrict our discussion of analysis of variance to fixed-effects models only. For information regarding the other two models, the interested reader is referred to *Designing Experiments and Analyzing Data* by Maxwell and Delaney (2004) and *Design and Analysis: A Researcher's Handbook* by Keppel (1991).

POST-HOC MULTIPLE COMPARISON TESTS

In Chapter 13, following a statistically significant omnibus F-test in the one-way ANOVA, we conducted a series of post-hoc tests to determine which specific means differed from which others. We shall do the same in the two-way anova. But, there is a slight difference. In the one-way ANOVA, there is only one omnibus F-test. In the two-way ANOVA, there are three, one for the row main effect, another for the column main effect, and a third for the interaction. Hence, in the two-way ANOVA we shall conduct a post-hoc test for each statistically significant effect with one caveat. If an interaction effect is found to be statistically significant, then we shall conduct the post-hoc test associated with the interaction first and then decide whether it is meaningful to conduct the post-hoc tests in connection with any statistically significant main effects.

In the presence of an interaction, we know that the relationship between the two factors and the dependent variable is more complex than is suggested by either of the two main effects alone. Accordingly, in the presence of an interaction effect, we postpone an in-depth analysis of main effects until we understand the more complex nature of the interaction. As we shall see, main effects are often not meaningful in the presence of an interaction effect. In such cases, we carry out post-hoc analyses on the interaction effect only and interpret accordingly.

As we have discussed, a main effect due to a factor is simply the average effect of that factor across all levels of the other factor and is reflected by differences among the population marginal means associated with that factor.

In our working example, there is a statistically significant main effect due to Treatment. This implies that the population means of the manual dexterity scores for Treatments I, II, and III, averaged across males and females, are not all equal. If there were no interaction, we could simply ignore Sex and conduct the post-hoc tests as described in Chapter 13 to determine which treatment means are different from which others. However, there is an interaction, as the nonparallel lines of Figure 14.6, reproduced from Figure 14.2, suggest.

According to the interaction of Figure 14.6, Treatment I appears to be more effective for males, Treatment II appears to be equally as effective for both genders, and Treatment III appears to be more effective for females. Because the main effect estimates the average effect of Treatment across both males and females, it does not convey the complexities that exist in the relationship between Treatment, Gender, and manual dexterity. To convey these complexities, we must analyze the effect due to Treatment for each gender separately. That is,

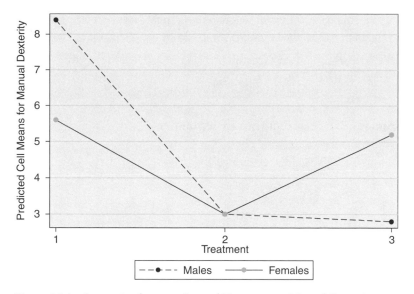

Figure 14.6 Interaction between Sex and Treatment on Manual Dexterity

we analyze the differences in treatment means represented by the solid line segments separately from the differences in treatment means represented by the dashed line segments. In so doing, we are analyzing what are called *simple effects*. If there were no interaction, the Treatment effect would be the same for males and females and there would be no reason to analyze the Treatment effect separately for males and females. In that case, we simply could investigate the Treatment effect averaged over males and females, because, in some sense, we can say, "one size fits all." Such average effects also are called marginal effects.

In more general terms, a *simple effect* is the effect of one factor at a given level of the other factor. There are as many simple effects of one factor as there are levels of the other factor.

In our working example, there are two simple effects due to Treatment because there are two levels of Sex. There is the Treatment effect for males (represented by the dashed line segments) and the Treatment effect for females (represented by the solid line segments). Given the interaction between Treatment and Gender, we need to analyze these two distinct simple effects to understand the true nature of the Treatment effect.

In testing for simple effects we increase the number of statistical tests conducted and potentially increase the probability of a family-wise Type I error. To control the family-wise error a popular approach is to use the Bonferroni adjustment for simple effects. To test the simple effects associated with the Row factor (e.g., Sex), use $\alpha = \alpha_{FW}/C$, where C is the number of levels of the column factor. Likewise, to test for simple effects associated with the Column factor (e.g., Treatment), use $\alpha = \alpha_{FW}/R$, where R is the number of levels of the row factor.

MORE Stata: To obtain the two tests of simple effects due to Treatment, one for males and one for females

We use the **margins** command, which produces a list of adjusted cell means (also called estimated marginal means) and their standard errors. The **post** option is needed to be able to carry out simple effects using the **test** command. Said differently, **post** saves or 'posts' the adjusted cell means needed to conduct the specified multiple comparisons using the **test** command.

anova ManualDex Treatment Sex Sex#Treatment
margins Sex#Treatment, post

The results from the margins command are as follows:

```
. margins Sex#Treatment, post

Adjusted predictions                                Number of obs    =       30

Expression      :  Linear prediction, predict()
```

	Margin	Delta-method Std. Err.	t	P > |t|	[95% Conf.	Interval]
Sex#Treatment						
Male#1	8.4	.4654747	18.05	0.000	7.439308	9.360692
Male#2	3	.4654747	6.45	0.000	2.039308	3.960692
Male#3	2.8	.4654747	6.02	0.000	1.839308	3.760692
Female#1	5.6	.4654747	12.03	0.000	4.639308	6.560692
Female#2	3	.4654747	6.45	0.000	2.039308	3.960692
Female#3	5.2	.4654747	11.17	0.000	4.239308	6.160692

From these results, we know that the adjusted cell mean for Males in Treatment 1 is 8.4 with standard error .465, and so on.

To test the simple effects for Treatment, we follow the **margins** command with the **test** command. Because there are three Treatment levels, each simple effect test has 3–1 or 2 degrees of freedom and so each test is composed of two contrasts, each enclosed within its own set of parentheses.

test (1.Sex#1.Treatment == 1.Sex#2.Treatment)(1.Sex#1.Treatment == 1.Sex#3.Treatment)

```
(1) 1bn.Sex #1bn.Treatment − 1bn.Sex #2.Treatment = 0
(2) 1bn.Sex #1bn. Treatment − 1bn.Sex #3.Treatment = 0

       F(2, 24)     =   46.58
       Prob > F     =   0.0000
```

test (2.Sex#1.Treatment == 2.Sex#2.Treatment)(2.Sex#1.Treatment == 2.Sex#3.Treatment)

```
(1) 2.Sex#1bn.Treatment − 2.Sex#2.Treatment = 0
(2) 2.Sex#1bn.Treatment − 2.Sex#3.Treatment = 0

       F (2, 24)    =    9.05
       Prob > F     =    0.0012
```

Each *F* test tests the simple effect of Treatment within each level of Sex. According to these results, both *F* tests are statistically significant using the Bonferroni adjustment α level (.05/2 = .025). Thus, we know that there are statistically significant treatment mean differences for both males and females.

☞ **Remark.** Conceptually, we may think of the two tests of simple effects as two one-way analyses of variance. That is, a one-way ANOVA on treatment mean differences based on males only and another one-way ANOVA on treatment mean differences based on females only. While conceptually they are similar, in actuality they are different because the one-way analyses of variance and the tests for simple effects use different error terms. The one-way ANOVA on males, for example, uses an error term based on males only. Likewise, the one-way ANOVA on females, uses an error term based on females only. These error terms are likely to be different as they are based on different groups. By contrast, the simple effect within males uses the error term from the two-way ANOVA and therefore is based on the data from both males and females combined. Likewise, the simple effect within females also uses the error term from the two-way ANOVA and is based on the data from both males and females combined. Hence, the error terms for both simple effects are equal. Use of this error term based on data from both males and females combined is most appropriate when the homogeneity of variance assumption is met. We should point out as well that when all relevant data are combined to form the estimate of the error term, the statistical power of the test is maximized.

We now examine the simple effects for Sex at each level of Treatment; i.e., whether males and females are different at each Treatment level. Because there are only 2 Sexes, each simple effect test has 2–1 or 1 degree of freedom and so each test is composed of a single contrast enclosed in a set of parentheses.

test (1.Sex#1.Treatment == 2.Sex#1.Treatment)
test (1.Sex#2.Treatment == 2.Sex#2.Treatment)
test (1.Sex#3.Treatment == 2.Sex#3.Treatment)

```
.test (1.Sex#1.Treatment == 2.Sex#1.Treatment)
(1) 1bn.Sex#1bn.Treatment – 2.Sex#1bn.Treatment = 0

                  F(1, 24)   =   18.09
                  Prob > F   =   0.0003

.test (1.Sex#2.Treatment == 2.Sex#2.Treatment)
(1) 1bn.Sex# 2.Treatment – 2.Sex#2.Treatment = 0

                  F(1, 24)   =   0.00
                  Prob > F   =   1.0000

.test (1.Sex#3.Treatment == 2.Sex#3.Treatment)
(1) 1bn.Sex#3.Treatment – 2.Sex#3.Treatment = 0

                  F(1, 24)   =   13.29
                  Prob > F   =   0.0013
```

These results suggest that males and females have significantly different Manual Dexterity means under Treatments 1 ($p = 0.0003$) and 3 ($p = 0.0013$), but not under Treatment 2 ($p = 1.000$). Here, we have used $\alpha = .05/3 = .017$ for our significance level.

We may further explore all pairwise differences between the adjusted cell means using the command **pwcompare**. The option **group** displays a table of means with codes that indicate which groups have means that are not significantly different from each other.

> **anova ManualDex Sex Treatment Sex#Treatment**
> **pwcompare Sex#Treatment, group**

The results from this command are as follows:

Pairwise comparisons of marginal linear predictions

Margins:	asbalanced		
Sex#Treatment	Margin	Std. Err.	Unadjusted Groups
Male#1	8.4	.4654747	
Male#2	3	.4654747	A
Male#3	2.8	.4654747	A
Female#1	5.6	.4654747	B
Female#2	3	.4654747	A
Female#3	5.2	.4654747	B

Note: Margins sharing a letter in the group label are not significantly different at the 5% level.

According to these results, we may note that males in Treatment 1 are significantly different from all other groups; that females in Treatments 1 and 3 are not different from each other, but are different from the other groups, and that females in Treatment 2 and males in Treatments 2 and 3 are not different from each other.

SUMMARY OF STEPS TO BE TAKEN IN A TWO-WAY ANOVA PROCEDURE

In summary, we may express the sequence of tests in a two-way analysis of variance as follows.

1. Conduct the two-way ANOVA using the ANOVA command with the interaction between the two categorical variables (i.e., Treatment#Sex) and the given α level.
2. If the interaction term and both main effects are not statistically significant, do not proceed with post hoc testing.
3. If the interaction term is not statistically significant, but one or both main effects are statistically significant, examine the marginal effects for each main effect that is statistically significant, adjusting the alpha level using the Bonferroni adjustment.
4. If the interaction term is statistically significant do the following steps as we did in our running example:
   a) Test for simple effects of the row factor within the column factor, and if desired, test for simple effects of the column factor within the row factor as well. To control the family-wise Type I error for testing simple effects associated with the Row factor, use $\alpha = \alpha_{FW}/C$ and for testing simple effects associated with the Column factor use $\alpha = \alpha_{FW}/R$.

b) Follow all tests of simple effects that are statistically significant with tests of pair-wise comparisons on the individual group means within each simple effect.

c) Finally, if meaningful, conduct all pairwise comparisons on the marginal means for each main effect that is statistically significant.

● ●

EXAMPLE 14.3. For this example we turn to the *Wages* data set. Given a sample of 100 males and 100 females randomly selected from the 534 cases that comprised the 1985 Current Population Survey in a way that controls for highest education level attained. The sample of 200 contains 20 males and 20 females with less than a high school diploma, 20 males and 20 females with a high school diploma, 20 males and 20 females with some college training, 20 males and 20 females with a college diploma, and 20 males and 20 females with some graduate school training. As such, the study may be described as a 2 x 5 (gender by education level) factorial design. Use the two-way ANOVA procedure to explore the relationship between gender (male, female), highest education level attained, and hourly wage. Specifically, investigate (a) whether there are differences in hourly wage by gender, and (b) by highest education level attained, and (c) whether there is an interaction between gender and highest education level attained on hourly wage. The data are contained in file *Wages*. The syntax used for this set of analyses may be found in the Do-file associated with this chapter.

Solution. Using a two-way ANOVA, with the variables sex and education as the independent variables and hourly wage as the dependent variable, we obtain the following descriptive statistics, and omnibus F test results for the two-way ANOVA.

. tabulate ed sex, summarize (wage)

Means, Standard Deviations and Frequencies of Wage
(dollars per hour)

Highest education level	sex		Total
	Male	Female	
Less than	7.3315	5.6145	6.473
	3.9287896	2.4767482	3.3755991
	40	40	80
High scho	8.3235	6.047	7.18525
	3.9158983	2.8644883	3.5962209
	40	40	80
Some coll	10.24	7.81	9.025
	4.9996318	2.8076379	4.2102719
	40	40	80
College d	12.3235	10.061	11.19225
	5.3958353	4.4041366	5.0244025
	40	40	80

(continued)

Graduate	13.1465	12.379	12.76275
	6.9973513	5.69452	6.3505307
	40	40	80
Total	10.273	8.3823	9.32765
	5.5891756	4.581561	5.1908832
	200	200	400

We may note that males earn more than females (mean hourly wage for males is $10.26 while for females it is $8.38) and that education level varies directly with hourly wage (as education level increases so does hourly wage, from $6.47, to $7.18, to $9.03, to $11.19, and to $12.76). Furthermore, we may note that the relationship between education level and hourly wage appears to be the same for males and females, suggesting that there is no interaction between gender and education level on hourly wage. The plot of mean values given below presents a visual account of these tentative conclusions.

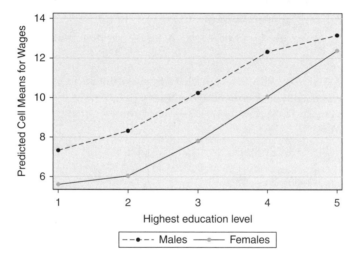

In particular, the mean hourly wage for males averaged across education levels is higher than the mean hourly wage for females averaged across education level. Also, the mean hourly wage for each level of education averaged across males and females increases as education level increases. Finally, while not exactly parallel, these two sets of line segments, one for males and one for females, are closely parallel suggesting the absence of an interaction between gender and education level on hourly wage.

Before looking at the results of the two-way ANOVA, we need to evaluate the tenability of the independence, equal cell sizes, normality and homogeneity of variance assumptions. The wages are independent because individuals were randomly selected separately for each cell. Each cell has size n = 40 so that the cell sizes are equal. The two-way ANOVA is robust to violations of the normality assumption because each cell contains more than 30 subjects.

In addition, because the sample sizes in each group are equal, however, the validity of the F test is not compromised and we may proceed with the analysis of variance to determine whether our observed results are significant of differences in the population.

The results of the two-way ANOVA are given below. As expected, these results indicate that while both main effects due to gender and education level are statistically significant, the interaction is not. We use post hoc comparisons to determine which specific means are different from which others. Because the interaction effect is not statistically significant, we are only interested in comparing the marginal means relative to education level and gender.

```
. anova wage ed sex ed#sex

                Number of obs    =      400     R-squared      =  0.2459
                Root MSE         =   4.5595     Adj R-squared  =  0.2285
```

Source	Partial SS	df	MS	F	Prob > F
Model	2643.4398	9	293.715533	14.13	0.0000
ed	2248.57173	4	562.142931	27.04	0.0000
sex	357.474649	1	357.474649	17.20	0.0000
ed#sex	37.393426	4	9.3483565	0.45	0.7726
Residual	8107.72219	390	20.7890313		
Total	10751.162	399	26.9452681		

Because the interaction is not statistically significant, we only need to conduct pairwise comparisons for each main effect that has more than two levels. Because the sex factor only has 2 levels, by virtue of the fact that it is statistically significant, we know that males differ from females in terms of wages and from the summary table, know that males' wages exceed those of females. To conduct the pairwise comparisons on education we use the pwcompare command, adjusting the multiple comparisons using the tukey adjustment. The effects option displays the table of contrasts (pairwise differences in this case) with confidence intervals and p-values.

We obtain the following results.

```
. pw compare ed, mcompare (tukey) effects

Pairwise comparisons of marginal linear predictions

Margins       :  asbalanced
```

	Number of Comparisons
ed	10

	Contrast	Std. Err.	Tukey t	P > |t|	Tukey [95% Conf.	Interval]
ed						
High school degree vs Less than h.s.degree	.71225	.7209201	0.99	0.861	−1.263492	2.687992
Some college vs Less than h.s.degree	2.552	.7209201	3.54	0.004	.5762584	4.527742
College degree vs Lessthan h.s.degree	4.71925	.7209201	6.55	0.000	2.743508	6.694992
Graduate school vs Lessthan h.s.degree	6.28975	.7209201	8.72	0.000	4.314008	8.265492
Some college vs High school degree	1.83975	.7209201	2.55	0.082	−.1359916	3.815492
College degree vs High school degree	4.007	.7209201	5.56	0.000	2.031258	5.982742
Graduate school vs High school degree	5.5775	.7209201	7.74	0.000	3.601758	7.553242
College degree vs Some college	2.16725	.7209201	3.01	0.023	.1915084	4.142992
Graduate school vs Some college	3.73775	.7209201	5.18	0.000	1.762008	5.713492
Graduate school vs College degree	1.5705	.7209201	2.18	0.190	−.4052416	3.546242

According to the results of the post hoc test on education level, the mean hourly wage for those with less than a high school degree is not statistically significantly different from the mean hourly wage for those with a high school degree, but it is statistically significantly lower than all other educational attainments. The mean hourly wage for those with a high school degree is not statistically significantly different from the mean hourly wage for those with a college degree, but it is statistically significantly lower than for those with a college degree or graduate school. All other pairwise differences are statistically significant with the population mean hourly wage for those with a graduate degree the highest, followed by those with a college degree, followed by those with some college.

SUMMARY OF STATA COMMANDS IN CHAPTER 14

For a complete listing of all Stata commands associated with this chapter, you may access the Do-file for Chapter 14 located on the text website.

Create	Command Lines
Generate a table of cell and marginal means, standard deviations and sample sizes. (Table 14.4)	**tabulate Sex Treatment, summarize(ManualDex)** Or **table Sex Treatment, contents(n ManualDex mean ManualDex sd ManualDex) row col format(%6.2f)**
Create a line graph of means to illustrate the two-way ANOVA of ManualDex by Sex and Treatment (Figure 14.2)	**anova ManualDex Sex Treatment Sex#Treatment predict yhat** **twoway (line yhat Treatment if Sex == 1, lpattern(dash)) (line yhat Treatment if Sex == 2, lpattern(solid)), legend(label(1 "Males") label(2 "Females")) ytitle("Predicted Cell Means for Manual Dexterity") xlabel(1 2 3)**
Create a clustered bar graph to illustrate the two-way ANOVA of ManualDex by Sex and Treatment (Figure 14.5)	**graph bar yhat, over(Sex) over(Treatment) asyvars ytitle("Predicted Cell Means for Manual Dexterity")**
Calculate within-cell skewness and other statistics	**statsby skew=r(skewness), by(Treatment Sex): summarize ManualDex, detail** **tabdisp Sex Treatment, cell(skew)** **Or** **by Sex Treatment, sort: summarize ManualDex, detail**
Generate descriptive statistics associated with the ANOVA for detecting mean differences in ManualDex by Treatment and Sex.	**statsby skew=r(skewness), by(Treatment Sex): summarize ManualDex, detail** **tabdisp Sex Treatment, cell(skew)** To obtain a more complete set of summary statistics:

Create	Command Lines
	by Sex Treatment, sort: summarize ManualDex, detail
	And, to obtain the skewness ratio, we type:
	summskewcell ManualDex Treatment Sex
To obtain the results of Levene's test associated with the two way ANOVA for detecting mean differences in ManualDex by Treatment and Sex	**egen cell = group(Treatment Sex)** **robvar ManualDex, by(cell)**
Perform the two way ANOVA for detecting mean differences in ManualDex by Treatment and Sex with interaction (Example 14.2)	**anova ManualDex Sex Treatment Sex#Treatment** **OR** **anova ManualDex Sex##Treatment**
Perform post hoc testing for mean difference main effects in the ANOVA if there is no interaction.	**anova ManualDex Treatment Sex Sex#Treatment** **margins Treatment, post** **pwmean ManualDex, over(Treatment)** **mcompare(bonferroni) effects** **OR** **pwcompare Treatment, mcompare(bonferroni) effects**
Perform post hoc testing for the interaction in the ANOVA for detecting mean differences in ManualDex by Treatment and Sex. (Example 14.2)	**anova ManualDex Treatment Sex Sex#Treatment** **margins Sex#Treatment, post** **test (1.Sex#1.Treatment == 1.Sex#2.Treatment)** **(1.Sex#1.Treatment == 1.Sex#3.Treatment)** **test (2.Sex#1.Treatment == 2.Sex#2.Treatment)** **(2.Sex#1.Treatment == 2.Sex#3.Treatment)** **Alternatively, we may use the contrast command as follows: contrast Treatment@Sex**

EXERCISES

*Create a .do file for each exercise that requires the use of Stata. Run the commands from the Do-file by highlighting them and hitting **Control+d**. Save each Do-file using a name associated with the Exercise for which it was created. It is recommended that you review the Do-file for* Chapter 14 *located on the textbook's website before completing these exercises. To facilitate doing each exercise, it may be helpful to copy and paste relevant commands from the Do-file for* Chapter 14 *into your own Do-file and modify them as needed.*

14.1. The following illustrations are of population means and are, therefore, not subject to sampling error. They are based on the results of a fictional study to determine whether there is a relationship between gender, teaching method, and achievement in reading.

Assume that each illustration represents a 2x3 between-subjects factorial design with equal cell sizes. Use the line graphs to answer the following questions.

For each graph:

    a) Is there a main effect due to gender? What mean values are compared to make this assessment?

    b) Is there a main effect due to teaching method? What mean values are compared to make this assessment?

    c) Is there an interaction effect? What mean values or differences in mean values are compared to make this assessment?

    d) Interpret the relative effectiveness of teaching method for males and females.

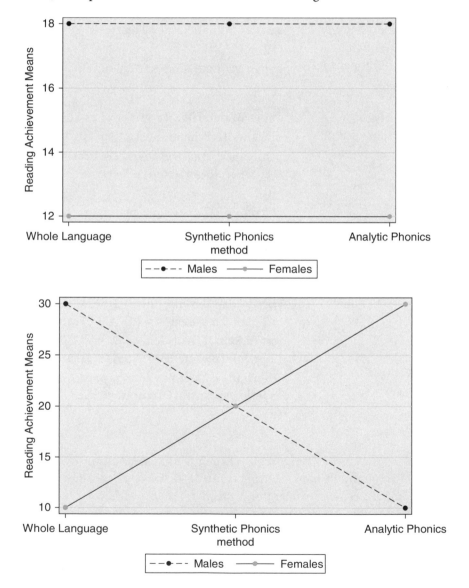

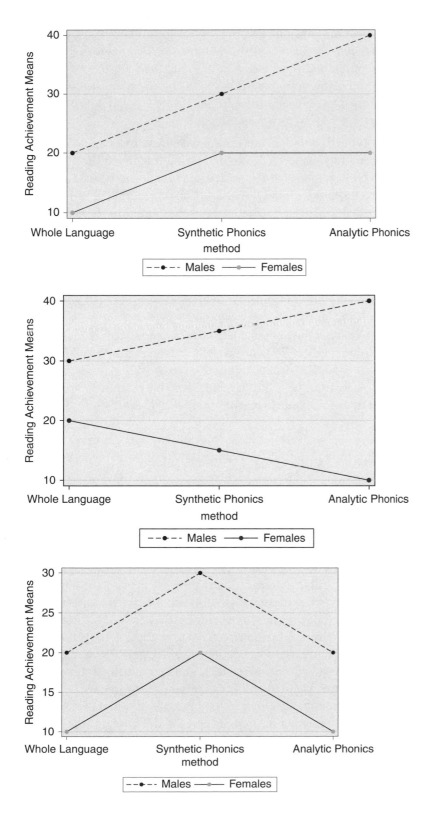

Exercises 14.2–14.3 involve Framingham data set. In this series of exercises, we, respectively, investigate whether body mass index and age varied as a function of gender, whether or not the person smoked cigarettes, and the interaction of gender and whether or not the person smoked cigarettes. For inferential purposes, as described in the study itself, we consider the people in the Framingham data set to be a random sample of the population of all noninstitutionalized adults. Use α = .05 for all significance tests.

14.2. The Body Mass Index is a tool for indicating weight status in adults. The following questions relate to using a two-way ANOVA to determine whether at the beginning of the Framingham study body mass index (BMI1) varied as a function of gender (SEX), whether the person smoked (CURSMOKE1), and the interaction of gender and smoking status.

    a) State the null and alternative hypotheses for each of the three tests associated with the ANOVA.

    b) Create a multiple line graph of the sample means. Based on this graph, does there appear to be a statistically significant interaction effect? A statistically significant main effect due to gender? A statistically significant main effect due to cigarette use?

    c) Evaluate the tenability of the normality assumption for these data or indicate why the assumption is not an issue for this analysis.

    d) Evaluate the tenability of the homogeneity of variance assumption for these data or indicate why the assumption is not an issue for this analysis.

    e) According to the ANOVA results, is there a statistically significant interaction effect? Is there a statistically significant main effect due to gender? Is there a statistically significant main effect due to cigarette use? Provide statistical support for your answer.

    f) Is *post-hoc* testing necessary in this case? Why or why not? Interpret results.

    g) Calculate and interpret the effect sizes of the statistically significant effects.

14.3. The following questions relate to using a two-way ANOVA to determine whether at the beginning of the Framingham study that age (AGE1) varied as a function of gender (SEX), whether a person smoked (CURSMOKE1), and the interaction of gender and smoking status. Given the nature of the study design, the ANOVA, in this case, is considered to be robust to both normality and homogeneity of variance assumptions.

    a) Create a multiple line graph of the sample means. Based on this graph, does there appear to be a statistically significant interaction effect? A statistically significant main effect due to gender? A statistically significant main effect due to cigarette use?

    b) According to the ANOVA results, is there a statistically significant interaction effect? A statistically significant main effect due to gender? A statistically significant main effect due to cigarette use? Provide statistical support for your answer.

    c) Given the statistically significant interaction, conduct and interpret simple effects, holding constant, in turn, cigarette use and then gender. If appropriate, conduct additional *post-hoc* tests as well. Note that in the presence of this statistically significant interaction, main effects are not meaningful and should not be interpreted per se.

    d) Calculate and interpret the effect sizes of the statistically significant effects.

Exercise 14.4 makes use of the Wages data set. In this exercise we are interested in whether number of years of work experience as of 1985 varies as a function of education level and gender. For inferential purposes, we consider the people in the Wages data set to be a random sample of the population of all adults living in America in 1985. Use α = .05 throughout this example.

14.4. The following questions relate to using a two-way ANOVA to determine whether the number of years of work experience as of 1985 (exper) varies as a function of gender (sex), education level (ed), or the interaction between gender and education level.

a) Create a multiple line graph of the sample means. Based on this graph, does there appear to be a statistically significant interaction effect? A statistically significant main effect due to gender? A statistically significant main effect due to education level?

b) Evaluate the tenability of the normality assumption for these data or indicate why the assumption is not an issue for this analysis.

c) Evaluate the tenability of the homogeneity of variance assumption for these data or indicate why the assumption is not an issue for this analysis.

d) According to the ANOVA results, is there a statistically significant interaction effect? A statistically significant main effect due to gender? A statistically significant main effect due to education? Provide statistical support for your answer.

e) Given the statistically significant disordinal interaction, conduct and interpret a test of simple effects, and additional *post-hoc* tests, if necessary.

f) Calculate and interpret the effect sizes of the statistically significant effects.

Exercises 14.5 and 14.6 require that you first enter the given data into Stata. Use $\alpha = .05$ for all significance tests.

14.5. Professor Dani teaches an undergraduate introductory statistics course. She teaches students from all four academic years in both morning and afternoon classes. She has reason to believe that either the grade level of the students or the time of the course or both may affect how well undergraduate students at her college do in her course. To test her conjecture, she randomly selects 40 of the students who register for her introductory statistics course the following term, 10 from each academic year, with 20 of those registered for the morning and 20 for the afternoon. At the end of the semester, she gives both classes the same final exam and arranges their final exam scores in a two-way analysis of variance design, as shown in the following table. Use it to answer the following questions.

		Factor B: Academic Year			
		Freshmen	**Sophomores**	**Juniors**	**Seniors**
Factor A:	Morning	80	85	93	100
Time of Course		80	80	90	98
		75	80	89	95
		70	83	87	93
		70	82	87	90
	Afternoon	70	75	85	88
		70	71	84	83
		65	70	80	80
		60	69	73	79
		60	65	72	75

a) Create a table of cell and marginal means and standard deviations.

b) Evaluate the tenability of the underlying normality and homogeneity of variance assumptions or indicate why the assumptions are not an issue for this analysis.

c) Are any of the effects statistically significant? If so, which ones? Provide statistical support for your answer.

d) What is the proportion of variance explained by each of the statistically significant effects?

e) Create a line graph of the cell means to illustrate the effects. Explain how the line graph corroborates the results of the significance tests.

f) Describe the nature of the main effect due to time and explain why a Tukey post hoc test is not necessary in this case.

g) Carry out a Tukey HSD *post-hoc* test on the main effect due to academic year to determine exactly which academic levels are different from which others with respect to final exam performance.

14.6. The data for this exercise are taken from the following website: http://lib.stat.cmu .edu/DASL/Datafiles/Stepping.html.

Students at Ohio State University conducted an experiment in the fall of 1993 to explore the nature of the relationship between a person's heart rate and the frequency at which that person stepped up and down on steps of various heights. The response variable, heart rate, was measured in beats per minute. For each person, the resting heart rate was measured before a trial (RestHR) and after stepping (HR). There were two different step heights (HEIGHT): 5.75 inches (coded as 0), and 11.5 inches (coded as 1). There were three rates of stepping (FREQUENCY): 14 steps/min. (coded as 0), 21 steps/min. (coded as 1), and 28 steps/min. (coded as 2). This resulted in six possible height/frequency combinations. Each subject performed the activity for three minutes. Subjects were kept on pace by the beat of an electric metronome. One experimenter counted the subject's heart rate, in beats per minute, for 20 seconds before and after each trial. The subject always rested between trials until her or his heart rate returned to close to the beginning rate. Another experimenter kept track of the time spent stepping. Each subject was always measured and timed by the same pair of experimenters to reduce variability in the experiment.

The data are saved in the file *Stepping.dta*. The following questions relate to using a two-way ANOVA to determine whether final heart rate (HRFinal) varies by stepping rate (Freq), step height (Height), and the interaction between the two.

Height	Freq	HRInit	HRFinal
0	0	60	75
0	1	63	84
1	2	69	135
1	0	69	108
0	2	69	93
1	1	96	141
1	0	87	120
0	0	90	99
1	2	93	153
0	2	87	129
1	1	72	99
0	1	69	93
1	0	78	93

Height	Freq	HRInit	HRFinal
0	2	72	99
1	2	78	129
0	0	87	93
1	1	87	111
1	2	81	120
0	2	75	123
0	1	81	96
1	0	84	99
1	0	84	99
1	1	90	129
0	1	75	90
0	0	78	87
0	0	84	84
0	1	90	108
0	2	78	96
1	1	84	90
1	2	90	147

a) Evaluate the tenability of the underlying normality and homogeneity of variance assumptions or indicate why the assumptions are not an issue for this analysis.

b) Is there a statistically significant interaction effect? Provide statistical support for your answer.

c) Is there a statistically significant main effect due to stepping rate? Provide statistical support for your answer.

d) Describe the nature of the main effect due to stepping rate.

e) Is there a statistically significant main effect due to step height? Provide statistical support for your answer.

f) Describe the nature of the main effect due to step height.

14.7. Three methods of dieting are compared for effectiveness in terms of pounds lost. Because it is believed that a person's gender may influence the relative effectiveness of the three methods, a two-way ANOVA balanced design with equal cell sizes is employed and the summary table is provided.

Tests of Between-Subjects Effects

Dependent Variable: Weight Loss

Source	Type III Sum of Squares	df	Mean Square	F	Sig.
Corrected Model	626.400[a]	5	125.280	18.514	.000
Intercept	4177.200	1	4177.200	617.320	.000
GENDER	48.133	1	48.133	7.113	.013
TREATMEN	453.800	2	226.900	33.532	.000
GENDER * TREATMEN	124.467	2	62.233	9.197	.001
Error	162.400	24	6.767		
Total	4966.000	30			
Corrected Total	788.800	29			

a. R Squared = .794 (Adjusted R Squared = .751)

a) Describe the design by filling in the blanks in the following sentence: The design is a ___ x ___ balanced ANOVA with ___ participants per cell.

b) Had we performed a one-way ANOVA to look at weight loss by treatment, ignoring gender, how would the results have differed? Complete the following table by filling in the values of the shaded boxes.

Weight Loss by Treatment

	Sum of Squares	df	Mean Square	F	Sig.
Between Groups					
Within Groups					
Total					

c) Which of the two types of design, the one-way or two-way, is the more powerful test of treatment, in this case? Explain.

14.8. A hypothetical study was conducted to determine whether weight differs by incidence of coronary heart disease (CHD) and cigarette use. One hundred people were randomly selected from among each of the four conditions: no CHD nonsmokers, no CHD smokers, CHD nonsmokers, and CHD smokers. The following line graph represents the results of the study.

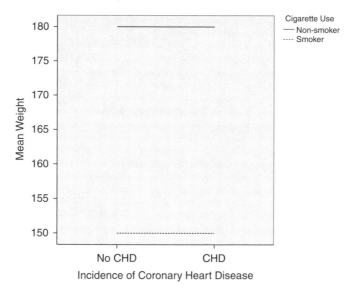

a) Does the line graph suggest a main effect due to Cigarette Use? If so, describe the nature of the effect.

b) Does the line graph suggest a main effect due to Incidence of Coronary Heart Disease? If so, describe the nature of the effect.

c) Does the line graph suggest an interaction effect? If so, describe the nature of the effect.

d) The factorial ANOVA design in this situation is orthogonal (or balanced) because
   (i) the lines representing the mean weights of the cells are parallel

(ii) the cell sizes are all equal

(iii) there are two factors represented (Cigarette Use and Incidence of Coronary Heart Disease (CHD)) in a 2×2 configuration

(iv) none of the above

e) Based on the results depicted in the line graph, complete the two-way ANOVA table by filling in the values of the shaded boxes.

Source of Variation	SS	df	MS	F-value	p-value
CHD					
Cigarette Use					
Interaction					
Error	35,000				
Total	76,000				

14.9. Is the number of sources of variance in a 2×3 ANOVA design different from the number of sources of variance in a 3×5 ANOVA design? What are these sources of variance?

14.10. Under what conditions, in general, is the two-way ANOVA more powerful than the one-way ANOVA?

CHAPTER FIFTEEN

Correlation and Simple Regression as Inferential Techniques

In Chapter 5, we discussed the Pearson Product Moment Correlation Coefficient used to assess the degree of linear relationship between two variables. Recall that in that chapter we assessed the degree of linear relationship between fat grams and calories by type of McDonald's hamburger as one example. In Chapter 6, we discussed how this linear relationship could be used to develop a linear prediction system (a linear regression equation) to predict the value of one variable when the value of the other variable is known. Recall that in that chapter we developed a linear regression equation for predicting the number of calories in a McDonald's hamburger from its fat grams.

In both situations, our discussions were limited to descriptive settings. That is, our measures of linear relationship and accuracy of prediction were confined to the data at hand. In this chapter, we discuss inferential techniques applicable to measures of relationship and linear regression that enable us to generalize our results from a sample to the population from which that sample was randomly selected.

As with other inferential techniques described in this text, the inferential techniques described in this chapter are based also on certain assumptions about the distribution of the parent population. Because the parent population relevant to measuring the linear relationship between two variables is comprised of *pairs of values*, the distribution of this parent population is described as a *joint distribution*, and, in particular, as a *bivariate distribution*. Extending the assumption of population normality in the case of inferential tests based on univariate distributions (e.g., tests of means), the major assumption underlying the inferential test of a linear relationship between two variables is that of *bivariate normality* in the population. That is, the parent population from which the sample of pairs of values has been randomly selected is assumed in this case to have a bivariate normal distribution.

THE BIVARIATE NORMAL DISTRIBUTION

A bivariate distribution is a special case of a joint distribution in which exactly two variables are considered simultaneously or jointly. If we call one variable X and the other variable Y, we can depict a bivariate distribution graphically by using a scatterplot with the two axes labeled X and Y, respectively. Figure 15.1 shows a bivariate distribution and its corresponding scatterplot.

While all pairs of values in Figure 15.1 occur with frequency of 1, in other situations, some of the pairs of values, if not all, can occur with frequency greater than 1. Figure 15.2 shows a bivariate distribution with some frequencies of pairs of values greater than 1 along with its scatterplot. In this scatterplot, the different frequencies of the pairs of values are represented by the relative sizes of the points.

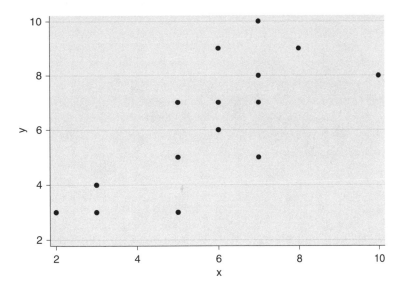

Figure 15.1 A bivariate distribution and its corresponding scatterplot.

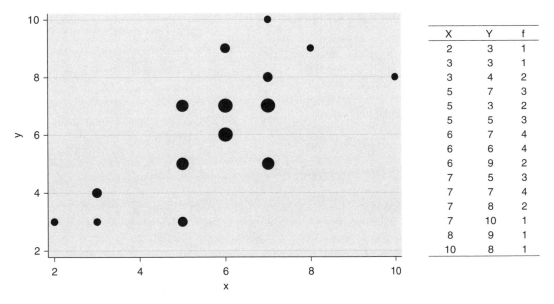

X	Y	f
2	3	1
3	3	1
3	4	2
5	7	3
5	3	2
5	5	3
6	7	4
6	6	4
6	9	2
7	5	3
7	7	4
7	8	2
7	10	1
8	9	1
10	8	1

Figure 15.2 A bivariate distribution and scatterplot with some frequencies greater than 1.

If X and Y are both continuous and they assume all possible values with varied frequencies, we can more effectively represent the frequencies as a third axis perpendicular to the X and Y axes. In this case, the bivariate frequency distribution of X and Y would be represented graphically as a continuous surface (kind of like a tent) sitting on top of the X, Y plane. In this chapter, we are interested in a specific type of bivariate distribution, a *bivariate normal distribution*. Such a distribution has the following seven characteristics.

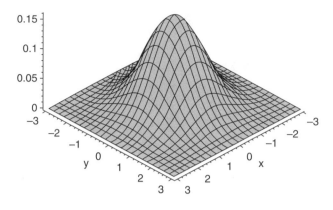

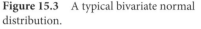

Figure 15.3 A typical bivariate normal distribution.

1. Taken separately, the X and Y variables are both normally distributed.
2. When X is held constant at any value (for example, $X = a$), the distribution of all those Y values corresponding to this value of X (called the conditional distribution of Y given $X = a$) is normally distributed.
3. When Y is held constant at any value (for example, $Y = b$), the distribution of all those X values corresponding to this value of Y (called the conditional distribution of X given $Y = b$) is normally distributed.
4. All the conditional distributions of Y given X have the same standard deviation $\sigma_{Y|X}$.
5. All the conditional distributions of X given Y have the same standard deviation $\sigma_{X|Y}$.
6. The means of all the conditional distributions of Y given X fall along a straight line.
7. The means of all the conditional distributions of X given Y fall along a straight line.

We may cluster the seven characteristics of the bivariate normal distribution into the following three properties:

Normality – Characteristics 1, 2, and 3
Homoscedasticity – Characteristics 4 and 5
Linearity – Characteristics 6 and 7

As we would expect from our experience with univariate normal distributions (normal distributions of one variable), all bivariate normal distributions give rise to frequency or relative frequency curves of a particular shape. This shape is often described as a bell that has been stretched in one direction sitting above the X, Y plane. Figure 15.3 shows a typical bivariate normal distribution curve when there is no stretching in either direction; that is, when the correlation between X and Y is zero. The bivariate normal distribution of Figure 15.3 may be described as a Hershey kiss with its top licked down a bit!

Figure 15.4 shows the same bivariate normal distribution curve composed of a series of cross sections or slices at particular values of X. Each slice is a conditional distribution of Y given X. Notice that all slices satisfy the conditional distribution characteristics of a bivariate normal distribution. They are normally distributed (*normality*) with the same standard deviation $\sigma_{Y|X}$ (*homoscedasticity*) and their means all fall along a straight line (*linearity*).

The assumption of bivariate normality (defined by the characteristics of linearity, homoscedasticity and normality) in the population is required for the tests of inference

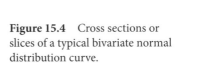

Figure 15.4 Cross sections or slices of a typical bivariate normal distribution curve.

introduced in this chapter regarding the Pearson Product Moment Correlation Coefficient. In this chapter we discuss methods to evaluate these assumptions. Correlation is a symmetric index. That is, the value of the correlation indicates the degree to which X relates to Y and the degree to which Y relates to X.

☞ **Remark.** Less restrictive assumptions are required for tests of inference regarding (simple) linear regression. The assumptions of linearity, homoscedasticity, and normality are still required but as they concern the population conditional Y distributions given X (the slices illustrated in Figure 15.4), and not the conditional X distributions given Y as well. Less restrictive assumptions are appropriate in simple linear regression because it is based on an asymmetric relationship between X and Y. The asymmetric relationship is created by the necessity of designating Y as the dependent variable, and in so doing, emphasizing the importance of Y over X.

TESTING WHETHER THE POPULATION PEARSON PRODUCT MOMENT CORRELATION EQUALS ZERO

Suppose you are making extra money one summer by selling ice cream on the beach and notice that a positive trend exists between the daily highest temperature and the number of ice cream bars you sell that day. Suppose also that you are an astute businessperson and do not want to have to carry and refrigerate more ice cream than you will be able to sell. Accordingly, you check the weather forecast each morning, and the higher the temperature is expected to be, the more ice cream bars you take out with you. In other words, you use the temperature to *predict* your ice cream sales.

But, we can be even more systematic than this in making our predictions. Table 15.1 contains the temperature and ice cream sales for 30 days randomly selected between May 15th and September 6th. It is saved as the file *Ice Cream.dta*.

Figure 15.5 presents the scatterplot of the bivariate distribution given in Table 15.1. The regression line for predicting sales from temperature is included in the plot as well.

TABLE 15.1. Temperature and ice cream sales for 30 randomly selected summer days

TEMP	BARSOLD
75	170
70	160
65	155
60	150
72	153
60	142
63	145
68	156
78	170
77	172
75	165
75	167
80	175
82	180
85	180
59	143
86	173
88	176
85	177
90	185
74	163
73	160
71	162
68	148
70	160
73	154
85	169
90	178
70	175
81	164

MORE Stata: To obtain a scatterplot with a regression line superimposed as in Figure 15.5, we use the following command:

twoway (scatter barsold temp) (lfit barsold temp)

The first part of this command creates the twoway scatterplot, and the second part plots the regression fit line over the scatterplot.

According to Figure 15.5, we may surmise that the linear relationship is a strong one as the points hug the regression line rather well. Furthermore, the nature of the relationship is positive – with each unit increase in temperature along the horizontal axis, there is a corresponding increase in sales along the vertical axis.

While this relationship appears to be a strong one, it is based only on 30 randomly selected days. Our question of true interest is whether this relationship based on 30 randomly selected days holds for all summer days during the time period sampled. In this context, we consider the sample correlation (r) as an estimate of the population correlation coefficient (*rho* or ρ) and apply an inferential test to determine whether the correlation between temperature and sales is greater than zero in the population. That is, whether the observed correlation coefficient r based on the sample data is greater enough from zero to infer that the corresponding population parameter ρ based on all summer days during the time period sampled is greater than zero as well.

Because our hypothesis is directional in this case, our null and alternative hypotheses are:

$H_0: \rho = 0$
$H_1: \rho > 0$

We assume that the parent population from which we have randomly sampled our 30 pairs of values has a bivariate normal distribution (as defined in the previous section). If the null hypothesis, $H_0: \rho = 0$ is true, then it can be shown mathematically that the appropriate sampling distribution is the t distribution presented earlier in connection with tests on means, and the appropriate t statistic is:

$$t = \frac{r - 0}{\sqrt{(1 - r^2)/(N - 2)}} \tag{15.1}$$

$$df = N - 2$$

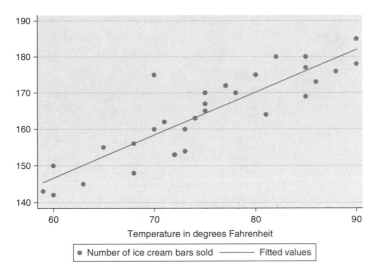

Figure 15.5 Scatterplot of bivariate distribution relating temperature to number of ice creams bars sold.

where r represents the sample Pearson Product Moment correlation coefficient and $N - 2$ equals the number of degrees of freedom, two less than the number of pairs of values in the sample.

As we have done in Chapter 5, we use Stata to calculate the Pearson Product Moment correlation. Before proceeding, however, we use the scatterplot of this small data set represented in Figure 15.5 to check informally whether the assumptions of linearity, homoscedasticity, and normality are viable. According to Figure 15.5, violations of these assumptions do not appear to exist. The points conform reasonably well to a linear pattern supporting the assumption of linearity; the spread of ice cream sales for each temperature value (the conditional distributions of ice cream sales given temperature) and the spread of temperature given ice cream sales (the conditional distributions of temperature given ice cream sales) appears similar, supporting the assumption of homoscedasticity; overall, there do not appear to be severe outliers either in the univariate or conditional distributions, supporting the assumption of normality.

MORE Stata: To obtain the Pearson Product Moment Correlation along with the significance level and the number of observations

pwcorr barsold temp, obs sig

We obtain the following output:

	barsold	temp
barsold	1.0000	
	30	
temp	0.8867	1.0000
	0.0000	
	30	30

The correlation between number of ice cream bars sold and temperature in degrees Fahrenheit is .887 based on the $N = 30$ pairs of values. The double asterisk indicates that the correlation is significant at the .01 level (1-tailed). A more exact p-value (.000) is given in the correlation matrix itself, suggesting that in fact $p < .0005$.

While the significance (p-value) of the correlation that is provided in the output is based on the t-statistic given as Equation 15.1, the t-value itself is not provided. We may calculate it, however, as:

$$t = \frac{r-0}{\sqrt{(1-r^2)/(N-2)}} = \frac{.887-0}{\sqrt{(1-.887^2)/(30-2)}} = \frac{.887}{\sqrt{.213/28}} = \frac{.887}{.087} = 10.20$$

We may also note that the degrees of freedom for this example are $N - 2 = 30 - 2 = 28$.

If we wish, we may use the obtained t-value and corresponding degrees of freedom to find the p-value using the Stata function ttail(df, t) or from Table 2 in Appendix C online, www.cambridge.org/Stats-Stata.

Using Stata, we find that **display ttail(28, 10.1) = 3.862e-11** = .0000000000386, justifying the value provided in the correlation matrix. Using Table 2, we obtain the estimate $p < .0005$.

☞ **Remark.** To confirm that the t-value is correct as calculated, we may use the following command, **regress**, to predict barsold from temp, and check the t-value for the b-weight for temp. This is because, according to Equation 6.6, in predicting barsold from temp, the value of the beta-weight for temp equals the value of the correlation between barsold and temp.

regress barsold temp, beta

USING A CONFIDENCE INTERVAL TO ESTIMATE THE SIZE OF THE POPULATION CORRELATION COEFFICIENT, ρ

We may construct by hand confidence intervals around r to estimate ρ using a method developed by R. A. Fisher. We construct these by hand because such intervals are not available through Stata. The method for constructing such confidence intervals is based on a transformation (called Fisher's Z transformation) that converts r to Z values using Equation 15.2.

$$Z_r = .5\ln\frac{1+r}{1-r} \tag{15.2}$$

A plot of the r to Z relationship is given in Figure 15.6. The Do-file associated with this chapter contains the Stata syntax used to create this figure.

Notice that from $r = -.50$ to $r = +.50$ the relationship is linear. Because this portion of the graph has slope equal to 1.00 and it passes through the origin, the transformation does not change correlation values that are originally between -0.50 and $+0.50$. The more the correlation diverges from zero, the greater the difference between r and Z. The net result of the Fisher r to Z transformation is to transform r values from an ordinal scale to an interval one.

Assuming that the population has a bivariate normal distribution, the equation for the upper and lower limits of the confidence interval estimate of ρ in terms of the Z-transformed values is

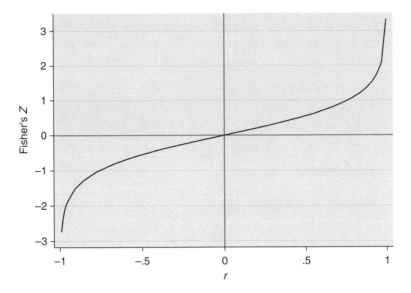

Figure 15.6 Relationship between r and Fisher's Z.

$$UpperLimit = Z_r + (z_{critical})\left(\frac{1}{\sqrt{N-3}}\right)$$
$$LowerLimit = Z_r - (z_{critical})\left(\frac{1}{\sqrt{N-3}}\right)$$

(15.3)

where

$z_{critical}$ = 1.645 for a 90% CI
= 1.960 for a 95% CI
= 2.576 for a 99% CI

Using this method, we may use the following steps to construct a 95% CI for ρ, the correlation between temperature in degrees Fahrenheit and ice cream sales in the population, in terms of Z-transformed values. The syntax for these steps also is given in the Do-file associated with this chapter.

1. Transform r = .887 to Z using the generate function in Stata. The Z value obtained is 1.408.

MORE Stata: To transform r = .887 to Z and obtain descriptives on Z

gen Z = .5*ln((1+.887)/(1-.887))
summarize Z

---

2. Compute the Upper Limit as: $1.408 + 1.96\left(\frac{1}{\sqrt{27}}\right) = 1.408 + 1.96(.192) = 1.785$.

3. Compute the Lower Limit as: $1.408 - 1.96\left(\frac{1}{\sqrt{27}}\right) = 1.408 - 1.96(.192) = 1.031$.

Therefore, the 95% CI for ρ in terms of the Fisher's Z values is $1.031 \leq Z_\rho \leq 1.785$.

To make this estimate more meaningful, we transform these upper and lower limits back into correlation values. To do so, we use Equation 15.4:

$$r = \frac{e^{2Z} - 1}{e^{2Z} + 1} \tag{15.4}$$

where the letter e represents a constant approximately equal to 2.718.

Using Equation 15.4 the r values corresponding to the Z values of 1.031 and 1.785 are respectively:

$$r = \frac{e^{2(1.031)} - 1}{e^{2(1.031)} + 1} = \frac{e^{2.062} - 1}{e^{2.062} + 1} = \frac{7.86 - 1}{7.86 + 1} = \frac{6.86}{8.86} = .774$$

$$r = \frac{e^{2(1.785)} - 1}{e^{2(1.785)} + 1} = \frac{e^{3.570} - 1}{e^{3.570} + 1} = \frac{35.52 - 1}{35.52 + 1} = \frac{34.52}{36.52} = .945$$

MORE Stata: To transform Z back to r and display results in the Output Window

display "rlower = " (exp(2*1.031) − 1)/(exp(2*1.031) + 1)
display "rupper = " (exp(2*1.785) − 1)/(exp(2*1.785) + 1)

Note: exp is Stata's function to denoting the constant e.

Using these values of r from the above analyses, we find that the 95% CI for ρ centered about r is $.774 \leq \rho \leq .945$, suggesting that the correlation between temperature and ice cream sales in the population from which our 30 days were randomly selected is very high and positive. We are using this confidence interval to estimate ρ, not to test the set of directional hypotheses given earlier. Confidence intervals are useful in testing nondirectional hypotheses only.

☞ **Remark.** Although confidence intervals for means are symmetric about the sample mean, $\overline{X}$, confidence intervals for correlations are not symmetric about the sample correlation, r.

• •

EXAMPLE 15.1. Use the *NELS* data set to determine whether there is a correlation between reading achievement and math achievement in twelfth grade in the population. Estimate the size of the population correlation by constructing a 95 percent CI about ρ.

Solution. Using the Stata **pwcorr** procedure we find that the Pearson Product Moment Correlation Coefficient, r, between achmat12 and achrdg12 equals .636. Because our question is whether the correlation is different from zero, a two-tailed test of significance is appropriate. According to our output, the correlation is statistically significantly different from zero ($p < .0005$), and we observe from the sign of the correlation that the relationship is positive. Using our definitions of effect size, we may also note that the relationship is a strong one.

To find the 95 percent confidence interval about r, we follow the procedure detailed earlier and type:

display "Z = " .5*ln((1 + .636)/(1 − .636))

We compute the Upper Limit in terms of the transformed Z score as:

$$.7514 + 1.96\left(\frac{1}{\sqrt{497}}\right) = .7514 + 1.96(.045) = .8396.$$

We next compute the Lower Limit in terms of the transformed Z score as:

$$.7514 - 1.96\left(\frac{1}{\sqrt{497}}\right) = .7514 - 1.96(.045) = .6632.$$

Finally, we transform the Upper and Lower Limits in terms of Z values into their respective r values using Equation 15.4 and display results.

display "r = " (exp(2*.8396) − 1)/(exp(2*.8396) + 1)

The upper limit in terms of r equals .69.

By following the same procedure, we obtain the lower limit in terms of r as $r = .58$. Accordingly, the 95% CI for r is: $.58 \le \rho \le .69$, suggesting that the population correlation is likely to fall between .58 and .69. Because zero does not fall within this interval, we know, once again, that the correlation is statistically significantly different from zero. Because the range is in the positive region, we know also that the relationship is positive. Furthermore, because .58 is substantially greater than zero, we can be confident that the effect size for this result is large.

REVISITING SIMPLE LINEAR REGRESSION FOR PREDICTION

The discovery of a linear relationship between highest daily temperature and ice cream sales (the higher the temperature, the greater the number of ice cream sales) is an important aspect of the process of setting up a linear regression equation to predict number of ice cream sales from temperature. The linear prediction equation for this example has number of ice cream sales as the dependent variable (otherwise called a *criterion variable*) and highest daily temperature as the independent variable (otherwise called a *predictor variable*).

Because there is only one independent variable, this type of regression is called *simple linear regression*. When there is more than one independent variable in the equation (for example, when we use both highest daily temperature *and* humidity to predict ice cream sales) we have what is called *multiple linear regression*. In the following chapter we discuss multiple linear regression and related issues.

Recall that in Chapter 6 we introduced simple linear regression for prediction in a descriptive context. In this chapter we introduce tests of inference in connection with simple linear prediction.

As we recall from Chapter 6, the linear regression (prediction) equation is:

$$\hat{Y} = bX + a \tag{15.5}$$

where

$$b = r\frac{S_Y}{S_X} \tag{15.6}$$

$$a = \bar{Y} - b\bar{X} \tag{15.7}$$

Equation 15.5 may be represented by a line that has slope b and intercept a. The slope b is also called the *regression coefficient* and is interpreted as the amount of change in Y, on average, for each unit increase in X. In short, b represents the *effect* that X has on Y. The intercept a is interpreted as the predicted Y value associated with $X = 0$. The intercept a is defined to allow the regression line to pass through the center of the bivariate distribution or scatterplot, $(\bar{X}, \bar{Y})$. If you are average on the X variable, you will be predicted to be average on the Y variable.

ESTIMATING THE POPULATION STANDARD ERROR OF PREDICTION, $\sigma_{Y|X}$

If the linear regression equation is based on a sample of values randomly selected from a bivariate normal population, then $\hat{Y}$ is an unbiased estimate of the mean of the conditional distribution of Y given X for all values of X within the sampling frame. That is, given that the population has a bivariate normal distribution, as shown in Figure 15.4, the slices of the bivariate distribution for each X value will be normally distributed in the population with mean $\bar{Y} = \hat{Y}$ and standard deviation $\sigma_{Y|X}$. Thus, if Carolyn has a value of $X = X_1$, then the linear regression equation will predict Carolyn's Y value to be equal to the mean of all the Y values for the individuals in the sample who, like Carolyn, have $X = X_1$.

This is a reasonable prediction because among other things, the mean of any normal distribution is that value having the largest frequency. While the prediction is reasonable, the possibility still exists that Carolyn's actual Y score is one of the other Y scores corresponding to $X = X_1$. The accuracy of the prediction will depend upon how closely the Y scores for all individuals who have $X = X_1$ are to one another and to their mean or, in other words, on the spread of the Y distribution for all individuals who have $X = X_1$. The spread of this conditional Y distribution given X_1 is measured by the standard deviation of this conditional Y distribution given X_1, and is denoted as $\sigma_{Y|X_1}$. The less the Y values deviate from their mean for all individuals with $X = X_1$, the smaller the error of prediction can be expected to be. The better the linear model fits the data, the closer $\hat{Y}$ will be to $\bar{Y}$ given $X = X_1$ and the smaller the expected error of prediction for $X = X_1$.

We may generalize from the case of $X = X_1$ to all values of X because of the bivariate normal distribution property of homoscedasticity. This property tells us that *all* the conditional distributions of Y given X have the same standard deviation as the Y distribution corresponding to $X = X_1$. Accordingly, we do not have to link the standard deviation of the conditional Y value given X to any particular X value, like X_1. We may use a more generic measure for the spread of the conditional Y distributions given X for the population at large. This measure is called the *standard error of prediction*, also called the *standard error of estimate*, denoted by $\sigma_{Y|X}$.

We may use the sample data on which the linear regression equation was developed to obtain an estimate of $\sigma_{Y|X}$. This estimate is denoted by $\hat{\sigma}_{Y|X}$ and is given by Equation 15.8.

$$\hat{\sigma}_{Y|X} = \sqrt{\frac{\sum (Y_i - \hat{Y}_i)^2}{N-2}} \tag{15.8}$$

where Y_i = the actual Y score of individual i in the sample

$\hat{Y}_i$ = the predicted Y score of individual i in the sample using the linear regression equation.

N = the number of pairs of values in the sample.

TESTING THE b-WEIGHT FOR STATISTICAL SIGNIFICANCE

$\hat{Y}$ is an unbiased estimate of the mean of the conditional distribution of Y given X for all values of X. In addition, the slope b of the regression (prediction) line is an unbiased estimate of the slope of the population regression line.

To test whether there is a relationship in the population between Y and the single predictor X, we may test the regression coefficient b for significance. As we shall see, this test is equivalent to the test for the significance of the correlation coefficient r presented earlier in this chapter.

The test of the regression coefficient b is

$$t = \frac{b-0}{\hat{\sigma}_b}$$

$$df = N - 2$$

(15.9)

where $\hat{\sigma}_b$ represents the standard error of b, the standard deviation of the sampling distribution of b weights based on random samples of the same size randomly drawn from the same population. This t value tests whether the b coefficient differs from 0 in the population. It has $N - 2$ degrees of freedom, two less than the number of pairs of scores.

As we shall see, the t-value, including the b coefficient and the standard error of the b coefficient, along with its two-tailed level of significance are given as part of the Stata regression output.

For completeness, the equation of the standard error of b is:

$$\hat{\sigma}_b = \sqrt{\frac{\frac{1}{N-2}\sum(Y_i - \hat{Y}_i)^2}{(N-1)\hat{\sigma}_X^2}}$$

(15.10)

Thus, the standard error of b is a function of the accuracy of the regression equation as measured by $\frac{1}{N-2}\sum(Y - \hat{Y})^2$ relative to (a function of) the variance estimate of X, $\hat{\sigma}_X^2$. In general, then, the standard error of the b coefficient of X in Equation 15.5 will be smaller when X has a larger variance.

• •

EXAMPLE 15.2. Construct the linear regression equation for predicting number of ice cream bars sold (barsold) from highest daily temperature (temp) for the whole summer. Interpret the equation as well as the various tests of significance reported in the output.

Solution.

MORE Stata: To perform a regression analysis including summary statistics

summarize barsold temp
pwcorr barsold temp, sig obs
regress barsold temp

The Stata output is reproduced below.

Variable	Obs	Mean	Std. Dev.	Min	Max
barsold	30	164.2333	11.90677	142	185
temp	30	74.93333	8.944015	59	90

	barsold	temp
barsold	1.0000	
	30	
temp	0.8867	1.0000
	0.0000	
	30	30

From the first table, we note that the analysis is based on $N = 30$ observations and that for these observations, the mean and standard deviation of the number of ice cream bars sold is approximately 164 and 12, respectively, and that the mean and standard deviation of highest daily temperature is approximately 75 and 9, respectively.

From the second table, we note that the correlation between temperature and ice cream sales is .887 with two-tailed level of significance $p < .001$.

Source	SS	df	MS			
				Number of obs	=	30
				F (1, 28)	=	103.00
Model	3232.59944	1	3232.59944	Prob > F	=	0.0000
Residual	878.767228	28	31.3845439	R-squared	=	0.7863
				Adj R-squared	=	0.7786
Total	4111.36667	29	141.771264	Root MSE	=	5.6022

barsold	Coef.	Std. Err.	t	P > |t|	[95% Conf.	Interval]
temp	1.180441	.1163125	10.15	0.000	.942186	1.418697
_cons	75.77892	8.775494	8.64	0.000	57.80314	93.75471

From the regression output table, we learn from the column of coefficients that the simple linear regression equation for predicting ice cream sales from highest daily temperature is:

Predicted barsold = 1.18*temp + 75.78

The *b*-coefficient for TEMP is 1.18, indicating that each additional one degree rise in temperature is associated with 1.18 more ice cream bars sold on average. The constant or intercept is 75.78. That is, when TEMP = 0, the number of ice creams that are predicted to be sold equals 75.78. While in some contexts the constant has a meaningful interpretation, in this one it does not because 0 degrees Fahrenheit is not a plausible or realistic temperature reading for the summer, the time period under study.

Recall that the intercept equals that value that allows the regression line to pass through the center of the scatterplot, $\overline{X}, \overline{Y}$. In this case, the center of the scatterplot is at 74.93, 164.23. When the highest daily temperature is equal to the mean temperature for the days sampled (74.93), the number of bars sold is predicted to equal to the mean number of bars sold for the days sampled (164.23).

To determine whether the slope (or b-coefficient or b-weight) is statistically significantly different from zero, we refer to the t-test with $N - 2$ degrees of freedom and its corresponding two-tailed significance level, or p-value from the Coefficients Table. In our example, $t(28) = 10.15$, $p < .001$, suggesting that, in fact, the regression weight is statistically significantly different from zero. Looking at the sign of b, in this case of simple linear regression, the relationship may be inferred to be positive. That is, the observed positive relationship between ice cream sales and temperature holds for the population of all summer days, not just for the 30 days that comprised our random sample.

We may calculate by hand the standard error of b using Equation 15.10,

$$\hat{\sigma}_b = \sqrt{\frac{\frac{1}{N-2}\sum(Y_i - \hat{Y}_i)^2}{(N-1)\hat{\sigma}_X^2}}.$$ To do so, we first compute $\frac{1}{N-2}\sum(Y_i - \hat{Y}_i)^2$, the mean squared

residual, MS_{RES}. In particular, we obtain the predicted Y values from Stata using the **predit yhat** command introduced in Chapter 6 of Example 6.2.

$$MS_{RES} = \frac{1}{28}\left(\frac{(170-164.31)^2 + (160-158.41)^2 + (155-152.51)^2}{+\cdots+(178-182.02)^2 + (175-158.41)^2 + (164-171.39)^2}\right) = 31.385.$$

From the table of Descriptive Statistics, we have the values for both N (30) and the standard deviation of X, Temperature in degrees Fahrenheit (8.94). Substituting these values and the value for MS_{RES} into Equation 15.10, we obtain:

$$\hat{\sigma}_b = \sqrt{\frac{31.385}{(30-1)(8.94)^2}} = .116,$$

which is the value printed in the Coefficients table for the standard error of b.

We may also verify that the t-value of 10.15 is obtained from Equation 15.8, the ratio of the b-coefficient divided by its standard error, $1.18/.116 = 10.15$.

Finally, we may note that in the case of simple regression, the test of significance for the regression coefficient b is equivalent to the test of significance for the correlation coefficient r. We may do so by noting that the t-values based on Equations 15.1 and 15.8 are the same ($t = 10.15$).

The t-test of the b-coefficient tells us whether the b coefficient in the population is statistically significantly different from zero. This is the same test of whether the correlation between barsold and temperature is statistically significantly different from zero. The 95% confidence interval about b gives us an estimate of the likely values of the b-coefficient in the population. From the printout we may note that reasonable estimates of the b-weight are between .942 and 1.419. That the interval does not include zero corroborates the result of the t-test that the b-coefficient is different from zero in the population. That the confidence interval includes only positive values suggests that the b-coefficient in the population is positive, that increases in daily temperature associates with increases in ice cream sales and decreases in daily temperature associates with decreases in ice cream sales.

To obtain a robust estimate of the standard error of the *b*-coefficient for temp, we use the bootstrap procedure as we have done in earlier chapters. The command with 1,000 replications and requesting no dots in the output and setting the **seed** to be equal to 1234 is:

MORE Stata: To obtain a bootstrap estimate of the standard error of the b-coefficient for variable temp and for the constant

bootstrap _b, reps(1000)nodots seed(1234): regress barsold temp

Note: The **seed** option sets the initial value of the random number generator used to begin the resampling process, and allows us to fix the sequence and composition of random samples drawn so that we may replicate our results in the future if we so desire.

Although we have chosen the number 1234 as the initial value, any number between 0 and 2^31-1 may be used (type **help set seed** in the Command Window for more detailed information about setting a seed).

Linear regression					Number of obs	=	30
					Replications	=	1000
					Wald chi2 (1)	=	142.41
					Prob > chi2	=	0.0000
					R-squared	=	0.7863
					Adj R-squared	=	0.7786
					Root MSE	=	5.6022

barsold	Observed Coef.	Bootstrap Std. Err.	z	P > |z|	Normal-based [95% Conf. Interval]	
temp	1.180441	.0989189	11.93	0.000	.986564	1.374319
_cons	75.77892	7.601232	9.97	0.000	60.88078	90.67706

The bootstrap estimate of the standard error for this *b*-coefficient is .099, which is a bit smaller than the theoretically-derived standard error of .097. Accordingly, the length of the 95% confidence interval for this *b*-coefficient is somewhat shorter at .987 to 1.374 versus .942 to 1.419. Although the results are somewhat different, the overall substantive conclusion remains the same.

MORE Stata: To rename a variable in a bootstrap procedure

If we are finding the bootstrap estimate of the standard error of only one term in the equation (in this case, the variable temp), we may rename that estimate simply as b, as follows:

bootstrap b = _b[temp], reps(1000) nodots seed(1234): regress barsold temp

In the Output Window, the row of the table that contains the results for temp would be labeled b instead of temp.

We also could rename both terms in the equation as b1 and b0 as follows:

bootstrap b1 = _b[temp] b0 = _b[_cons], reps(1000) nodots seed(1234): regress barsold temp

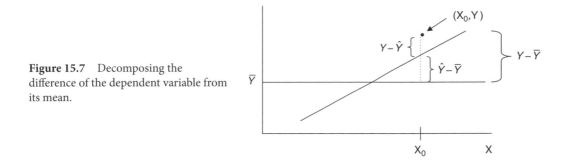

Figure 15.7 Decomposing the difference of the dependent variable from its mean.

We turn now to another explanation of simple regression that is based on a decomposition of total sums of squares about the mean. This explanation links simple regression to the analysis of variance framework and enables us to understand additional regression output provided by Stata and other computer programs.

EXPLAINING SIMPLE REGRESSION USING AN ANALYSIS OF VARIANCE FRAMEWORK

Recall that in one-way analysis of variance the total variability (SS_T) of the dependent variable may be decomposed in into two unrelated (orthogonal) components: variability due to the between groups effect (SS_B) and variability due to a within effect (SS_W). In the context of regression, SS_B is referred to as SS_{REG}, sum of squares due to regression and SS_W is referred to as SS_{RES}, the sum of squares due to residual or error. Analogously, we may decompose or partition the total variability of the dependent variable in simple regression. We begin with $Y - \overline{Y}$, which is the error in predicting Y if we were to use $\overline{Y}$ to predict Y. The questions is: How much closer can we get to Y by predicting Y from a new variable X using a regression equation?

As shown in Figure 15.7, $Y - \overline{Y}$, the total difference between an actual Y value and its mean, may be expressed as the sum of the two nonoverlapping components, $\hat{Y} - \overline{Y}$ and $Y - \hat{Y}$.

$$Y - \overline{Y} = (\hat{Y} - \overline{Y}) + Y - \hat{Y}) \tag{15.11}$$

The first component represents that part of the total difference that is explained or accounted for by the relationship of Y with X; the other component represents that part of the total difference that remains after accounting for the relationship of Y with X.

If both sides of Equation 15.10 are squared, then summed, and simplified using properties of the regression equation, we obtain Equation 15.12.

$$\Sigma(Y - \overline{Y})^2 = \Sigma(\hat{Y} - \overline{Y})^2 + \Sigma(Y - \hat{Y})^2 \tag{15.12}$$

The term on the left hand side of Equation 15.12 equals the sum of squared deviations of the actual (as opposed to predicted) values of Y about its mean and is what we have called the *total sum of squares* (SS_{TOT}) of Y. The first term on the right hand side of (15.12) equals the sum of squared deviations of the predicted values of Y, $\hat{Y}$, about the mean of the actual values of Y. Because it represents that part of Y's variability that is due to Y's relation to X (symbolized by $\hat{Y}$), this term is called the *sum of squares due to the regression* (SS_{REG}). The second term on the right hand side of Equation 15.12 is the sum of the squared deviations between the actual and predicted values of Y. Because it represents that part of Y's variability that is left over after accounting for Y's relation to X (symbolized by $\hat{Y}$), this term is called the sum of squares due to residual (SS_{RES}). We may note that the sum of squares due to residual is related to the standard error of prediction as they are both based on the sum of the squared differences between the actual and predicted Y values.

In diagram form we may illustrate this decomposition as follows:

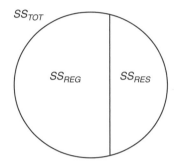

And we may rewrite Equation 15.12 as:

$$SS_{TOT} = SS_{REG} + SS_{RES} \tag{15.13}$$

In like manner, the degrees of freedom associated with SS_{TOT} (df_{TOT}) may be decomposed as the sum of df_{REG} and df_{RES} as follows:

$$df_{TOT} = df_{REG} + df_{RES} \tag{15.14}$$

$$N - 1 = P + N - P - 1$$

where P = the number of predictors in the regression equation. In the case of simple regression, $P = 1$.

We are now in a position to understand an Analysis of Variance summary table for regression that is part of a Stata regression analysis printout. This summary table provides a test of the statistical significance of the overall fit of the regression model. The table from the temperature/ice cream sales example is given below.

Source	SS	df	MS			
				Number of obs	=	30
				F (1, 28)	=	103.00
Model	3232.59944	1	3232.59944	Prob > F	=	0.0000
Residual	878.767228	28	31.3845439	R-squared	=	0.7863
				Adj R-squared	=	0.7786
Total	4111.36667	29	141.771264	Root MSE	=	5.6022

Notice that the sum of SS_{REG} (3232.599) and SS_{RES} (878.767) equals SS_{TOT} (4111.367). Notice also that the sum of df_{REG} ($P = 1$) and df_{RES} ($N - P - 1 = 30 - 1 - 1 = 28$) equals df_{TOT} ($N - 1 = 29$). As discussed in Chapters 13 and 14 on the analysis of variance, each Mean Square term equals the ratio of the corresponding Sum of Squares term to its corresponding degrees of freedom, and the F-ratio is obtained as MS_{REG}/MS_{RES}.

In the case of simple regression, when $P = 1$, the F-ratio for the regression equals the t-ratio for the b coefficient squared (i.e., $F = t^2$ when the numerator degrees of freedom for the F-ratio equals 1). In our example, we may note that $103 = 10.15^2$.

Thus, in summary, in the case of simple regression, the t-test of the significance of r is equivalent to the t-test of the significance of b, and these two t-tests are equivalent to the F-test of the overall regression model. Hence, in the case of simple regression, when r is not statistically significant, b will not be statistically significant, nor will the overall regression equation be statistically significant.

MEASURING THE FIT OF THE OVERALL REGRESSION EQUATION: USING R AND R^2

A measure of the fit of the overall regression equation is given by R, the correlation between the actual values of the dependent variable and the values of the dependent variable predicted from the linear model; that is, as the correlation between Y and $\hat{Y}$. This information is provided by Stata in the Model Summary table as part of the regression output. This table is reproduced here as follows:

Source	SS	df	MS			
				Number of obs	=	30
				F (1, 28)	=	103.00
Model	3232.59944	1	3232.59944	Prob > F	=	0.0000
Residual	878.767228	28	31.3845439	R-squared	=	0.7863
				Adj R-squared	=	0.7786
Total	4111.36667	29	141.771264	Root MSE	=	5.6022

The Root MSE (*standard error of estimate*), given in the Model Summary table, is defined earlier by Equation 15.8. Its value for this example is 5.60 according to the Model Summary table entry. We may also find it from the Analysis of Variance table as the square root of MS_{RES}, the mean square due to residual or error. That is,

$$\sqrt{MS_{RES}} = \sqrt{SS_{RES} / (N-2)} = \sqrt{\sum (Y - \hat{Y})^2 / (N-2)} = \hat{\sigma}_{Y|X} = \sqrt{31.385} = 5.60.$$

Recall that in Chapter 6 we defined the effect size for regression in terms of the Pearson Product Moment correlation, r, and in terms of the correlation between the actual and predicted values, R. An alternative measure of effect size, or overall fit of the regression equation, is r^2 or R^2. In the case of simple regression, these two measures are equivalent.

We may link the measure of overall fit, R^2, to the analysis of variance framework and in so doing, explain R^2 as the proportion of Y variance accounted for by X. To do so we divide Equation 15.12 through by SS_{TOT} and obtain Equation 15.15.

$$1 = \frac{SS_{REG}}{SS_{TOT}} + \frac{SS_{RES}}{SS_{TOT}} \tag{15.15}$$

The total variability of Y, represented by the whole value 1, is decomposed into two nonoverlapping components: that proportion due to the regression equation (i.e., that proportion explained by X) and that proportion due to the residual (i.e., that proportion unexplained by X).

For our example,

$$1 = \frac{3232.599}{4111.367} + \frac{878.767}{4111.367}$$

$$= .786 + .214$$

$$= R^2 + (1 - R^2).$$

This result is true not only for our example, but it is true in general as well. That is,

$$R^2 = \frac{SS_{REG}}{SS_{TOT}} \tag{15.16}$$

$$1 - R^2 = \frac{SS_{RES}}{SS_{TOT}} \tag{15.17}$$

RELATING R^2 TO $\sigma^2_{Y|X}$

Given the assumption of homoscedasticity, we may express the relationship in the population between R^2, the proportion of Y variance explained by X, and $\sigma^2_{Y|X}$, the common variance of all the conditional Y distributions. In particular, when all conditional Y distributions have the same variance in the population, then it can be shown, from Equation 15.17, that

$$\sigma^2_{Y|X} = \sigma^2_Y (1 - R^2_{POP}) \tag{15.18}$$

where $\sigma^2_{Y|X}$ is the common variance of all conditional Y distributions in the population

σ^2_Y is the variance of the Y values in the population

R^2_{POP} is the population squared correlation coefficient between X and Y.

We illustrate Equation 15.18 with a concrete situation. For simplicity, assume that X represents gender, a dichotomous variable, and Y represents mathematics achievement. Suppose the scores on the test of mathematical achievement are known to range from 20 to 90 with a variance of 100 in the population. Suppose also that we separate these scores into two distinct groups, male and female, and find that the scores for females range only from 50 to 90 with a variance of 51 and that the scores for males range only from 20 to 60 with a variance of 51. By controlling for gender, we obtain a consequent reduction in the variance of math scores from $\sigma^2_Y = 100$, to $\sigma^2_{Y|X} = 51$, almost half of what it was originally. Said differently, each of the two cross sections of slices of the bivariate distribution, one for males and the other for females, has a variance of 51. Taken together, however, the total variance of math scores is almost doubled.

To find what the correlation between gender and math achievement must be in order to observe such a dramatic reduction in variance we use Equation 15.18.

$$51 = 100(1 - R^2) \rightarrow 51 = 100 - 100R^2 \rightarrow 49 = 100R^2 \rightarrow R^2 = .49 \rightarrow R = .70$$

Thus, in order to explain, or account for, 49 percent of the total variance of a variable by another variable, the two variables must correlate .70.

In the ice cream example, because $R^2 = .786$, we know that highest daily temperature accounts for 78.6 percent of the variance in ice cream sales. This implies that 21.4 percent of ice cream sales variance remains unexplained by highest daily temperature. In the next chapter, we discuss an approach, called multiple regression, which allows us to include other independent variables into the equation, like humidity, for example. Such other variables may account for some of the variance in Y that remains unexplained, and in so doing, allow us to predict more accurately daily ice cream sales.

TESTING R^2 FOR STATISTICAL SIGNIFICANCE

In the case of simple regression, we have described three different, yet equivalent, ways to test the statistical significance of the regression model: The t-test of the significance of r, the t-test of the significance of b, and the ANOVA F-test of the overall regression model. A fourth, equivalent test is the test of the significance of R^2. Conceptually this makes sense because in the case of simple regression, the magnitude of r, the correlation between the single predictor and Y, equals the magnitude of R, the correlation between the actual and predicted values of Y.

The equation for testing R^2 for statistical significance is:

$$F_{P,N-P-1} = \frac{R^2/P}{(1-R^2)/(N-P-1)} \tag{15.19}$$

where P = the number of predictors in the regression equation

(Note: in the case of simple regression, $P = 1$. In the next chapter, P will be greater than 1.)

N = the sample size

P and $N - P - 1$ = the F numerator and denominator degrees of freedom, respectively. In the case of simple regression, these are 1 and $N - 2$, respectively.

For the ice cream sales example, we may note that $F = \dfrac{.786/1}{.214/28} = \dfrac{.786}{.0076} = 103.00$. This is the same value that appears in the analysis of variance table and suggests that R^2 is statistically greater than zero in the population, or equivalently, that the fit of the overall regression model to the data is statistically significant.

☞ **Remark.** For the interested reader we provide the algebraic link between the F-test of R^2 as given by Equation 15.15 and the F-test in the analysis of variance table.

$$F = \frac{MS_{REG}}{MS_{RES}} = \frac{SS_{REG}/P}{SS_{RES}/(N-P-1)} = \frac{SS_{REG}/P}{SS_{RES}/(N-P-1)} \times \frac{SS_{TOT}}{SS_{TOT}}$$

$$= \frac{\dfrac{SS_{REG}/SS_{TOT}}{P}}{\dfrac{SS_{RES}/SS_{TOT}}{N-P-1}} = \frac{R^2/P}{(1-R^2)/(N-P-1)}$$

with numerator and denominator degrees of freedom equal to P and $N - P - 1$, respectively.

ESTIMATING THE TRUE POPULATION R^2: THE ADJUSTED R^2

Although the slope b of the regression (prediction) line was described as an unbiased estimate of the slope of the population regression line, the sample R^2 is not an unbiased estimate of the true population R^2, denoted R^2_{POP}. Rather, it's biased upwards; that is, the sample R^2 overestimates the population R^2, R^2_{POP}.

Said differently, when $R^2_{POP} = 0$, then, on average, the sample R^2 will be greater than 0. It will be equal to $P/(N-1)$.

For example, given $R^2_{POP} = 0$, if $P = 1$ and $N = 9$, then, on average, the sample R^2 will equal $1/8 = .125$; if $P = 1$ and $N = 5$, then, on average, the sample R^2 will equal $1/4 = .25$.

The degree to which the sample R^2 overestimates the population R^2 depends upon both the number of predictors in the equation, P, and the size of the sample, N. The larger P is relative to N, the more the sample R^2 will overestimate the population R^2; the smaller P is relative to N, the less the sample R^2 will overestimate the population R^2.

☞ **Remark.** When $P = N - 1$, the sample R^2 will be equal to one regardless of the size of the population R^2. That is, if you constructed a regression equation with the number of predictors equal to one less than the total sample size (e.g., if $P = 1$ and $N = 2$), the sample R^2 would be one, indicating perfect fit in the population! But certainly, this would not be the case. With $P = 1$ and $N = 2$, the scatterplot consists of only two (X,Y) points, and a line can always be drawn connecting the two, or passing through both. Therefore, your result of $R^2 = 1$ should be taken merely as a reminder of just how upwardly biased the sample R^2 can be when the number of variables is large relative to the sample size.

A more accurate estimate of the population R^2 may be obtained by adjusting the sample R^2 using the following Equation:

$$R^2_{ADJ} = 1 - (1 - R^2)\frac{(N-1)}{N-P-1} \tag{15.20}$$

For the ice cream sales example, we have

$$R^2_{ADJ} = 1 - (1 - R^2)\frac{(N-1)}{N-P-1} = 1 - (1 - .786)\frac{30-1}{30-1-1}$$
$$= 1 - .214\frac{29}{28} = 1 - .221 = .779.$$

This is the *adjusted* R^2 value given in the Model Summary table presented earlier, and represents a more accurate estimate of the population R^2 than the original, unadjusted R^2. Because in this case, however, the ratio of predictors to sample size ($P:N$) is relatively large, 1:30, .786 is trivially different from .779.

☞ **Remark.** In general, as a rule of thumb, when the ratio of $P:N$ is greater than or equal to 1:30, there will be little difference between the adjusted and unadjusted R^2. When, however, the ratio of $P:N$ is less than or equal to 1:10, the difference between the adjusted and unadjusted R^2 will tend to be large.

☞ **Remark.** The adjusted R^2 is used to provide a more accurate estimate of the population R^2. The original, unadjusted R^2, however, is used in Equation 15.20 for testing R^2 for statistical significance.

EXPLORING THE GOODNESS OF FIT OF THE REGRESSION EQUATION: USING REGRESSION DIAGNOSTICS

Throughout this book we have made the point that summary statistics may be misleading if the data they are purported to characterize are anomalous; if, for example, they contain outliers or do not, in other ways, satisfy the explicit or implicit distributional assumptions upon which these statistics are based. Because the simple regression model serves to characterize, in summary form, the linear relationship between two variables as a line with intercept and slope, it too may be misleading, or in some way, fail to capture the salient features of the data. To be convinced that the resulting intercept and slope are not distorted by outliers and other influential observations contained in the sample, we need to explore ways to validate our linear regression model. To do so, we return to the Anscombe data presented in Chapter 6.

Consider the four panels of Anscombe data reproduced here as Figure 15.8 along with their associated summary statistics. (The syntax to generate Figure 15.8 may be found in the Do-file associated with this chapter.) Notice that for all panels, the slope, intercept, correlation, standard error, and t-value are the same. Yet, if we look at the four scatterplots that visually represent these four panels of data, we see to what extent they are different from one another.

y1	Coef.	Std. Err.	t	P > |t|	[95% Conf.	Interval]
x1	.5000909	.1179055	4.24	0.002	.2333701	.7668117
_cons	3.000091	1.124747	2.67	0.026	.4557369	5.544445

y2	Coef.	Std. Err.	t	P > |t|	[95% Conf.	Interval]
x2	.5	.1179637	4.24	0.002	.2331475	.7668525
_cons	3.000909	1.125302	2.67	0.026	.4552982	5.54652

y3	Coef.	Std. Err.	t	P > |t|	[95% Conf.	Interval]
x3	.4997273	.1178777	4.24	0.002	.2330695	.7663851
_cons	3.002455	1.124481	2.67	0.026	.4587013	5.546208

y4	Coef.	Std. Err.	t	P > |t|	[95% Conf.	Interval]
x4	.4999091	.1178189	4.24	0.002	.2333841	.7664341
_cons	3.001727	1.123921	2.67	0.026	.4592412	5.544213

Notice that in only one case, in Panel I, does the linear model provide a good characterization of the underlying data. In Panel II, the data show a nonlinear relationship, yet the model that is used to characterize these data is not nonlinear; it is linear. In Panel III, the outlier gives rise to a linear regression model that is quite different from the perfectly fitting regression line that would have been created in the absence of the outlier. In Panel IV, the outlier creates a systematic relationship between the dependent and independent variables and allows a line to be fit to the data that otherwise would not have been able to be fit in the absence of the outlier. That the linear regression models in Panels III and IV

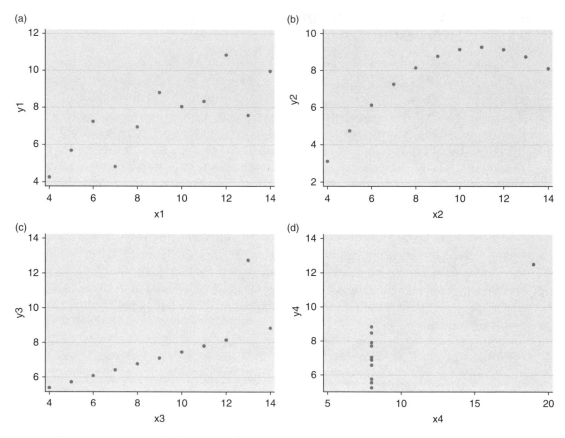

Figure 15.8   Anscombe data revisited.

are the direct result of a single outlier raises questions about the confidence we may place in these models.

Regression diagnostics are tools with which to explore our data to uncover such anomalies. As we shall see, these tools are useful for determining whether our regression models are in fact meaningful and appropriate characterizations of our data and for suggesting ways to modify our models to improve them if necessary.

RESIDUAL PLOTS: EVALUATING THE ASSUMPTIONS UNDERLYING REGRESSION

From our work on regression, we know that error (also called residual error) is defined for each individual (or more generally, for each case) as the difference between an individual's actual value on the dependent variable, Y, and his or her predicted value, $\hat{Y}$, predicted from the linear regression model. As such, $Y - \hat{Y}$ represents that part of Y that is left over after its linear association with X has been removed.

If the assumptions underlying the linear regression model are met, then the plot of residual values along the vertical axis versus the original values of X along the horizontal axis will be rectangular in shape. A rectangular scatterplot suggests that the relationship between X and Y is a wholly linear one; that after the linear relationship between X and Y is

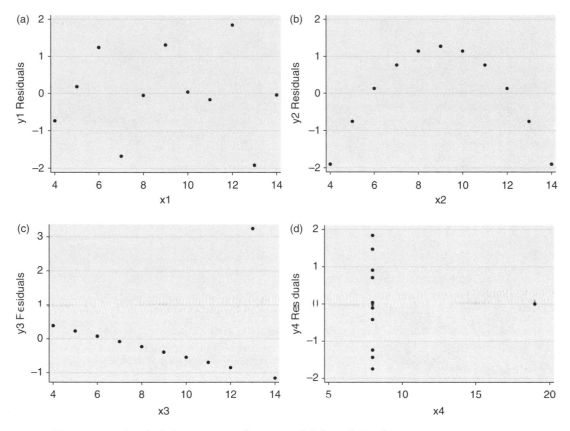

Figure 15.9 Residual plots corresponding to panels I through IV of Figure 15.8.

removed, no systematic relationship between X and Y remains. If the relationship between X and Y is not wholly linear, then the scatterplot of the residual values will not be rectangular in shape. An examination of the scatterplot may reveal the presence of a nonlinear relationship between X and Y or the violation of one or more of the other assumptions underlying the linear regression model (normality and homoscedasticity).

Residual plots for the four panels of Anscombe's data, I through IV, that appear in Figure 15.8 are given in Figure 15.9.

MORE Stata: To obtain the residual scatterplot of Panel I of Figure 15.9

regress y1 x1
predict y1_resid, residuals
twoway scatter y1_resid x1, ytitle("y1 Residuals")

The syntax to generate all of the remaining figures of this chapter may be found in the Do-file associated with this chapter.

Notice that in Panel I, the points in the scatterplot are rectangular in shape indicating that once the linear relationship between X and Y is removed, there is no other systematic relationship between these two variables.

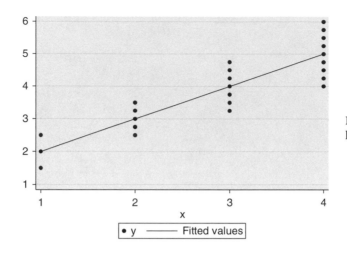

Figure 15.10   Scatterplot with heteroscedasticity.

The situation for Panel II is quite different. In this case, after the linear relationship between X and Y is removed, a clearly discernible nonlinear relationship remains between X and Y. The nature of the nonlinear relationship is quadratic. That is, that part of Y that remains after accounting for Y's linear association with X is a function of X^2. What this implies is that in addition to an X term, an X^2 term should be included in the regression model to obtain a more accurate model for predicting Y. We shall see how this may be done in the next chapter on multiple regression.

The residual plot of Panel III highlights the existence of the outlier, which, if removed, would make the relationship between X and Y perfect. The residual plot of Panel IV highlights the existence of the outlier which, if removed, would make the concept of a relationship between X and Y meaningless because without the outlier, X would be a constant.

Figure 15.10 contains a scatterplot of X versus Y from a fabricated data set. Notice that while there is a systematic linear relationship between X and Y ($r_{X,Y} = 0.89$), the variances of the conditional Y distributions given X are not constant as stipulated by the assumption of homoscedasticity, a condition of bivariate normality. In particular, the conditional Y distributions of Figure 15.10 increase with increasing values of X. For example, the variance of the three Y values corresponding to $X = 1$ is smaller than the variance of the five Y values corresponding to $X = 2$, and so on. This funnel shape in the residual plot is indicative of heteroscedasticity.

Figure 15.11 contains the scatterplot of the unstandardized residual plot X versus $Y - \hat{Y}$ corresponding to the data of Figure 15.10.

Notice that once that part of X linearly related to Y is removed, no relationship remains ($r = 0$). Thus, while the assumption of linearity appears to be met by these data, the assumption of homoscedasticity is quite clearly violated.

We may transform our data nonlinearly to rectify violations of the assumptions of bivariate normality and to achieve a better fitting model. In this case, the type of transformation we want is one that will produce a constant residual variance. The logarithmic transformation of Y does the trick as shown in Figure 15.12. Not only are the conditional Y distributions of Figure 15.12 homoscedastic, but the linear regression model now provides a slightly better fit to the data ($r_{X,\log(Y)} = 0.90$).

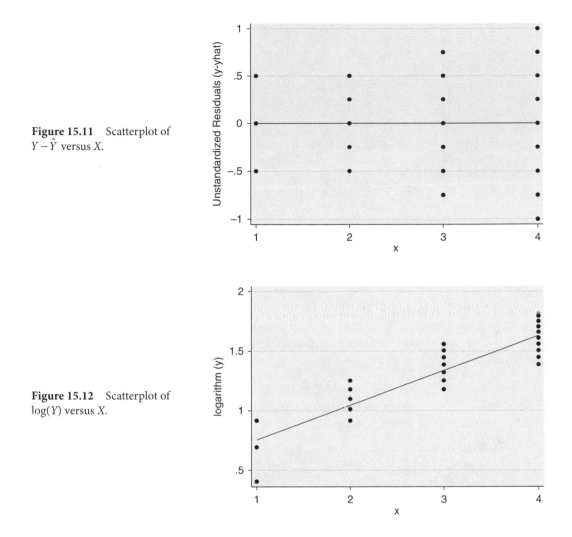

Figure 15.11 Scatterplot of $Y - \hat{Y}$ versus X.

Figure 15.12 Scatterplot of $\log(Y)$ versus X.

In addition to residual plots, other diagnostic tools are available for helping to improve the fit of a regression model to data.

DETECTING INFLUENTIAL OBSERVATIONS: DISCREPANCY AND LEVERAGE

In Chapters 2 and 4, we discussed the importance of identifying univariate outliers through the use of boxplots or z-scores. In this section, we expand that discussion to the case of bivariate distributions and introduce ways to identify bivariate outliers in a regression context. For this discussion, a bivariate outlier is a point in the scatterplot that behaves differently from the other points.

Outliers which unduly influence the slope and/or intercept of our regression model are called *influential observations*. Not all outliers are influential observations. Figures 15.13 and 15.14 both contain an outlier, yet in neither case does the outlier unduly influence the parameters of the regression equation.

In Figure 15.13, because the regression outlier is near the mean of $\overline{X}$ it does not affect the slope of the regression line at all, and affects the intercept only slightly. The presence of

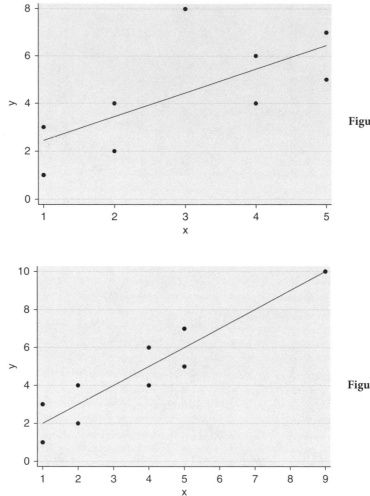

Figure 15.13   Outlier near $\bar{X}$.

Figure 15.14   Outlier far from $\bar{X}$.

the outlier raises the regression line to be slightly closer to the points (1, 3), (2, 4), (4, 6), and (5, 7) than it would otherwise. In Figure 15.14, the regression outlier, while far from $\bar{X}$, does not affect the slope or the intercept of the regression line because it falls directly in line with the regression line.

Thus, while the vertical distance of the outlier from the regression line in Figure 15.13 and the horizontal distance of the outlier from $\bar{X}$ in Figure 15.14 characterize both points as outliers, in neither case are these outliers influential observations; in neither case do these points actually influence the slope and/or intercept of the regression model.

The vertical distance of a point from a regression line is called its *residual, discrepancy, or deviation*. A function of the horizontal distance of a point from the X mean is called its *leverage*. In general, only when a point has both discrepancy and leverage, as noted in Figure 15.15, does a point influence the slope of a regression equation.

We may express the influence of a point on the slope of a regression equation as a function of discrepancy and leverage as shown in Equation 15.21:

$$\text{Influence} \approx \text{Discrepancy*Leverage} \qquad (15.21)$$

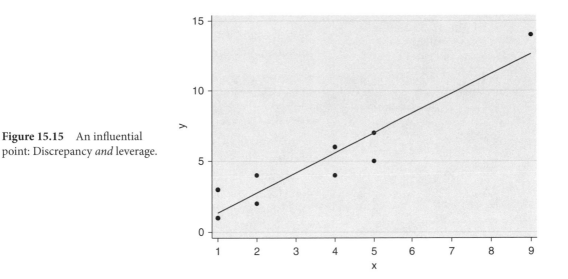

Figure 15.15 An influential point: Discrepancy *and* leverage.

Several diagnostic tools are available In Stata to measure the degree to which each point in a data set influences the coefficients of a regression equation.

USING STATA TO OBTAIN LEVERAGE

The leverage of a point is the distance of a point from $\overline{X}$ in simple regression. Mathematically it is computed as the squared distance of the point from $\overline{X}$ relative to the sum of squared deviations of all points in the data set from $\overline{X}$.

MORE Stata: To obtain the leverage of a data point

regress y x
predict lev, leverage

TABLE 15.2. Leverage values for the nine points of Figure 15.15

X,Y values	Leverage
1,1	.2479
1,3	.2479
2,2	.1645
2,4	.1645
4,4	.1132
4,6	.1132
5,5	.1453
5,7	.1453
9,14	.6581

Table 15.2 contains the leverage of all nine points of Figure 15.15. Not surprisingly, the leverage of the last point (9, 14) is the highest because this point is farthest from $\overline{X}$ in this data set.

USING STATA TO OBTAIN DISCREPANCY

The discrepancy of a point is the vertical distance of the point from the regression line. While discrepancy may be measured as a residual value, for reasons we will not go into here, a better approach is measure discrepancy as a *Studentized residual value*. The Studentized residual value of a point is the residual value of the point relative to an estimate of the standard deviation of all residual values for the entire data set. Studentized residual values follow a *t*-distribution with $N - P - 2$ degrees of freedom.

TABLE 15.3. Studentized residual values for the nine points of Figure 15.13

X, Y values	Studentized residual
1,1	−.9730
1,3	.3514
2,2	−.8696
2,4	.3178
3,8	3.2660
4,4	−.8696
4,6	−.3178
5,5	−.9730
5,7	.3514

TABLE 15.4. Cook's influence values for the nine points of Figure 15.15

X, Y values	Cook's influence
1,1	.0140
1,3	.3098
2,2	.0354
2,4	.0941
4,4	.0936
4,6	.0066
5,5	.2050
5,7	.0000
9,14	2.7360

MORE Stata: To obtain the Studentized residual value for each data point (x,y)

regress y x

predict stres, rstudent

To exemplify, Table 15.3 contains the Studentized residual values of all nine points of Figure 15.13.

As we would expect, the Studentized residual value of the point (3, 8) is highest because this point has the greatest vertical distance from the regression line as shown in Figure 15.13.

USING STATA TO OBTAIN INFLUENCE

The influence of a point is the amount by which the slope of the regression line (the regression coefficient) will change when that point is removed from the data set and we compute a new slope. The amount of change may be scaled by an index developed by Cook, based loosely on the F-statistic, so that we may evaluate which changes are relatively small, moderate, or large.

Many researchers treat cases with Cook's influence scores that are larger than 1 as outliers. We will make particular note of such cases in our analyses.

MORE Stata: To obtain Cook's influence value for a data point (x,y)

regress y x

predict influence, cooksd

Table 15.4 contains the Cook's influence values of all nine points of Figure 15.15. As expected, the last value in the data set (9, 14) has the highest value of Cook's influence (called Cook's distance by Stata), indicating that this point influences the slope of the regression equation more than any other point in the data set. It also has a Cook's value that is quite a bit larger than 1.00 so that it is classified as an outlier.

Table 15.5 presents the results of the regression analysis based on the total set of nine points in the data set and on the nine subsets of size eight each with one point removed. Notice that Cook's influence is zero for point (5, 7). Notice also that the regression line based on the sample without this point is identical to the regression line based on the sample that includes this point. Hence, as Cook's influence value suggests, the analysis is not at all influenced by the presence of this point. With or without this point, the results are the same. Notice, however, that as Cook's influence value also suggests, the point with the greatest influence on the equation is point (9, 14). The equation based on the subsample with point (9, 14) removed is quite different from all other equations that are based on samples that include point (9, 14) as one of the points in the sample.

TABLE 15.5. Regression results based on all nine points and on all subsets of eight points eliminating one point each time.

Analysis	Point removed	Sample size	Regression equation
1	1,1	8	$\hat{Y} = 1.386X - .080$
2	1,3	8	$\hat{Y} = 1.523X - .720$
3	2,2	8	$\hat{Y} = 1.381X + .148$
4	2,4	8	$\hat{Y} = 1.458X - .399$
5	4,4	8	$\hat{Y} = 1.422X - .096$
6	4,6	8	$\hat{Y} = 1.407X - .101$
7	5,5	8	$\hat{Y} = 1.470X - .020$
8	5,7	8	$\hat{Y} = 1.410X - .060$
9	9,14	8	$\hat{Y} = 1.000X - 1.00$
10	none	9	$\hat{Y} = 1.410X - .060$

Other measures of influence exist and are called in Stata, Dfl3eta(s), Standardized DfBeta(s), DfFit, Standardized DfFit, and Covariance ratio. The use of Cook's distance alone is usually sufficient to measure influence.

In summary, anomalies in our data may distort the results of our regression analyses. While some anomalies may be corrected easily (e.g., they are the result of data entry mistakes), others may not. Several outliers may be found to cluster together in a data set, in which case, a separate regression line fit to those points may be warranted. In other cases, transformations of the data may be used to reduce the influence of the outliers. Because the particular course of action taken with regard to outliers will vary with the circumstance of the problem, it is incumbent upon the researcher to provide a clear justification of whatever course of action he or she chooses to use in a particular case.

USING DIAGNOSTICS TO EVALUATE THE ICE CREAM SALES EXAMPLE

We complete the ice cream example with an examination of our data for possible anomalies that may compromise the utility of our regression model. We begin with a scatterplot of X (temp) by Y (barsold) with case id numbers listed (see Fig. 15.16).

MORE Stata: To create a scatterplot that is labeled by ID numbers, we run the following command:

twoway (scatter barsold temp, mlabel(id))

With the exception of case number 29, all points fall fairly close to the regression line and the residual plot, $Y - \hat{Y}$ versus X, given below is fairly rectangular in shape, suggesting that the assumptions of linear regression are met and that transformations of the variables are not needed. Case number 29 warrants further attention (Fig. 15.17).

Accordingly, we investigate the vertical discrepancy (as measured by the Studentized residuals), the horizontal leverage, and finally, the influence of all cases in this analysis. Boxplots of these statistics are provided below in Figures 15.18 through 15.20, respectively.

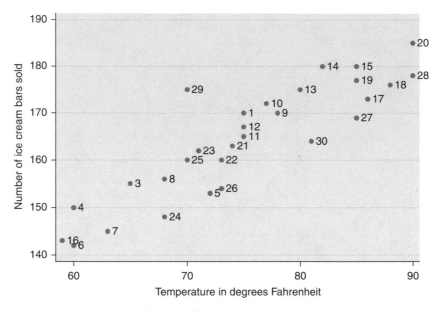

Figure 15.16   Scatterplot of temp by barsold with case id numbers.

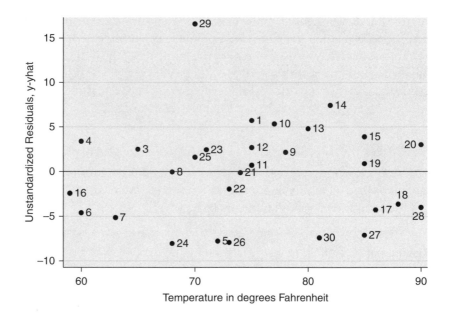

Figure 15.17   Residual plot of $Y - \hat{Y}$ versus X.

As expected from Figures 15.16 and 15.17, and as illustrated in Figure 15.18, case number 29 has the greatest vertical distance from the regression line as measured by the Studentized residual. Because case number 29 is close to the mean temperature value, it does not show up as an outlier with respect to leverage or horizontal distance from the X

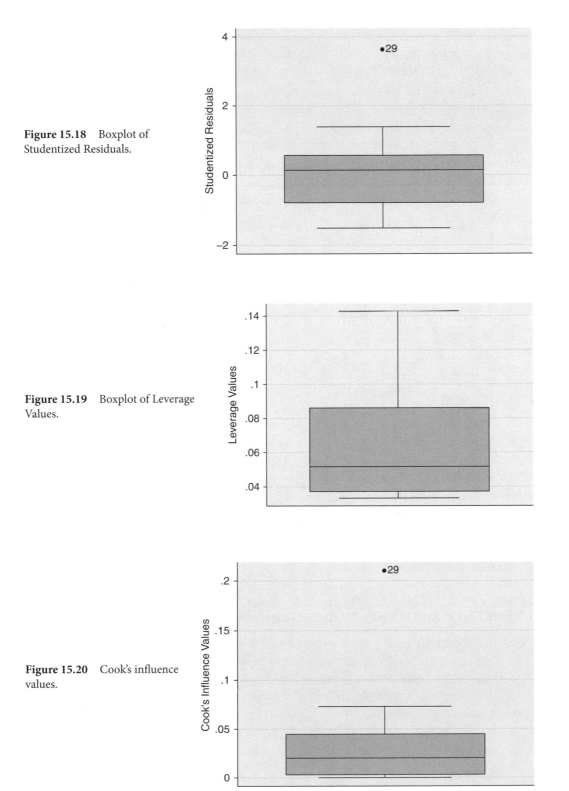

Figure 15.18 Boxplot of Studentized Residuals.

Figure 15.19 Boxplot of Leverage Values.

Figure 15.20 Cook's influence values.

mean. Although it does show up as an outlier with respect to influence, the influence value itself is close to 0 (at .2) and suggests negligible influence on the regression slope. To confirm this, however, we redo the regression analysis without case number 29 and obtain the following result.

Source	SS	df	MS			
				Number of obs	=	29
				F (1, 27)	=	155.38
Model	3400.52983	1	3400.52983	Prob > F	=	0.0000
Residual	590.918447	27	21.8858684	R-squared	=	0.8520
				Adj R-squared	=	0.8465
Total	3991.44828	28	142.551724	Root MSE	=	4.6782

barsold	Coef.	Std. Err.	t	P > |t|	[95% Conf.	Interval]
temp	1.217338	.0976607	12.46	0.000	1.016955	1.417722
_cons	72.43576	7.385924	9.81	0.000	57.28109	87.59042

That is, without case number 29, the linear regression equation for predicting barsold from temp is Predicted barsold = 1.22(temp) + 72.44, which has a b-weight that is negligibly different from the b-weight of the original equation obtained with case number 29 included: Predicted barsold = 1.18(temp) + 75.78.

Notice that the intercept is lower without case number 29 than with case number 29. This is to be expected because of where case number 29 sits relative to the other points in the sample. Case number 29 is near the X mean indicating that it will not affect the b-weight by very much, but it is high above the regression line indicating that it will raise the level of the regression line and increase the Y-intercept as shown.

As one might expect, without case number 29 in the sample, the fit of the regression line to the points is improved (from R^2 = .786 with case number 29 to R^2 = .852 without case number 29). However, because there is no compelling reason to eliminate case number 29 from the analysis, we leave it in and acknowledge its influence on our results, albeit small.

USING THE PREDICTION MODEL TO PREDICT ICE CREAM SALES

Now that we have shown that our model was appropriately fit to our data using diagnostics and that the result was statistically significant, we can be confident in using our regression equation to predict ice cream sales from temperature. Simply stated, to predict the number of ice cream sales on a particular day with a given forecasted highest daily temperature, we use

Predicted barsold = 1.18(temp) + 75.78.

Thus, if the highest daily temperature is forecasted to be 78 for a particular day, we would take Predicted barsold = 1.18(78) + 75.78 = 167.82, or 168 bars to the beach.

Given how well our model fits our data ($R^2 = .786$), we can expect our equation to yield reasonably accurate estimates of ice cream sales given particular daily highest temperatures. However, the accuracy of a particular prediction (that we will sell exactly 168 ice cream bars when the daily highest temperature is forecast to reach 78 degrees, for example) will depend on several factors. One factor is the distance between the given forecasted daily high (e.g., 78 in this case) and the mean daily highest temperature for our sample of data (e.g., 75 for these data). Simply stated, the accuracy of our prediction will be better the closer the particular X value is to $\overline{X}$. Thus, in the context of our example, we can expect our prediction of ice cream sales to be more accurate on days when the highest daily temperature is forecast to be around 75 than far from 75.

SIMPLE REGRESSION WHEN THE PREDICTOR IS DICHOTOMOUS

In Example 11.8 (in Chapter 11) we used the independent samples t-test on the *NELS* data set to determine whether gender differences exist in the number of units of mathematics taken in high school among college-bound students from the southern United States. In this problem, gender, a dichotomous variable, may be considered as the independent variable and number of units of mathematics taken in high school as the dependent variable. In this section we compare the result of the independent samples t-test to that of the t-test on the b-weight for predicting units of math taken in high school from gender, and show that they are equivalent.

The Stata result of the independent samples t-test for this example is reproduced below.

Group	Obs	Mean	Std. Err.	Std. Dev.	[95% Conf.	Interval]
Male	66	3.916667	.0907	.7368505	3.735526	4.097807
Female	84	3.664048	.0788377	.7225592	3.507243	3.820853
combined	150	3.7752	.060195	.7372356	3.656254	3.894146
diff		.252619	.1198904		.015701	.4895371

diff = mean (Male) − mean (Female)   t =   2.1071
Ho: diff = 0   degrees of freedom =   148

Ha: diff < 0   Ha: diff ! = 0   Ha: diff > 0
Pr (T < t) = 0.9816   Pr (|T| > |t|) = 0.0368   Pr (T > t) = 0.0184

As discussed in Chapter 11, and as noted in the tables above, the mean gender difference in math courses taken of .25 is statistically significant, indicating that males in the south take statistically significantly more math than females in the south ($t(148) = 2.11$, $p = .04$).

The Coefficients table from the simple linear regression analysis to predict units of math taken from gender is given below.

Source	SS	df	MS				
Model	2.35865352	1	2.35865352		Number of obs	=	150
Residual	78.6252905	148	.531251963		F(1, 148)	=	4.44
					Prob > F	=	0.0368
					R–squared	=	0.0291
Total	80.983944	149	.543516403		Adj R–squared	=	0.0226
					Root MSE	=	.72887

unitmath	Coef.	Std. Err.	t	P > |t|	[95% Conf.	Interval]
gender	−.252619	.1198904	−2.11	0.037	−.4895371	−.015701
_cons	3.916667	.0897177	43.66	0.000	3.739373	4.09396

Notice that the t-test of the b-weight is identical (except for the sign) to the t-test of the mean difference ($t = -2.11$, $p = .04$). The sign change in the t-value simply reflects the fact that in one approach, the mean units of math taken by males is subtracted from the mean units of math taken by females, while in the other approach the reverse is the case. Notice that the b-weight of −.253 equals the difference in means between males and females, once again allowing for a sign change due to the way the subtraction is carried out.

Whenever a dichotomous independent variable is coded 0 for one group (e.g., males) and 1 for the other (e.g., females), the b-weight will reflect the difference in means on the dependent variable between the two groups. Furthermore, the constant (3.917 in this case) will equal the mean on the dependent variable of the group coded 0. Hence, we can learn from the regression equation alone that the mean number of math units taken by males is 3.917 and by females is 3.917 − .253, or 3.664, which we know to be the case from the descriptive statistics associated with the t-test on means of independent samples. Because X takes only two values, $\hat{Y}$ takes only two, also.

We already have pointed out that the t-test of the b-weight is equivalent to the t-test of the correlation between independent and dependent variables. The Stata correlation output given below corroborates that fact.

	unitmath	gender
unitmath	1.0000	
	150	
gender	−0.1707	1.0000
	0.0368	
	150	150

Notice that the correlation between gender and units of math taken is $r = -.17$, which is statistically significant. The t-test on the correlation (note that the t-value is not reported) has a two-tailed p-value of $p = .0368$, which is exactly the value given in connection with the t-test on the b-weight and the t-test on the means of the two independent groups.

SUMMARY OF STATA COMMANDS IN CHAPTER 15

For a complete listing of all Stata commands associated with this chapter, you may access the Do-file for Chapter 15 located on the text website.

Create	Command Lines
To obtain a scatterplot with a regression line superimposed (Figure 15.5)	**twoway (scatter barsold temp) (lfit barsold temp)**
To create a scatterplot that is labeled by ID numbers (Figure 15.16)	**twoway (scatter barsold temp, mlabel(id))**
To obtain the residual scatterplot (Figure 15.9)	**regress y1 x1**
	predict y1_resid, residuals
	twoway scatter y1_resid x1, ytitle("y1 Residuals")
Pearson Product Moment Correlation along with the significance level and the number of observations	**pwcorr barsold temp, obs sig**
To transform r = .887 to Z and obtain descriptives on Z	**gen Z = .5*ln((1+.887)/(1-.887))**
	summarize Z
To transform Z back to r and display results in the Output Window	**display "rlower = " (exp(2*1.031) − 1)/ (exp(2*1.031) + 1)**
	display "rupper = " (exp(2*1.785) − 1)/(exp(2*1.785) + 1)
To perform a regression analysis including summary statistics (Example 15.2)	**summarize barsold temp**
	pwcorr barsold temp, sig obs
	regress barsold temp
To obtain a bootstrap estimate of the standard error of the b-coefficient	**bootstrap _b, reps(1000)nodots seed(1234): regress barsold temp**
To obtain the leverage of a data point (Table 15.2)	**regress y x**
	predict lev, leverage
To obtain the Studentized residual value for each data point (x,y) (Table 15.3)	**regress y x**
	predict stres, rstudent
To obtain Cook's influence value for a data point (x,y) (Table 15.4)	**regress y x**
	predict influence, cooksd

EXERCISES

*Create a Do-file for each exercise that requires the use of Stata. Run the commands from the Do-file by highlighting them and hitting **Control+d**. Save each Do-file using a name associated with the Exercise for which it was created. It is recommended that you review the Do-file for Chapter 15 located on the textbook's website before completing these exercises. To facilitate doing each exercise, it may be helpful to copy and paste relevant commands from the Do-file for Chapter 15 into your own Do-file and modify them as needed.*

Exercises 15.1 and 15.2 involve correlation and simple linear regression analyses with interval or ratio leveled independent variables from the Learndis data set. For inferential purposes, we consider the children in the data set to be a random sample of all children attending public elementary school in a certain city who have been diagnosed with learning disabilities. Use α = .05 for all significance tests.

15.1. Perform correlation analyses to investigate whether grade level (grade), intellectual ability (iq), placement type (placemen, where 0 = Part time resource room and 1 = Full-time self-contained classroom) are statistically significantly associated with reading achievement (readcomp). For now, assume that the underlying assumptions have been verified.

    a) What are the null and alternative hypotheses for testing the linear relationship between reading comprehension and intellectual ability?

    b) Is the linear relationship between reading comprehension and intellectual ability statistically significant? If so, describe its nature and magnitude.

    c) Is the linear relationship between reading comprehension and grade level statistically significant? If so, describe its nature and magnitude.

    d) Is there a statistically significant difference in reading comprehension scores, on average, between the two placement types? If so, describe the nature and magnitude of the difference.

    e) Although data were collected on 105 children attending public school in the urban area who had been diagnosed with learning disabilities, reading comprehension scores were not available for 29 of the students. By using the Stata default of list-wise deletion of missing data, the scores of only 76 children were included in the analyses. Describe how this method of dealing with missing data might impact the obtained results. Because a discussion of the many possible ways of handling missing data is beyond the scope of this text, all solutions to problems with missing data are handled as if the data did not have missing values.

15.2. Perform a correlation and simple linear regression analysis to understand how mathematics comprehension (mathcomp) may be explained by intellectual ability (iq).

    a) Find the 95 percent confidence interval for ρ.

    b) Find the 95 percent confidence interval for the population b.

    c) Is the regression model statistically significant? Explain.

    d) Describe, to the extent possible, the nature of the linear relationship between reading comprehension and math comprehension.

    e) Describe, to the extent possible, the strength of the linear relationship between reading comprehension and math comprehension, using Cohen's scale as a guide.

Exercises 15.3 and 15.4 involve correlation and simple linear regression analyses with interval or ratio leveled independent variables from the NELS data set. For inferential purposes, we consider the students in the data set to be a random sample of the population of all college-bound students who have always been at grade level. Use α = .05 for all significance tests.

15.3. Among college-bound students in an urban setting, what is the relationship between family size (famsize) and twelfth grade self-concept (slfcnc12)?

    a) Select cases so that urban = 1 (students included in the analysis are from an urban setting only). Create a scatterplot between family size (famsize) and twelfth grade self-concept (slfcnc12). The Stata command for obtaining the scatterplot with the appropriate cases selected is: **twoway (scatter slfcnc12 famsize) (lfit slfcnc12**

famsize) if urban ==1. Use the scatterplot to comment upon the appropriateness of a correlation analysis.

b) Find the correlation between famsize and slfcnc12 and indicate whether or not it is statistically significant.

c) Find the 95 percent confidence interval for the correlation between famsize and slfcnc12. Use it to determine whether or not the correlation between famsize and slfcnc12 is statistically significant.

d) According to Cohen's scale, what is the strength of the linear relationship between famsize and slfcnc12 in the population? Which is more useful for making the determination, the correlation, or the confidence interval?

15.4. Construct a regression model to predict twelfth grade math achievement (achmat12) from socioeconomic status (ses), reported in eighth grade.

a) Is the regression model statistically significant?

b) What is the regression equation for predicting achmat12 (Y) from ses (X).

c) What is the interpretation of the slope of the regression equation in the context of this analysis?

d) Interpret the y-intercept or constant within the context of this analysis, or explain why it would not be meaningful to do so.

e) Report and interpret a measure of effect size for the relationship.

Exercises 15.5 and 15.6 involve simple linear regression analyses with dichotomous independent variables from the Learndis data set. For inferential purposes, we consider the children in the data set to be a random sample of all children attending public elementary school in a certain city who have been diagnosed with learning disabilities. Use α = .05 for all significance tests.

15.5. Perform a simple linear regression analysis to understand how intellectual ability (iq) may be predicted from gender. Use it to answer the following questions.

a) Is the regression model statistically significant? Explain and indicate what part of the output you used to determine the significance of the model.

b) Explain why, in this case, it is not appropriate to report the regression equation and its components.

15.6. Perform a simple linear regression analysis to determine the proportion of reading comprehension (readcomp) variance explained by type of placement (placemen). For these data, there are two types of placement, part-time resource room, coded 0, and full-time self-contained classroom, coded 1. Use your analysis to answer the following questions.

a) Is the regression model statistically significant? Explain and indicate what part of the output you used to determine the significance of the model.

b) What is the regression equation for predicting reading comprehension scores (Y) from the type of placement (X)?

c) What is the interpretation of the slope of the regression equation in the context of this analysis?

d) Interpret the y-intercept or constant within the context of this analysis, or explain why it would not be meaningful to do so.

e) Based on the regression model, what would you predict the reading comprehension score to be for a student within the resource room? Can the predicted score be interpreted as the mean reading comprehension score for all students within the resource room?

f) Use the regression model to predict the reading comprehension score for a student within the self-contained classroom.

g) What percentage of the variance in reading comprehension scores is explained by placement type? Explain and indicate what part of the output you used to determine this effect size.

h) What other inferential test could have been performed to determine how reading comprehension may be predicted from type of placement?

Exercise 15.7 involves simple linear regression analyses with dichotomous independent variables from the NELS data set. For inferential purposes, we consider the students in the data set to be a random sample of the population of all college-bound students who have always been at grade level. Use $\alpha = .05$ for all significance tests.

15.7. Develop a regression model to predict twelfth grade math achievement (achmat12) from computer ownership (computer), as reported in eighth grade?

a) Is the regression model statistically significant?

b) Report the regression equation for predicting achmat12 (Y) from computer (X).

c) What is the interpretation of the slope of the regression equation in the context of this analysis?

d) Interpret the y-intercept or constant within the context of this analysis, or explain why it is not meaningful.

e) Report and interpret two different measures of effect size for the relationship.

Exercise 15.8 involves correlation and simple linear regression analyses with variables from the Brainsz data set. Recall that the population of students for this study consisted only of those with either extremely high or extremely low intelligence. For inferential purposes, we consider the students in the data set to be a random sample of all college students with extremely low or high intelligence. Use $\alpha = .05$ for all significance tests.

15.8. Perform correlation analyses to investigate whether gender and brain size (mri) are statistically significantly associated with intelligence as measured by the Full-Scale IQ score of the WAIS-R test (fsiq). Use these analyses to answer the following questions.

a) Is the linear relationship between intelligence and brain size statistically significant? If so, describe its nature and magnitude.

b) Is there a statistically significant relationship between intelligence and gender? If so, describe its nature and magnitude.

c) Comment upon the effect of the sampling design on the correlation computed in part a).

d) Construct a scatterplot of these two variables with FSIQ on the vertical axis and brain size as measured by the MRI on the horizontal axis.

e) Explain why there are two clouds of points in the scatterplot.

f) Regress fsiq on mri using a single regression model for the entire sample. Comment on the significance and fit of this model.

g) Regress fsiq on mri using two regression models, one fit to extremely high fsiq group and the other fit to the extremely low fsiq group. Comment on the fit of each model and compare these values to the fit of the model developed on the entire sample and obtained in part (f).

Exercises 15.9–15.12 focus on regression diagnostics using the Learndis data set. For inferential purposes, we consider the children in the data set to be a random sample of all children attending public elementary school in a certain city who have been diagnosed with learning disabilities. Use α = .05 for all significance tests.

15.9. Create a scatterplot that could be used to predict reading comprehension (readcomp) from grade level (grade) for the students in the data set, labeling the points by the case numbers. Use the scatterplot to answer the following questions.

a) Do any of the assumptions (normality, homoscedasticity, and linearity) underlying the correlation analysis between reading comprehension and grade level appear to be violated? Explain.

b) Which case number has the data point with the largest residual (in magnitude)? Is that residual negative or positive? That is, is that case over- or under-predicted by the model? Note that if you used any Stata procedures that re-sorted the data set, your case numbers may not be the same as those given in the scatterplot.

c) Give an example of a case number with relatively large leverage.

d) Give an example of a case number with relatively large discrepancy (in magnitude).

e) Give an example of a case number with relatively large influence.

15.10. Perform a simple linear regression analysis with reading comprehension (readcomp) as the dependent variable and grade (grade) as the independent variable. Create a residual plot that gives the residuals associated with that analysis by grade, labeling the points by their case numbers. Use the residual plot to answer the following questions.

a) Do any of the assumptions (normality, homoscedasticity, and linearity) underlying the correlation analysis between reading comprehension and grade level appear to be violated? Explain.

b) Which case number has the data point with the largest residual (in magnitude)? Is that residual negative or positive? That is, is that case over- or under-predicted by the model? Note that if you used any Stata procedures that re-sorted the data set, your case numbers may not be the same as those given in the scatterplot.

c) Give an example of a case number with relatively large leverage.

d) Give an example of a case number with relatively large discrepancy (in magnitude).

e) Give an example of a case number with relatively large influence.

f) Compare the residual plot of Exercise 15.3 to the scatterplot of Exercise 15.2. In your opinion, which more clearly depicts the appropriateness of the regression model?

15.11. Perform a simple linear regression analysis with math comprehension (mathcomp) as the dependent variable and reading comprehension (readcomp) as the independent variable. Create a residual plot for the analysis that is labeled by case number. Use the residual plot to answer the following questions.

a) Do any of the assumptions (normality, homoscedasticity, and linearity) underlying the regression analysis between the dependent variable math comprehension and the independent variable reading comprehension appear to be violated? Explain.

    b) Which case number has the data point with the largest residual (in magnitude)? Is that residual negative or positive? That is, is that case over- or under-predicted by the model?

    c) Give an example of a case number with relatively large influence.

15.12. In Exercise 15.11, we identified case number 43 as being potentially influential in the model predicting math comprehension from reading comprehension. In this exercise, we compare the models with and without that case number. This type of analysis is called a sensitivity analysis.

    a) What is the regression equation for predicting math comprehension scores (Y) from reading comprehension scores (X) according to the model without case number 43? What is the regression equation for predicting math comprehension scores (Y) from reading comprehension scores (X) according to the model with all cases? How different are the parameter estimates?

    b) Are the regression models with and without case number 43 statistically significant (i.e., are both b-weights statistically significantly different from zero)?

    c) Compare the fit of each model to the underlying, respective datat sets, with and without case 43.

    d) Is the y-intercept or constant meaningful within the context of this analysis?.

    e) Interpret the b-weights in each model.

    f) Use both models to predict the math comprehension score for a student with a reading comprehension score of 75.

    g) Which model should one ultimately report and use?

    h) Where should one look in the regression output to find the number of scores used in the analysis?

    i) Compare the value for R^2 to the value for the adjusted R^2 using the model based on all cases. Why are these two values so similar?

Exercises 15.13–15.14 involve regression diagnostics with variables from the NELS data set. For inferential purposes, we consider the students in the data set to be a random sample of the population of all college-bound students who have always been at grade level. Use $\alpha = .05$ for all significance tests.

15.13. Comment on the appropriateness of using simple linear regression for predicting achmat12 from computer, as we did in Exercise 15.7.

15.14. In Exercise 15.4, we developed a simple regression model to predict achmat12 from ses. In this exercise, we follow-up with some regression diagnostics to verify the appropriateness of the model.

    a) Create a scatterplot of the regression for predicting achmat12 from ses. Does the scatterplot suggest a linear relationship between these two variables with no apparent violation of underlying assumptions?

    b) Calculate the studentized residuals and create a residual scatterplot and frequency distribution. What are the lowest and highest values of the studentized residuals? What do these values indicate about the appropriateness of the model?

    c) Calculate the Cook's influence scores and create a boxplot of the distribution. What are the lowest and highest values of the Cook's influence scores? What do these values indicate about the appropriateness of the model?

    d) Using the obtained regression model, what is the value of the predicted twelfth grade math achievement score for the first person in the data set (with id = 1)?

e) Using the obtained regression model, what is the unstandardized residual value of the twelfth grade math achievement score for the first person in the data set (with id = 1)?

f) Which unstandardized residual value has the greatest magnitude? What is its associated id number?

Exercise 15.15 involves a small data set.

15.15. Dr. Michelle Knapp, a research pediatrician, is interested in predicting the birth weight of first-born infants (Y) from the amount of weight gained by the mother during her pregnancy (X) for the population of middle-class individuals. She therefore randomly selects 15 middle-class mothers, pregnant for the first time, and follows them through pregnancy. After the mothers give birth, she records their weight gains in pounds and the birth weights of their offspring in pounds. The data are given in the following table. Use them to answer the associated questions.

X Weight gain of Mother (Pounds)	Y Birth Weight of Infant (Pounds)
14	6.2
23	6.8
28	7.5
27	7.3
12	6.0
19	6.2
25	7.0
24	6.3
34	8.0
21	6.0
30	8.0
32	8.2
26	7.5
27	7.5
23	6.8

a) Create a scatterplot and, if necessary, a diagnostic analysis, and use them to show that a correlation and simple linear regression analysis is appropriate for these data.

b) Construct a 95 percent confidence interval for the population correlation, ρ between the birth weight of the infant and the weight gain of the mother. According to the confidence interval, is the correlation statistically significant? If so, describe its nature and strength.

c) Construct the linear regression equation for predicting the birth weight of the infant (Y) from the weight gain of the mother (X).

d) Is the linear regression model statistically significant? Use $\alpha = .05$. Explain.

e) What is the predicted birth weight of a first-born infant whose mother gained 25 pounds during her pregnancy?

f) Calculate the overall standard error of estimate when using the linear regression equation to predict Y from X in the population.

g) Interpret the standard error of estimate and estimate with approximately 95% accuracy the weight of an infant whose mother gained 25 pounds during pregnancy.

Exercises 15.16–15.32 are conceptual in nature and do not require the use of Stata.

15.16. The b-weight for predicting Y from X is computed in a sample of size 200 drawn randomly from a bivariate population. If this process is repeated 2,000 times, the standard deviation of the 2,000 b-weights is approximately equal to:

a) the standard deviation of X.

b) the standard deviation of Y.

c) the standard error of b for $N = 200$.

d) the standard error of b for $N = 2,000$.

e) none of the above

15.17. Given a simple regression equation for predicting Y from X, $\hat{Y} = bX + a$. When will Var(Y) equal Var(residual)? [HINT: The residual is that part of Y that remains after accounting for X, or $Y - \hat{Y}$.]

a) when the correlation between X and Y is equal to zero.

b) when the correlation between X and Y is not equal to zero.

c) when the correlation between X and Y is positive, but not when it's negative.

d) always

e) never

f) none of the above

15.18. Given a simple regression equation for predicting Y from X, $\hat{Y} = bX + a$. When will Var(Y) be less than Var(residual)?

a) when the correlation between X and Y equal to zero.

b) when the correlation between X and Y not equal to zero.

c) when the correlation between X and Y is positive, but not when it's negative.

d) always

e) never

f) none of the above

Exercises 15.19–15.23 relate to the following scatterplot. The regression line has been added and the points are labeled by their case numbers.

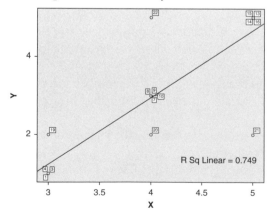

15.19. The value 3 may be described most closely as
a) $\overline{X}$, the mean of X
b) $\overline{Y}$, the mean of Y
c) both (a) and (b)
d) neither (a) nor (b)

15.20. The point with the greatest residual corresponds to case number
a) 19   b) 20   c) 21   d) 22

15.21. The point with the greatest influence corresponds to case number
a) 19   b) 20   c) 21   d) 22

15.22. The slope of the regression equation, in this case is
a) positive
b) negative
c) zero

15.23. The y-intercept of the regression equation, in this case is
a) positive
b) negative
c) zero

15.24. Which regression assumption is most likely violated in the following scatterplot?

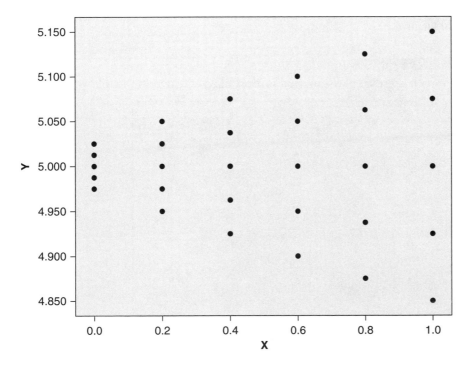

a) linearity
b) normality
c) homoscedasticity

15.25. Which regression assumption is most likely violated in the following scatterplot?

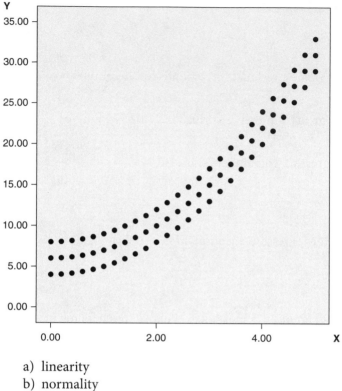

a) linearity
b) normality
c) homoscedasticity

15.26. Which regression assumption is most likely violated in the following scatterplot?

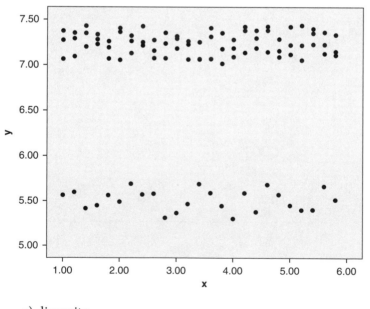

a) linearity
b) normality
c) homoscedasticity

15.27. Which regression assumption is most likely violated in the following scatterplot that depicts the Y scores of 300 Boys and 300 Girls?

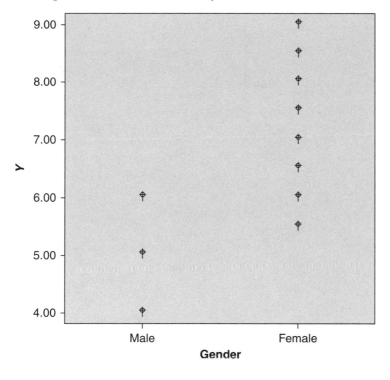

a) linearity
b) normality
c) homoscedasticity

Exercises 15.28–15.31 come from Becker and Kennedy (1992). Use the following graph to determine the most correct response to the multiple-choice questions.

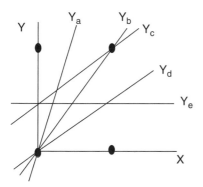

15.28. For the four sample points, which line best represents the average of the Y data? (Note that the point (0, 0) is one of the observations.)
    a) Y_a b) Y_b c) Y_c d) Y_d e) Y_e

15.29. For the four sample points, which line best represents the regression line?
    a) Y_a b) Y_b c) Y_c d) Y_d e) Y_e

15.30. The value of R^2 for the regression line is:
   a) less than 0
   b) 0
   c) between 0 and .5
   d) .5
   e) greater than .5

15.31. Verify that the mean of the residuals is 0 for any simple linear regression analysis.

CHAPTER SIXTEEN

An Introduction to Multiple Regression

In Chapter 15, we were concerned with predicting the number of ice cream bars we could expect to sell at the beach from the daily highest temperature. Our goal was to predict that number as accurately as possible so that we would neither take too much ice cream to the beach or too little. Because of the linear shape depicted in the scatterplot and the strong relationship between number of ice cream sales and daily highest temperature ($r = .887$), we were able to construct a reasonably accurate simple linear regression equation for prediction with $R^2 = .78$. But, we can try to do even better. That is, we can consider ways to predict ice cream sales even more accurately.

Alternatively, we can shift our focus away from prediction and consider ways to *explain* the observed variability in ice cream sales. That is, rather than use multiple regression for prediction, we may use it to understand and explain phenomena of interest to us and to study the effects that individual independent variables have on these phenomena. That is, we can use multiple regression to understand the factors that contribute to ice cream sales at the beach rather than to predict the number of ice cream sales we can expect on a particular day at the beach. Clearly, we have already defined temperature as one explanatory factor. We now seek to identify another factor, in addition to temperature, that explains why people buy ice cream at the beach.

Assuming that our beach example takes place in the northeastern part of the United States, another factor might be relative humidity. Like increases in temperature, increases in relative humidity make us feel more uncomfortably hot. Yet, because relative humidity does not correlate highly with temperature when we consider only the summer months in the northeast, relative humidity offers the potential for tapping a set of reasons related to ice cream sales that is different from temperature. Because temperature and humidity are not highly correlated, we say that they are not *redundant* of each other. In general, to optimize the explanatory power of a multiple regression equation, we seek to add new variables to the equation that do not highly correlate with the other independent variables already in the equation and that do highly correlate with the dependent variable.

While multiple regression, in general, allows for the inclusion of many independent variables in the equation, we shall restrict our discussion to the case of only two independent variables. We do so for simplicity and because the principles and concepts that apply in the case of only two independent variables in the equation generalize easily to the case of more than two independent variables in the equation. While five or six or more independent variables are not uncommon in a regression equation, in practice, it is often difficult to identify more than three independent variables that each contributes new explanatory information over and above the others. Said differently, in general, R will tend not to increase dramatically as the number of independent variables increases beyond even a few because the new variables will tend to be redundant with those already in the equation.

THE BASIC EQUATION WITH TWO PREDICTORS

When there are two independent variables (for example, temperature and humidity) and a dependent variable Y (for example, ice cream sales) in a multiple regression equation, the equation has the following form (notice that we have renamed the constant a as b_0):

$$\hat{Y} = b_1 X_1 + b_2 X_2 + b_0 \tag{16.1}$$

As in the simple linear regression case, the b's are coefficients of the X variables and b_0 is an additive constant. The right side of Equation 16.1 is called a *linear composite of the X variables*. As Equation 16.1 suggests, the linear composite is obtained by multiplying X_1 by b_1 and X_2 by b_2 and by adding these two products together with the additive constant b_0 to obtain $\hat{Y}$, the predicted value of Y.

The b's of Equation 16.1 are determined to produce the largest possible correlation between the actual value of Y and the linear composite $\hat{Y}$. Once the b's are determined, the constant b_0 is determined so that on average, the predicted value of Y will equal the actual value of Y. That is, so that the mean of $\hat{Y}$ will equal the mean of Y, $\overline{\hat{Y}} = \overline{Y}$. The additive constant b_0 has the following equation:

$$b_0 = \overline{Y} - (b_1 \overline{X}_1 + b_2 \overline{X}_2) \tag{16.2}$$

The linear composite and additive constant of Equations 16.1 and 16.2 are based on raw or unstandardized scores. When, on the other hand, the independent variables are standardized to have mean zero and standard deviation one (when they are in z-score form), we may re-express Equation 16.1 as Equation 16.3:

$$\hat{z}_Y = \beta_1 z_1 + \beta_2 z_2 \tag{16.3}$$

β's (betas) as opposed to b's are used in Equation 16.3 to indicate that the linear composite is based on z-scores as opposed to raw scores. Because this equation is based on z-scores, the additive constant, b_0, is zero.

☞ **Remark.** Because z_Y, z_1, and z_2 are in standardized form, $\overline{z}_Y = \overline{z}_1 = \overline{z}_2 = 0$. If we substitute these means of zero into Equation 15.2 we find that $b_0 = 0$. Regression equations based on z, or standardized, scores all have additive constants equal to zero.

If the independent X variables are converted to z-scores, then the linear composite of the z-scores, z_Y, may be obtained using Equation 16.3. One simply multiplies β_1 and β_2 by z_1 and z_2, respectively, and computes the sum of these two products.

As in simple linear regression, the correlation between Y and $\hat{Y}$, or between z_Y and z_Y, is denoted by R. In the context of multiple regression, however, R is called a *multiple correlation*. R is also denoted as $R_{Y,\hat{Y}}$ or as $R_{Y.12}$. The latter notation explicitly conveys the fact that $\hat{Y}$ is estimated from an equation that contains two predictor variables, X_1 and X_2.

In the next two sections we give the equations for b, β, and R. In the first of these sections we consider the case when the two predictors are not correlated. In the second, we consider the more general case when the two predictors are correlated.

EQUATIONS FOR b, β, AND $R_{Y.12}$ WHEN THE PREDICTORS ARE NOT CORRELATED

When the two predictors in the regression equation are not correlated (i.e., when $r_{X_1,X_2} = 0$), then b_1 and b_2 are expressed simply as Equation 16.4.

$$b_1 = r_{Y,X_1} \frac{S_Y}{S_{X_1}}$$

$$b_2 = r_{Y,X_2} \frac{S_Y}{S_{X_2}}$$

(16.4)

Notice that as Equation 16.4 suggests, when the two predictors are uncorrelated, the b-weight for each predictor is simply the b-weight that would be obtained if that predictor were the only one in the equation. That is, the b-weight of a predictor in an equation with two (or more) uncorrelated predictors is obtained simply by ignoring the remaining predictor(s) and calculating the b-weight as though that predictor were the only one in the equation (as in the case of simple linear regression).

The same, of course, applies when the two predictors are uncorrelated and all variables are standardized. The Equations for β_1 and β_2 are given by Equation 16.5.

$$\beta_1 = r_{Y,X_1}$$
$$\beta_2 = r_{Y,X_2}$$

(16.5)

Here again, each beta-weight is determined as if its corresponding predictor were the only one in the equation, as in the case of simple linear regression.

We may find $R_{Y.12}$ by taking the square root of $R_{Y.12}^2$ using Equation 16.6.

$$R_{Y.12}^2 = r_{Y,X_1}^2 + r_{Y,X_2}^2$$

(16.6)

As Equation 16.6 suggests, when the two predictors are uncorrelated, the squared multiple correlation, $R_{Y.12}^2$, is simply equal to the sum of the squared correlations between each predictor and the dependent variable.

☞ **Remark.** The correlations r_{Y,X_1} and r_{Y,X_2} are called *zero-order correlations* to distinguish them from the other types of correlation we encounter in multiple regression. For notational simplicity, we shall follow common procedure and express r_{Y,X_1} as r_{Y1} and r_{Y,X_2} as r_{Y2}. Likewise, we shall also express the correlation between predictors r_{X_1,X_2} as r_{12} and the standard deviation of X_1, S_{X_1} as S_1, and so on for S_{X_2}.

In previous work we have noted that R^2 (or r^2) is a measure of overall fit of the regression model to the data, and is interpreted more specifically as the proportion of Y variance explained by the regression. Accordingly, we may use Figure 16.1 to illustrate Equation 16.6.

In Figure 16.1, each circle represents the variance of one of the variables in the equation, Y, X_1, and X_2 and the amount of overlap between two circles represents their squared correlation. Because X_1 and X_2 are uncorrelated, their circles are nonoverlapping. By contrast, X_1 overlaps with Y, and X_2 overlaps with Y, indicating that these two pairs of variables are correlated. The two overlapping areas are shaded and labeled appropriately, r_{Y1}^2 and r_{Y2}^2. When X_1 and X_2 are uncorrelated, we may observe quite clearly that the sum of the shaded areas, r_{Y1}^2 and r_{Y2}^2, represents the overlap between Y and the two variables taken together, and as such, equals $R_{Y.12}^2$, the proportion of Y variance that is explained by the regression containing X_1 and X_2.

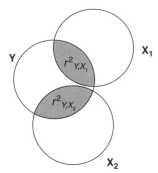

Figure 16.1 The proportion of Y variance explained by the regression when predictors are uncorrelated

EQUATIONS FOR b, β, AND $R_{Y.12}$ WHEN THE PREDICTORS ARE CORRELATED

When the predictors are correlated, one cannot ignore the other predictor in the equation when calculating a regression coefficient or the multiple correlation as was the case in the previous section. As a result, the equations for the b-weights and $R_{Y.12}$ are a bit more complex than those given in the previous section. The equation for the b-weights is given in Equation 16.7.

$$b_1 = \frac{r_{Y1} - r_{Y2}r_{12}}{1 - r_{12}^2} \times \frac{S_Y}{S_1}$$

$$b_2 = \frac{r_{Y2} - r_{Y1}r_{12}}{1 - r_{12}^2} \times \frac{S_Y}{S_2}$$

(16.7)

Equation 16.7 tells us that when the two predictors are correlated, the value of b_1 (both its magnitude and sign) depends upon the correlation between X_1 and Y, r_{Y1}, the correlation between X_2 and Y, r_{Y2}, and the intercorrelation between X_1 and X_2, r_{12}. The same is true for b_2.

☞ **Remark.** When the two predictors are not correlated, when $r_{12} = 0$, Equation 16.7 reduces to Equation 16.4.

Thus, when the predictors of a multiple regression equation are correlated, we do not have the luxury of ignoring the second predictor in the equation when interpreting the importance of the first predictor, and vice versa.

Equation 16.7 reduces to Equation 16.8 when all variables are in standardized form. Once again, β's are used in place of b's.

$$\beta_1 = \frac{r_{Y1} - r_{Y2}r_{12}}{1 - r_{12}^2}$$

$$\beta_2 = \frac{r_{Y2} - r_{Y1}r_{12}}{1 - r_{12}^2}$$

(16.8)

To help conceptualize the equation for R^2, we present Figure 16.2(a) and (b) which each illustrate the relationships between the correlated independent variables and the dependent variable. In Figure 16.2 (a), the proportion of Y variance explained is expressed as the sum of what is due to X_1 (the shaded part) plus what is due to that part of X_2 unrelated to X_1 (the cross-hatched part). In Figure 16.2 (b), the proportion of Y variance explained is

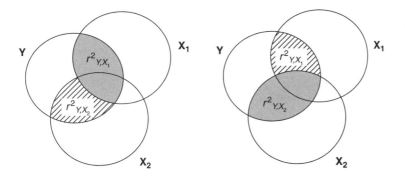

Figure 16.2 (a) The proportion of Y variance explained by X_1 (shaded part) and that part of X_2 unrelated to X_1 (cross-hatched part). (b) The proportion of Y variance explained by X_2 (shaded part) and that part of X_1 unrelated to X_2 (cross-hatched part).

expressed as the sum of what is due to X_2 (the shaded part) plus what is due to that part of X_1 unrelated to X_2 (the cross-hatched part).

Equations 16.9 (a) and (b) translate what is illustrated, respectively, in Figures 16.2(a) and (b) into an Equation for $R^2_{Y.12}$. Equation 16.9(a) is a direct translation of Figure 16.2(a) and Equation 16.9(b) is a direct translation of Figure 16.2 (b). For both Equations, $R_{Y.12}$ is obtained by simply taking the square root.

$$R^2_{Y.12} = r^2_{Y1} + r^2_{Y,2(1)} \tag{16.9a}$$

where r^2_{Y1} equals the proportion of Y variance explained by X_1

$r^2_{Y,2(1)}$ equals the proportion of Y variance explained by X_2 beyond that explained by X_1

$$R^2_{Y.12} = r^2_{Y2} + r^2_{Y,1(2)} \tag{16.9b}$$

where r^2_{Y2} equals the proportion of Y variance explained by X_2

$r^2_{Y,1(2)}$ equals the proportion of Y variance explained by X_1 beyond that explained by X_2

☞ **Remark.** Both $r_{Y,1(2)}$ and $r_{Y,2(1)}$ are called *semipartial (aka part) correlations*. In particular, $r^2_{Y,1(2)}$ is the semipartial correlation of X_1 squared and may be interpreted as the amount R^2 would drop if X_1 were removed from the equation. Likewise, $r^2_{Y,2(1)}$ is the semipartial correlation of X_2 squared and may be interpreted as the amount R^2 would drop if X_2 were removed from the equation. As we will discuss in more detail later, the semipartial correlation squared is a highly useful measure of the importance of a predictor variable in an equation and we shall use it as such in our examples in this chapter.

☞ **Remark.** The semipartial correlation of X_1 squared may also be thought of as the *unique contribution* of X_1 to R^2 in the context of the remaining variable in the equation, X_2. An analogous statement may be made for X_2.

SUMMARIZING AND EXPANDING ON SOME IMPORTANT PRINCIPLES OF MULTIPLE REGRESSION

1. R will be high when the independent variables are each highly correlated with the dependent variable.

2. R will not be less than the highest correlation between any of the independent variables and the dependent variable.

3. R will be larger when the independent variables are not redundant of one another, when their intercorrelations are relatively low.

4. R is difficult to estimate from eyeballing the simple, zero-order correlation matrix when the number of independent variables is large.

5. R does not increase dramatically in practice as the number of independent variables increases because the independent variables tend to become redundant of one another as they increase in number.

6. R based on sample data tends to overestimate the population R. Said differently, the sample R is upwardly biased. The smaller the sample size relative to the number of independent variables, the more R will be inflated. In situations of prediction, the best way to estimate the extent of inflation is to cross-validate results on a new sample randomly selected from the same population. When there are more than 30 subjects for each independent variable in the equation, the difference between the sample and cross-validated R's will tend to be small. When, there are fewer than 10 subjects for each independent variable in the equation, the difference between the sample and cross-validated R will tend to be large.

7. The importance of an independent variable in an equation is best measured by the amount R^2 would drop if that variable were removed from the equation. This amount may be measured by the squared semi-partial (or part) correlation of that variable.

8. The importance of an independent variable in an equation depends upon what other variables are included in the equation along with that variable. When other variables are included in the equation that correlate strongly with that variable, these other variables will "rob" that variable of some of its unique contribution. As a result, that variable will not appear to be so important in the equation. Of course, if all independent variables in an equation are highly intercorrelated, none of them will appear to be so important in that equation because they will each "rob" one another of its unique contribution.

9. b_1 measures the *net or marginal effect* of X_1 partialling out or holding constant X_2. Likewise, b_2 measures the net or marginal effect of X_2 partialling out or holding constant X_1. Accordingly, these coefficients are called *partial regression coefficients*. Said differently, the net effect of X_1 equals the *average effect* of X_1 for any given value of X_2; the net effect of X_2 equals the *average effect* of X_2 for any given value of X_1.

10. b_1 and b_2 are calculated on unstandardized values. As a result, the net effects associated with them are measured in terms of the original units of measure for the variables (e.g., in degrees Fahrenheit, in percentage points of relative humidity).

11. β_1 is a standardized partial regression coefficient and measures the net effect of $z1$ partialling out or holding constant z_2. Likewise, β_2 is also a standardized partial regression coefficient and measures the net effect of z_2 partialling out or holding constant z_1.

12. β_1 and β_2 coefficients are calculated on standardized values. As a result, the net effects associated with them are measured in standard deviation units rather than in the original units of measure for the variables.

13. In multiple regression, both b and β can be greater than 1 or less than −1, even though in the case of simple linear regression, when there is only one independent variable, β must be between −1 and 1.

Example 16.1 illustrates the points we have made so far in this chapter using our ice cream sales example with humidity included as an independent variable in addition to temperature.

• •

EXAMPLE 16.1. Given the scenario described in Chapter 15 using the dataset, *Ice Cream. dta*, construct a regression equation with both temperature and relative humidity as independent variables and ice cream sales as the dependent variable. Said differently, construct an equation that regresses ice cream sales on both temperature and relative humidity. The data below contain relative humidity values in addition to daily highest temperature and number of bars sold for each of the thirty days sampled. Interpret the equation as well as the various tests of significance reported in the output.

barsold	temp	relhumid
170	75	70
160	70	72
155	65	73
150	60	72
153	72	70
142	60	72
145	63	60
156	68	70
170	78	73
172	77	85
165	75	70
167	75	70
175	80	89
180	82	95
180	85	98
143	59	75
173	86	82
176	88	88
177	85	93
185	90	97
163	74	70
160	73	75
162	71	73
148	68	68
160	70	78
154	73	72
169	85	72
178	90	95
175	70	88
164	81	65

Solution.

MORE Stata: To perform a multiple regression analysis

We build on the syntax we have used earlier to run a simple linear regression. The general form of the syntax for a multiple regression is:

regress *y* x1 x2 ...... x10

where *y* is the dependent variable and the *x*'s are the predictor variables (also called independent variables and regressors). In the current example, the command would be: (See the Do-file associated with this chapter for an annotated listing of all Stata commands used in this chapter.)

regress barsold temp relhumid

To obtain additional statistics related to our regression analysis:

summarize barsold temp relhumid
pwcorr barsold temp relhumid, obs star(5)

The Stata output is reproduced and described below.

(1) From **summarize barsold temp relhumid**

Variable	Obs	Mean	Std. Dev.	Min	Max
barsold	30	164.2333	11.90677	142	185
temp	30	74.93333	8.944015	59	90
relhumid	30	77.66667	10.49904	60	98

We note that, as expected, the analysis is based on a sample of size $N = 30$. The mean number of ice cream bars sold is approximately 164 with standard deviation 12, the mean temperature is approximately 75 degrees Fahrenheit with standard deviation 9, and the mean relative humidity is approximately 78 with standard deviation 10.5.

(2) From **pwcorr barsold temp relhumid, obs star(5)**

	barsold	temp	relhumid
barsold	1.0000 30		
temp	0.8867* 30	1.0000 30	
relhumid	0.7782* 30	0.6494* 30	1.0000 30

We note that the correlations between the dependent variable barsold and the two independent variables, temp and relhumid, are .887 and .778, respectively, and that $p < .05$ indicating that these relationships are statistically significant. Thus, we may conclude that both independent variables relate strongly to barsold.

We also may note that temp and relhumid are not uncorrelated as their correlation is .649. If we square .649, we obtain that approximately 42 percent of the variance of each these variables is explained by the other.

When we combine the two independent variables, temp and relhumid, into a regression equation predicting barsold, we can, therefore, expect R to be no smaller than .887, the higher of the two correlations with the dependent variable. And, because the two independent variables are only moderately correlated, we can expect R to exceed .887 by a nonnegligible amount.

(3) From **regress barsold temp relhumid**

Source	SS	df	MS		
				Number of obs	= 30
				F(2, 27)	= 80.99
Model	3523.95292	2	1761.97646	Prob > F	= 0.0000
Residual	587.413748	27	21.7560647	R-squared	= 0.8571
				Adj R-squared	= 0.8465
Total	4111.36667	29	141.771264	Root MSE	= 4.6643

According to these regression results, $R^2 = .857$ $(R = .926)$. Thus, temperature and relative humidity *collectively* account for 85.7 percent of ice cream sales variance. While the sample R^2 value is .857, we may note that the adjusted R^2 value is .847. The small amount of shrinkage from sample to adjusted R^2 is due to the fact that the ratio of subjects to independent variables exceeds 10:1. For this example, this ratio is 30:2 or 15:1.

We may note as well that R is statistically significant $(F(2, 27) = 80.988, p < .0005)$. The degrees of freedom of 2 and 27 represent, respectively, the number of independent variables in the equation $(P = 2)$ and the sample size minus the number of independent variables minus 1 $(N - P - 1 = 30 - 2 - 1 = 27)$.

barsold	Coef.	Std. Err.	t	P > |t|	[95% Conf.	Interval]
temp	.8778386	.1273412	6.89	0.000	.616556	1.139121
relhumid	.3969829	.1084806	3.66	0.001	.1743992	.6195666
_cons	67.62162	7.638874	8.85	0.000	51.94795	83.29529

Given this table of coefficients, we note that the multiple regression equation for predicting ice cream sales from both temperature and relative humidity is:

Estimated barsold = .878*temp + .397*relhumid + 67.622

We may interpret $b_1 = .878$ as follows: For days with a given or specified relative humidity (X_2), each increase in temperature by one degree Fahrenheit is associated with an average increase of .878 ice cream bars sold. In this sense, b_1 represents the net effect of X_1 (temperature) holding X_2 (relative humidity) constant.

Analogously, we may interpret $b_2 = .397$ as follows: For days with a given or specified temperature (X_1), each increase in relative humidity by one percentage point is associated with an average increase of .397 ice cream bars sold. In this sense, b_2 represents the net effect of X_2 (relative humidity) holding X_1 (temperature) constant.

A multiple regression equation with one predictor may be represented as a two-dimensional line; with two predictors, it may be represented as a three-dimensional

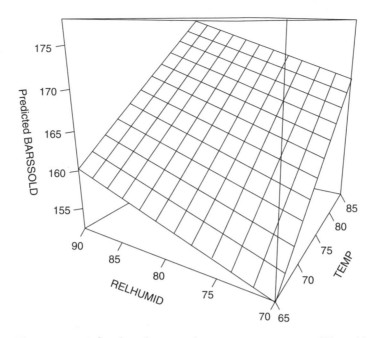

Figure 16.3   A flat plane depicting the regression equation, est'd barsold = .878(temp) + .397(relhumid) + 67.622

plane as shown in Figure 16.3. As denoted by the plane, which is flat as denoted by the series of parallel lines depicted in it, the slopes of the lines representing the relationship between temp and barsold remain constant at .878 across all values of relhumid. Likewise, the slopes of the lines representing the relationship between relhumid and barsold remain constant at .397 across all values of temp. For this reason, it makes sense to think of the b-weight of temp (.878) as representing the *average* increase in barsold associated with each unit increase in temp, averaged across the full range of values (levels) of relhumid; and, to think of the b-weight of relhumid (.397) as representing the *average* increase in barsold associated with each unit increase in relhumid, averaged across the full range of values (levels) of temp.

From Equation 16.7, we may note that the relative values of the *b coefficients* are a function of the relative values of the standard deviations of X_1 and X_2. In particular, the size of a variable's b-coefficient varies inversely with that variable's standard deviation; it will be small when its variable's standard deviation is large and large when its variable's standard deviation is small. Accordingly, because a b-coefficient is confounded by its variable's standard deviation, b-coefficients are not a pure measure of the relative importance of the variables in an equation and cannot be used as such.

To assess the relative importance of variables in an equation, beta coefficients (aka beta weights) are usually more useful because they are based on the standardized values, with each variable having an equal standard deviation of 1.00. To obtain the standardized beta weights of a regression equation, we need to add **beta** as an option in the **regress** command as follows:

```
regress barsold temp relhumid, beta
```

barsold	Coef.	Std. Err.	t	P > |t|	Beta
temp	.8778386	.1273412	6.89	0.000	.6594063
relhumid	.3969829	.1084806	3.66	0.001	.3500478
_cons	67.62162	7.638874	8.85	0.000	.

From this coefficients table, we may note that the standardized form of the multiple regression equation is: $z_{\hat{y}} = .659z_1 + .350z_2$. According to this equation, we also may note that temperature is relatively more important than relative humidity in predicting ice cream sales because it receives a higher beta weight.

☞ **Remark.** In general, when there are more than two predictors, the beta weights are not the best measure of relative importance of the variables. The beta weights are not so easily interpreted when the independent variables are correlated.

☞ **Remark.** Note that for this example the same general conclusion regarding the relative importance of the independent variables may be obtained from either a comparison of b-weights or the beta weights. This is because, in this example, the standard deviation of temperature (11.94) is similar in value to the standard deviation of relative humidity (10.50). That is, the ratio of the two standard deviations is approximately 1:1.

TESTING THE b-WEIGHTS FOR STATISTICAL SIGNIFICANCE

Following the same procedures described in Chapter 15, we may test each of the partial regression coefficients for statistical significance by way of the t-ratio:

$$t = \frac{b}{\hat{\sigma}_b} \qquad (16.10)$$

where $\hat{\sigma}_b$ equals the standard error of b, the standard deviation of the sampling distribution of b-weights based on random samples of the same size randomly drawn from the same population. This t-ratio tests whether the b-coefficient differs from 0 in the population. With P independent variables in the equation, the t-test has $N - P - 1$ degrees of freedom. (In Chapter 15, we considered the case of only one independent variable in the equation. Thus, P equaled 1 and the degrees of freedom for the t-test of the b-weight were noted as being $N - 2$). If a b-coefficient differs significantly from 0, the variable associated with that b contributes significantly to the prediction over and above the contribution of the other variables.

We may obtain the t-ratios for b_1 and b_2 from the table of Coefficients in Example 16.1. The t-ratio for b_1 is 6.894 (derived from the t-ratio .878/.127) is statistically significant ($p < .0005$) and suggests that b_1 is different from zero in the population. We conclude that the temperature is a statistically significant predictor of the number of ice cream bars sold over what is predicted by relative humidity. Likewise, the t-ratio for b_2 is 3.659 (derived from the t-ratio .397/.108) is statistically significant ($p = .001$) and suggests that b_2 is different from zero in the population. We conclude that the relative humidity is a statistically significant predictor of the number of ice cream bars sold over what is predicted by temperature.

From the results of the ANOVA, we noted that the overall regression equation containing both temperature and relative humidity is statistically significant and that, therefore, temperature and relative humidity *collectively* predict ice cream sales. From the *t*-test results, we now know that *individually* temperature and relative humidity each contributes uniquely to the prediction of ice cream sales.

To estimate the respective values of the *b* coefficients in the population we may use confidence intervals as described in Chapter 15. The interested reader may refer back to Equation 15.3 in Chapter 15 for the equations of the upper and lower limits of the confidence interval for *b*.

The two-tailed 95 percent confidence intervals for b_1 and b_2 in Example 16.1 may be obtained from the table of coefficients associated with the **regress** command. We may note that reasonable estimates of b_1 in the population are between .617 and 1.139 while reasonable estimates of b_2 in the population are between .174 and .620. While there is some overlap between the two estimates, b_1 is likely to be the larger of the two weights in the population.

To check the accuracy of the obtained theoretically-derived results, we use the bootstrap procedure as we have done previously to obtain robust, empirically-driven estimates of the standard errors of the b-coefficients. In Stata, b-coefficients are referred to by the variable name, _b, and this command will output bootstrap standard errors for all the coefficients in the model. As before, we use the **nodots** option, and the **seed** option in the event that we would like to reproduce these results in the future.

MORE Stata: To obtain the bootstrap-derived standard errors of the b-coefficients

bootstrap _b, reps(1000) nodots seed(2576): regress barsold temp relhumid

---

The bootstrap results for the *b*-coefficients of our regression equation are given as follows:

Linear regression						
					Number of obs	= 30
					Replications	= 1000
					Wald chi2 (2)	= 189.64
					Prob > chi2	= 0.0000
					R-squared	= 0.8571
					Adj R-squared	= 0.8465
					Root MSE	= 4.6643

barsold	Observed Coef.	Bootstrap Std. Err.	z	P > |z|	Normal-based [95% Conf.	Interval]
temp	.8778386	.1485555	5.91	0.000	.5866751	1.169002
relhumid	.3969829	.1213075	3.27	0.001	.1592246	.6347412
_cons	67.62162	7.263347	9.31	0.000	53.38572	81.85752

Compared to the theoretically-driven standard error estimates of temperature and relative humidity (.127 and .108, respectively), the bootstrap estimates of .149 and .121 are a bit larger. Nonetheless, because the significance of the b-weights remain the same, our substantive conclusions remain the same as well.

ASSESSING THE RELATIVE IMPORTANCE OF THE INDEPENDENT VARIABLES IN THE EQUATION

As noted earlier, while the beta weights are often useful in assessing the relative importance of the independent variables in an equation, a preferred approach is to use the amount R^2 will drop when that variable is removed from the equation, or equivalently, the amount R^2 will increase when that variable is added to the equation last.

The amount R^2 will drop when X_2, for example, is removed from an equation that contains both X_1 and X_2 equals the cross-hatched area of Figure 16.2(a). Likewise, the amount R^2 will drop when X_1 is removed from the equation that contains both X_1 and X_2 equals the cross-hatched area of Figure 16.2(b).

Without X_2, R^2 would only be equal to r_{Y1}^2 as it would no longer include the cross-hatched area of Figure 16.2(a). Without X_1, R^2 would only be equal to r_{Y2}^2 as it would no longer include the cross-hatched area of Figure 16.2(b).

From Equation 16.9(a), we know that the cross-hatched area of Figure 16.2(a) may be expressed directly as $r_{Y,2(1)}^2$, defined earlier as the square of the semipartial (or part) correlation of X_2. From Equation 16.9(b), we know that the cross-hatched area of Figure 16.2(b) may be expressed directly as $r_{Y,1(2)}^2$, defined earlier as the square of the semi-partial (or part) correlation of X_1.

☞ **Remark.** As the cross-hatched area of Figure 16.2(a) suggests, the square of the semi-partial (aka part) correlation of X_2 may be defined more explicitly as the square of the correlation between Y and that part of X_2 uncorrelated with (or orthogonal to) X_1. The part of X_2 uncorrelated with (or orthogonal to) X_1 is that part of X_2 that remains after removing the linear relationship of X_2 with X_1, likewise for the semi-partial correlation of X_1.

Thus, to assess the relative importance of temperature and relative humidity in Example 16.1 we may use the values of their semipartial correlations, which may be obtained using the **pcorr** command as follows:

```
pcorr barsold temp relhumid
```

Partial and semipartial correlations of barsold with

Variable	Partial Corr.	Semipartial Corr.	Partial Corr.^2	Semipartial Corr.^2	Significance Value
temp	0.7986	0.5015	0.6377	0.2515	0.0000
relhumid	0.5758	0.2662	0.3315	0.0709	0.0011

From these results, we note that the semipartial correlations of temperature (X_1) and relative humidity (X_2), are respectively, .501 and .266, and semipartial correlations squared are .251 and .071 respectively. Therefore, the amount that the overall R^2 of .857 would drop if temperature were removed from the equation is .251 and the amount that the overall R^2 of .857 would drop if relative humidity were removed from the equation is .071. From these statistics, it is clear that temperature is the more important variable of the two.

☞ **Remark.** The above table of coefficients also includes an index called the partial correlation. Partial correlations are closely related to semipartial correlations and will provide the same rank order of variables in terms of their importance. Because, however, semipartial correlations are useful in the regression context in that they can be interpreted directly in terms of a drop in R^2, while partial correlations cannot, we shall confine our discussion to semipartial correlations in this text. The interested reader is referred to a more advanced treatment of regression to learn more about partial correlations (Cohen, Cohen, West, & Aiken; 2003).

MEASURING THE DROP IN R^2 DIRECTLY: AN ALTERNATIVE TO THE SQUARED SEMIPARTIAL CORRELATION

If we so choose, we may carry out a series of regression analyses to obtain the amount that R^2 will drop when a variable is removed from the equation. In particular, to find the amount that R^2 will drop when temperature is removed from the equation with both temperature and humidity, we construct one regression equation with both temperature and humidity to obtain $R^2_{Y.12}$. We then construct another equation without temperature to obtain $R^2_{Y.2}$. The difference, $R^2_{Y.12} - R^2_{Y.2}$ is the amount by which $R^2_{Y.12}$ will drop when temperature is removed from the equation.

For our example, we find that $R^2_{Y.12} = .857$ and $R^2_{Y.2} = .605$, and that therefore, $R^2_{Y.12} - R^2_{Y.2} = .252$, which is the amount R^2 drops when temperature is removed from the equation. Notice that, within rounding error, this amount equals $(.501)^2$, the square of the part correlation for temperature.

We may use an analogous procedure to find $R^2_{Y.12} - R^2_{Y.1}$, the drop in R^2 when humidity is removed from the equation. As before, this amount equals the part correlation of humidity squared.

EVALUATING THE STATISTICAL SIGNIFICANCE OF THE CHANGE IN R^2

Intuitively, it should make sense that whenever the b-weight of an independent variable is statistically significant, the increase in R^2 obtained when that variable is added last to the equation will also be statistically significant. It can be shown that the t-test of the statistical significance of the b-weight of an independent variable is equivalent to the corresponding F-test associated with the increase in R^2 when that variable is added last to the equation.

Consider the following two equations, the first with only X_1 and the second with both X_1 and X_2.

$$\hat{Y} = b_1 X_1 + b_0$$
$$\hat{Y} = b_1 X_1 + b_2 X_2 + b_0 \tag{16.11}$$

Because the two models represented in 16.11 are different, in general, we would expect the b_1 and b_0 values to be different in the two equations as well.

The squared multiple correlations of the first and second equations are designated $R^2_{Y.1}$ and $R^2_{Y.12}$, respectively. As discussed earlier, a test of whether the effect of X_2 (relative humidity), controlling for X_1 (temperature), is statistically significant is given by the t-test of b_2 that appears in the table of coefficients ($t(27) = 3.659$, $p = .001$) associated with the **regress** command. Alternatively, it is given by the following associated F-test of the increment in R^2 due to X_2.

$$F_{(1, N-2-1)} = \frac{(R^2_{Y.12} - R^2_{Y.1})/1}{(1 - R^2_{Y.12})/(N-2-1)} \tag{16.12}$$

For our ice cream example, we have $R^2_{Y.12} = .857$, $R^2_{Y.1} = .787$ and $N = 30$. Substituting these values into Equation 16.12 and simplifying we find that $F_{(1,27)} = \dfrac{.07}{.143/27} = \dfrac{.07}{.00529} = 13.22$ which equals within rounding error $t^2 = 3.659^2 = 13.39$.

Likewise, the t-test on the b weight of temperature, b_1 in our equation, is equivalent to the F-test associated with the increase in R^2 when temperature is added last to the equation (when it is added to the equation that already includes relative humidity).

MORE Stata: To test the statistical significance of the change in R^2 of two nested equations

Because the first equation (16.11) includes only X_1 and the second equation includes both X_1 and X_2, the first equation is said to be *nested* within the second equation. Accordingly, to evaluate the statistical significance of the change in R^2 for these two nested equations, we may use the **nestreg** command.

nestreg: regress barsold (temp) (relhumid)

Note: This command will run two separate regressions. The first will regress barsold on temp. The second will regress barsold on both temp and relhumid. The command will also test whether the change in R^2 between the first and second models is statistically significant. One may think of the two sets of ()'s as defining Block 1 (Model 1) and Block 2 (Model 2), respectively. For this example, temp constitutes Block 1 and is entered first and relhumid constitutes Block 2 and is entered next. Although only one variable constitutes each Block in this example, in general, more than one variable may constitute a Block. In that case, all the variables in a Block are entered simultaneously. Given that there is only one variable per Block in this example, and each variable accounts for 1 *df*, this explains why each Block noted in the output contains has 1 *df* associated with it.

The relevant output for each Block follows:

```
Block 1: temp

barsold |  Coef.  Std. Err.      t     P>|t|    [95% Conf.      Interval]
temp    |  1.180441  .1163125  10.15   0.000     .942186       1.418697
_cons   | 75.77892  8.775494    8.64   0.000   57.8031493.75471

Block 2: relhumid

barsold  | Coef.  Std. Err.        t     P>|t|     [95% Conf.Interval]
temp     |  .8778386  .1273412    6.89   0.000     .616556    1.139121
relhumid |  .3969829  .1084806    3.66   0.001     .1743992    .6195666
_cons    | 67.62162  7.638874     8.85   0.000   51.9479583.29529
```

		Block	Residual		Change	
	Block	F	df	Pr > F	R2	in R2
	1	103.00	1	28 0.0000	0.7863	
	2	13.39	1	27 0.0011	0.8571	0.0709

The output for each Block is reported under the headings Block 1: temp and Block 2: relhumid. The R^2 values in the Block Residual table for Blocks 1 and 2 correspond to the

Figure 16.4 (a) That part of X_1 unrelated (orthogonal) to X_2. (b). That part of X_2 unrelated (orthogonal) to X_1.

values that we computed as $R^2_{Y.1}$ .786 and $R^2_{Y.12}$ = .857. That is, we see that R^2 for Block 1 (aka Model 1) is .786, so that we may conclude that 78.6 percent of the variance in ice cream sales can be explained by temperature. The R^2 for Block or Model 2 is .857, so that we may conclude that 85.7 percent of the variance in ice cream sales can be explained by both temperature and relative humidity. According to the value of the R^2 change statistic due to the addition of relhumidity in Block 2 (.071), we see that relative humidity explains 7.1 percent of the variance in ice cream sales over and above the percentage of variance explained by temperature.

The change statistics for Block 2 contain the results of the significance test on the change in R^2 between the model that contains only temperature to the model that contains both temperature and relative humidity. We have $F(1, 27) = 13.39$ with $p = .001$. We conclude that relative humidity explains a statistically significant proportion of variance in ice cream sales over and above what was explained by temperature.

THE *b*-WEIGHT AS A PARTIAL SLOPE IN MULTIPLE REGRESSION

Recall that in the case of simple regression, the single *b*-weight or regression coefficient is interpreted as a slope that signifies the expected change in the dependent variable, *Y*, for each unit increase in the independent variable, *X*. Just as *b* is the slope of the line that relates *Y* to *X*, we can also describe b_1 and b_2 as slopes, or more precisely, as *partial slopes*. In particular, b_1 can be described as the slope of the line that relates *Y* to X_1 *is partialled from* X_1. Likewise, b_2 can be described as the slope of the line that relates *Y* to X_2 after X_1 *is partialled from* X_2. X_1 with X_2 partialled from it may be represented graphically as the shaded area of Figure 15.3(a). Likewise, X_2 with X_1 partialled from it may be represented graphically as the shaded area of Figure 16.4(b). As Figures 16.4(a) and (b) indicate, what remains of X_1 after X_2 is partialled from it is that part of X_1 unrelated (or orthogonal) to X_2 and what remains of X_2 after X_1 is partialled from it is that part of X_2 unrelated (or orthogonal) to X_1.

If we wanted to create a new variable that represents the shaded part of Figure 16.4(a), for example, we may do so by setting up a simple regression equation to predict X_1 from X_2 as shown in Equation 16.13.

$$\hat{X}_1 = bX_2 + b_0 \tag{16.3}$$

and then compute $X_1 - \hat{X}_1$. Recall that $X_1 - \hat{X}_1$ is also called the residual of X_1 after accounting for X_2 and may be denoted as $X_{1.2}$. It is that part of X_1 (temp) orthogonal to X_2 (relhumid). Analogously, to find $X_{2.1}$ we compute $X_2 - \hat{X}_2$ where $\hat{X}_2$ is obtained from Equation 16.4.

$$\hat{X}_2 = bX_1 + b_0 \tag{16.4}$$

Relating this discussion to our ice cream example, X_1 represents temperature and X_2 represents relative humidity. We may create the new variables $X_{1.2}$ and $X_{2.1}$ by constructing the respective simple regression equations (16.3) and (16.4), and obtaining the two respective residuals $X_1 - \hat{X}_1$ and $X_2 - \hat{X}_2$. In so doing we will be creating that part of temperature unrelated to humidity ($X_{1.2}$) and that part of humidity unrelated to temperature ($X_{2.1}$). Note that the correlation between ($X_{1.2}$) and ($X_{2.1}$) is 0.

We shall use Stata to create the new variable $X_{1.2}$ and show that b_1, which equals .878, is simply the slope of the regression line that predicts Y from $X_{1.2}$. In Exercise 16.12 you will show that b_2, which equals .397, is simply the slope of the regression line that predicts Y from $X_{2.1}$.

MORE Stata: To create the variable $X_{1.2}$ that depicts that part of X_1 orthogonal to X_2.

We use the **regress** command to regress one independent variable X_1 (temp) on X_2 (relhumid). We then generate the set of unstandardized residuals, representing that part of X_1 (temp) that is orthogonal to X_2 (relhumid).

regress temp relhumid
predict x1orthx2, residuals

Table 16.1 contains the results of the Stata analysis that we use to show that b_1, which is .878, equals the b weight in the simple regression equation that predicts ice cream sales (Y) from that part of temperature unrelated or orthogonal to humidity ($X_{1.2}$). In so doing, we can begin to appreciate why b_1 is described as a *partial slope*.

• •

EXAMPLE 16.2. Use the data of Table 16.1 to predict ice cream sales (Y) from that part of temperature unrelated to humidity ($X_{1.2}$) and show that the *b*-weight of $X_{1.2}$ is equal to b_1, the *b*-weight associated with temperature in the regression equation containing both temperature and humidity. For this to be the case, the simple *b*-weight from this analysis should equal .878.

Solution. To find the slope, *b*, of the simple regression equation that predicts number of ice cream sales from that part of temperature unrelated to humidity, we use the linear regression procedure with ice cream sales as the dependent variable and $X_{1.2}$, the unstandardized residual, as the independent variable. The following table of Coefficients is obtained as part of our results:

Source	SS	df	MS			
				Number of obs	=	30
				F (1, 28)	=	9.41
Model	1033.88355	1	1033.88355	Prob > F	=	0.0048
Residual	3077.48312	28	109.910111	R-squared	=	0.2515
				Adj R-squared	=	0.2247
Total	4111.36667	29	141.771264	Root MSE	=	10.484

barsold	Coef.	Std. Err.	t	P > |t|	[95% Conf.	Interval]
x1orthx2	.8778386	.2862185	3.07	0.005	.2915466	1.464131
_cons	164.2333	1.914072	85.80	0.000	160.3125	168.1541

Notice that, as expected, *b* = .878.

Notice that, as expected, *b* = .878.

TABLE 16.1. Data to illustrate that b_1 is a partial slope

Ice cream bars sold (Y)	Temperature (X_1)	That part of temperature unrelated to humidity ($X_{1.2} = X_1 - \hat{X}_1$)
170	75	4.30772
160	70	−1.79864
155	65	−7.35182
150	60	−11.79864
153	72	1.30772
142	60	−11.79864
145	63	−2.16048
156	68	−2.69228
170	78	5.64818
172	77	−1.98999
165	75	4.30772
167	75	4.30772
175	80	−1.20271
180	82	−2.52179
180	85	−1.18133
143	59	−14.45819
173	86	8.66955
176	88	7.35047
177	85	1.58457
185	90	4.37185
163	74	3.30772
160	73	−.45819
162	71	−1.35182
148	68	−1.58592
160	70	−5.11773
154	73	1.20136
169	85	13.20136
178	90	5.47821
175	70	−10.64953
164	81	13.07362

MULTIPLE REGRESSION WHEN ONE OF THE TWO INDEPENDENT VARIABLES IS DICHOTOMOUS

In the examples presented thus far in this chapter, the independent variables, temperature and relative humidity, were at least interval-leveled. We consider in Example 16.3 the situation in which one of the two independent variables is dichotomous.

• •

EXAMPLE 16.3. Using the *NELS* data set, regress twelfth grade self-concept (slfcnc12) on both eighth grade self-concept (SLFCNC08) and gender. In doing so, determine the extent to which twelfth grade self-concept variance is explained collectively by eighth grade self-concept and gender. In addition, determine whether eighth grade self-concept has an effect on twelfth grade self-concept after gender is controlled and whether gender has an effect on twelfth grade self-concept after eighth grade self-concept is controlled.

Solution. Using the same commands as for Example 16.1, we obtain the following results:

Variable	Obs	Mean	Std. Dev.	Min	Max
slfcnc12	500	31.48	7.231195	0	43
slfcnc08	500	21.062	5.971052	0	32
gender	500	.546	.4983781	0	1

From the table of descriptive statistics, we note that the mean and standard deviation of self-concept for twelfth graders is 31.48 and 7.23, respectively, and for eighth graders it is 21.06 and 5.97, respectively. Gender has a mean of .55 which implies that 55 percent of the sample is female because females are coded 1 and males are coded 0.

	slfcnc12	slfcnc08	gender
slfcnc12	1.0000		
	500		
slfcnc08	0.4436*	1.0000	
	500	500	
gender	−0.1607*	−0.1912*	1.0000
	500	500	500

The table of correlations suggests a statistically significant moderate positive correlation between twelfth grade and eighth grade self-concept ($r = .444$, $p < .001$) and a statistically significant, yet low correlation between twelfth grade self-concept and gender ($r = −.161$, $p < .001$). The first correlation indicates that students who had relatively low self-concept in eighth grade tended also to have relatively low self-concept in twelfth grade and that students who had relatively high self-concept in eighth grade tended also to have relatively high self-concept in twelfth grade. Given the coding for gender, the negative correlation implies that on average males have higher self-concept scores than females in twelfth grade. The statistically significant intercorrelation between the two independent variables is also low ($r = −.191$) and implies, as before, that on average males have higher scores than girls in eighth grade as well.

Source	SS	df	MS			
				Number of obs	=	500
				F (2, 497)	=	63.19
Model	5290.03014	2	2645.01507	Prob > F	=	0.0000
Residual	20802.7699	497	41.8566798	R-squared	=	0.2027
				Adj R-squared	=	0.1995
Total	26092.8	499	52.2901804	Root MSE	=	6.4697

The fact that R-squared equals 0.2027, we know that R = .450; namely, that a linear composite of gender and eighth grade self-concept maximally correlates $R = .450$ with twelfth grade self-concept. Because .450 is only marginally greater than .444, the simple, zero-order correlation between twelfth grade and eighth grade self-concept, we can infer that gender is likely to be contributing little, if anything at all, to the equation over and above eighth grade self-concept. Said differently, gender does not appear to relate to twelfth grade self-concept after eighth grade self-concept is accounted for.

We may determine the proportion of variance accounted for by gender over and above eighth grade self-concept by examining the R^2 values. We know that the overall R^2 with both eighth grade self-concept and gender in the equation is .203. Thus, collectively, eighth grade self-concept and gender account for 20.3 percent of twelfth grade self-concept variation. (We may also obtain this measure of effect size by dividing the SS due to the Model by SS Total ($5,290/26,093.8 = .203$).) From the Correlation Table, we know that eighth grade self-concept, by itself, accounts for $r^2 = .444^2 = .197$ of twelfth grade self-concept variance. The difference between .203 and .197 is the proportion of twelfth grade self-concept variance due to gender after eighth grade self-concept is accounted for. This difference, at .006, is certainly negligible, suggesting again, that gender does not have much explanatory power over and above eighth grade self-concept.

slfcnc12	Coef.	Std. Err.	t	P > |t|	[95% Conf.	Interval]
slfcnc08	.5189408	.0494161	10.50	0.000	.4218505	.616031
gender	−1.14327	.5920529	−1.93	0.054	−2.306505	.0199646
_cons	21.1743	1.183276	17.89	0.000	18.84946	23.49913

To assess the statistical significance of the individual, unique contribution of each variable and to obtain the regression equation itself, we consult the above Table of Coefficients.

The unstandardized regression equation is:

Estimated slfcnc12 = (.519)(slfcnc08) − (1.143)(gender) + 21.174

Likewise, the standardized regression equation is:

Estimated slfcnc12 = (.429)($z_{slfcnc08}$) − (.079)(z_{gender})

According to the significance values associated with the t-tests on the regression coefficients, we may note that while eighth grade self-concept is statistically significant, gender is not. This result is consistent with what our earlier analysis based on the correlations showed.

According to the standardized regression equation, we may note that slfcnc08 receives the higher beta weight because it is more important than gender in predicting slfcnc12.

Because the b-weight associated with eighth grade self-concept is statistically significant, we may say that controlling for gender, every one point increase in eighth grade self-concept associates with a .519 point increase in twelfth grade self-concept on average. Because the b-weight associated with gender is not statistically significant, we know that after controlling for eighth grade self-concept the magnitude of the difference in twelfth grade self-concept between males and females is not likely to be different from zero. That is, the gender difference in twelfth grade self-concept represented by the statistically significant zero-order correlation coefficient between gender and twelfth grade self-concept appears to be explained by the difference in self-concept in eighth grade. Said differently, gender differences in twelfth grade self-concept do not exist after partialling out or controlling for eighth grade self-concept.

We may use the unstandardized regression equation to estimate the overall twelfth grade self-concept mean as well as the separate means for males and females by substituting the relevant independent variable mean values into the equation.

The overall twelfth grade mean is obtained by substituting the respective eighth grade self-concept and gender means into the equation as follows:

Estimated twelfth grade self-concept mean = (.519)(21.06) − (1.143)(.55) + 21.174 = 31.48.

Note that this is the twelfth grade self-concept mean value printed in the table of summary statistics.

The twelfth grade self-concept mean for males may be obtained by substituting into the equation the eighth grade self-concept mean and the value of 0 for gender (because males are coded 0) as follows:

Estimated twelfth grade self-concept mean for males = (.519)(21.06) − (1.143)(0) + 21.174 = 32.104.

Likewise, the twelfth grade self-concept mean for females is obtained by substituting the value of 1 for gender:

Estimated twelfth grade self-concept mean for females = (.519)(21.06) − (1.143)(1) + 21.174 = 30.961.

☞ **Remark.** Notice that if we subtract the male mean from the female mean we obtain −1.143, the value of the *b*-weight associated with gender. Hence, as noted earlier, the *b*-weight associated with the dichotomous variable equals the difference between the dependent variable means for the two groups represented by the dichotomy. In our example, it equals the difference between the twelfth grade self-concept means for males and females (30.961 − 32.104 = −1.143). Because the *b*-weight associated with gender is not statistically significant, we know that after controlling for eighth grade self-concept, the populations of males and females are not different, on average, in terms of twelfth grade self-concept.

EXAMPLE 16.4. The Basketball data set contains data regarding the top 20 scoring professional basketball players in the United States for the 2013–2014 season. The commands used to obtain the results for this problem are in the Solution to this Example. They also may be found in the Do-file associated with this chapter.

a) Obtain summary statistics for average number of points scored per game (points) and weight in pounds (weightlb) as well as the correlation between these two variables. Obtain the regression equation for predicting points from weightlb.
b) Interpret the regression equation.
c) If you were a scout for a professional basketball team, this result would imply that you should recommend hiring as team members heavier players over lighter ones. Does this conclusion make sense?
d) Construct a scatterplot with points on the vertical axis and weightlb on the horizontal axis. Superimpose the fitted regression line on this scatterplot. Verify that the regression line passes through the point (21.95, 202.70), the respective means of the variables, points and weightlb.
e) Re-do the scatterplot labeling each observation by gender using the following command, which generates three graphs on our coordinate axes (1) a scatterplot of all points labelled by gender, (2) a regression line fitted to the female points, and (3) a regression line fitted to the male points.
f) Describe the slope of each of the regression lines? Do they convey the same positive relationship that the total regression line did?
g) Obtain the regression equation for predicting points from both weightlb and gender. Is the coefficient for weightlb still positive and statistically significant?
h) What is the moral of this example?

Solution.

a) We use the following commands to answer part(a):

> **summarize points weightlb gender**
> **pwcorr points weightlb gender, obs star(5)**
> **regress points weightlb**

The mean and standard deviation of the variables points and weightlb respectively are: mean = 21.95, sd = 4.47 and mean = 202.70, sd = 38.28. Corr(points, weightlb) = 0.709.

The regression equation is: Pred'd Points = .083weightlb + 5.153.

The t-value associated with the coefficient for weightlb is $t = 4.266$, $p < .0005$, suggesting that the relationship between weight in pounds and points scored per game is highly statistically significant.

b) According to the b-coefficient, each pound increase in a player's weight is associated with an average of .083 additional points scored per game.

c) Something seems awry with this result, as such a conclusion does not make sense. Perhaps an important variable has been omitted from the regression model that results in a biased estimate of the coefficient for weightlb.

d) We use the command (Note: legend(order(2)) stipulates that we only want the legend associated with the 2nd graphic, the line, in this case, to appear, but not the legend associated with the 1st graphic, the scatterplot):

> **twoway (scatter points weightlb) (lfit points weightlb), ytitle("Total Points Scored")**
> **legend(order(2))**

Yes, from the graphic, we note that the regression line does pass through (21.95, 202.70), the respective means of points and weightlb.

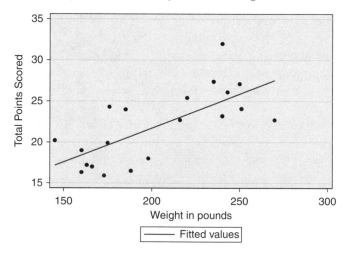

e) To generate the following graph, we use the command,

> **twoway (scatter points weightlb, mlabel(gender))(lfit points weightlb if gender == 1,**
> **lpattern(dash))(lfit points weightlb if gender == 0, lpattern(solid)),legend(row(1)**
> **order(2 3) label(2 Female) label(3 Male)) ytitle("Total Points Scored")**

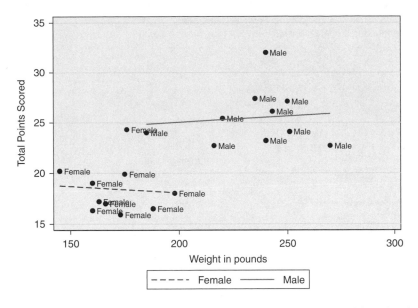

f)   The slope of the regression line for males is positive, although close to zero, and the slope of the regression line for females is negative, although also close to zero, suggesting that when gender is held constant, the magnitude of the relationship between points and weight is near zero. The partial relationship between points and weightlb controlling for gender makes more sense than the earlier result based on the total set of points, without controlling for gender. As suggested by the scatterplot of part e), the earlier positive coefficient for weightlb based on the total set of scores is a result of having combined the two genders into a single analysis, and the fact that one gender, females, has both lower weight and lower average points scored than the male gender.

g)   We use the command: **regress points weightlb gender** to obtain the regression equation with both regressors in the equation: Predicted points = .005weightlb – 6.73gender + 24.358.
     The t-value associated with the coefficient for weightlb is $t = .142$, $p = .889$, suggesting that the (partial) relationship between weight in pounds and points scored per game after controlling for gender is no longer statistically significant.

h)   By omitting from a regression equation a variable that correlates with the dependent variable as well as with a regressor in the equation in whose coefficient we are interested in estimating, we obtain a biased estimate of that coefficient; that is, the coefficient will be either too big or too small. In this example, omitting gender from the regression equation resulted in an estimate of the coefficient of weightlb that was too big. We have seen another instance of "the omitted variable problem" in our kidney stone example in Chapter 12. In that example, the severity of the kidney stone was the omitted variable, which we called a confounder.

THE CONCEPT OF INTERACTION BETWEEN TWO VARIABLES THAT ARE AT LEAST INTERVAL-LEVELED

Thus far we have considered temperature and humidity as variables that individually and collectively affect ice cream sales at the beach. Suppose we notice, however, that when the

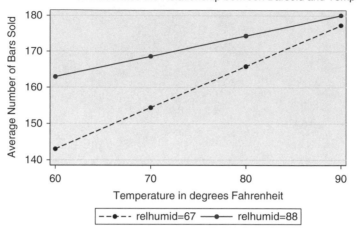

Figure 16.5   The relationship between ice cream sales and temperature varies with humidity

temperature is low, the humidity influences ice cream sales to a greater extent than when the temperature is high. That is, when temperature is relatively low, ice cream sales are much stronger when humidity is relatively high (at 88%) rather than when it is relatively low (at 67%). When temperature is relatively high, however, ice cream sales are reasonably strong regardless of whether humidity is relatively low or relatively high. Figure 16.5 illustrates this sales scenario.

As Figure 16.5 shows, the increase in ice cream sales as temperature increases is more dramatic under conditions of relatively low humidity than under conditions of relatively high humidity. Thus, the relationship between temperature and ice cream sales varies as a function of humidity. When humidity is relatively low, the relationship between temperature and ice cream sales is stronger than when humidity is relatively high. Based on our discussion of interaction in Chapter 14 in connection with two-way ANOVA, we may note that Figure 16.5 depicts an interaction between temperature and humidity on ice cream sales, that humidity *moderates* the relationship between temperature and ice cream sales. When a variable, like humidity, moderates the relationship between two other variables, that variable is said to be a *moderator*. The moderator variable and the variable whose relationship it moderates with the dependent variable are also called *interacting* variables.

In a multiple regression equation, interactions involving two variables (two-way interactions) are represented as the product of the two interacting variables. Thus, if the two variables in the equation are X_1 and X_2, the interaction between X_1 and X_2 is represented as $X_1 \cdot X_2$. The multiple regression model that includes X_1 and X_2 and their interaction is given in Equation 16.12.

$$\hat{Y} = b_1 X_1 + b_2 X_2 + b_3 X_1 \cdot X_2 + b_0 \tag{16.12}$$

By rearranging terms in Equation 16.12, we can show how the product term in Equation 16.12 represents situations like Figure 16.4 in which the slope of the line relating X_1 (temperature) to Y (ice cream sales) varies with the value of X_2 (humidity).

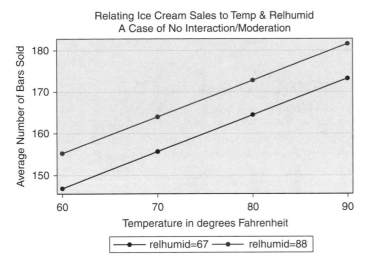

Figure 16.6 The relationship between ice cream sales and temperature does not vary with humidity $(b_3 = 0)$

$$\hat{Y} = b_1 X_1 + b_2 X_2 + b_3 X_1 \cdot X_2 + b_0$$
$$= b_1 X_1 + b_3 X_1 \cdot X_2 + b_2 X_2 + b_0 \qquad (16.13)$$
$$= \left(b_1 + b_3 X_2\right) X_1 + b_2 X_2 + b_0$$

In Equation 16.13, the slope of X_1 (temperature) is not simply b_1, but rather it is $b_1 + b_3 X_2$. If it were simply b_1 then we would know that the slope of the line relating X_1 to Y would remain constant regardless of the value of X_2 (humidity). Because the slope is $b_1 + b_3 X_2$, we know that the slope of the line relating X_1 to Y depends on what the value of X_2 is. Figure 16.5 gives an example of this situation.

From Equation 16.13, we know that when $b_3 = 0$, the slope of the line relating X_1 to Y would remain constant regardless of the value of X_2. An illustration of this situation is given in Figure 16.6.

The parallel lines in Figure 16.6, depicting a constant relationship between X_1 and Y regardless of the value of X_2, imply no interaction between X_1 and X_2. In Figure 16.4, there is an interaction between X_1 and X_2 and $b_3 \neq 0$. In Figure 16.5, there is no interaction between X_1 and X_2 and $b_3 = 0$. In short, therefore, an interaction exists in the population if and only if $b_3 \neq 0$ in the population. As before, we use the t-ratio to test whether b_3 is different from zero in the population. This t-ratio is given in Equation 16.10.

☞ **Remark.** We may interpret b_1 and b_2 in Equation 16.12 as follows: b_1 represents the slope of the line that describes the relationship between Y and X_1 when X_2 is zero; b_2 represents the slope of the line that describes the relationship between Y and X_2 when X_1 is zero. *If an interaction term is in the equation, b_1 and b_2 are easily interpreted as long as the value of zero is a meaningful one for X_1 and X_2.* If an interaction term is *not* in the equation, b_1 represents the average effect of X_1 averaged across the full range of values (levels) of X_2 and b_2 represents the average effect of X_2 averaged across the full range of values (levels) of X_1.

☞ **Remark.** We may interpret b_3 in Equation 16.12 as follows: For every unit change in X_1, the slope of the line that describes the relationship between Y and X_2 changes by b_3 units.

Likewise, for every unit change in X_2 the slope of the line that describes the relationship between Y and X_1 changes by b_3 units. A graphical illustration of this point is given in the next section.

TESTING THE STATISTICAL SIGNIFICANCE OF AN INTERACTION USING STATA

EXAMPLE 16.5. Test whether there is an interaction between temperature and humidity on ice cream sales. If there is an interaction, what proportion of ice cream sales variance does it explain?

Solution.

Use the Stata **generate** command to compute the product of temperature and relative humidity and give that new variable the name, product (note that any other variable name would do equally as well).

gen product = temp*relhumid

This new variable carries the interaction between temperature and relative humidity and we now include it as an independent variable in the **regress** command that regresses barsold on temp (x_1) and relhumid (x_2). The syntax for this analysis (which includes summary statistics and bivariate correlations) is:

summarize barsold temp relhumid product
pwcorr temp barsold relhumid product, obs star(5)
regress barsold temp relhumid product

Variable	Obs	Mean	Std. Dev.	Min	Max
barsold	30	164.2333	11.90677	142	185
temp	30	74.93333	8.944015	59	90
relhumid	30	77.66667	10.49904	60	98
product	30	5878.767	1392.111	3780	8730

☞ **Remark.** It should come as no surprise that the mean and standard deviation of the variable product are both very large since it is formed by multiplying the values of temp and relhumid.

	temp	barsold	relhumid	product
temp	1.0000 30			
barsold	0.8867* 30	1.0000 30		
relhumid	0.6494* 30	0.7782* 30	1.0000 30	
product	0.8861* 30	0.8991* 30	0.9255* 30	1.0000 30

☞ **Remark.** We may note that the correlations between the product term and its component parts are both very high. The correlation between product and temp is $r = .886$; the correlation between product and relhumid is $r = .926$. The reason for these high correlations is that the variable, product, carries within it some of the main (or *first-order*) effects of its component parts (temperature and relative humidity). In order for the product term to truly represent an interaction, it must represent the multiplicative effects of temp and relhumid after the additive effects of temp and relhumid are controlled for or partialled out. As such, authors have referred to the interaction as a *partialled product*. In the case of two independent variables, the partialled product is simply obtained by entering the product term into an equation that already contains its two component, first-order effects. The test of the b-weight associated with the product term is then a test of the unique contribution of the product term after controlling for the two first-order effects that are already in the equation. In the context of this problem, a test of the b-weight associated with the product term is a test of the interaction between temperature and relative humidity on ice cream sales *as long as both first-order component terms are already in the equation*.

barsold	Coef.	Std. Err.	t	P > |t|	[95% Conf.	Interval]
temp	2.967853	.8164026	3.64	0.001	1.289714	4.645993
relhumid	2.583397	.8511625	3.04	0.005	.8338077	4.332987
product	−.0272381	.0105323	−2.59	0.016	−.0488875	−.0055886
_cons	−98.67536	64.67668	−1.53	0.139	−231.6202	34.26947

The unstandardized regression equation for estimating ice cream sales (Y) from temperature (temp), relative humidity (relhumid), and their interaction (product = temp*relhumid) is:

$$\hat{Y} = 2.968(\text{temp}) + 2.583(\text{relhumid}) - .0272(\text{product}) - 98.675$$

The b-weight associated with the product term is statistically significant ($p = .016$), suggesting that there is an interaction between temperature and relative humidity on ice cream sales; that the relationship between temperature and ice cream sales varies as a function of relative humidity, or that the relationship between relative humidity and ice cream sales varies as a function of temperature.

Source	SS	df	MS			
				Number of obs	=	30
				F (3, 26)	=	67.60
Model	3644.14061	3	1214.71354	Prob > F	=	0.0000
Residual	467.226052	26	17.9702328	R-squared	=	0.8864
				Adj R-squared	=	0.8732
Total	4111.36667	29	141.771264	Root MSE	=	4.2391

To assess the overall goodness of fit of the model that contains the two main effects and the interaction term we may consult the table of model summary statistics. By dividing SS_{Model} by SS_{Total} (3,644/4,111) we find that approximately 89 percent of the ice cream sales variance is accounted for by temperature, relative humidity, and their interaction.

We also may use the hierarchical multiple regression approach to test the statistical significance of the interaction term by evaluating the statistical significance of the change in R^2 when the interaction term is introduced to the model. In this approach, the main effects of temp and relhumid are entered simultaneously in the first block and then the interaction term product is entered in the second block.

MORE Stata: To use **nestreg** to test the significance of the interaction term

nestreg: regress barsold (temp relhumid) (product)

Note: Model 1 contains the predictors temp and relhumid; Model 2 contains all three predictors with the product term having been added to Model 1. Accordingly, Model 1 is nested within Model 2. **The command nestreg** tests the significance in the change in R^2 when the product term is added to Model 1.

We obtain the following results:

Block	Block Residual					Change in R2
	F	df	df	Pr > F	R2	
1	80.99	2	27	0.0000	0.8571	
2	6.69	1	26	0.0157	0.8864	0.0292

The change in R^2 associated with introducing the interaction term into the equation is $R^2_{Change} = .029$, and is statistically significant ($F(1, 26) = 6.69$, $p = .016$). Thus, as we noted before from the t-test value associated with the product term, there is an interaction between temperature and relative humidity on ice cream sales. The R^2_{Change} statistic informs us that the interaction accounts for approximately 3 percent of ice cream sales variance over and above first-order effects. We emphasize the fact that the F-test on R^2_{Change} is identical to the t-test of the b-weight associated with the product term. Note that both have p-values equal to .016 and by squaring the t-value of –2.586 we obtain the F-value of 6.688. Recall that with 1 degree of freedom in the numerator, $F = t^2$. Finally, we note once again that the overall R^2 equals .886, suggesting that approximately 89 percent of the ice cream sales variance is accounted for by all three terms in the equation, temperature, relative humidity, and their interaction.

Figure 16.5 illustrates the regression equation, including the interaction, as a three-dimensional plane. As we noted earlier, with one predictor, we may plot the regression equation as a two-dimensional line, but with two predictors, we need one more dimension to plot the equation.

By contrast to the flat plane of Figure 16.3, the plane of Figure 16.7 is warped. Consistent with the flat plane of Figure 16.3, the slopes of the lines relating temp to barsold are equal across all values (levels) of relhumid, and the lines themselves are parallel. In the warped

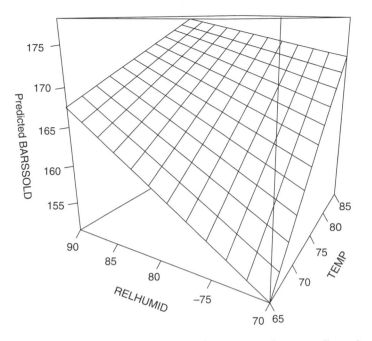

Figure 16.7   Warped plane depicting the interaction between relhumid and temp.

plane of Figure 16.7, however, these slopes are not equal across values of relhumid, and the lines are not parallel. Rather, when relhumid is low (e.g., at 70 and vicinity) the slopes are more steep and when relhumid is high (e.g., at 90 and vicinity) they are less steep. In particular, with each unit increase in relhumid, the b-weight for temp changes by the value of the b-weight for the interaction (product) term (–.0272). Likewise, with each unit increase in temp, the b-weight for relhumid changes by –.0272 as well. Because in the presence of an interaction, the slope of the line relating temp to barsold is different for each value of relhumid, one cannot say that the b-weight for temp represents the average effect of temp on barsold, averaged across all values (levels) of relhumid. Rather, we say that the b-weight for temp is *conditional on* the value of relhumid and must be interpreted with respect to specific values of relhumid.

As in previous chapters, we now obtain bootstrap estimates of the standard errors of the *b*-coefficients for both Models 1 and 2 to see to what extent the robust standard errors from this nonparametric procedure agree with those based on the parametric assumptions underlying ordinary least squares (OLS) regression analysis. We combine the **bootstrap** command with the command **nestreg** and refer to the b-coefficients by using Stata's name for these coefficients, **_b**.

MORE Stata: To obtain bootstrap estimates of the standard errors of the b-coefficients

bootstrap _b, reps(1000) nodots seed(3027): nestreg: regress barsold (temp relhumid) (product)

. bootstrap_b, reps (1000) nodots: nestreg: regress barsold (temp relhumid)

Linear regression					Number of obs	=	30
					Replications	=	1000
					Wald chi2 (2)	=	201.78
					Prob > chi2	=	0.0000
					R-squared	=	0.8571
					Adj R-squared	=	0.8465
					Root MSE	=	4.6643

barsold	Observed Coef.	Bootstrap Std. Err.	z	P > |z|	Normal-based [95% Conf.	Interval]
temp	.8778386	.1544175	5.68	0.000	.5751858	1.180491
relhumid	.3969829	.1266374	3.13	0.002	.1487782	.6451877
_cons	67.62162	7.060342	9.58	0.000	53.7836	81.45964

. bootstrap_b, reps (1000) nodots: nestreg: regress barsold (temp relhumid) (product)

Linear regression					Number of obs	=	30
					Replications	=	1000
					Wald chi2 (3)	=	227.48
					Prob > chi2	=	0.0000
					R-squared	=	0.8864
					Adj R-squared	=	0.8732
					Root MSE	=	4.2391

barsold	Observed Coef.	Bootstrap Std. Err.	z	P > |z|	Normal-based [95% Conf.	Interval]
temp	2.967853	1.005096	2.95	0.003	.9979005	4.937806
relhumid	2.583397	1.066474	2.42	0.015	.4931458	4.673648
product	−.0272381	.012992	−2.10	0.036	−.0527019	−.0017743
_cons	−98.67536	81.05986	−1.22	0.223	−257.5498	60.19904

According to these results, although the bootstrap estimates of the b-coefficient standard errors are all larger than the theoretically-derived estimates, nonetheless, our substantive conclusions remain the same overall.

☞ **Remark.** When the interaction term is not statistically significant, the regression analysis should be rerun without the product term and the resulting regression equation with only main effects reported. If the analysis is carried out using blocks, as in this example, the regression equation on the main effects may be obtained simply as the equation based on the variables in the first block only. Analyses that are carried out using blocks are called *hierarchical analyses* because they rely on a hierarchy or order of entry of terms into the equation. In this example, that order was main effects entered as the first block, followed by the interaction or product term entered as the second block.

CENTERING FIRST-ORDER EFFECTS TO ACHIEVE MEANINGFUL INTERPRETATIONS OF b-WEIGHTS

If an equation contains a product term, the interpretation of the b-weights associated with the first-order effect variables is a bit more complicated than if the equation does not contain a product term. In our example, the b-weight associated with temperature represents the slope of the line that describes the relationship between ice cream sales and temperature when relative humidity is 0; the b-weight associated with relative humidity represents the slope of the line that describes the relationship between ice cream sales and relative humidity when temperature is 0. Because both zero temperature and zero relative humidity are not meaningful in the context of this problem set in the northeast during the summer months, the interpretation of these b-weights is also not meaningful.

To impart meaning to the b-weights of first-order effect variables in an equation that contains a product term, we may rescale each of the first-order effect variables so as to make the value of zero in each variable correspond to something meaningful. A reasonable choice is to set the mean of each rescaled variable at zero by subtracting the mean from each variable value. Such rescaling is called *centering* and the newly rescaled variables are called *centered variables*. Another advantage to centering is that it allows us to test the inter-action term with greater power than if we had not centered the variables (Cohen, Cohen, West, & Aiken; 2003). In general, a product term that is based on centered first-order effect variables will correlate less strongly with each of the centered first-order variables already in the equation than a product term that is not based on centered first-order variables will correlate with each of the uncentered first-order effect variables already in the equation. As a result, the product term will have a greater unique contribution to make over and above the first-order effect variables, and we will be able to test the interaction with greater power. To find the centered temperature variable, we subtract the mean temperature (74.93) from each temperature value in the distribution; to find the centered relative humidity variable, we subtract the mean relative humidity (77.67) from each relative humidity value in the distribution. The product term would then be the product of each centered variable. The analysis of the interaction from Example 16.5 using the centered temperature and relative humidity variables is left for the reader to complete as Exercise 16.17.

UNDERSTANDING THE NATURE OF A STATISTICALLY SIGNIFICANT TWO-WAY INTERACTION

A statistically significant two-way interaction informs us that the effect of X_1 (temperature) is not the same across all levels of X_2 (relative humidity) and likewise the effect of X_2 is not the same across all levels of X_1. But, beyond that, the significant t-ratio tells us nothing about the nature of the interaction. There are at least two ways to determine the nature of the interaction: by plotting discrete predicted values and by computing simple slopes. The first method, which is the only one that we shall describe in this text, does not incorporate the use of significance testing. The interested reader is referred to Cohen, Cohen, Aiken, and West (2003) or Darlington (1990) for a discussion of simple slopes, which incorporates significance testing on the nature of the interaction.

A good way to describe the interaction is to plot it. To do so, we need to examine the estimated Y values for each combination of meaningful X_1 and X_2 values. The estimated Y values are the equivalent of cell means that we will use to obtain a plot like Figure 15.4. To obtain a 2 × 2 array of cell means, we often identify as meaningful values those con-sidered to be low and high for each of the two variables X_1 and X_2. These values are often interpreted to be at one standard deviation below the mean (−1sd) and at one standard deviation above the mean (+1sd).

For example, with respect to our ice cream data, we may ask "what is the average number of ice cream sales for days with low and high humidity and low and high temperature?" To answer this question, we compute $\hat{Y}$ for each combination of low and high values of our independent variables using the regression equation obtained from the solution to Example 16.3. This equation is:

Estimated Sales = –98.68 + 2.97(Temp) + 2.58(Humid) – .027(Temp*Humidity)

To clarify the nature of the interaction, estimated ice cream sales at one standard deviation below the mean and at one standard deviation above the mean are obtained as follows and are plotted in Figure 16.8.

Based on calculations using the means and standard deviations from our summary statistics, we obtain the values at one standard deviation below the mean and at one standard deviation above the mean for Temperature and Humidity.

Variable	Mean	StDev	One SD Below, –1sd (Low)	One SD Above, +1sd (High)
Temperature	74.93	8.94	65.99	83.87
Humidity	77.67	10.50	67.17	88.17
Interaction	5878.77	1392.11		

Substituting each combination of low and high values for these variables into the regression equation produces the following 2 x 2 table of cell means that gives $\hat{Y}$ values at each of the four pairs of temperature and humidity values.

		Humidity	
		Low	High
Temperature	High	170.32	176.59
	Low	149.97	166.46

A plot of these values is given in Figure 16.8. For heuristic reasons, we present how we plot these values as a two-step process, and describe in the Do-file associated with this chapter, two other Stata commands, **margins** and **marginsplot,** that were more recently added to the Stata package that simplify this process considerably.

Using the two-step approach, we first enter the four calculated values associated with the 2 × 2 table into a new data set, and then next create the graph from these values.

To form the new data set containing the 2 × 2 table values, we need three columns, one for temperature with value labels, 1 = Low and 2 = High, another for humidity with value labels, 1 = Low and 2 = High, and a third column for sales, labelled "predicted ice cream sales". If done correctly, the completed dataset, saved to a new data file, (e.g., Data Set of Temp X Humidity Interaction) will have the following form:

temperature	humidity	sales
1	1	149.97
1	2	166.46
2	1	170.32
2	2	176.59

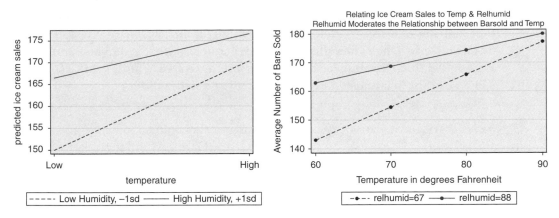

Figure 16.8   (a) Plot of the interaction between temperature and humidity. (b) Plot of the interaction between temperature and humidity.

MORE Stata: To create the line graphs shown in Figures 16.8(a) & (b) based on the values in the above table.

twoway (line sales humidity if temperature == 1, lpattern(dash)) (line sales humidity if temperature == 2, lpattern(solid)), legend(label(1 "Low Temperature, –1sd") label(2 "High Temperature, +1sd")) xlabel(1 "Low" 2 "High")

twoway (line sales humidity if temperature == 1, lpattern(dash)) (line sales temperature if humidity == 2, lpattern(solid)), legend(label(1 "Low Humidity, –1sd") label(2 "High Humidity, +1sd")) xlabel(1 "Low" 2 "High")

MORE Stata: To use the **margins** and **marginsplot** commands to generate a version of Figure 16.8(b) more efficiently (See also the Do-file associated with this chapter.). The margins command computes the predicted values for each of the specified cases designated within the option, **at**. In the example, we find the predicted values of barsold when temp = 60, 75, and 90 and when relhumid = 67 and 88. As a result, 3x2=6 predicted values will be computed by the margins command. The first marginsplot command plots these values with temp on the x-axis, and the second marginsplot command plots these values with relhumid on the x-axis. In order to use the margins and marginsplot commands, the regress command must be in terms of factor variables. Because both temp and relhumid are continuous variables, we preface them with **c.** as shown below.

quietly regress barsold c.temp c.relhumid c.temp#c.relhumid
set more off
margins, at(temp = (60 (15) 90) relhumid = (67 88)) vsquish
marginsplot, xdimension(temp) xlabel(60 (15) 90) plot1opt(lpattern(dash)) plot2opt(lpattern(solid)) noci ytitle ("Average Number of Bars Sold") title("Relating Ice Cream Sales to Temp & Relhumid") subtitle("Relhumid Moderates the Relationship between Barsold and Temp")

To obtain a graph with relhumid on the x-axis, the following command would be appropriate:

marginsplot, xdimension(relhumid) xlabel(67 88) plot1opt(lpattern(dash)) plot2opt(lpattern(solid)) plot3opt(lpattern(longdash)) legend(row(1) order(1 2 3) label(1 low) label(2 middle) label(3 high)) noci ytitle ("Average Number of Bars Sold") title("Relating Ice Cream Sales to Temp & Relhumid") subtitle("Temp Moderates the Relationship between Barsold and Relhumid")

The results of our analysis of ice cream sales suggest that both temperature and humidity influence summer ice cream sales at the beach in the Northeast and that relative humidity moderates the influence that temperature has on ice cream sales. The pattern for the predicted values depicted in the line graph suggests that the relationship between ice cream sales and temperature is greater when humidity is relatively low rather than when it is relatively high. Ice cream sales on days with relatively high temperature and relatively low humidity are similar to ice cream sales on days with relatively high temperature and relatively high humidity. On such days, ice cream sales are strong. However, on days with relatively low temperature, ice cream sales are much stronger when humidity is relatively high than when it is relatively low.

In completing this analysis, we should also have paid attention to the diagnostics we discussed in the previous chapter to verify that our model was not influenced unduly by outliers and that the assumptions underlying the procedure are met. Often, to determine to what extent outliers influence the results of a regression analysis, the analysis is carried out both with and without outliers and changes in results are noted and evaluated. Such analyses are called "sensitivity analyses" because they are measuring the sensitivity of the results to what appear to be critical changes in the data set. We ask you to complete this aspect of the analysis in Exercise 16.18.

INTERACTION WHEN ONE OF THE INDEPENDENT VARIABLES IS DICHOTOMOUS AND THE OTHER IS CONTINUOUS

In Example 16.3, we examined the extent to which eighth grade self-concept and gender collectively and individually explained twelfth grade self-concept. In this section we extend Example 16.3 and examine whether there is an interaction between eighth grade self-concept and gender on twelfth grade self-concept. That is, whether the relationship between eighth grade self-concept and twelfth grade self-concept varies as a function of gender.

• •

EXAMPLE 16.6. Determine whether there is an interaction between eighth grade self-concept and gender on twelfth grade self-concept. Construct a plot to facilitate the interpretation of the interaction, if one exists.

Solution. In the solution to this example we shall center the eighth grade self-concept variable to have a mean of zero to illustrate how to carry out an analysis of interactions using centered variables. By centering, the value of zero on the self-concept scale will be a meaningful quantity for interpretation purposes. We do not need to center gender because the value of 0 on the gender scale is already meaningful as it is the code for males.

Prior to conducting the regression analysis, we center the interval-leveled variable and form the product term to represent the interaction. To center eighth grade self-concept, we generate a new variable, called ctrslf08, by subtracting the mean of slfcnc08 from every score of slfcnc08. The syntax for doing this is:

MORE Stata: To center the variables, generate the product term that carries the interaction, and conduct the regression analysis

***To center the variables, for greater precision we use the mean value stored in r(mean) as computed by the summarize command.

summarize slfcnc08
gen ctrslf08 = slfcnc08 – r(mean)

OR

gen ctrslf08 = slfcnc08–21.06

***To generate the product term

gen product = ctrslf08 * gender

***To run the regression analysis

sum slfcnc12 ctrslf08 gender product
pwcorr slfcnc12 ctrslf08 gender product, obs star(5)
regress slfcnc12 ctrslf08 gender product

The results of the regression analysis reproduced and analyzed below.

Variable	Obs	Mean	Std. Dev.	Min	Max
slfcnc12	500	31.48	7.231195	0	43
ctrslf08	500	.002	5.971052	−21.06	10.94
gender	500	.546	.4983781	0	1
product	500	−.56676	4.751841	−21.06	10.94

	slfcnc12	ctrslf08	gender	product
slfcnc12	1.0000 500			
ctrslf08	0.4436* 500	1.0000 500		
gender	−0.1607* 500	−0.1912* 500	1.0000 500	
product	0.4010* 500	0.8072* 500	−0.1089* 500*	1.0000 500

Notice, that as expected, the mean of the centered eighth grade self-concept variable is virtually zero. The means of the gender and twelfth grade self-concept are the same as they were earlier because neither of these variables was centered.

Because centering is a translation, a form of linear transformation that does not involve reflection, the correlations between the first-order effect variables remain the same. The correlations of product with its component parts are nonzero, suggesting once again that the product term, by itself, is not the interaction. Rather, the interaction is the *partialled product*, the product with its component parts removed or partialled out.

Source	SS	df	MS			
				Number of obs	=	500
				F(3, 496)	=	43.68
Model	5453.09798	3	1817.69933	Prob > F	=	0.0000
Residual	20639.702	496	41.6123025	R-squared	=	0.2090
				Adj R-squared	=	0.2042
Total	26092.8	499	52.2901804	Root MSE	=	6.4508

Model summary statistics inform us that the overall model, consisting of the product, gender, and centered eighth grade self-concept variables, is statistically significant ($p < .0005$). Both the ratio SS_{MODEL}/SS_{TOTAL} and the R-squared value inform us that 20.9 percent of twelfth grade self-concept variance is explained by this model.

slfcnc12	Coef.	Std. Err.	t	P > |t|	[95% Conf.	Interval]
ctrslf08	.3861487	.0832318	4.64	0.000	.2226183	.5496792
gender	−1.235263	.5921483	−2.09	0.037	−2.398691	−.0718346
product	.2044342	.1032715	1.98	0.048	.0015308	.4073377
_cons	32.26955	.440666	73.23	0.000	31.40374	33.13535

Given that the overall model is statistically significant, we construct the regression equation using the unstandardized weights and to determine whether the interaction is statistically significant.

The unstandardized regression equation for $\hat{Y}$ = predicted twelfth grade self-concept (slfcnc12) is:

$$\hat{Y} = .386(\text{ctrslf08}) - 1.235(\text{gender}) + .204(\text{product}) + 32.27$$

or equivalently

$$\hat{Y} = .386(\text{ctrslf08}) - 1.235(\text{gender}) + .204(\text{ctrslf08} * \text{gender}) + 32.27$$

Because the *b*-weight associated with the product term is statistically significant ($p = .048$), the interaction is statistically significant. Therefore, the relationship between eighth grade and twelfth grade self-concept is not constant for males and females; rather, it varies as a function of gender. Because the relationship between eighth grade self-concept and twelfth grade self-concept is different for males and females in the population, we can create two separate regression equations, one for each gender.

To find the regression equation for males, we substitute gender = 0 into

$$\hat{Y} = .386(\text{ctrslf08}) - 1.235(\text{gender}) + .204(\text{ctrslf08} * \text{gender}) + 32.27$$

$$\hat{Y} = .386(\text{ctrslf08}) - 1.235(0) + .204(\text{ctrslf08} * 0) + 32.27$$

$$\hat{Y} = .386(\text{ctrslf08}) + 32.27$$

To find the regression equation for females, we substitute GENDER = 1 into

$$\hat{Y} = .386(\text{ctrslf08}) - 1.235(\text{gender}) + .204(\text{ctrslf08}*\text{gender}) + 32.27$$

$$\hat{Y} = .386(\text{ctrslf08}) - 1.235(1) + .204(\text{ctrslf08}*1) + 32.27$$

$$\hat{Y} = .386(\text{ctrslf08}) - 1.235 + .204(\text{ctrslf08}) + 32.27$$

$$\hat{Y} = .590(\text{ctrslf08}) + 31.035$$

Looking at the two slopes, we see that for males, every one point increase in eighth grade self-concept is associated with a .386 point increase in twelfth grade self-concept, whereas for females, every one point increase in eighth grade self-concept is associated with a .590 point increase in twelfth grade self-concept. The statistical significance of the interaction term tells us that these two slopes are significantly different from each other. That the slope for females, .591, is greater than the slope for males, .386, suggests that females exhibit greater growth in self-concept than males between grades 8 and 12.

We illustrate the interaction by plotting the scatterplot of twelfth grade self-concept by eighth grade self-concept and superimposing on it two regression lines, one for females and the other for males. The plot of the interaction is given in Figure 16.9 using the boxed syntax. This syntax also may be found in the annotated Do-file associated with this chapter. To produce Figure 16.9 with additional bells and whistles using the margins and marginsplot commands, refer to the Do-file associated with this chapter. The output produced by this syntax will include 95% confidence intervals constructed at particular values of slfcnc08 so that we may see at which values males and females differ from each other in terms of slfcnc12.

Note that jitter(10) in the below command adds some small random value to each point in the scatterplot so as to help separate the points in the scatterplot from one another and reduce the amount of overlap between points.

MORE Stata: To plot the twoway scatterplot of Figure 16.9. Of course, we also could use the margins and marginsplot using the procedure presented earlier.

twoway (scatter slfcnc12 slfcnc08, jitter(10))(lfit slfcnc12 slfcnc08 if gender == 1, lpattern(dash))(lfit slfcnc12 slfcnc08 if gender == 0, lpattern(solid)), legend(label(1) label(2 Female) label(3 Male)) ytitle("Twelfth Grade Self Concept")

The results of these analyses suggest that while females have lower self-concept than males, on average, in eighth grade, by twelfth grade they appear to catch up. Thus, females appear to sustain a greater increase in self-concept across the grades than males. If there were no interaction, the rate of growth across the grades would have been the same for both males and females.

SUMMARY OF STATA COMMANDS IN CHAPTER 16

For a complete listing of all Stata commands associated with this chapter, you may access the Do-file for Chapter 16 located on the text website.

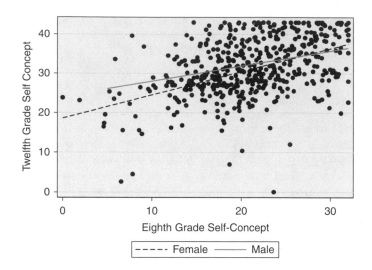

Figure 16.9   Plot of the interaction between 8th grade self-concept and gender

Create	Command Lines
Perform a multiple regression of barsold on temp and relhumid (Example 16.1)	**regress barsold temp relhumid** **summarize barsold temp relhumid** **pwcorr barsold temp relhumid, obs** **star(5)**
Obtain the bootstrap-derived standard errors of the b-coefficients	**bootstrap _b, reps(1000) nodots** **seed(2576): regress barsold temp** **relhumid**
To test the statistical significance of the change in R^2 of two nested equations where the first equation includes only X_1 and the second equation includes both X_1 and X_2,	**nestreg: regress barsold (temp)** **(relhumid)**
Regress one independent variable X_1 (temp) on X_2 (relhumid), then generate the set of unstandardized residuals, representing that part of X_1 (temp) that is orthogonal to X_2 (relhumid). (Example 16.2)	**regress temp relhumid** **predict x1orthx2, residuals**
Construct a scatterplot with points on the vertical axis and weightlb on the horizontal axis. Superimpose the fitted regression line on this scatterplot. (Example 16.4)	**twoway (scatter points weightlb) (lfit** **points weightlb), ytitle("Total Points** **Scored") legend(order(2))**
Adapt the scatterplot labeling each observation by gender using the following command, which generates three graphs on our coordinate axes (1) a scatterplot of all points labelled by gender, (2) a regression line fitted to the female points, and (3) a regression line fitted to the male points (Example 16.4)	**twoway (scatter points weightlb,** **mlabel(gender))(lfit points weightlb** **if gender == 1, lpattern(dash))** **(lfit points weightlb if gender ==** **0, lpattern(solid)),legend(row(1)** **order(2 3) label(2 Female) label(3** **Male)) ytitle("Total Points Scored")**

Create	Command Lines
Compute the product of temperature and relative humidity and give that new variable the name, product (Example 16.5)	**gen product = temp*relhumid)**
Perform a multiple regression of barsold on temp and relhumid with the interaction term (Example 16.5)	**summarize barsold temp relhumid product**
	pwcorr temp barsold relhumid product, obs star(5)
	regress barsold temp relhumid product
Use a nested regression to test the statistical significance of the interaction term (Example 16.5)	**nestreg: regress barsold (temp relhumid) (product)**
To obtain bootstrap estimates of the standard errors of the *b*-coefficients (Example 16.5)	**bootstrap _b, reps(1000) nodots seed(3027): nestreg: regress barsold (temp relhumid) (product)**
Create the graph of the interaction between two scale variables (Figure 16.8 b)	**twoway (line sales humidity if temperature == 1, lpattern(dash)) (line sales temperature if humidity == 2, lpattern(solid)), legend(label(1 "Low Humidity, -1sd") label(2 "High Humidity, +1sd")) xlabel(1 "Low" 2 "High")**
To center the variables, form the product term that carries the interaction, and conduct the regression analysis (Example 16.6).	**summarize slfcnc08**
	gen ctrslf08 = slfcnc08 – r(mean)
	gen product = ctrslf08 * gender
	sum slfcnc12 ctrslf08 gender product
	pwcorr slfcnc12 ctrslf08 gender product, obs star(5)
	regress slfcnc12 ctrslf08 gender product
To create the scatterplot depicting the interaction between a scale and a dichotomous variable (Figure 16.9)	**twoway (scatter slfcnc12 slfcnc08, jitter(10))(lfit slfcnc12 slfcnc08 if gender == 1, lpattern(dash))(lfit slfcnc12 slfcnc08 if gender == 0, lpattern(solid)), legend(label(1 label(2 Female) label(3 Male)) ytitle("Twelfth Grade Self Concept")**

EXERCISES

Create a Do-file for each exercise that requires the use of Stata. Run the commands from the Do-file by highlighting them and hitting **Control+d**. *Save each Do-file using a name associated with the Exercise for which it was created. It is recommended that you review the Do-file for* Chapter 16 *located on the textbook's website before completing these exercises. To facilitate* *doing each exercise, it may be helpful to copy and paste relevant commands from the Do-file for* Chapter 16 *into your own Do-file and modify them as needed.*

Exercises 16.1–16.2 make use of the NELS data set. For inferential purposes, we consider the students in the data set to be a random sample of the population of all college-bound students who have always been at grade level. Use $\alpha = .05$ *for all significance tests.*

16.1. In this exercise, we will use multiple regression to determine whether there is a gender (gender) difference in twelfth grade math achievement (achmat12) after controlling for amount of math taken (unitmath) and to investigate related questions.

     a) Conduct initial univariate and bivariate analyses of the variables involved in the multiple regression model.

     b) Is the regression model for predicting achmat12 from gender and unitmath statistically significant? Provide statistical support for your answer.

     c) Report and interpret the value of R^2.

     d) Write down the regression equation for predicting achmat12 from gender and unitmath.

     e) Use the regression equation to predict the twelfth grade math achievement score of a male who took 4 NAEP units of math in high school.

     f) Which of the two independent variables makes a greater unique contribution to the regression model? Explain and provide statistical support for your answer.

     g) Interpret the value of the y-intercept or indicate why it would not be appropriate to do so.

     h) Interpret the value of the coefficient (slope) of unitmath in the regression equation.

     i) Interpret the value of the coefficient (slope) of gender in the regression equation.

     j) After controlling for number of years of math taken, is there a gender difference in twelfth grade math achievement among college-bound students who are always at grade level? If so, what is the nature of the gender difference? Explain and provide statistical support for your answer.

16.2. In this exercise, we will see that independent variables each by themselves may be statistically significantly correlated to the dependent variable in the bivariate sense, but when examined together in the same regression equation, both may not be statistically significant. Perform a multiple regression analysis to determine whether twelfth grade self-concept (slfcnc12) is related to mathematics achievement as measured by both twelfth grade math achievement (achmat12) and the number of units of mathematics taken in high school (unitmath). Exercise 16.7 utilizes regression diagnostics to determine aspects of model fit and whether underlying assumptions appear to be met.

     a) Conduct initial univariate and bivariate analyses of the variables involved in the multiple regression model.

     b) Perform a multiple regression analysis with slfcnc12 as the dependent variable and achmat12 and unitmath as independent variables. Is the regression model statistically significant? Provide statistical support for your answer.

     c) What proportion of variance in slfcnc12 is explained by both independent variables?

     d) Which, if any, of the independent variables make a statistically significant unique contribution to the regression model? Provide statistical support for your response.

e) Interpret the value of the y-intercept or indicate why it would not be appropriate to do so.

f) Interpret the value of the statistically significant b-weight coefficient (slope) of achmat12 in the regression equation.

Exercises 16.3–16.4 make use the Learndis data set. For inferential purposes, we consider the children in the data set to be a random sample of all children attending public school in the urban area who have been diagnosed with learning disabilities. Many students in the data set have missing values for either math or reading comprehension, or both. Such omissions can lead to problems when generalizing results. There are statistical remedies for missing data that are beyond the scope of this text. For these exercises, we will assume that there is no pattern to the missing values, and that our sample is representative of the population. Use α = .05 for all significance tests.

16.3. Recall that students diagnosed with learning disabilities in this urban area are placed in one of two classroom situations: resource room for part of the day (coded as 0) or in a full-time self-contained classroom (coded as 1). Use multiple regression analysis to determine whether reading comprehension (readcomp) variance can be explained by math comprehension (mathcomp) and type of placement (placemen).

a) Conduct initial univariate and bivariate analyses of the variables involved in the multiple regression model.

b) Is the regression model for predicting readcomp from mathcomp and placemen statistically significant? Are the independent variables statistically significant in the equation? Provide statistical support for your response.

c) Report and interpret the value of $R^2_{adjusted}$.

d) Compare the values of R^2 and $R^2_{adjusted}$. Explain why they are similar or different.

e) What is the regression equation for predicting readcomp from mathcomp and placemen?

f) Interpret value of the y-intercept or indicate why it would not be meaningful to do so.

g) Controlling for type of placement, are higher math comprehension scores associated with higher or lower reading comprehension scores? Provide statistical support for your response.

h) Interpret the value of the slope of mathcomp.

i) Controlling for math comprehension, does reading comprehension statistically significantly differ for children attending public school in the urban area who have been diagnosed with learning disabilities depending on placement type? Provide statistical support for your response. If there is a difference, describe its nature.

j) Interpret the value of the slope of placemen.

k) Use your regression equation to predict the reading comprehension score of a student in a resource room placement who has a mathcomp score of 84.

l) Explain why you should not use the regression equation to predict the reading comprehension score student in a resource room placement who has a mathcomp score of 40.

16.4. In this exercise, we look at the individual and unique contributions of mathcomp and iq in explaining readcomp variance.

a) What proportion of the variance in reading comprehension scores can be explained by intellectual ability? Is this proportion statistically significant? Explain and provide statistical support for your response.

b) What proportion of the variance in reading comprehension scores can be explained by math comprehension? Is this proportion statistically significant? Explain and provide statistical support for your response.

c) What is the intercorrelation between IQ and mathcomp? Is it statistically significant?

d) What proportion of the variance in reading comprehension scores can be explained by math comprehension after controlling for intellectual ability? Said differently, what proportion of reading comprehension variance can be explained uniquely by math comprehension? Is this proportion statistically significant? Explain and provide statistical support for your response.

e) What proportion of the variance in reading comprehension scores can be explained by intellectual ability controlling for math ability? Said differently, what proportion of reading comprehension variance can be explained uniquely by intellectual ability? Is this proportion statistically significant? Explain and provide statistical support for your response.

f) What is another way to determine whether the proportion of variance in reading comprehension scores that can be explained by intellectual ability controlling for math ability is statistically significant?

g) Why is it that the proportion of variance in reading comprehension that can be explained by intellectual ability is larger than the proportion of variance in reading comprehension that can be explained by intellectual ability after *controlling for math comprehension*?

h) Explain why R^2 for the model with both independent variables is less than $r^2_{\text{Readng Comprehension,IQ}} + r^2_{\text{Reading Comprehension, Math Comprehension}}$.

Exercise 16.5 makes use of the Framingham data set. For inferential purposes, we consider the people in the Framingham data set to be a random sample of the population of all noninstitutionalized adults. Use $\alpha = .05$ for all significance tests.

16.5. In this exercise we use regression to model total serum cholesterol at time 3 (TOTCHOL3) using initial systolic blood pressure at time 1 (SYSBP1) and diastolic blood pressure at time 1 (DIABP1).

a) Conduct initial univariate and bivariate analyses of the variables involved in the multiple regression model.

b) Is the regression model for predicting TOTCHOL3 from SYSBP1 and DIABP1 statistically significant? Is the individual contribution of any of the variables statistically significant?

c) Why do you suppose the model is statistically significant, but none of the independent variables is?

d) What is an appropriate model for predicting TOTCHOL3?

e) Compare the proportion of variance in TOTCHOL3 explained by DIABP1 alone to that explained by the combination of DIABP1 and SYSBP1.

Exercises 16.6–16.8 involve regression diagnostics and nonlinear transformations using the NELS data set. For inferential purposes, we consider the students in the data set to be a *random sample of the population of all college-bound students who have always been at grade level. Use $\alpha = .05$ for all significance tests.*

16.6. In Exercise 16.1, we created a model to predict twelfth grade math achievement (achmat12) from gender and the number of NAEP units of math taken in high school (unitmath). In this exercise, we will conduct a series of residual analyses to examine more closely the fit of the model to these data.

a) Create a partial plot between the residual scores and the continuous regressor. Examine this plot for evidence of nonlinearity.

b) Name two cases that have relatively high positive residuals and two cases that have relatively high negative residuals. What do the residuals say about these four cases?

c) Create boxplots of Cook's distance and leverage values. What do they tell you about the appropriateness of the regression model?

d) Based on these diagnostic analyses, comment on the appropriateness of this regression equation.

16.7. In Exercise 16.2, we created a model to predict twelfth grade self-concept (slfcnc12) from twelfth grade math achievement (achmat12) and NAEP units of math taken in high school (unitmath). In this exercise, we will perform regression diagnostics on the model to determine whether it can be improved.

a) Create partial plots between the residual scores and the two continuous regressors. Examine these plots for evidence of nonlinearity.

b) Determine whether there are any bivariate outliers in the model, that is, points whose standardized residual is greater than 2 in magnitude. Indicate the number of such points and give their case numbers.

c) Create boxplots of Cook's distance and leverage values. What do they tell you about the appropriateness of the regression model?

e) Based on these diagnostic analyses, comment on the appropriateness of this regression equation.

16.8. In this exercise, we will create a multiple regression model to determine how expected income at age 30 (expinc30) can be explained by gender and socioeconomic status (ses).

a) Conduct initial univariate and bivariate analyses of the variables involved in the multiple regression model.

b) Because of its severe positive skew, transform expinc30 using both the square root and log transformations to try to reduce that skew. In both cases, translate first by adding 1, so that the log is defined for all values. Which of the two transformations is more effective in symmetrizing expinc30?

c) Conduct bivariate analyses using the square root transformed expected income at age 30.

d) Conduct the multiple regression analysis with the square root transformed expinc30 as the dependent variable and ses and gender as the independent variables. Is the model statistically significant? Provide statistical support for your response.

e) Compare the proportion of variance explained with the untransformed and the transformed expinc30.

f) Write down the regression for predicting expinc30 from ses and gender.

g) Use your model to predict the expected income at age 30 of a male with ses 15.

Exercise 16.9 involves regression diagnostics and nonlinear transformations using the Learndis data set. In this chapter, we consider the children in the data set to be a random sample of all children attending public school in the urban area who have been diagnosed with learning disabilities. Use α = .05 for all significance tests.

16.9. In Exercise 16.3, we created a model to predict readcomp from mathcomp and placemen. In this exercise, we perform regression diagnostics on the model to determine whether it can be improved.

a) Create a partial plot between the residual scores and the continuous regressor. Examine this plot for evidence of nonlinearity.
b) What are the Stata commands for creating the variables mathcompctrd, which is the centered mathcomp, and mathcompctrdsqd which is the square of the centered mathcomp? Create these new variables.
c) What is the regression equation for predicting readcomp from placemen, mathcompctrd and mathcompctrdsqd?
d) Overall, is the regression model for predicting readcomp from placemen, mathcompctrd and mathcompctrdsqd statistically significant? In particular, is the squared term statistically significant? Provide statistical support for your responses.
e) What proportion of the variance in readcomp is explained by the squared term over and above that explained by the other variables?
f) Construct a residual plot and boxplots of Cook's distance and leverage values for the model including the squared term. What do they tell you about the appropriateness of the regression model?

Exercises 16.10–16.14 involve interactions in the NELS data set. For inferential purposes, we consider the students in the data set to be a random sample of the population of all college-bound students who have always been at grade level. Use α = .05 for all significance tests.

16.10. Predict twelfth grade math achievement (achmat12) from whether or not the student attended public school (schtypdi), whether or not the student took advanced math in eighth grade (advmath8), and the interaction of the two. This is a multi-step analysis that involves creating new variables, so conduct your analysis using a Do-file to track your steps for parts a) – e).

a) Use the Recode procedure in Transform to create schtypdi, a variable with 0 = Public and 1 = private (both religious and nonreligious) from the variable schtyp8. How many students attended private school?
b) Create a multiple line graph using the command twoway scatter to depict the predicted twelfth grade math achievement by schtypdi and advmat8 and use it to anticipate the results.
c) Create the product term of the two independent variables.
d) Is the overall model that predicts achmat12 from schtypdi, advmat8, and their interaction statistically significant?
e) Is the interaction statistically significant?
f) What percentage of the variance in twelfth grade math achievement can be explained by the two main effect variables and their interaction? What percentage can be explained by the interaction alone? (HINT: Use nestreg to obtain this answer.)

g) Write out the full regression equation that includes main and interaction effects?

h) Describe the nature of the interaction by writing down and interpreting separate regression equations for predicting twelfth grade math achievement from school type for those who did not take advanced math in eighth grade and for those who did.

i) Interpret the slope of school type for these two equations.

j) Print out the contents of your Do-file file.

16.11. In this exercise, we expand on Exercise 16.1 by investigating whether there is an interaction between gender and unitmath on achmat12.

a) Center the variable unitmath by computing a new variable, unitmatc (unitmatc = unitmath – 3.637, where 3.637 is the mean of unitmath for those values included in the analysis). Rather than subtracting 3.637, you may run summarize unitmath and subtract r(mean) from unitmath to generate unitmatc. Verify that the mean of the centered variable, unitmatc, is 0.

b) Create the interaction term, product, as unitmatc*gender. What is the mean of this product term?

c) To determine if there is an interaction, use nestreg to conduct a hierarchical multiple regression analysis with achmat12 as the dependent variable, unitmatc and gender in the first block, and product in the second block. Is there a statistically significant interaction between gender and number of years of math taken on achievement in math? Explain.

d) What can you conclude from the results of the test of significance of the interaction?

16.12. In Exercise 16.8, we constructed a regression model to predict the square root of expected income at age 30 plus one, created using the Stata command **gen expincsq = sqrt(expinc30+)**, from gender and socioeconomic status (ses). In this exercise, we will investigate whether it is appropriate to include an interaction term in the model.

a) Create a scatterplot of points for the entire sample. Superimpose two fit lines, one for males and the other for females. Based on the scatterplot, do you anticipate that there is a statistically significant interaction between the two independent variables on the dependent variable? Explain.

b) Use nestreg to determine if the interaction is statistically significant. Provide statistical support for your answer using both the relevant b-weight and the F-change statistic.

16.13. In this exercise, we will use multiple regression to determine if expected income at age 30 (expinc30) can be explained by eighth grade self-concept (slfcnc08), socioeconomic status (ses) and their interaction.

a) Conduct initial univariate and bivariate analyses of the variables involved in the multiple regression model.

b) Center the variable slfcnc08 by computing a new variable, slfc8c, that is defined as slfcnc08 – 20.94 (20.94 is the mean of slfcnc08 for those values included in the analysis, or you may subtract r(mean) following the command summarize slfcnc08). Center the variable ses by computing a new variable, sesc, that is defined as ses – 18.52 (where 18.52 is the mean of ses for those values included in the analysis, or you may subtract r(mean) following the command summarize ses). Create the product term that carries the interaction, product, as slfc8c*sesc. Use nestreg to conduct a hierarchical multiple regression analysis with expinc30 as the dependent variable, slfc8c and sesc in the first block, and product in the second block. Is the interaction, represented by product statistically significant? Provide statistical support for your response.

c) What is the regression equation for the full model that includes the interaction?

d) Clarify the nature of the interaction by using the regression equation to estimate the expected income at age 30 at one standard deviation above and one standard deviation below 0 (0 is the mean because the variables have been centered) for both slfc8c and sesc.

e) Replicate the results in (d) by using the margins command. To use the margins command, you will need to run the regression using factor variables.

f) Create a line graph like that of Figure 16.6, which is a summary of the interaction based on the four estimates obtained in parts d and e.

g) Describe the nature of the interaction.

16.14. Perform a multiple regression analysis to determine whether ses can be explained by the NAEP units of mathematics taken in high school (unitmath), nursery school attendance (nursery) and their interaction.

a) Construct a correlation matrix between all pairs of variables and their corresponding scatterplots.

b) Run the summarize command for unitmath.

c) Using r(mean) from the summarize command, center unitmath (call it unitmatc) and create the product term between unitmatc and nursery that carries the interaction.

d) Conduct a simultaneous regression analysis with the three independent variables. Is the full regression model including the interaction term statistically significant? Is the interaction term statistically significant? Provide statistical support for your answer.

e) Write out the regression equation for the full model that includes the interaction.

f) For those who attended nursery school, write out the regression equation for predicting ses from unitmath?

g) For those who did not attend nursery school, write out the regression equation for predicting ses from unitmath.

h) Are the slopes of unitmath from the regression equations given in parts (g) and (h) statistically significantly different from each other? How can you tell?

i) Create a multiple line graph that depicts the interaction. Use the margins and marginsplot commands (which means that you will have to re-run the regression analysis using factor variables).

j) Describe the nature of the interaction.

Exercises 16.15–16.16 involve interactions in the Learndis data set. In this chapter, we consider the children in the data set to be a random sample of all children attending public school in the urban area who have been diagnosed with learning disabilities. Use $\alpha = .05$ for all significance tests.

16.15. Perform a multiple regression analysis to determine whether reading comprehension (readcomp) can be explained by a combination of math comprehension (mathcomp), grade level (grade), and their interaction. Prior to the analysis, center the variables math comprehension and grade level. Create the variable product as the product of centered math comprehension and centered grade, to facilitate the evaluation of the interaction between the independent variables.

a) What is the average reading comprehension score for public school students diagnosed with learning disabilities in this urban area?

b) Is the standard deviation of the centered math comprehension variable (14.59) different from the standard deviation of the original noncentered math comprehension variable? Explain.

c) Look at the three dimensional picture of the regression equation. Does there appear to be an interaction? How can you tell?

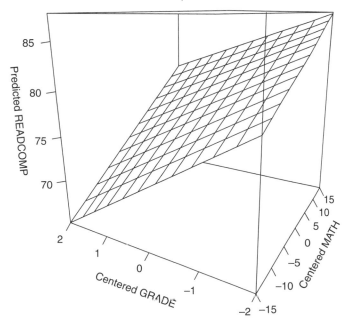

d) Is the interaction effect statistically significant? Explain.

e) What is the regression equation with main effects only? Are these main effects statistically significant? Why is the regression equation that includes only main effects a better model for these data?

f) Using the equation with main effects only, interpret b_1, the b-weight for centered math comprehension, within the context of the problem.

g) Using the equation with main effects only, interpret b_2, the b-weight for centered grade, within the context of the problem.

h) What is the proportion of dependent variable variance explained by these two variables?

i) What is the proportion of dependent variable variance explained by math comprehension, controlling for grade?

j) What is the proportion of dependent variable variance explained by grade, controlling for math comprehension?

k) What is the relative importance of the two regressors? Support your answer.

16.16. This exercise makes use of the data in the file Exercise, Food Intake and Weight Loss. This exercise illustrates the importance of controlling for confounding variables in a regression equation to achieve b-weight estimates that are less clearly biased and more credible. This exercise is adapted from Darlington (1990). *Food Intake* is defined as the average daily number of calories consumed in one particular week that is more than a baseline of 1,000 calories as measured in increments of 100 calories. That is, for example, a person who has a score of 2 on the Food Intake variable has consumed a daily average of 1,200 calories; namely, 200 more than the baseline number of 1,000 calories for that week. *Weight Loss* is defined as the number of pounds lost in that week. *Exercise* is defined as the average daily number of hours exercised in that week.

a) Obtain the regression equation for predicting Weight Loss (WeightLoss) from Food Intake (FoodIntake). Compute the correlation between Weight Loss and Food Intake as well as the means of these two variables.

b) Write out the regression equation and interpret the b-weight for Food Intake. Is the value of this b-weight consistent with what you would have expected? Might the problem be an omitted variable that, in its absence, causes this b-weight to be biased?

c) Construct a scatterplot with Weight Loss on the vertical axis and Food Intake on the horizontal axis and include the fitted regression line on this scatterplot. Verify that the regression line passes through the point $(\bar{X}, \bar{Y})$.

d) Re-do the scatterplot using the option, mlabel(Exercise) so that each point in the scatterplot indicates the number of hours each person exercised (0, 2, or 4). Include three fitted regression lines on this scatterplot, one for each exercise group.

e) Do these three regression lines of Weight Loss on Food Intake controlling for Exercise, have positive or negative slopes? Said differently, is the (partial) relationship between Food Intake and Weight Loss controlling for Exercise, positive or negative? Is this result consistent with what you would have expected?

f) What is the omnibus F-test associated with the regression equation containing both Food Intake and Exercise? Is it statistically significant?

g) Obtain the regression equation for predicting Weight Loss from both Food Intake and Exercise. Is the partial regression coefficient (b-weight) for Food Intake (controlling for Exercise) positive or negative? Is it consistent with what you would have expected? Obtain robust estimates of the standard errors of the b-weights for this problem using a bootstrap analysis. Compare the bootstrap results to the theoretically-driven results to see if substantive conclusions remain the same.

h) Use nestreg to test whether the contribution of Food Intake over and above Exercise is statistically significant. Test this in two ways: by the t-test associated with the b-weight for Food Intake based on the model that contains both Exercise and Food Intake, and by the F-test associated with the change in R^2 resulting from adding Food Intake to the equation that contains only Exercise. These two tests will produce identical results in this situation.

Exercises 16.17–16.19 relate to examples from the chapter.

16.17. In the section entitled, "The b-weight as a partial slope in multiple regression", we used Stata to create the new variable $X_{1.2}$ and showed that b_1, which equals .878, is simply the slope of the regression line that predicts Y from $X_{1.2}$. For this exercise, show that b_2, which equals .397, is simply the slope of the regression line that predicts Y from $X_{2.1}$.

16.18. In this chapter, we analyzed the relationship between ice cream sales, temperature, relative humidity, and the interaction between temperature and relative humidity. We did not center the variables before conducting our analysis. For this exercise, rerun the analysis using the centered variables and compare these results to those obtained in the chapter based on the noncentered variables.

a) Use the Icecream data set. Center temp. Center relhumid. Create the product term to represent the interaction. Using the centered variables, test whether there is an interaction between temperature and relative humidity on ice cream sales. What proportion of variance in ice cream sales is explained by the model including the interaction term? How do your results compare to those obtained in Example 16.4 based on noncentered variables?

b) Interpret the coefficient of centered temperature in the regression equation.

c) Interpret the coefficient of centered relative humidity in the regression equation.

d) Explain why the plot of the interaction between temperature and relative humidity, given in Figure 16.6, is the same for the two analyses.

16.19. In completing the analysis of the relationship between ice cream sales, temperature, relative humidity, and the interaction between temperature and relative humidity, we should also have paid attention to the diagnostics we discussed in the previous chapter to verify that our model was not influenced unduly by outliers and that the assumptions underlying the procedure are met. We ask you to complete this aspect of the analysis in this exercise. Use the centered variables that you created in Exercise 16.17.

a) Once you have re-done the regression analysis from Exercise 16.17, use the predict command to obtain standardized residuals and Cook's distances. Are any of the standardized residuals less than -2 or greater than 2? Are any of the values for Cook's distance greater than 1?

b) Construct two scatterplots, one with centered temp vs. the standardized residuals and one with centered relhumid vs. the standardized residuals. Place the residuals on the vertical axis. Do any of the assumptions (normality, homoscedasticity, and linearity) underlying the multiple regression analysis appear to be violated? Explain.

The following exercises are conceptual and are not based on a specific data set.

16.20. Given the regression equation, $\hat{Y} = 1.2X_1 + .6X_2 + 10$.

a) X_1 is more important than X_2

b) X_1 is less important than X_2

c) X_1 is equally as important as X_2

d) One cannot tell the relative importance of X_1 and X_2 from the information given

16.21. In general, higher R^2 values will arise when the correlation between each regressor and Y is _____ and the intercorrelation between the regressors is _____.

a) high, high

b) high, low

c) low, high

d) low, low

16.22. Given a regression equation with two regressors: $\hat{Y} = b_1X_1 + b_2X_2 + a$. If b_1 is *not* statistically significant, then _____ will also *not* be statistically significant.

a) R

b) r_{Y1}

c) $r_{Y1(2)}$

d) none of the above

16.23. Given a regression equation with two regressors: $\hat{Y} = b_1 X_1 + b_2 X_2 + a$. The largest discrepancy between R^2 and $R^2_{adjusted}$ will occur when

    a) $N = 100$

    b) $N = 10$

    c) $N = 5$

    d) cannot tell from the information given

16.24. Given Y and two different X variables, X_1 and X_2, with the following two different scatterplots, A and B. Assume the Y Sum of Squares equals 100 ($SS_Y = 100$) in both situations.

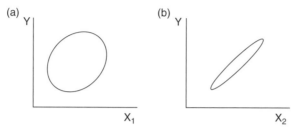

If we construct two regression equations, one for predicting Y from X_1 and another for predicting Y from X_2, which is most descriptive of situations A and B.

    a) For (A), $SS_{REG} = 90$ and $SS_{ERROR} = 10$; For (B), $SS_{REG} = 60$ and $SS_{ERROR} = 40$

    b) For (A), $SS_{REG} = 60$ and $SS_{ERROR} = 40$; For (B), $SS_{REG} = 90$ and $SS_{ERROR} = 10$

    c) For (A), $SS_{REG} = 50$ and $SS_{ERROR} = 50$; For (B), $SS_{REG} = 50$ and $SS_{ERROR} = 50$

    d) For (A), $SS_{REG} = 90$ and $SS_{ERROR} = 60$; For (B), $SS_{REG} = 10$ and $SS_{ERROR} = 40$

16.25. Under what circumstances would the weights for variables X_1 and X_2 not change when a third variable X_3 is added to the multiple regression equation?

Nonparametric Methods

In the situations of statistical inference that we have discussed regarding the mean and the variance, the dependent variable Y was tacitly assumed to be at the interval level of measurement. In addition, the statistical tests (e.g., t and F) required the assumptions of normality and homogeneity of variance of the parent population distributions. In the situations of statistical inference regarding correlation and regression, both variables X and Y were tacitly assumed to be at the interval level of measurement and the statistical tests required the assumption of homogeneous variances and bivariate normality of the parent population distribution. When one or more of these assumptions regarding the population distributions and parameters are not reasonable, alternative methods of statistical inference must be employed. The focus of this chapter is on the development and use of such alternative methods.

PARAMETRIC VERSUS NONPARAMETRIC METHODS

Because the validity of the inferential tests we have discussed so far in this book rely on explicit assumptions about population distributions and parameters, they are called "parametric" or "distribution-tied" methods. There are occasions, however, when the use of parametric methods is not warranted. One such instance occurs when the dependent variable is not at the interval level of measurement, but rather at the nominal or ordinal levels of measurement as in the case of categorical or ranked data. Another instance occurs when one or more of the required assumptions regarding the parent population distributions are not reasonable, as in the case of studying the mean of a nonnormal population using a small sample of data.

In situations where the use of parametric or distribution-tied methods is inappropriate, alternative methods called "nonparametric" or "distribution-free" may be employed. In this chapter, we first present nonparametric techniques that can be used for nominal-leveled variables and then we present techniques that can be used for ordinal-leveled variables.

Although nonparametric methods have the advantage of being relatively free from assumptions about population distributions and parameters, they have the disadvantage of having lower power generally than comparable parametric methods when these parametric methods do apply. It should also be pointed out that the hypotheses tested using nonparametric methods are not exactly the same as the hypotheses tested using parametric methods. For example, although the parametric two-group t-test specifically tests a hypothesis about the equality of two population means, the comparable nonparametric alternative (to be discussed later in this chapter) tests a hypothesis about the equality of two population distributions, providing information about the equality of the two medians as a by-product.

NONPARAMETRIC METHODS WHEN THE DEPENDENT VARIABLE IS AT THE NOMINAL LEVEL

In this section, we present two commonly used nonparametric techniques of statistical inference based on the chi-square distribution, which are applicable when the dependent variable is at the nominal level of measurement. The first method, the chi-square goodness-of-fit test can be used to analyze the distribution of subjects among the categories of a nominal-leveled variable. For example, it can be used to answer questions such as "Is the distribution of car sales in the eastern United States in the current year for Nissans, Mazdas, Toyotas, and Hondas the same as the known distribution of the previous year?" and "Are college-bound students who are always at grade level equally divided among the four regions of the United States?" The second method, the chi-square test of independence can be used to determine whether two at most ordinal-leveled variables are related. For example, it can be used to answer questions such as "Is there a relationship between gender and political party affiliation in the United States?," "Among college-bound students in the South who are always at grade level, is there a relationship between nursery school attendance and gender?," and "Among college bound students who are always at grade level, does computer ownership differ by region of residence?."

THE CHI-SQUARE DISTRIBUTION (χ^2)

Given a *normal* distribution with mean μ and variance σ^2, we select at random a value X from this population. We then form the corresponding z-score and square it to obtain z^2, as follows:

$$z^2 = \left(\frac{X-\mu}{\sigma}\right)^2 = \frac{(X-\mu)^2}{\sigma^2}$$

The distribution of all z^2 values that could be obtained in this way is shown in Figure 17.1. This distribution is called a chi-square distribution with one degree of freedom, and it is denoted by the symbol $\chi^2_{(1)}$.

If instead of drawing a single value at random from the population, we select two values at random from the population and for each value compute the corresponding z^2, we obtain

$$z_1^2 = \frac{(X_1-\mu)^2}{\sigma^2} \text{ and } z_2^2 = \frac{(X_2-\mu)^2}{\sigma^2}$$

If we now add these two z^2 values together and plot the distribution of all such sums that could be obtained in this way (from the given population), we have what is called a chi-square distribution with two degrees of freedom. It is denoted by the symbol $\chi^2_{(2)}$. This distribution is shown in Figure 17.2. Note that, as before, all $\chi^2_{(2)}$ values are nonnegative, because the $\chi^2_{(2)}$ values are sums of z^2 values, and all squared values are nonnegative.

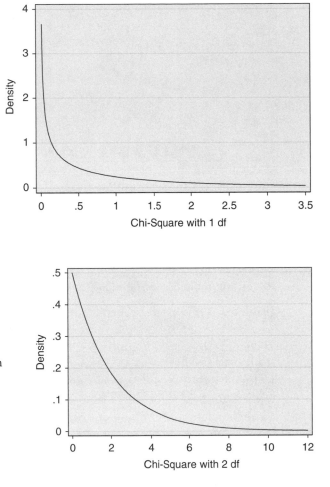

Figure 17.1 The chi-square distribution with 1 *df*.

Figure 17.2 The chi-square distribution with 2 *df*.

In general, the values of a chi-square distribution with N degrees of freedom are of the form

$$\chi^2_{(N)} = \sum_{i=1}^{N} z_i^2 = \sum_{i=1}^{N} \frac{(X_i - \mu)^2}{\sigma^2}$$

where $X_1, X_2, X_3, \ldots, X_N$ is a random sample of size N drawn from a given normally distributed population with mean μ and variance σ^2.

Figure 17.3 illustrates two chi-square distributions with 4 and 9 degrees of freedom, respectively.

In terms of summary statistics, the mean, mode, and standard deviation of the chi-square distribution are all functions of its degrees of freedom (*df*). The chi-square distribution has mean equal to *df*, mode equal to $df - 2$ (as long as $df > 2$), and standard deviation $= \sqrt{2(df)}$.

At this point, we turn to the question of how to use this chi-square distribution (really a family of distributions, just like the *t*-distributions) to find p values. To do so, we may use either the Stata function **chi2tail(df, x)**, which gives the right-tail probability of a chi-square distribution for x or Table 5 in Appendix C online, www.cambridge.org/Stats-Stata, which also gives the chi-square distribution for right-tailed areas.

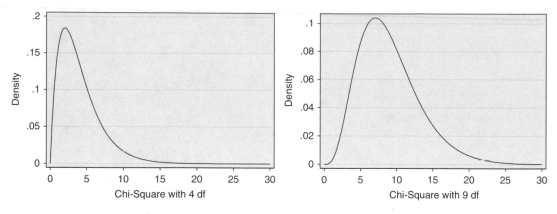

Figure 17.3   Two chi-square distributions.

• •

EXAMPLE 17.1. Estimate the p-value associated with $\chi_3^2 = 23.18$, first using Stata syntax and then using Table 5 in Appendix C online, www.cambridge.org/Stats-Stata.

Solution. Executing **display chi2tail(3, 23.19)** leads to the estimate $p = 0.00003686$, which may be rounded to 0.00004.

Turning to Table 5 in Appendix C online, www.cambridge.org/Stats-Stata, we see that the degrees of freedom are listed down the leftmost column and that they range from 1 to 100 inclusive. Listed across the top row of Table 5 are selected probability values corresponding to the right tails of the curve. That is, these probability values refer to the amount of area located under the chi-square distribution curve that falls to the right of the chi-square value listed in the table. In our example, we look at the row with $df = 3$. To find the p-value associated with $\chi_3^2 = 23.18$, we find that the closest χ^2 value to 23.18 is 16.27 and we conclude that $p < .001$. Note that the two methods, using Stata and the table, lead to consistent answers, but that the value obtained from Stata is a more precise estimate.

If the number of degrees of freedom is not listed in the table, the conservative approach is to take the chi-square value closest to, but lower than, the desired degrees of freedom value. Alternately, the Stata function **chi2tail** may be used.

THE CHI-SQUARE GOODNESS-OF-FIT TEST

Consider the problem of determining whether the distribution of car sales in the eastern United States in the current year for Nissans, Mazdas, Toyotas, and Hondas is the same as the known distribution of the previous year, which is given hypothetically in Table 17.1.

Setting this question up as a hypothesis test, we have as our null and alternative hypotheses:

H$_0$: The current year's sales distribution is the same as that of the previous year (Nissan: 18 percent, Mazda: 10 percent, Toyota: 35 percent, Honda: 37 percent).
H$_1$: The current year's sales distribution is not the same as that of the previous year.

From Motor Vehicle Bureau records, we select a random sample of 1,000 families resid-ing in the eastern United States who have purchased one of these four types of foreign cars

TABLE 17.1. Previous year's sales distribution of selected foreign cars in the eastern United States

Type of Car	Percentage
Nissan	18%
Mazda	10%
Toyota	35%
Honda	37%

TABLE 17.2. Current sales distribution of selected foreign cars in the eastern United States (sample size = 1,000)

Type of Car	Frequency
Nissan	150
Mazda	65
Toyota	385
Honda	400

in the current year, and we note which type of car was purchased. From this information, we arrive at the sample distribution given in Table 17.2.

If H_0 is true, we would *expect* approximately 18 percent of this sample to have bought Nissans (18 percent of 1,000 = .18x1000 = 180); approximately 10 percent to have bought Mazdas (10 percent of 1,000 = $0.10 \times 1,000$ = 100); approximately 35 percent to have bought Toyotas (35 percent of 1,000 = $0.35 \times 1,000$ = 350); and approximately 37 percent to have bought Hondas (37 percent of 1,000 = $0.37 \times 1,000$ = 370). We create Table 17.3 to compare the sales frequencies *observed* in this sample of 1,000 (as given in Table 17.2) to the sales frequencies *expected* if the hypothesis is true.

Making use of a procedure developed by Karl Pearson in 1900 (Pearson, 1900), we may now determine how unlikely it is for the observed values (O_i) to differ as much as they do from the expected values (E_i), given that the null hypothesis is true. If we compare the observed and expected frequencies shown in Table 17.3 according to the equation

$$\chi^2_{K-1} = \sum_{i=1}^{K} \frac{(O_i - E_i)^2}{E_i} \qquad (17.1)$$

the obtained value will be distributed as a chi-square with $df = K - 1$ degrees of freedom, where K is the number of cells (or categories). We can then use the chi-square distribution to calculate the associate p-value to decide whether to retain the null hypothesis that the current year's sales distribution is the same as that of the previous year. The test is always a one-tailed (and in particular a right-tailed) test, because only large, positive values of χ^2 indicate a significant discrepancy between observed and expected values.

Using the data given in Table 17.3 and Equation 17.1, we test our hypothesis that the current year's distribution of foreign car sales is the same as the previous year's distribution of foreign car sales at significance level $\alpha = .05$.

TABLE 17.3. Comparison of observed and expected car sales in our sample of 1,000

Type of Car	Observed frequency (O_i)	Expected frequency (E_i)
Nissan	150	180
Mazda	65	100
Toyota	385	350
Honda	400	370

We calculate the observed chi-square as

$$\chi_3^2 = \sum_{i=1}^{4} \frac{(O_i - E_i)^2}{E_i} = \frac{(O_1 - E_1)^2}{E_1} + \frac{(O_2 - E_2)^2}{E_2} + \frac{(O_3 - E_3)^2}{E_3} + \frac{(O_4 - E_4)^2}{E_4}$$

$$= \frac{(150 - 180)^2}{180} + \frac{(65 - 100)^2}{100} + \frac{(385 - 350)^2}{350} + \frac{(400 - 370)^2}{370}$$

$$= \frac{(-30)^2}{180} + \frac{(-35)^2}{100} + \frac{(35)^2}{350} + \frac{(30)^2}{370} = \frac{900}{180} + \frac{1225}{100} + \frac{1225}{350} + \frac{900}{370}$$

$$= 5.00 + 12.25 + 3.50 + 2.43 = 23.18$$

To find the associated p-value, we may use Table 5 in Appendix C online, www.cambridge.org/Stats-Stata, as illustrated in Example 17.1 or Stata as described below.

MORE Stata: To find the p-value associated with a chi-squared goodness of fit test
We use the **chi2tail** function and type:

display chi2tail(3, 23.19)

The obtained result is $p = .00004$. That is, if the distribution of sales is the same as in the previous year, the probability of obtaining the observed sample distribution is approximately .00004. Thus, our decision is to reject H_0 and switch to H_1. We conclude that the current year's distribution of foreign car sales for these selected types is not the same as that of the previous year.

We carried out the hypothesis test by hand for heuristic reasons. We now use Stata.

Given the values in Table 17.2, we may enter the data in tabulated form to create our dataset.

TABLE 17.4. The tabulated data set associated with the data of Table 17.2.

car_type	freq
1	150
2	65
3	385
4	400

MORE Stata: To enter tabulated data

We may highlight and run the relevant command lines in the Do-file for Chapter 17, that follow the line, ***To input the data for the Chi-Square Goodness of Fit test on Tabulated Data

OR

We may open a new Stata Data Editor in edit mode and enter the values of Table 17.4 as two columns of data. Click on each variable in turn in the Variables box on the top right and while each is highlighted move to the Properties box at the bottom right and assign var1 the name "car_type" and var2 the name "freq." To give the four values of the variable car_type labels, we first define the labels for each value of this variable by typing in the Command Window **label define car 1 "Nissan" 2 "Mazda" 3 "Toyota" 4 "Honda"** and then we assign these labels to the variable car_type by typing **label value car_type car**. To verify that car_type has now been labeled correctly, we type **codebook** in the Command Window.

MORE Stata: To perform the chi-square goodness-of-fit test on tabulated data

We type **findit csgof** to find and then install the user-defined **csgof** command by following the prompts to install this program into your version of Stata, by clicking on the relevant link in the Viewer Window.

Because **csgof** expects there to be one observation per subject in the dataset, and because our data set is in tabulated form, it does not conform to the requirements of the **csgof** command. We, therefore, convert our data to be in the appropriate form (with only one observation per subject – that is, with 150 rows of type 1 cars, 65 rows of type 2 cars, 385 rows of type 3 cars, and 400 rows of type 4 cars), we use the command **expand** prior to **csgof**, as follows:

expand freq
csgof car_type, expperc(18 10 35 37)

Note: The values in ()'s represent the expected percentage of each car type. By default, without the **expperc** option, expected percentages are assumed to be all equal. This syntax is provided in the Do-file associated with this chapter.

The first part of the output gives the observed and expected frequencies and agrees with the results of Table 17.3.

car_type	expperc	expfreq	obsfreq
Nissan	18	180	150
Mazda	10	100	65
Toyota	35	350	385
Honda	37	370	400

The second part reports the observed χ^2 value, its associated degrees of freedom, and p-value, chisq(3) is 23.18, p = 0.

These values agree with those obtained by hand and we conclude, as before, that the current year's distribution of foreign car sales for these selected types is not the same as that of the previous year.

Note that we rejected the null hypothesis in favor of the alternative because the fit between the observed and the expected cell values was not good enough. For this reason, this type of chi-square test is known as the *chi-square goodness-of-fit test*.

As discussed previously, because the chi-square goodness-of-fit test is a nonparametric method, its validity does not rely on assumptions about the population from which the sample is selected. The validity of the test, however, does rely on several assumptions about the sample and the treatment of the sample data. First, the cells must be mutually exclusive and exhaustive; that is, each observed piece of information must fit into one and only one of the cells. Second, the observations must be independent of each other; that is, the result of any one observation must tell us nothing about the result of any other observation. Third, the *expected* frequency in each cell must be at least 5. Fourth and last, the sum of the expected frequencies must equal the sum of the observed frequencies. To justify the use of $K - 1$ degrees of freedom rather than K, the number of cells, we note that the sum of the observed cell frequencies must be equal to the sample size, so that once the first $K - 1$ observed frequencies are known, the Kth is completely determined.

In the special case where the number of degrees of freedom is 1 (when there are two cells), the distribution of values obtained from Equation 17.1 departs markedly from a chi-square distribution. A correction called Yates' correction is used when $df = 1$ to enhance the validity of the test. When $df = 1$, the equation for the observed chi-square value is

$$\chi^2_{(1)} = \frac{(|O_1 - E_1| - .5)^2}{E_1} + \frac{(|O_2 - E_2| - .5)^2}{E_2} \tag{17.2}$$

Note that the absolute value of the difference $O_i - E_i$ is taken *before* subtracting 0.5 and squaring.

• •

EXAMPLE 17.2. Are college-bound high school students who have always been at grade level in the United States equally divided among the four census regions? That is, do the students in the *NELS* data set come from a population in which 25 percent of the students are in each region? Use $\alpha = .05$.

Solution. In this case, we solve using Stata only.
The null and alternative hypotheses in this problem are

H_0: The distribution by region is uniform (25 percent in each region).
H_1: The distribution by region is not uniform.

MORE Stata: To perform the chi-square goodness-of-fit test on raw data

W once again use **csgof**. In this case, because our data already had one observation per subject, we may bypass the use of the **expand** command. In addition, because the expected percentages are all equal, we do not need to include the **csgof** option **expperc**.

csgof region

We obtain the following table with observed and expected frequencies. The observed frequencies are based on the 500 students in the *NELS* data set. The expected frequencies for each region are found by multiplying the proportion (or percentage) expected for that region by the total sample size. In this example, each of the four regions has an expected percentage of 25 percent (or 0.25). To find the expected frequency for each region, we multiply 0.25 by the sample size 500 to obtain 0.25 x 500 = 125.

region	expperc	expfreq	obsfreq
Northeast	25	125	106
North Cent	25	125	151
South	25	125	150
West	25	125	93

The next table gives the results of the chi-square goodness-of-fit test. Note that because there are four regions, the degrees of freedom equal 4 − 1 or 3.

Chisq (3) is 21.49, p =.0001

We see that in this case, our obtained chi-square value is $\chi^2_3 = 21.49$, which has $p < .0005$. Because $p < \alpha$, we conclude that such students in the U.S. are not uniformly distributed among the four regions.

THE CHI-SQUARE TEST OF INDEPENDENCE

In this section, we present another application of the Pearson chi-square distribution, one that enables us to determine whether two categorical variables are related. For example, suppose we were interested in determining whether the gender (Male, Female) and ppa (Political Party Affiliation [Democrat, Republican, Neither]) are related (dependent). If they are related, then knowing the gender of an individual would predict the individual's political party affiliation, otherwise not.

Suppose that a random sample of 200 individuals drawn from a population of interest, produces the following observed frequencies, organized in Table 17.5 as what is called a bivariate contingency table or crosstabulation.

If we can determine the expected frequency in each cell given that the two variables are mutually independent, then, as in the chi-square goodness-of-fit test, we can compare observed with expected cell frequencies. We do so by using Equation 17.3.

$$\chi^2_{(C-1)(R-1)} = \sum_{i,j} \frac{(0_{ij} - E_{ij})^2}{E_{ij}} \qquad (17.3)$$

which gives values that are distributed as a chi-square with $(C − 1)(R − 1)$ degrees of freedom, where C is the number of columns and R is the number of rows in the contingency table. In Table 17.5, there are three columns and two rows, so the number of degrees of freedom is $df = (C − 1)(R − 1) = (3 − 1)(2 − 1) = (2 \times 1) = 2$. We compute p based on this chi-square value to determine how unlikely it is for the observed frequencies (O_{ij}) to differ as much as they do from the expected frequencies (E_{ij}), given that the null hypothesis is true, that the two variables are mutually independent.

The p-value is the area to the right of the observed chi-square value. If the fit between observed and expected values is poor, then the observed chi-square value will be large and we will reject the hypothesis of independence. We show how to determine the expected cell frequencies for all cells using the data (observed cell frequencies) of Table 17.5.

We first sum all the frequencies in each row to find the row marginal frequencies. We also sum all the frequencies in each column to find the column marginal frequencies. The marginal frequencies are given in Table 17.6. The marginal frequency for the first row (Males) is 40 + 10 + 50 = 100; the marginal frequency for the second row (Females) is 60 + 20 + 20 = 100; the marginal frequency for the first column (Democrat) is 40 + 60 = 100; the marginal frequency of the second column (Republican) is 10 + 20 = 30; and, the marginal frequency of the third column (Neither) is 50 + 20 = 70. The marginal frequencies tell us that there are 100 males and 100 females in the

TABLE 17.5. Political party affiliation by gender

	Democrat	Republican	Neither
Male	40	10	50
Female	60	20	20

TABLE 17.6. Crosstabulation of political party affiliation by gender with marginal frequencies

gender	ppa			
	Democrat	Republican	Neither	Total
Male	40	10	50	100
Female	60	20	20	100
Total	100	30	70	

TABLE 17.7. Observed and expected frequencies for political party affiliation by gender

	Democrat	Republican	Neither
Male	O = 40	O = 10	O = 50
	E = 50	E = 15	E = 35
Female	O = 60	O = 20	O = 20
	E = 50	E = 15	E = 35

entire sample of 200 individuals and that there are 100 Democrats, 30 Republicans, and 70 of neither party in the same sample of 200 individuals.

If the two variables gender and political party affiliation truly are independent of each other, because we have the same number of males and females in the sample, we would expect the number of male Democrats to equal the number of female Democrats, the number of male Republicans to equal the number of female Republicans, and the number of males of neither party to equal the number of females of neither party. That is, because there are a total of 100 Democrats, we would expect 50 of them to be male and 50 of them to be female. Because there are a total of 30 Republicans, we would expect 15 of them to be male and 15 of them to be female. And because there are a total of 70 of neither party we would expect 35 of them to be male and 35 of them to be female.

These expected frequencies, along with the observed frequencies, are given in Table 17.7.

A more formal method for finding the expected frequency of a given cell is simply to multiply the marginal frequency of the row the cell is in by the marginal frequency of the column the cell is in, and divide by the total sample size N.

For example, to find the expected frequency for "Male Democrats," the cell in row 1 and column 1 of Table 17.6, we multiply the marginal frequency of row 1 (100) by the marginal frequency of column 1 (100) to obtain $100 \times 100 = 10,000$. We then divide this product by the total sample size $N = 200$ to obtain an expected frequency of $10,000/200 = 50$, the value we obtained earlier in Table 17.7. Similarly, to find the expected frequency for "Male Republicans," the cell in row 1 and column 2 in Table 17.6, we multiply the marginal frequency of row 1 (100) by the marginal frequency of column 2 (30) to obtain $100 \times 30 = 3,000$. We then divide this product by the total sample size $N = 200$ to obtain an expected frequency of $3,000/200 = 15$, the value we obtained earlier in Table 17.7.

Given these expected frequencies, we now test the null and alternative hypotheses.

H_0: Gender and political party affiliation are independent.
H_1: Gender and political party affiliation are dependent.

Because there are two rows and three columns in this example, the number of degrees of freedom is $df = (C - 1)(R - 1) = (3 - 1)(2 - 1) = (2 \times 1) = 2$.

Using Equation 17.3, we obtain the following observed chi-square value:

$$\chi^2_{(2)} = \sum_{i,j} \frac{(O_{ij} - E_{ij})^2}{E_{ij}}$$

$$= \frac{(40-50)^2}{50} + \frac{(10-15)^2}{15} + \frac{(50-35)^2}{35} + \frac{(60-50)^2}{50} + \frac{(20-15)^2}{15} + \frac{(20-35)^2}{35}$$

$$= \frac{100}{50} + \frac{25}{15} + \frac{225}{35} + \frac{100}{50} + \frac{25}{15} + \frac{225}{35} = \frac{200}{50} + \frac{50}{15} + \frac{450}{35} = 4 + 3.33 + 12.86$$

$$= 20.19.$$

To find the associated p-value, we use Stata or the chi-square table in Appendix C online, www.cambridge.org/Stats-Stata. In this case, the Stata syntax **display chi2tail(2, 20.19)** gives $p = .00004$. Alternatively, the estimated p-value using Table 5 in Appendix C online is $p < .001$.

Thus, if there were no relationship between political party affiliation and gender, the probability of obtaining the observed sample data is approximately .00004. Accordingly, we reject H_0 in favor of H_1, that gender and political party affiliation are related, for the population under study. Said differently, the distribution of political party affiliation for males is different from that for females. The data of Table 17.5 indicate that while females tend to be Democrats, males are more evenly split between Democrats and neither political party.

We now illustrate how to perform the chi-square test of independence using Stata.

We begin by entering the tabulated data of Table 17.5 into a dataset using either the procedure used earlier with respect to the car data or by highlighting and running the relevant command lines in the Do-file for Chapter 17. For this example, we use the following variable names and codes: We name the first variable gender, with value labels 1 = male and 2 = female, the second variable ppa, to stand for "political party affiliation" with value labels, 1 = Democrat, 2 = Republican, and 3 = Neither, and the third variable freq with variable label "frequency". Table 17.8 shows how the cross-tabulated data between gender and political party affiliation should appear in our Stata dataset.

MORE Stata: To perform the chi-square test of independence

We use the command **tabulate**, specifying that **fweight = freq** to ensure that each combination of gender by ppa values is weighted by its frequency of occurrence.

tabulate gender ppa [fweight = freq], chi2

TABLE 17.8. The tabulated data set associated with the data of Table 17.5.

gender	ppa	freq
1	1	40
2	1	60
1	2	10
2	2	20
1	3	50
2	3	20

The output gives the contingency table or cross-tabulation with marginal frequencies followed by the results of the chi-square test of independence.

gender	political party affiliation			Total
	1	2	3	
1	40	10	50	100
2	60	20	20	100
Total	100	30	70	200

Pearson chi2 (2)   =   20.1905   Pr = 0.000

The Pearson Chi-Square results from Stata are consistent with those obtained by hand in that $\chi^2_{(2)} = 20.19$ with $p < .0005$. As before, we conclude that the distribution of political party affiliation for males is different from that for females.

MORE Stata: Immediate commands

The **tabi** command, ending with the letter i, is what is called an *immediate command* in Stata. Immediate commands are those that operate on data typed at the same time (or immediately) after the command itself, as opposed to on data stored in memory. To carry out the chi-square test of independence using the immediate command, see the Do-file associated with this chapter.

Assumptions of the Chi-Square Test of Independence

The basic assumptions underlying the use of the chi-square test of independence are as follows:

1. The individual observations are independent of each other (no observation has any effect on any other observation).
2. The expected cell frequencies are not too small (the minimum expected cell frequency required in a particular problem depends on the significance level α and how similar in size the expected cell frequencies are to each other). In general, however, a good minimum expected cell frequency is 5; that is, each cell should have an expected frequency of 5 or more.

For the analysis of the relationship between gender and political party affiliation, we see that the first assumption was met by the sampling design. The Stata output for the test indicates that the second assumption was met as well. Below the results of the hypothesis test there is a note about the minimum expected cell frequency.

EXAMPLE 17.3. Using the *NELS* data set, is there a relationship between nursery school attendance and gender among college-bound high school students from the South who are always at grade level?

Solution. Note that in Example 5.6(1), we asked whether there is a relationship between nursery school attendance and gender among students in the *NELS* data set. To answer this descriptively, we used both the correlation (phi coefficient, in this case) and the contingency table. We now answer this question inferentially and draw conclusions to the larger population from which the students in the *NELS* data set have been selected.

The null and alternative hypotheses are

H_0: There is no relationship between nursery school attendance and gender in the population (they are independent).

H_1: There is a relationship between nursery school attendance and gender in the population (they are dependent).

MORE Stata: To perform the chi-square test of independence with raw (nontabulated) data

tabulate gender nursery, chi2

Note: tab may be used as the shorthand form of tabulate

The output gives the contingency table followed by the p-value associated with the chi-square test of independence. In this case, $\chi^2_{(1)} = .36$, $p = .55$, indicating that we should retain the null hypothesis. We conclude that there is no relationship between gender and nursery school attendance among college bound high school students from the south who are always at grade level.

Gender	Nursery School Attended? No	Yes	Total
Male	62	134	196
Female	77	147	224
Total	139	281	420

Pearson chi2 (1) =   0.3550   Pr = 0.551

In a situation such as this one that has two dichotomous variables, there is an alternative approach to determine whether there is a relationship between nursery school attendance and gender among college-bound high school students from the South who are always at grade level. That approach is via the use of the Pearson correlation coefficient.

MORE Stata: To have the chi-square test of independence results include the expected values and to obtain the correlation between the two variables as well

tabulate gender nursery, chi2 expected
pwcorr nursery gender, obs star(5)

The following table is included with the earlier output from the tab command:

	nursery	gender
nursery	1.0000 420	
gender	−0.0291 420	1.0000 500

We see that $r = -.029$ with $p > .05$, corroborating the results of the chi-square test of independence.

FISHER'S EXACT TEST

The p-values obtained through the chi-square test of independence are only approximations to the true or exact p-values. In the case of a 2 x 2 contingency table, an approach that does provide exact p-values is the Fisher's Exact Test. The approximate p-values of the chi-square test of independence depart from the true or exact p-values especially when sample sizes are small, and in such cases, the Fisher's Exact Test result should be used as it provides the more accurate result.

The Fisher's Exact Test was first proposed in 1934 by R.A. Fisher (Fisher, 1934) and makes use of a probability distribution called the hypergeometric probability distribution for obtaining the exact probability values associated with the observed outcome or an outcome that is more extreme than the observed outcome, given that the null hypothesis is true.

By contrast to the Pearson chi-square test, the calculation of exact probabilities using the hypergeometric probability distribution is quite laborious even when sample sizes are small. We illustrate this fact with an example that makes use of the same variables as in Example 17.3, but with a far smaller sample size. In practice, however, we simply may rely on the computer to obtain these Fisher's exact probability values using Stata.

• •

EXAMPLE 17.3a. Is there a relationship between nursery school attendance and gender given a sample of size $N = 12$, randomly selected without replacement from a relatively small population of college-bound high school students from one particular area in the South?

In Example 17.3, notice that the ratio of those who attended nursery school to those who did not is approximately 2:1. Likewise, the ratio of males to females is approximately 1:1. For comparability, these same ratios will be used in the current example. That is, for this example, we assume that of the 12 students randomly selected, 8 have attended nursery school and 4 have not; and that 6 are male and 6 are female. Accordingly, the marginal values of our 2 X 2 contingency table are as follows:

	Male	**Female**	**Total**
Nursery School – No			8
Nursery School – Yes			4
Total	6	6	12

Given these marginal values, the Fisher's Exact Test provides the exact probability of whether the observed, or even more extreme, distribution of the proportion of males and females who attend nursery school is consistent with the null hypothesis that there is no difference between the proportion of males and females who attend nursery school.

Assume that we have observed the following number of males and females to have attended nursery school or not:

TABLE 17.A

	Male	Female	Total
Nursery School – No	2	6	8
Nursery School – Yes	4	0	4
Total	6	6	12

MORE Stata: To perform the Fisher's Exact Test in addition to the chi-square test of independence

tabulate gender nursery [fweight = freq], chi2 exact

Note: **tabulate** makes use of already input and saved data. Instead we may use the immediate command **tabi** and input data immediately after the command itself. The values 2 and 6 form the first column of data and 4 and 0, by following the backslash (\), form the second column of data.

tabi 2 6 \4 0, chi2 exact

Using either of these procedures, we obtain the following results:

gender	nursery 1	2	Total
1	2	4	6
2	6	0	6
Total	8	4	12

```
        Pearson chi2 (1)   =     6.0000   Pr = 0.014
           Fisher's exact   =                  0.061
  1-sided Fisher's exact    =                  0.030
```

For this example, while the (asymptotic or approximate) 2-sided probability associated with the Pearson Chi-Square test is $p = .014$, resulting in the rejection of the null hypothesis that there is no relationship between gender and nursery school attendance in favor of the alternative that there is a relationship between these two variables, the Fisher's Exact Test 2-sided probability is $p = .061$, resulting in the opposite conclusion not to reject the null hypothesis. As noted earlier, the result of the Fisher Exact Test is the more accurate of the two, and should be the one used.

Calculating the Fisher Exact Test by Hand Using the Hypergeometric Distribution

For those interested, in this section we provide the general form of the Fisher Exact Test for the 2×2 case using the hypergeometric distribution.

Given N subjects categorized into a 2 X 2 contingency table as follows:

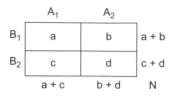

If the marginal values are considered fixed, and sampling is without replacement from a relatively small population, the 1-sided exact probability of observing the relative frequencies, a, b, c, and d in the 2 x 2 table is given by the hypergeometric distribution as follows:

$$\frac{\binom{a+c}{a}\binom{b+d}{b}}{\binom{N}{a+b}} = \frac{(a+b)!(c+d)!(a+c)!(b+d)!}{N!a!b!c!d!} \tag{17.4}$$

Given the observed nursery school/gender results provided by Table 17.A, using Equation (17.4), we find that the 1-sided exact probability of obtaining this particular set of frequencies, with the marginal values considered fixed, is (see the Do-file for Chapter 17 to see how to compute this value using the **display** function in Stata):

$$\frac{8!4!6!6!}{12!2!6!4!0!} = \frac{1}{33} = 0.0303$$

Doubling this value, we obtain the 2-sided exact probability to be .0606, or .061 as given by Stata in its rounded form.

This is the exact probability of obtaining by chance the observed outcome or an outcome more extreme, given the null hypothesis is true. Accordingly, since .0606 exceeds the .05 significance level, we cannot reject the null hypothesis in favor of the alternative. We conclude that there appears to be no relationship between nursery school attendance and sex based on this example.

☞ **Remark.** Because the observed result given in Table 17.A is as extreme as possible in one direction (we know this to be the case because of the presence of the 0 in one of the cells), we needed only to compute the hypergeometric probability for this one case. Given that a test of the null hypothesis addresses the generic question: "What is the probability, given the null hypothesis is true, of obtaining the result observed or results even less consistent with the null hypothesis (i.e., more extreme)?", the calculation of the exact probability in question must consider not only the result observed, but also all possible results that are more extreme (or more disproportionate) than the result observed (if the result is not already most extreme, as it was in our example). Simply stated, the calculation of the exact probability in question must be based not only on the result observed, but also on all possible results that may be observed that are increasingly more extreme (increasingly less consistent with the null hypothesis of no relationship) than the result observed, until the smallest cell frequency is 0; the exact probability equals the sum of the hypergeometric probabilities of all such possible increasingly more extreme results, beginning with the result observed. We illustrate by assuming that the observed result is given in Table 17.B, rather than in Table 17.A.

TABLE 17.B

	Male	Female	Total
Nursery School – No	3	5	8
Nursery School – Yes	3	1	4
Total	6	6	12

Given the marginal values of 8 and 4, and 6 and 6, respectively, we may note that the cell frequencies of Table 17.B are more consistent with the null hypothesis of no relationship between nursery school attendance and sex (and therefore less extreme) than those of Table 17.A.

Using Equation 17.4, we find that the 1-sided exact probability of obtaining the particular set of cell frequencies given in Table 17.B, with the marginal values considered fixed, to be (see the do-file associated with this chapter to see how to compute this value using the **display** function in Stata):

$$\frac{8!4!6!6!}{12!3!5!3!1!} = \frac{8}{33} = 0.2424$$

Adding this probability value to the probability value associated with the more extreme result given in Table 17A, yields the following 1-sided exact probability value $p = .2424 + .0303 = .2727$. Doubling this value we find the 2-sided exact probability value to be $p = .5454$, which is the value given by the following Stata output obtained using the previously-used Stata input and tabulate commands (see the do-file associated with this chapter for the specific commands).

gender	nursery 1	2	Total
1	3	3	6
2	5	1	6
Total	8	4	12

Pearson chi2 (1) =	1.5000	Pr =	0.221
Fisher's exact =			0.545
1-sided Fisher's exact =			0.273

Because the exact probability ($p = .545$) of obtaining by chance the observed outcome of Table 17.B, or an outcome more extreme, given the null hypothesis is true, exceeds the .05 significance level, we cannot reject the null hypothesis in favor of the alternative in this case. We conclude, therefore, that there appears to be no relationship between nursery school attendance and sex based on the observed result given in this example.

• •

EXAMPLE 17.4. Do families of eighth graders who are college bound and always at grade level differ on computer ownership according to the region of the country in which they reside?

Solution. Note that we answered this question descriptively in Example 5.9, confining our conclusions to the 500 individuals in our *NELS* data set. We now answer this question inferentially and draw inferences to the larger population from which the students in the *NELS* data set have been selected.

The null and alternative hypotheses are

H₀: There is no relationship between region and computer ownership in the population (they are independent).

H₁: There is a relationship between region and computer ownership in the population (they are dependent).

MORE Stata: To perform the chi-square test of independence using raw data

tabulate region computer, chi2

The Output gives the results of the Pearson chi-square test of independence. In this case, $\chi^2_{(3)} = 9.45$, $p = .02$, indicating that we should reject the null hypothesis as implausible in favor of the alternative. We conclude that there is a relationship between region and computer ownership among college bound high school students from the south who are always at grade level. According to the contingency table, we see that while in the northeast and west, students are more likely than not to own a computer, in the north central and south the opposite is true.

Geographic Region of School	Computer Owned by Family in 8th Grade?		
	No	Yes	Total
Northeast	46	60	106
North Central	89	62	151
South	86	64	150
West	42	51	93
Total	263	237	500

Pearson chi2 (3) =   9.4481   Pr = 0.024

☞ **Remark.** Although it is too advanced for inclusion in this book, we should mention the existence of a general technique called log-linear analysis that can be used to estimate and test complex models involving dependent variables measured at the nominal level. The model for log-linear analysis is similar to the model for analysis of variance in that it allows for the estimation and testing of both main and interaction effects. The interested reader should consult a more advanced book that covers this topic in detail (Marascuilo & Busk, 1987; Marascuilo & Serlin, 1988).

NONPARAMETRIC METHODS WHEN THE DEPENDENT VARIABLE IS ORDINAL-LEVELED

In this section, we present a few commonly used nonparametric techniques that are applicable when the dependent variable is at the ordinal level of measurement. In particular, we present the Wilcoxon sign test for matched pairs, the nonparametric analog to the *t*-test on Means for dependent groups; the Mann-Whitney U test, the nonparametric analog to the t-test on means for independent groups; and the Kruskal-Wallis "Analysis of Variance," the nonparametric analog of the one-way ANOVA. These tests were first introduced in the mid to late 1940's.

☞ **Remark.** Frank Wilcoxon, then a chemist at American Cyanimid, published a revolutionary paper, "Individual Comparisons by Ranking Methods," in 1945 (Wilcoxon, 1945) that introduced the notion that statistical hypothesis tests do not necessarily need to be based on estimates of distribution parameters (e.g., the mean, variance, or correlation), but rather could be based more simply on assigning ranks to the observed data and comparing those ranks to ranks that would be expected randomly, or by chance. As noted earlier, because such tests do not require the estimation of a parameter, they are called *nonparametric* tests. Working independently, and in the same vein, Henry B. Mann, an economist, and D. Ransom Whitney, a graduate student in statistics at Ohio State University, published a paper two years later that served to continue a focus on nonparametric tests (Mann & Whitney, 1947). As noted by Salsburg (2001, p. 164), "[t]he work of Wilcoxon and Mann and Whitney had opened a new window of mathematical investigation by directing attention to the underlying nature of ordered ranks." One such later example is the paper by Kruskal and Wallis (1952).

A nonparametric measure of association between two variables, each in rank order form, is the Spearman Rank Correlation Coefficient. Recall that this measure of association was discussed and illustrated in Chapter 5 as a special case of the Pearson Correlation Coefficient. Consequently, although the Spearman Rank Correlation Coefficient is a nonparametric technique, it will not be presented in this chapter.

WILCOXON SIGN TEST

Perhaps the simplest nonparametric procedure is the sign test for matched pairs. The sign test tests the null hypothesis that two population distributions are identical. It is used with pairwise matched (or related) samples to determine whether or not two conditions (or treatments) have identical population distributions for the dependent variable. The proportion in the population is denoted π.

The sign test assumes that there is no difference between conditions, and consequently that chance alone determines whether the difference between scores on the dependent variable for each sample pair is positive or negative. If the signs of the pairwise differences are due to chance alone, then the probability that any particular pairwise difference is positive (or negative) is .50, and the probabilities of all possible outcomes of the experiment (i.e., the number of positive pairwise differences, *Pos*) may be represented by a binomial model with $p = .50$ and N equal to the number of matched pairs. In the event of ties (i.e., pairwise differences of 0), the procedure is to drop the tied pairs from the sample and to reduce the sample size accordingly. The null hypothesis of equal treatment effects in the population ($H_0: \pi = .50$) is tested using the binomial distribution. We carry out the sign test procedure by hand and then by Stata in Example 17.5.

• •
EXAMPLE 17.5. In a study to determine if weights recorded on packaged snack food items (muffins, cookies, cakes, candy bars, potato chips, and pretzels) are accurate, two of each

item type was randomly selected, removed from its packaging, and weighed on a high precision scale. Recorded package weights and obtained (actual) weights in ounces are given pairwise below.

Sample 1 (recorded weights): 11.5, 10.0, 17.0, 16.0, 12.5, 9.0, 8.75, 6.0, 8.0, 20.5, 5.75, 16.0
Sample 2 (actual weights): 11.8, 10.0, 16.5, 16.0, 13.0, 9.5, 9.00, 6.0, 8.2, 19.5, 6.20, 16.2

Because the data are ratio, the paired samples t-test could be appropriate, in this case. We assume, for the purposes of this example, that at least one of the assumptions underlying the paired samples t-test is not tenable (namely, that either the two parent populations are not normally distributed or that they do not have equal variances). Accordingly, we employ instead its nonparametric analog, the sign test. We use a .05 level of significance. Because a direction of difference is not specified, the test is two-tailed.

Solution. The data are reproduced and the signs of the differences between the recorded and actual weights are noted as well.

Sample 1 (recorded weights): 11.5, 10.0, 17.0, 16.0, 12.5, 9.0, 8.75, 6.0, 8.0, 20.5, 5.75, 16.0
Sample 2 (actual weights): 11.8, 10.0, 16.5, 16.0, 13.0, 9.5, 9.00, 6.0, 8.2, 19.5, 6.20, 16.2

Sign of difference(recorded-actual): $-$ 0 $+$ 0 $-$ $-$ $-$ 0 $-$ $+$ $-$ $-$

Because there are three tied pairs (sign of difference = 0), we eliminate these pairs and reduce the sample size from $N = 12$ to $N = 9$. Using Table 2 of the binomial probability distribution with $N = 9$ and $p = .50$, we find the two-tailed rejection region to be 0, 1, 8, or 9 positive differences. We observe that the number of positive pairwise differences as $Pos = 2$. Because 2 is not in the rejection region, we cannot reject the null hypothesis of equal weights and we conclude that weights recorded on such packaged snack food items are accurate; they are not statistically significantly different from actual weights.

We may note also from the binomial distribution table with $N = 9$ and $p = .50$ that the probability of obtaining 2 or more extreme positive differences is

Prob(0 or 1 or 2 or 7 or 8 or 9)
= Prob(0) + Prob(1) + Prob(2) + Prob(7) + Prob(8) + Prob(9)
= .002 + .0176 + .0703 + .0703 + .0176 + .002 = .1798 or .18.

Because .18 exceeds .05, our conclusion, once again, is not to reject the null hypothesis in favor of the alternative.

MORE Stata: To carry out the sign test.

Once the data are entered as twelve records of two variables each (recordwt and actualwt) (see the Do-file for Chapter 17 for an approach that may be used to enter these data), we use the following command:

signtest recordwt = actualwt

The results corroborate with those obtained above.

Sign test

sign	observed	expected
positive	2	4.5
negative	7	4.5
zero	3	3
all	12	12

One-sided tests:
    Ho: median of recordwt – actualwt = 0 vs.
    Ha: median of recordwt – actualwt > 0
        Pr (#positive >= 2) =
            Binomial (n = 9, x> = 2, p = 0.5) = 0.9805

    Ho: median of recordwt – actualwt = 0 vs.
    Ha: median of recordwt – actualwt < 0
        Pr (#negative >= 7) =
            Binomial (n = 9, x >= 7, p = 0.5) = 0.0898

Two–sided test:
    Ho: median of recordwt – actualwt = 0 vs.
    Ha: median of recordwt – actualwt ! = 0
        Pr (#positive > = 7 or #negative > =7)=
            min (1,2* Binomial (n = 9, x >= 7, p = 0.5)) = 0.1797

As mentioned earlier, the *t*-test on related samples is the parametric alternative to the sign test. When the parametric assumptions underlying the *t*-test are true, the power of the *t*-test will be greater than that of the corresponding nonparametric sign test. Consequently, if the underlying assumptions of the parametric test are satisfied, we should use the more powerful parametric procedure, the *t*-test on related groups, in this case. If one or more of the assumptions are not satisfied, however, then the nonparametric procedure, the sign test for matched pairs, in this case, is the best available alternative.

Remark. As noted in Chapter 8, when Np and Nq both exceed 5, the binomial distribution is well approximated by the normal. Because $p = .50$ for the sign test, N must exceed 10 to use the normal as an approximation of the binomial. In this case, the normal distribution has mean and standard deviation given by Equation 17.5.

$$\text{Mean} = \mu_{Pos} = Np = N(.5) = \frac{N}{2} \tag{17.5}$$

$$\text{Standard Deviation} = \sigma_{Pos} = \sqrt{Npq} = \sqrt{N(.5)(.5)} = \sqrt{N}(.5) = \frac{\sqrt{N}}{2}$$

We may determine the significance of an observed value of *Pos* by transforming it to a *z*-value using Equation 17.6.

$$z = \frac{2Pos - N + C}{\sqrt{N}} \tag{17.6}$$

where

$C = +1$ if $(2\text{Pos} - N) < 0$
$C = -1$ if $(2\text{Pos} - N) > 0$.

The z-value obtained in Equation 17.5 may be compared to an appropriate critical z-value to determine its statistical significance. The letter C in this Equation is a correction for continuity factor, which is included to enhance the fit between the binomial model (which is discrete) and the normal model (which is continuous).

THE MANN-WHITNEY U TEST

Like the sign test, the Mann-Whitney U test tests the null hypothesis that two population distributions are identical. Unlike the sign test, however, the Mann-Whitney U test is designed for use with unrelated or independent samples, and uses the ranks of the sample scores rather than the scores themselves.

The Mann-Whitney U test assumes that there is no difference between populations, and consequently, if both populations were combined into one large group, there would be a complete intermingling of scores. If we select a random sample from each population, and combine both samples into one large group, we would expect a complete intermingling of sample scores similar to that of the population scores, but with some separation due to sampling error. The question is whether the observed separation between samples is significant of a true separation in the population, or can be accounted for by chance factors alone.

What we need is a measure of the extent to which the two groups are not completely intermingled; that is, the extent to which the scores of one group is generally smaller than, equal to, or larger than the scores of the other group. What is also needed is a sampling distribution against which to compare this measure to determine if the difference between the two groups is statistically significant. Such a measure is provided by the U statistic, which is defined as the number of times a score from one group is smaller than a score from the other group. For simplicity, we shall assume that all scores are unique and that there are no ties. For situations in which there are tie scores, the interested reader is referred to Siegel, Sidney, and Castellan (1988), a more advanced book on this topic. We illustrate with an example.

EXAMPLE 17.6. Use the Mann-Whitney U test to determine whether a random sample of four boys and a random sample of five girls who participate in varsity college soccer come from identical populations when one considers the number of injuries sustained in a season of play. Use a .05 level of significance. The data are given below.

Boys: 14	17	18	25	
Girls: 7	13	15	16	12

Solution. We will compute U as the number of times a value in the sample of boys is smaller than a value in the sample of girls. Looking at the data, we see that 14 is smaller than two values in the sample of girls; 17 is smaller than none of the five values in the sample of girls; 18 is smaller than none of the five values, and likewise for 25. Consequently, $U = 2+0+0+0 = 2$.

☞ **Remark.** It may be noted that the value of U will always be between 0 and $(N_1)(N_2)$. A value of U near 0 indicates that the values in the first group are generally larger than the values in the second group. A value of U near the middle of the range, $(N_1)(N_2)/2$, indicates that the values in the first group are generally intermingled with the values in the second group. A value of U near $(N_1)(N_2)$ indicates that the values in the first group are generally smaller than the values in the second group.

In this example, U can range between 0 and $(N_1)(N_2) = (4)(5) = 20$, so the obtained U value of 2 suggests that the number of injuries sustained by the sample of boys is generally larger than the number of injuries sustained by the sample of girls.

To determine whether the sample data are consistent with the null hypothesis that the two population distributions are identical, we compare the obtained value of U to an appropriate sampling distribution of U values. We reject the null hypothesis of identical population distributions if the obtained value of U is in the rejection region, otherwise we do not.

A table of critical U values, organized by rows and columns, is given in Table 6 of Appendix C online, www.cambridge.org/Stats-Stata. The rows are indexed by N_1, the size of Sample 1, and the columns are indexed by N_2, the size of Sample 2.

In this example, $N_1 = 4$ and $N_2 = 5$. Therefore, the critical values, contained in the column labeled $N_1 = 4$ and the row labeled $N_2 = 5$, for $\alpha = .05$, two-tailed, are 1 and 19 and the rejection region for U is 0, 1, 19, 20. Because the obtained U value of 18 is not in the rejection region, we retain belief in the null hypothesis that the two population distributions are identical.

An alternative method for obtaining the U statistic that is based on the ranks of the scores is given in Equation 17.7.

$$U = N_1 N_2 + \frac{N_1(N_1 + 1)}{2} - R_1 \tag{17.7}$$

where N_1 is the size of Sample 1, N_2 is the size of Sample 2, and R_1 is the sum of the ranks of Sample 1 when all scores from both samples are combined and rank-ordered from smallest (assigned a rank of 1) to largest (assigned a rank of $N_1 + N_2$).

We illustrate the use of Equation 17.6 using the data of Example 17.7.

The nine scores rank ordered from smallest to largest are:

Raw Score:	7	12	13	14	15	16	17	18	25
Rank:	1	2	3	4	5	6	7	8	9

The sum of Sample 1 ranks is: $R_1 = 4 + 7 + 8 + 9 = 28$. Substituting the relevant values into Equation 17.6, we obtain:

$$U = (4)(5) + \frac{(4)(4 + 1)}{2} - 28 = 2,$$

the same value obtained in connection with the approach presented previously.

Our conclusion, once again, is not to reject the null hypothesis in favor of the alternative.

MORE Stata: To carry out the Mann-Whitney U test.

Once the data are entered as two variables called sample (a dichotomous variable that distinguishes Sample 1, Boys, from Sample 2, Girls) and score (see the Do-file for Chapter 17 for data entry instructions), we use the following syntax to execute the test:

ranksum score, by(sample)

Using Stata, we obtain the following results, which corroborate with those obtained above.

Two-sample Wilcoxon rank-sum (Mann-Whitney) test			
sample	obs	rank sum	expected
1	4	28	20
2	5	17	25
combined	9	45	45

unadjusted variance   16.67
adjustment for ties   0.00
                        _____
adjusted variance   16.67

Ho: score (sample == 1) = score (sample == 2)
                z =   1.960
        Prob > |z| =   0.0500

Notice that Stata agrees with our results insofar as the sum of the ranks for Sample 1 is 28.

However, rather than use the U distribution to determine whether the result is statistically significant, Stata approximates the U distribution by the normal distribution even when N_1 and N_2 are small, as in this example. The mean and standard deviation of the normal distribution that approximates the U distribution are given by Equation 17.8,

$$\text{Mean} = \mu_U = \frac{(N_1)(N_2)}{2} \tag{17.8}$$

$$\text{Standard Deviation} = \sigma_U = \sqrt{\frac{(N_1)(N_2)(N_1 + N_2 + 1)}{12}}$$

and the observed z-value is calculated using Equation 17.9.

$$z = \frac{U - \mu_U}{\sigma_U} \tag{17.9}$$

Based on these equations, we find that $\mu_U = 10$, $\sigma_U2 = 16.67$, $\sigma_U = 4.08$, and $z = (2 - 10)/4.08 = 8/4.08 = 1.96$, which, in this case, is just statistically significant at $\alpha=.05$. Because this result is based only on an approximation of the U distribution by the normal distribution, it is likely to be less accurate than a result based directly on the U distribution. Accordingly, in this case, where the two results lead to two different conclusions, one nonstatistically significant and the other statistically significant, we should place more confidence in the one that is nonstatistically significant because it is based on the U distribution, not on an approximation to it.

EXAMPLE 17.7. In a small study to determine whether boys have a more positive attitude than girls toward organized baseball at a co-ed summer camp, eight boys and five girls of the same age were randomly selected from a particular summer camp and given an attitude questionnaire on this topic. The following data were obtained. Higher scores indicate more positive attitudes.

Boys	25	32	16	11	29	31	22	15
Girls	9	10	12	26	24			

Use a Mann-Whitney U test with the stated hypothesis at $\alpha = .05$.

Solution. The null hypothesis is that the distributions of boys' attitude scores and girls' attitude scores are identical in the population. Because the alternative hypothesis is directional, we use a one-tailed test. Arbitrarily, we let the boys be Sample 1 and the girls Sample 2. Because the value of U measures the degree to which the scores in Sample 1 are smaller than the scores in Sample 2 (that is, higher values of U suggest that boys score lower than girls, in this case), the one-tailed test for this example is left-tailed.

A combined ranking for all 13 participants is:

Score	9	10	11	12	15	16	22	24	25	26	29	31	32
Rank	1	2	3	4	5	6	7	8	9	10	11	12	13

$R_1 = 3+5+6+7+9+11+12+13 = 66$. Substituting the relevant values into Equation 17.3 we obtain:

$$U = (8)(5) + \frac{(8)(9)}{2} - 66 = 40 + 36 - 66 = 10$$

Because the range of possible values of U in this example is from 0 to $(8)(5) = 40$, with midpoint 20, the obtained U value of 10 indicates that, in general, for these data boys' attitude scores are higher than girls' attitude scores. We consult Table X in Appendix C online, www.cambridge.org/Stats-Stata, to determine whether the obtained U value is statistically significant at the chosen level of alpha.

From column $N_1 = 8$ and $N_2 = 5$, we find the left critical value for $\alpha = .05$ to be 6 and the rejection region is $U \le 6$. Hence, our obtained value of U, $U = 10$, does not fall in the rejection region and our conclusion is not to reject the null hypothesis that the boys' and girls' attitude distributions in the population are identical.

Using Stata, we may obtain the following one-tailed p-value = .1432/2 = .0716) as shown below.

Two–sample Wilcoxon rank–sum (Mann–Whitney) test

sample	obs	rank sum	expected
1	8	66	56
2	5	25	35
combined	13	91	91

unadjusted variance	46.67
adjustment for ties	−0.00
adjusted variance	46.67

Ho: score (sample==1) = score (sample == 2)

z = 1.464

Prob > |z| = 0.1432

☞ **Remark.** Had we arbitrarily designated the boys as Sample 2 and the girls as Sample 1, the test would be right-tailed because a larger value of U in this case would suggest, as hypothesized, that girls score lower than boys. In this case, $R_1 = 25$ and U, from Equation 17.6, equals

$$U = (5)(8) + \frac{(5)(6)}{2} - 25 = 40 + 15 - 25 = 30$$

The right tail critical value from Table 7 in Appendix C online for $N_1 = 5$ and $N_2 = 8$ is $U = 34$ and the rejection region is therefore, $U \geq 34$. Notice that the sum of the left and right tail critical U values equals the product of N_1 and N_2, or 5 and 8, or 40, in this case. Because $U = 30$ is not in the rejection region, we reach the same conclusion as before.

☞ **Remark.** We should note that by reassigning boys to Sample 2 and girls to Sample 1, our conclusion based on Stata also will remain unchanged.

THE KRUSKAL-WALLIS ANALYSIS OF VARIANCE

The Kruskal-Wallis Analysis of Variance may be considered an extension of the Mann-Whitney U test to three or more populations using unrelated samples. It tests the null hypothesis that all population distributions are identical, against the nondirectional alternative that at least one of the population distributions is different from at least one of the others.

As with the Mann-Whitney U test, the Kruskal-Wallis test is carried out using the ranks of the scores when they are all combined into a single group. To determine whether the differences among the samples are due to more than chance factors, we compare the obtained measure of separation, in this case referred to as H, against an appropriate sampling distribution. As long as the size of each group is at least five, the chi-square distribution with $K - 1$ degrees of freedom is a good approximation to the appropriate sampling distribution, where K is the number of groups or samples. Because H is a measure of separation, H is compared to a right-tail rejection region. Like the Mann-Whitney, H relies on the sum of the ranks in each of the K groups. H is given by Equation 17.10.

$$H = \frac{12}{N(N+1)} \sum_{j=1}^{K} \frac{R_j^2}{N_j} - 3(N+1) \tag{17.10}$$

where

  K = number of groups
  N_j = size of Sample j
  N = total number of scores from all samples
  R_j = sum of ranks for the scores in Sample j

For simplicity, we shall assume that all scores are unique and that there are no ties. For situations in which there are tie scores, the interested reader is referred to a more advanced book on this topic (e.g., Siegel & Castellan, 1988). We illustrate with an example.

• •

EXAMPLE 17.8. In a study to determine whether there is a relationship between age and time spent on the internet, eight college students, ten adults between the ages of 35 and 45, and seven adults between the ages of 60 and 70 were randomly selected from their respective populations of known internet users. Participants were asked to indicate on a survey the average number of minutes they spent each day on the internet. The data are given below. Use the Kruskal-Wallis test to test the null hypothesis that the three population distributions of time are identical. Set $\alpha = .05$.

College students	Adults aged 35 to 45	Adults aged 60 to 70
48	28	15
42	33	19
40	26	20
46	34	25
35	29	18
39	36	27
32	31	16
41	22	
	21	
	17	

Solution. Grouping all 25 times together and rank-ordering them, we obtain:

15 16 17 18 19 20 21 22 25 26 27 28 29 31 32 33 34 35 36 39 40 41 42 46 48	Times
1 2 3 4 5 6 7 8 9 10 11 12 13 14 15 16 17 18 19 20 21 22 23 24 25	Ranking
3 3 2 3 3 3 2 2 3 2 3 2 2 2 1 2 2 1 2 1 1 1 1 1 1	Group

$N_1 = 8$ $N_2 = 10$ $N_3 = 7$ $N = 25$

$R_1 = 168$ $R_2 = 119$ $R_3 = 38$ $K = 3$

Substituting these values into Equation 17.10, we obtain

$$H = \frac{12}{(25)(26)}\left[\frac{168^2}{8} + \frac{119^2}{10} + \frac{38^2}{7}\right] - 3(26) = (0.01846)(5150.3857) = 95.08 - 78 = 17.08$$

From Table 5 in Appendix C online, www.cambridge.org/Stats-Stata, we note that a chi-square value closest, but less than, 17.08 with $K - 1 = 2$ degrees of freedom is 13.82. This value marks off area 0.001 to its right, suggesting that the probability of observing 13.82 or higher is less than 0.001. Since 0.001 is less than 0.05, our conclusion is to reject the null hypothesis in favor of the alternative that the populations from which these samples were drawn do not have identical distributions in terms of average daily time spent on the internet.

MORE Stata: To carry out the Kruskal-Wallis test

Once the data are entered as two variables; group (a trichotomous variable that distinguishes the three groups from one another) and time (see the Do-file for Chapter 17 for data entry instructions), we use the following syntax to execute the test:

kwallis time, by(group)

We obtain the following results, which corroborate those obtained above.

```
Kruskal-Wallis equality-of-populations rank test

┌─────────┬───────┬──────────────┐
│  group  │  Obs  │   Rank Sum   │
├─────────┼───────┼──────────────┤
│    1    │   8   │   168.00     │
│    2    │  10   │   119.00     │
│    3    │   7   │    38.00     │
└─────────┴───────┴──────────────┘

chi-squared = 17.084 with 2 d.f.
probability = 0.0002

chi-squared with ties = 17.084 with 2 d.f.
probability = 0.0002
```

SUMMARY OF STATA COMMANDS IN CHAPTER 17

For a complete listing of all Stata commands associated with this chapter, you may access the Do-file for Chapter 17 located on the text website.

Create	Command Lines
Estimate the p-value associated with $\chi_3^2 = 23.18$ (Example 17.1)	**display chi2tail(3, 23.19)**
Perform the chi square goodness of fit test for tabulated or summary data (Assuming csgof is installed)	**expand freq** **csgof car_type, expperc(18 10 35 37)**
Perform the chi square goodness of fit test for raw data (Example 17.2) (Assuming csgof is installed)	**csgof region**
Perform the chi square goodness of fit test for tabulated or summary data	**tabulate gender ppa [fweight = freq], chi2**
Perform the chi square test of independence for raw data (Example 17.3)	**tabulate gender nursery, chi2**
Have the chi-square test of independence results include the expected values and to obtain the correlation between the two variables (Example 17.3)	**tabulate gender nursery, chi2 expected** **pwcorr nursery gender, obs star(5)**
Perform the Fisher's Exact Test in addition to the chi-square test of independence (Example 17.3a)	**tabulate gender nursery [fweight = freq], chi2 exact**
Carry out the sign test (Example 17.5)	**signtest recordwt = actualwt**
To carry out the Mann-Whitney U test (Example 17.6)	**ranksum score, by(sample)**
To carry out the Kruskal-Wallis test (example 17.8)	**kwallis time, by(group)**

EXERCISES

*Create a Do-file for each exercise that requires the use of Stata. Run the commands from the Do-file by highlighting them and hitting **Control+d**. Save each Do-file using a name associated with the Exercise for which it was created. It is recommended that you review the Do-file for Chapter 17 located on the textbook's website before completing these exercises. To facilitate doing each exercise, it may be helpful to copy and paste relevant commands from the Do-file for Chapter 17 into your own Do-file and modify them as needed.*

Exercises 17.1–17.5 relate to the Learndis data set. For inferential purposes, we consider the children in the data set to be a random sample of all children attending public school in the urban area who have been diagnosed with learning disabilities. Use $\alpha = .05$ for all significance tests.

17.1. There are two different types of placement for these students diagnosed with learning disabilities: resource room for part of the day and full-time self-contained classroom (placemen). Perform a chi-square goodness of fit test to determine whether children attending public school in this urban area who have been diagnosed with learning disabilities are equally likely to be in either type of placement or whether one of the two placements is statistically significantly more prevalent than the other. Explain the results.

17.2. Are there gender differences in the type of placement assigned to public school children in this urban area who have been diagnosed with learning disabilities? Perform a chi-square test of independence to make the determination.

    a) According to the chi-square test of independence, are there gender differences in the type of placement assigned to public school children in this urban area who have been diagnosed with learning disabilities?

    b) What type of graph is appropriate to display these data?

    c) What other statistical significance test could we have performed to determine whether there gender differences in the type of placement assigned to public school children in this urban area who have been diagnosed with learning disabilities?

17.3. In Exercise 11.22, we used a paired samples *t*-test to determine whether elementary school children in the city diagnosed with learning disabilities perform better in math comprehension or in reading comprehension. According to the descriptive statistics, the skewness ratio for math comprehension is 2.25 and the skewness ratio for reading comprehension is –3.77, indicating that both variables are statistically significantly skewed. Because the sample size was adequate, $N = 74$, we determined that the paired samples *t*-test was robust to the violation of the normality assumption. In this exercise, use an alternative approach, the sign test to answer the same question.

    a) According to the results of the sign test, do elementary school children in the city diagnosed with learning disabilities perform better in math comprehension or in reading comprehension? Explain.

    b) Do these results corroborate those obtained in Exercise 11.22?

17.4. Is there a statistically significant difference in reading comprehension depending on type of placement?

    a) Why might someone question the appropriateness of the independent samples *t*-test, in this case?

b) Conduct the Mann-Whitney *U*-test. Is there a statistically significant difference in reading achievement depending on type of placement? What is the nature of the difference?

17.5. Are there statistically significant differences in reading comprehension by grade? Calculate relevant descriptive statistics and conduct the Kruskal-Wallis analysis of variance. Use your results to answer the following questions.

a) Why might one question the use of a one-way ANOVA to determine whether there is a statistically significant difference in reading achievement by grade?

b) Using the results of the Kruskal-Wallis test, is there a statistically significant difference in reading achievement by grade? Explain.

17.6. Data were gathered on a random sample of 200 people visiting the Museum of Natural History in New York City in order to understand the background of visitors to the museum. The variable descriptions of the various measures taken are contained in the following table.

Variable Name	What the Variable Measures	How the Variable Measures It
EDLEVEL	Highest educational level achieved	1 = Less than H.S.
		2 = H.S Graduate
		3 = B.A. or more
MUSEUMS	Annual charitable contributions to museums	1 = $0
		2 = $0.01–$100
		3 = $100.01–$500
		4 > $500
WILDLIFE	Annual charitable contributions to wildlife conservation	1 = $0
		2 = $0.01–$100
		3 = $100.01–$500
		4 > $500
LOCATION		1 = Resident of NYC
		2 = Tourist
MEMBER	Whether the person is a member of the Museum of Natural History	0 = No
		1 = Yes

For each of the following questions based on this data set, select an appropriate statistical procedure from the list below to answer each of the following questions based on this data set. A nonparametric analysis is to be used. In some instances, more than one procedure many be appropriate. Also, procedures may be selected more than once. Note that you do not have to perform any analyses to complete this exercise, just specify the analyses that should be performed.

Procedures:
(1) Chi-square goodness-of-fit test
(2) Chi-square test of independence
(3) Sign test

(4) Mann-Whitney U-test

(5) Kruskal-Wallis analysis of variance

Questions:
  a) Which is typically higher, charitable contributions to museums, or charitable contributions to wildlife preservation?
  b) Is there a difference in charitable contributions to museums according to the highest educational level achieved?
  c) Is the distribution of charitable contributions to museums between tourists and residents different from the distribution of charitable contributions to wildlife preservation between tourists and residents?
  d) Is the amount of charitable contributions to museums higher among tourists or among residents?
  e) Are visitors to the museum evenly divided between tourists and residents?
  f) Is there a difference in the highest educational level attained between tourists and residents?
  g) Is there a relationship between highest educational level attained and membership in the museum?

Exercises 17.7–17.11 relate to the NELS data set. For inferential purposes, we consider the students in the data set to be a random sample of the population of all college-bound students who have always been at grade level. Use $\alpha = .05$ for all significance tests.

17.7. Using crosstabulation introduced in Chapter 5, we may determine descriptively that there is a relationship between region and urban.
  a) What nonparametric test is appropriate to determine whether this relationship is statistically significant?
  b) Use this test to determine whether this relationship is statistically significant.

17.8. Is there a statistically significant difference in the frequency of cut classes by seniors (cuts12) and the frequency of missed school by seniors (absent12)? If so, which occurs more often?
  a) What nonparametric test is appropriate to determine whether this difference is statistically significant?
  b) Why is the test specified in your answer to part (a) more appropriate than a paired-samples t-test, in this case?
  c) Is the nonparametric test statistically significant? What is the nature of the difference?

17.9. Is there a statistically significant difference in perceived teacher interest (tcherint) between those students taking a challenging curriculum and those taking a less challenging curriculum (advmath8)?
  a) What two nonparametric tests are appropriate to determine whether this difference is statistically significant?
  b) Are these tests statistically significant? What is the nature of the difference in perceived teacher interest?

17.10. In the *Marijuan* data set, we see that in 1992, 32.6 percent of high school seniors in the United States reported smoking marijuana at least once. The same information was measured for the college-bound students in the *NELS* data set, when they were seniors in

604   STATISTICS USING STATA: AN INTEGRATIVE APPROACH

1992. For those students, 92 reported that they had tried marijuana, while 408 reported that they never had. Do college-bound students report the same incidence of marijuana use as that of the population of all high school seniors?

    a) What nonparametric test is appropriate to determine whether college-bound students report the same incidence of marijuana use as that of the population of all high school seniors?

    b) Conduct the test specified in your answer to part (a). Use $\alpha = .05$.

17.11. Does time spent on homework outside school by high school seniors (hwkout12) vary by urbanicity (urban)?

    a) Explain why a nonparametric test is appropriate, in this case.

    b) Which nonparametric test would you use?

    c) Conduct the test specified in your answer to part (b). Use $\alpha = .05$.

17.12. According to an article in the *New York Times* on June 1, 2000, the New York State health commissioner suspended the licenses of two doctors who were accused of falsifying mammogram test results for poor women. These radiologists, who screened approximately 10,000 women in the Bronx for breast cancer over the course of five years, were accused of providing faulty tests and billing for tests that they did not perform. The problem was detected by looking at the rate at which the two doctors reported abnormal mammogram results and comparing it to the average rate for all doctors in New York State. Of the 10,000 women evaluated by these doctors, only 13 screened positive for breast cancer, while the rate for the rest of the state is 52 positive screens per 10,000 patients. Conduct a hypothesis test at $\alpha = .05$ to determine whether the difference in rates is statistically significant.

17.13. According to data from the Department of Health and Human Services, there is an association between estrogen use and cardiovascular death rates. To corroborate these results, 1,500 people were randomly selected from the population of female Americans over 50; 750 took estrogen supplements and 750 did not. The results are summarized in the following table. Use them to conduct a nonparametric hypothesis test of the association between estrogen use and cardiovascular death rates. Use $\alpha = .05$.

		Status Alive	Dead
Takes estrogen supplements?	Yes	746	4
	No	740	10

17.14. A researcher is studying whether the education level of first-born sons in a small rural community in the Midwest is higher than the education level of their fathers. Accordingly, the researcher randomly selects 15 adult males from this community who are first-born sons and asks them to indicate on a questionnaire the highest level of education attained by themselves and by their fathers. To measure the variable, highest level of education attained, the following scale is used:

    1 = graduated from elementary school
    2 = graduated from middle school
    3 = graduated from high school
    4 = graduated from two-year college
    5 = graduated from four-year college
    6 = at least some graduate training

The data are as follows:

Highest Level of Education Attained

Sons	3	3	3	5	6	4	3	5	2	4	4	1	4	3	6
Fathers	1	2	1	3	3	2	3	4	3	3	2	1	2	2	4

Run an appropriate nonparametric analysis on these data at $\alpha = .05$. Interpret your results within the context of the problem.

17.15. A researcher is interested in determining the degree of overall competitiveness between high-school-aged siblings from two-child families. In particular, she is interested in determining whether siblings of the same sex are more competitive overall than siblings of the opposite sex. Accordingly, she selects at random 10 high-school aged students with younger siblings of the same sex in high school and 10 high-school-aged students with younger siblings of the opposite sex in high school. Each student selected is asked to respond to a questionnaire in which degree of perceived competitiveness with younger siblings is sought in each of four areas (academic, athletic, personal appearance, and social). Each area is to be rated on a scale from 0 (no competition) to 10 (extreme competition). A total score of perceived overall competitiveness is obtained by summing the individual responses in each of the four areas. Assume that this competitiveness score is measured on an ordinal scale.

Same sex siblings	15	23	38	35	29	22	31	26	39	36
Opposite sex siblings	24	25	16	10	13	18	9	37	27	33

Perform an appropriate nonparametric analysis at $\alpha = .05$. Interpret your results within the context of the problem.

17.16. In a study to interpret the effects of music on mood, 12 adults are asked to spend 30 minutes in a room into which one of three different types of music is piped (slow classical, soft rock, or hard rock). At the end of the 30 minutes, participants are asked to complete a questionnaire designed to measure mood. Low scores on this test suggest a relaxed mood, whereas high scores suggest a relatively tense mood. Assume that these mood scores are measured at the ordinal level. The 12 participants are randomly assigned to one of the three music conditions. The data are as follows:

Slow Classical	1	3	4	2
Soft Rock	5	8	6	7
Hard Rock	9	12	11	10

Perform an appropriate nonparametric analysis at $\alpha = .05$ to determine whether mood differed depending on music type. Interpret your results within the context of the problem.

Data Set Descriptions

Anscombe

This data set is used to illustrate the importance of statistical display as an adjunct to summary statistics. Anscombe (1973) fabricated four different bivariate data sets such that, for all data sets, the respective X and Y means, X and Y standard deviations, and correlations, slopes, intercepts, and standard errors of estimate are equal. Accordingly, without a visual representation of these four panels, one might assume that the data values for all four data sets are the same. Scatterplots illustrate, however, the extent to which these data sets are different from one another.

Basketball

The data set consists of the heights and weights of the 24 scoring leaders, 12 each from the U.S. Women's and Men's National Basketball Association, for the 2014–2015 season. These data are taken from the ESPN website at espn.go.com.

Variable Name	Variable Label	Additional Description
PLAYER	Player name	0 = Male; 1 = Female
GENDER		
HEIGHTIN	Height in inches	
WEIGHTLB	Weight in pounds	
GAMES	Games played	
MINUTESGAME	Minutes per game	
POINTS	Average total points scored per game	

Blood

The data were collected to determine whether an increase in calcium intake reduces blood pressure among African-American adult males. The data are based on a sample of 21 African-American adult males selected randomly from the population of African-American adult males. These data come from the Data and Story Library (DASL) website. Ten of the 21 men were randomly assigned to a treatment condition that required them to take a calcium supplement for 12 weeks. The remaining 11 men received a placebo for the 12 weeks. At both the beginning and the end of this time period, systolic blood pressure readings of all men were recorded.

Variable Name	Variable Label	Additional Description
ID		
SYSTOLC1	Initial blood pressure	
SYSTOLC2	Final blood pressure	
TREATMEN	Treatment	0 = Placebo; 1 = Calcium

Brainsz

The data set and description are taken from the DASL (Data Sets and Story Library) website. The data are based on a study by Willerman et al. (1991) of the relationships between brain size, gender, and intelligence. The research participants consisted of 40 right-handed introductory psychology students with no history of alcoholism, unconsciousness, brain damage, epilepsy, or heart disease who were selected from a larger pool of introductory psychology students with total Scholastic Aptitude Test Scores higher than 1350 or lower than 940. The students in the study took four subtests (Vocabulary, Similarities, Block Design, and Picture Completion) of the Wechsler (1981) Adult Intelligence Scale-Revised. Among the students with Wechsler full-scale IQ's less than 103, 10 males and 10 females were randomly selected. Similarly, among the students with Wechsler full-scale IQ's greater than 130, 10 males and 10 females were randomly selected, yielding a randomized blocks design. MRI Scans were performed at the same facility for all 40 research participants to measure brain size. The scans consisted for 18 horizontal MRI images. The computer counted all pixels with non-zero gray scale in each of the 18 images and the total count served as an index for brain size.

Variable Name	Variable Label	Additional Description
ID		
GENDER		0 = Male; 1 = Female
FSIQ	Full Scale IQ Score based on WAIS-R	
VIQ	Verbal IQ Score	
PIQ	Performance IQ Score	
MRI		
IQDI		0 = Lower IQ; 1 = Higher IQ

Currency

This data set contains, for the smaller bill denominations, the value of the bill and the total value in circulation. The source for these data is *The World Almanac and Book of Facts 2014*.

Variable Name	Variable Label
BILLVALU	Denomination
CIRC	Total currency in circulation

Exercise, Food Intake, and Weight Loss

A fabricated data set constructed by Darlington (1990) to demonstrate the importance of including all relevant variables in an analysis. This data set contains information about exercise, food intake, and weight loss for a fictional set of dieters.

Variable Name	Variable Label	Additional Description
FOOD	Food intake	**The average daily number of calories consumed in one particular week that is more than a baseline of 1,000 calories as measured in increments of 100 calories**
WEIGHTLOSS	Weight loss	The number of pounds lost in that week
EXERCISE	Exercise	The average daily number of hours exercised in that week

Framingham

The Framingham Heart Study is a long term prospective study of the etiology of cardiovascular disease among a population of noninstitutionalized people in the community of Framingham, Massachusetts. The Framingham Heart Study was a landmark study in epidemiology in that it was the first prospective study of cardiovascular disease and identified the concept of risk factors and their joint effects. The study began in 1956 and 5,209 subjects were initially enrolled in the study. In our data set, we included variables from the first examination in 1956 and the third examination, in 1968. Clinic examination data has included cardiovascular disease risk factors and markers of disease such as blood pressure, blood chemistry, lung function, smoking history, health behaviors, ECG tracings, Echocardiography, and medication use. Through regular surveillance of area hospitals, participant contact, and death certificates, the Framingham Heart Study reviews and adjudicates events for the occurrence of any of the following types of coronary heart disease (CHD): Angina Pectoris, Myocardial Infarction, Heart Failure, and Cerebrovascular disease.

The associated dataset is a subset of the data collected as part of the Framingham study and includes laboratory, clinic, questionnaire, and adjudicated event data on 400 participants. These participants for the data set have been chosen so that among all male participants, 100 smokers and 100 non-smokers were selected at random. A similar procedure resulted in 100 female smokers and 100 female nonsmokers. This procedure resulted in an over-sampling of smokers. The data for each participant is on one row. People who had any type of CHD in the initial examination period are not included in the dataset.

Variable Name	Variable Label	Additional Description
ID		
SEX	Sex	1 = Men; 2 = Women
TOTCHOL1	Serum Cholesterol mg/dL (1)	
AGE1	Age (years) at examination (1)	
SYSBP1	Systolic BP mmHg (1)	

Variable Name	Variable Label	Additional Description
DIABP1	Diastolic BP mmHg (1)	
CURSMOKE1	Current Cig Smoker Y/N (1)	0 = No; 1 = Yes
CIGPDAY1	Cigarettes per day (1)	
BMI1	Body Mass Index (kg/(M*M) (1)	
DIABETES1	Diabetic Y/N (1)	0 = Not a diabetic; 1 = Diabetic
BPMEDS1	Anti-hypertensive meds Y/N (1)	0 = Not currently used; 1 = Currently used
HEARTRTE1	Ventricular Rate (beats/min) (1)	
GLUCOSE1	Casual Glucose mg/dL (1)	
PREVCHD1	Prevalent CHD (MI,AP,CI) (1)	0 = Free of CHD; 1 = Prevalence of CHD
TIME1	Days since Index Exam (1)	
TIMECHD1	Days Baseline-Inc Any CHD (1)	
TOTCHOL3	Serum Cholesterol mg/dL (3)	
AGE3	Age (years) at examination (3)	
SYSBP3	Systolic BP mmHg (3)	
DIABP3	Diastolic BP mmHg (3)	
CURSMOKE3	Current Cig Smoker Y/N (3)	0 = No; 1 = Yes
CIGPDAY3	Cigarettes per day (3)	
BMI3	Body Mass Index (kg/(M*M) (3)	
DIABETES3	Diabetic Y/N (3)	0 = Not a diabetic; 1 = Diabetic
BPMEDS3	Antihypertensive meds Y/N (3)	0 = Not currently used; 1 = Currently used
HEARTRTE3	Ventricular Rate (beats/min) (3)	
GLUCOSE3	Casual Glucose mg/dL (3)	
PREVCHD3	Prevalent CHD (MI,AP,CI) (3)	0 = Free of CHD; 1 = Prevalence of CHD
TIME3	Days since Index Exam (3)	
HDLC3	HDL Cholesterol mg/dL (3)	
LDLC3	LDL Cholesterol mg/dL (3)	
TIMECHD3	Days Baseline-Inc Any CHD (3)	
ANYCHD4	Incident Hosp MI, AP, CI, Fatal CHD by the end of the study	0 = CHD event did not occur; 1 = CHD even did occur

Hamburg

This data set contains the fat grams and calories associated with the different types of hamburger sold by McDonald's. The data are from McDonald's Nutrition Information Center.

Variable Name	Variable Label	Additional Description
CALORIES		
CHEESE	Cheese Added?	0 = No; 1 = Yes
FAT	Grams of fat	
NAME	Type of burger	

Ice Cream

This data set contains fabricated data for the temperature, relative humidity and ice cream sales for 30 days randomly selected between May 15th and September 6th.

Variable Name	Variable Label	Additional Description
ID		
BARSOLD	Number of ice cream bars sold	
TEMP	Temperature in degrees Fahrenheit	
RELHUMID	Relative humidity	

Impeach

On February 12, 1999, for only the second time in the nation's history, the U.S. Senate voted on whether to remove a president, based on impeachment articles passed by the U.S. House. Professor Alan Reifman of Texas Tech University created the data set consisting of descriptions of each senator that can be used to understand some of the reasons that the senators voted the way they did. The data are taken from the Journal of Statistics Education [online].

Variable Name	Variable Label	Additional Description
NAME	**Senator's name**	
STATE	State the senator represents	
REGION		1 = Northeast; 2 = Midwest; 3 = South; 4 = West
VOTE1	Vote on perjury	0 = Not guilty; 1 = Guilty
VOTE2	Vote on obstruction of justice	0 = Not guilty; 1 = Guilty
GUILTY	Number of guilty votes	0 = Democrat; 1 = Republican
PARTY		
CONSERVA	Conservatism score	The senator's degree of ideological conservatism is based on 1997 voting records as judged by the American Conservative Union, where the scores ranged from 0 to 100 and 100 is most conservative

Variable Name	Variable Label	Additional Description
SUPPORTC	State voter support for Clinton	The percent of the vote Clinton received in the 1996 Presidential election in the senator's state
REELECT	Year the senator's seat is up for reelection	2000, 2002, or 2004
NEWBIE	First-term senator?	0 = No; 1 = Yes

Learndis

What is the profile of students classified as learning disabled? The questions on this exam relate to a subset of data from a study by Susan Tomasi and Sharon L. Weinberg (1999). According to Public Law 94.142, enacted in 1976, a team may determine that a child has a learning disability (LD) if a severe discrepancy exists between a child's actual achievement in, for example, math or reading, and his or her intellectual ability. The data set consists of six variables, described below, on 105 elementary school children from an urban area who were classified as LD and who, as a result, had been receiving special education services for at least three years. Of the 105 children, 42 are female and 63 are male. There are two main types of placements for these students: part-time resource room placements in which the students get additional instruction to supplement regular classroom instruction and self-contained classroom placements in which students are segregated full time. In this data set 66 students are in resource room placements while 39 are in self-contained classroom placements. For inferential purposes, we consider the children in the data set to be a random sample of all children attending public elementary school in a certain city who have been diagnosed with learning disabilities. Many students in the data set have missing values for either math or reading comprehension, or both. Such omissions can lead to problems when generalizing results. There are statistical remedies for missing data that are beyond the scope of this text. In this case, we will assume that there is no pattern to the missing values, so that our sample is representative of the population.

Variable Name	Variable Label	Additional Description
GENDER	**Gender**	**0 = Male; 1 = Female**
GRADE	Grade level	1, 2, 3, 4, or 5
IQ	Intellectual ability	Higher scores ↔ greater IQ Scores could range from 0 to 200
MATHCOMP	Math comprehension	Higher scores ↔ greater math comprehension Scores could range from 0 to 200
PLACEMEN	Type of placement	0 = Part-time in resource room; 1 = Full-time in self-contained classroom
READCOMP		Higher scores ↔ greater reading comprehension Scores could range from 0 to 200

Mandex

This fictional data set contains the treatment group number and the manual dexterity scores for 30 individuals selected by the director of a drug rehabilitation center. There are three treatments and the individuals are randomly assigned ten to a treatment. After five weeks of treatment, a manual dexterity test is administered for which a higher score indicates greater manual dexterity.

Variable Name	Variable Label
SCORE	
TREATMEN	Manual Dexterity Score

Marijuana

The data set contains the year and percentage of twelfth graders who have ever used marijuana for several recent years. The source for these data is *The World Almanac and Book of Facts 2014*.

Variable Name	Variable Label
YEAR	
MARIJ	Percentage of twelfth graders who reported that they have ever used marijuana

Nels

In response to pressure from federal and state agencies to monitor school effectiveness in the United States, the National Center of Education Statistics (NCES) of the U.S. Department of Education conducted a survey in the spring of 1988. The participants consisted of a nationally representative sample of approximately 25,000 eighth graders to measure achievement outcomes in four core subject areas (English, history, mathematics, and science), in addition to personal, familial, social, institutional, and cultural factors that might relate to these outcomes. Details on the design and initial analysis of this survey may be referenced in Horn, Hafner, and Owings (1992). A follow-up of these students was conducted during tenth grade in the spring of 1990; a second follow-up was conducted during the twelfth grade in the spring of 1992; and, finally, a third follow-up was conducted in the spring of 1994.

For this book, we have selected a subsample of 500 cases and 50 variables. The cases were sampled randomly from the approximately 5,000 students who responded to all four administrations of the survey, who were always at grade level (neither repeated nor skipped a grade) and who pursued some form of postsecondary education. The particular variables were selected to explore the relationships between student and home background variables, self-concept, educational and income aspirations, academic motivation, risk-taking behavior, and academic achievement.

Variable Name	Variable Label	Additional Description
ABSENT12	Number of Times Missed School	**0 = Never; 1 = 1–2 Times; 2 = 3–6 Times; 3 = 7–9 Times; 4 = 10–15 Times; 5 = Over 15 Times**

Variable Name	Variable Label	Additional Description
ACHMAT08	Math Achievement in Eighth Grade	Similar to ACHRDG08
ACHMAT10	Math Achievement in Tenth Grade	Similar to ACHRDG08
ACHMAT12	Math Achievement in Twelfth Grade	Similar to ACHRDG08
ACHRDG08	Reading Achievement in Eighth Grade	Gives a score for the student's performance in eighth grade on a standardized test of reading achievement. Actual values range from 36.61 to 77.2, from low to high achievement. 99.98 = Missing; 99.99 = Missing
ACHRDG10	Reading Achievement in Tenth Grade	Similar to ACHRDG08
ACHRDG12	Reading Achievement in Twelfth Grade	Similar to ACHRDG08
ACHSCI08	Science Achievement in Eighth Grade	Similar to ACHRDG08
ACHSCI10	Science Achievement in Tenth Grade	Similar to ACHRDG08
ACHSCI12	Science Achievement in Twelfth Grade	Similar to ACHRDG08
ACHSLS08	Social Studies Achievement in Eighth Grade	Similar to ACHRDG08
ACHSLS10	Social Studies Achievement in Tenth Grade	Similar to ACHRDG08
ACHSLS12	Social Studies Achievement in Twelfth Grade	Similar to ACHRDG08
ADVMATH8	Advanced Math Taken in Eighth Grade	**0 = No; 1 = Yes; 8 = Missing**
ALCBINGE	Binged on Alcohol Ever?	**0 = Never; 1 = Yes**
ALGEBRA8	Algebra Taken in Eighth Grade?	**0 = No; 1 = Yes**
APOFFER	Number of Advanced Placement Courses Offered by School	98 = Missing
APPROG	Advanced Placement Program Taken?	**0 = No; 1 = Yes; 6 = Missing; 8 = Missing**
CIGARETT	Smoked Cigarettes Ever?	**0 = Never; 1 = Yes**
COMPUTER	Computer Owned by Family in Eighth Grade?	**0 = No; 1 = Yes**
CUTS12	Number of Times Skipped/ Cut Classes in Twelfth Grade	**0 = Never; 1 = 1–2 Times; 2 = 3–6 Times; 3 = 7–9 Times; 4 = 10–15 Times; 5 = Over 15 Times**

Variable Name	Variable Label	Additional Description
EDEXPECT	Highest level of education expected	1 = Less than College Degree; 2 = Bachelor's Degree; 3 = Master's Degree; 4 = Ph.D., MD, JD, etc.
EXCURR12	Time Spent Weekly on Extra-Curricular Activities in Twelfth Grade	0 = None; 1 = Less than 1 Hour; 2 = 1–4 Hours; 3 = 5–9 Hours; 4 = 10–14 Hours; 5 = 15–19 Hours; 6 = 20–24 Hours; 7 = 25 or More Hours
EXPINC30	Expected income at age 30	–6 = Missing, –9 = Missing
FAMSIZE	Family Size	98 = Missing
FINANAID	Received Financial Aid in College	0 = No; 1 = Yes; –9 = Missing; –8 = Missing; –7 = Missing; –6 = Missing
GENDER	Gender	0 = Male; 1 = Female
HOMELANG	Home Language Background	1 = Non-English Only; 2= Non-English Dominant; 3 = English Dominant; 4 = English Only
HSPROG	Type of High School Program	1= Rigorous Academic; 2 = Academic; 3 = Some Vocational; 4 = Other
HWKIN12	Time Spent on Homework Weekly in School Per Week in Twelfth Grade	0 = None; 1 = Less than 1 Hour; 2 = 1–3 Hours; 3 = 4–6 Hours; 4 = 7–9 Hours; 5 = 10–12 Hours; 6 = 13–15 Hours; 7 = 16–20 Hours; 8 = Over 20 Hours; 98 = Missing
HWKOUT12	Time Spent on Homework out of School per Week in Twelfth Grade	0 = None; 1 = Less than 1 Hour; 2 = 1–3 Hours; 3 = 4–6 Hours; 4 = 7–9 Hours; 5 = 10–12 Hours; 6 = 13–15 Hours; 7 = 16–20 Hours; 8 = Over 20 Hours; 98 = Missing
ID	Case Number	
IMPTEDUC	How Important is a Good Education?	1 = Not Important; 2 = Somewhat Important; 3 = Very Important
LATE12	Number Times Late for School in Twelfth Grade	0 = Never; 1 = 1–2 Times; 2 = 3–6 Times; 3 = 7–9 Times; 4 = 10–15 Times; 5 = Over 15 Times
MARIJUAN	Smoked Marijuana Ever?	0 = Never; 1 = Yes
NUMINST	Number postsecondary institutions attended	
NURSERY	Nursery School Attended?	0 = No; 1 = Yes; 8 = Missing

Variable Name	Variable Label	Additional Description
PARMARL8	Parents' Marital Status in Eighth Grade	**1 = Divorced; 2 = Widowed; 3 = Separated; 4= Never Married; 5 = Marriage-Like Relationship; 6 = Married; 98 = Missing**
REGION	Geographic Region of School	**1= Northeast; 2 = North Central; 3 = South; 4 = West**
SCHATTRT	School Average Daily Attendance Rate	Gives the average daily attendance rate for the secondary school the student attends. 998 = Missing
SCHTYP8	School Type in Eighth Grade	Classifies the type of school each student attended in eighth grade where 1 = Public; 2 = Private, Religious; 3 = Private, Non-Religious
SES	Socio-Economic Status	Gives a score representing the socioeconomic status (SES) of the student, a composite of father's education level, mother's education level, father's occupation, mother's education, and family income. Values range from 0 to 35, from low to high SES.
SLFCNC08	Self-Concept in Eighth Grade	Similar to SLFCNC12
SLFCNC10	Self-Concept in Tenth Grade	Similar to SLFCNC12
SLFCNC12	Self-Concept in Twelfth Grade	Gives a score for student self-concept in twelfth grade. Values range from 0 to 43. Self-concept is defined as a person's self-perceptions, or how a person feels about himself or herself. Four items comprise the self-concept scale in the NELS questionnaire: I feel good about myself; I feel I am a person of worth, the equal of other people; I am able to do things as well as most other people; and, on the whole, I am satisfied with myself. A self-concept score, based on the sum of scores on each of these items, is used to measure

Variable Name	Variable Label	Additional Description
		self-concept in the NELS study. Higher scores associate with higher self-concept and lower scores associate with lower self-concept.
TCHERINT	My Teachers are Interested in Students	Classifies student agreement with the statement "My teachers are interested in students" using the Likert scale 1 = Strongly agree; 2 = Agree; 3 = disagree; 4 = strongly disagree
UNITCALC	Units in Calculus (NAEP)	Number of years of Calculus taken in high school
UNITENGL	Units in English (NAEP)	**Number of years of English taken in high school**
UNITMATH	Units in Mathematics (NAEP)	**Number of years of Math taken in high school**
URBAN	Urbanicity	**Classifies the type of environment in which each student lives where 1 = "Urban", 2 = "Suburban", and 3 = "Rural".**
ABSENT12	Number of Times Missed School	

Skulls

Four size measurements are taken on 150 male skulls, 30 from each of 5 different time periods between 4000 B.C.E. and 150 C.E. The data include the time period and the four size measurements. These data come from the Data and Story Library (DASL) website.

Variable Name	Variable Label	Additional Description
BH	**Basibregmatic Height of Skull**	
BL	Basialveolar Length of Skull	
MB	Maximal Breadth of Skull	
NH	Nasal Height of Skull	
YEAR	Approximate Year of Skull Formation	

States

This data set includes different measures of the 50 states and Washington, DC. These data are from *The 2014 World Almanac and Book of Facts*.

Variable Name	Variable Label	Additional Description
EDUCEXPE	Expenditure per Pupil, on Average, 2011–2012	
ENROLLMT	Total Public School Enrollment 2011–2012	
PERTAK	Percentage of Eligible Students Taking the SAT 2012	
REGION	The region of the country in which the state is located	1 = Northeast; 2 = Midwest; 3 = South; 4 = West
SATCR	Average SAT Critical Reading 2013	
SATM	Average SAT Math 2013	
SATW	Average SAT Writing 2013	
STATE	Name of state	
STUTEACH	Pupils per Teacher, on Average 2011–2012	
TEACHPAY	Average Annual Salary for Public School Teachers 2011–2012	

Stepping

The data set and description are taken from the DASL (Data Sets and Story Library) website. Students at Ohio State University conducted an experiment in the fall of 1993 to explore the nature of the relationship between a person's heart rate and the frequency at which that person stepped up and down on steps of various heights. The response variable, heart rate, was measured in beats per minute. For each person, the resting heart rate was measured before a trial (RestHR) and after stepping (HR). There were two different step heights (HEIGHT): 5.75 inches (coded as 0), and 11.5 inches (coded as 1). There were three rates of stepping (FREQUENCY): 14 steps/min. (coded as 0), 21 steps/min. (coded as 1), and 28 steps/min. (coded as 2). This resulted in six possible height/frequency combinations. Each subject performed the activity for three minutes. Subjects were kept on pace by the beat of an electric metronome. One experimenter counted the subject's heart rate, in beats per minute, for 20 seconds before and after each trial. The subject always rested between trials until her or his heart rate returned to close to the beginning rate. Another experimenter kept track of the time spent stepping. Each subject was always measured and timed by the same pair of experimenters to reduce variability in the experiment.

Variable Name	Variable Label	Additional Description
ORDER	The overall performance order of the trial	
BLOCK	The subject and experimenters' block number	

Variable Name	Variable Label	Additional Description
HEIGHT	Step Height	0 = Low; 1 = High
FREQ	Rate of stepping	0 = Slow; 1 = Medium; 2 = Fast
HRINIT	The resting heart rate of the subject before a trial, in beats per minute	
HRFINAL	The final heart rate of the subject after a trial, in beats per minute	

Temp

This data set gives the average monthly temperatures (in Fahrenheit) for Springfield, MO and San Francisco, CA. These data are from Burrill and Hopensperger (1993).

Variable Name	Variable Label	Additional Description
CITY		1 = Springfield, MO; 2 = San Francisco, CA
TEMP	Average monthly temperature	

Wages

This is a subsample of 100 males and 100 females randomly selected from the 534 cases that comprised the 1985 Current Population Survey in a way that controls for highest education level attained. The sample of 200 contains 20 males and 20 females with less than a high school diploma, 20 males and 20 females with a high school diploma, 20 males and 20 females with some college training, 20 males and 20 females with a college diploma, and 20 males and 20 females with some graduate school training. The data include information about gender, highest education level attained, and hourly wage.

Variable Name	Variable Label	Additional Description
ED	Highest education level	1 = Less than a HS degree; 2 = HS degree; 3 = Some college; 4 = College degree; 5 = Graduate school
EDUC	Number of years of education	
EXPER	Number of years of work experience	
ID		
MARR	Marital status	0 = Not married; 1 = Married

Variable Name	Variable Label	Additional Description
OCCUP		1 = Management; 2 = Sales; 3 = Clerical; 4 = Service; 5 = Professional; 6 = Other
SEX		0 = Male; 1 = Female
SOUTH		0 = Does not live in South; 1 = Lives in South
WAGE	Wage (dollars per hour)	

Stata .do Files and Data Sets in Stata Format

www.cambridge.org/Stats-Stata

Statistical Tables

TABLE 1. Areas under the standard normal curve (to the right of the z-score)

[For example, the area to the right of $z = 1.96$ is found by decomposing 1.96 as 1.9 + .06 and referencing the entry in the row labeled 1.9 and the column labeled .06. This right-tailed area is .0250. To obtain the area to the left, calculate 1 − .0250. The left-tailed area equals .9750. Because the normal curve is symmetric about its mean, the area to the left of $z = -1.96$ is equal to the area to the right of $z = 1.96$.]

	0	0.01	0.02	0.03	0.04	0.05	0.06	0.07	0.08	0.09
0.0	.5000	.4960	.4920	.4880	.4840	.4801	.4761	.4721	.4681	.4641
0.1	.4602	.4562	.4522	.4483	.4443	.4404	.4364	.4325	.4286	.4247
0.2	.4207	.4168	.4129	.4090	.4052	.4013	.3974	.3936	.3897	.3859
0.3	.3821	.3783	.3745	.3707	.3669	.3632	.3594	.3557	.3520	.3483
0.4	.3446	.3409	.3372	.3336	.3300	.3264	.3228	.3192	.3156	.3121
0.5	.3085	.3050	.3015	.2981	.2946	.2912	.2877	.2843	.2810	.2776
0.6	.2743	.2709	.2676	.2643	.2611	.2578	.2546	.2514	.2483	.2451
0.7	.2420	.2389	.2358	.2327	.2296	.2266	.2236	.2206	.2177	.2148
0.8	.2119	.2090	.2061	.2033	.2005	.1977	.1949	.1922	.1894	.1867
0.9	.1841	.1814	.1788	.1762	.1736	.1711	.1685	.1660	.1635	.1611
1.0	.1587	.1562	.1539	.1515	.1492	.1469	.1446	.1423	.1401	.1379
1.1	.1357	.1335	.1314	.1292	.1271	.1251	.1230	.1210	.1190	.1170
1.2	.1151	.1131	.1112	.1093	.1075	.1056	.1038	.1020	.1003	.0985
1.3	.0968	.0951	.0934	.0918	.0901	.0885	.0869	.0853	.0838	.0823
1.4	.0808	.0793	.0778	.0764	.0749	.0735	.0721	.0708	.0694	.0681
1.5	.0668	.0655	.0643	.0630	.0618	.0606	.0594	.0582	.0571	.0559
1.6	.0548	.0537	.0526	.0516	.0505	.0495	.0485	.0475	.0465	.0455
1.7	.0446	.0436	.0427	.0418	.0409	.0401	.0392	.0384	.0375	.0367
1.8	.0359	.0351	.0344	.0336	.0329	.0322	.0314	.0307	.0301	.0294
1.9	.0287	.0281	.0274	.0268	.0262	.0256	.0250	.0244	.0239	.0233
2.0	.0228	.0222	.0217	.0212	.0207	.0202	.0197	.0192	.0188	.0183
2.1	.0179	.0174	.0170	.0166	.0162	.0158	.0154	.0150	.0146	.0143
2.2	.0139	.0136	.0132	.0129	.0125	.0122	.0119	.0116	.0113	.0110
2.3	.0107	.0104	.0102	.0099	.0096	.0094	.0091	.0089	.0087	.0084
2.4	.0082	.0080	.0078	.0075	.0073	.0071	.0069	.0068	.0066	.0064
2.5	.0062	.0060	.0059	.0057	.0055	.0054	.0052	.0051	.0049	.0048
2.6	.0047	.0045	.0044	.0043	.0041	.0040	.0039	.0038	.0037	.0036
2.7	.0035	.0034	.0033	.0032	.0031	.0030	.0029	.0028	.0027	.0026
2.8	.0026	.0025	.0024	.0023	.0023	.0022	.0021	.0021	.0020	.0019
2.9	.0019	.0018	.0018	.0017	.0016	.0016	.0015	.0015	.0014	.0014
3.0	.0013	.0013	.0013	.0012	.0012	.0011	.0011	.0011	.0010	.0010
3.1	.0010	.0009	.0009	.0009	.0008	.0008	.0008	.0008	.0007	.0007
3.2	.0007	.0007	.0006	.0006	.0006	.0006	.0006	.0005	.0005	.0005
3.3	.0005	.0005	.0005	.0004	.0004	.0004	.0004	.0004	.0004	.0003
3.4	.0003	.0003	.0003	.0003	.0003	.0003	.0003	.0003	.0003	.0002
3.5	.0002	.0002	.0002	.0002	.0002	.0002	.0002	.0002	.0002	.0002

TABLE 2. *t* distribution values for right-tail areas
[For example, the *t*-value with 22 degrees of freedom that has to its right an area of .05 is found at the intersection of the row labeled *df* = 22 and column labeled .05. The t-value is 1.717. Because the t curve is symmetric about its mean, the t-value with 22 degrees of freedom that has to its left an area of .05 is −1.717. The table also may be used to find approximate p-values corresponding to given t-values. For example, to estimate the p-value associated with a t value of 8.42 with 83 degrees of freedom, we look at the line corresponding to the *df* value that is closest to and smaller than or equal to 83. In this case, we estimate the answer using 80 degrees of freedom. On the line corresponding to 80 degrees of freedom, we find the *t*-value that is closest to, but smaller than 8.42. In this case, the value is 3.416. We conclude that $p < .0005$. If the t-value had been .5, with 83 degrees of freedom, we would see that there are no values smaller than or equal to .5 on the line and we would conclude that $p > .25$.]

df	.25	.20	.15	.10	.05	.025	.02	.01	.005	.001	.0005
1	1.000	1.376	1.963	3.078	6.314	12.706	15.894	31.821	63.656	318.289	636.578
2	0.816	1.061	1.386	1.886	2.920	4.303	4.849	6.965	9.925	22.328	31.600
3	0.765	0.978	1.250	1.638	2.353	3.182	3.482	4.541	5.841	10.214	12.924
4	0.741	0.941	1.190	1.533	2.132	2.776	2.999	3.747	4.604	7.173	8.610
5	0.727	0.920	1.156	1.476	2.015	2.571	2.757	3.365	4.032	5.894	6.869
6	0.718	0.906	1.134	1.440	1.943	2.447	2.612	3.143	3.707	5.208	5.959
7	0.711	0.896	1.119	1.415	1.895	2.365	2.517	2.998	3.499	4.785	5.408
8	0.706	0.889	1.108	1.397	1.860	2.306	2.449	2.896	3.355	4.501	5.041
9	0.703	0.883	1.100	1.383	1.833	2.262	2.398	2.821	3.250	4.297	4.781
10	0.700	0.879	1.093	1.372	1.812	2.228	2.359	2.764	3.169	4.144	4.587
11	0.697	0.876	1.088	1.363	1.796	2.201	2.328	2.718	3.106	4.025	4.437
12	0.695	0.873	1.083	1.356	1.782	2.179	2.303	2.681	3.055	3.930	4.318
13	0.694	0.870	1.079	1.350	1.771	2.160	2.282	2.650	3.012	3.852	4.221
14	0.692	0.868	1.076	1.345	1.761	2.145	2.264	2.624	2.977	3.787	4.140
15	0.691	0.866	1.074	1.341	1.753	2.131	2.249	2.602	2.947	3.733	4.073
16	0.690	0.865	1.071	1.337	1.746	2.120	2.235	2.583	2.921	3.686	4.015
17	0.689	0.863	1.069	1.333	1.740	2.110	2.224	2.567	2.898	3.646	3.965
18	0.688	0.862	1.067	1.330	1.734	2.101	2.214	2.552	2.878	3.610	3.922
19	0.688	0.861	1.066	1.328	1.729	2.093	2.205	2.539	2.861	3.579	3.883
20	0.687	0.860	1.064	1.325	1.725	2.086	2.197	2.528	2.845	3.552	3.850
21	0.686	0.859	1.063	1.323	1.721	2.080	2.189	2.518	2.831	3.527	3.819
22	0.686	0.858	1.061	1.321	1.717	2.074	2.183	2.508	2.819	3.505	3.792
23	0.685	0.858	1.060	1.319	1.714	2.069	2.177	2.500	2.807	3.485	3.768
24	0.685	0.857	1.059	1.318	1.711	2.064	2.172	2.492	2.797	3.467	3.745
25	0.684	0.856	1.058	1.316	1.708	2.060	2.167	2.485	2.787	3.450	3.725
26	0.684	0.856	1.058	1.315	1.706	2.056	2.162	2.479	2.779	3.435	3.707
27	0.684	0.855	1.057	1.314	1.703	2.052	2.158	2.473	2.771	3.421	3.689
28	0.683	0.855	1.056	1.313	1.701	2.048	2.154	2.467	2.763	3.408	3.674
29	0.683	0.854	1.055	1.311	1.699	2.045	2.150	2.462	2.756	3.396	3.660
30	0.683	0.854	1.055	1.310	1.697	2.042	2.147	2.457	2.750	3.385	3.646
35	0.682	0.852	1.052	1.306	1.690	2.030	2.133	2.438	2.724	3.340	3.591
40	0.681	0.851	1.050	1.303	1.684	2.021	2.123	2.423	2.704	3.307	3.551
50	0.679	0.849	1.047	1.299	1.676	2.009	2.109	2.403	2.678	3.261	3.496
60	0.679	0.848	1.045	1.296	1.671	2.000	2.099	2.390	2.660	3.232	3.460
70	0.678	0.847	1.044	1.294	1.667	1.994	2.093	2.381	2.648	3.211	3.435
80	0.678	0.846	1.043	1.292	1.664	1.990	2.088	2.374	2.639	3.195	3.416
90	0.677	0.846	1.042	1.291	1.662	1.987	2.084	2.368	2.632	3.183	3.402
100	0.677	0.845	1.042	1.290	1.660	1.984	2.081	2.364	2.626	3.174	3.390
500	0.675	0.842	1.038	1.283	1.648	1.965	2.059	2.334	2.586	3.107	3.310
1000	0.675	0.842	1.037	1.282	1.646	1.962	2.056	2.330	2.581	3.098	3.300
∞	0.674	0.841	1.036	1.282	1.645	1.960	2.054	2.326	2.576	3.091	3.291

TABLE 3. *F* distribution values for right-tail areas

[For example, the *F* value with numerator degrees of freedom 2 and denominator degrees of freedom 3 that has to its right an area of .05 is found at the intersection of the row with *df* FOR DENOM =3 and α = .05 and column with *df* FOR NUMERATOR = 2. The *F*-value is 9.55. The table may also be used to find approximate p-values corresponding to given *F* values. For example, to find the *p*-value associated with *F* = 8.66 with numerator degrees of freedom = 2 and denominator degrees of freedom = 3, we find all of the values associated with *df* FOR DENOM = 3 and *df* FOR NUMERATOR = 2. We find that the *F* values that are closest to *F* = 8.66 are *F* = 5.46 and *F* = 9.55. The area to the right of *F* = 5.46 is .10 and the area to the right of *F* = 9.55 is .05. The p-value, or the area to the right of *F* = 8.66 is less than .10 but larger than .05. We have the estimate .05 < *p* <.10. If however, given the same degrees of freedom, we wished to find the p-value associated with *F* = 1.56, we find that the *F* value that is closest to *F* = 1.56 is *F* = 2.28. The area to the right of *F* = 2.28 is .25. The *p*-value, or the area to the right of *Fi* = 1.56 is greater than .25. We have the estimate *p* > .25.]

		df FOR NUMERATOR							
df FOR DENOM	α	1	2	3	4	5	6	7	8
1	0.25	5.83	7.50	8.20	8.58	8.82	8.98	9.10	9.19
1	0.10	39.86	49.50	53.59	55.83	57.24	58.20	58.91	59.44
1	0.05	161.45	199.50	215.71	224.58	230.16	233.99	236.77	238.88
1	0.03	647.79	799.48	864.15	899.60	921.83	937.11	948.20	956.64
1	0.01	4.E+03	5.E+03	5.E+03	6.E+03	6.E+03	6.E+03	6.E+03	6.E+03
1	0.001	4.E+05	5.E+05	5.E+05	6.E+05	6.E+05	6.E+05	6.E+05	6.E+05
2	0.25	2.57	3.00	3.15	3.23	3.28	3.31	3.34	3.35
2	0.10	8.53	9.00	9.16	9.24	9.29	9.33	9.35	9.37
2	0.05	18.51	19.00	19.16	19.25	19.30	19.33	19.35	19.37
2	0.03	38.51	39.00	39.17	39.25	39.30	39.33	39.36	39.37
2	0.01	98.50	99.00	99.16	99.25	99.30	99.33	99.36	99.38
2	0.001	998.38	998.84	999.31	999.31	999.31	999.31	999.31	999.31
3	0.25	2.02	2.28	2.36	2.39	2.41	2.42	2.43	2.44
3	0.10	5.54	5.46	5.39	5.34	5.31	5.28	5.27	5.25
3	0.05	10.13	9.55	9.28	9.12	9.01	8.94	8.89	8.85
3	0.03	17.44	16.04	15.44	15.10	14.88	14.73	14.62	14.54
3	0.01	34.12	30.82	29.46	28.71	28.24	27.91	27.67	27.49
3	0.001	167.06	148.49	141.10	137.08	134.58	132.83	131.61	130.62

9	10	12	15	20	24	30	40	60	120	10000
9.26	9.32	9.41	9.49	9.58	9.63	9.67	9.71	9.76	9.80	9.85
59.86	60.19	60.71	61.22	61.74	62.00	62.26	62.53	62.79	63.06	63.32
240.54	241.88	243.90	245.95	248.02	249.05	250.10	251.14	252.20	253.25	254.30
963.28	968.63	976.72	984.87	993.08	997.27	1.0E+03	1.0E+03	1.0E+03	1.0E+03	1.0E+03
6.E+03	6.E+03	6.E+03	6.E+03	6.E+03	6.E+03	6.E+03	6.E+03	6.E+03	6.E+03	6.E+03
6.E+05	6.E+05	6.E+05	6.E+05	6.E+05	6.E+05	6.E+05	6.E+05	6.E+05	6.E+05	6.E+05
3.37	3.38	3.39	3.41	3.43	3.43	3.44	3.45	3.46	3.47	3.48
9.38	9.39	9.41	9.42	9.44	9.45	9.46	9.47	9.47	9.48	9.49
19.38	19.40	19.41	19.43	19.45	19.45	19.46	19.47	19.48	19.49	19.50
39.39	39.40	39.41	39.43	39.45	39.46	39.46	39.47	39.48	39.49	39.50
99.39	99.40	99.42	99.43	99.45	99.46	99.47	99.48	99.48	99.49	99.50
999.31	999.31	999.31	999.31	999.31	999.31	999.31	999.31	999.31	999.31	999.31
2.44	2.44	2.45	2.46	2.46	2.46	2.47	2.47	2.47	2.47	2.47
5.24	5.23	5.22	5.20	5.18	5.18	5.17	5.16	5.15	5.14	5.13
8.81	8.79	8.74	8.70	8.66	8.64	8.62	8.59	8.57	8.55	8.53
14.47	14.42	14.34	14.25	14.17	14.12	14.08	14.04	13.99	13.95	13.90
27.34	27.23	27.05	26.87	26.69	26.60	26.50	26.41	26.32	26.22	26.13
129.86	129.22	128.32	127.36	126.43	125.93	125.44	124.97	124.45	123.98	123.46

df FOR NUMERATOR

df FOR DENOM	α	1	2	3	4	5	6	7	8	9	10	12	15	20	24	30	40	60	120	10000
4	0.25	1.81	2.00	2.05	2.06	2.07	2.08	2.08	2.08	2.08	2.08	2.08	2.08	2.08	2.08	2.08	2.08	2.08	2.08	2.08
4	0.10	4.54	4.32	4.19	4.11	4.05	4.01	3.98	3.95	3.94	3.92	3.90	3.87	3.84	3.83	3.82	3.80	3.79	3.78	3.76
4	0.05	7.71	6.94	6.59	6.39	6.26	6.16	6.09	6.04	6.00	5.96	5.91	5.86	5.80	5.77	5.75	5.72	5.69	5.66	5.63
4	0.03	12.22	10.65	9.98	9.60	9.36	9.20	9.07	8.98	8.90	8.84	8.75	8.66	8.56	8.51	8.46	8.41	8.36	8.31	8.26
4	0.01	21.20	18.00	16.69	15.98	15.52	15.21	14.98	14.80	14.66	14.55	14.37	14.20	14.02	13.93	13.84	13.75	13.65	13.56	13.46
4	0.001	74.13	61.25	56.17	53.43	51.72	50.52	49.65	49.00	48.47	48.05	47.41	46.76	46.10	45.77	45.43	45.08	44.75	44.40	44.05
5	0.25	1.69	1.85	1.88	1.89	1.89	1.89	1.89	1.89	1.89	1.89	1.89	1.89	1.88	1.88	1.88	1.88	1.87	1.87	1.87
5	0.10	4.06	3.78	3.62	3.52	3.45	3.40	3.37	3.34	3.32	3.30	3.27	3.24	3.21	3.19	3.17	3.16	3.14	3.12	3.11
5	0.05	6.61	5.79	5.41	5.19	5.05	4.95	4.88	4.82	4.77	4.74	4.68	4.62	4.56	4.53	4.50	4.46	4.43	4.40	4.37
5	0.03	10.01	8.43	7.76	7.39	7.15	6.98	6.85	6.76	6.68	6.62	6.52	6.43	6.33	6.28	6.23	6.18	6.12	6.07	6.02
5	0.01	16.26	13.27	12.06	11.39	10.97	10.67	10.46	10.29	10.16	10.05	9.89	9.72	9.55	9.47	9.38	9.29	9.20	9.11	9.02
5	0.001	47.18	37.12	33.20	31.08	29.75	28.83	28.17	27.65	27.24	26.91	26.42	25.91	25.39	25.13	24.87	24.60	24.33	24.06	23.79
6	0.25	1.62	1.76	1.78	1.79	1.79	1.78	1.78	1.78	1.77	1.77	1.77	1.76	1.76	1.75	1.75	1.75	1.74	1.74	1.74
6	0.10	3.78	3.46	3.29	3.18	3.11	3.05	3.01	2.98	2.96	2.94	2.90	2.87	2.84	2.82	2.80	2.78	2.76	2.74	2.72
6	0.05	5.99	5.14	4.76	4.53	4.39	4.28	4.21	4.15	4.10	4.06	4.00	3.94	3.87	3.84	3.81	3.77	3.74	3.70	3.67
6	0.03	8.81	7.26	6.60	6.23	5.99	5.82	5.70	5.60	5.52	5.46	5.37	5.27	5.17	5.12	5.07	5.01	4.96	4.90	4.85
6	0.01	13.75	10.92	9.78	9.15	8.75	8.47	8.26	8.10	7.98	7.87	7.72	7.56	7.40	7.31	7.23	7.14	7.06	6.97	6.88
6	0.001	35.51	27.00	23.71	21.92	20.80	20.03	19.46	19.03	18.69	18.41	17.99	17.56	17.12	16.90	16.67	16.44	16.21	15.98	15.75
7	0.25	1.57	1.70	1.72	1.72	1.71	1.71	1.70	1.70	1.69	1.69	1.68	1.68	1.67	1.67	1.66	1.66	1.65	1.65	1.65
7	0.10	3.59	3.26	3.07	2.96	2.88	2.83	2.78	2.75	2.72	2.70	2.67	2.63	2.59	2.58	2.56	2.54	2.51	2.49	2.47
7	0.05	5.59	4.74	4.35	4.12	3.97	3.87	3.79	3.73	3.68	3.64	3.57	3.51	3.44	3.41	3.38	3.34	3.30	3.27	3.23
7	0.03	8.07	6.54	5.89	5.52	5.29	5.12	4.99	4.90	4.82	4.76	4.67	4.57	4.47	4.41	4.36	4.31	4.25	4.20	4.14
7	0.01	12.25	9.55	8.45	7.85	7.46	7.19	6.99	6.84	6.72	6.62	6.47	6.31	6.16	6.07	5.99	5.91	5.82	5.74	5.65
7	0.001	29.25	21.69	18.77	17.20	16.21	15.52	15.02	14.63	14.33	14.08	13.71	13.32	12.93	12.73	12.53	12.33	12.12	11.91	11.70

8	0.25	1.54	1.66	1.67	1.66	1.66	1.65	1.64	1.64	1.63	1.63	1.62	1.62	1.61	1.60	1.60	1.59	1.59	1.58	1.58
8	0.10	3.46	3.11	2.92	2.81	2.73	2.67	2.62	2.59	2.56	2.54	2.50	2.46	2.42	2.40	2.38	2.36	2.34	2.32	2.29
8	0.05	5.32	4.46	4.07	3.84	3.69	3.58	3.50	3.44	3.39	3.35	3.28	3.22	3.15	3.12	3.08	3.04	3.01	2.97	2.93
8	0.03	7.57	6.06	5.42	5.05	4.82	4.65	4.53	4.43	4.36	4.30	4.20	4.10	4.00	3.95	3.89	3.84	3.78	3.73	3.67
8	0.01	11.26	8.65	7.59	7.01	6.63	6.37	6.18	6.03	5.91	5.81	5.67	5.52	5.36	5.28	5.20	5.12	5.03	4.95	4.86
8	0.001	25.41	18.49	15.83	14.39	13.48	12.86	12.40	12.05	11.77	11.54	11.19	10.84	10.48	10.30	10.11	9.92	9.73	9.53	9.34
9	0.25	1.51	1.62	1.63	1.63	1.62	1.61	1.60	1.60	1.59	1.59	1.58	1.57	1.56	1.56	1.55	1.54	1.54	1.53	1.53
9	0.10	3.36	3.01	2.81	2.69	2.61	2.55	2.51	2.47	2.44	2.42	2.38	2.34	2.30	2.28	2.25	2.23	2.21	2.18	2.16
9	0.05	5.12	4.26	3.86	3.63	3.48	3.37	3.29	3.23	3.18	3.14	3.07	3.01	2.94	2.90	2.86	2.83	2.79	2.75	2.71
9	0.03	7.21	5.71	5.08	4.72	4.48	4.32	4.20	4.10	4.03	3.96	3.87	3.77	3.67	3.61	3.56	3.51	3.45	3.39	3.33
9	0.01	10.56	8.02	6.99	6.42	6.06	5.80	5.61	5.47	5.35	5.26	5.11	4.96	4.81	4.73	4.65	4.57	4.48	4.40	4.31
9	0.001	22.86	16.39	13.90	12.56	11.71	11.13	10.70	10.37	10.11	9.89	9.57	9.24	8.90	8.72	8.55	8.37	8.19	8.00	7.82
10	0.25	1.49	1.60	1.60	1.59	1.59	1.58	1.57	1.56	1.56	1.55	1.54	1.53	1.52	1.52	1.51	1.51	1.50	1.49	1.48
10	0.10	3.29	2.92	2.73	2.61	2.52	2.46	2.41	2.38	2.35	2.32	2.28	2.24	2.20	2.18	2.16	2.13	2.11	2.08	2.06
10	0.05	4.96	4.10	3.71	3.48	3.33	3.22	3.14	3.07	3.02	2.98	2.91	2.85	2.77	2.74	2.70	2.66	2.62	2.58	2.54
10	0.03	6.94	5.46	4.83	4.47	4.24	4.07	3.95	3.85	3.78	3.72	3.62	3.52	3.42	3.37	3.31	3.26	3.20	3.14	3.08
10	0.01	10.04	7.56	6.55	5.99	5.64	5.39	5.20	5.06	4.94	4.85	4.71	4.56	4.41	4.33	4.25	4.17	4.08	4.00	3.91
10	0.001	21.04	14.90	12.55	11.28	10.48	9.93	9.52	9.20	8.96	8.75	8.45	8.13	7.80	7.64	7.47	7.30	7.12	6.94	6.76
11	0.25	1.47	1.58	1.58	1.57	1.56	1.55	1.54	1.53	1.53	1.52	1.51	1.50	1.49	1.49	1.48	1.47	1.47	1.46	1.45
11	0.10	3.23	2.86	2.66	2.54	2.45	2.39	2.34	2.30	2.27	2.25	2.21	2.17	2.12	2.10	2.08	2.05	2.03	2.00	1.97
11	0.05	4.84	3.98	3.59	3.36	3.20	3.09	3.01	2.95	2.90	2.85	2.79	2.72	2.65	2.61	2.57	2.53	2.49	2.45	2.41
11	0.03	6.72	5.26	4.63	4.28	4.04	3.88	3.76	3.66	3.59	3.53	3.43	3.33	3.23	3.17	3.12	3.06	3.00	2.94	2.88
11	0.01	9.65	7.21	6.22	5.67	5.32	5.07	4.89	4.74	4.63	4.54	4.40	4.25	4.10	4.02	3.94	3.86	3.78	3.69	3.60
11	0.001	19.69	13.81	11.56	10.35	9.58	9.05	8.65	8.35	8.12	7.92	7.63	7.32	7.01	6.85	6.68	6.52	6.35	6.18	6.00

(continued)

df FOR NUMERATOR

df FOR DENOM	α	1	2	3	4	5	6	7	8	9	10	12	15	20	24	30	40	50	120	10000
12	0.25	1.46	1.56	1.56	1.55	1.54	1.53	1.52	1.51	1.51	1.50	1.49	1.48	1.47	1.46	1.45	1.45	1.44	1.43	1.42
12	0.10	3.18	2.81	2.61	2.48	2.39	2.33	2.28	2.24	2.21	2.19	2.15	2.10	2.06	2.04	2.01	1.99	1.96	1.93	1.90
12	0.05	4.75	3.89	3.49	3.26	3.11	3.00	2.91	2.85	2.80	2.75	2.69	2.62	2.54	2.51	2.47	2.43	2.38	2.34	2.30
12	0.03	6.55	5.10	4.47	4.12	3.89	3.73	3.61	3.51	3.44	3.37	3.28	3.18	3.07	3.02	2.96	2.91	2.85	2.79	2.73
12	0.01	9.33	6.93	5.95	5.41	5.06	4.82	4.64	4.50	4.39	4.30	4.16	4.01	3.86	3.78	3.70	3.62	3.54	3.45	3.36
12	0.001	18.64	12.97	10.80	9.63	8.89	8.38	8.00	7.71	7.48	7.29	7.00	6.71	6.40	6.25	6.09	5.93	5.76	5.59	5.42
13	0.25	1.45	1.55	1.55	1.53	1.52	1.51	1.50	1.49	1.49	1.48	1.47	1.46	1.45	1.44	1.43	1.42	1.42	1.41	1.40
13	0.10	3.14	2.76	2.56	2.43	2.35	2.28	2.23	2.20	2.16	2.14	2.10	2.05	2.01	1.98	1.96	1.93	1.90	1.88	1.85
13	0.05	4.67	3.81	3.41	3.18	3.03	2.92	2.83	2.77	2.71	2.67	2.60	2.53	2.46	2.42	2.38	2.34	2.30	2.25	2.21
13	0.03	6.41	4.97	4.35	4.00	3.77	3.60	3.48	3.39	3.31	3.25	3.15	3.05	2.95	2.89	2.84	2.78	2.72	2.66	2.60
13	0.01	9.07	6.70	5.74	5.21	4.86	4.62	4.44	4.30	4.19	4.10	3.96	3.82	3.66	3.59	3.51	3.43	3.34	3.25	3.17
13	0.001	17.82	12.31	10.21	9.07	8.35	7.86	7.49	7.21	6.98	6.80	6.52	6.23	5.93	5.78	5.63	5.47	5.30	5.14	4.97
14	0.25	1.44	1.53	1.53	1.52	1.51	1.50	1.49	1.48	1.47	1.46	1.45	1.44	1.43	1.42	1.41	1.41	1.40	1.39	1.38
14	0.10	3.10	2.73	2.52	2.39	2.31	2.24	2.19	2.15	2.12	2.10	2.05	2.01	1.96	1.94	1.91	1.89	1.86	1.83	1.80
14	0.05	4.60	3.74	3.34	3.11	2.96	2.85	2.76	2.70	2.65	2.60	2.53	2.46	2.39	2.35	2.31	2.27	2.22	2.18	2.13
14	0.03	6.30	4.86	4.24	3.89	3.66	3.50	3.38	3.29	3.21	3.15	3.05	2.95	2.84	2.79	2.73	2.67	2.61	2.55	2.49
14	0.01	8.86	6.51	5.56	5.04	4.69	4.46	4.28	4.14	4.03	3.94	3.80	3.66	3.51	3.43	3.35	3.27	3.18	3.09	3.01
14	0.001	17.14	11.78	9.73	8.62	7.92	7.44	7.08	6.80	6.58	6.40	6.13	5.85	5.56	5.41	5.25	5.10	4.94	4.77	4.61
15	0.25	1.43	1.52	1.52	1.51	1.49	1.48	1.47	1.46	1.46	1.45	1.44	1.43	1.41	1.41	1.40	1.39	1.38	1.37	1.36
15	0.10	3.07	2.70	2.49	2.36	2.27	2.21	2.16	2.12	2.09	2.06	2.02	1.97	1.92	1.90	1.87	1.85	1.82	1.79	1.76
15	0.05	4.54	3.68	3.29	3.06	2.90	2.79	2.71	2.64	2.59	2.54	2.48	2.40	2.33	2.29	2.25	2.20	2.16	2.11	2.07
15	0.03	6.20	4.77	4.15	3.80	3.58	3.41	3.29	3.20	3.12	3.06	2.96	2.86	2.76	2.70	2.64	2.59	2.52	2.46	2.40
15	0.01	8.68	6.36	5.42	4.89	4.56	4.32	4.14	4.00	3.89	3.80	3.67	3.52	3.37	3.29	3.21	3.13	3.05	2.96	2.87
15	0.001	16.59	11.34	9.34	8.25	7.57	7.09	6.74	6.47	6.26	6.08	5.81	5.54	5.25	5.10	4.95	4.80	4.64	4.48	4.31

16	0.25	1.42	1.51	1.51	1.50	1.48	1.47	1.46	1.45	1.44	1.44	1.43	1.41	1.40	1.39	1.38	1.37	1.36	1.35	1.34
16	0.10	3.05	2.67	2.46	2.33	2.24	2.18	2.13	2.09	2.06	2.03	1.99	1.94	1.89	1.87	1.84	1.81	1.78	1.75	1.72
16	0.05	4.49	3.63	3.24	3.01	2.85	2.74	2.66	2.59	2.54	2.49	2.42	2.35	2.28	2.24	2.19	2.15	2.11	2.06	2.01
16	0.03	6.12	4.69	4.08	3.73	3.50	3.34	3.22	3.12	3.05	2.99	2.89	2.79	2.68	2.63	2.57	2.51	2.45	2.38	2.32
16	0.01	8.53	6.23	5.29	4.77	4.44	4.20	4.03	3.89	3.78	3.69	3.55	3.41	3.26	3.18	3.10	3.02	2.93	2.84	2.75
16	0.001	16.12	10.97	9.01	7.94	7.27	6.80	6.46	6.20	5.98	5.81	5.55	5.27	4.99	4.85	4.70	4.54	4.39	4.23	4.06
17	0.25	1.42	1.51	1.50	1.49	1.47	1.46	1.45	1.44	1.43	1.43	1.41	1.40	1.39	1.38	1.37	1.36	1.35	1.34	1.33
17	0.10	3.03	2.64	2.44	2.31	2.22	2.15	2.10	2.06	2.03	2.00	1.96	1.91	1.86	1.84	1.81	1.78	1.75	1.72	1.69
17	0.05	4.45	3.59	3.20	2.96	2.81	2.70	2.61	2.55	2.49	2.45	2.38	2.31	2.23	2.19	2.15	2.10	2.06	2.01	1.96
17	0.03	6.04	4.62	4.01	3.66	3.44	3.28	3.16	3.06	2.98	2.92	2.82	2.72	2.62	2.56	2.50	2.44	2.38	2.32	2.25
17	0.01	8.40	6.11	5.19	4.67	4.34	4.10	3.93	3.79	3.68	3.59	3.46	3.31	3.16	3.08	3.00	2.92	2.83	2.75	2.65
17	0.001	15.72	10.66	8.73	7.68	7.02	6.56	6.22	5.96	5.75	5.58	5.32	5.05	4.78	4.63	4.48	4.33	4.18	4.02	3.85
18	0.25	1.41	1.50	1.49	1.48	1.46	1.45	1.44	1.43	1.42	1.42	1.40	1.39	1.38	1.37	1.36	1.35	1.34	1.33	1.32
18	0.10	3.01	2.62	2.42	2.29	2.20	2.13	2.08	2.04	2.00	1.98	1.93	1.89	1.84	1.81	1.78	1.75	1.72	1.69	1.66
18	0.05	4.41	3.55	3.16	2.93	2.77	2.66	2.58	2.51	2.46	2.41	2.34	2.27	2.19	2.15	2.11	2.06	2.02	1.97	1.92
18	0.03	5.98	4.56	3.95	3.61	3.38	3.22	3.10	3.01	2.93	2.87	2.77	2.67	2.56	2.50	2.44	2.38	2.32	2.26	2.19
18	0.01	8.29	6.01	5.09	4.58	4.25	4.01	3.84	3.71	3.60	3.51	3.37	3.23	3.08	3.00	2.92	2.84	2.75	2.66	2.57
18	0.001	15.38	10.39	8.49	7.46	6.81	6.35	6.02	5.76	5.56	5.39	5.13	4.87	4.59	4.45	4.30	4.15	4.00	3.84	3.67
19	0.25	1.41	1.49	1.49	1.47	1.46	1.44	1.43	1.42	1.41	1.41	1.40	1.38	1.37	1.36	1.35	1.34	1.33	1.32	1.30
19	0.10	2.99	2.61	2.40	2.27	2.18	2.11	2.06	2.02	1.98	1.96	1.91	1.86	1.81	1.79	1.76	1.73	1.70	1.67	1.63
19	0.05	4.38	3.52	3.13	2.90	2.74	2.63	2.54	2.48	2.42	2.38	2.31	2.23	2.16	2.11	2.07	2.03	1.98	1.93	1.88
19	0.03	5.92	4.51	3.90	3.56	3.33	3.17	3.05	2.96	2.88	2.82	2.72	2.62	2.51	2.45	2.39	2.33	2.27	2.20	2.13
19	0.01	8.18	5.93	5.01	4.50	4.17	3.94	3.77	3.63	3.52	3.43	3.30	3.15	3.00	2.92	2.84	2.76	2.67	2.58	2.49
19	0.001	15.08	10.16	8.28	7.27	6.62	6.18	5.85	5.59	5.39	5.22	4.97	4.70	4.43	4.29	4.14	3.99	3.84	3.68	3.52

(continued)

df FOR NUMERATOR

df FOR DENOM	α	1	2	3	4	5	6	7	8	9	10	12	15	20	24	30	40	50	120	10000
20	0.25	1.40	1.49	1.48	1.47	1.45	1.44	1.43	1.42	1.41	1.40	1.39	1.37	1.36	1.35	1.34	1.33	.32	1.31	1.29
20	0.10	2.97	2.59	2.38	2.25	2.16	2.09	2.04	2.00	1.96	1.94	1.89	1.84	1.79	1.77	1.74	1.71	.68	1.64	1.61
20	0.05	4.35	3.49	3.10	2.87	2.71	2.60	2.51	2.45	2.39	2.35	2.28	2.20	2.12	2.08	2.04	1.99	.95	1.90	1.84
20	0.03	5.87	4.46	3.86	3.51	3.29	3.13	3.01	2.91	2.84	2.77	2.68	2.57	2.46	2.41	2.35	2.29	2.22	2.16	2.09
20	0.01	8.10	5.85	4.94	4.43	4.10	3.87	3.70	3.56	3.46	3.37	3.23	3.09	2.94	2.86	2.78	2.69	.61	2.52	2.42
20	0.001	14.82	9.95	8.10	7.10	6.46	6.02	5.69	5.44	5.24	5.08	4.82	4.56	4.29	4.15	4.00	3.86	.70	3.54	3.38
22	0.25	1.40	1.48	1.47	1.45	1.44	1.42	1.41	1.40	1.39	1.39	1.37	1.36	1.34	1.33	1.32	1.31	.30	1.29	1.28
22	0.10	2.95	2.56	2.35	2.22	2.13	2.06	2.01	1.97	1.93	1.90	1.86	1.81	1.76	1.73	1.70	1.67	.64	1.60	1.57
22	0.05	4.30	3.44	3.05	2.82	2.66	2.55	2.46	2.40	2.34	2.30	2.23	2.15	2.07	2.03	1.98	1.94	.89	1.84	1.78
22	0.03	5.79	4.38	3.78	3.44	3.22	3.05	2.93	2.84	2.76	2.70	2.60	2.50	2.39	2.33	2.27	2.21	.14	2.08	2.00
22	0.01	7.95	5.72	4.82	4.31	3.99	3.76	3.59	3.45	3.35	3.26	3.12	2.98	2.83	2.75	2.67	2.58	.50	2.40	2.31
22	0.001	14.38	9.61	7.80	6.81	6.19	5.76	5.44	5.19	4.99	4.83	4.58	4.33	4.06	3.92	3.78	3.63	.48	3.32	3.15
24	0.25	1.39	1.47	1.46	1.44	1.43	1.41	1.40	1.39	1.38	1.38	1.36	1.35	1.33	1.32	1.31	1.30	.29	1.28	1.26
24	0.10	2.93	2.54	2.33	2.19	2.10	2.04	1.98	1.94	1.91	1.88	1.83	1.78	1.73	1.70	1.67	1.64	.61	1.57	1.53
24	0.05	4.26	3.40	3.01	2.78	2.62	2.51	2.42	2.36	2.30	2.25	2.18	2.11	2.03	1.98	1.94	1.89	.84	1.79	1.73
24	0.03	5.72	4.32	3.72	3.38	3.15	2.99	2.87	2.78	2.70	2.64	2.54	2.44	2.33	2.27	2.21	2.15	.08	2.01	1.94
24	0.01	7.82	5.61	4.72	4.22	3.90	3.67	3.50	3.36	3.26	3.17	3.03	2.89	2.74	2.66	2.58	2.49	.40	2.31	2.21
24	0.001	14.03	9.34	7.55	6.59	5.98	5.55	5.24	4.99	4.80	4.64	4.39	4.14	3.87	3.74	3.59	3.45	3.29	3.14	2.97
26	0.25	1.38	1.46	1.45	1.44	1.42	1.41	1.39	1.38	1.37	1.37	1.35	1.34	1.32	1.31	1.30	1.29	1.28	1.26	1.25
26	0.10	2.91	2.52	2.31	2.17	2.08	2.01	1.96	1.92	1.88	1.86	1.81	1.76	1.71	1.68	1.65	1.61	1.58	1.54	1.50
26	0.05	4.23	3.37	2.98	2.74	2.59	2.47	2.39	2.32	2.27	2.22	2.15	2.07	1.99	1.95	1.90	1.85	1.80	1.75	1.69
26	0.03	5.66	4.27	3.67	3.33	3.10	2.94	2.82	2.73	2.65	2.59	2.49	2.39	2.28	2.22	2.16	2.09	2.03	1.95	1.88
26	0.01	7.72	5.53	4.64	4.14	3.82	3.59	3.42	3.29	3.18	3.09	2.96	2.81	2.66	2.58	2.50	2.42	2.33	2.23	2.13
26	0.001	13.74	9.12	7.36	6.41	5.80	5.38	5.07	4.83	4.64	4.48	4.24	3.99	3.72	3.59	3.44	3.30	3.15	2.99	2.82

df	α																			
28	0.25	1.24	1.25	1.27	1.28	1.29	1.30	1.31	1.33	1.34	1.36	1.37	1.38	1.39	1.40	1.41	1.43	1.45	1.46	1.38
28	0.10	1.48	1.52	1.56	1.59	1.63	1.66	1.69	1.74	1.79	1.84	1.87	1.90	1.94	2.00	2.06	2.16	2.29	2.50	2.89
28	0.05	1.65	1.71	1.77	1.82	1.87	1.91	1.96	2.04	2.12	2.19	2.24	2.29	2.36	2.45	2.56	2.71	2.95	3.34	4.20
28	0.03	1.83	1.91	1.98	2.05	2.11	2.17	2.23	2.34	2.45	2.55	2.61	2.69	2.78	2.90	3.06	3.29	3.63	4.22	5.61
28	0.01	2.07	2.17	2.26	2.35	2.44	2.52	2.60	2.75	2.90	3.03	3.12	3.23	3.36	3.53	3.75	4.07	4.57	5.45	7.64
28	0.001	2.70	2.86	3.02	3.18	3.32	3.46	3.60	3.86	4.11	4.35	4.50	4.69	4.93	5.24	5.66	6.25	7.19	8.93	13.50
30	0.25	1.23	1.24	1.26	1.27	1.28	1.29	1.30	1.32	1.34	1.35	1.36	1.37	1.38	1.39	1.41	1.42	1.44	1.45	1.38
30	0.10	1.46	1.50	1.54	1.57	1.61	1.64	1.67	1.72	1.77	1.82	1.85	1.88	1.93	1.98	2.05	2.14	2.28	2.49	2.88
30	0.05	1.62	1.68	1.74	1.79	1.84	1.89	1.93	2.01	2.09	2.16	2.21	2.27	2.33	2.42	2.53	2.69	2.92	3.32	4.17
30	0.03	1.79	1.87	1.94	2.01	2.07	2.14	2.20	2.31	2.41	2.51	2.57	2.65	2.75	2.87	3.03	3.25	3.59	4.18	5.57
30	0.01	2.01	2.11	2.21	2.30	2.39	2.47	2.55	2.70	2.84	2.98	3.07	3.17	3.30	3.47	3.70	4.02	4.51	5.39	7.56
30	0.001	2.59	2.76	2.92	3.07	3.22	3.36	3.49	3.75	4.00	4.24	4.39	4.58	4.82	5.12	5.53	6.12	7.05	8.77	13.29
40	0.25	1.19	1.21	1.22	1.24	1.25	1.26	1.28	1.30	1.31	1.33	1.34	1.35	1.36	1.37	1.39	1.40	1.42	1.44	1.36
40	0.10	1.38	1.42	1.47	1.51	1.54	1.57	1.61	1.66	1.71	1.76	1.79	1.83	1.87	1.93	2.00	2.09	2.23	2.44	2.84
40	0.05	1.51	1.58	1.64	1.69	1.74	1.79	1.84	1.92	2.00	2.08	2.12	2.18	2.25	2.34	2.45	2.61	2.84	3.23	4.08
40	0.03	1.64	1.72	1.80	1.88	1.94	2.01	2.07	2.18	2.29	2.39	2.45	2.53	2.62	2.74	2.90	3.13	3.46	4.05	5.42
40	0.01	1.81	1.92	2.02	2.11	2.20	2.29	2.37	2.52	2.66	2.80	2.89	2.99	3.12	3.29	3.51	3.83	4.31	5.18	7.31
40	0.001	2.23	2.41	2.57	2.73	2.87	3.01	3.15	3.40	3.64	3.87	4.02	4.21	4.44	4.73	5.13	5.70	6.59	8.25	12.61
60	0.25	1.15	1.17	1.19	1.21	1.22	1.24	1.25	1.27	1.29	1.30	1.31	1.32	1.33	1.35	1.37	1.38	1.41	1.42	1.35
60	0.10	1.29	1.35	1.40	1.44	1.48	1.51	1.54	1.60	1.66	1.71	1.74	1.77	1.82	1.87	1.95	2.04	2.18	2.39	2.79
60	0.05	1.39	1.47	1.53	1.59	1.65	1.70	1.75	1.84	1.92	1.99	2.04	2.10	2.17	2.25	2.37	2.53	2.76	3.15	4.00
60	0.03	1.48	1.58	1.67	1.74	1.82	1.88	1.94	2.06	2.17	2.27	2.33	2.41	2.51	2.63	2.79	3.01	3.34	3.93	5.29
60	0.01	1.60	1.73	1.84	1.94	2.03	2.12	2.20	2.35	2.50	2.63	2.72	2.82	2.95	3.12	3.34	3.65	4.13	4.98	7.08
60	0.001	1.89	2.08	2.25	2.41	2.55	2.69	2.83	3.08	3.32	3.54	3.69	3.86	4.09	4.37	4.76	5.31	6.17	7.77	11.97

(continued)

df FOR NUMERATOR

df FOR DENOM	α	1	2	3	4	5	6	7	8	9	10	12	15	20	24	30	40	60	120	10000
120	0.25	1.34	1.40	1.39	1.37	1.35	1.33	1.31	1.30	1.29	1.28	1.26	1.24	1.22	1.21	1.19	1.18	1.16	1.13	1.10
120	0.10	2.75	2.35	2.13	1.99	1.90	1.82	1.77	1.72	1.68	1.65	1.60	1.55	1.48	1.45	1.41	1.37	1.32	1.26	1.19
120	0.05	3.92	3.07	2.68	2.45	2.29	2.18	2.09	2.02	1.96	1.91	1.83	1.75	1.66	1.61	1.55	1.50	1.43	1.35	1.26
120	0.03	5.15	3.80	3.23	2.89	2.67	2.52	2.39	2.30	2.22	2.16	2.05	1.94	1.82	1.76	1.69	1.61	1.53	1.43	1.31
120	0.01	6.85	4.79	3.95	3.48	3.17	2.96	2.79	2.66	2.56	2.47	2.34	2.19	2.03	1.95	1.86	1.76	1.66	1.53	1.38
120	0.001	11.38	7.32	5.78	4.95	4.42	4.04	3.77	3.55	3.38	3.24	3.02	2.78	2.53	2.40	2.26	2.11	1.95	1.77	1.55
10000	0.25	1.32	1.39	1.37	1.35	1.33	1.31	1.29	1.28	1.27	1.26	1.24	1.22	1.19	1.18	1.16	1.14	1.12	1.08	1.01
10000	0.10	2.71	2.30	2.08	1.95	1.85	1.77	1.72	1.67	1.63	1.60	1.55	1.49	1.42	1.38	1.34	1.30	1.24	1.17	1.03
10000	0.05	3.84	3.00	2.61	2.37	2.21	2.10	2.01	1.94	1.88	1.83	1.75	1.67	1.57	1.52	1.46	1.40	1.32	1.22	1.03
10000	0.03	5.03	3.69	3.12	2.79	2.57	2.41	2.29	2.19	2.11	2.05	1.95	1.83	1.71	1.64	1.57	1.49	1.39	1.27	1.04
10000	0.01	6.64	4.61	3.78	3.32	3.02	2.80	2.64	2.51	2.41	2.32	2.19	2.04	1.88	1.79	1.70	1.59	1.48	1.33	1.05
10000	0.001	10.83	6.91	5.43	4.62	4.11	3.75	3.48	3.27	3.10	2.96	2.75	2.52	2.27	2.14	1.99	1.84	1.66	1.45	1.06

TABLE 4. Binomial Distribution Table

The entries in the table below give the probability of K successes in N trials where p is the probability of success on a single trial. For example, to find the probability of obtaining 2 heads in 3 coin tosses, we have $N = 3$, $K = 2$, and $p = .5$. The probability of obtaining 2 heads in 3 coin tosses is .375.

N	K	P									
		0.05	**0.10**	**0.15**	**0.20**	**0.25**	**0.30**	**0.35**	**0.40**	**0.45**	**0.50**
2	0	0.9025	0.8100	0.7225	0.6400	0.5625	0.4900	0.4225	0.3600	0.3025	0.2500
	1	0.0950	0.1800	0.2550	0.3200	0.3750	0.4200	0.4550	0.4800	0.4950	0.5000
	2	0.0025	0.0100	0.0225	0.0400	0.0625	0.0900	0.1225	0.1600	0.2025	0.2500
3	0	0.8574	0.7290	0.6141	0.5120	0.4219	0.3430	0.2746	0.2160	0.1664	0.1250
	1	0.1354	0.2430	0.3251	0.3840	0.4219	0.4410	0.4436	0.4320	0.4084	0.3750
	2	0.0071	0.0270	0.0574	0.0960	0.1406	0.1890	0.2389	0.2880	0.3341	0.3750
	3	0.0001	0.0010	0.0034	0.0080	0.0156	0.0270	0.0429	0.0640	0.0911	0.1250
4	0	0.8145	0.6561	0.5220	0.4096	0.3164	0.2401	0.1785	0.1296	0.0915	0.0625
	1	0.1715	0.2916	0.3685	0.4096	0.4219	0.4116	0.3845	0.3456	0.2995	0.2500
	2	0.0135	0.0486	0.0975	0.1536	0.2109	0.2646	0.3105	0.3456	0.3675	0.3750
	3	0.0005	0.0036	0.0115	0.0256	0.0469	0.0756	0.1115	0.1536	0.2005	0.2500
	4	0.0000	0.0001	0.0005	0.0016	0.0039	0.0081	0.0150	0.0256	0.0410	0.0625
5	0	0.7738	0.5905	0.4437	0.3277	0.2373	0.1681	0.1160	0.0778	0.0503	0.0313
	1	0.2036	0.3281	0.3915	0.4096	0.3955	0.3602	0.3124	0.2592	0.2059	0.1563
	2	0.0214	0.0729	0.1382	0.2048	0.2637	0.3087	0.3364	0.3456	0.3369	0.3125
	3	0.0011	0.0081	0.0244	0.0512	0.0879	0.1323	0.1811	0.2304	0.2757	0.3125
	4	0.0000	0.0005	0.0022	0.0064	0.0146	0.0284	0.0488	0.0768	0.1128	0.1563
	5	0.0000	0.0000	0.0001	0.0003	0.0010	0.0024	0.0053	0.0102	0.0185	0.0313
6	0	0.7351	0.5314	0.3771	0.2621	0.1780	0.1176	0.0754	0.0467	0.0277	0.0156
	1	0.2321	0.3543	0.3993	0.3932	0.3560	0.3025	0.2437	0.1866	0.1359	0.0938
	2	0.0305	0.0984	0.1762	0.2458	0.2966	0.3241	0.3280	0.3110	0.2780	0.2344
	3	0.0021	0.0146	0.0415	0.0819	0.1318	0.1852	0.2355	0.2765	0.3032	0.3125
	4	0.0001	0.0012	0.0055	0.0154	0.0330	0.0595	0.0951	0.1382	0.1861	0.2344
	5	0.0000	0.0001	0.0004	0.0015	0.0044	0.0102	0.0205	0.0369	0.0609	0.0938
	6	0.0000	0.0000	0.0000	0.0001	0.0002	0.0007	0.0018	0.0041	0.0083	0.0156
7	0	0.6983	0.4783	0.3206	0.2097	0.1335	0.0824	0.0490	0.0280	0.0152	0.0078
	1	0.2573	0.3720	0.3960	0.3670	0.3115	0.2471	0.1848	0.1306	0.0872	0.0547
	2	0.0406	0.1240	0.2097	0.2753	0.3115	0.3177	0.2985	0.2613	0.2140	0.1641
	3	0.0036	0.0230	0.0617	0.1147	0.1730	0.2269	0.2679	0.2903	0.2918	0.2734
	4	0.0002	0.0026	0.0109	0.0287	0.0577	0.0972	0.1442	0.1935	0.2388	0.2734
	5	0.0000	0.0002	0.0012	0.0043	0.0115	0.0250	0.0466	0.0774	0.1172	0.1641
	6	0.0000	0.0000	0.0001	0.0004	0.0013	0.0036	0.0084	0.0172	0.0320	0.0547
	7	0.0000	0.0000	0.0000	0.0000	0.0001	0.0002	0.0006	0.0016	0.0037	0.0078
8	0	0.6634	0.4305	0.2725	0.1678	0.1001	0.0576	0.0319	0.0168	0.0084	0.0039
	1	0.2793	0.3826	0.3847	0.3355	0.2670	0.1977	0.1373	0.0896	0.0548	0.0313
	2	0.0515	0.1488	0.2376	0.2936	0.3115	0.2965	0.2587	0.2090	0.1569	0.1094
	3	0.0054	0.0331	0.0839	0.1468	0.2076	0.2541	0.2786	0.2787	0.2568	0.2188
	4	0.0004	0.0046	0.0185	0.0459	0.0865	0.1361	0.1875	0.2322	0.2627	0.2734
	5	0.0000	0.0004	0.0026	0.0092	0.0231	0.0467	0.0808	0.1239	0.1719	0.2188
	6	0.0000	0.0000	0.0002	0.0011	0.0038	0.0100	0.0217	0.0413	0.0703	0.1094
	7	0.0000	0.0000	0.0000	0.0001	0.0004	0.0012	0.0033	0.0079	0.0164	0.0313
	8	0.0000	0.0000	0.0000	0.0000	0.0000	0.0001	0.0002	0.0007	0.0017	0.0039

(*continued*)

N	K	P									
		0.05	**0.10**	**0.15**	**0.20**	**0.25**	**0.30**	**0.35**	**0.40**	**0.45**	**0.50**
9	0	0.6302	0.3874	0.2316	0.1342	0.0751	0.0404	0.0207	0.0101	0.0046	0.0020
	1	0.2985	0.3874	0.3679	0.3020	0.2253	0.1556	0.1004	0.0605	0.0339	0.0176
	2	0.0629	0.1722	0.2597	0.3020	0.3003	0.2668	0.2162	0.1612	0.1110	0.0703
	3	0.0077	0.0446	0.1069	0.1762	0.2336	0.2668	0.2716	0.2508	0.2119	0.1641
	4	0.0006	0.0074	0.0283	0.0661	0.1168	0.1715	0.2194	0.2508	0.2600	0.2461
	5	0.0000	0.0008	0.0050	0.0165	0.0389	0.0735	0.1181	0.1672	0.2128	0.2461
	6	0.0000	0.0001	0.0006	0.0028	0.0087	0.0210	0.0424	0.0743	0.1160	0.1641
	7	0.0000	0.0000	0.0000	0.0003	0.0012	0.0039	0.0098	0.0212	0.0407	0.0703
	8	0.0000	0.0000	0.0000	0.0000	0.0001	0.0004	0.0013	0.0035	0.0083	0.0176
	9	0.0000	0.0000	0.0000	0.0000	0.0000	0.0000	0.0001	0.0003	0.0008	0.0020
10	0	0.5987	0.3487	0.1969	0.1074	0.0563	0.0282	0.0135	0.0060	0.0025	0.0010
	1	0.3151	0.3874	0.3474	0.2684	0.1877	0.1211	0.0725	0.0403	0.0207	0.0098
	2	0.0746	0.1937	0.2759	0.3020	0.2816	0.2335	0.1757	0.1209	0.0763	0.0439
	3	0.0105	0.0574	0.1298	0.2013	0.2503	0.2668	0.2522	0.2150	0.1665	0.1172
	4	0.0010	0.0112	0.0401	0.0881	0.1460	0.2001	0.2377	0.2508	0.2384	0.2051
	5	0.0001	0.0015	0.0085	0.0264	0.0584	0.1029	0.1536	0.2007	0.2340	0.2461
	6	0.0000	0.0001	0.0012	0.0055	0.0162	0.0368	0.0689	0.1115	0.1596	0.2051
	7	0.0000	0.0000	0.0001	0.0008	0.0031	0.0090	0.0212	0.0425	0.0746	0.1172
	8	0.0000	0.0000	0.0000	0.0001	0.0004	0.0014	0.0043	0.0106	0.0229	0.0439
	9	0.0000	0.0000	0.0000	0.0000	0.0000	0.0001	0.0005	0.0016	0.0042	0.0098
	10	0.0000	0.0000	0.0000	0.0000	0.0000	0.0000	0.0000	0.0001	0.0003	0.0010
11	0	0.5688	0.3138	0.1673	0.0859	0.0422	0.0198	0.0088	0.0036	0.0014	0.0005
	1	0.3293	0.3835	0.3248	0.2362	0.1549	0.0932	0.0518	0.0266	0.0125	0.0054
	2	0.0867	0.2131	0.2866	0.2953	0.2581	0.1998	0.1395	0.0887	0.0513	0.0269
	3	0.0137	0.0710	0.1517	0.2215	0.2581	0.2568	0.2254	0.1774	0.1259	0.0806
	4	0.0014	0.0158	0.0536	0.1107	0.1721	0.2201	0.2428	0.2365	0.2060	0.1611
	5	0.0001	0.0025	0.0132	0.0388	0.0803	0.1321	0.1830	0.2207	0.2360	0.2256
	6	0.0000	0.0003	0.0023	0.0097	0.0268	0.0566	0.0985	0.1471	0.1931	0.2256
	7	0.0000	0.0000	0.0003	0.0017	0.0064	0.0173	0.0379	0.0701	0.1128	0.1611
	8	0.0000	0.0000	0.0000	0.0002	0.0011	0.0037	0.0102	0.0234	0.0462	0.0806
	9	0.0000	0.0000	0.0000	0.0000	0.0001	0.0005	0.0018	0.0052	0.0126	0.0269
	10	0.0000	0.0000	0.0000	0.0000	0.0000	0.0000	0.0002	0.0007	0.0021	0.0054
	11	0.0000	0.0000	0.0000	0.0000	0.0000	0.0000	0.0000	0.0000	0.0002	0.0005
12	0	0.5404	0.2824	0.1422	0.0687	0.0317	0.0138	0.0057	0.0022	0.0008	0.0002
	1	0.3413	0.3766	0.3012	0.2062	0.1267	0.0712	0.0368	0.0174	0.0075	0.0029
	2	0.0988	0.2301	0.2924	0.2835	0.2323	0.1678	0.1088	0.0639	0.0339	0.0161
	3	0.0173	0.0852	0.1720	0.2362	0.2581	0.2397	0.1954	0.1419	0.0923	0.0537
	4	0.0021	0.0213	0.0683	0.1329	0.1936	0.2311	0.2367	0.2128	0.1700	0.1208
	5	0.0002	0.0038	0.0193	0.0532	0.1032	0.1585	0.2039	0.2270	0.2225	0.1934
	6	0.0000	0.0005	0.0040	0.0155	0.0401	0.0792	0.1281	0.1766	0.2124	0.2256
	7	0.0000	0.0000	0.0006	0.0033	0.0115	0.0291	0.0591	0.1009	0.1489	0.1934
	8	0.0000	0.0000	0.0001	0.0005	0.0024	0.0078	0.0199	0.0420	0.0762	0.1208
	9	0.0000	0.0000	0.0000	0.0001	0.0004	0.0015	0.0048	0.0125	0.0277	0.0537
	10	0.0000	0.0000	0.0000	0.0000	0.0000	0.0002	0.0008	0.0025	0.0068	0.0161
	11	0.0000	0.0000	0.0000	0.0000	0.0000	0.0000	0.0001	0.0003	0.0010	0.0029
	12	0.0000	0.0000	0.0000	0.0000	0.0000	0.0000	0.0000	0.0000	0.0001	0.0002

N	K	0.05	0.10	0.15	0.20	0.25	0.30	0.35	0.40	0.45	0.50
13	0	0.5133	0.2542	0.1209	0.0550	0.0238	0.0097	0.0037	0.0013	0.0004	0.0001
	1	0.3512	0.3672	0.2774	0.1787	0.1029	0.0540	0.0259	0.0113	0.0045	0.0016
	2	0.1109	0.2448	0.2937	0.2680	0.2059	0.1388	0.0836	0.0453	0.0220	0.0095
	3	0.0214	0.0997	0.1900	0.2457	0.2517	0.2181	0.1651	0.1107	0.0660	0.0349
	4	0.0028	0.0277	0.0838	0.1535	0.2097	0.2337	0.2222	0.1845	0.1350	0.0873
	5	0.0003	0.0055	0.0266	0.0691	0.1258	0.1803	0.2154	0.2214	0.1989	0.1571
	6	0.0000	0.0008	0.0063	0.0230	0.0559	0.1030	0.1546	0.1968	0.2169	0.2095
	7	0.0000	0.0001	0.0011	0.0058	0.0186	0.0442	0.0833	0.1312	0.1775	0.2095
	8	0.0000	0.0000	0.0001	0.0011	0.0047	0.0142	0.0336	0.0656	0.1089	0.1571
	9	0.0000	0.0000	0.0000	0.0001	0.0009	0.0034	0.0101	0.0243	0.0495	0.0873
	10	0.0000	0.0000	0.0000	0.0000	0.0001	0.0006	0.0022	0.0065	0.0162	0.0349
	11	0.0000	0.0000	0.0000	0.0000	0.0000	0.0001	0.0003	0.0012	0.0036	0.0095
	12	0.0000	0.0000	0.0000	0.0000	0.0000	0.0000	0.0000	0.0001	0.0005	0.0016
	13	0.0000	0.0000	0.0000	0.0000	0.0000	0.0000	0.0000	0.0000	0.0000	0.0001
14	0	0.4877	0.2288	0.1028	0.0440	0.0178	0.0068	0.0024	0.0008	0.0002	0.0001
	1	0.3593	0.3559	0.2539	0.1539	0.0832	0.0407	0.0181	0.0073	0.0027	0.0009
	2	0.1229	0.2570	0.2912	0.2501	0.1802	0.1134	0.0634	0.0317	0.0141	0.0056
	3	0.0259	0.1142	0.2056	0.2501	0.2402	0.1943	0.1366	0.0845	0.0462	0.0222
	4	0.0037	0.0349	0.0998	0.1720	0.2202	0.2290	0.2022	0.1549	0.1040	0.0611
	5	0.0004	0.0078	0.0352	0.0860	0.1468	0.1963	0.2178	0.2066	0.1701	0.1222
	6	0.0000	0.0013	0.0093	0.0322	0.0734	0.1262	0.1759	0.2066	0.2088	0.1833
	7	0.0000	0.0002	0.0019	0.0092	0.0280	0.0618	0.1082	0.1574	0.1952	0.2095
	8	0.0000	0.0000	0.0003	0.0020	0.0082	0.0232	0.0510	0.0918	0.1398	0.1833
	9	0.0000	0.0000	0.0000	0.0003	0.0018	0.0066	0.0183	0.0408	0.0762	0.1222
	10	0.0000	0.0000	0.0000	0.0000	0.0003	0.0014	0.0049	0.0136	0.0312	0.0611
	11	0.0000	0.0000	0.0000	0.0000	0.0000	0.0002	0.0010	0.0033	0.0093	0.0222
	12	0.0000	0.0000	0.0000	0.0000	0.0000	0.0000	0.0001	0.0005	0.0019	0.0056
	13	0.0000	0.0000	0.0000	0.0000	0.0000	0.0000	0.0000	0.0001	0.0002	0.0009
	14	0.0000	0.0000	0.0000	0.0000	0.0000	0.0000	0.0000	0.0000	0.0000	0.0001
15	0	0.4633	0.2059	0.0874	0.0352	0.0134	0.0047	0.0016	0.0005	0.0001	0.0000
	1	0.3658	0.3432	0.2312	0.1319	0.0668	0.0305	0.0126	0.0047	0.0016	0.0005
	2	0.1348	0.2669	0.2856	0.2309	0.1559	0.0916	0.0476	0.0219	0.0090	0.0032
	3	0.0307	0.1285	0.2184	0.2501	0.2252	0.1700	0.1110	0.0634	0.0318	0.0139
	4	0.0049	0.0428	0.1156	0.1876	0.2252	0.2186	0.1792	0.1268	0.0780	0.0417
	5	0.0006	0.0105	0.0449	0.1032	0.1651	0.2061	0.2123	0.1859	0.1404	0.0916
	6	0.0000	0.0019	0.0132	0.0430	0.0917	0.1472	0.1906	0.2066	0.1914	0.1527
	7	0.0000	0.0003	0.0030	0.0138	0.0393	0.0811	0.1319	0.1771	0.2013	0.1964
	8	0.0000	0.0000	0.0005	0.0035	0.0131	0.0348	0.0710	0.1181	0.1647	0.1964
	9	0.0000	0.0000	0.0001	0.0007	0.0034	0.0116	0.0298	0.0612	0.1048	0.1527
	10	0.0000	0.0000	0.0000	0.0001	0.0007	0.0030	0.0096	0.0245	0.0515	0.0916
	11	0.0000	0.0000	0.0000	0.0000	0.0001	0.0006	0.0024	0.0074	0.0191	0.0417
	12	0.0000	0.0000	0.0000	0.0000	0.0000	0.0001	0.0004	0.0016	0.0052	0.0139
	13	0.0000	0.0000	0.0000	0.0000	0.0000	0.0000	0.0001	0.0003	0.0010	0.0032
	14	0.0000	0.0000	0.0000	0.0000	0.0000	0.0000	0.0000	0.0000	0.0001	0.0005
	15	0.0000	0.0000	0.0000	0.0000	0.0000	0.0000	0.0000	0.0000	0.0000	0.0000

(*continued*)

N	K	0.05	0.10	0.15	0.20	0.25	0.30	0.35	0.40	0.45	0.50
						P					
16	0	0.4401	0.1853	0.0743	0.0281	0.0100	0.0033	0.0010	0.0003	0.0001	0.0000
	1	0.3706	0.3294	0.2097	0.1126	0.0535	0.0228	0.0087	0.0030	0.0009	0.0002
	2	0.1463	0.2745	0.2775	0.2111	0.1336	0.0732	0.0353	0.0150	0.0056	0.0018
	3	0.0359	0.1423	0.2285	0.2463	0.2079	0.1465	0.0888	0.0468	0.0215	0.0085
	4	0.0061	0.0514	0.1311	0.2001	0.2252	0.2040	0.1553	0.1014	0.0572	0.0278
	5	0.0008	0.0137	0.0555	0.1201	0.1802	0.2099	0.2008	0.1623	0.1123	0.0667
	6	0.0001	0.0028	0.0180	0.0550	0.1101	0.1649	0.1982	0.1983	0.1684	0.1222
	7	0.0000	0.0004	0.0045	0.0197	0.0524	0.1010	0.1524	0.1889	0.1969	0.1746
	8	0.0000	0.0001	0.0009	0.0055	0.0197	0.0487	0.0923	0.1417	0.1812	0.1964
	9	0.0000	0.0000	0.0001	0.0012	0.0058	0.0185	0.0442	0.0840	0.1318	0.1746
	10	0.0000	0.0000	0.0000	0.0002	0.0014	0.0056	0.0167	0.0392	0.0755	0.1222
	11	0.0000	0.0000	0.0000	0.0000	0.0002	0.0013	0.0049	0.0142	0.0337	0.0667
	12	0.0000	0.0000	0.0000	0.0000	0.0000	0.0002	0.0011	0.0040	0.0115	0.0278
	13	0.0000	0.0000	0.0000	0.0000	0.0000	0.0000	0.0002	0.0008	0.0029	0.0085
	14	0.0000	0.0000	0.0000	0.0000	0.0000	0.0000	0.0000	0.0001	0.0005	0.0018
	15	0.0000	0.0000	0.0000	0.0000	0.0000	0.0000	0.0000	0.0000	0.0001	0.0002
	16	0.0000	0.0000	0.0000	0.0000	0.0000	0.0000	0.0000	0.0000	0.0000	0.0000
17	0	0.4181	0.1668	0.0631	0.0225	0.0075	0.0023	0.0007	0.0002	0.0000	0.0000
	1	0.3741	0.3150	0.1893	0.0957	0.0426	0.0169	0.0060	0.0019	0.0005	0.0001
	2	0.1575	0.2800	0.2673	0.1914	0.1136	0.0581	0.0260	0.0102	0.0035	0.0010
	3	0.0415	0.1556	0.2359	0.2393	0.1893	0.1245	0.0701	0.0341	0.0144	0.0052
	4	0.0076	0.0605	0.1457	0.2093	0.2209	0.1868	0.1320	0.0796	0.0411	0.0182
	5	0.0010	0.0175	0.0668	0.1361	0.1914	0.2081	0.1849	0.1379	0.0875	0.0472
	6	0.0001	0.0039	0.0236	0.0680	0.1276	0.1784	0.1991	0.1839	0.1432	0.0944
	7	0.0000	0.0007	0.0065	0.0267	0.0668	0.1201	0.1685	0.1927	0.1841	0.1484
	8	0.0000	0.0001	0.0014	0.0084	0.0279	0.0644	0.1134	0.1606	0.1883	0.1855
	9	0.0000	0.0000	0.0003	0.0021	0.0093	0.0276	0.0611	0.1070	0.1540	0.1855
	10	0.0000	0.0000	0.0000	0.0004	0.0025	0.0095	0.0263	0.0571	0.1008	0.1484
	11	0.0000	0.0000	0.0000	0.0001	0.0005	0.0026	0.0090	0.0242	0.0525	0.0944
	12	0.0000	0.0000	0.0000	0.0000	0.0001	0.0006	0.0024	0.0081	0.0215	0.0472
	13	0.0000	0.0000	0.0000	0.0000	0.0000	0.0001	0.0005	0.0021	0.0068	0.0182
	14	0.0000	0.0000	0.0000	0.0000	0.0000	0.0000	0.0001	0.0004	0.0016	0.0052
	15	0.0000	0.0000	0.0000	0.0000	0.0000	0.0000	0.0000	0.0001	0.0003	0.0010
	16	0.0000	0.0000	0.0000	0.0000	0.0000	0.0000	0.0000	0.0000	0.0000	0.0001
	17	0.0000	0.0000	0.0000	0.0000	0.0000	0.0000	0.0000	0.0000	0.0000	0.0000
18	0	0.3972	0.1501	0.0536	0.0180	0.0056	0.0016	0.0004	0.0001	0.0000	0.0000
	1	0.3763	0.3002	0.1704	0.0811	0.0338	0.0126	0.0042	0.0012	0.0003	0.0001
	2	0.1683	0.2835	0.2556	0.1723	0.0958	0.0458	0.0190	0.0069	0.0022	0.0006
	3	0.0473	0.1680	0.2406	0.2297	0.1704	0.1046	0.0547	0.0246	0.0095	0.0031
	4	0.0093	0.0700	0.1592	0.2153	0.2130	0.1681	0.1104	0.0614	0.0291	0.0117
	5	0.0014	0.0218	0.0787	0.1507	0.1988	0.2017	0.1664	0.1146	0.0666	0.0327
	6	0.0002	0.0052	0.0301	0.0816	0.1436	0.1873	0.1941	0.1655	0.1181	0.0708
	7	0.0000	0.0010	0.0091	0.0350	0.0820	0.1376	0.1792	0.1892	0.1657	0.1214
	8	0.0000	0.0002	0.0022	0.0120	0.0376	0.0811	0.1327	0.1734	0.1864	0.1669

N	K					P					
		0.05	**0.10**	**0.15**	**0.20**	**0.25**	**0.30**	**0.35**	**0.40**	**0.45**	**0.50**
	9	0.0000	0.0000	0.0004	0.0033	0.0139	0.0386	0.0794	0.1284	0.1694	0.1855
	10	0.0000	0.0000	0.0001	0.0008	0.0042	0.0149	0.0385	0.0771	0.1248	0.1669
	11	0.0000	0.0000	0.0000	0.0001	0.0010	0.0046	0.0151	0.0374	0.0742	0.1214
	12	0.0000	0.0000	0.0000	0.0000	0.0002	0.0012	0.0047	0.0145	0.0354	0.0708
	13	0.0000	0.0000	0.0000	0.0000	0.0000	0.0002	0.0012	0.0045	0.0134	0.0327
	14	0.0000	0.0000	0.0000	0.0000	0.0000	0.0000	0.0002	0.0011	0.0039	0.0117
	15	0.0000	0.0000	0.0000	0.0000	0.0000	0.0000	0.0000	0.0002	0.0009	0.0031
	16	0.0000	0.0000	0.0000	0.0000	0.0000	0.0000	0.0000	0.0000	0.0001	0.0006
	17	0.0000	0.0000	0.0000	0.0000	0.0000	0.0000	0.0000	0.0000	0.0000	0.0001
	18	0.0000	0.0000	0.0000	0.0000	0.0000	0.0000	0.0000	0.0000	0.0000	0.0000
19	0	0.3774	0.1351	0.0456	0.0144	0.0042	0.0011	0.0003	0.0001	0.0000	0.0000
	1	0.3774	0.2852	0.1529	0.0685	0.0268	0.0093	0.0029	0.0008	0.0002	0.0000
	2	0.1787	0.2852	0.2428	0.1540	0.0803	0.0358	0.0138	0.0046	0.0013	0.0003
	3	0.0533	0.1796	0.2428	0.2182	0.1517	0.0869	0.0422	0.0175	0.0062	0.0018
	4	0.0112	0.0798	0.1714	0.2182	0.2023	0.1491	0.0909	0.0467	0.0203	0.0074
	5	0.0018	0.0266	0.0907	0.1636	0.2023	0.1916	0.1468	0.0933	0.0497	0.0222
	6	0.0002	0.0069	0.0374	0.0955	0.1574	0.1916	0.1844	0.1451	0.0949	0.0518
	7	0.0000	0.0014	0.0122	0.0443	0.0974	0.1525	0.1844	0.1797	0.1443	0.0961
	8	0.0000	0.0002	0.0032	0.0166	0.0487	0.0981	0.1489	0.1797	0.1771	0.1442
	9	0.0000	0.0000	0.0007	0.0051	0.0198	0.0514	0.0980	0.1464	0.1771	0.1762
	10	0.0000	0.0000	0.0001	0.0013	0.0066	0.0220	0.0528	0.0976	0.1449	0.1762
	11	0.0000	0.0000	0.0000	0.0003	0.0018	0.0077	0.0233	0.0532	0.0970	0.1442
	12	0.0000	0.0000	0.0000	0.0000	0.0004	0.0022	0.0083	0.0237	0.0529	0.0961
	13	0.0000	0.0000	0.0000	0.0000	0.0001	0.0005	0.0024	0.0085	0.0233	0.0518
	14	0.0000	0.0000	0.0000	0.0000	0.0000	0.0001	0.0006	0.0024	0.0082	0.0222
	15	0.0000	0.0000	0.0000	0.0000	0.0000	0.0000	0.0001	0.0005	0.0022	0.0074
	16	0.0000	0.0000	0.0000	0.0000	0.0000	0.0000	0.0000	0.0001	0.0005	0.0018
	17	0.0000	0.0000	0.0000	0.0000	0.0000	0.0000	0.0000	0.0000	0.0001	0.0003
	18	0.0000	0.0000	0.0000	0.0000	0.0000	0.0000	0.0000	0.0000	0.0000	0.0000
	19	0.0000	0.0000	0.0000	0.0000	0.0000	0.0000	0.0000	0.0000	0.0000	0.0000
20	0	0.3585	0.1216	0.0388	0.0115	0.0032	0.0008	0.0002	0.0000	0.0000	0.0000
	1	0.3774	0.2702	0.1368	0.0576	0.0211	0.0068	0.0020	0.0005	0.0001	0.0000
	2	0.1887	0.2852	0.2293	0.1369	0.0669	0.0278	0.0100	0.0031	0.0008	0.0002
	3	0.0596	0.1901	0.2428	0.2054	0.1339	0.0716	0.0323	0.0123	0.0040	0.0011
	4	0.0133	0.0898	0.1821	0.2182	0.1897	0.1304	0.0738	0.0350	0.0139	0.0046
	5	0.0022	0.0319	0.1028	0.1746	0.2023	0.1789	0.1272	0.0746	0.0365	0.0148
	6	0.0003	0.0089	0.0454	0.1091	0.1686	0.1916	0.1712	0.1244	0.0746	0.0370
	7	0.0000	0.0020	0.0160	0.0545	0.1124	0.1643	0.1844	0.1659	0.1221	0.0739
	8	0.0000	0.0004	0.0046	0.0222	0.0609	0.1144	0.1614	0.1797	0.1623	0.1201
	9	0.0000	0.0001	0.0011	0.0074	0.0271	0.0654	0.1158	0.1597	0.1771	0.1602
	10	0.0000	0.0000	0.0002	0.0020	0.0099	0.0308	0.0686	0.1171	0.1593	0.1762
	11	0.0000	0.0000	0.0000	0.0005	0.0030	0.0120	0.0336	0.0710	0.1185	0.1602
	12	0.0000	0.0000	0.0000	0.0001	0.0008	0.0039	0.0136	0.0355	0.0727	0.1201
	13	0.0000	0.0000	0.0000	0.0000	0.0002	0.0010	0.0045	0.0146	0.0366	0.0739

(continued)

N	K	P									
		0.05	0.10	0.15	0.20	0.25	0.30	0.35	0.40	0.45	0.50
	14	0.0000	0.0000	0.0000	0.0000	0.0000	0.0002	0.0012	0.0049	0.0150	0.0370
	15	0.0000	0.0000	0.0000	0.0000	0.0000	0.0000	0.0003	0.0013	0.0049	0.0148
	16	0.0000	0.0000	0.0000	0.0000	0.0000	0.0000	0.0000	0.0003	0.0013	0.0046
	17	0.0000	0.0000	0.0000	0.0000	0.0000	0.0000	0.0000	0.0000	0.0002	0.0011
	18	0.0000	0.0000	0.0000	0.0000	0.0000	0.0000	0.0000	0.0000	0.0002	0.0011
	19	0.0000	0.0000	0.0000	0.0000	0.0000	0.0000	0.0000	0.0000	0.0000	0.0000
	20	0.0000	0.0000	0.0000	0.0000	0.0000	0.0000	0.0000	0.0000	0.0000	0.0000

TABLE 5. Chi-square distribution values for right-tailed areas
[For example, the area to the right of $\chi^2 = 3.841$ with $df = 1$ is .05.]

df	0.10	0.05	0.025	0.01	0.001
1	2.706	3.841	5.024	6.635	10.83
2	4.605	5.991	7.378	9.210	13.82
3	6.251	7.815	9.348	11.34	16.27
4	7.779	9.488	11.14	13.28	18.47
5	9.236	11.07	12.83	15.09	20.51
6	10.64	12.59	14.45	16.81	22.46
7	12.02	14.07	16.01	18.48	24.32
8	13.36	15.51	17.53	20.09	26.12
9	14.68	16.92	19.02	21.67	27.88
10	15.99	18.31	20.48	23.21	29.59
11	17.28	19.68	21.92	24.73	31.26
12	18.55	21.03	23.34	26.22	32.91
13	19.81	22.36	24.74	27.69	34.53
14	21.06	23.68	26.12	29.14	36.12
15	22.31	25.00	27.49	30.58	37.70
16	23.54	26.30	28.85	32.00	39.25
17	24.77	27.59	30.19	33.41	40.79
18	25.99	28.87	31.53	34.81	42.31
19	27.20	30.14	32.85	36.19	43.82
20	28.41	31.41	34.17	37.57	45.31
21	29.62	32.67	35.48	38.93	46.80
22	30.81	33.92	36.78	40.29	48.27
23	32.01	35.17	38.08	41.64	49.73
24	33.20	36.42	39.36	42.98	51.18
25	34.38	37.65	40.65	44.31	52.62
26	35.56	38.89	41.92	45.64	54.05
27	36.74	40.11	43.19	46.96	55.48
28	37.92	41.34	44.46	48.28	56.89
29	39.09	42.56	45.72	49.59	58.30
30	40.26	43.77	46.98	50.89	59.70
32	42.58	46.19	49.48	53.49	62.49
34	44.90	48.60	51.97	56.06	65.25
36	47.21	51.00	54.44	58.62	67.98
38	49.51	53.38	56.90	61.16	70.70

df	0.10	0.05	0.025	0.01	0.001
40	51.81	55.76	59.34	63.69	73.40
50	63.17	67.50	71.42	76.15	86.66
60	74.40	79.08	83.30	88.38	99.61
70	85.53	90.53	95.02	100.4	112.3
80	96.58	101.9	106.6	112.3	124.8
90	107.6	113.1	118.1	124.1	137.2
100	118.5	124.3	129.6	135.8	149.4

Table 6. The critical q-values[a]

df_w	α	\multicolumn{10}{c}{K (number of groups)}

df_w	α	2	3	4	5	6	7	8	9	10	11
5	.05	3.64	4.60	5.22	5.67	6.03	6.33	6.58	6.80	6.99	7.17
	.01	5.70	6.98	7.80	8.42	8.91	9.32	9.67	9.97	10.24	10.48
6	.05	3.46	4.34	4.90	5.30	5.63	5.90	6.12	6.32	6.49	6.65
	.01	5.24	6.33	7.03	7.56	7.97	8.32	8.61	8.87	9.10	9.30
7	.05	3.34	4.16	4.68	5.06	5.36	5.61	5.82	6.00	6.16	6.30
	.01	4.95	5.92	6.54	7.01	7.37	7.68	7.94	8.17	8.37	8.55
8	.05	3.26	4.04	4.53	4.89	5.17	5.40	5.60	5.77	5.92	6.05
	.01	4.75	5.64	6.20	6.62	6.96	7.24	7.47	7.68	7.86	8.03
9	.05	3.20	3.95	4.41	4.76	5.02	5.24	5.43	5.59	5.74	5.87
	.01	4.60	5.43	5.96	6.35	6.66	6.91	7.13	7.33	7.49	7.65
10	.05	3.15	3.88	4.33	4.65	4.91	5.12	5.30	5.46	5.60	5.72
	.01	4.48	5.27	5.77	6.14	6.43	6.67	6.87	7.05	7.21	7.36
11	.05	3.11	3.82	4.26	4.57	4.82	5.03	5.20	5.35	5.49	5.61
	.01	4.39	5.15	5.62	5.97	6.25	6.48	6.67	6.84	6.99	7.13
12	.05	3.08	3.77	4.20	4.51	4.75	4.95	5.12	5.27	5.39	5.51
	.01	4.32	5.05	5.50	5.84	6.10	6.32	6.51	6.67	6.81	6.94
13	.05	3.06	3.73	4.15	4.45	4.69	4.88	5.05	5.19	5.32	5.43
	.01	4.26	4.96	5.40	5.73	5.98	6.19	6.37	6.53	6.67	6.79
14	.05	3.03	3.70	4.11	4.41	4.64	4.83	4.99	5.13	5.25	5.36
	.01	4.21	4.89	5.32	5.63	5.88	6.08	6.26	6.41	6.54	6.66
15	.05	3.01	3.67	4.08	4.37	4.59	4.78	4.94	5.08	5.20	5.31
	.01	4.17	4.84	5.25	5.56	5.80	5.99	6.16	6.31	6.44	6.55
16	.05	3.00	3.65	4.05	4.33	4.56	4.74	4.90	5.03	5.15	5.26
	.01	4.13	4.79	5.19	5.49	5.72	5.92	6.08	6.22	6.35	6.46
17	.05	2.98	3.63	4.02	4.30	4.52	4.70	4.86	4.99	5.11	5.21
	.01	4.10	4.74	5.14	5.43	5.66	5.85	6.01	6.15	6.27	6.38
18	.05	2.97	3.61	4.00	4.28	4.49	4.67	4.82	4.96	5.07	5.17
	.01	4.07	4.70	5.09	5.38	5.60	5.79	5.94	6.08	6.20	6.31
19	.05	2.96	3.59	3.98	4.25	4.47	4.65	4.79	4.92	5.04	5.14
	.01	4.05	4.67	5.05	5.33	5.55	5.73	5.89	6.02	6.14	6.25
20	.05	2.95	3.58	3.96	4.23	4.45	4.62	4.77	4.90	5.01	5.11
	.01	4.02	4.64	5.02	5.29	5.51	5.69	5.84	5.97	6.09	6.19
24	.05	2.92	3.53	3.90	4.17	4.37	4.54	4.68	4.81	4.92	5.01
	.01	3.96	4.55	4.91	5.17	5.37	5.54	5.69	5.81	5.92	6.02
30	.05	2.89	3.49	3.85	4.10	4.30	4.46	4.60	4.72	4.82	4.92
	.01	3.89	4.45	4.80	5.05	5.24	5.40	5.54	5.65	5.76	5.85
40	.05	2.86	3.44	3.79	4.04	4.23	4.39	4.52	4.63	4.73	4.82
	.01	3.82	4.37	4.70	4.93	5.11	5.26	5.39	5.50	5.60	5.69
60	.05	2.83	3.40	3.74	3.98	4.16	4.31	4.44	4.55	4.65	4.73
	.01	3.76	4.28	4.59	4.82	4.99	5.13	5.25	5.36	5.45	5.53
120	.05	2.80	3.36	3.68	3.92	4.10	4.24	4.36	4.47	4.56	4.64
	.01	3.70	4.20	4.50	4.71	4.87	5.01	5.12	5.21	5.30	5.37
∞	.05	2.77	3.31	3.63	3.86	4.03	4.17	4.29	4.39	4.47	4.55
	.01	3.64	4.12	4.40	4.60	4.76	4.88	4.99	5.08	5.16	5.23

[a]Adapted from E. S. Pearson and H. O. Hartley (eds.), *Biometrika Tables for Statisticians.* New York: Cambridge University Press, 1966, Vol. 1, Table 29. Used by permission.

Table 7. The critical *U*-values

Critical values of the U distribution (.01 level, two-tailed)[a]

	1	2	3	4	5	6	7	8	9	10	11	12	13	14	15	16	17	18	19	20
	—	—	—	—	—	—	—	—	—	—	—	—	—	—	—	—	—	—	—	—
2	—	—	—	—	—	—	—	—	—	—	—	—	—	—	—	—	—	—	0	0
																			38	40
	—	—	—	—	—	—	—	—	0	0	0	1	1	1	2	2	2	2	3	3
									27	30	33	35	38	41	43	46	49	52	54	57
4	—	—	—	—	—	0	0	1	1	2	2	3	3	4	5	5	6	6	7	8
						24	28	31	35	38	42	45	49	52	55	59	62	66	69	72
5	—	—	—	—	0	1	1	2	3	4	5	6	7	7	8	9	10	11	12	13
					25	29	34	38	42	46	50	54	58	63	67	71	75	79	83	87
	—	—	—	0	1	2	3	4	5	6	7	9	10	11	12	13	15	16	17	18
				24	29	34	39	44	49	54	59	63	68	73	78	83	87	92	97	102
7	—	—	—	0	1	3	4	6	7	9	10	12	13	15	16	18	19	21	22	24
				28	34	39	45	50	56	61	67	72	78	83	89	94	100	105	111	116
	—	—	—	1	2	4	6	7	9	11	13	15	17	18	20	22	24	26	28	30
				31	38	44	50	57	63	69	75	81	87	94	100	106	112	118	124	130
	—	—	0	1	3	5	7	9	11	13	16	18	20	22	24	27	29	31	33	36
			27	35	42	49	56	63	70	77	83	90	97	104	111	117	124	131	138	144
10	—	—	0	2	4	6	9	11	13	16	18	21	24	26	29	31	34	37	39	42
			30	38	46	54	61	69	77	84	92	99	106	114	121	129	136	143	151	158
11	—	—	0	2	5	7	10	13	16	18	21	24	27	30	33	36	39	42	45	48
			33	42	50	59	67	75	83	92	100	108	116	124	132	140	148	156	164	172
	—	—	1	3	6	9	12	15	18	21	24	27	31	34	37	41	44	47	51	54
			35	45	54	63	72	81	90	99	108	117	125	134	143	151	160	169	177	186
13	—	—	1	3	7	10	13	17	20	24	27	31	34	38	42	45	49	53	56	60
			38	49	58	68	78	87	97	106	116	125	134	144	153	163	172	181	191	200
	—	—	1	4	7	11	15	18	22	26	30	34	38	42	46	50	54	58	63	67
			41	52	63	73	83	94	104	114	124	134	144	154	164	174	184	194	203	213
	—	—	2	5	8	12	16	20	24	29	33	37	42	46	51	55	60	64	69	73
			43	55	67	78	89	100	111	121	132	143	153	164	174	185	195	206	216	227
16	—	—	2	5	9	13	18	22	27	31	36	41	45	50	55	60	65	70	74	79
			46	59	71	83	94	106	117	129	140	151	163	174	185	196	207	218	230	241
	—	—	2	6	10	15	19	24	29	34	39	44	49	54	60	65	70	75	81	86
			49	62	75	87	100	112	124	136	148	160	172	184	195	207	219	231	242	254
18	—	—	2	6	11	16	21	26	31	37	42	47	53	58	64	70	75	81	87	92
			52	66	79	92	105	118	131	143	156	169	181	194	206	218	231	243	255	268
19	—	0	3	7	12	17	22	28	33	39	45	51	56	63	69	74	81	87	93	99
		38	54	69	83	97	111	124	138	151	164	177	191	203	216	230	242	255	268	281
	—	0	3	8	13	18	24	30	36	42	48	54	60	67	73	79	86	92	99	105
		40	57	72	87	102	116	130	144	158	172	186	200	213	227	241	254	268	281	295

[a] **Adapted** from D. V. Lindley and W. F. Scott, *New Cambridge Elementary Statistical Tables.* London: Cambridge University Press, 1984, Table 21. **Used** by permission.

Critical Values of the U distribution (.01 level, one-tailed) (continued)

1	2	3	4	5	6	7	8	9	10	11	12	13	14	15	16	17	18	19	20
–	–	–	–	–	–	–	–	–	–	–	–	–	–	–	–	–	–	–	–
–	–	–	–	–	–	–	–	–	–	–	–	0	0	0	0	0	0	1	1
												26	28	30	32	34	36	37	39
–	–	–	–	–	–	0	0	1	1	1	2	2	2	3	3	4	4	4	5
						21	24	26	29	32	34	37	40	42	45	47	50	52	55
–	–	–	–	0	1	1	2	3	3	4	5	5	6	7	7	8	9	9	10
				20	23	27	30	33	37	40	43	47	50	53	57	60	63	67	70
–	–	–	0	1	2	3	4	5	6	7	8	9	10	11	12	13	14	15	16
			20	24	28	32	36	40	44	48	52	56	60	64	68	72	76	80	84
–	–	–	1	2	3	4	6	7	8	9	11	12	13	15	16	18	19	20	22
			23	28	33	38	42	47	52	57	61	66	71	75	80	84	89	94	98
–	–	0	1	3	4	6	7	9	11	12	14	16	17	19	21	23	24	26	28
		21	27	32	38	43	49	54	59	65	70	75	81	86	91	96	102	107	112
–	–	0	2	4	6	7	9	11	13	15	17	20	22	24	26	28	30	32	34
		24	30	36	42	49	55	61	67	73	79	84	90	96	102	108	114	120	126
–	–	1	3	5	7	9	11	14	16	18	21	23	26	28	31	33	36	38	40
		26	33	40	47	54	61	67	74	81	87	94	100	107	113	120	126	133	140
–	–	1	3	6	8	11	13	16	19	22	24	27	30	33	36	38	41	44	47
		29	37	44	52	59	67	74	81	88	96	103	110	117	124	132	139	146	153
–	–	1	4	7	9	12	15	18	22	25	28	31	34	37	41	44	47	50	53
		32	40	48	57	65	73	81	88	96	104	112	120	128	135	143	151	159	167
–	–	2	5	8	11	14	17	21	24	28	31	35	38	42	46	49	53	56	60
		34	43	52	61	70	79	87	96	104	113	121	130	138	146	155	163	172	180
–	0	2	5	9	12	16	20	23	27	31	35	39	43	47	51	55	59	63	67
	26	37	47	56	66	75	84	94	103	112	121	130	139	148	157	166	175	184	193
–	0	2	6	10	13	17	22	26	30	34	38	43	47	51	56	60	65	69	73
	28	40	50	60	71	81	90	100	110	120	130	139	149	159	168	178	187	197	207
–	0	3	7	11	15	19	24	28	33	37	42	47	51	56	61	66	70	75	80
	30	42	53	64	75	86	96	107	117	128	138	148	159	169	179	189	200	210	220
–	0	3	7	12	16	21	26	31	36	41	46	51	56	61	66	71	76	82	87
	32	45	57	68	80	91	102	113	124	135	146	157	168	179	190	201	212	222	233
–	0	4	8	13	18	23	28	33	38	44	49	55	60	66	71	77	82	88	93
	34	47	60	72	84	96	108	120	132	143	155	166	178	189	201	212	224	234	247
–	0	4	9	14	19	24	30	36	41	47	53	59	65	70	76	82	88	94	100
	36	50	63	76	89	102	114	126	139	151	163	175	187	200	212	224	236	248	260
–	1	4	9	15	20	26	32	38	44	50	56	63	69	75	82	88	94	101	107
	37	53	67	80	94	107	120	133	146	159	172	184	197	210	222	235	248	260	273
–	1	5	10	16	22	28	34	40	47	53	60	67	73	80	87	93	100	107	114
	39	55	70	84	98	112	126	140	153	167	180	193	207	220	233	247	260	273	286

(continued)

Critical Values of the U distribution (.05 level, two-tailed) (continued)

	1	2	3	4	5	6	7	8	9	10	11	12	13	14	15	16	17	18	19	20
	–	–	–	–	–	–	–	–	–	–	–	–	–	–	–	–	–	–	–	–
2	–	–	–	–	–	–	–	0	0	0	0	1	1	1	1	1	2	2	2	2
								16	18	20	22	23	25	27	29	31	32	34	36	38
	–	–	–	–	0	1	1	2	2	3	3	4	4	5	5	6	6	7	7	8
					15	17	20	22	25	27	30	32	35	37	40	42	45	47	50	52
4	–	–	–	0	1	2	3	4	4	5	6	7	8	9	10	11	11	12	13	13
				16	19	22	25	28	32	35	38	41	44	47	50	53	57	60	63	67
5	–	–	0	1	2	3	5	6	7	8	9	11	12	13	14	15	17	18	19	20
			15	19	23	27	30	34	38	42	46	49	53	57	61	65	68	72	76	80
	–	–	1	2	3	5	6	8	10	11	13	14	16	17	19	21	22	24	25	27
			17	22	27	31	36	40	44	49	53	58	62	67	71	75	80	84	89	93
7	–	–	1	3	5	6	8	10	12	14	16	18	20	22	24	26	28	30	32	34
			20	25	30	36	41	46	51	56	61	66	71	76	81	86	91	96	101	106
	–	0	2	4	6	8	10	13	15	17	19	22	24	26	29	31	34	36	38	41
		16	22	28	34	40	46	51	57	63	69	74	80	86	91	97	102	108	111	119
	–	0	2	4	7	10	12	15	17	20	23	26	28	31	34	37	39	42	45	48
		18	25	32	38	44	51	57	64	70	76	82	89	95	101	107	114	120	126	132
10	–	0	3	5	8	11	14	17	20	23	26	29	33	36	39	42	45	48	52	55
		20	27	35	42	49	56	63	70	77	84	91	97	104	111	118	125	132	138	145
11	–	0	3	6	9	13	16	19	23	26	30	33	37	40	44	47	51	55	58	62
		22	30	38	46	53	61	69	76	84	91	99	106	114	121	129	136	143	151	158
	–	1	4	7	11	14	18	22	26	29	33	37	41	45	49	53	57	61	65	69
		23	32	41	49	58	66	74	82	91	99	107	115	123	131	139	147	155	163	171
13	–	1	4	8	12	16	20	24	28	33	37	41	45	50	54	59	63	67	72	76
		25	35	44	53	62	71	80	89	97	106	115	124	132	141	149	158	167	175	184
	–	1	5	9	13	17	22	26	31	36	40	45	50	55	59	64	67	74	78	83
		27	37	47	51	67	76	86	95	104	114	123	132	141	151	160	171	178	188	197
	–	1	5	10	14	19	24	29	34	39	44	49	54	59	64	70	75	80	85	90
		29	40	50	61	71	81	91	101	111	121	131	141	151	161	170	180	190	200	210
16	–	1	6	11	15	21	26	31	37	42	47	53	59	64	70	75	81	86	92	98
		31	42	53	65	75	86	97	107	118	129	139	149	160	170	181	191	202	212	222
	–	2	6	11	17	22	28	34	39	45	51	57	63	67	75	81	87	93	99	105
		32	45	57	68	80	91	102	114	125	136	147	158	171	180	191	202	213	224	235
	–	2	7	12	18	24	30	36	42	48	55	61	67	74	80	86	93	99	106	112
		34	47	60	72	84	96	108	120	132	143	155	167	178	190	202	213	225	236	248
19	–	2	7	13	19	25	32	38	45	52	58	65	72	78	85	92	99	106	113	119
		36	50	63	76	89	101	114	126	138	151	163	175	188	200	212	224	236	248	261
	–	2	8	13	20	27	34	41	48	55	62	69	76	83	90	98	105	112	119	127
		38	52	67	80	93	106	119	132	145	158	171	184	197	210	222	235	248	261	273

Critical Values of the U distribution (.05 level, one-tailed) (continued)

	1	2	3	4	5	6	7	8	9	10	11	12	13	14	15	16	17	18	19	20
1	–	–	–	–	–	–	–	–	–	–	–	–	–	–	–	–	–	–	0	0
																			19	20
2	–	–	–	–	0	0	0	1	1	1	1	2	2	2	3	3	3	4	4	4
					10	12	14	15	17	19	21	22	24	26	27	29	31	32	34	36
3	–	–	0	0	1	2	2	3	3	4	5	5	6	7	7	8	9	9	10	11
			9	12	14	16	19	21	24	26	28	31	33	35	38	40	42	45	47	49
4	–	–	0	1	2	3	4	5	6	7	8	9	10	11	12	14	15	16	17	18
			12	15	18	21	24	27	30	33	36	39	42	45	48	50	53	56	59	62
5	–	0	1	2	4	5	6	8	9	11	12	13	15	16	18	19	20	22	23	25
		10	14	18	21	25	29	32	36	39	43	47	50	54	57	61	65	68	72	75
6	–	0	2	3	5	7	8	10	12	14	16	17	19	21	23	25	26	28	30	32
		12	16	21	25	29	34	38	42	46	50	55	59	63	67	71	76	80	84	88
7	–	0	2	4	6	8	11	13	15	17	19	21	24	26	28	30	33	35	37	39
		14	19	24	29	34	38	43	48	53	58	63	67	72	77	82	86	91	96	101
8	–	1	3	5	8	10	13	15	18	20	23	26	28	31	33	36	39	41	44	47
		15	21	27	32	38	43	49	54	60	65	70	76	81	87	92	97	103	108	113
9	–	1	3	6	9	12	15	18	21	24	27	30	33	36	39	42	45	48	51	54
		17	24	30	36	42	48	54	60	66	72	78	84	90	96	102	108	114	120	126
10	–	1	4	7	11	14	17	20	24	27	31	34	37	41	44	48	51	55	58	62
		19	26	33	39	46	53	60	66	73	79	86	93	99	106	112	119	125	132	138
11	–	1	5	8	12	16	19	23	27	31	34	38	42	46	50	54	57	61	65	69
		21	28	36	43	50	58	65	72	79	87	94	101	108	115	122	130	137	144	151
12	–	2	5	9	13	17	21	26	30	34	38	42	47	51	55	60	64	68	72	77
		22	31	39	47	55	63	70	78	86	94	102	109	117	125	132	140	148	156	163
13	–	2	6	10	15	19	24	28	33	37	42	47	51	56	61	65	70	75	80	84
		24	33	42	50	59	67	76	84	93	101	109	118	126	134	143	151	159	167	176
14	–	2	7	11	16	21	26	31	36	41	46	51	56	61	66	71	77	82	87	92
		26	35	45	54	63	72	81	90	99	108	117	126	135	144	153	161	170	179	188
15	–	3	7	12	18	23	28	33	39	44	50	55	61	66	72	77	83	88	94	100
		27	38	48	57	67	77	87	96	106	115	125	134	144	153	163	172	182	191	200
16	–	3	8	14	19	25	30	36	42	48	54	60	65	71	77	83	89	95	101	107
		29	40	50	61	71	82	92	102	112	122	132	143	153	163	173	183	193	203	213
17	–	3	9	15	20	26	33	39	45	51	57	64	70	77	83	89	96	102	109	115
		31	42	53	65	76	86	97	108	119	130	140	151	161	172	183	193	204	214	225
18	–	4	9	16	22	28	35	41	48	55	61	68	75	82	88	95	102	109	116	123
		32	45	56	68	80	91	103	114	123	137	148	159	170	182	193	204	215	226	237
19	0	4	10	17	23	30	37	44	51	58	65	72	80	87	94	101	109	116	123	130
	19	34	47	59	72	84	96	108	120	132	144	156	167	179	191	203	214	226	238	250
20	0	4	11	18	25	32	39	47	54	62	69	77	84	92	100	107	115	123	130	138
	20	36	49	62	75	88	101	113	126	138	151	163	176	188	200	213	225	237	250	262

References

Bakan, D. (1966). The test of significance in psychological research. *Psychological Bulletin,* 66(6), 423–437.

Becker, W., & Kennedy, P. (1992). A lesson in least squares and R squared. *The American Statistician,* 46(4), 282–283.

Bem, S. L. (1977). *Bem Sex-Role Inventory Professional Manual.* California: Consulting Psychologists Press, Inc.

Bloom, H. (2009). *Modern Regression Discontinuity Analysis.* An MDRC publication. www.mdrc.org/publication/modern-regression-discontinuity-analysis.

Burrill, G., & Hopensperger, P. (1993). *Exploring Statistics with the T1-81.* Reading, Massachusetts: Addison-Wesley.

Campbell, D. T., & Stanley, J. C. (1963). Experimental and quasi-experimental designs for research on teaching. In N. L. Gage (Ed.), *Handbook of Research on Teaching,* (pp. 171–246). 24, Chicago, IL: Rand McNally.

Card, David. (1995). Using geographic variation in college proximity to estimate the return to schooling. National Bureau of Economic Research Working Paper No. 4483. Doi: 10.3386/w4483.

Carver, R. P. (1978). The case against statistical significance testing. *Harvard Educational Review,* 48(3), 378–398.

Charig, C. R., Webb, D. R., Payne, S. R., & Wickham, O. E. (March 1986). Comparison of treatment of renal calculi by operative surgery, percutaneous nephrolithotomy, and extracorporeal shock wave lithotripsy. *British Medical Journal (Clin Res Ed),* 292 (6524): 879–882.

Cohen, J. (1994). The earth is round (*p* < .05). *American Psychologist,* 49(12), 997–1003.

(1990). Things I have learned (so far). *American Psychologist,* 45, 1304–1312.

(1988). *Statistical Power Analysis for the Behavioral Sciences* (2nd edition.). Hillsdale, NJ: Lawrence Erlbaum Associates.

Cohen, J., Cohen, P., West, S.G., & Aiken, L.S. (2003). *Applied Multiple Regression/Correlation Analysis for the Behavioral Sciences, 3rd Edition.* Hillsdale, NJ: Lawrence Erlbaum Associates.

Cohen, R.J., & Swerdlik, M. (2005). *Psychological Testing and Assessment: An Introduction to Tests and Measurement, 6th Edition.* Boston, MA: McGraw Hill.

Cohen, R. J., Swerdlik, M., & Sturman, E. (2012). *Psychological Testing and Assessment: An Introduction to Tests and Measurement.* Boston, MA: McGraw-Hill Education.

Cook, T. D., & Campbell, D. T. (1979). *Quasi-Experimentation: Design & Analysis Issues for Field Settings.* Boston, MA: Houghton-Mifflin.

Darlington, R. B. (1990). *Regression and linear models.* New York: McGraw Hill.

de Moivre, A. (1756). *The Doctrine of Chances, 3rd edition.* London: Millar.

Elmore, J. et. al. (1998). Ten-year risk of false positive screening mammograms and clinical breast examinations. *The New England Journal of Medicine,* 338(16), 1089–1096.

Efron, B. 1979. Bootstrap methods: Another look at the jackknife. *Annals of Statistics* 7: 1–26.

Efron, B. 1982. *The Jackknife, the Bootstrap and Other Resampling Plans*. Philadelphia: Society for Industrial and Applied Mathematics.

Falk, R., & Greenbaum, C. W. (1995). Significance tests die hard. The amazing persistence of a probabilistic misconception. *Theory and Psychology*, 5(1), 75–98.

Fisher, R.A. (1934). *Statistical Methods for Research Workers*. Edinburgh, Scotland: Oliver & Boyd. 319 pp.

Fisher, R. A. (1959). *Statistical methods and scientific inference* (2nd ed.). Edinburgh, Scotland: Oliver and Boyd.

Galton, F. (1886). Regression towards mediocrity in hereditary stature. *The Journal of the Anthropological Institute of Great Britain and Ireland* 15: 246–263.

Gelman, A. & Hill, J. (2007). *Data analysis using regression and multilevel/hierarchical models*, New York, NY: Cambridge University Press.

Glass, G.V., Peckham, P.D., & Sanders, J.R. (1972). Consequences of Failure to Meet Assumptions Underlying the Fixed Effects Analyses of Variance and Covariance, *Review of Educational Research* 42(3), pp. 237–288.

Gough, P. (1996). How children learn to read and why they fail. *Annals of Dyslexia*, 46(1), 1–20.

Groves, R. M., F. J. Fowler Jr., M. P. Couper, J. M. Lepkowski, E. Singer, & R. Tourangeau. (2009). *Survey Methodology*, 2nd ed. Hoboken, New Jersey: John Wiley & Sons.

Hagen, R. L. (1997). In praise of the null hypothesis statistical test. *American Psychologist*, 52, 15–24.

Harlow, L. L., Mulaik, S. A., & Steiger, J. H. (eds.) (1997). *What if there were no significance tests?* Mahwah, NJ: Lawrence Erlbaum Associates.

Hays, W. L. (1973). *Statistics for the social sciences*. 2nd ed. New York: Holt, Rinehart, and Winston.

Holland, P. W., & Rubin, D. B. (1982). On Lord's paradox. In H. Wainer & S. Messick (Eds.), *Principles of modern psychological measurement: A festschrift for Frederick Lord* (pp. 3–25). Hillsdale, NJ: Lawrence Erlbaum Associates.

Horn, L., Hafner, A., & Owings, J. (1992). A profile of American eighth-grade mathematics and science instruction. National Education Longitudinal Study of 1988. Statistical Analysis Report. ERIC Document (ERIC Document Reproduction Service No. ED337094).

Imbens, G. W., & Lemieux, T. (2008). Regression discontinuity designs: A guide to practice. *Journal of Economics*, (142): 615–635.

Julious, S. A., & Mullee, M. A. (1994). Confounding and Simpson's paradox. *British Medical Journal*, 309 (6967): 1480–1481.

Kaplan, A. (1964). *The conduct of inquiry: Methodology for behavioral science*. San Francisco, CA: Chandler Publishing Company.

Keppel, G. (1991). *Design and analysis: A researcher's handbook*. Englewood, NJ: Prentice Hall.

Kirk, R. E. (1996). Practical significance: A concept whose time has come. *Educational and psychological measurement*, 56(5), 746–759.

Kivimaki, M., Ferrie, J. E., Brunner, E., Head, J., Shipley, M. J., Vahtera, J., & Marmot, M. G. (October 24, 2005). Justice at work and reduced risk of coronary heart disease among employees. *Archives of Internal Medicine*, 2245–2251.

Kruskal, W.H. & Wallis, W.A. (1952). Use of ranks in one-criterion variance analysis. *Journal of the American Statistical Association* 47(260), 583–621.

Lord, F. M. (1967) A paradox in the interpretation of group comparisons. *Psychological Bulletin*, 68, 304–305.

Lykken, D. T. (1968). Statistical significance in psychological research. *Psychological Bulletin, 70,* 151–159.

Mann, H.B. & Whitney, D.R. (1947). On a test of whether one of two random variables is stochastically larger than the other. *The Annals of Mathematical Statistics, 18,* 50–60.

Marascuilo, L. A., & Busk, P. L. (1987). Loglinear models: A way to study main effects and interactions for multidimensional contingency tables with categorical data. *Journal of Counseling Psychology, 34,* 443-455.

Marascuilo, L. A., & Serlin, R. C. (1988). *Statistical Methods for the Behavioral Sciences. New York:* W. H. Freeman.

Maxwell, S. E., & Delaney, H. D. (2004). *Designing experiments and analyzing data: A model comparison perspective.* (2nd ed.). Mahwah, NJ: Lawrence Erlbaum Associates.

Meehl, P. E. (1967). Theory testing in psychology and physics: A methodological paradox. *Philosophy of Science, 34,* 103–115.

Nagourney, Eric. (November 1, 2005). Injustices at work may harm men's hearts. Vital Signs Column, *The New York Times.*

Pearson, K. (1900). On the criterion that a given system of deviations from the probably in the case of a correlated system of variables is such that it can be reasonable supposed to have arisen from random sampling. *Phil. Mag. (5)* 50, 157–175. Reprinted in K Pearson (1956), pp. 339–357.

Rosenbaum, P. R., & Rubin, D. B. (1983). The central role of the propensity score in observational studies for causal effects. *Biometrika* 70(1): 41–55.

Rosnow, R. L., & Rosenthal, R. (1989). Statistical procedures and the justification of knowledge in psychological science. *American Psychologist, 44,* 1276–1284.

Rozeboom, W. W. (1960). The fallacy of the null hypothesis significance test. *Psychological Bulletin, 57,* 416–428.

Salsburg, David. (2001). The Lady Tasting Tea: How statistics revolutionized science in the twentieth century. New York: W.H. Freeman and Company.

Satterthwaite, F. W. (1946). An approximate distribution of estimates of variance components. *Biometrics Bulletin, 2,* 100–144.

Schau, C., Stevens, J., Dauphinee, T., & Del Vecchio, A. (1995). The development and validation of the Survey of Attitudes toward Statistics. *Educational & Psychological Measurement, 55(5),* 868–876.

Shadish, W. R., Cook, T. D., & Campbell, D. T. (2002). *Experimental and quasi-experimental designs for generalized causal inference.* Boston, MA: Houghton Mifflin.

Shadish, W. R., Galindo, R., Wong, V.C., Steiner, P. M., & Cook, T. D. (2011). A randomized experiment comparing random and cutoff-based assignment. *Psychological Methods, 16(2),* 179–191.

Siegel, Sidney, & Castellan, Jr., N. J. (1988). *Nonparametric statistics for the behavioral sciences.* New York: McGraw-Hill.

Stanton, J. (2001). Galton, Pearson, and the Peas: A Brief History of Linear Regression for Statistics Instructors. *Journal of Statistics Education, 9* (3).

Stevens, S. S. (1946). On the theory of scales of measurement. *Science, 103,* 677–680.

Stevens, S. S. (1951). Mathematics, Measurement, and Psychophysics. In S. S. Stevens (Ed.), *Handbook of Experimental Psychology.* New York: John Wiley & Sons.

Stigler, S. M. (1986). *The History of Statistics: The measurement of uncertainty before 1900.* Cambridge, MA: Harvard University Press.

Stigler, S. M. (1997). Regression toward the mean, historically considered. *Statistical Methods in Medical Research* 6 (2): 103–114.

Thompson, B. (1994). The concept of statistical significance testing. *ERIC/AE Digest.* ERIC Document (ERIC Document Reproduction Service No. ED366654).

(1996). AERA editorial policies regarding statistical significance testing: Three suggested reforms. *Educational Researcher,* 25, 26–30.

Thorndike, R. L., & Hagen, E. P. (1969). *Measurement and Evaluation in Psychology and Education.* New York: John Wiley & Sons.

Tomasi, S., & Weinberg, S. L. (1999). Classifying children as learning disabled: An analysis of current practice in an urban setting. *Learning Disability Quarterly,* 22, 31–42.

Tukey, J. (1977). *Exploratory Data Analysis.* Reading, MA: Addison-Wesley.

Wainer, H. (2011). *Uneducated guesses: Using evidence to uncover misguided education policies. Princeton, NJ:* Princeton University Press.

Weinberg, S. L., Carroll, J. D., & Cohen, H. S. (1984). Confidence regions for INDSCAL using the jackknife and bootstrap techniques. *Psychometrika,* 49, 475–491.

Wechsler, D. (1981). *Manual for the Wechsler Adult Intelligence Scale-Revised.* New York: Psychological Corporation.

Willerman, L., Schultz, R., Rutledge, J. N., and Bigler, E. (1991). In vivo brain size and intelligence. *Intelligence* 15, 223–228.

Wilcoxon, F. (1945). Individual comparisons by ranking methods. *Biometrics Bulletin,* 1, *pp.* 80–83.

Wilcoxon, F. *The World Almanac and Book of Facts 2006.* (2014). New Jersey: World Almanac Books.

Solutions

www.cambridge.org/Stats-Stata

Index